Paths to Freedom

THE CAROLINA LOWCOUNTRY AND THE ATLANTIC WORLD
Sponsored by the Carolina Lowcountry and
Atlantic World Program of the College of Charleston

Paths to Freedom

Manumission in the Atlantic World

Edited by

Rosemary Brana-Shute *and* Randy J. Sparks

THE UNIVERSITY OF SOUTH CAROLINA PRESS

Published by the University of South Carolina Press
Columbia, South Carolina 29208

www.sc.edu/uscpress

Manufactured in the United States of America

17 16 15 14 13 12 11 10 09 08
10 9 8 7 6 5 4 3 2 1

Library of Congress Cataloging-in-Publication Data

Paths to freedom : manumission in the Atlantic world / edited by Rosemary Brana-Shute and
Randy J. Sparks.
     p. cm.
   Includes bibliographical references and index.
   ISBN 978-1-57003-774-0 (cloth : alk. paper)
   1. Slaves—Emancipation. 2. Slavery—History. I. Brana-Shute, Rosemary, 1944– II. Sparks,
Randy J.
   HT1031.P37 2009
   306.3'6209—dc22   2008051929

This book was printed on Glatfelter Natures, a recycled paper with 30 percent
postconsumer waste content.

Contents

Editors' Note

Despite the outpouring of scholarly work on the institution of slavery over the past several decades, manumission—the act of freeing individual slaves while the institution of slavery continues—has not received the same scholarly attention. In an attempt to focus more attention on this important subject, we present this volume. We begin in early modern Iberia, where the Spanish and Portugese began exploring the western coast of Africa and returning with slaves. We follow the emerging system of slavery across the Atlantic and throughout the Americas, where the European powers developed closely related but distinct laws governing their slave systems. All Atlantic slave societies had some form of manumission, making it an ideal topic for comparative study. Through this window, we can see into the slave system, for who could manumit, who could be manumitted, and how this act could be achieved offer important insights into the workings of the institution of slavery. But manumission also highlights one of the most significant moments in the life of an enslaved individual—the passage from an enslaved person to a free person and, in the eyes of the law, from chattel to personhood. In that sense, manumission is also a process, not simply an act, and one laden with meaning and significance for the relatively small number of slaves who managed to achieve it.

As this collection demonstrates, there were many paths to freedom and many variables that governed the process. In some societies there were very few such paths, in others there were several. For instance, in some societies only masters had the authority to manumit slaves. In others the state might also free individuals, and in still others slaves enjoyed the legal right to purchase their freedom. Such variables as gender, age, service, family, and urbanization play important roles in determining who could or would be freed. Obviously manumission also raises questions about the status of freed slaves and the creation of free black communities. Once freed, former slaves often set to work to bring family members out of slavery. In some societies manumitted slaves entered into a well-established free black community which often helped individual slaves achieve their freedom. In more restrictive societies manumitted slaves were forced to leave the state once they had won their freedom. Complexities abound as we begin to look carefully at the workings of the many and varied slave systems in the Atlantic world. We should note here one glaring omission from the volume: any study of manumission in African slave societies. We received no submission from any scholar of African slavery, and while we attempted to locate someone interested in this topic in West Africa, we had no success. We hope that this volume will help advance scholarly interest in the topic in Africa and throughout the Atlantic world.

In the process of editing this book we have accrued many debts. First, we thank all of the scholars who agreed to include their studies in this volume for their patience with the lengthy editing process. We also thank the Avery Research Center for African American History and Culture at the College of Charleston and the National Endowment for the Humanities for their financial support. We owe an additional debt of gratitude to Anne Hawks, who provided editorial assistance as the project entered its final stages, and to Simon Lewis, director of the Program in the Carolina Lowcountry and the Atlantic World. Last, but certainly not least, we would like to thank Alexander Moore, acquisitions editor at the University of South Carolina Press. Alex was instrumental in creating the Carolina Lowcountry and Atlantic World series with us, and he has been tireless in his efforts to see this volume to publication.

Introduction

—∿—

This collection will modify and reshape many preconceived ideas about manumission and pose many questions for future research. If there is a lingering belief that manumission was a disinterested practice that humanized the institution of slavery, or even negated it, then it will need to be reconsidered in the light of the arguments and evidence in this book. Authors from Alexander Humboldt in 1806 to Frank Tannenbaum in 1946 saw the practice of manumission in the Spanish colonies as sharply contrasted with the rigid slave conditions found in the Dutch and English colonies.[1] The stress in such understandings was on law, culture, and religion. Carl Degler's work on Brazil also drew attention to a legal and cultural ethos which allowed for manumission as a "mulatto escape hatch" from slavery.[2] Although law and culture undoubtedly help to create a contrast between "Anglo" and "Latin" regimes of slavery and manumission in the Americas, they interact with other variables, notably the extent of plantation development and urbanization and the slave owners' need for social allies in maintaining the subjugation of the enslaved.

The studies published in this volume concern either New World systems of slavery or Old World slaveholding practices which directly contributed to the evolution of the Atlantic pattern. Stretching from medieval times to the late nineteenth century, they cover an epoch which embraces the rise of Western capitalism and the rise and fall of European colonial empires in the Americas. The traditional slaveholding practices noted in the first three essays focused on domestic service or artisan employment and allowed manumission as a reward for good service or as a consequence of self-purchase. With the rise of plantations in the seventeenth and eighteenth centuries, slave labor became of great economic importance and possibilities of manumission were generally, though never completely, foreclosed. The Atlantic boom of 1650–1770 riveted more firmly the chains of slavery, but it eventually set the scene for political and social struggles which were once again to favor manumission, in ways indicated in some of the later essays.

The essays in this book show that New World slavery adopted but transformed the "traditional" Old World regime of slavery. They include two studies mainly focused on the manumission practices of medieval Europe (Phillips and Blumenthal); one on manumission in the Jewish communities of the Levant, Europe, and the New World (Schorsch); three studies of Dutch colonial slavery; one essay each on the English and Spanish Caribbean; five essays on the post–Revolutionary War and antebellum United States; and three studies on slavery and manumission in Brazil. While it would have been good to have a study of manumission in Spanish and French America, the fact remains that these essays furnish a wide range of varied perspectives which together illuminate the differing role of manumission across most of the history of the New World slave systems. The essays also offer insights which transcend the particular time and region they concern, illuminating wider patterns of slavery and manumission. It has often been claimed that female slaves were always more likely to be manumitted than male slaves, that many of those manumitted were offspring of slave owners, that there were wide variations in manumission rates in the Americas, and that manumission could achieve sufficient critical mass to undermine slavery. While these views are not completely wrong, they do need to be qualified. Generally, female slaves—especially those attached to the household or resident in urban areas—were indeed more likely to achieve manumission. But the essays on the early U.S. Republic by Eva Sheppard Wolfe and Sean Condon show that in North America male slaves were as likely as female slaves to achieve manumission, while several essays, especially the study by Rosemary Brana-Shute, furnish evidence that the high female proportion elsewhere has a gendered rather than sexual explanation (I will return to this).

We do not yet have the comprehensive comparative account of manumission for which Orlando Patterson calls, but a number of the patterns and puzzles will be found in these studies. They show fluctuations in the rate of manumission—further aspects of these contrasts will be noted later—but several suggest that manumission levels were everywhere rather low, affecting at most one slave in every five hundred or thousand per year and very often much less than that. It is difficult to offer a precise manumission rate for the ancient or medieval worlds because we do not know the exact size of the slave population. In his essay William Phillips nevertheless reports that "many scholars are suggesting that the number of cases [of manumission in Imperial Rome] was always small and that the majority of Roman slaves never won their freedom." It has always been thought that the slavery of the medieval and early modern Europe was marked by high manumission rates. Slaves were owned in small groups, and plantation slavery was found on the Atlantic islands but not the mainland. The Siete Partidas, the influential legal code drawn up by Alfonso the Wise in thirteenth-century Spain, clearly described slavery as contrary to natural freedom and furnished several routes to manumission. Yet Debra Blumenthal cites a figure for Granada of two hundred manumissions across the whole of the sixteenth century—or two a year. Since there were probably a few thousand slaves at any one time in Granada, the manumission rate was probably around one in a thousand annually. Mary Cravens computes a manumission rate of slightly over one per thousand slaves a year for the Dutch East India Company's slave lodge at the Cape of Good Hope. Given that these slaves lived in an urban setting, with the possibilities of manumission that often flowed from that, this is not a very high rate. Eva Sheppard Wolfe finds that during the two decades immediately following the American Revolutionary War—a period far more favorable to manumission than those which preceded or succeeded it—a total of only 11,000 slaves were freed by manumission. In a way this is a high figure, but not when compared to the size of Virginia's slave population, which ran at 293,000 in 1790, giving the state a peak annual rate of only two manumissions per thousand slaves annually. The upper end of the spectrum is furnished by Curaçao, where Willem Klooster estimates a manumission rate of 0.5 percent, or five per thousand slaves around the same time.

These rates were not high from the individual slave's viewpoint. Assuming that the average slave life expectancy was around thirty-five years, an annual manumission rate of one per thousand would mean that 3.5 percent of all slaves would be manumitted at some point in their lives, 7 percent at the rate of two per thousand, and so on.

While these rates still condemned the great majority of slaves to lifetime servitude, they did create the possibility—at the higher rates and given the characteristics of those manumitted—of a rising proportion of freedmen and freedwomen in the population over half a century or more. The slaves most likely to be manumitted, these essays confirm, included creoles and, outside North America, females. Women born in the Americas, whether slave or free, were much more fertile than those born in Africa. They had not experienced the traumas of enslavement and of the Middle Passage, and their dietary history was more favorable to reproduction. So the high proportion of females and of creoles among those manumitted made for high reproduction rates, especially when compared with the enslaved. While the slave population outside North America had negative reproduction rates, this was not true of the free people of color. In Brazil and many parts of Spanish America the urban slaves would be matched, after half a century of so, by a population of free people of color of similar size. In seventeenth-century Rio de Janeiro, Lima, Mexico City, Veracruz, and Havana, the slaves and free people of color comprised roughly half the population or more, and the two groups were of roughly equal size. Iberian America, to begin with, used African captives mainly in an urban context and was heavily influenced in doing so by medieval European slaveholding practices. William Phillips makes it clear that in medieval and early modern Europe the importance of manumission was qualitative rather than quantitative. Masters liked the power to manumit because it opened up several advantageous possibilities. It enabled them to reward slaves to whom they felt a special gratitude. It allowed them to encourage good behavior by dangling the prospect of freedom. And it enabled them to strike advantageous bargains with slaves who would pay above the market price for their freedom because it was worth more to them than to anybody else. Of course, the latter depended on slaves possessing earning power, especially earning power the owner found difficulty in monitoring. Masters who hired out skilled slaves, or allowed them to ply a trade, could not always easily keep track of their earnings. A manumission agreement enabled them to extract extra gain from slave ownership and to acquire the purchase price of a new slave by the time manumission was complete. But as Debra Blumenthal shows in her essay on manumission in Valencia, owners who had made such calculated offers of freedom would subsequently seek to retract them. Once a manumission agreement had been made, especially if it had been written down and formalized, then according to the laws of the Spanish kingdoms, a contract had been made and the manumitted person had some legal personality. For their part the owners might claim that the slave had not delivered the further years of good service or had absconded or raised a hand against a free person. In the most transparent cases she cites the masters even claimed that the offer was invalid because not they but their spouse was the true owner when the original agreement had been made. Because owners were better able to assemble witnesses and pay for legal representation, they may often have succeeded in nullifying contracts of manumission. But as Blumenthal indicates, the record does show slaves having recourse to the law and sometimes gaining their point.

Both Blumenthal and Phillips note the importance of religion to the institution of slavery and the practice of manumission. By law Muslims or Jews were forbidden to own Christian slaves. This helped to encourage Muslims and Jews to convert. Slaves who converted to Christianity might hope to claim their liberty if their owners did not convert too but would be more likely to bring about their sale to a Christian. Basing himself partly on the responsa of medieval rabbis, Jonathan Schorsch's study of Jewish practices of slavery and manumission shows they were transformed by contact with the New World systems of racial slavery. Traditionally, manumission had often been encouraged and could lead to the slave's integration as a member of the Jewish community. But in the New World manumission became more difficult and no longer led to integration for the freedperson.

The fact that the rise of the plantation systems made slavery a more concentrated, menial, and permanent condition inexorably meant that it cast a much heavier racial shadow. The "ruralization" of slavery, connected to the rise of plantation agriculture and the need for a great mass of menial gang laborers, was associated with a reduction of manumission rates and the growth of more racializing practices of enslavement (Jonathan Schorsch's essay furnishes a particularly good account of the pressures associated with the new context of plantation development). But over a generation or two, even plantation slavery itself gave rise to a problem of order—how to maintain the subjection of the numerous enslaved mass. And this could be met—to an extent which depended on the over overall balance between free and enslaved, white and colored—by offering privileges to a slave elite or to a layer of free people of color.

All slave regimes involve stigmatization of the other, whether conceived in ethnic, religious, or civilizational terms. But there can be little doubt that the New World slave systems produced a peculiarly intense and racialized identity, condemning not only the first-generation African captives but also their descendants to enslavement. In the new plantations of the seventeenth and eighteenth centuries there was generally little need for manumission as an incentive or mechanism of social control. The dynamic system of plantation slavery, based on the European consumers' limitless appetite for sugar, tobacco, coffee, and cotton, both stimulated the demand for tied labor and rested on a labor process that could be easily supervised. There were skilled slave craftsmen and drivers who received small privileges, but it did not seem to the planters that their productivity could be boosted if they were free. Indeed, if the slave carpenters, wheelwrights, and coopers had been free, they would have been able to bid up their wages considerably. Slaves sometimes earned small cash sums received as an incentive payment or for the sale of surplus produce or foodstuffs. However, the planters generally kept such arrangement far short of a situation allowing the slaves to buy their own freedom. Manumission offered few advantages and some inconveniences. But laws to prevent or tighten manumission are another matter, which cannot be explained in this way.

Slave owners who lacked the power freely to manumit suffered a diminution in their absolute dominion which could be galling. Slave owners practiced manumission where they were left to their own devices. The colonial state often saw reasons of policy for maintaining the racial order and for preventing the emergence of a free colored stratum that might weaken it. The free people of color might encourage slave pilfering or harbor runaways, for example. Because of such problems, slave owners themselves could resent manumissions granted by other slave owners. A further fear cited in many of these essays was that the emancipated slave could become a charge upon the community in sickness or old age. To obviate this slave owners were required to prove that this would not happen and, if necessary, to supply their freedmen and women with property to ensure they would not become a burden on others. Assemblies of slave owners were prone to fear that the growth of the free population of color would weaken the racial hierarchy and furnish ready-made allies to rebellious slaves.

In early-eighteenth-century North America, as the planters became mainly reliant on a slave labor force, the planter-dominated assemblies had put stiff obstacles in the way of manumission. The penalties and difficulties involved were to be lifted in the immediate post–Revolutionary War period for a decade or two. But the authorities, while greatly discouraging manumission, were unable completely to prevent the emergence of a free colored stratum. While some free people of color may have been descendants of runaways, or even of the tiny number of free Africans who had never been enslaved, manumission must have been the main source of these populations. In North America the free people of color were at all times greatly outnumbered by both the slave and the free white population. In 1790 the U.S. census recorded 59,000 free people of color and 698,000 slaves, with few as yet having been freed by northern emancipation laws where they existed because they freed only the children born to slave mothers and hence took a long time to come into effect. By 1860 there were 488,000 free people of color and 3,954,000 slaves. The northern emancipation laws or judgments would have contributed greatly to the 226,000 free colored population of the northern states but not at all to the 262,000 free colored population of the southern states, a community largely created by manumission, notwithstanding the prevalence of laws throughout the slave states making it difficult and costly and often requiring the removal of the freed person from the state. Indeed, given the hostility to manumission in English North America and in the antebellum U.S. South, the emergence of a free colored community at all testified more to the slaves' untiring efforts to free themselves and to the help they received from a few free people.

With his brilliant flair for synthesis, Orlando Patterson sets out for us not only the variables that have to be borne in mind when studying manumission but also a number of the most characteristic patterns.[5] Most of these patterns manage to combine the "gift" of a limited freedom to a particular individual with the reaffirmation of the master's superiority and of the social relations of slavery. And many characteristic patterns not only reaffirm slavery in the sphere of values but also furnish the slaveholders with the means to acquire new slaves. Thus slave soldiers offered their freedom would be used in Africa, especially Islamic Africa, as the means to make new captives, some of whom would, in their turn, become slave soldiers aspiring to free themselves. As noted above, the essays by William Phillips and Debra Blumenthal show that slaves who plied a trade could be allowed to buy their freedom over a lengthy period—and for a price which would enable more slaves to be purchased. Patterson sees the beginnings of a capitalist logic in this commercial reproduction of slavery.

Some of the key manumission patterns identified by Patterson were largely absent in New World colonial societies (Native American practices of traditional slavery being another question). In the pattern he calls "domestic assimilation," slaves themselves might have little chance of ever being manumitted, but their children would become junior members of the masters' household. Where matrilineal kinship rules were dominant, as in parts of West Africa, acquisition of a slave allowed masters to strengthen their own rather than their spouses' lineage because slave women had no kin identity or lineage of their own. Since none of the European cultures had matrilineal descent rules, the incentive for this type of "circumvention" did not exist. Paradoxically the slave owners of the Americas adopted the rule of matrilineal descent only for the slave condition. By adopting this approach—similar to that obtaining for domestic animals and beasts of burden—slave owners established a gulf between themselves and their human chattels and made the possibility of manumission the more problematic.

In some cases, especially in the earlier period, European masters still practiced a species of "domestic assimilation" when they sponsored the freedom of slave concubines and their children. This encouraged the view that manumission of this type was the main explanation for the emergence of free colored populations in the Americas. The essays in this book confirm that a few masters did seek to free their slave children and the latter's slave mothers. But Rosemary Brana-Shute brings forward compelling evidence that neither sexual relations between free men and slave women nor the appearance of offspring, necessarily, or even typically, led to manumission. Brana-Shute is convinced that in the case of the plantation society of Dutch colonial Suriname, this species of sponsored manumission could explain no more than a third, and possibly much less, of all acts of manumission. Indeed, many cases of manumission—for example of adult males, black infants and youths, or those involving lengthy self-purchase—are unlikely to involve the white masters' gratitude or paternal pride. Brana-Shute reminds us that sexual exploitation of slave women was far more frequent than any disposition to recognize offspring. Furthermore, obtaining manumission could be difficult and costly. The manumission of slaves did crucially depend on sponsorship by free people, but on the evidence furnished in this book, it is clear that these were often free people of color related in some way to the enslaved person.

Slave owners enjoyed an extraordinary power which they did not lightly give up. John F. Campbell draws our attention to the case of Thomas Thistlewood in eighteenth-century Jamaica, an estate manager who had sex with many slave women and who would have had some offspring as a result. But in only one case, that of Phibba, the slave housekeeper who became his concubine, did he strive to obtain manumission for mother and child. Yet for many years Phibba's master would neither sell her nor hire her out to Thistlewood, instead using his attachment to her to retain Thistlewood's valued services as a manager. In this case denial of manumission enabled the owner to achieve extra leverage over his manager as well as over his slave Phibba.[6]

Slave owners' unwillingness to give up their extraordinary dominion was compounded by its conceptual and legal difficulty. Since the power of the master over his slave was complete, and the slave a social zero, it was impossible for the former to negotiate with the latter. The act of manumission, even if paid for, overflowed any possible price and thus had to be conceptualized as a "gift." Yet as anthropologists have stressed since the classic work of Marcel Mauss, the gift relationship is inherently unequal and leaves the recipient with obligations to the donor commensurate with the importance of the gift. The powerful negative associations of New World slavery could not be washed away by manumission but instead remained a burden. This was especially true so long as many of African descent remained in slavery—but remained as a legacy even after general emancipation.

Patterson urges us to consider the scope for somewhat higher manumission rates opened up by "plantocratic cooptation" in the Caribbean, where the slaves hugely outnumbered the free white population. To begin with, the racial character of the New World slave systems—the fact that only Africans and their descendants were enslaved—militated against high manumission rates and degraded the status of the free people of color. But eventually, where whites were a tiny minority, the emergence of even a small population of free people of color could become a major consideration in a complex equation of power. This logic eventually led to concessions to free people of color in most parts of the Caribbean and in Brazil but not in the United States, where there was a large white population in the slave zone. While in the Caribbean the problem of runaways led to the arming of black slave catchers, in North America the free colored were excluded from the patrols and the militia.

In general the planters in the British Caribbean islands only gradually become aware of the need to allow the free people of color enough latitude to make them into reliable defenders of the slave order. In Jamaica, as Campbell emphasizes, the condition of the manumitted person long remained barely above that of the slave. But as Patterson points out, both colonial authorities and planters found the greatest difficulty in maintaining order and suppressing the maroons, so they eventually recognized the latter and sought to employ them in defense of the slave regime. As Patterson also observes, by 1790 or thereabouts the British planters and colonial authorities saw the necessity of elevating the condition of some free people of color as a way of underpinning both slavery and British control. Spain and Portugal had long envisaged "military manumission," the freeing of slaves who fought to defend the established power. In the 1790s the British army, locked in a punishing struggle with revolutionary France, purchased slave soldiers and promised them their freedom. Eventually, as Patterson notes, there was a disposition to concede more—rights to all free people of color in the British West Indies.

The contributions confirm Orlando Patterson's thesis that the variable characteristics of any slave regime are thrown into sharp relief by the possibilities of manumission that it offers, or fails to offer, and that the paths to manumission condition the quality of freedom eventually gained. Some slave regimes conceded a little more scope for manumission than others. Manumission as a legal act could be promoted or discouraged by the state, but the actual negotiation of offers of freedom by masters and slaves sometimes anticipated, qualified, or even flouted the law. Masters claiming ownership of slaves often believed themselves to enjoy an untrammeled authority to dispose of their property as they wished. This could clash with the claims of the sovereign power, even if the latter was responding to the fears of other slave owners.

Manumission was conceived of as a gift, even when the slave had tendered decades of service or had paid for it with hard-earned cash. Like other gifts, it left the recipient of freedom deeply beholden. In Roman law the former slave was to owe a debt of gratitude and respect to the former owner that could never be discharged. The servile relationship was transmuted into that of patron to client. The mere existence of paths to manumission would offer, perhaps, a spark of hope to other slaves. The exercise of the power of manumission could confirm the legitimacy and benevolence of master and sovereign power.

Manumission, Brana-Shute observes, should be seen as a process rather than an isolated act. Slaves who might aspire to manumission would know that this was likely to take many years and that it would require their constant and faithful service. Those most eligible for manumission were either those in direct contact with their owner—a consideration that favored domestics and members of the slave elite but excluded field slaves—or those who, as Patterson puts it, had "direct control of [their] earnings and occupation."

While plantation owners came under pressure to free elite slaves, these were the very people on whom they were most dependent for maintaining output and income. Domestic slaves were sometimes seen in a different light, especially if they were willing to remain as servants or were in anyway aged. In a typical sequence noted in several of the essays, the slave might be promised eventual freedom as a result of an owner's gratitude or uneasiness over slavery. Slave domestics who nursed a master or family member when they were badly ill might receive such a promise. However, manumission would be deferred until they were older or until their owner died. Slaves freed by testament also still had to secure legal execution of the bequest. The will might be contested by the owner's heirs or might fail to conform to the full requirements for manumission. In the English and Dutch colonies the authorities were likely to be concerned that the freedperson should not become a burden on the public in sickness or old age. Several essays note laws requiring that freedpeople be endowed with property or required to leave the colony (the latter stipulation being motivated by the desire to prevent a growing free population of color as well as economic motives, of course). Agreements allowing self-purchase would stretch over many years and require great tenacity from the slave purchaser. The complexity of any negotiation over manumission would usually be very great, with owners changing their minds or changing preconditions and invariably enjoying better access to the relevant authorities or judicial processes. Only slaves who had determined sponsors among the free population were liable to gain their freedom at the end of it.

However, while an owner's willingness to negotiate manumission would reflect individual motives, the possibility that these would lead to this particular conclusion was very much dependent on the wider context. The essays on the United States by Eva Sheppard Wolfe, Ellen Eslinger, and Sean Condon bring this out clearly. Between 1782 and 1806 manumission became far easier in Virginia than it had been before or was subsequently to be. The values of the revolutionary epoch and the keenness of Methodists, Quakers, and Baptists to demonstrate their own commitment to right conduct at this time were both favorable to a higher rate of manumission. They prompted both new legislation and a climate of opinion in particular regions and communities that led to high manumission rates. The 1780s and 1790s also saw some abatement of economic pressure to maintain slavery since the tobacco economy was in a weakened state. But the great slave rebellion in Saint-Domingue and the impact of its example on African Americans evident in Gabriel's conspiracy (1800) fostered a white panic that was not favorable to manumission in the U.S. South. The new vitality of the cotton economy following the introduction of the cotton gin also made manumission less attractive.

Eric Burin and Ellen Eslinger note that southern supporters of manumission were drawn to the advantages of "colonization," or ensuring that those freed by manumission returned to Africa. Notwithstanding the great attractions of freedom, many of the enslaved found the prospect of achieving it at the cost of separation from loved ones too great a price a pay. And antebellum slavery was largely rural, not urban, and thus, according to Eslinger, stony ground for hopes of manumission because masters had less need of this tactic to control their slaves. In an urban setting relatives helped one another through the complicated hoops of manumission, while in the countryside family attachments complicated matters since emancipation meant leaving the plantation. Familial ties among both masters and slave complicated and often prevented the individual act of manumission. A master could be very uneasy about slavery but still deem it wrong to deprive his children of their inheritance, just as a slave might refuse to be parted from kin even to attain freedom. And even if a master deeded the manumission of his slaves in his will, his heirs or executors might neglect or challenge his wishes. Finally, Scott Hancock also shows us that the wider social and political context also shaped African American aspirations as they discovered a New World identity which counteracted the colonization effort.

Manumission rates in the Brazilian empire also reflected shifts in the political conjuncture and in social conditions. In the 1830s and 1840s the dismal fate of the libertos related by Beatriz Gallotti Mamigonian showed a pitiless appetite for slave labor. The libertos were slaves who had been cargo aboard slave-trading vessels captured by naval patrols established by the treaties between Britain and Brazil aimed at suppressing the slave traffic. If captured near Brazilian waters, these slaves were turned over to the Brazilian authorities, who were supposed to make arrangements for their custody and eventual freedom. But in practice the libertos were hired out as unfree toilers to the benefit of the public treasury or required to work for government institutions or ministers. Eventually, a few libertos were able to sue for their freedom, but often with little success. Keila Grinberg's study of the hearing of freedom suits by the Rio de Janeiro Court of Appeals shows a rise from about thirty-five suits per decade in the period 1823 to 1850 to a rate of one hundred per decade in the years 1850 to 1870. In the second half of the century matters improved slowly and unsteadily, first with the final suppression of slave imports in the 1850s and then in 1860s and 1870s with legislation which made it easier to manumit. But it was not until the 1880s that social pressure on owners led to widespread manumission, especially in the declining northeast outside the dynamic plantation zone, prior to abolition in 1888. Grinberg shows that the court of appeals was more likely to overturn a lower court judgment favorable to manumission than one favorable to slavery, essentially because the lower courts were so vulnerable to direct representations from slave owners. While the judges in the capital tended to be more enlightened, only small numbers gained access to the appeals court.

Most of the studies published here point out that manumission was designed to strengthen slavery, and usually it did so. But most also show the extraordinary efforts required from slaves and their free supporters if they wished really to benefit from the offers and possibilities dangled in from of them. While there was a great gulf between manumission and acts of emancipation, there were also indirect ways in which the former eventually helped to set the scene for the latter. Manumission theoretically applied to an individual but often affected other members of a family or estate. Success usually required the support of free relatives, friends, and work mates. Where masters sought to weasel out of their promises—there are many examples in the essays which follow—the result was often a "freedom suit," which made even greater demands on the courage and resources of the manumittee's friends and family. On occasion such cases aroused a wider public opinion or could lead to judicial decisions which critically weakened the powers of the slaveholder. On a few notable occasions from parts of Europe and North America in the 1760s to

Brazil's Northeast in the 1880s, acts of manumission, whether contested or not, helped to establish a wider public opinion hostile to slavery. Free people of color, many of them manumittees, played a key role in these developments. This does not contradict the observation that manumission was quite different from emancipation, but it does show that the enslaved and their supporters did eventually find a way of linking the one to the other.

The cultural consequences of manumission emerge from these studies as a topic that will have to be further explored. Instead of diminishing racial sentiment, manumission sometimes confirmed it since the manumittees remained marked as former slaves and as clients of their former masters or of the sovereign power. The Brazilian emperor would enact ceremonial manumissions on his birthday as if this was a proof of his sovereign power. When democratic and republic assemblies enacted manumission or emancipation, this was also a proof of sovereignty. Instead of being the property of an individual slave owner, the freed individual might be deemed to stand in a subordinate position to all those citizens who had, as it were, given them their freedom. This abject condition was not acceptable to the freemen and women and they sought means of alleviating it. In early Spanish and Portuguese America the former slave would find a new identity in membership of a religious brotherhood. In the antebellum United States free people of color played a large part in the founding of black churches and in supporting the abolitionist movement. In the postbellum United States, and in some of the South American republics, organizations of black veterans embodied the claim to civic dignity.

Orlando Patterson has written about the momentous contribution of the manumitted and their descendants in the ancient world to the spread of Pauline Christianity and its distinctive notion of freedom. We should consider the possibility that New World manumissions helped to nourish a milieu which gave birth to a variety of religious and political movements that embodied aspirations for a new birth of liberty appropriate to a New World setting. The origins of African American music, storytelling, religion, and politics are nearly everywhere reflective not only of the slave community and of African traditions but also of the travail of the manumitted and of other free people of color. The reader will find many examples of this cumulative and many-faceted phenomenon in the essays that follow.

NOTES

1. Frank Tannenbaum, *Slave and Citizen: The Negro in the Americas* (New York: Knopf, 1947).

2. Carl Degler, *Neither Black nor White: Slavery and Race Relations in Brazil and the United States* (New York: Macmillan, 1971; reprint, Madison: University of Wisconsin Press, 1986).

3. Charles Frostin, *Les Révoltes blanches à Saint-Domingue aux XVIIe et XVIIIe siècles: Haïti avant 1789* (Paris: l'École, 1966).

4. Ira Berlin, *Slaves Without Masters: The Free Negro in the Antebellum South* (New York: New Press, 1974).

5. Orlando Patterson summarizes and develops his analysis in his essay in this volume. His earlier formulations remain very much worth consulting; see also Orlando Patterson, *Slavery and Social Death: A Comparative Study* (Cambridge, Mass.: Harvard University Press, 1982), 209–296.

6. Douglas Hall, ed., *In Miserable Slavery: Thomas Thistlewood on Jamaica, 1750–86* (London: Macmillan, 1989; Kingston: University of the West Indies Press, 1999), 66–67, 148.

7. Orlando Patterson, *Freedom in the Making of Western Culture,* vol. 1 of *Freedom* (New York: Basic Books, 1991), esp. 316–345.

ORLANDO PATTERSON

Three Notes of Freedom

—ɯ—

The Nature and Consequences of Manumission

Manumission has been one of the most important institutions in the history of the West both because of its role in ancient and modern slavery and because it is the social source of the two most important shapers of Western culture: the ideal of freedom and the religion of Christianity. In the ancient and medieval world it was the critical institution in the invention of freedom. But what is less well known is the fact that it was decisive in the development of Christian thought and doctrine. First I define manumission and the problems it poses. Then I move to a discussion individual manumission and its frequency within and between societies. Third, I refine a framework for understanding how manumission rates and freedmen status interact to create various kinds of manumission systems. And finally, I discuss the major consequences of manumission in modern postslavery Western societies.

What is manumission? In the simplest dictionary terms it means the release from slavery; the word derives from the Latin *manumittere*—literally, to let go from the hand or set at liberty. Manumission, however, was easier said than conceived of or done. In nearly all slave societies manumission posed the same set of conceptual and ideological problems: If the slave completely belongs to the master, how is he to be released? To understand why this is a problem, one must first grasp the nature of slavery itself. Slavery is more than simply a matter of ownership of one person by another.[1] All slaves are owned, but not all owned people are slaves, as children, women, and certain categories of men in many societies will attest.

Rather, slavery is a relation of domination in which one person claims total power over another and achieves this by the act of natal alienation. The slave, that is, is totally deracinated and does not belong in any legitimate way to the community in which he lives. The master's power inheres in the absence of all legitimate claims of the slave on the part of other people. Reciprocally, the slave has no claims of, or protection from, others, not even his closest kinsmen. Almost everywhere this condition is a form of social death. This concept was not something I imposed on the comparative data; rather, it was something that emerged inductively, indeed, that literally screamed at me in nearly every case I observed from one end of the universe of slave societies to the other, and especially those of the Atlantic world.

The slave was a man possessed who was incapable of possession, and this included, quintessentially, the possession of self. This being so, attempting to release someone from slavery posed at least three problems. One was the problem of alienation from the master. The most familiar instances of this were found in more advanced societies in which property played an important role in the economy and self-purchase was a major means of release. How was it possible for the slave to buy himself since everything he owned belonged to the master? Actually, this was not the really interesting problem, since slave societies have found all sorts of rough-and-ready means of getting around this in purely practical terms—the Roman *peculium* and its modern derivations, especially in Latin America, being the best-known means.

Far more interesting was the fact that both ancient and modern legal theorists have had a hard time coming up with a legal conception of the manumission process. The temptation is to conceive of it as a conveyance, but a moment's reflection shows that it is no such thing, since conveyancing involves the passing of something or the title of something from a seller or conveyancer to a buyer of conveyance, and what the latter receives is that which the former parts with. This, however, was not what happened in a manumission transaction since the master did not pass his power or dominion over to the slave. What the master gave up—his power over the slave—was not what the slave received.

The real mystery of manumission was that it involved the social construction, by master and slave, of something entirely new. Equally problematic was the fact that the slave was essentially a nonperson, someone without a will of his own, a mere surrogate of another. How did a nonperson become a person? If one is to believe the master's claim—that his slaves were mere surrogates of his own will—how did it happen that one of these surrogates suddenly became a person with a will of his own?

This immediately raises yet another problem, perhaps the most serious for all parties contemplating manumitting. Manumission was a private act with immediate social and public consequences. For this reason, in all slaveholding societies, third parties—nonslaveholding freemen—took a keen interest in the act of manumission and what it brought into being, that is, the freedman. It may be one thing for the master to decide that his slave was no longer a socially dead nonperson but quite another for third parties who usually had nothing to gain from the transaction—in contrast with the master, who often profited handsomely—to suddenly change their views on the subject. Indeed, the problem for many slave societies was that many slaves who were manumitted by the master remained slaves to nonmasters. In many small, kin-based societies such as the Tupinamba of northeastern Brazil, the idea of the freed slave was so abhorrent, so socially inconceivable, that their only fate was to be sacrificed and in some cases eaten. But this was no remote problem confined to kin-based ancient and premodern societies. As Ira Berlin and others have shown, freed slaves in America were truly slaves without masters.[2] And it should come as no surprise that the most brutal period of African American history was the three-quarters of a century between the end of Reconstruction and World War II, when the sacrificial culture of lynching—the defining communal ritual of the postslavery South—finally drew to a close.

How was this problem of alienation solved? Were there common patterns in the approach used by peoples in different parts of the world and, in particular, the Atlantic world? I think there were. Slave societies generally used the cultural strategy of the gift exchange to both express and negotiate the manumission transaction. Note that what we are concerned with here is the sociocultural problem of manumission—the means by which it was interpreted, explained, and legitimized to all three parties involved: master, slave, and free person. The actual mechanics of manumission, the means of compensation and the negotiated terms of the release, was another, far less complex issue, which will be discussed below.

All over the Atlantic world, as elsewhere, manumission was culturally interpreted as a gift from the master to the slave—a gift, however, that completed one triad of social exchanges and initiated another. Manumission stood in the midst of a series of processes that, in ideological and cultural terms, began with enslavement, which was the ultimate form of separation and alienation, whether attained by capture, purchase, or birth. The slave's social death was itself the primal exchange; the master imagined himself giving physical life and sustenance for the slave's degradation into social death, his total obedience to the master's will. The slave reciprocated with the gift of faithful service. The master completes the first triad by giving the slave the gift of social life in exchange for faithful service. His gift is a double negation—the negation of the negation of his social death. This, in turn, begins a new round of exchanges, for in nearly all societies the former slave is expected to remain forever grateful to the former master, who has now become his patron. The fee the slave or his redeemer pays is a mere token, an expression of gratitude for the master's freely given decision to release the slave from his eternal bondage.

This, as noted earlier, was a cultural process, the way in which the transaction was made meaningful, explained, and rationalized. In reality we can see what actually transpired in most slave societies. The whole transaction was often horribly exploitative. The master and the master class gained throughout. For what manumission, or rather the prospect of manumission, did was to solve the chronic problem created by slavery: that of motivation—how to get an utterly degraded and socially dead person to serve faithfully and productively. While psychologists call this problem one of motivation, economists call it a problem of incentive. By whatever definition, slavery ended up as a seemingly hopeless contradiction. For many theorists, the contradiction was without resolution. Hence, what arose—among other theories—was the celebrated view of Adam Smith that slavery had to collapse of its own accord, especially in a capitalist society, since it was absurd to expect so degraded and demoralized a worker to do anything else but shirk and, at every turn, undermine his owner's desire for efficiency. Many economists and social theorists from Adam Smith through John Cairnes right down to Eugene Genovese have been infatuated with this seemingly unassailable logic.[3]

We now know that they were wrong. For the empirical reality was that slavery worked. And not only did it work, but it worked tragically well. Whole civilizations have prospered on it: ancient Greece and Rome for centuries, Visigothic Spain, Merovingian France, the premodern advanced states of Ashanti and Dahomey, the many advanced city-states of the Yorubas, the numerous warrior states of the Sahel (Songhay, Mali, and Timbuktu), and more recently the Fulani, the Hausas, and the Tuaregs. The rise of Islam was made possible by this institution, as were the trading states of the Vikings and other Scandinavians. And we now know from the work of the cliometricians and others that capitalism, far from being inherently incompatible with slavery, thrived on it. The New World slave systems, as scholars from Eric Williams to Robin Blackburn have demonstrated, were not aberrations in the onward march of capitalism toward freedom but a critical and historically fundamental version of the rise and spread of capitalism, complementing and substantially propelling its free-labor version.[4]

Why was slavery so successful in spite of its inherent contradictions? The answer, quite simply, was that with a few major exceptions, its incentive problem was solved by the institutional process of manumission. Manumission, I am saying, was an integral and necessary part of the process of slavery in all but a few advanced slave societies. This was the naked reality. Still, the iron fist of oppression had to be gloved even with—especially with—this most extreme and total form of the relations of domination. In Rousseau's words ways had to be found of "transforming force into right and obedience into duty."[5] Culture was the means by which this was achieved. And in the case of slavery, as in many other forms of domination, the culture of the gift exchange was the symbolic process by which slavery was clothed, interpreted, and resolved in the interest of the master class.

If you are skeptical of all this, it may come as a shock to you to learn that the culture of the gift exchange is still alive and well in the United States, arguably the world's most advanced capitalist society. If you are reluctant to take the word of a historical sociologist discussing the behavior of slaves and masters on this matter, let me digress for a moment and bring to your attention the current work of one of the world's most distinguished economists. In a brilliant series of papers the Berkeley economist and recent Nobel Laureate George Akerlof has argued that the modern U.S. labor contract can be best interpreted as a "partial gift exchange." Firms, especially those in the primary sector, he argues, "willingly pay workers in excess of the market-clearing wage; in return they expect workers to supply more effort than they would if equivalent jobs could be readily obtained (as is the case if wages are just at market clearing)." Traditional neoclassical theories of wages, based on the laws of demand and supply, simply cannot explain the seeming paradox of why a profit-motivated employer would want to pay more than the clearing wage. Nor can it explain the well-documented fact that workers often contribute far more than what is required by their employment contract and the norms set by the firm.[6]

Akerlof uses gift-exchange theory to show how "the loyalty of workers is exchanged for high wages, and this loyalty can be translated via effective management into high productivity." Here is how he sums up, in plain English, his mathematically derived model of the capitalist gift exchange:

> The giving of gifts is almost always determined by norms of behavior. In most cases the gift given is approximately in the range of what the recipient expects, and he reciprocates in kind. The norms of gift giving are determined by the relationship between the parties; thus, for example, it is expected that an increase in workers' productivity will be rewarded by increased wages to the workers. Much of union wage negotiations concern the question of what constitutes a *fair* wage. To an economist who believes that wages are market-clearing or only determined by the relative bargaining power of the contractual parties, long discussions about the "fair wage" should have no bearing on the final settlement. But this notion neglects the fact that the average worker works harder than necessary according to the firm's rules, and in return for this donation of goodwill and effort, he expects a fair wage from the firm.[7]

In more recent work Akerlof has bolstered his theory of gift exchange by drawing on the industrial studies of the sociologist Michael Burawoy, who demonstrates how a culture of gaming and equity among workers, engaged in by them in order to make their lives more bearable, is translated into higher productivity and profit for firms.[8]

The theory of gift exchange, it should be noted, was first developed by anthropologist Marcel Mauss in his study of preliterate societies.[9] Slaves, precisely because they had no power, resorted to this most fundamental form of interaction between human beings. They had no choice, but neither did the master caught in the crisis of motivation. Playing the gift-exchange game was somewhat analogous to communicating in pidgin where both parties needed desperately to communicate and so resorted to the most basic linguistic processes that made it possible.

The ritual of the gift exchange was the ideological elaboration of the whole series of linked processes that began with enslavement, proceeded through the brutal dialectics of enslavement, continued in the ritual of manumission, and culminated in the dependency relationship between freedman and former master. In this way manumission—far from being a termination or undermining of slavery—became in most cases an integral part of the system of slavery and, in most slave societies, not only nicely resolved its inherent contradictions but also was a major basis of support for the entire system.

Two things followed from this. One was that manumission had little to do with the abolition of slavery. Thus it is incorrect to expect that a slave system with a high rate of manumission was in any way on the path to abolition. The often-repeated expression of amazement that almost no one even hinted at the abolition of slavery in the ancient world, and that Christianity and Islam both condoned it, is really an expression of naïveté, when not wholly anachronistic. Second, manumitted people, while they nearly always cherished their freedom, rarely developed any hostility to the institution of slavery. To the contrary, what the successful freedman in most slave societies usually most desired was to achieve the status of master, of slaveholder himself. This was overwhelmingly the case in ancient Rome, as Petronius's wickedly satirical novel about the freedman Trimalchio makes clear. But it was equally true of the slave systems of Atlantic Africa, as it was of Latin America and, sad to say, even the United States (among the few who were freed and who had the resources to purchase fellow human beings). To the modern person this may seem perverse. We want to believe that the former slave behaved consistently and honorably, if not heroically. We desperately want to view these people as heroes who defied the system that had oppressed them and sought to relieve those left behind from the shackles of thralldom. But with the exception of a few former slaves in the antebellum United States, such as the truly heroic Frederick Douglass, most former slaves were thoroughly coopted by the system of slavery. All over the Atlantic world—including the U.S. South but especially in places such as Brazil, Saint-Domingue, Cuba, and the slave-based city states of the Ibibios in the Niger delta and South Africa—all successful former slaves seized the first opportunity to get their own slaves.

And what was true of those who achieved their freedom by legitimate means held equally for those who achieved it through rebellion and maroonage. Many years ago I studied the series of slave revolts in Jamaica that were collectively known as the First Maroon Wars.[10] These wonderful rebels not only fiercely fought the British for over eighty years but also eventually forced the imperial power to sue for peace and to humiliatingly accept a state-within-a state arrangement—the maroon communities of Jamaica. And what did these heroic rebels do with their freedom? Well, among the clauses of the treaty signed with the British was one in which the maroons agreed to return or hunt down runaway slaves for a bounty to be paid by the master class. Indeed, it is very likely that, had it not been for the maroons, Jamaica would have long preceded Haiti as the country with the first truly successful slave revolt.

Both the social problems posed by manumission and the gift-exchange process by which it was culturally negotiated and rationalized explain the otherwise puzzling array of means used to manumit slaves throughout the Atlantic world. While self-purchase was to become a major means of manumission in the more advanced capitalistic slave systems, especially in Brazil and the United States, it was not the most widespread, and in many slave regimes, especially in Africa, it was rather unusual. Instead, we find in addition to self-purchase, means of manumission such as the postmortem or testamentary mode, the cohabitational or concubinal mode, adoption, political or state manumission, various forms of collusive manumission, and occasionally, especially in Africa, forms of sacral manumission similar to those found in Delphi.

I have discussed these modes of manumission at great length in *Slavery and Social Death* and have only a few passing remarks to make on them here. Postmortem manumission was of enormous cultural significance in most slave societies and was invariably associated with religious doctrine and ritual. It was perhaps one of the earliest modes of manumitting slaves. In many African and pre-Columbian slave societies it was a surrogate for earlier practices of sacrificing slaves on the death of their masters, and indeed it continued to exist with the practice of sacrificing slaves in many parts of West Africa. It takes little anthropological knowledge to see how the testamentary freeing of slaves was intimately related to notions of gift exchange between both the living and the dead and the dead master and his god. Since the slave was socially dead, it made sense that the master's own death was the occasion for the slave's release from death. People everywhere strived to make their deaths meaningful by associating it with life—whether in doctrines of immortality or in notions of ancestral spirits guarding the household. What more obvious a symbol of death as life giving is there than to make the master's death the occasion for the slave's rebirth into social life? It not only placed an awesome burden on the slave to repay the gift of life by honoring the memory of the master and serving his heirs faithfully but also was also a gift to the gods, a sacrificial surrogate meant for the spiritual masters whom the master himself was about to meet. All the great world religions eventually came to view manumission as a special act of piety, especially Islam, which is explicit in its doctrinal advocacy of such acts.

Manumission as a result of sexual relations with slaves and the fathering of children with them was another major means of release from slavery. Slaves were sexually exploited everywhere that slavery existed. However, as many of the essays in this volume show, the Atlantic slave systems varied greatly in the degree to which such relationships were recognized and the tendency to which concubines or the children of concubines were manumitted: from the Islamic slave systems of Africa at one extreme, through precapitalist Latin America, to the U.S. South at the other extreme. Recent studies have also greatly increased our knowledge of the extent to which state or political manumission operated in the Americas. In the 1970s and early 1980s, when I did research for *Slavery and Social Death*, I came away with the impression that this was an isolated mode, used rarely and very reluctantly during periods of crisis. We now know, thanks to many fine recent studies, some of them in this volume, that this practice was far more widely distributed than previously thought.

Another major area of concern among students of manumission is the explanation of the incidence of manumission and the varying rates between different slave regimes. We must be careful to distinguish these two, a point too often missed by several scholars. Explaining why certain kinds of individuals in a given slave society were more likely to be manumitted is not the same thing as explaining why some slave societies have higher rates than others, even if the variables tend to overlap. One is an individual-level explanation, the other calls for a macro-level analysis, and one easily commits what sociologist call the ecological fallacy if we fail to distinguish between the two kinds of explanations.

Regarding the incidence of manumission—the isolation of those attributes of individuals which explain their greater propensity to be released from slavery—the many studies on the subject have generated a number of variables, the most important being gender, parental status, relation to the master, somatic factors such as "race" and/or color, age, whether local or foreign born, means of acquisition, ethnicity, occupation, and control of earnings and location (whether urban, mining, rural small farm, plantation or latifundia). Many of these variables are closely interrelated, and indeed it is possible to do a principal component analysis of them so as to reduce their number without losing explanatory power. One hypothesized reduction renders gender, parental status, relation to master, and the color or "race" of the individual as a single component which may be termed "status"; a second reduces age, whether local or foreign born, means of acquisition, and ethnicity to a demographic component; and a third component reduces occupation, control of earnings, and location to a single economic factor.

And my own earlier work, along with those of others, have suggested some surprising noneffects. Color, for example, was far less important than appeared at first sight, once we take account of location, occupation, and relation to master. A principal component analysis would almost certainly show it to have very low uniqueness value, and the same may well hold for the urbanism variable. On the other hand, control of earnings and occupation, both related to some degree, may well be the most powerful variables in explaining individual variations in manumission. Turning now to the question of varying rates of manumission across slave societies, my review of recent studies, plus those conducted earlier, indicates a large number of potential variables (see table 1).

TABLE 1. Main variables in the explanation of manumission rates
          and freedman status

Type of slave economy	% Slaves
Economic cycle	% Free
Replacement cost of slave	% Freedmen
External availability of slaves	% Of free who are freedmen
% Slave owners absentee	% Whites
Religion	% Mixed race
Legal system	% Black
Sexual attitudes	Sex ratio of masters
Racial attitudes	Sex ratio of slaves
Wala [patron-client] relationship	Native/foreign ratio among slaves
Political autonomy	Native/foreign ratio among free
Regime type: settler democracy or not?	Slave rate of reproduction
External military threats	Free rate of reproduction
Domestic security threats: maroonage	Freed rate of reproduction

Different scholars have emphasized different clusters of these variables, but we have not gotten very far for the simple reason that there is often no good reason given for the particular configuration of variables chosen, other than the whim or special interests of the scholar. I strongly urge students of manumission to use one or other of the variable reduction statistical techniques to make their work more manageable and to employ factor analysis to sort out the explanatory problem. Simply dipping into this bag of variables and offering up whatever configuration comes to mind will no longer do. In spite of the large number of studies on this subject, there is as yet no half-decent theory of manumission rates. And there never will be one if we continue using current eyeballing, trial-and-error methods of analysis.

I will not have much to say about the status of freedmen for two reasons. First, this is not a volume about freedmen and their status but about manumission. Second—and contrary to what some scholars imagine—there is no necessary relationship between manumission rates and the status of freedmen. There were societies with high manumission rates in which the status of freedmen, by any measure, was dreadful—as in many of the mining and urban areas of Brazil, but most notably in Curaçao, where massive unemployment among the freed led to chronic urban poverty and gang warfare among the freed in a freakish precursor of modern shanty towns and ghettos. At the other extreme we find societies that were hostile to manumission with generally low rates in which the freed had relatively good status. The best example here is early nineteenth-century Jamaica, where the small freed population was able to win full civil liberties at the same time as the Jews, even in the face of a hostile planter class.

There also were slave societies in which manumission was high and the condition of freedmen relatively good, as was true of the pre-plantation Latin Caribbean and the southern cone region of South America, especially Buenos Aries. At the other extreme there were cases where the rates were low, the planter class was hostile, and the condition of freedmen were generally dreadful, if not impossible, the most obvious case being the U.S. South, but also places such as eighteenth-century Suriname. The variables mentioned earlier are also those that explain these patterns and outcomes. Take as an example the pattern in which manumission rates were low but the status of freedmen relatively good. This pattern I call the system of *plantocratic cooptation*. Here the critical variables were the low percentage of whites, the low ratio of free to slave, the high risk of slave revolts, the existence of maroon communities, and the high rate of foreign-born people among both the slave population and the white and master class. All of these factors created a situation favorable to the free colored group. The free coloreds of the British Caribbean are cases in point.

Spanish Louisiana was typical of the pattern I call *pre-capitalist assimilation*. Here we find that a combination of high urbanism, high levels of dependence on slaves for skilled tasks, high levels of imperial control, a high rate of miscegenation, an institutionalization of the postmanumission patron-client relationship, and above all considerable risk of invasion from foreign nations created an environment that favored both high manumission rates and relatively high status of freedmen—high, that is, in relation to freedmen elsewhere. In the societies of Atlantic Africa other factors were important in determining particular configurations of manumission and freed status. In earlier work I have the four basic patterns found there: *domestic assimilation, matrilineal circumvention, predatory circulation*, and *commercial reproduction*. Let me say a brief word on a couple of these manumission regimes or patterns. *Domestic assimilation* was the most common. The slave population was small and intragenerational manumission low. However, the children of female slaves were eventually assimilated into free status as junior members of their master-father's household so that intergenerational manumission was actually quite high. Most of the lineage-based societies of Africa fall into this pattern.

In sharp contrast are those Atlantic African slaveholding societies in which the matrilineal rule of descent prevailed. Manumission rates were low here, both intra- and intergenerationally. Slaves were sometimes recruited for economic reasons, as among the Ashanti, but the main motive was that it provided powerful men with a way of circumventing the matrilineal rule whereby a man's natural children belong to, and inherited from their mother's brothers. The natural children of slave women, on the other hand, belong to the man and his household and, as such, they could be used to build up a strong following. However, for this reason, such children had no legitimate claims on any lineage and in this respect remained social outsiders forever.

Finally, there is the manumission regime I have called *predatory circulation*; here slaves were pivotal in what were economically more complex societies and were used as both reproducers as well as major producers of wealth for the elites. As retainers they also directly supported their power. The wealth slaves generated was used to acquire yet more slaves and as retainers for slaves and freedmen who actually assisted their masters in raids for slaves. There was a high level of both intra- and intergenerational manumission in these regimes. This was due to several factors: high levels of concubinage and the assimilation of concubines and their children into free status, the dependence of the free on agricultural and pastoral slaves who largely worked on their own, and the generally high level of availability of outside sources of slaves, which lowered the replacement cost of those already enslaved. Islamic slave doctrine, where it existed, also played an important role in explaining both the rate of manumission and the status of freedpeople. I include in the predatory circulation regime almost all the Islamic societies of Atlantic Africa and the Sahel. Among non-Islamic West Africans I include most of the Yoruba slave regimes and those of the Ibibios of the Oil Rivers in what is now Nigeria.

I move now to issues concerning the major consequences of manumission. One of these is that the patterns of race and racism that were to emerge in, and continue to bedevil, New World societies were largely determined by the kind of manumission regimes that existed in former slaveholding societies. Again, space allows me to discuss this in only the briefest terms. As students of comparative race relations have long pointed out, several patterns of "race" and racism existed in the Americas. There is the American binary pattern based on notions of racial purity and the notorious one-drop rule of racial definition. There is the South American pattern, best exemplified by Brazil, which has a more fluid conception of race and in which class and color are intertwined in a system of "whitening" that has had devastatingly reactionary consequences for the mass of people of African ancestry in South America, even as the elites cynically gloat about their systems of racial democracy. In these societies there is much intermingling of different colors and "races" the lower down the social ladder one goes, but there is a sharp "racial" ceiling over which only European-ancestry people are found.

There is, third, a Latin Caribbean pattern which has produced perhaps the most mixed group of people in the world, Puerto Rico being the best example. There is the pattern found in Central America, which anthropologist Marvin Harris has called, somewhat awkwardly, a system of "social race," best exemplified by Mexico.[11] And there is the African Caribbean system in places such as Jamaica and Barbados, where color gradations have nearly complete replaced any sharp racial boundaries but in which the political elites and a growing proportion of the economic elites are of African ancestry. All of these systems can be shown to have been directly and powerfully influenced by the pattern of manumission and freedman status that existed during the period of slavery.

I began this essay by stating that manumission has been one of the most important institutions in the history of Western culture, and I would like to conclude by indicating, however briefly, what I meant. In *Freedom in the Making of Western Culture* and subsequent work, I have argued that slavery, in particular, the manumission process, was centrally involved in the invention and social construction of the most important secular value in Western civilization, namely, freedom.[12] It not only was the sociohistorical source of this value but also shaped its character in ways that have persisted to the present. Freedom is a tripartite value, a cultural chord composed of three notes: *personal or negative freedom, civic freedom,* and *positive or sovereignal freedom.* Personal or negative freedom is the absence of constraint on our desire to do whatever it is we please, so long as we do no harm to others; positive freedom is the capacity, the power, to do whatever we want, especially in our relations with others. It is control of one's body and one's inner self as well as power in and over others. And then there is civic freedom, democracy, participating in the government of one's community. Note that there is a simple yet powerful coherence in the three notes of freedom. Perhaps counterintuitively it is power that gives it its focus. The three notes of freedom are merely aspects of the experience of power. One is free to the degree that one exercises power, to the degree that one is not under the power of another, and to the degree that one shares in the collective power of one's state. I have argued, along with a few others, that this unusual configuration of ideas and its extreme valorization emerged in the large-scale slave formations of the ancient world.

Freedom as power was rooted in the unprecedented power of the master; negative freedom originated in the desperate desire of the slave to be manumitted, and the thing that the master gave him we now see was what came to be known as freedom. And democracy emerged in the relation between slaveholder and native nonslave members of their communities who, by the simple existence of slavery, were transformed into something they had not been before: free men. Democracy was first and foremost an emerging bond of solidarity between slave masters and native Greek free men, in contradistinction to alien slaves, métis, and excluded Greek women.

Once we grasp the manner in which freedom was socially constructed, we come to understand its fundamental character, that it is a tension between three ways of relating to power. We also understand how different classes of people will come to emphasize one or other note in the chord. In particular we understand how, to the ruling classes of the West until the rise of industrial capitalism, freedom meant primarily power and control over oneself and over others, which is not to say that they did not hold negative freedom and freedom as participation as secondary notes. At the other extreme we understand how this same freedom could be cherished by slaves and former slaves who came to emphasize the note of the chord that originated in the process of manumission—freedom as liberation.

Ironically the slave and manumitive origins of freedom explain one of the greatest puzzles of New World, especially American history. And I want to close by focusing on this puzzle with special reference to one part of the Americas, the slave South. One of the greatest puzzles in American history was how it was that the southern plantocracy, and southerners in general, fought a brutal civil war that eventually led to the devastation of their way of life, in the name of freedom. Many people have marveled at what seemed the sheer hypocrisy and insanity of their defense. How could one fight a war to defend a slave system in the name of liberty? Yet we know that these slaveholders, whatever their many faults and evils, were not being hypocrites when they claimed to be defending their liberty, including their liberty to hold others in slavery. Indeed, only a generation and a half earlier, these very slaveholders were the source of another great mystery in American history, what I have called the puzzle of the confounding fathers: the fact that nearly every one of the major leaders of the American revolution, and the people who fought hardest to fashion the United States' concept of liberty and enact its Bill of Rights, were large-scale slaveholders.

How was this possible? We can solve the puzzle only when we understand how central slavery and manumission were in determining the character of freedom. For the simple truth of the matter is that the southern view of freedom was utterly consistent with the Western origins and tradition of freedom. Freedom as power—the idea that the more power a man exercised over himself, his household, and his community, the more freedom he possessed—was a central part of the Western conception of freedom and had always been the note of the chord emphasized by Western elites. It was the northern capitalist elite that had shifted ground in its emphasis on negative freedom, the freedom of the manumitted, a shift determined by the cultural demands of industrial capitalism and the supremacy of the market.

Did the collapse of slavery in America and the other parts of the Americas mean the end of the notion of freedom as power and the final triumph of the freedman's view of freedom? Not in the least. Freedom as power—the note of the chord that originated in the master's view of freedom—is alive and well. Only now, as Marx long ago indicated, instead of control of wealth being exercised through control of people—the old way, to which the southern planter class clung to the bitter end—capitalism inverted the equation to one in which power over people is exercised through control and power over property.

Things change, and things remain the same. Freedom remains triumphant and as a value is now sweeping the world. Nonetheless it remains true that to understand its inner meaning, to come to a full grasp of its inner tensions and its protean, paradoxical character, we have to understand its roots in the condition of slavery and in that critical institution that slavery necessitated for its own survival, that double negation—the negation of the negation that was social death—that is the complex, fascinating process this volume explores.

TABLE 2. Intersocietal patterns of manumission and freedman status

1. Domestic assimilation
2. Matrilineal circumvention
3. Predatory circulation
4. Commercial reproduction
5. Pre-capitalist assimilation
6. Plantocratic cooptation
7. Plantocratic exclusion

TABLE 3. Principal component model of incidence of manumission

Status
    Gender
    Parental status
    Relation to master
    Color/race
Demographic
    Age
    Local/foreign born
    Means of acquisition
    Ethnicity
Economics
    Occupation
    Control of earnings
    Location

NOTES

1. Orlando Patterson, *Slavery and Social Death: A Comparative Study* (Cambridge, Mass.: Harvard University Press, 1982).

2. Ira Berlin, *Slaves without Masters: The Free Negro in the Antebellum South* (New York: Free Press, 1992). See also John Hope Franklin, *The Free Negro in North Carolina, 1790–1860* (Chapel Hill: University of North Carolina Press, 1995); Larry Koger, *Free Black Slave Masters in South Carolina, 1790–1860* (Columbia: University of South Carolina Press, 1995); Jay Kinsbruner, *Not of Pure Blood: The Free People of Color and Racial Prejudice in Nineteenth-Century Puerto Rico* (Durham, N.C.: Duke University Press, 1996); and Robin Blackburn, *The Making of New World Slavery: From the Baroque to the Modern, 1492–1800* (London: Verso Press, 1997), 4, 147, 213, 265–266, 291, 302–303, 312, 362, 396, 404–408, 439–443, 419, 474, 489–492, 497–499.

3. Adam Smith, *The Wealth of Nations* (New York: Bantam Classics, 2003); Tom Boylan, ed., *John Elliott Cairnes: Collected Works* (London: Routledge, 2003); Eugene Genovese, *The Political Economy of Slavery* (New York: Vintage Books, 1965); Eugene Genovese, *The World the Slaveholders Made: Two Essays in Interpretation* (Middletown, Conn.: Wesleyan University Press, 1988).

4. Blackburn, *Making of New World Slavery*; Eric Williams, *Capitalism and Slavery* (Chapel Hill: University of North Carolina Press, 1994).

5. Rousseau quoted in Patterson, *Slavery and Social Death*, 2.

6. George A. Akerlof, "Gift Exchange and Efficiency-Wage Theory: Four Views," *American Economic Review* 78 (May 1984): 79.

7. George A. Akerlof, "Labor Contracts as Partial Gift Exchange," *Quarterly Journal of Economics* 97 (November 1982): 550.

8. George A. Akerlof, *An Economic Theorist's Book of Tales* (Cambridge: Cambridge University Press, 1984).

9. Marcel Mauss, *The Gift: Forms and Functions of Exchange in Archaic Societies* (London: Cohen and West, 1954).

10. Orlando Patterson, *The Sociology of Slavery: An Analysis of the Origins, Development, and Structure of Negro Slave Society in Jamaica* (Cranbury, N.J.: Associated University Presses, 1969).

11. Marvin Harris, *Theories of Culture in Postmodern Times* (Lanham, Md.: AltaMira Press, 1998), 73–76, 113–114.

12. Orlando Patterson, *Freedom in the Making of Western Culture* (London: Basic Books, 1991).

William D. Phillips Jr.

Manumission in Metropolitan Spain and the Canaries in the Fifteenth and Sixteenth Centuries

—⚏—

> For, as slavery is the vilest thing in this world except sin, and the most despised, so, on the other hand, is freedom the dearest and most valuable of all benefits.
>
> Las Siete Partidas, Partida IV, título 22, ley 8

Slavery persisted in Mediterranean Europe throughout the Middle Ages and the early modern period.[1] Spain, Portugal, Italy,[2] and southern France during that time witnessed the presence of slaves and a functioning slave trade. Slaves were brought in relatively small numbers to work mainly as domestics and occasionally as auxiliaries in urban workshops and on farms. The system of slavery in the medieval and early modern Mediterranean was on a small scale, with nothing like the gang slavery of classical Rome or the colonial Americas. The kingdoms of Iberia were societies with slaves, not slave societies.[3] The ethnicity of the slaves varied and included eastern Europeans, North Africans, and sub-Saharan Africans. Religion often was a significant difference separating slaves from their owners.

When Europeans reached the Americas and began to develop their enterprise there, they easily transferred their fifteenth- and sixteenth-century experience in Iberia and the Atlantic islands to the fields, mines, and cloth factories of the Caribbean, Mexico, and Peru (and, somewhat later, Brazil). By then the Portuguese had a network for the acquisition of slaves on the African coast, experience with a seaborne delivery system for the slaves they acquired, and a ready market for slaves in the new Spanish colonies. Many components of Old World slavery crossed the Atlantic with the Iberians, including manumission, one aspect of the experience of slaves in the transitional period of the fifteenth and sixteenth centuries in metropolitan Spain and in the Canaries.

Manumission is a normal component of most slave systems. The complete pattern includes a progression from freedom to slavery and back to freedom. After a free person became a slave, usually by capture in war or a raid, the movement back to freedom could be rapid. The captive might be ransomed or exchanged and returned home, having experienced only a brief period of enslavement. More commonly the captured person lived as a slave in the society of the owner. If lucky, the slave then received freedom by manumission and either returned home or, more usually, integrated into the host society as a freed person with rights similar to the rights of a free person in that society. In this simple form such a progression could take place in a single lifetime. But not all slaves obtained freedom, and many people were born and died as slaves. The path to freedom was complicated and often unfolded over several generations. The captive and the captive's children might have had to live as slaves, and manumission might occur only in subsequent generations. Assimilation into the host society often lasted for a generation or more. Nevertheless, manumission is a feature of most systems of slavery, and the harshest of them tend to be those in which access to manumission is most restricted and the assimilation of the freed slaves is the most protracted or incomplete.

Slavery and the manumission of slaves were both well established in metropolitan Spain and its Canarian colonies in the fifteenth and sixteenth centuries. The historical and legal roots were in the experience and legislation of the classical Romans. Because of the striking elements of continuity in the legal sphere from ancient to modern slavery, an account of manumission in Spain and the Canaries must begin by examining the Roman precedents. In the Roman case manumission was usually the prerogative of the masters, who decided to emancipate for a variety of reasons: in gratitude for long service, for the money a slave had saved to purchase freedom, to free a woman slave for marriage, or to grant a dying slave a last request. Most manumissions were not free gifts. Slaves bought their freedom by their own savings or from funds provided by friends or relatives. Masters sometimes freed their slaves for cynical reasons. A master realized that slaves were expensive to maintain, and even if he freed them, they still owed him well-defined obligations. Freed slaves, as Roman citizens, were eligible for the free public distribution of food, and the masters no longer had to feed them. The depths were reached when masters manumitted aged or disabled slaves, in effect granting them the freedom to be maintained by the state or starve in the streets.[4]

Roman masters could choose to manumit during their lifetimes or by testament after their deaths. Manumissions during the master's life required the master and the slave to present themselves before a public official who declared the slave to be legally freed. Manumission by testament could be a pious act or it could be calculated to keep the prospective freed people in a state of anxious anticipation and to encourage them to behave as the owner wished. The failures of the deceased's heirs or agents to fulfill the stipulations of the will were common enough for the legal system to provide means of redress. While the law held slaves to be legally incompetent and barred them from the courts except as witnesses, they could seek legal action in cases regarding manumission and could obtain legal rulings concerning their status.[5]

Aside from voluntary acts by the masters, Roman slaves could gain their freedom through the direct intervention of the state, which can be separated into two broad categories: as a reward for a slave's meritorious service to the state and as a consequence of a master's punishment for crimes. Castration, for example, was a crime in Roman territory. The perpetrator was punished, and in a fifth-century law the victim was freed. Masters could not expose sick slaves or make prostitutes of their chattels; in both these cases the state could prosecute the owner and free the slave.[6]

Until recently scholars assumed that manumission was popular in imperial Rome, both with the slaves and with their owners, and that cases of manumission increased with time. Now many scholars are suggesting that the number of cases was always small and that the majority of Roman slaves never won their freedom.[7] Whatever the actual figures were, manumission continued over the centuries of the Roman Empire, at times accompanied by gifts or bequests to the newly freed for their support.[8]

In many instances citizenship did not follow automatically from the act of manumission. Even with the new status the freed person still suffered under legal disabilities and social discrimination. Freedmen could not hold public office nor officer rank in the army. All freed slaves owed respect to the former master and his family, and often labor or money. If the master were less than twenty years of age and the slave less than thirty, the new freedman became a Junian Latin, not a Roman citizen, with limitations on his legal status.[9] Children born after their parents were manumitted were free, but those born before their parents' freeing were still the slaves of the master.

In the sixth century, when slavery was still significant in Roman society, the emperor Justinian (527–565) embarked on a course designed to restore the empire to its former glory. Many of his initiatives, such as the effort to recover the lands of the former western empire, failed or were only partially successful, but he did have some solid accomplishments, especially in law. At Justinian's behest a panel of legal scholars produced the Corpus Juris Civilis, the body of the civil law, commonly called the Code of Justinian.[10] Roman law before Justinian lacked order and cohesion and was a complicated mixture of senatorial legislation, imperial decrees, and the opinions of jurists. Justinian's code brought order to the system and provided a finely worked instrument for Byzantine administration throughout the Middle Ages. Rediscovered in Western Europe in the eleventh century, it spread widely there and formed the basis of the legal codes of many European kingdoms. Rediscovery of the Corpus Juris Civilis provided Western lawyers and legislators with an easily available manual for the administration of a slave system and significantly influenced the subsequent history of slavery in the Western world.

Most relevant to our concerns, Alfonso X of Castile in the thirteenth century produced a new code for his kingdom known as the Siete Partidas; with heavy influences of Roman law, it had great influence on subsequent legislation for Spain and its colonies.[11] Its provisions on slavery in general and manumission in particular, derived in large part from the Code of Justinian, offered advantages to the slave and for the slave's emancipation. The authors of the Siete Partidas accepted slavery as a fact of human life but, at the same time, recognized its true nature. As the introduction to the section on manumission put it, "All creatures in the world naturally love and desire liberty, and much more do men, who have intelligence superior to that of the others."[12] One law in the same section stated, "For, as slavery is the vilest thing in this world except sin, and the most despised, so, on the other hand, is freedom the dearest and most valuable of all benefits."[13] But slaves who had wanted freedom had to defer to their owners, who in normal circumstances were the only ones able to grant freedom. The Siete Partidas specified the ways the master could free his slaves: "This liberty can be granted by a master to his slave, in church or out of it, before a judge, or anywhere else, by will or without a will, or by a written instrument. He should, however, do this himself, and not by an attorney, except where he orders some of those in his direct line to do so. It is necessary when he frees a slave by a written instrument, or in the presence of his friends, to do so before five witnesses."[14] These legal provisions, incorporated into later legislation in Spain and in the Spanish colonies, offered some protection to the slaves from their complete dependence on their masters. We know, nonetheless, that legal codes are not always an accurate guide to actual behavior, and now we must turn to what we know about the historical experience of slaves and their owners and about how closely that reality coincided with the laws.

The special case of capture and ransom comes first. Raids by Christian forces into Muslim territory still produced captives who were enslaved when they were not ransomed. Muslims raided Christian territories and enslaved those they captured. Their *razzias* often yielded booty in the form of Christian captives, who usually received harsh treatment at the hands of their Muslim captors. Both sides routinely exchanged prisoners immediately after the battles. Peace treaties between Christian and Muslim states frequently specified mutual repatriation of prisoners, and public and private exchanges took place periodically. The prime responsibility for securing the release of long-term prisoners devolved to the families of the prisoners, and both church and state devised means to help them. In both Castile and Aragon in the twelfth century, there were identical procedures for those who wished to ransom a prisoner from the Muslims. In the twelfth century Alfonso VIII of Castile directed the military orders to redeem captives. Family members could requisition a Muslim slave belonging to another Christian, and after having paid the owner one and one-third of the slave's value as compensation, they could use the Muslim slave to exchange for their relative. Before long, however, specialized officials and deputized merchants began to deal with arranging and effecting the exchange of captives. The public officials called *exeas* took both ransomed Muslims and Muslim slaves into Muslim territory and returned with Christians whose ransoms were paid or who were exchanged for Muslims. They could also arrange to ransom prisoners on their own account. In all events these agents, either merchants or at times crown officials, received compensation for their activities. Cuenca and other cities regularly taxed their citizens to raise funds for ransoms, and the monks of Santo Domingo de Silos ransomed captives in the kingdom of Granada and in North African ports. By the thirteenth century two religious orders, the Trinitarians and the Mercedarians, assumed a major role in redemptionism, and they coordinated fund raising for that purpose.[15] Yet individual ransoming continued. Examples include Juan Batlle, a native of the kingdom of Valencia who had a brother held captive in North Africa. In 1491 he bought a Muslim slave from a Christian merchant and arranged with the merchant to take the slave to North Africa, find the brother, and exchange the slave for him. In 1494 Francisca Bos sent a Muslim slave to Oran in a German vessel, with the slave to be exchanged for her husband, who was being held there.[16]

Clearly captivity through war and raids has been a constant feature of world history, but ransoming was not the same as manumission. Nor was simple flight. Slaves always had the option to flee, but to attain freedom in that way led to only two possible successful outcomes. The fugitives could either reach their home country or try to remain undetected in the land of their captors. The Siete Partidas provided laws about obtaining freedom through lapse of time. If a slave believed himself to be free and acted as if he were free for ten years, if his master was in the country—or twenty years, if the master were out of the country—and if the master makes no claim on him, the slave could be considered free. All this assumed the slave was acting in good faith, but even if he were not, he could be considered free after thirty years.[17] One suspects that few slaves actually benefited from these provisions.

Still, slaves constantly tried to flee. So concerned were masters in late medieval Barcelona that they purchased insurance against their losses when slaves fled. Often slaves used false documents of manumission, which had their own black market. Most fugitives were North Africans, who sought to return to their homes. Valencia's Muslim slaves often attempted to flee to the coast and, if they were fortunate, contact a Muslim ship. Muslim fugitives could also seek refuge in the kingdom of Granada before it came under Christian control in 1492. They also could seek aid in the Muslim communities of Valencia, and after 1492 there were isolated Muslim or morisco (Christian converts of Muslim origin) communities in the mountains of Granada where they might seek help. For the Africans and other slaves from distant origins, there was little or no hope of escaping and getting back to their homelands. In the Americas from the sixteenth century onward, runaways formed successful communities and held out for decades. Nothing like that was possible in mainland Spain, though slaves tried it in the Canaries, despite the odds against them. On the islands they could not hope to evade capture for long, and sure safety lay only in reaching Africa. That, however, required a voyage. Stealing boats was not easy, and even if the fugitives secured a vessel, they had to know how to sail and to navigate it. Few of the many slaves in the Canaries achieved freedom by flight.[18]

How often did fugitive slaves attain freedom? Their numbers cannot be counted because records were most often produced when fugitives were captured rather than when they were successful.[19] The question of freedom by flight does not really fit into the category of manumission.

Manumission was the means by which long-term slaves reached free status. In our discussion of manumission we will concentrate on the crown of Castile because of its American connection, but we will not neglect examples from the crown of Aragon. Manumission in late medieval and early modern Castilian was call *ahorramiento*. Freed slaves were called *horros,* and the documents granting their freedom were called *cartas de ahorría* or *cartas de horro*. These words came from Arabic, in which *hurr* meant "free," *harrar* meant to "free," and *harra* meant "to free oneself" or "to be free."[20]

As in Roman times, the granting of freedom was almost always the master's prerogative, but there were some exceptions. The Siete Partidas followed Roman law in providing for the emancipation of slaves without the master's approval in cases of the master's misdeeds or of the slave's service to the kingdom. Masters who placed women slaves in prostitution could have their slaves confiscated and freed.[21] Some authors report that masters who castrated their men slaves would be punished and their slaves freed. In fact, the Siete Partidas provided less for the slave. Those who castrated free men were to be punished as if they had committed homicide, but if a master castrated a slave, he could only be punished by the confiscation of the slave. The slave in turn would become the property of the royal treasury, not freed.[22] Services to the kingdom for which a slave could be freed included reporting the rape or abduction of a virgin, denouncing a counterfeiter, informing on frontier guards who abandoned their posts. In these cases the master would be compensated for his loss of the slave. Slaves who denounced the murder of their masters or revealed treason against the state could be freed with no compensation to their masters.[23]

Public and church authorities could and did free slaves when they determined that the circumstances warranted. The European captains in the fifteenth century who visited the Canaries, armed with Castilian crown patents, found the islands inhabited by neolithic people whom scholars believe to have been related to the Berbers of northwestern Africa. Primarily herders, only on Grand Canary had the natives developed an agriculture. They were organized politically into bands, and the leaders of the European expeditions made treaties with some of the bands and conquered others. Members of the bands that signed treaties were thereby legally exempt from enslavement, but members of the conquered groups could be enslaved as captives of "good war." Members of allied bands who later rebelled or refused to carry out the terms of their treaties could be enslaved as "captives of second war." Despite watchfulness by royal officials, the conquerors at times violated the rules and enslaved members of the treaty bands. The Spanish monarchs Fernando and Isabel had their officials in the islands investigate and free those improperly enslaved, many of whom had advocates in the local bishops or their own families, who hired attorneys to take the plea to the royal court.[24] As an example, in 1491 the royal council compensated Fernando González, the fortress governor of Gibraltar, for his loss when the bishop of the Canary Islands declared a Canarian slave that González had purchased to be free.[25] Similar misunderstandings could find Muslims enslaved in the Canaries. About 1501 a group of some twenty-four Moroccan Muslims went to the island of Gran Canaria with a guarantee of free movement through the island granted by the governor. Within two years a new governor made them captives, including some members of the group who had converted to Christianity. They appealed to Queen Juana, whose government responded by declaring that all the Christians of the group were to be free. The remaining Muslims could take thirty days to decide if they wished to convert as well. If they did convert, they could remain in the islands. If they chose not to convert, they could freely return to North Africa.[26]

Similar practices operated in the Crown of Aragon, where the laws were based as well on Roman legal practice.[27] Valencia was the favored market in the Crown of Aragon because of the fifteenth-century decline of Barcelona. Merchants brought slaves from many origins to Valencia, but before they could be sold, an official called the chief bailiff (*bayle general*) had to register them and collected the royal tax of 20 percent on their sales. At the time of registration the bailiff's officers interviewed the slaves, using translators if necessary, concerning their origin and the circumstances of their enslavement. The sellers had to swear that their slaves had been legally purchased or acquired as a result of good war or just war.[28] Some slaves used the occasion of the bailiff's interview to assert that they were really free and should not be sold. Those who could prove their cases were freed; those who could not were sold.[29]

Even the Spanish Inquisition could become interested in the fate of individual slaves. In the middle of the seventeenth century the officials of the Inquisition in the Canaries petitioned the king to allow them to free a black slave named Herbas. His master was Duarte Enríquez, whom the Inquisition had convicted of secretly practicing Judaism while outwardly living as a Christian.

The slave, though, was thoroughly Christian, and the officials sought a royal order to free him "because in these islands no one knows that Christian slaves become free because of the heresy of their owners, and accordingly the said slave had not sought his freedom nor talked to anyone about it."[30]

These laws and the actions of public officials based on them probably produced only a limited number of freed slaves over the long run. Most slaves who reached freedom did so because their owners chose to manumit them. Even though the decision to grant freedom was the master's, there were methods that slaves could use to try to reach freedom. All slaves had some degree of agency, and many worked hard to maximize their chances of obtaining freedom.

If we look at the strategies that slaves might adopt to attain freedom, one of the first steps was to adopt the dominant religion: Christianity.[31] If a Jewish or Muslim slave became a Christian, however, that did not automatically mean freedom. Castilian laws enforced society's norms and expectations about holding of slaves across religious lines. Non-Christians could not hold Christian slaves, and for knowingly violating the rule a non-Christian master could be executed and all his property confiscated by the state. If non-Christian masters held non-Christian slaves who converted to Christianity, they could see their slaves go free and could expect no compensation. Even if the master subsequently became a Christian, he would lose any slaves who converted before he did.[32]

The religious diversity in Valencia—with the uneasy coexistence there of Christians, Jews, and Muslims—and the official favor for Christianity posed complications for slavery. The crown would not permit non-Christian masters to hold Christian slaves. If a Muslim slave of a Jewish owner converted to Christianity, royal officials took the slave from his owner and assigned the baptized Moor to work for a Christian until he could pay for his manumission. If he could not do so within two months, the officials could arrange to have the new convert work for the king until he had repaid his ransom. If Christian masters owned non-Christian slaves, baptism alone would not free them; their master still had to agree to their manumission.[33]

Nothing obliged Christian masters to free slaves who converted. They could continue to hold converted slaves, and many did. On the other hand, a slave's conversion was a necessary first step toward manumission. Owners might sell their Muslim slaves or allow them to buy their freedom, but the slaves freed by testament were almost exclusively Christians, converted or having been baptized as infants in the case of those born in the home.[34]

Seville's slave owners considered Muslim and morisco slaves recalcitrant, hostile, and liable to run away. African slaves, on the other hand, just as in Portugal at the same time, had a much better reputation. Religion seems to have been the operative factor. With the increasingly hostile relations between

Islamic and Christian states in the Mediterranean in the fifteenth and sixteenth centuries, the Christians directed considerable mistrust toward Muslims and even toward moriscos. Despite their conversion, the latter were suspected of continuing to practice Islam in a clandestine fashion. African blacks received conversion to Christianity either before or soon after they reached Spain. Those who had come from pagan areas and who had not formerly been Muslim usually became faithful Christians. This meant that the whites accepted them more readily and also enabled them to become acculturated more easily. The higher regard for blacks was translated into generally better treatment. Masters and their white friends acted as godparents for the children of slaves, and black slaves were buried in Christian cemeteries and at times even in family vaults in the churches. Slaves, especially those in the second and later generations, were often sincerely pious and active in religious matters. Their religious devotion and participation in the religious life and festivals increased their acceptance.[35]

According to the Siete Partidas, slaves who received holy orders could be freed if the master knew and consented. If he neither knew nor consented, things became more complicated. He had a year and no longer to complain. If the slave had become a subdeacon, the master could claim him and return him to slavery. If the slave had become a deacon or a priest, the master could not reclaim him as a slave, but the former slave had to pay the master a sum equivalent to his price at the time of ordination or provide him with another slave of equal value. If the slave became a bishop, he would have to provide his master with two slaves, each of his own value when he was ordained.[36] I suspect that the jurists who wrote the Siete Partidas were merely repeating earlier provisions dating back to the early centuries of Christianity. In practical terms few if any late medieval slaves won their freedom in this way.

In the vast majority of cases of manumission slaves attained freedom because the owner chose to grant that freedom. Frequently the owner arranged that the slave would provide compensation either by money or by continued service. Freedom by purchase was a common pattern, especially for manumissions made during the lifetime of the owner, rather than by will. The price demanded was usually high, normally above market prices, and the prices of women slaves were usually higher than for men.[37]

Some slaves bought their own freedom. Anything the slave had legally belonged to the master, including any money he or she earned. In these circumstances, how did they get the money to pay for their manumission? They often earned extra money from working outside the home with the master's permission. In fifteenth-century Mallorca owners allowed some of their slaves to live as "setmaners," who lived independently and paid a portion of their income to the owner until the price of freedom was reached.[38] If they could not raise the full amount, they could also borrow what was necessary, either from the master or from a third party, and they could pay it back by payments over time. Many of the installment contracts called for manumission only after all the money had been paid, but there were others in which the manumission took place before the slave paid the full amount.[39] For example, the mulatto slave Gabriel, born in Granada in the home of his mistress, purchased his freedom in 1567 when he was twenty-seven years old. He agreed to pay a ducat each month for four years, and if he failed to keep up the payments, he would return to being a slave.[40] In 1552 a member of the city council of Lucena offered freedom on the installment plan to his slave Magdalena for fifty ducats, with half down and half to be paid over ten years while she still worked for him. Thus the owner got assured labor for ten years as well as the price of his slave.[41]

Other slaves raised money for their manumissions by begging.[42] In late medieval Alicante the chief bailiff could grant slaves a license to beg, under an arrangement called *acapte,* until the money was raised for the manumission.[43] Throughout the kingdom of Valencia, Mudejars (Muslims living under Christian rule) could receive permission to seek alms to secure their own freedom or the freedom of their kin.[44] In 1510 the widow of a silversmith in Córdoba gave her white slave María, fifty years of age, permission to go begging for seven months in the hope of raising the sixty-five hundred maravedís she still owned on her price of manumission of ten thousand maravedís.[45] In the case of a similar agreement a slave took the opportunity to flee once she obtained the permission to beg. In 1511 Isabel Fernández of Seville complained that she had allowed her white slave Isabel, thirty-five years old and a native of Málaga, to seek alms for a period of a year and a half to pay for her manumission. The slave went to a small town near Málaga and did not return, even though her time limit had passed.[46] In the Canaries in 1536 there were complaints that slaves were robbing to secure the money for their manumissions.[47]

If the slave could not pay, others could. To achieve freedom a slave frequently needed the financial assistance of relatives or others. Mothers often bought the freedom of their slave children, as did fathers of their own slave children.[48] As an example, in 1549 García de Paredes, a free man of Baza in the kingdom of Granada, purchased the freedom of his son Gabriel, aged fifteen months, for fifteen ducats from the widow Catalina de Cordoncillo, who owned the child's mother, Isabel.[49] In the Canaries free men could purchase and free their children by slave women, either by outright purchase, by substituting a slave of similar value, or by providing the owner with labor services.[50] Perhaps some of these purchases by free men were designed to save the reputation of the owner who was the true father of the child in question. Men paid for manumission of future wives. The Siete Partidas provided that a slave, man or woman, could become free by marrying a free person if the master knew and approved of the match. When a master married his own slave, she became free.

Interestingly, nothing in the law provided for a slave man to be free if he married the woman who owned him.[51]

Free Canarians constantly aided their enslaved compatriots to obtain freedom. In numerous wills, for example, Canarians left money to executors charged with the redemption of Canarian slaves. The executor could purchase the slave outright or purchase a black slave and exchange him or her for the Canarian. Such exchanges were more easily arranged for slaves who remained in the islands because relatives could not easily determine the whereabouts of those who had been sold in European markets.[52]

Slaves could also persuade their masters to free them by the terms of a last will and testament. Some slaves did so overtly through behavior designed to win the approval of their owners. Other slaves won approval because of who they were: children born in the household, for example, especially if the master were the father. The provisions for manumissions in wills usually contained pious statements that the manumission was due to the great love that the owner had for the slave. We should be wary about accepting these statements at face value, for many of the testators placed conditions on the manumission. Some wills required a monetary payment in exchange for the slave's freedom. More often they required the slave to continue rendering service for a number of years. On the other hand wills often provided for liberations without conditions and even with small inheritances.[53] On the island of Mallorca testators frequently left money to slaves to help them to purchase their freedom.[54] In Tenerife in the early sixteenth century one master made an agreement with his white woman slave, a morisca, to serve him in honest work while he lived. In return he would provide her with food, clothing, shoes, and an honest life. After he died, the slave would be free.[55]

Many freed slaves ended up poor and had to depend on charity. As women slaves were not usually prepared to hold salaried jobs after they became free, the perceived danger was that they would fall into illegal activities once manumitted if alternative provisions were not made. Thus when their owners wrote in their wills that slave women should be freed, they often provided a dowry to enable the new freedwomen to marry or to live honestly.[56] In the early seventeenth century in the town of Lucena, Juan Hurtado de Val left a fine legacy in his will to his slave Leonor, a North African of forty years of age with two children of twenty-one and ten. She was to receive a new house, vineyards, olive groves, wheat land, the chest that she used to store her clothes, and two hundred ducats. She was charged to pray for the souls of her masters. A potential for Leonor was that all this would not come to her until Hurtado del Val's wife died.[57] Slave children born in the home were often well integrated into the life of the family, even more than their mothers, and there are examples of such children being freed when their mothers were not. This was the case of the slave Inés, daughter of the slave Juana, owned by a widow, Doña Beatriz de Angulo of Córdoba, who left instructions for Inés's well-being in her will of 1524. When Inés reached fifteen years of age, she was to be freed and given ten thousand maravedís and a bed. Until she reached fifteen she was to live in the household of Beatriz's sister in Écija.[58] Sometimes freedom was not an unmixed blessing. In 1526 the pregnant slave Catalina was about to leave for Cuba with her master, the priest Alvaro de Castro. Castro freed Catalina's unborn child because the mother would have to be separated from her husband, also Castro's slave, who had to stay behind in Seville.[59]

The rate of manumission was generally low, despite the availability of the many paths to freedom. Alfonso Franco Silva called the rate of manumission "frequent."[60] For Granada in the sixteenth century, Aurelia Martín Casares, after an exhaustive search of the documents, found a total of sixteen hundred documents recording slave sales but only two hundred manumissions.[61] In early-seventeenth-century Córdoba Albert N'Damba Kabongo uncovered references to 2,684 slaves and only 198 freeings.[62] For the town of Martos, Manuel López Molina found 211 cases of slavery in the documents and only 13 cases in which freedom was attained. For Jaén in the late seventeenth century, the same historian found ninety cases of slavery in the documents and only eight slaves who became free, all by the concession of the master.[63] For the town of Lucena, Françoise Orsini-Avila found a clear evolution over the century and a half after 1500. In the period 1550–70 no manumissions appeared in the remaining documents. From 1570 to 1600 there were very few, and all involved the aged. In the first half of the seventeenth century, with slavery declining, the number of manumissions grew. In the second half of the century slavery declined even more, and manumissions grew accordingly, often of second and third generation slaves born in the household.[64]

Few slaves could expect to be freed in their prime adult years. For Granada, Martín Casares found that most of the manumitted were children under ten years of age or adults over thirty. Franco Silva found that most of those manumitted in Seville were people below the age of eighteen or over thirty.[65] Thus it seems that masters freed slaves who were of little immediate economic benefit and held on to slaves in their working prime. There is a long list of those who criticized freeing aged and infirm slaves, stretching back to classical times. The master's motive for freeing his slave is not clear from the wording of this document: "And he has served me for over forty years with good and loyal service, and in respect to that, and for the love and good will that I have toward him."[66] The "love and good will" might be genuine, but we can also assume that after forty years the slave had little service left to give. In Seville in 1525 the slave Inés, white and forty-four years old, gained her freedom, as her master reported, "because she is of great age and sick and of little use and because she gave eighteen ducats for her freedom."[67] In 1617 the merchant Juan de Bargas acceded to the request of his Moorish slave Jamete to be freed.

Jamete was about thirty-six years old, missing an upper tooth, and marked with a brand on his right arm. At the time he was sick and so lame he could not stand on his feet. Obviously he could not work, and Bargas freed him after seeking and failing to find a buyer for him.[68] A clear example of the mixture of religious and economic motivations is the case of Pedro de Vergara, who in 1528 freed two Guanche slaves, Pedro and Juan de Abona, because they had become Christians and because each had paid him sixty Castilian doblas.[69]

Slaves could go to court or seek the aid of public officials if promised freedom not delivered. In Valencia the chief bailiff or his agents investigated each slave sale and interviewed each slave. Some slaves declared themselves to be free, as did the black woman Inés, whose story illustrates the difficulty some slaves had in getting their freedom even after it had been given. Her Valencian master, Pedro González Docón, freed her by the terms of his will, but his heir sold her to a man from Málaga. When she told the purchaser that she was free, he returned her to a man named Frutos, who had guaranteed the sale. Thereafter she lived with Frutos for four years until he gave her to a merchant for sale again in Valencia. This time she told the market examiner that she was really free, and the general bailiff kept her from being sold until the facts could be determined.[70] The Siete Partidas said that if a slave were owned by more than one master and if only one of the masters wanted to free the slave, the slave could be freed.[71]

From Roman times masters and legislators expected freed slaves to render complete respect to their former masters and the masters' families. A law in the Siete Partidas explained what this "pietistic obsequience" meant: "They should humble themselves and salute whenever they appear before him and his children, and every time their master comes where they are, if they are seated, they should rise and welcome him pleasantly." In practical matters the freed person should not take the former masters into court, save with a judge's permission, and should do what was necessary to protect the former master's property. If the master fell on hard times the freed person "should go to his assistance, and give him food, drink, clothing, and shoes according to his means and ability."[72] The thirteenth-century jurists backed this up with a law providing that the freed person could be returned to slavery for failure to carry out the provisions regarding obsequience.[73]

Examples of reenslavement are very rare, but in the early seventeenth century Bartolomé de Albillos, a lawyer in the town of Martos, revoked the manumission of his former slave and explicitly cited the Siete Partidas: "Law [9], title 22, of the fourth Partida gives the former master the ability to revoke the manumission and reduce to servitude the slave whom he had freed. . . . The said Ana has been ungrateful for the favor that I granted her and on numerous occasions she has sorely wounded me by word and also hitting me with her hands because I am seen to be old, sick, and weak and I cannot control or punish her. . . . [Therefore] I revoke the manumission document for the reasons I have declared . . . and reduce her to her former state of servitude and slavery."[74] The questions of the lives of the newly manumitted slaves and the degree of their integration into the larger society are obviously crucial in the study of the history of slavery.[75] The major focus of the present study is manumission, but we cannot conclude without mentioning a few words about the brotherhoods of people of sub-Saharan origin in Spain. Many of the former slaves of North African or Spanish Muslim origin left for Granada or North Africa after they received manumission. Others of them blended into the larger white community, as did those of eastern European origin. For the sub-Saharan Africans and their progeny the situation was different. They found their acceptance incomplete, in part because of their skin color or other indications of their origins. Yet they did what they could to blend in through their work—which in most cases was no different from that of whites of similar incomes and social standing—and through religion. Religious practice and the communal bonds associated with it allowed African Spaniards to achieve their most complete acceptance by the wider community.

Seville had the largest black community, and in the late fourteenth century local church authorities set up the Hospital of Our Lady to serve the African and mixed-race people of the parish of San Bernardo. A black *cofradía* (religious brotherhood) emerged a few years later to run the hospital. By the mid-fifteenth century a special city official (called the *mayoral*, or "steward") settled problems involving his fellow blacks, including relations with their masters and the judiciary. By 1475 the African and mixed-race population, both slave and free, was large enough for the monarchs Fernando and Isabel to make the *mayoral* a royal official. The first incumbent was Juan de Valladolid, who was commonly called "the Negro count." By the late sixteenth century many blacks and mulattos also lived in the parish of San Ildefonso, where they also had a religious brotherhood and where a street was named the "Street of Mulattos."[76]

Other Spanish cities also had religious brotherhoods of Africans and African Spaniards. In 1472 black freedmen in Barcelona established a religious brotherhood, the *cofradía* of Nuestra Señora de Gracia, to dispense charity to the poor and sick and to provide religious fellowship for its members. The members of the brotherhood held their meetings in a chapter house they owned, and they made annual pilgrimages to the nearby monastery of San Agustín.[77] In the sixteenth century Granada had two brotherhoods for people of African descent: In the church of San Justo y Pastor, there was the brotherhood of Nuestra Señora de la Encarnación y Paciencia de Cristo, and in the church of Santa Escolástica, the *cofradía* of San Benito de Palermo.[78] In Málaga slaves of North African origin joined with Africans and African Spaniards to form the Hermandad de la Misericordia.[79]

The experience of fifteenth- and sixteenth-century metropolitan Spain and the Canaries is vitally important for the later history of slavery in Iberoamerica and, to an important degree, everywhere in the Americas. From this examination of the process of manumission in Spain and the Canaries, we can easily see the precedents that were set for the actions of the slaves and the slave owners across the Atlantic.

NOTES

1. For surveys of slavery in the medieval Mediterranean world, see William D. Phillips Jr., *Slavery from Roman Times to the Early Transatlantic Trade* (Minneapolis: University of Minnesota Press, 1985); Jacques Heers, *Esclaves et domestiques au Moyen Age dans le monde méditerranéen* (Paris: Hachette/Pluriel, 1996). For slavery in medieval Spain see Charles Verlinden, *L'esclavage dans l'Europe médiévale,* in *Péninsule ibérique—France,* vol. 1 (Bruges: De Tempel, 1955); William D. Phillips Jr., *Historia de la Esclavitud en España* (Madrid: Playor, 1990). I am currently updating and thoroughly revising my two slavery books for publication by the University of Pennsylvania Press.

2. The terms "Spain" and "Italy" are used for convenience. There was a kingdom of Portugal in that period, but neither Spain nor Italy was a political unit until later.

3. The concept of a slave society is now common in the historical literature. It implies an elevated percentage of slaves in the population. Most scholars put the figure at a third, others at a fifth, of the total population. Additionally, the economy must be dominated by what the slaves produced. In societies with slaves, free people provided most of the labor, the numbers of slaves were not great, and their economic role was restricted. Though the definition of slave societies originated earlier, Moses Finley popularized it in various works culminating with *Ancient Slavery and Modern Ideology* (New York: Viking, 1980). A recent example of the use of the concept is Ira Berlin, *Many Thousands Gone: The First Two Centuries of Slavery in North America* (Cambridge, Mass.: Belknap Press of Harvard University Press, 1998), esp. 7–9.

4. For a recent survey of Greek and Roman slavery, see Thomas E. J. Wiedemann, *Slavery,* New Surveys in the Classics, no. 19 (Oxford: Oxford University Press, 1992). For manumission in the Roman world, see the classic works by William L. Westermann, *The Slave Systems of Greek and Roman Antiquity* (Philadelphia: American Philosophical Society, 1955) and W. W. Buckland, *The Roman Law of Slavery: The Conditions of the Slave in Private Law from Augustus to Justinian* (Cambridge: Cambridge University Press, 1908). Recent reprints demonstrate the continuing utility of Buckland's book: Holmes Beach, Fla.: W. W. Gaunt, 1994; and Union, N.J.: Lawbook Exchange, 2000. For more recent works, see David Daube, "Two Early Patterns of Manumission," in *Collected Studies in Roman Law,* ed. David Cohen and Dieter Simon (Frankfurt: Vittorio Klostermann, 1991): 165–191; Thomas E. J. Wiedemann, "The Regularity of Manumission at Rome," *Classical Quarterly* 35, no. 1 (1985): 162–175; J. Albert Harrill, *The Manumission of Slaves in Early Christianity* (Tübigen: J. C. B. Mohr, 1995); Keith R. Bradley, *Slaves and Masters in the Roman Empire: A Study in Social Control* (New York: Oxford University Press, 1987); and Keith R. Bradley, "Roman Slavery and Roman Law," *Historical Reflections / Réflexions historiques* 15, no. 3 (1988): 477–495.

5. Thomas E. J. Wiedemann, ed., *Greek and Roman Slavery* (Baltimore: Johns Hopkins University Press, 1981), selection 32, *Digest,* 40, 1, 52.

6. Buckland, *Roman Law of Slavery,* 598–603.

7. While the state on occasion attempted to restrict the right of masters to manumit and to permit the freed to be reenslaved, such measures were seldom enacted. The most famous

limitations of manumissions were those of Augustus. See Wiedemann, *Greek and Roman Slavery*, selections 6, 29–30, 71–73.

8. Pliny provided a farm and later a manager for it to his former nurse. Wiedemann, *Greek and Roman Slavery*, selection 136, 129–130.

9. Pedro López Barja de Quiroga, "La dependencia económica de los libertos en el Alto Imperio Romano," *Gerión* 9 (1991): 163–174; Pedro López Barja de Quiroga, "Freedmen [*sic*] Social Mobility in Roman Italy," *Historia: Zeitschrift für Altegeschichte* 44, no. 3 (1995): 326–348; Pedro López Barja de Quiroga, "Latinus Iunianus: 'Status' jurídico y realidad historica," in *Esclavos y semilibres en la antigüedad clasica*, ed. Universidad Complutense de Madrid, Facultad de Geografía e Historia (Madrid: Editorial de la Universidad Complutense, 1989): 85–89; R. C. Weaver, "Where Have All the Junian Latins Gone? Nomenclature and Status in the Early Empire," *Chiron* 20 (1990): 275–305.

10. Justinian's code contained the Digest, the Institutes, and the Novels, or new laws. *The Digest of Justinian*, trans. Charles H. Munro, 2 vols. (Cambridge: Cambridge University Press, 1904–9). See also Alan Watson's new English translation of the Digest (Philadelphia: University of Pennsylvania Press, 1998); *The Institutes of Justinian*, trans. L. B. Moyle, 5th ed. (Oxford: Clarendon Press, 1913); *The Civil Law, Including the Twelve Tables, the Institutes of Gaius, the Rules of Ulpian, the Opinions of Paulus, the Enactments of Justinian, and the Constitutions of Leo*, ed. S. P. Scott (Cincinnati: Central Trust, 1932; reprint, New York: AMS Press, 1973).

11. See the new edition of the English translation of the Siete Partidas. Robert I. Burns, S.J., ed., *Las Siete Partidas*, trans. Samuel Parsons Scott, 5 vols. (Philadelphia: University of Pennsylvania Press, 2001). The first volume includes introductory material by Burns, a historical essay on Alfonso X and the Partidas by Joseph F. O'Callaghan, and bibliographical notes by Jerry R. Craddock.

12. Siete Partidas, Partida IV, título 22, in Burns, *Siete Partidas* 4:981.

13. Siete Partidas, Partida IV, título 22, ley 8, in ibid. 4:983.

14. Siete Partidas, Partida IV, título 22, ley 1, in ibid. 4:981. That law contained special provisions for masters under the age of twenty who freed slaves.

15. José María de Cossío, "Cautivos de moros en el siglo XIII: El texto de de Pero Marín," *Al Andalus* 7 (1942): 49–112; Verlinden, "Esclavage," 152–156, 159, 165–168, 546–548; James William Brodman, "Military Redemptionism and the Castilian Reconquest, 1180–1250," *Military Affairs* 44 (1980): 24–27; James William Brodman, "Municipal Ransoming Law on the Medieval Spanish Frontier," *Speculum* 60 (1985): 318–330; James William Brodman, *Ransoming Captives in Crusader Spain: The Order of Merced on the Christian-Islamic Frontier* (Philadelphia: University of Pennsylvania Press, 1986); J. E. López de Coca Castañer, "Institutions on the Castilian-Granadan Frontier, 1369–1482," in *Medieval Frontier Societies*, ed. R. Bartlett and A. MacKay (Oxford: Claredon Press, 1989): 135–141; María Isabel Jiménez Jurado, "Cautiverio y rescate de moriscos almerienses," *Almería entre culturas, siglos XIII–XVI (actas del coloquio, 19–21 de abril de 1990)* (Almería: Instituto de Estudios Almerienses de la Diputación de Almería, 1990): 577–586; A. López Dapena, "Cautiverio y rescate de D. Juan Manrique, capitán de la fontera castellana, 1456–1457," *Cuadernos de estudios medievales* 12–13 (1984): 243–253; María de los Llanos Mártez Carrillo, "Rescate de cautivos—comercio de esclavos: Murcia siglos XIV–XV," *Estudios de historia de España* 47, no. 141 (1993): 21–47; Alfonso Franco Silva, *La esclavitud en Andalucia, 1450–1550* (Granada: Universidad de Granada, 1992). *Exeas* existed in both Castile and Aragon. *Exea* meant both the exchange and the person who conducted the exchange. Ocaña Argente del Castillo, "Los

cautivos en la frontera entre Jaén y Granada," and Emilio Cabrera Muños, "Cautivos cristianos en el reino de Granada durante la segunda mitad del siglo XV," in *Relaciones exteriores del Reino de Granada—IV Coloquio de historia medieval andaluza*, ed. Cristina Segura Graiño (Almería: Instituto de Estudios Almerienses, 1988): 211–225 and 227–236, respectively; George Camamis, *Estudios sobre el cautiverio en el Siglo de Oro* (Madrid: Editorial Gredos, 1977).

16. Vicenta Cortés Alonso, *La esclavitud en Valencia durante el reinado de los Reyes Católicos, 1479–1516* (Valencia: Ayuntamiento de Valencia, 1964), 140.

17. Siete Partidas, Partida III, título 29, ley 23, and Partida IV, título 22, ley 7, both in Burns, *Siete Partidas* 4:983.

18. Manuel Lobo Cabrera, *La esclavitud en las Canarias orientales en el siglo XVI: Negros, Moros, y Moriscos* (Gran Canaria: Cabildo Insular de Gran Canaria, 1982), 250, 280–281; Mateo Antonio Páez García, "Notas en torno a aspectos sociales de la esclavitud en Córdoba a comienzos del siglo XVI," in *Historia Medieval,* vol. 2 of *Actas del II Congreso de Historia de Andalucía,* 10 vols. (Córdoba: Cajasur, 1994), 211; Alfonso Franco Silva, *La esclavitud en Sevilla y su tierra a fines de la edad media* (Seville: Diputación Provincial de Sevilla, 1979), 203–210; Miguel Gual Camarena, "Un seguro contra crímines de esclavos en el siglo XV," *Anuario de Historia de Derecho Española* 23 (1953): 247–258; Roser Salicrú i Lluch, *Esclaus i propietaris d'esclaus a la Cataluyna del segle XV: L'assegurança contra fugues* (Barcelona: Consejo Superior de Investigaciones Científicas, 1998).

19. For the early seventeenth century in the town of Martos, Manuel López Molina found no successful cases of flight, and three in which those who attempted to flee were caught and returned. "Cartas de horro y libertad de esclavos en Martos: 1610–1630," in *Comunicaciones presentadas al XI Congreso de Profesores-Investigadores: Palos del la Frontera, 21–24 September 1992* (Granada: Asociación de Profesores de Geografía e Historia de Bachillerato de Andalucia "Hespérides," 1994), 146. The black slave Francisco fled his master in Córdoba in April 1611 and reached as the kingdom of Murcia before being caught and returned in November 1613. Albert N'Damba Kabongo, "Les esclaves à Cordoue au début du XVIIe siècle (1600–1621): Provenance et condition sociale" (Ph.D. dissertation, University of Toulouse–Le Mirail, 1975), annex 6, unpaginated.

20. Aurelia Martín Casares, *La esclavitud en la Granada del siglo XVI: Género, raza, y religión* (Granada: Universidad de Granada, 2000), 435. Freed slaves could run into real difficulty if they could not produce the proper documents, and they and their former masters made sure that the manumission documents were available. In 1533 the widow Contaza Núñez of Baza went before a notary to reconfirm the freeing of her former slave Leonor de Alcaraz, because the papers of the notary who registered the original manumission had been dispersed following his death. Carlos Asenjo Sedano, *Sociedad y esclavitud en el Reino de Granada, siglo XVI: Las tierras de Guadix y Baza* (Granada: Ilustre Colegio Notarial de Granada, 1997), 66. Aurelia Martín Casare, "Free and Freed Black Africans in Granada in the Time of the Spanish Renaissance," in *Black Africans in Renaissance Europe,* ed. T. F. Earle and K. J. P. Lowe (Cambridge: Cambridge University Press, 2005), 247–60.

21. Siete Partidas, Partida IV, título 22, ley 4, in Burns, *Siete Partidas* 4:982.

22. Siete Partidas, Partida VII, título 8, ley 13, in ibid. 5:1349.

23. Siete Partidas, Partida IV, título 22, ley 3, in ibid. 4:982.

24. Manuela Marrero Rodríguez, *La esclavitud en Tenerife a raíz de la conquista* (La Laguna de Tenerife: Instituto de Estudios Canarios, 1966), 17–18, 23–24, 26–27; Lobo, *Esclavitud en las Canarias,* 259; Franco Silva, *Esclavitud en Sevilla,* 248–249.

25. Archivo General de Simancas, Registro General del Sello, January 21, 1491, fol. 74.

26. Lobo, *Esclavitud en las Canarias*, 259–260.

27. The Siete Partidas were Castilian and as such not operative in the Crown of Aragon.

28. Cortés, *Esclavitud en Valencia*, 65–70, 87, 99, 107, 114–115, 118, 120; Vicente Graullera Sanz, *La esclavitud en Valencia en los siglos XVI y XVII* (Valencia: Instituto Valenciano de Estudios Históricos, 1978), 57–68.

29. Cortés, *Esclavitud en Valencia*, 121–122.

30. Lobo, *Esclavitud en las Canarias*, 258. The response of the Crown is not recorded in this case.

31. I purposely omit discussion of slavery in the Islamic kingdom of Granada before its demise in 1492. François Soyer, "Muslim Freedmen in León, Castile and Portugal," *Al-Masaq: Islam and Medieval Mediterranean* 18 (2006): 129–43.

32. Siete Partidas, Partida IV, título 21, ley 8, in Burns, *Siete Partidas* 4:979–980. The loss of converted slaves applied to those slaves held for service to a master, not to the trade slaves he might control. If a trade slave became a Christian, the master had three months to sell him; afterward, he would see the slave confiscated. Similar regulations operated in the Crown of Aragon. See Verlinden, "Esclavage," 300.

33. Cortés, *Esclavitud en Valencia*, 136–137.

34. Lobo, *Esclavitud en las Canarias*, 260–261.

35. Ruth Pike, *Aristocrats and Traders: Sevillian Society in the Sixteenth Century* (Ithaca, N.Y.: Cornell University Press, 1972), 173, 186–188; Juan Aranda Doncel, "Estructura de la población morisca en tres parroquias sevillanas: San Julián, San Román, y Santa Lucía," *Boletín de la Real Academia de Córdoba de Ciencias, Bellas Artes y Nobles Artes* 45 (1976): 77–78. The masters of the town of Martos showed the same preference for blacks in the early seventeenth century. Manuel López Molina, "Cartas de horro y libertad de esclavos en Martos: 1610–1630," in *Comunicaciones Presentadas al XI Congreso de Profesores-Investigadores, Palos del la Frontera, 21–24 September 1992* (Granada: Asociación de Profesores de Geografía e Historia de Bachillerato de Andalucia "Hespérides," 1994), 154.

36. Siete Partidas, Partida IV, título 22, ley 6, in Burns, *Siete Partidas* 4:983.

37. Franco Silva, *Esclavitud en Sevilla*, 246–247; Lobo, *Esclavitud en las Canarias*, 257–277. Josep Hernando, *Els esclaus islàmics a Barcelona: Blancs, negres, llors i turcs; De l'esclavitud a la llibertat (s. xiv)* (Barcelona: Institució Milà i Fontanels, 2003).

38. Onofre Vaquer Bennàssar, *L'esclavitud a Mallorca, 1448–1500* (Palma de Mallorca: Institut d'Estudis Baleàrics, Govern Balear, Conselleria d'Educació, Cultura i Esports; Consell Insular de Mallorca, Comissió de Cultura i Patrimoni, 1997), 79.

39. Marrero Rodríguez, *Esclavitud en Tenerife*, 95.

40. Martín Casares, *Esclavitud en Granada*, 444–445.

41. Françoise Orsini-Avila, *Les esclaves de Lucena 1539–1700* (Paris: Publications de la Sorbonne, Presses de la Sorbonne Nouvelle, 1998), 104.

42. Cortés, *Esclavitud en Valencia*, 139.

43. José Hinojosa Montalvo, *Esclavos, nobles y corsarios en el Alicante medieval* (Alicante: Universidad, 2000), 111.

44. Mark D. Meyerson, "Slavery and the Social Order: Mudejars and Christians in the Kingdom of Valencia," *Medieval Encounters* 1, no.1 (1995): 169–171.

45. Páez García, "Esclavitud en Córdoba," 206.

46. Franco Silva, *Esclavitud en Sevilla*, 244.

47. Lobo, *Esclavitud en las Canarias*, 259. Similar complaints appeared elsewhere.

48. Marrero, *Esclavitud en Tenerife*, 95–96; Franco Silva, *Esclavitud en Sevilla*, 253–254.

49. Acing Sedano, *Sociedad y esclavitud en el Reino de Granada*, 123.

50. Lobo, *Esclavitud en las Canarias*, 264–265.

51. Siete Partidas, Partida IV, título 22, ley 5, in Burns, *Siete Partidas* 4:982.

52. Marrero, *Esclavitud en Tenerife*, 80–81, 84, 88, 96, 104; John Mercer, *The Canary Islanders: Their Prehistory, Conquest and Survival* (London: Collins, 1980), 233–34; Felipe Fernández-Armesto, *The Canary Islands after the Conquest: The Making of a Colonial Society in the Early Sixteenth Century* (Oxford: Oxford University Press, 1982), 39–40.

53. Martín, *Esclavitud en Granada*, 438–439; 449–450; Orsini-Avila, *Esclaves de Lucena*, 103.

54. Vaquer Bennàssar, *Esclavitud a Mallorca*, 79.

55. Marrero, *Esclavitud en Tenerife*, 93.

56. Martín, *Esclavitud en Granada*, 452.

57. Orsini-Avila, *Esclaves de Lucena*, 103.

58. Páez García, "Esclavitud en Córdoba," 211.

59. Ruth Pike, "Sevillian Society in the Sixteenth Century: Slaves and Freedmen," *Hispanic American Historical Review* 47 (1967): 344–359.

60. Franco Silva, *Esclavitud en Sevilla*, 243.

61. Martín, *Esclavitud en Granada*, 437. Granada's documents include forced liberations and those done by the morisco community in the aftermath of the rebellion that saw many of the defeated enslaved and later freed by members of the community. Without those counted Martín assumed that manumissions would equal only 6 percent of sales.

62. N'Damba Kabongo, "Esclaves à Cordoue," 228, 273.

63. Manuel López Molina, *Una década de esclavitud en Jaén, 1675–1685* (Jaén: Ayuntamiento de Jaén, 1995), 193; López Molina, "Cartas de horro," 151.

64. Orsini-Avila, *Esclaves de Lucena*, 100–101.

65. Martín, *Esclavitud en Granada*, 446; Franco Silva, *Esclavitud en Sevilla*, 249. López Molina found similar statistics for the town of Martos. "Cartas de horro," 154.

66. Martín, *Esclavitud en Granada*, 447.

67. Franco Silva, *Esclavitud en Sevilla*, 250.

68. N'Damba, "Esclaves à Cordoue," 220.

69. Marrero, *Esclavitud en Tenerife*, 29, 34–35.

70. Cortés, *Esclavitud en Valencia*, 121–122. The documents state that Inés was later sent to Castile, but whether as free or slave, we do not know.

71. Siete Partidas, Partida IV, título 22, ley 2, in Burns, *Siete Partidas* 4:981.

72. Siete Partidas, Partida IV, título 22, ley 8, in ibid. 4:983–984.

73. Siete Partidas, Partida IV, título 22, ley 9, in ibid. 4:984.

74. López Molina, "Cartas de horro," 151–152. Abillos went on to state that Ana would be freed again on his death. Ana was pregnant when reenslaved, and Abillos stated that the child she produced would be free from birth.

75. Libertos (freed slaves) were free citizens and could make wills. Martín, *Esclavitud en Granada*, 453–454. She found only three such wills in her Granadan documents.

76. Pike, *Aristocrats and Traders*, 173–174, 180–181, 186–188; Pike, "Sevillan Society," 344–359; Juan Aranda Doncel, "Estructura de la población morisca en tres parroquias sevillanas: San Julián, San Román y Santa Lucía," *Boletín de la Real Academia de Córdoba de Ciencias, Bellas Artes y Nobles Artes* 45 (1976): 77–84; Alfonso Franco Silva, "Precedentes de la abolición de la esclavitud: Los libertos andaluces en los siglos XV y XVI," in *Esclavitud y derechos humanos: La lucha por la libertad del negro en el siglo XIX*, ed. Francisco de Solano and Agustín Guimerá (Madrid: Consejo Superior de Investigaciones Científicas, 1990); Isidoro

Moreno Navarro, *La antigua hermandad de los negros de Sevilla: Etnicidad, poder y sociedad en 600 años de historia* (Seville: Universidad de Sevilla, 1997).

77. Miguel Gual Camarena, "Una cofradía de negros libertos en el siglo XV," *Estudios de la Edad Media en la Corona de Aragón* 5 (1952): 457–466.

78. Martín, *Esclavitud en Granada*, 422–423. San Benedetto (Benito in Castilian) de Palermo was a Sicilian saint whose parents were black slaves. Stephen A. Epstein, *Speaking of Slavery: Color, Ethnicity, and Human Bondage in Italy* (Ithaca, N.Y.: Cornell University Press, 2001), 16–17.

79. María del Carmen Gómez García and Juan María Martín Vergara, *La esclavitud en Málaga entre los siglos XVII y XVIII* (Málaga: Servicio de Publicaciones, Diputación Provincial de Málaga, 1993), 44–46.

The Promise of Freedom in Late Medieval Valencia

—ɯ—

Shortly after Christmas 1461 Joan Rossell, a Valencian merchant, lay on his deathbed, surrounded by his wife, Ysabel; his brother Dionis; and his slave Maria. Fearful of what lay ahead of her following her master's death, Maria seized this opportunity to make one final plea for her liberation. Climbing into her master's bed in order to help him get into a more comfortable position, Maria reportedly broke into tears and begged her master to "make me free and see to it that I do not come into the hands of anyone else." While other accounts of this incident feature a more assertive Maria pointedly questioning her master, "Lord, am I to stay like this forever?" Or "Lord, don't you have *any-thing* to say to me?" By all accounts Joan's response to his slave's plea had been one and the same: a firm assurance of a prompt liberation. Joan soothed his slave's fears by stating, "Don't worry, Maria. I have already told my brother to see to it that you are well taken care of. I have told everyone that I am leaving you free to act according to your will and I have asked Benet Salvador (a notary) to record this in writing." Grateful for this act of lordly munificence, Maria kissed her master's hands (as was customary) and, according to one observer, joyfully exclaimed, "God grant you salvation!"[1]

The aforementioned deathbed manumission scene taken from the civil court records of fifteenth-century Valencia conforms quite nicely with the prevailing image of the slave experience in the late medieval Mediterranean world: manumission (effective upon one's master's or mistress's death)[2] was frequent and expected. Slavery, for most, was but a temporary condition, and once freed, former slaves successfully integrated themselves into their communities by marrying, setting up households, and contracting out their own labor.[3]

More recent research, particularly by scholars investigating the fate of slaves in the more ethnically and religiously pluralistic slave populations of the Iberian peninsula, however, has revealed that the practice of outright manumission during the fifteenth and sixteenth centuries was not nearly as widespread as previously had been assumed. In her study of slavery in sixteenth-century Granada, for instance, Aurelia Martín Casares found that only about 12 percent of the overall slave population received charters of freedom and that these lucky few often were obliged to pay exorbitant redemption fees in return.[4]

My own research in the archives of Valencia likewise reveals that (in the latter half of the fifteenth century) resales and transferals of slaves far outnumbered grants of freedom in extant notarial records. In contrast with the 417 contracts of sale I encountered in a randomly selected sample of notarial records dating from 1464 to 1504, I found but 57 charters of freedom. Moreover, while 27 of the grantees were granted their liberty immediately "without any retention or condition (*absque aliqua retencione sine condicione*)," the remaining 30 would enjoy their freedom only after they had fulfilled certain requirements. Twenty-four were obliged to complete terms of service ranging from "set" terms of three, seven, or ten-plus years to "indefinite" terms such as the lifetime of the surviving spouse, relative, or some other third party. One master stipulated that his female slave's manumission would not take effect until a suitable spouse was found for her. The remaining six were obliged to pay redemption fees ranging from 25 pounds to 3,000 sous (roughly 150 pounds). Although some slaves managed to pay the fee immediately in one lump sum, in most cases it was paid off in installments over a period of several years, during which time, depending on the terms of the charter, the slave often was obliged to continue providing service, if not remain in his or her owner's household. Thus although the formularies for charters of freedom invariably represent manumission as a "gift,"[5] closer examination of these "gifts" reveals lots of small print: labor obligations, redemption fees, and even morality clauses.[6] More than half (thirty) of the fifty-seven charters of liberty encountered made the slave's freedom contingent upon him/her continuing to provide service, without compensation, for substantial periods of time.[7]

It bears noting that recent studies have also shown that a slave's access to freedom varied significantly according to such factors as gender, ethnic origin, and/or religious identity as well as the socioeconomic status of a slave's master and/or mistress.[8] In assessing the ability slaves had to secure their freedom, it is absolutely essential for historians to differentiate between male and female, Muslim and Christian, black and white.

Hence in the past few years scholars have begun to reevaluate the somewhat benign image of medieval slavery sketched out by Ridolfo Livi and to a certain extent perpetuated by Jacques Heers and others. In stressing the great diversity of slave experience in the late medieval Mediterranean world, they have pointed out the deficiencies of prior generalizations, revealing that the obstacles slaves faced in regaining their freedom were not only significant but variable.

However, one further obstacle slaves faced in recovering their liberty—which has not been adequately addressed—was securing recognition of legitimate and hard-earned claims to freedom in the event that masters and mistresses had a change of heart or heirs proved unwilling to relinquish their claims on what they perceived as a valuable portion of their inheritance. According to the kingdom of Valencia's legal code (the Furs de Valencia), a valid and legally binding manumission could be effected in one of three ways: an oral statement before witnesses, as a clause in a last will and testament or by means of a document drawn up by their masters or mistresses specifically for this purpose, or a charter of liberty (*instrumentum franquitatis*). All three modes of enfranchisement were deemed equally effective (*haia valor*).[9] While these statutes as well as the formularies for charters of liberty and last wills and testaments almost invariably represent manumission as a gift, we have already noted how slaves were only in very rare cases granted their freedom immediately and with no strings attached. For a slave actually to be able to "enjoy" these "gifts," masters and mistresses imposed obligations of terms of service and/or payment of a redemption fee. A quick perusal of contemporary civil court records, moreover, reveals that grants of liberty were hardly ironclad agreements. If not renounced by masters and mistresses themselves while they were still living, manumissions often were ignored, challenged, or rejected by the slave owner's heirs after their deaths.

Indeed, despite all her master's assurances to the contrary, the aforementioned Maria's death-bed manumission was later contested by her master's brother and heir following Joan's death. Emphatically denying that his brother ever made such a promise, Dionis maintained that even if he had, such a promise could not have been sincere. Noting how masters habitually extended promises of freedom as a means to induce their slaves to provide them with better service, Dionis insisted that if his brother had, in fact, ever made such a promise, he would have "said these words to Maria only in order to persuade her to serve him well during his illness, putting her in [the false] expectation that he would make her free." For, Dionis continued, if his brother had truly wanted to make Maria free, he would have not only promised it orally (*de paraula*) but would have "really put it into effect (*realment ho haguera posat en execucio*)," issuing her a charter of freedom (*carta de franquea*).[10]

This essay considers the promise of freedom in late medieval Valencian society—how it was regarded and interpreted by masters, slaves, and their contemporaries and how it was treated in contemporary courts. For this we have an incredibly rich group of source materials to consult: civil court records, suits in which masters and slaves accused one another of violating the terms of manumission agreements. In particular I examine two types of lawsuits filed before municipal and Crown magistrates in the city of Valencia: suits filed by masters and/or mistresses seeking the nullification of grants of liberty on a variety of different grounds and suits filed by slaves seeking the court's assistance in forcing masters and/or their heirs to honor and implement promises of liberty— be they oral promises, testamentary clauses, or redemption agreements. What is particularly surprising about these cases, however, is not that slaves were complaining that promises of freedom, once extended, were not always honored and respected, but that slaves—admittedly only a handful—had the ability to take their masters to court. In other words, this consideration of disputed manumissions encountered in civil court records of the city of Valencia, dating from the latter half of the fifteenth century, will highlight the means at both the masters' and the slaves' disposal to promote their interests and protect their rights. In stark contrast with the gift rhetoric used in notarial documents recording grants of liberty, promises of freedom, whether oral or written, were regarded and treated explicitly in courts of law as contracts in which masters and slaves had both responsibilities and rights.

On an early autumn day in 1472, Bernat Gilabert, a Valencian merchant, took his two male slaves, Nadal and Johan, to his wine cellar. The two slaves—one white, the other black—were to assist Bernat in bottling his most recent vintage. Yet when Bernat directed his white slave Nadal to begin bottling the wine, Nadal, in his mid-twenties, grabbed his master, threw him to the ground, and pummeled him with some "powerful blows." Aiming to finish the job, Nadal then tried to hurl his master into a huge vat of wine. A widow who witnessed the struggle stated that the vat had been filled with wine at a depth of "more than the height of a man." According to Bernat's complaint and the testimony of several witnesses, had not Bernat's black slave Johan and others nearby immediately come to his assistance, Nadal would have succeeded in his "deliberate plot" to drown his master in a tub of wine.

Only a few months prior, in response to the pleas of "friends and well-wishers," Bernat had tentatively agreed to grant Nadal his freedom. The document promising Nadal his freedom had been contractual in nature—Bernat granting and Nadal "accepting and receiving" his liberty in accordance with certain mutually agreed upon terms. Nadal's ultimate liberation was conditional upon him serving Bernat "well and faithfully" for five more years. According to Bernat's present complaint, Nadal's act of rebellion had reversed and invalidated this partial liberation. Hardly providing "good and faithful service," Nadal's attempt on his master's life rendered the contract of manumission null and void.

What is remarkable about this episode—beyond the fact that a slave allegedly attempted to drown his master in a vat of wine—is that we only learn of this encounter because Bernat sought official confirmation of his right to maintain Nadal in slavery. Bernat was not pressing criminal charges against his slave. He was not asking the justice of the city of Valencia to administer any sort of corporal punishment. Rather, he was appearing before the civil court of the city of Valencia to ask the justice to confirm his right to sell Nadal to another, no doubt unwitting, master. He wished the justice to lend his authority and back up his claim that Nadal's act of rebellion invalidated any rights he previously may have had to freedom.

Whether or not we can accept Bernat's account of this episode as true and accurate and whether or not Nadal in fact attempted to drown his master in a vat of wine, Bernat's avowed scrupulous attention to the legal process is revealing of how the dominance of a master over his slave was established, justified, and understood in fifteenth-century Valencia. Slavery in fifteenth-century Valencia was an institution regulated by a well-defined set of legal procedures.

Considered in isolation, Bernat's efforts to block his slave's enfranchisement might not seem all that noteworthy. While the degree to which masters relied upon the courts to back up their claims is perhaps somewhat striking, that the Valencian legal system would affirm a master's right to keep a "rebellious" slave in captivity is not terribly startling. Yet when Bernat's request is considered in conjunction with eighty-six demands for liberty filed before Crown courts between 1450 and 1500, Bernat's allegations take on added significance. It becomes evident that Bernat's actions were likely motivated by more than legal scrupulousness. His actions appear more defensive in nature, demonstrative of an awareness among masters that to a limited extent, slaves too had access to the courts.

A formal promise of freedom, even if it could not be realized until far off into the future, brought slaves special rights, if not a distinct legal status. They became a new category of person: the provisionally freed—or, in contemporary documentation, a "sclau/sclava . . . constituhida en gracia de libertat."[11] Principally, this seems to have meant that they had the right to defend their claims to freedom in royal and municipal courts. In the event that a legitimate claim to freedom was ignored, provisionally freed slaves could contest their masters' and mistresses' right to keep them in servitude, citing the legally binding terms of a manumission agreement.

Indeed, when Dionis refused to recognize Maria's freed status, Maria took him to court, filing—with the help of the "procurator of the miserable"—a demand for liberty (*demanda de libertat*) before the court of the governor. Several months later, after hearing testimony from witnesses appearing on behalf of both Maria and Dionis, the governor issued a ruling in Maria's favor "condemning" Dionis to give Maria her liberty and awarding her freed status.[12]

To file a demand for liberty slaves typically sought out the assistance of a municipal official known as the procurator of the miserable.[13] The procurator was an annually elected municipal official entrusted with overseeing conditions in the city prison, making sure that its inmates were properly fed, clothed, and provided with suitable bedding. More important, however, he seems to have been responsible for seeing to it that prisoners were not detained there indefinitely at the municipality's expense. In connection with this latter responsibility the procurator of the miserable came to play a role somewhat akin to that of a court-appointed attorney. In return for a nominal salary paid by the municipality, the procurator saw to it that the poor and indigent of Valencia would receive a fair and timely hearing in the city's courts. Thus on behalf of the so-called miserable, the procurator collected testimony, filed motions, and appeared at court hearings, all free of charge.

A slave's ability to seek the procurator of the miserable's counsel in filing a demand for liberty, as well as having access to his services throughout the course of the trial, was guaranteed and upheld by the courts. Upon filing a demand for liberty, slaves typically turned themselves over into the protective custody of the court. Thereupon they would be placed either in the city's prison or in a designated safe house. While in some instances slaves remained there until the dispute with their masters had satisfactorily been resolved, in most instances slaves would be released back into their masters' custody. The court would only do so, however, upon receipt of sworn assurances from the slave's master or mistress that they would not harm the slave physically or remove him/her from the city limits.[14] In this way the court tried to defend a purportedly freed slave's right to pursue justice, protecting them from being bullied into renouncing their claims.[15] More strikingly still, however, in order to regain custody of their slaves, masters and mistresses had to promise the court that they would permit them continued access to the services of the procurator of the miserable. For example, when a female slave named Juliana filed a demand for liberty in 1456, her mistress was unable to regain custody of her until she promised the court that she would not maltreat Juliana "like a slave" and that she would allow her to continue meeting with the procurator of the miserable. The bail-bond specified that Juliana would be permitted "to go speak to and consult the Procurator two days a week—that is, for one hour after suppertime every Tuesday and Friday."[16]

Some masters, not surprisingly, contested the very authority of the courts to intervene in these disputes. From their perspective slaves were their private property (*cosa propria*) such that how, when, and whether slaves won their freedom was entirely up to them. Promises or no promises, they argued, the court had no right to interfere in the disposition of their own personal property. In 1488 a female slave named Magdalena filed a *demanda de libertat* against her master alleging that he had promised her freedom in exchange for sexual favors and a redemption fee of fifty-seven pounds. When her master, a Genoese merchant, was called before the court of the governor to respond to Magdalena's charges, Raffel Gentil protested, declaring that "justice will not tolerate" a slave winning freedom against the will of her master.[17] Similarly, in 1478 a slave-owning mason complained, "Truly it is a thing of bad example that female slaves found in a state of servitude, by merely *claiming* that they have an agreement with their masters by which they could free themselves in exchange for a certain quantity, have the capacity to go wherever they like and demand their liberty [emphasis added]."[18]

Nevertheless, although some masters contested the court's authority to intervene in manumission disputes, many more masters (like slaves) actively sought out the court's assistance in protecting their rights and promoting their interests. Both parties turned to royal and municipal courts to adjudicate what seem to have been generally treated as contract (as opposed to property) disputes. Despite the fact that this was not always acknowledged in the formulary of the notarial documents recording these promises, these court records indicate that under the terms of a manumission agreement both parties—slave and free—had duties and obligations to the other. While slave plaintiffs took great pains to show how masters or mistresses were reneging on their promises of freedom by ignoring, denying, or not complying with the terms of the agreement, masters and mistresses likewise accused slaves of "bad faith" in these agreements, pointing out their failure to provide good service, their misdemeanors, and, in the most extreme cases, acts of violent insubordination.

Certainly, both masters and slaves attempted to evade the obligations imposed in these contracts. For example, rather than complete the term of service stipulated in a manumission agreement, a slave might instead opt for taking flight. Two years after his master, a sugar refiner named Johan Rufach, promised him freedom contingent upon ten more years of service, a black slave named Geronim tried (unsuccessfully) to take a short cut.[19] Geronim fled his master's service after being approached by a group of slaves who told him that if he ran away with them to France he would win his freedom automatically after a period of only four days.[20] Another way a "provisionally freed" slave might attempt to expedite the process would be to kill his master. Although his master had promised him liberty upon his death, a slave named Jacme Ros allegedly was too impatient to wait for nature to take its course. When Jacme, immediately subsequent to his master's demise, filed a demand for liberty before the court of the governor, the executors of his master's last will and testament accused him of poisoning his master's drinking water. The executors claimed that the slave had secretly been depositing higher and higher concentrations of lead in his master's drinking water.[21]

Masters and mistresses in turn engaged in some rather elaborate legal finagling to get out of these agreements—reflective of the seriousness with which such promises of freedom were regarded. Rather than simply renouncing their slaves' claims outright, masters, mistresses, and their heirs exploited loopholes to retain custody and authority over their slaves. One of the most common tactics used to counter a slave's demands was to argue that the person who promised the slave his or her freedom lacked the authority (i.e., legal title) to do so. For example, in 1484, when a slave named Beatriu demanded her liberty, claiming, among other things, that her master had promised her freedom after a three-year term of service, her master, a sugar merchant named Francesch de Cas, did not deny having done so. Instead he effectively invalidated her claim by "admitting" that he had had no real authority to grant the slave her freedom since, "in truth," she belonged to his wife.[22]

Similarly, in 1498 a black slave named Lucia filed a demand for liberty against Ursola, the daughter of a coppersmith (now deceased), seeking the implementation of the promise of freedom Ursola's father had extended to her that had been contingent upon a six-year term of service. Ursola's husband, Pere Miro, immediately contested Lucia's claim, arguing that the promise of freedom (ostensibly made in 1492) was invalid because at the time it was granted the coppersmith no longer had title over the slave. Producing an earlier document (dated 1483) in which the coppersmith transferred all of his worldly possessions over to his new son-in-law, Pere maintained that this *donatio inter vivos* had included Lucia. Hence, Pere reasoned, Lucia's claim to freedom "did not proceed from justice since said grant of liberty could not have been made lawfully since said Miquel Miro was no longer her master."[23]

Reflective of the rather precarious status of freedmen during this period, a former slave named Miquel appeared before the court of the governor in 1499 to seek its assistance in putting an end to his master's attempts to recover him. Although Miquel possessed a charter of freedom (*carta de franquea*) and had been living and working in Valencia for the past four months as a freedman, his former master, Jaume Assensi, denied the legitimacy of his manumission, arguing that the *carta de franquea* had been issued by his wife, Agnes, without his consent.[24]

In other instances, rather than try to "weasel out" of these agreements masters and mistresses countered a slave's demand for freedom by adopting almost the exact opposite tactic: affirming the manumission agreement's legally binding character. In these cases masters and mistresses contrasted their scrupulous observation of its various terms and stipulations unfavorably with their slaves' multiple violations. Recounting instances of theft and/or flight and acts of ingratitude, if not open rebellion, they maintained that these slaves—through their own actions—had effectively invalidated their claims to freedom. In 1471 the nobleman Johan Roiz de Corella appeared before the Justicia Civil seeking its permission to sell a conditionally freed black male slave whom he claimed had violated each and every term of his manumission "contract" as outlined in his brother's last will and testament. According to this last will and testament the black man's freedom was contingent upon him serving Johan Roiz "well and faithfully" for ten years following his master's death. Roiz contended that the slave had run off only a few days following his brother's death. Although he eventually did manage to recover him, Johan Roiz complained that the slave went on to take flight no fewer than three more times. Furthermore, the nobleman continued, the slave was a chronic thief, stealing items not only from his own household but from households across the city. Worst of all this black man was impudent and disobedient, "serving him bad and obeying him little." Not only had he verbally abused him on several occasions, but on one occasion, the nobleman recounted, the black male had actually threatened him physically. For these reasons, the nobleman insisted—and the Justicia Civil agreed—that it was not only within his rights but absolutely essential for him to dissolve the manumission contract and resell the slave to another household since the slave had put it "in great peril."[25]

While in the aforementioned instance the slave owner was "on the offensive," seeking the official nullification of a promise of freedom before the slave had a chance to demand its implementation, in most other instances slave owners were on the defensive, refuting demands for liberty that had been filed against them by their slaves. In 1480 Elvira de Ladro, the widow of the former viscount of Vilanova, rejected the demand for liberty filed by her husband's black male slave on the grounds that the slave was a chronic thief. Though Elvira readily acknowledged that her husband had promised the slave (named Johan) his freedom contingent upon completion of a term of service in his last will and testament, she emphasized how this grant had also been subject to a certain "pact and condition and in no other manner." That is, Johan was obliged to serve his master's heirs *well and faithfully* for a period of five years" (emphasis added). Indeed, Elvira's advocate noted that her husband had explicitly stated in his last will and testament that if the slave failed to provide the requisite service, "in such a case I will and order that said Johan Ferrandez not be freed but remain a captive." Hence it cannot be doubted, Elvira's advocate confidently argued, that given the slave's multiple crimes of theft, Johan had failed to live up to the terms of this manumission agreement, effectively invalidating it as well as any claim he may have had to freedom.[26]

In 1471 a notary utilized a similar type of argument in his efforts to refute the demand for liberty filed against him by a Tartar male slave who had been in his service for more than eighteen years (since he was about seven years old). The notary, Miguel Puigmiga, admitted that more than ten years previously he had issued the slave a charter of liberty, promising him freedom after eight more years of service. But Miguel maintained that the slave's almost constant misbehavior had invalidated the grant since it had been contingent not only upon the slave serving Miguel "well, faithfully and legally" but also upon an understanding that the slave would never flee "from his service, household or dominion" nor would he "beat or mistreat his livestock."[27] In the past ten years, Miguel contended, Anthoni had violated each and every one of these stipulations. To bolster his own complaints that the slave provided him with poor service and, indeed, had run away on several different occasions, Miguel produced numerous witnesses who could testify that the slave verbally abused his master, repeatedly dishonored his mistress, and sadistically beat his master's livestock.[28]

In his demand for liberty, of course, the Tartar male presented himself as the very paragon of the faithful Christian slave, serving his master for the requisite eight-year period "well and loyally, without any fraud and never departing from his master's service." Indeed, Anthoni maintained, when it came time for him to claim his freedom, he had been somewhat hesitant to do so, "not wishing to appear ungrateful and not wishing to depart from Miguel de Puigmiga's service and household since he did not wish to lose the love and companionship which he had received there." Nevertheless, Anthoni did eventually ask his master to make good on his promise, humbly informing him, "Lord, the eight year term of service that I was obliged to provide to you has been completed. I have served it in full so that I am now free and released from all yoke of servitude. Would you please give me license to depart?" Miguel, however, "having forgotten what he had done," refused to comply with their earlier agreement. Miguel allegedly replied that "this would please him not at all"and told Anthoni that he would *never* give him license to depart. At that point, to hear Anthoni tell it, the slave was left with no choice but to "free himself," departing from Miguel's household to manage his own affairs as a free person. Anthoni expressed no qualms whatsoever about the actions he had taken, insisting that, whether or not his master acknowledged it, he had legitimately earned his freedom. Indeed, he viewed his arrest and detention in the municipal prison as most unjust.

Ultimately the governor found the master's (Miguel's) account the more compelling, perhaps because he was able to present no fewer than thirteen witnesses who corroborated his story. The governor issued a ruling declaring Anthoni's charter of freedom null and void and proclaiming Anthoni to be Miguel's slave for perpetuity.[29]

Although in this particular case, the slave's efforts to recover his freedom proved unsuccessful, it nonetheless serves as an example which illustrates quite well how masters were not the only ones using the courts to defend and further their interests. Slaves likewise turned to the courts to promote their interests and protect their claims.

Already "freed" slaves turned to the court of the governor for assistance in protecting their freed status. The most important instrument a freed slave had to protect his or her liberty was the "charter of freedom," an official, written document attesting to their hard-earned status as a freed person.[30] In 1468 a freed Tartar by the name of Anthoni traveled all the way from Genoa to Barcelona in order to secure one. Although he had been living and working in Genoa for the past ten years as a freed person, before moving to a new city (Valencia) where he intended to work as an apprentice, Anthoni took the precaution of making a detour back to his former master's household in Barcelona to get a "carta de franquea."[31] Reflective of its central importance in securing recognition of a slave's freed status is the fact that in many manumission agreements, the issuance of a charter of freedom upon a slave's fulfillment of the stipulated requirements figures prominently among the obligations enjoined upon the master. For example, a Majorcan merchant promised to issue his Tartar female slave a *carta de franquea* upon receipt of her redemption fee.[32] Likewise, in their last will and testaments we encounter masters and mistresses granting their slaves *cartas de franquea* alongside pious bequests of clothing, bed linens, and sums of money. In this way masters and mistresses attempted to help their former slaves ease into their new lives as free people, providing them with all the things they would need to live independently and set up their own households. For example, in a last will and testament drawn up in 1477, Maria "the Galician" left her black female slave named Luisa not only her freedom but also a *carta de franquea* and "the bed where she was accustomed to sleep along with all of its linens."[33]

In some cases even *before* they had effectively earned their freedom, slaves appealed to the court of the governor for help in protecting their status as provisionally freed slaves. In 1478 a conditionally freed black slave named Lucia appealed to the governor for assistance in vouchsafing her claim to freedom. Fearing that her claim to liberty had been severely compromised as a consequence of her being transferred from her master's household on the island of Sardinia into the custody of a merchant in Valencia, Lucia asked the governor to issue a ruling ordering her immediate return to Sardinia and stipulating that she be allowed to complete the term of service required for her liberation in her former master's household in Caller. The governor acceded to her request and Lucia was transferred back into the custody of her master's household in Caller.[34] While the governor perhaps was motivated by an interest in cutting down on his paperwork, attempting to prevent a *demanda de libertat* from being filed in the future, these provisionally freed slaves seem more concerned that in these "far-off lands" it would be extremely difficult, if not next to impossible, to get their claims recognized.

In 1488 another conditionally freed black female slave named Lucia appeared before the governor seeking protection of her claim to freedom. In this instance Lucia complained that despite the fact that she was "constituhida en gracia de libertat," her mistress was plotting to resell her in far-off lands "fraudulently, to the disadvantage and detriment of said Lucia and the liberty that had been promised her." Lucia feared that once she had been sent to "strange and far-off lands and kingdoms," she would "lose the rights and claim she had to freedom." At the very least, her advocate reasoned, given the distance it would put between her and her former mistress and supporters, it would make it considerably more difficult for her to get these claims recognized in the even that they happened to be contested.[35] As in all of these cases the governor acceded to the provisionally freed slave's request, instructing the local magistrate not to release Lucia back into her mistress's custody "until said

Lucia be sufficiently assured with good promises and documents that during the remainder of said four-year term of service, said Lucia would not be alienated, transported, or pledged such that she would be taken out of or separated from the kingdoms and lands that our lord king rules (i.e., the territories of the Crown of Aragon: the kingdoms of Aragon and Valencia, the principality of Catalonia, and the lands the Crown controlled "overseas")." In this way the governor took pains to enforce the terms of the legally constituted contract of manumission, ordering Lucia's mistress to allow her slave to perform the term of service required for her freedom "without any impediment, not being pestered, vexed, or inconveniences by being transported to lands and kingdoms where she would not be able to obtain justice."[36]

Considering what we have already seen of the efforts masters and mistresses made to "back out" of these agreements in conjunction with the example that follows, it would seem that these conditionally freed slaves' fears were well justified. Sometime around the year 1450 a Majorcan merchant and his wife assembled several people "worthy of faith" to publicly affirm a promise they made to a Tartar female slave of theirs named Marta. Marta was promised that her master and mistress would have a notary draw up a "charter of liberty" (*carta de libertat*) for her as soon as she paid a redemption fee of fifty pounds "mallorquines." In the presence of the aforementioned witnesses Marta was awarded provisionally freed status (*statu liber*) and granted her license to go live and work wherever she pleased. According to Marta's perspective, from that day forward, the only claim her master and mistress retained over her person was that she give them a certain portion of whatever she earned each week— and even that claim, once the redemption fee had been paid in full, was only temporary and eventually would lapse.

And yet we only learn of this oral promise of freedom because several years later, Marta filed a demand for liberty in the court of the governor of Valencia. (Interestingly enough, it is the second such suit she filed; she reportedly had another *demanda de libertat* pending back "home" in Majorca). Marta complained that after she had collected *and paid* about thirty pounds of her redemption fee, her mistress did an "about face" and now denied ever having agreed to grant her her liberty. Hardly without recourse, Marta took her mistress to court, filing a demand for liberty before the governor of the kingdom of Majorca. And yet, Marta tells us, "in gross violation of her freed status and in an effort to prevent her from obtaining justice," her mistress arranged for her to be kidnapped and shipped off to Valencia. Under the ruse of sending her on an "errand," Marta's mistress instructed her to deliver a jar of preserves to a vessel docked in the port of Majorca. Once Marta arrived at the port, however, she was violently seized and forced aboard a ship bound for Valencia.

The above-cited examples reveal how the promise of freedom in late medieval Valencia was legally binding at the same time as it was tenuous.

While it is perhaps not terribly surprising to discover that the terms of a manumission were at times ignored, challenged, or rejected by slaves as well as masters, it is somewhat more surprising to see slaves—as well as masters—exploiting the legal channels available to them to ensure that these contracts were implemented in accordance to their interests. And yet we must consider this striking display of slave agency in perspective. What at first glance seems a powerful weapon with which slaves could demand their liberty was by the same token wielded by their masters to maintain the vast majority of slaves in servitude under an aura of fairness and legality. By providing access to the courts to a small segment of the slave population, masters were able to legitimize the subjugation of thousands. That being said, the ability of those slaves who were able to take their masters to court and successfully demand their liberty becomes all the more striking.

NOTES

1. Gobernación 2304: M. 2:26v, M. 7:47r–48v, M. 8:1r–v; 2305: M. 12:43r–44v; 2306: M. 25:7r, Archivo del Reino de Valencia (hereafter cited as ARV). Testimony of the tailor Jofré Ripoll: "En veritat sta que passades festes de nadal propassat ell testimoni essent en la cambra del dit Johan Rossell apres que lo agueren per noliat stant axi lo dit en Johan Rossell crida a la dita Maria. E li dix vine aci Maria gita'm e ella gita'l e adoba'l e feu co que ell volia laudas dix la dita Maria senyor no'm dius res. E lo dit en Johan Rossell respos que vols que't digua. E ella dix plorant senyor que'm dexes franqua que no vaga a mans de negu e ell dit Johan Rossell respos ja't dexe franqua a totes tes voluntats e a ta libertat e axiu ha fet scriure aci Benet Salvador e encara ho dit a mon frare e a tots los de casa que no vull que vages a mans de negu. E llavors la dita Maria dix e respos senyor deu te do salut."

2. Jacques Heers posits that the practice of granting slaves their freedom effective upon their masters' or mistresses' deaths is characteristic of domestic slavery. The practice "corresponde perfectamente a la idea de un servicio doméstico 'personal.' E esclavo es afecto a su amo, al cual sirve; cuando el amo muere, el lazo se rompe. . . . Se trataba en efecto, de un lazo personal, el cual no es fácilmente transferible en beneficio de otro." Jacques Heers, *Esclavos y sirvientes en las sociedades metierráneas durante la Edad Media* (Valencia: Edicións Alfons el Magnànim. Institució Valenciana d'Estudis i Investigació, 1989), 234–235.

3. Stephen Bensch put it best when he observed that "recent scholarship has looked upon urban slavery, at least in comparison to the massive brutality of the later transatlantic slave trade, as a rather benign institution, a form of forced social integration that brought Mediterranean peoples into close contact. The slave blocks of Venice and Genoa, and even Valencia and Mallorca, have begun to take on the character of miniature Ellis Islands." Stephen Bensch, "From Prizes of War to Domestic Merchandise: The Changing Face of Slavery in Catalonia and Aragon, 1000–1300," *Viator* 25 (1994): 85.

4. While Alfonso Franco Silva has claimed that "en la sociedad andaluza de fines del Medioevo fue bastante frecuente la concesión de libertad al esclavo. La liberación era el premio que recibía aquel esclavo cuyo comporatmiento hacie el amo había sido fiel, cariñoso, obediente, y respetuoso." Martín, in contrast, argues that "en general, ni cristianos, ni moriscos propietarios de mano de obra esclava muestran intenciones de liberar gratuitamente a sus dependientes. Al contrario, el número de liberaciones es reducido, y a menudo se demandan rescates desorbitados." Comparing the number of charters of freedom encountered in

sixteenth-century Grandan notarial records with the number of slave sales, Martín found that only about 12 percent of the overall slave population was ever granted their freedom. To further buttress her conclusions, Martín cites similar findings in recent studies of slave populations in Jaén and Córdoba. Aurelia Martín Casares, *La esclavitud en la Granada del siglo XVI* (Granada: Universidad de Granada, 2000), 438–440. See also Alfonso Franco Silva, *Esclavitud en Andalucía 1450–1550* (Granada: Universidad de Granada, 1992); Juan Aranda Doncel, "Los esclavos de Jaén durante el último tercio del siglo XVI," in *Homenaje a Antonio Domínguez Ortiz* (Madrid: Ministerio de Educación general de y Ciencia, 1981), 233–251; and Albert N'Damba Kabongo, "Les esclaves à Cordue au début du XVII siècle (1600–1621)" (Ph.D. diss., University of Toulouse–Le Mirail, 1975).

5. Charters of liberty characteristically begin with masters and mistresses proclaiming that "out of reverence for our lord God," "for the redemption of my soul and for the remission of my sins," and/or "in recognition of many years of faithful service," they were returning their slaves to "their natural born state of freedom" such that henceforth they would be treated "as if they had never been slaves." No matter what sorts of obligations and/or payments the grant of freedom entailed, they characteristically conclude with the slave humbly accepting the "gift" of freedom, expressing his or her gratitude by kissing the master's and/or mistress's hands. Orlando Patterson has observed that even when a slave "pays" in either service or cash a significant amount for his or her redemption, these gestures are invariably represented as mere token offerings. As in most gift exchanges, with regard to a slave's manumission there is often a marked contrast between the actual balance of the exchange and how it was represented ideologically. Whatever the slave may have provided in return, the act of manumission is always presented as an act of largesse, the master giving "something great (freedom) in exchange for something small." Orlando Patterson, *Slavery and Social Death: A Comparative Study* (Cambridge, Mass.: Harvard University Press, 1982), 209–219.

6. The saddle maker Marti Vilalba made his mulatto male slave's freedom contingent not only on nine more years of service but also on the slave's continued good behavior. During said term the slave not only was forbidden to "take flight from his service, household or lordship" or to "steal anything, whether from his household or anyone else's" but also had to promise "not to drink wine." Protocolos 1913 (Miguel Puigmicha Jr.), February 3, 1473, ARV. "Hanc vero preinsertam libertatem et alforriam tibi dicto Ferdinando facio et concedo sub hiis modis formis et condicionibus et non sine ipsis nech aliter nech alter. Videlicet quod tu tenearis michi et meis servire per tempus novem annorum a nativitate domini proxime preteriti in antea computandorum bene fideliter ac legaliter. Item quod durante dicto tempore non fugies a servicio et domo ac dominio meo. Item quod durante dicto tempore non bibas vinum. Item quod durante dicto tempore non fures aliquid tam de domo mea quam aliqua persone."

7. See chapter 6 ("Paths to Freedom") of my Ph.D. dissertation. Debra G. Blumenthal, "Implements of Labor, Instruments of Honor: Muslim, Eastern and Black African Slaves in Fifteenth-Century Valencia" (Ph.D. diss., University of Toronto, 2000).

8. See the recent volume of conference proceedings published by the Consejo Superior d'Investigacions Cientificas (CSIC) titled *Esclavitud y Libertad en la Corona d'Arago*, especially the article by Fabiana Plazolles Guillén, "Trayecotrias Sociales de los libertos musulmanes y negroafricanos en la Barcelona tardomedieval," and the article by Teresa Vinyoles i Vidal, "Integració de les llibertes a la societat Barcelona baixmedieval."

9. *Furs de València*, ed. Germà Colon and Arcadi Garcia (Barcelona: Editorial Barcino, 1990), 5:147. Llibre 6, rúbrica 4, 5: "Aquels qui donaran libertat als seus servus o als seus catius donen-la ab carta o ab testimonis. E si la donaran en testament, aquela franchea haja valor."

10. "Diu es dit en Dionis Rossell en lo dit nom que la dita demanda e lo articulant en aquella es tant inutil e impertinent que deu esser per vos dit magniffich tinent loch de governador lancada . . . . Diu lo dit en Dionis Rossell en lo nom qui dessus que no es recordant que lo dit en Johan Rossell jerma seu li haia dit en absencia del dit testimoni ne en presencia de aquell paraules continents en efecte que volia que la dita Maria fos en sa libertat. . . . Diu lo dit en Dionis Rossel en lo dit nom que lo dit en Johan Rossell frare de aquell nunqua li dix tals paraules ne les feu scriure al dit en Benet Salvador ans se mostra que lo dit en Johan Rossell no deya les dites paraules a la dita Maria sino per prozuduyir la que'l servis be en la dita malaltia metent la en speranca que la faria francha car si hagues tengut voluntat de fer la francha no ho haguera dit de paraula ans realment ho haguera posat en execucio fahent li carta de franquea."Gobernación 2304: M. 2:26v, M. 7:47r–48v, M. 8:1r–v; 2305: M. 12:43r–44v; 2306: M. 25:7r, ARV.

11. For one example among many, see Gobernación 2385: M. 9:16r, ARV. "E diu que ab carta publica feta en la present ciutat de Valencia a XIIII dies del mes de agost del any mil CCCCLXXXVI rebuda per lo discret en Johan Verancha notari la magnifica na Angela muller del magnifich en Berthomeu Cuteda donzell natural de la ciutat de Mallorques e domiciliat en lo castell de Caller del Regne de Cerdenya atorga libertat e franquea a Lucia negra cativa o sclava que solia esser de aquella en aquesta forma que servint quatre anys a la dita na Angela o a qui aquella volgues passats los dits quatre anys la dita Lucia fos libera franqua e alfora de tot jou de servitut. E jatsia per la dita carta la dita Luca fos e sia constituhida en gracia de libertat e passats los dits quatre anys nunch pro tunch li sia ja conferida e donada libertat empero la sobre dita na Angela apres de la dita constitucio de gracia e libertat atorgada a la dita Lucia ha cominat e encara comina alienar absegar e transportar la dita Lucia en frau prejuhi e dan de la dita Lucia e de la libertat a aquella atorgada e ha entes e enten en tal manera transportar e alienar la dita Lucia e en parts e regnes stranys e lunyadans que aquella dita Lucia perda los drets e justicia que te de la sua libertat o al menys per la distancia o lunyheha dels regnes e terres en los quals la vol transportar o alienar sia feta difficil la justicia de la dita Lucia o no la puixa haver ne obtenir."

12. Gobernación 23005: M. 12:44r, ARV. "E actenent que la dita demanda es fundada be e sufficientment per tant et als pronuncia e declara la dita demanda proceyr e ab la present condempna lo dit en Dionis Rossell en lo dit nom en donar libertat a la dita Maria en quant aquella haia obs de la dita libertat a aquella jaquida per lo dit en Johan Rossell esser donada per lo dit en Dionis Rossell en lo dit nom en forma que la dita Maria de tot en tot sua solts delliura de tot carrech de servitut no obstant res dit en contrari."

13. For a brief overview of the role and functions assigned to the *Procurador dels Miserables,* see F. Carreres I de Calatayud, "El Procurador dels Miserables: Notes per a la seua històrica," *Anales del Centrol de Cultura de Valenciana* 8 (193): 41–53.

14. Upon regaining custody of their slaves who had filed claims of freed status, masters and mistresses were ordered by court officials "que no la tragues de Valenica ni la venes ni maltractas." For one example among many, see Gobernación 2317: M. 35:32r, ARV.

15. The governor's efforts to secure a slave's protection, however, did not always meet with success. A Russian female slave named Anna, for instance, would complain that her master, upon regaining custody of her, whipped her naked body with a hempen rope "cruelly and with little piety." Not confident that he had fully cowed her into submission, Anna's master, likewise in violation of the governor's orders, snuck the slave out of town "so that she . . . would not be able to demand said liberty." Unfortunately, Anna does not reveal how she made it back to Valencia in order to pursue her claim. Gobernación 2317: M. 35:32r–33v, ARV.

16. Upon recovering custody of Juliana, her mistress promised—under a fine of two hundred florins—to uphold the terms of the following agreement: "Encara promes es obliga de no maltractar aquella axi com si no fos sclava e aco sots pena de docents florins aplicadors als cofrens del dit molt alt senyor rey e encara promes e obliga en poder del dit honorable tinent loch de governador que lexava aquella ho permetra que dos dies de la setmana co es lo dimarts e divendres en lo apres dinar una hora en cascu dels dits dies que aquella puxa venir a parlar e comunicar ab lo procurador e advocat per la present causa. E per co attendre e complir obliga en poder del dit honorable tinent loch de governador e lo dit notari scriva ut supra stipulant e rehebent tots sos bens e accions mobles inmobles priviligiats e non priviligiats hauts e per haver hon que sien ho seran." Gobernación 2287: M. 16:19r–21v, ARV.

17. Gobernación 2386: M. 12:40r–43r, ARV.

18. Gobernación 2348: M. 7:1r–2v; 36r–v, ARV. "Es cosa de mal exemple que les sclaves constituhides en stat de servitut per dir que tenen concordia ab lurs senyors de quitar se per certa quantitat stant tingue a ceruiment de anar s'en e proclamar en libertat."

19. "In order that the slave serve him more eagerly and more willingly (*ab milor cor e voluntat*)," Johan Rufach had agreed to grant Geronim his freedom. According to the terms of the agreement, however, he had done so not only under the condition that Geronim provide him with ten more years service but also under the proviso that during said term the slave would never abandon his service or his household. The agreement further stipulated that any failure on Geronim's part to live up to these terms would result in the automatic nullification of the agreement. Gobernación 2399: M. 20:28r–31r, ARV.

20. Geronim's partners in flight had convinced him that the freedom they secured in France would be recognized automatically everywhere such that, afterward, he could return to Valencia with impunity as a free man—"donant li a entendre que de continent que fosen en Francia quatre dies apres tots serien franchs e que puix fosen franchs apres porien venir aci en Valencia e pus no serien catius." When Geronim returned to Valencia a few years later, however, he discovered that in the eyes of his master and former neighbors, his status had not changed. His master assembled a veritable posse to recover him. After a rather spectacular standoff in which Geronim reportedly attacked (or in Geronim's perspective, defended himself against) his master with a sword in each hand, Geronim was subdued and returned to his master's household "bound and injured." Interestingly enough, this is not the end of the story. In scrupulous compliance with legal procedure, Johan Rufach appeared before the court of the governor to have Geronim's contract of manumission declared null and void. The governor, not surprisingly, complied, nullifying the contract not only on the grounds that the slave, by taking flight, had contravened the terms of the manumission agreement (*contravenint als pactes e condicions en lo dit contracte apposats*), but also, somewhat more important, because he had taken up "violent hands" against his lord (*manus violentiae progecit in dominum*)." Gobernación 2398: M. 3:1v; 2399: M. 20:28r–31r, ARV.

21. Although the executors insisted that Jacme's master had never definitively promised to grant him his freedom, they argued that even if he had, such an act of ingratitude effectively invalidated any claim to freedom he may have had. Unfortunately, the governor's final ruling in this case is not known. Gobernación 2285: M. 13:27r–29r, ARV.

22. In one fell swoop Francesch rather ingeniously invalidated both of Beatriu's claims to liberty. For in addition to citing Francesch's alleged promise to free her after three more years of service, Beatriu claimed that she was entitled to an automatic manumission as a consequence of bearing her master's child. By arguing that Lucia's "real" owner was Francesch's wife, Francesch effectively killed two birds with one stone. The promise to free her was invalid

because Francesch lacked the legal title to grant her freedom. Likewise, whether or not Francesch was the father of Beatriu's baby became inconsequential since a female slave was entitled to an automatic manumission only if she could prove that her owner was the child's father. Gobernación 2371: M. 3:14r; 2372: M. 13:38r–42r, ARV. Unfortunately, we do not know the governor's ultimate ruling on this case.

23. Gobernación 2405: M. 28:11r–13r, ARV: "Aquell no procex de justicia per co com lo dit en Miquel Miro no podia vendre ni alienar la dita Lucia ni apposat pacte e condicio de libertat e aco per quant lo dit en Miquel Miro ab carta rebuda per en Pere Soler notari a quinze de jener any mil quatrecent huytanta tres feu donacio al dit en Pere Miro a tots sos bens hauts e per aver en lo temps de la dita donacio o apres. . . . E per la dita raho la dita demanda de libertat no procehira de justicia com la dita inposeccio e donacio de libertat nos podia fer per co com lo dit en Miquel Miro no esser senyor de la dita . . . no podia donar ni imposar la dita libertat en prejuhi del dit en Pere Miro donatar." The governor's ultimate ruling on this case was a compromise. Lucia was obliged to provide Pere with two more years of service, after which Pere was obliged to grant Lucia her freedom.

24. In the end, however, Miquel was able to assemble three witnesses who could testify on his behalf that Jaume, even though he had not been physically present at the time of the charter's composition, had publicly acknowledged that he and his wife had granted Miquel his freedom. The governor ruled in Miquel's favor, proclaiming Miquel "freed" and ordering Jaume to stop harassing him. Gobernación 2406: M. 1:25v, M. 8:5r–6v, ARV.

25. Justicia Civil 923: M. 13:44r–48r, M. 14:11r–12v, ARV. In the end the Justicia Civil ruled in Johan Roiz de Corella's favor, declaring that "said slave ought not to be granted his freedom . . . either before or after the ten years indicated in the aforestated testament." Declaring "said Johan Roiz de Corella to be the absolute and eternal lord of said slave," the Justicia Civil gave him "license, faculty and complete authority to sell and/or alienate said slave absolutely and in perpetuity as his property."

26. Since Johan in turn denied that he had ever stolen anything and insisted that he had been seized unlawfully less than a month after his master's death on trumped up charges of theft, it is rather unfortunate that the governor's final ruling on this case did not survive. Gobernación 2354: M. 1:27r; 2357: M. 28:24r, ARV.

27. Excerpt from the charter of freedom, issued on May 18, 1461: "Hanc autem franquitatem manumissionem quittacionem et alforiam tibi facio et concedo tibi sub hiis tamen condicionibus et non alias videlicet quod tu tenearis michi et meis servire per temps octo annorum a presenti die in antea computandorum bene fideliter ac legaliter et durante dicto tempore non fugiens a servicio et domo ac dominio meo ni batre ni mal tractare les besties mies. Quibus quidem octo annis completiis et dictis condicionibus ad plenum omnibus servatis als si contra dictas condiciones et unam quancumque venies nunch pro tunch et tunch pro nunch revoco et pro revocata cassi nulla et irrita habeo presentem franquitatem libertatem et alforiam et sis servus meus et in mea potestate sicut eras ante." Gobernación 2331: M. 20:41r–42v, ARV.

28. Gobernación 2332: M. 27:3r–12v, ARV.

29. Gobernación 2331: M. 20:41r–42v; 2332: M. 27:3r–12v, ARV.

30. Further evidence of the importance of "cartas de franquea" in securing freed status are the numerous reports of slaves counterfeiting them. In her study of slavery in sixteenth-century Granada, Aurelia Martín Casares found that there was a veritable black market for them. She cites one case from 1672 in which two men, Don Antonio de Cantos and Don Pedro Benavides, were exiled from Granada (as well as from Sevilla, Llerena, Murcia, and Madrid) and

condemned to four years of galley service for "hazer cartas de libertad para los esclavos y que con ellas y firmas y sellos falsos del Santo Oficio abían dado libertad a casi todos los berberiscos de Andaluzía para que pasasen a su tierra." Martín further notes how the Cortes of 1552 issued a statue forbidding the trafficking in charters of freedom, warning that "otrosí que como los esclavos quieren ser libres, en siendo libres procuran de hacer malos a todos los esclavos acogiéndolos en sus casas y les dan sus cartas de horro y ansí se hacen muchos fugitivos." Martín Casares, *Esclavitud en la Granada,* 436–437.

31. Gobernación 2332: M. 30:30r–v, ARV. Unfortunately for Anthoni, the charter of freedom was completely ineffective in protecting his "freed status." The procurador fischal of Valencia deemed it "worthless" on the grounds that it had been issued by an illegitimate authority, a Catalan rebel against the Crown. Anthoni was arrested and imprisoned in the "preso comuna" of the city, whereupon he appealed to the governor for assistance. The governor accepted the case, but his final ruling on the matter did not survive.

32. The merchant Marti Gual and his wife Pereta promised Maria that they would sign and give her a "carta de libertat e de franquessa" as soon as she paid her fifty-pound redemption fee in full. Gobernación 2296: M. 24:37r–39v, ARV.

33. For one example among many, see Protocolos 2240 (Jaume Tolosa), March 21, 1477, ARV. "Item leix a Luisa negra o lora esclava mia franqua e quita de tota servitut e jou de aquella et que per la dita marmessora li sia feta carta de franquea. Item leix a aquella matexa lo lit on aquella jau e tota la roba de aquella."

34. Gobernación 2348: M. 3:42r, ARV. In particular Lucia feared that this third party would "resell" her for a term of service in excess to the term of service required for her liberation. "E essent en poder del dit en Johan Fort tement que aquella no fos venuda a mes temps del que deuia servir reclama e recorregut al illustrisimo senyor infant."

35. Gobernación 2385: M. 1:20v, M. 9:16r–17v, ARV. Lucia's advocate complained that "jatsia per la dita carta la dita Lucia fos e sia constituhida en gracia de libertat e passats los dits quatre anys nunch pro tunch li sia ja conferida e donada libertat empero la sobredita na Angela apres de la dita constitucio de gracia e libertat atorgada a la dita Lucia ha conviat e encara convia alienar absegar e transportar la dita Lucia en frau prejuhi e dan de la dita Lucia e de la libertat a aquella atorgada e ha entes e enten en tal manera transportar e alienar la dita Lucia en parts e regnes stranys e lunyadans que aquella Lucia perda los drets e justicia que te de la sua libertat o al menys per la distancia o lunyheda dels regnes e terres en los quals la vol transportar o alienar sia feta difficil la justicia de la dita Lucia o no la puixa haver ne obtenir."

36. Gobernación 2385: M. 1:20v, M. 9:16r–17v, ARV. Lucia was not to be released into her mistress's custody "fins e tro a tant la dita Lucia sia asegurada be sufficientment et ab bones seguretats obligacions e fermances que durant lo temps restant dels dits quatre anys que ha de servir la dita Lucia no sia alienada transportada empenyorada ni absegada ni encara treta e separada dels regnes o terres del rey nostre senyor que te deca mar ni dels regnes de Arago Valencia e principat de Catalunya a fi que passat lo dit temps restant dels dits quatre anys la dita Lucia sens empaig o impediment algu puixa usar e alegrar se de la sua libertat e no li sia feta dificultosa ni turbacio per alienacio o absegacio e per transportar la en part o regnes que no puixa haver ni obtenir la sua justicia."

JONATHAN SCHORSCH

Transformations in the Manumission of Slaves by Jews from East to West

—ᴍ—

Pressures from the Atlantic Slave Trade

This essay traces some of the changes wrought in the methods by which Jews liberated their slaves under the influence of the racialized slave system and economy forged in the Atlantic world from the fifteenth century into the eighteenth.[1] From the early Middle Ages Jews constituted a numerically insignificant and frequently persecuted segment of the population of the Mediterranean and European countries in which they resided. Nonetheless, Jewish elites— merchants and pseudo-aristocrats—like their non-Jewish counterparts, owned slaves and shared the surrounding attitudes toward slaves. In Muslim regions Jews were often allowed to possess pagan and Christian slaves, while in Christian lands they were frequently permitted to own pagan and Muslim slaves. While one might expect Jews to have behaved in accord with a fairly constant "Jewish" framework based on the scriptural and legal tradition (Torah and Halakha), a more detailed historical survey shows that the constant in "Jewish" behavior regarding slaves instead lay in the emulation of the subculture of slaveholding of each particular host country or region. Jewish slave owners, that is, were still Jews in many facets of their religious and daily lives but also lived out components of their lives within a rubric shared by the general local culture. Throughout the medieval and early modern Mediterranean region, slavery was a domestic affair; the servants and slaves of Jews tended to be women. But whatever the gender, these slaves seem generally to have been converted and manumitted ritually according to halakhic norms and, when manumitted, absorbed in some fashion within the Jewish community. Beginning in seventeenth-century northwestern European countries (the Netherlands, England), these practices began to recede, while in the Americas, they nearly disappeared entirely.

A note should be said regarding the responsa literature, which serves as the major source for information on Jews and their slaves east of the Atlantic. Responsa constitute queries addressed to rabbis concerning proper practice, which arose out of the daily life of Jewish communities. The voluminous literature of collections of such responsa—every famous rabbi (and some not so famous rabbis) or his pupils would publish a collection of the queries put to him and his responses—comprises a treasure trove of material for scholars. But they also present hermeneutic dangers. Like all legal records, without additional external sources, they provide only the most artificial and curtailed glimpse into living situations. In the process of publication the queries were made anonymous, often lacking any mention of locale or dates. The names used in the cases discussed were almost always masked, the Hebrew equivalents of John Doe: Shim'on was in the market one day . . . , Re'uven sent his slave to tell his uncle . . . , Levi had a wife whose slave mistakenly mixed milk and meat . . . , and so on. Perhaps more significant, the queries were probably edited; the originals in most cases cannot be found. Attendant to the shortcomings of these historical sources, however, one can put them to great use.

There is, of course, circular reasoning in concluding that queries to rabbis evince halakhic concerns on the part of Jewish laypeople. Still, as will be seen, the mere existence of such a high degree of halakhic consideration on the part of those turning to rabbis contrasts sharply with western Europe and the Americas, where responsa dealing with the practical halakhic issues of slavery are rare. Several factors play a role in the creation of this difference. For one thing, the sociological segmentation of the Jewish and non-Jewish judicial system in the Muslim Mediterranean promoted jurisdiction by rabbis and rabbinic courts over both the content of legal questions regarding slaves and the form or methodology in which such questions would be asked and resolved. Though many individual Jews brought their cases before non-Jewish courts, the rabbinic and communal leadership continued to prohibit the turning to non-Jewish courts.[1] In western Europe and the Americas, not only did individual Jews show themselves more ready to consult the general court system and to internalize its modes of legal reasoning but also the leadership encouraged the abandonment of halakhic fora for slave-related issues. A responsum of Rabbi Meir b. Shem Tov Melamed (early seventeenth century; Salonika [the Jewish name for Thessaloniki]) ruled that a maidservant to whom her master had bequeathed much of his property could not inherit it, as the will had been made in a non-Jewish Egyptian court and was therefore not halakhically valid or binding.[2] I have not seen any statement from western Europe that so discriminated against non-Jewish courts when it came to slaves. Perhaps this is what the seventeenth-century Rabbi Avraham b. Eliezer ha-Levi of Jerusalem meant when he described how the many important conversos flocking to Amsterdam "conduct themselves like Christian merchants in matters of business, wills and donations."[3] The difference between behavior regarding slaves east and west of the Atlantic is not to be found in the behavior of Jewish individuals, however, but rather in the contrasting positions of community leaders.

This is not to say that all Mediterranean Jewish slave owners followed halakhic procedure. Indeed, many rabbis complained about the very opposite problem. Some Jews simply took things into their own hands. According to the responsa of one Salonikan rabbi, one Jew, whose non-Jewish slave woman's son begged him for liberation, simply recited the formula for manumission and told the slave to go immerse himself before a rabbinic court, whereas Halakha required the master's participation at and surrounding the immersion.[4] A case brought to another Salonikan rabbi involved a slave woman who immersed for the sake of conversion to Judaism at the instigation of her master, without even bothering about the rabbinic court.[5] Shmuel de Medina of Salonika complained that the slaves and maidservants bought by Jews often ended up converting and marrying Jews after their liberation, without anyone bothering to check whether they had been manumitted properly or at all.[6]

EAST OF THE ATLANTIC

In almost every respect the manumission of slaves by Jewish owners followed the contours of the practice in the surrounding culture. Practices and attitudes regarding slaves were of course not identical from one religious community to another, but the differences paled in comparison to the pervasive conceptual fluidity between them.

Early modern Jews did not automatically convert their slaves immediately upon acquisition, as had been the halakhic norm in rabbinic thought until perhaps the ninth or tenth centuries. Already in the writing of Maimonides it was assumed that conversion occurred with the slave's manumission rather than with his purchase, and sociologically this seems to have become common. Yet Rabbi David Ibn Zimra (Egypt; 1479–1573) stated that the Egyptian Jews *did* immerse their slaves, both at purchase for the sake of enslavement and upon liberation for the sake of conversion.[7] That is, the halakhic norms themselves, not the behavior of individuals, had undergone changes. Yet it seems clear from the responsa literature that many Jews worried about getting the halakhic procedure of manumission right.[8] Indeed, the responsa literature is filled with queries regarding manumissions; these queries represented, of course, only those cases which led to halakhic problems.

Manumission was not something a servant or slave could necessarily expect. The majority of manumissions by Jews of which we have evidence came in the masters' last will and testament. As Ruth Pike insightfully commented, "Manumission by will had advantages, for the master retained the services of the slaves as long as he needed them; the prospect of freedom encouraged good conduct on the part of the slave; and the slaveholder could depart this life with a freer conscience."[9] Manumissions during the lifetime of the master of course occurred, but their rarity is proven by the manner in which they are described in the sources. Of one eighteenth-century rabbi of Constantinople, who had a bought a maidservant from among war captives, we read: "And after a time his spirit moved him . . . and he liberated her before [a Jewish] court according to Jewish law and practice."[10] The spirit moving him, though idiomatic, alludes ultimately to Exodus 35:21 and the voluntary donation of goods for the new tabernacle, implying that the liberation of his maidservant constituted not only an act of personal piety but of rarity.

Statistically the accumulation of anecdotes about manumissions and failures to manumit leads nowhere. There is no evidence that Jews freed their slaves more or less readily or generously than did non-Jews. One Spanish traveler noted slightly before 1555 that in Valladolid, then capitol of Castile, slaves were often given their liberty in their masters' wills.[11] Historian Ovadia Salama, writing about Ottoman Jerusalem, stated that "the liberation of slaves [was] considered a religious obligation within all of the communities, and in general it is so as well in the Christian community."[12] He proceeded to gives some wonderful examples, from the 1570s through the 1860s, of Greek Orthodox monks freeing slaves immediately after purchase and "for the sake of heaven."

As in Muslim and Christian cultures, the Jewish attitude toward slaves and their liberation came fraught with ambivalence. Many rabbis and laypeople held that non-Jewish, that is, so-called Canaanite, slaves were never to be freed. One of the chief rabbis of Salonika, Yoseph ben David (1662–1736), reported that in his time some Jews thought that freeing non-Jewish slaves meant transgressing a positive commandment to work them forever (Lev. 26:46), a view based on opinions attributed in the Babylonian Talmud (tractate Gitin 38b) to R. Judah in the name of Samuel and R. Eliezer.[13]

A number of rabbinic responsa indicate that slave women often sought entry to their Jewish host communities and often managed to achieve such in both halakhic and solely de facto manner, regardless of whether or not they were properly freed. These responsa reveal as well the differing layers of social practice and religious understanding involved in such cases. We will now examine a few such cases.

A Sephardic woman named Doña Paloma owned a black maidservant ("Kushite" in the texts) named Simha (meaning "happiness") whom she had given to her daughter, Dina. Simha had been imported by Doña Paloma's brother to Portugal, whence the family had moved to Ferrara some thirty years before, in about 1553. The brother had given her to his mother, who passed her on to Doña Paloma. Doña Paloma testified in 1583 before a rabbinic court in Ferrara, Italy, about the serving woman. When the daughter married,

> she went to the bathing house and also this the said maidservant Simha who wanted to go bathe in order to be a Jewess [went]. We [the rabbinic court] asked [Dina's mother Paloma] whether she [the maidservant Simha] had

accepted the commandments of the Jews in front of 3 Jewish witnesses and [Doña Paloma] answered that she had not accepted anything in front of anyone. We asked her if the mistress, the said Dina had been present when [Simha] bathed and she answered that she had not been but that she knew that [Simha] desired to bathe and she also said that [Simha] was punctilious about Jewish practice and observed the Sabbath.[14]

One cannot discount the possibility that the mother of the mistress exaggerated the serving woman's Jewish loyalties in order to remove blame from her daughter and herself for the improper manner of her ritual immersion and the fact that she had been living since then as if she were Jewish. The family members very possibly did not understand the correct sequence of ritual procedures and their significance. For example, there is no mention of a previous immersion, which would have been for the sake of slavery, to make this (second) immersion one for the sake of conversion, just as there is no mention of the maidservant Simha's having been manumitted, as would have also been necessary to make her a full Jew.

Not content, the rabbinic court interviewed another old woman, Doña Confrada, asking her if she remembered the events: "She answered that she remembers that she [the maidservant] came to the bathing house with the daughter of her mistress and bathed before her eyes [Doña Confrada] properly and correctly in order to become Jewish. We asked her if she knew whether [Simha] had accepted the commandments before 3 people and she answered that she had not seen that she had accepted anything. . . . We asked her how many times she went to the bathing house and she answered, that one time only she went down to bathe."[15] This Spanish woman, who might have been the bathing house attendant or a family friend, defended the maidservant Simha's immersion against halakhic requirements for 3 witnesses, as she had served as the only witness. Doña Confrada's stance hints at contestation, possibly gendered, between varying layers of functionaries. Some time later Simha bore a child to a Sephardic Jew also living in Ferrara, who had the boy circumcised.[16] Perhaps Simha had lied about her status or simply misunderstood it. One sees throughout this case the disjunction between halakhic requirements and the actual practice of those involved, with the latter consistently erring on the side of inclusion. Rabbi Boton, on the other hand, ruled that the maidservant could not be considered a Jewess.[17] Finally, it should be noted that nowhere here do we have the voice of Simha herself, so that her mistress's assertions about her desires to enter the Jewish community cannot be taken for granted.

Women such as Simha fold into the not-insignificant number of slaves who remained attached in one way or another to the Jewish community.[18] Many former maidservants married into the community.[19] In a 1721 case treated by

Rabbi Hayyim Moshe b. Shlomo Amarillo (1695–1748; Salonika, Constantinople), a maidservant belonging to two Jewish brothers had a daughter (of unstated paternity) who years later was immersed and converted by the new Jewish owners, who had inherited her mother and married off to a Jewish man.[20] One gentile maidservant who had been born in Salonika or its environs into the Jewish home of three business partners was immersed for conversion while still a girl, then married off to a Jewish man after four or five years.[21] No doubt these marriages held socioeconomic benefits for both parties. This most prominent form of manumission conforms to what Orlando Patterson has labeled "domestic assimilation."[22]

Even beyond marriage many former slave women affiliated with a Jewish community. One woman who had been brought as a non-Jewish captive of war to Constantinople and bought there by a rabbi eventually received her freedom from him. She converted at her manumission and maintained affiliation with the Jewish community, coming at a later date (1702) before a rabbinical court, where her trustworthiness (and that of her former master) convinced the court to vouch for her manumission and conversion despite her having lost all of the pertinent documents.[23] A non-Jewish serving woman sold by her Jewish master to another Jew was sent to the latter by sea, where she was captured by privateers. Landed at Leghorn, Italy (known to Jews as Livorno), the Jewish community redeemed her, and there she converted to Judaism.[24] Cases such as this last one tell us little about the slave's motivations, which could have been spiritual (sincere affection for Judaism), pragmatic (a convenient means of gaining liberty), or a combination of factors. One case brought to Rabbi Shmuel de Medina shows that some former slaves made their way into the Jewish community quite willingly. One maidservant bore a son to her master and had him circumcised.

> She brought the son to her master before a judge of the city, from the government, and claimed that she was [her master's] wife and became pregnant from him and gave birth, and the judge compelled him to sustain and maintain her, [the judge] also did for her [the ceremony called] *kaibin* according to their [Muslim] religion (and since he did *kaibin* [the master] cannot sell her, for she is like his wife in all regards, according to what I heard and learned from experts in their custom). And this woman remained some years in the [master's] house on her own. Even after the death of the master there was no one who could tell her anything [regarding the matter], to say to her that she is a maidservant, and she would observe the teaching of Moses and of a Jewess like the kosher women of Israel, until she was made a midwife by/to the Hebrews, and she had some little money and she passed it to the *gazbarim* to distribute, part to the land of Israel, may it be built speedily in our day, and part for inheritance and part to the

burial society. And after her death the master's heirs came to claim the money for themselves.[25]

The extent of this woman's participation in her adopted community was tremendous and entirely voluntary. She maintained Jewish ritual practices, worked for and among Jews, and even left money to some of the kinds of causes typically patronized by philanthropic Jews.

We know nothing of the backgrounds of many of these maidservants. Chances are that most of them would not have been in a position to return home on being liberated, even if they had known whence they came. Certainly the widespread negative pressure on "pagans" among believers of all the three major monotheistic religions engendered the desire in the mostly pagan slaves to avoid serving the dominant majority. Rabbi David ibn Zimra testified that in Egypt he saw that "all the maidservants at this time do not accept the *mitzvot* [commandments] on their own accord, and even though they say they do, it is but insincerely, since they are from the sect of pagans and seek not to be sold to Muslims."[26] Spanish Christian servants, as appear in some of the responsa, presumably would also have felt more compatible with Iberian Jews than in a Muslim Turkish home.

The immersion of a maidservant or manservant was to take place in front of the master, probably so that he could ensure the efficacy of the ritual. Rabbi Shlomo b. Avraham ha-Cohen treated a case that originally had been brought to another rabbi about a maidservant who immersed, but not in front of her master, and doubt existed over whether the immersion was done for the slave of slavery or for conversion.[27] This provided another good reason for the master to supervise the proceedings. Ushering the slave into the Jewish community, manumission was often performed in a public sphere. During the first three centuries of the common era, Jews in the Hellenized Bosporus region executed the manumission of their slaves in the prayer house.[28] Rabbi Yosef David mentioned a case in which the masters of a serving girl "had her immersed for the sake of conversion in her youth by means of a rabbinical court and the majority of local residents as was customary."[29] The public eye would also prevent a situation like the one put before Rabbi Shmuel b. Moshe Kalai in which the leader of a Jewish community was suspected of having an affair with his maidservant, who had been converted quietly such that no one in the community knew who had immersed her.[30] One clearly sees here how the rite of immersion served, in the words of Meyer Fortes, as the "ritual mobiliz[ing] incontrovertible authority behind the granting of office and status and this guarantees its legitimacy and imposes accountability for its proper exercise."[31]

The rite of manumission must have had a powerful impact on the slave. Wrote Rabbi David ha-Cohen (Corfu; d. ca. 1530), "When a slave becomes free he is like every other Jew."[32] According to Halakha, the master or mistress would bring the slave or maidservant before a rabbinical court and briefly inform him or her concerning some of the minor and major commandments that would soon become obligatory. In a case dealt with by the Salonika rabbi Aharon b. Hayyim Avraham ha-Cohen Perahya, one master freed "the son of a Christian maidservant who had not immersed for the sake of slavery. And his master says to him, 'In order to fulfil your request and carry out your will, I hereby release you and remove all of the power and right that I have over you. Go acquire the rights to yourself and immerse for the sake of freedom before a rabbinic court and be free. And you are your own [lit., for yourself] and I have no claim over you nor servitude.'"[33] These words constitute a performative speech act in the sense made classic by J. L. Austen: words whose effect in a certain setting bear efficacy to change things in the real world. Perhaps in an effort to escape from the doubts often tied up with manumission, one famous rabbi, Hayyim Abulafia, seems to have required a ceremony carried out before himself at which he would dispense to the slave or maidservant two coins, one with which to buy her freedom from her master.[34] Ritual immersion followed. The excitement and enthusiasm generated by this ritual cleansing away of the servile status in some cases burst out beyond the decorous confines in which it usually was performed. Rabbi Aharon b. Hayyim Avraham ha-Cohen Perahya of Salonika was asked whether the following spontaneous immersion ceremony was kosher:

> One [man] came to convert his maidservant and to free her, and brought her before the rabbinical court. . . . And when they came to immerse her, which needs to be before a court of three rabbis, the Turkish bath owner would not permit them to enter, and in the [Jewish] ritual bath men were occupied. Since the ritual bath for women is at the bath house where the Turkish and other non-Jewish women bathe, and there is no other ritual bath other than at the bath house where the women immerse after their period, many kosher women went there [with the maidservant] to bathe her. And she immersed in front of them.[35]

Despite halakhic understandings that a freed slave or maidservant assumed a rank absolutely equal to that of any other Jew, the social reality did not always agree. The canonical sixteenth-century legal compendium Shulkhan Arukh marked an advance of sorts. The textual contiguity of the laws pertaining to slaves, with those of converts (immediately preceding them) and circumcision (immediately following), projected the ideal of absorption; in Maimonides' multivolume code, the laws of circumcision and converts had come in the section titled "Love / Ahava," those of slaves in the section titled "Purchase" or "Acquisition of Things / Kinyan." The reality no doubt varied from slave to slave and between one host community and another. "Ever after shall I be known as a former slave—a freed-man," complained a slave who had inherited his master's wealth in a play composed around 1550 by the Jewish Italian writer Leone de' Sommi (or Sommo).[36] Indeed, Jacob Katz aptly called circumcised and converted slaves "'half' Jews."[37] Such snobbery derived from traditional attitudes toward slaves and slavery. Talmudic opinion on slaves, though complicated and containing significant tendencies of kindness, held slaves in as low esteem as Greek or Roman law. Slaves were stripped of the natural and human relationships into which they were born. Indeed, not all Jewish authorities accepted freed slaves into the community. One seventeenth-century Ashkenazic rabbi cited the popular anthology Yalkut Shimoni to the effect that converts and manumitted slaves do not merit inheritance in the land of Israel.[38] Hence manumission did not always necessitate conversion to Judaism. In his responsa chief rabbi of Salonika Yitshak b. Eliahu Shangi (d. 1761) produced the text of a contract (*get*) of liberation which was not for the purpose of conversion.[39] Clearly some slaves and masters chose a path leading elsewhere than the Jewish community.

Still many of the published cases indicate that even in situations where doubts arose concerning whether a slave's manumission had been properly executed, a rabbi was consulted, since the owners or slave evidently desired the slave to be allowed into the community, often through marriage.[40] As we have seen, many reasons caused room for doubt. Most cases point to the inclusion of former slaves into the Jewish community, even if rulings (especially in inheritance cases) often disfavored them and their descendants. This accords well with evidence from non-Jewish eastern Mediterranean communities.

INTO THE COLONIES

The desire to convert slaves to Judaism underwent a certain amount of repression in the early modern West at the hands of community leaders. Similarly, the manumission of slaves by Jews came to occur not in halakhic contexts but through non-Jewish state institutions. By the seventeenth and eighteenth centuries the circumcision of male slaves and the conversion of all slaves to Judaism seem to have become undesirable and unpracticed in Jewish communities in Holland, England, and their American colonies. Communal practices, including religious ones, experience natural up and down swings, and circumcision poses no exception. According to Israel Abrahams, the "tendency to enforce [circumcision of slaves] grows with the middle ages" so that "the sixteenth century finds Jews more resolute in this matter than the tenth century found them."[41] The decline after the sixteenth century in part stemmed from general political and religious pressures against conversion to Judaism, especially in the English orbit. It also derived from general trends of Jewish acculturation and falling away from halakhic living, especially in the Americas. But this transformation also reflected a more intimate nexus with the increasing identity of servitude and blackness: (1) an increasing propensity to follow halakhic opinion holding that the laws of slavery no longer obtained or to disregard halakhic thinking completely when it came to slaves, and (2) the growing use value of "racial" notions in the vocabulary of Jewish leaders and thinkers.

The seventeenth century was a liminal period during which these practices began to be ignored. It seems that at first many of the black slaves belonging to Jews indeed underwent the rituals necessary to work in Jewish homes. This can be inferred from cemetery records as well as other sources. But many of the most prominent western Sephardi communities either banned the circumcision of bought slaves—first in Recife in Dutch Brazil (1649) and then in Amsterdam (1650)—or ignored it in practice. Additional evidence from Amsterdam, London, and the Dutch and English colonies regarding means of ritual absorption into the Jewish community also fails to indicate the consistent circumcision of male slaves or the proper ritual immersion of either female or male slaves, much less their conversion. I am not arguing that some Jews in these places did not continue to circumcise and/or immerse their slaves, but that more Jews began not doing so (unlike in eastern Mediterranean regions) and that communal leaders discouraged the conversion of nonwhite slaves.[42] The very instability of the pertinent seventeenth-century discourse and actions reflects this shift.

The distinct transformation in the discourse around circumcision can be read in several texts, all of which derive from Amsterdam. The starkest such indication of change is Rabbi David Pardo's simple and brief translation of the Shulkhan Arukh into Spanish from 1689, which completely fails to mention that male slaves are to be circumcised, unlike its source text, whose first edition's section on laws pertaining to slaves opens with the heading, "One who takes a slave, to him it is forbidden to maintain [the slave] uncircumcised," though Pardo's translation goes to the trouble of listing the minor point from its source that slaves can perform circumcisions under the close supervision of their owner.[43] Other authors, in particular those from Amsterdam, also ignored without explanation this seemingly critical and clear biblical commandment, including many prominent rabbis: a 1683 Hebrew compendium of the commandments by R. Selomoh de Oliveyra; the list of commandments at the back of a 1695 Spanish translation of the Five Books of Moses; a 1713 compendium of the commandments; a similar Hebrew compendium from 1753; a 1763 verse rendition of the commandments according to Rambam; and a 1768 circumcision booklet.[44]

Again, I am not seeking to prove that the religious absorption of slaves disappeared, but that so many rabbis could overlook it indicates that something other than general pressure against Halakha was operative. After all, these western Sephardic communities continued to be highly ritually observant in many ways throughout the seventeenth century, if not later. These silences cannot all be mere oversights. It would seem that many leading Sephardic rabbis entered an unpublicized campaign to suppress the practice of circumcising slaves. These examples, all from the second half of the seventeenth century, were probably motivated by the general prohibition in 1650 of the circumcision of blacks and mulattos by the Amsterdam Sephardic Mahamad, the communal governing body. The Amsterdam ban in turn may very well have stemmed from the ordinance passed only the previous year by the Mahamad in Recife, Brazil, declaring that slaves could only be circumcised *after* their liberation. We will further discuss the forces motivating this sea change below.

Legislation in western Sephardic communities accompanied the discursive move away from the ritual absorption of slaves. The 1649 *haskamot* (communal ordinances) of Recife explicitly addressed the issue of circumcising slaves. No doubt, as in Amsterdam, these *haskamot* proceeded from a specific local cause; Jonathan Israel mentioned, without citing a source, that in early Dutch Brazil "a few of the Jews were mulatto half-castes."[45] Instead of banning conversions of slaves (and not slaves alone) the Mahamad attempted to control them: "No person shall—except with the permission of the Gentlemen of the Mahamad—circumcise a stranger or admit a strange woman to the Theuilah, under penalty of being separated from the nation and fined fifty florins. And if that person be a slave, he shall not be circumcised without first having been freed by his master, so that the master shall not be able to sell him from the moment the slave will have bound himself [to Judaism]."[46] The last provision constitutes a nimble response to the specific exigencies of the Brazilian slave economy in which Jewish merchants routinely possessed enormous numbers of slaves temporarily before selling them off. Yet halakhic reasoning had long before permitted the temporary possession of uncircumcised slaves. The provision ensured the potential convert—slaves belonging to Jewish masters, urban and rural—that his or her conversion would guarantee manumission but effectively penalized any master who circumcised his slaves. Whether protective of the slave's interest or exclusive for the sake of the Jewish community, the provision went directly contrary to the Shulkhan Arukh and would have placed a hardship on observant masters in a slave economy such as Brazil.

Even Jews in supposedly traditional and observant communities in the Mediterranean region often failed to observe *halakhot* pertaining to the circumcision and/or immersion of slaves. What differs in the movement westward, then, is that communal leaders and rabbis stopped insisting on the necessity of these same *halakhot*, if not actively discouraged their practice. If circumcision of slaves occurred at all, it was only in the rare cases of the slave's conversion to Judaism, not at purchase, as required by most halakhists except in certain extenuating circumstances.[47] The Halakha in practice among Sephardim in western Europe and the colonies seems to have made this merely a circumcision performed upon voluntary conversion. To understand why this was so, we turn to issues never brought up in the literature treating the question of whether or not to circumcise one's slaves: the increasing correlation of servitude and skin color. Indeed, a certain irony attends the trend of westward movement with the suppression of circumcision. While in Europe external pressures operated against the conversion or circumcision of Christians, who might be servants in Jewish households, across the Atlantic far less concern existed about the conversion or circumcision of black slaves to Judaism, since the Christianization of these slaves itself remained an ambivalent goal.

In the mid–seventeenth century the "Portuguese" Jewish community of Amsterdam instituted some communal ordinances which reflected and constructed the desired "ethnic" transformation of the Jews into "whites." It is this legislation that explains the transformation of attitudes toward the conversion and circumcision of slaves and the drastic decrease of both practices. These cases adumbrate the process through which whiteness became an operative principle in the organization of Jewish communal life in these two locations.

Perhaps the first exclusionary practice emerged in 1624. Since according to Halakha, Judaism is transmitted by the mother, the Mahamad tried to encourage formal conversion to Judaism among returning conversos with dubiously Jewish ancestors (i.e., Old Christians) by denying Jewish burial "to any person of any quality who might in the feminine line be of the race of *goys* [non-Jews]."[48] Three years later, in 1627, an ordinance was passed restricting access to burial at the community's cemetery, officially opened only in 1618: "No black person nor mulato will be able to be buried in the cemetary, except for those who had buried in it a Jewish mother. . . . None shall persuade any of the said blacks and mulatos, man or woman, or any other person who is not of the nation of Israel to be made Jews."[49] While the prohibition intended all foreigners, the specification of blacks and mulattos reflected both the reality of their presence as slaves or servants in the Amsterdam Jewish community as well as the degree to which they were seen to draw negative attention. An ordinance passed in 1614 with the initial purchase of the Ouderkerk cemetery had already established a separate section "intended especially for the burial of slaves, servants and 'Jewish girls, who are not of our Nation.'"[50] Though the motivation in 1627 still was halakhic, the language had in twelve years become explicitly "racial." Archival records in the Gemeentearchief Amsterdam reflect the perception that "of the first few blacks living in Amsterdam, most belonged to Portuguese Jews."[51]

Other exclusionary ordinances soon followed within the seventeenth-century Amsterdam Sephardic community. All drew on similar ordinances from the Iberian Catholic colonial world and reflect trends beginning to appear as well in the northern European Protestant colonial orbit. In 1640 the Amsterdam Sephardic communal board ordered that black and mulatto girls be allowed to sit in the synagogue's women's gallery only from the eighth row and farther back. At the same time the Mahamad decreed that the doors to the women's section of the sanctuary were not to be opened before six in the morning in order to prevent the congregating of these slave women and other servants on the street.[52] Four years later the men of the communal board decreed that "circumcised Negro Jews" were not to be called to the Torah or given any honorary commandment to perform in the synagogue, "for such is fitting for the reputation of the congregation and its good government."[53] Dutch Protestant planters in Brazil had been making it difficult for their slaves to attend church services as early as if not earlier than a 1636 report to that effect by a Dutch Protestant pastor.[54] In 1647 a separate section of the Sephardic cemetery was established for "all the Jewish Negroes and mulattoes." Exceptions were limited to those "who were born in Judaism, [their parents] having [been married] with *quedosim* [with *kiddushin*, that is, properly, according to Jewish law], or those who were married to whites with *quedosim*."[55] In other words *very* few if any blacks or mulattos would have qualified for burial in the Jewish cemetery proper. That so many blacks and mulattos *did* receive burial in the segregated section of the Jewish cemetery after this ordinance reflects a communal rift when it came to treatment of slaves. While the Mahamad wished to terminate the inclusion of blacks and mulattos in Jewish life, individual owners clearly saw fit to continue including them. In 1658 the Mahamad decided that mulatto boys would no longer be admitted for study in the Amsterdam yeshiva of the Sephardim.[56] Based on a view expressed in the Talmud, some early medieval rabbis, as well as Maimonides, prohibited the teaching of Torah to one's slave and ruled that such knowledge did not cause his liberation. These seventeenth-century mulattos were not identified as slaves, however; the issue was their background. Such an exclusion of "Others" considered unworthy had other general precedents. The Jesuit College of St. Peter and St. Paul in Mexico City, founded in 1582, had included in its constitution a clause expressly forbidding the admission of blacks and mulattos.[57] Indeed, since the mid-1500s, full-blooded American Indians and blacks were not allowed to receive holy orders or hold sacerdotal office in the viceroyalties of Mexico or Peru.[58] By the early seventeenth century, exceptions aside, the Jesuits and other religious orders working in the Kongo and Angola "refused to admit either blacks or mulattos to their own ranks, though they did train them at [their] colleges to enter the secular priesthood."[59]

Though only one Sephardic community outside of Amsterdam, Suriname, produced ordinances with similarly explicit exclusions, it seems that most such communities in the Americas followed them in practice.[60] By the eighteenth century Surinamese Sephardim at Jodensavane had promulgated similar legislation limiting the participation of colored Jewish.

David Brion Davis already came to the conclusion that as participants in the sugar industry, then the world's most advanced field of industrial agriculture, some, mostly elite Jews, immersed themselves in the requisite modes of production and social engineering.[61] Amsterdam produced a quasi-colonial constellation for these newly Jewish, Christian-born Iberian exiles, a constellation whose polyglot metropolitan mingling reinforced the "boundary-building" needs of this fledgling group far—experientially and geographically—from both the motherland and from other compatriot communities. The exclusionary ordinances and attitudes of these Sephardim comprise the reactions of settlers in a Jewish colonial territory within the Iberian empire.

No community or individual produced a halakhic reaction to any of these Sephardic ordinances, however, and in some cases rabbis supported them. According to the language of the minutes of the Mahamad, for instance, the 1647 expansion of the separate row for colored Jews had the approval of the community's scholars, though without specifying whether all or some of them. If the Dutch and English Sephardim banned conversion to Judaism and, explicitly or implicitly, the conversion or circumcision of slaves/servants, a rabbinic authority could have justified this, as had been done earlier elsewhere, ruling that since the law of the land (*dina de malkhuta*) forbids these proselytizing efforts, Halakha permits Jews to possess uncircumcised slaves. But the conversion of pagan slaves by Jews mattered little to the Protestant authorities. And to the best of my knowledge, no rabbi ever issued such a straightforward and acceptable ruling. Not all the ordinances went "against" Halakha, as some scholars have maintained. These ordinances reflect the notion of "the Law Merchant," an autonomous realm of customary practice carved out by Jewish merchants away from the jurisdiction of rabbinic authorities.[62] Practice regarding slaves seems to have generally fallen under such a customary rubric.

Slave Life West of the Atlantic

Humphrey E. Lamur's complaint that "very little is known about the religion of slaves in the Western Hemisphere" holds at least as true for slaves of Jews.[63] While for the Mediterranean region and Europe we possess probably several hundred responsa directly relating to slaves, a meager handful of similar documents (possibly) stemming from the Americas exists for the whole seventeenth and eighteenth centuries. This removes an entire area of information about and insight into the halakhic issues with which slave owners or community members, and to a lesser extent slaves, grappled. Aside from two responsa from Pri Ets Hayim, the eighteenth-century Amsterdam responsa collection, one study found that the "interval of 'no questions asked' appears to have been in force until the beginning of the Russian-Jewish settlement" in the 1850s.[64] Next to nothing is known about the religious life of slaves belonging to Jews in Dutch Brazil, Barbados, or Jamaica, for instance. No communal ordinance regarding slaves survives from Barbados, Jamaica, or the other smaller Jewish communities, while Curaçao and Suriname, both with larger numbers of Jews holding slaves and engaging in plantation agriculture, produced such legislation, traces of which remain extant. It appears likely, in any event, that like their non-Jewish peers throughout the Dutch and English colonies Jews for the most part kept their religion from the great majority of their slaves.[65]

It seems highly unlikely that the Sephardim of Curaçao routinely absorbed their slaves into the community. Both Protestants and Jews "mostly had their slaves christened as Catholics."[66] Like the Protestant population, the Jewish community "would not recognize colored persons as members."[67] According to Jacob Rader Marcus the Jews of Curaçao did not circumcise their male slaves, though he thinks that Surinamese Jews did. Writing about the Jews of Curaçao, he noted in passing that "unlike their Surinamese coreligionists, . . . [they] did not initiate their slaves into the covenant of Abraham."[68] The attitude toward the circumcision of slaves among Caribbean Sephardim can probably be accurately gauged from Rabbi Selomoh Levy Maduro's Brit Yitshak, a compendium of texts to be read the night before a circumcision and guide to the order of the ceremony, contains the blessings for circumcising a slave, but prefaces it with the heading: "The order for circumcising and immersing a slave *at the time the Temple was in existence.*" The ceremony's first instructions reiterate this declaration: "A Jew in buying a slave *used to be obligated* to bless."[69] Levy Maduro made this commandment obsolete,[70] despite the fact that many Sephardic rabbis held that the laws of slavery continued to be operative and that responsa from Amsterdam make it clear that some Jews even in "the West" continued to own slaves according to the halakhic, not just social, nomenclature and category. He evidently thought like those Sephardic rabbis who argued that the laws relating to Canaanite slaves no longer obtained. The author could not have been unaware of the social fact of Jewish slave owning; the book's final pages consist of a list of *mohelim* in the colonies of Curaçao and Suriname, among other Sephardic habitations. A connection probably exists between Levy Maduro's stance on the circumcision of slaves and his belonging to a family boasting prominent members in Curaçao, where male slaves were not circumcised.[71] Indeed, a Selomoh L. Maduro, no doubt our author, appeared in contemporary records as the owner of an unnamed plantation in 1722.[72]

Primary sources make it seem unlikely that the Jews of Suriname regularly circumcised their slaves.[73] I have so far been unable to locate any circumcision registers from Suriname, however, which might be able help resolve the question of whether slaves were circumcised. But the generalization of circumcision seems doubtful for many reasons. A 1794 letter written by some of the Sephardic leaders to the colony's governor attempted to explain their position regarding recent controversies involving the group of Jewish mulattos (congregation Darhe Jesarim) who desired rights equal to those of the white Jews.

Describing the genesis of this mulatto group, they write: "Several among the Portuguese Jewish Nation, out of private affection begot children with some of their female slaves or mulattos. Out of particular love for the Jewish Religion the boys were properly circumcised and the girls instructed by a teacher, as were their descendants."[74] I infer from the language used here that only these children of "private affection" were circumcised, not every slave. (Though the language, at least of the translation, leaves unclear whose private affection acted here.) If these Sephardic settlers followed the communal ordinance from Zur Israel in Recife, the circumcisions would have been performed only after manumission. Certainly the majority of the slaves belonging to Surinamese Jews were not circumcised or converted to Judaism. The mulatto children brought about through relations with their slave women constituted the only Jewish slaves or former slaves in the colony, and not even all such mulatto offspring became Jewish. One can infer from this that the community considered only these mulatto slaves born to Jewish fathers to be *yelidei bayit* (house-born slaves) according to Genesis 17:13 and halakhic principle, as opposed to *every* child born of one's slaves, and that in Suriname only these slaves with Jewish fathers received circumcision, though I have not come across any explicit statement that such was the community's policy. I have also not found any halakhic precedent for this understanding. Such a practice would, if calculated generously, yield a total of perhaps two hundred circumcised slaves (contemporary documentation recorded only twenty-seven colored Jews of both genders in 1762 and nearly one hundred in 1788), compared with the well over ten thousand uncircumcised slaves who belonged to Surinamese Jews during the seventeenth and eighteenth centuries, or under 2 percent.

The religious dynamics pertaining to the slaves of Jewish masters in Suriname would seem to have run no differently than with those of Christians. Rosemary Brana-Shute calculated that only 8 percent of the 1,346 slaves nominated for manumission from 1760 to 1828 "indicated any experience of, education in, or commitment to Christianity."[75] The *Historical Essay* (1788), produced by leading members of the Sephardic Surinamese community, made distinctions between Jewish and non-Jewish slaves. Speaking of the losses incurred on a 1749 expedition against the maroons, the authors mentioned "Abm. de Britton, a mulatto Jew, and three of four . . . good slaves."[76] The latter, that is, had not been converted, as must have been true of the overwhelming majority of the slaves of these Jews.

If so few male slaves were circumcised in Suriname, it could not have been due to ignorance. Suriname was not a completely isolated hinterlands when it came to religious culture. For example, a 1739 list of the Hebrew books held in the Ets Hayim school at Jodensavane makes it clear that enough halakhic sources existed in Suriname from which to draw a proper picture of duties regarding slaves.[77] People with rabbinic knowledge and training lived in the colony as early as 1642 and throughout the eighteenth century.[78]

Slaves in the colonial territories, then, remained unconverted, but more important, because of their high numbers and concomitantly increased social segregation, they constituted a significant class of people for the most part no longer admissible into the community. In 1793 the London rabbinic court reported receiving a letter from the Jewish congregation in Philadelphia, Mikveh Israel, asking "how to proceed in the matter of a *Yahid* [member] who wishes to have converted, so that he may marry her, a servant with whom he has lived and by whom he has begotten children. The [London] Mahamad discreetly advised the Beth Din that it is impolitic to give instructions in such a case."[79] Note the distance between this response—so sensitive as to require behind-the-scenes treatment—and the perfectly explicit and halakhic reactions of earlier and Mediterranean rabbis to marriages between former servants and free Jews mentioned in the previous essay. Other cases of conversion to Judaism had occurred by 1793 in England and its colonies; was the Mahamad's discretion due entirely to political fears about converts in general?

COLONIAL MANUMISSION

The contours of the practice of manumission enable us to say something more about the religious aspects of Jewish masters and their slaves. Given the labor "need" created by the possibility of slavery, manumission should not be overplayed. Even in periods of crisis, that is, when the government or masters most require the services of their slaves, manumission proved to be the exception, not the rule, in the lives of most slaves, as every other essay in this volume demonstrates. In any case manumission came all too rarely. Rosemary Brana-Shute found "the chances of ever having a request [for manumission] submitted [to the authorities in Suriname] in one's behalf very, very poor." She tabulated that only 1,346 slaves merited nomination for manumission between 1760 and 1826, at no time over 0.8 percent of the slave population, though of those nominated, more than 97 percent received their freedom.[80] It was the masters then who resisted the liberation of their slaves. Of the manumissions performed in Suriname from 1760 to 1826, blacks and colored owners sponsored more than 23 percent, far more than the Jewish percentage, for instance.[81]

Most Jewish owners in the colonies did not manumit their slaves. Yet scholars engaging in apologetics continue to assert that "it was customary for Jews to emancipate several blacks in their wills."[82] Perhaps true, but it was far *more* customary *not* to manumit slaves. In fact, rates of manumission by Jews did not differ significantly from those of non-Jews. In a random study of thirty-six eighteenth-century wills of Jews of Barbados, Joanna Westphal found that in "18 bequests, a total of 110 slaves are mentioned," while of these, "108 are given to heirs and beneficiaries, and 2 are manumitted (set free for a payment to the local parish)," less than 1 percent.[83] Counting the 57 Sephardic wills from seventeenth- and eighteenth-century Barbados presented in studies by Wilfred Samuel and Bertram Wallace Korn, I found 125 slaves mentioned, 4 manumissions without conditions, and 2 with conditions, a rate of 4.8 or 3.2 percent, depending on whether one includes the manumissions with restrictive conditions.[84] This rate is certainly higher than that for Suriname discussed by Brana-Shute, but more akin to rates in urban areas, where slavery had a more solely domestic face. This accords with the opinion of Frederick Bowser, who thought that manumission "was largely an urban phenomenon," a reward for favored slaves who had managed to get close enough to the master to earn recognition as a person.[85] Wim Klooster found, based on the number of free blacks and mulattos, that manumission rates in "distinctly urban" Curaçao had reached 5.6 percent of the slave population by 1717.[86]

Jews do not seem to have manumitted their slaves, other than in their wills, according to Halakha. The wills met halakhic criteria as the intention of the master expressed therein was considered legally binding on any heirs.[87] In ideal case wills bore the signatures of two witnesses, making them valid for confirmation by a *beit din* (rabbinic court). I have not found any indication of the existence of a *beit din* or an equivalent anywhere in the Caribbean, staffed by rabbis or other qualified laymen, which performed the functions ordained by Halakha in the liberation of slaves. I have not come across any mention that owners granted slaves a *get* (contract of emancipation) or that manumitted slaves were brought to the *mikve* for ritual immersion; presumably unconverted slaves possessed outside the framework of Halakha needed no such rituals. In 1780 requirements of manumission and declaration of paternity were established by the *parnasim*, the Surinamese Sephardic community leaders, as mentioned by Robert Cohen, but he failed to provide their content.[88]

Until 1722 in Suriname, manumission constituted a private transaction between owner and slave. In that year the colonial authorities—the Court of Policy and Criminal Justice—began intervening, regulating, and administering manumissions.[89] According to Brana-Shute, this legislation insisted that masters "have [the freed slave] educated and brought up in the Christian religion."[90] Since this legislation effectively removed the power to give liberty to one's slaves, it might explain why Sephardic authorities after 1733 made no manumissions on halakhic authority. Brana-Shute stated as much: "Neither Christian nor Jewish communicants in Suriname had the right to follow the dictates of religious conscience . . . unless they obtained the state's authorization."[91] I have not come across any mention of protest from the *parnasim*, however, nor any grants for the special authorization described. Should one assume that manumissions given in wills executed before Jewish notaries or parnasim needed and received authorization from the court? Repeated issuance of legislation concerning slave manumissions indicates that the population of owners, no doubt Jews included, failed to satisfactorily comply. But I have not seen any evidence that would indicate whether this loss of control became an issue for the Sephardim or had any impact; and if, so what kind on their practice of granting liberty to slaves. It is surprising that the Sephardim, so jealous of their rights, would not have fought for the prerogative of raising slaves in their own religion. Also difficult is squaring the governmental intrusion regarding manumission with what Rosemary Brana-Shute wrote about the Paramaribo Moravians of the early nineteenth century, who were permitted to preach to and convert their own slaves, "as no one could object," as if the religion of one's slaves was a private matter.[92] Generally, that is, the Dutch colonial owners and managers did not intervene in the religious affairs of the Jews and their slaves. The Sephardim themselves probably saw in the governmental regulations concerning manumission a fine excuse for their own de facto (and perhaps de jure) policy of preventing the absorption of slaves into the Jewish community.

As in the Mediterranean world, manumissions of slaves by colonial Jews conformed closely to local practices. Of the manumissions committed to writing, only a rare few occurred before the death of the owner. In Barbados in 1711 one Manuel Na[h]mias "release[d] for ever one negro boy named Jack."[93] Most manumissions came as part of the "last will and testament" of owners, as was true among non-Jewish owners, at least in Suriname.[94] Though these often were put to paper long before the actual death of the owner, they contained the intention or promise (and even that not always effected in reality) to liberate, not its enactment. Brana-Shute noted that even slaves manumitted in a last will and testament might not be "able muster the kind of support necessary to force executors to comply with the wishes of a late owner."[95] Still, there is no gainsaying the significance of emancipation for the slave. Brana-Shute noted that the most frequently cited reason owners gave for manumitting a slave entailed the wish to reward a slave for loyal or trustworthy service and/or because the owner felt a special affection toward the slave.[96] Hence some manumitted slaves received in addition gifts from their masters. Josseph de Samuel Nassy, in his will of 1757, gave pensions of 30 florins each to several slaves.[97]

Manumissions by Jews were essentially an act of mercy. The will of Josseph Gabay Farro elaborated a generous scenario of unconditional liberation for two mulattas, Jael and Simha.[98] Other manumissions bore less generosity. The last will and testament of one Barbados owner beqeathed to his blind son a slave, who might be freed at the son's death only if he had remained blind.[99] The freedom of the slave depended solely and precariously on the master's favor. Though beneficent, an owner's act of manumission reconfirmed the legal inequality making the slave system possible, as made particularly clear by the language of another Barbados will in which liberty was eventually to be granted to a slave woman, Consciencia, "without any person or persons, heirs of myself or my wife, having the right to keep her captive."[100] The white owner, then, could demand terms respectful of the very rights whose trampling allowed her initial enslavement, kept her enslaved despite the protests of her own (legally unrecognized) person, and would keep her enslaved until the death of the white man's wife to whom she was being given.

Slaves were usually handed down to the next generation. Slaves with personal familiarity with a family and its children were often given to the children of owners. One parent from Barbados presented to each of his children the help deemed necessary to maintain a household: his daughter Rebecca was to receive "one Mallatta Woo by name jubah with her son Ventur," his son David "one Negro boy by name Cuffy," and his daughter Sarah "one Negroe Woman by name Mally."[101] A woman of the same island divvied up her slaves among her children as follows: To her son Hezekiah, "two negro boys, called Robin and Johnny"; to Esther, "two negro slaves by name Esperansa & Peggy, women"; to Rachel, "a negro woman called Ruth"; to Hannah, "a negro woman called Franky"; and to Rebecca, "two negro slaves by name Phillis, a woman, and little Esperansa a girl."[102]

One Surinamese man lacking a son of his own bequeathed to his nephew at his coming of age "four Blacks newly off the boat," which his heirs were ordered to purchase for the nephew.[103] Another bequeathed "three pieces of slaves," or the equivalent of three adult slaves, to his aunt "for her service."[104] Jewish masters, like their non-Jewish counterparts, tried to ensure in their last wills and testaments that their children would receive the continued services of well-liked, devoted slaves. Sometimes manumission was given on condition that the slave to be freed would not cease providing the same services to the manumitting owner.[105] Those who had grown dependent on the luxury of slave assistance found it hard to renounce.

As property, slaves bequeathed to a relative stood at the mercy of that relative's desires. She might choose to sell them or give them over to yet another person. A clause from a 1767 Surinamese will in which a husband allowed his wife to dispose of any inherited slaves as she might see fit entailed a not uncommon condition.[106] Another Surinamese will from the same era provided the estate's executors with the authority to sell two slaves to pay off debts but stipulated the condition that they may not select slaves who have their mother, father, or siblings still alive on the plantation.[107] Wills often contained a clause reverting the possession of inherited slaves to other relatives should the heir die without children of their own.[108]

The last such stipulations indicate the economic value of slaves but may also show that those who insisted on inserting these clauses into their testaments believed that slaves *must* be passed down by Jewish law. If so, here we see at work not some eternal Jewish view but the functional and self-interested invocation of a particular earlier halakhic opinion, (re)constructed for new times. As mentioned previously, this view had many adherents among the Jews of the Mediterranean region. Such too was the opinion of Rabbi Abraham Gabay Yzidro (eighteenth century), who served various communal functions in Suriname and then Barbados.[109] In his verse rendition of the 613 commandments according to Maimonides, published posthumously by his widow in 1763, Gabay Yzidro explicitly juxtaposed the freeing of a Hebrew slave with the eternal employment of a non-Jewish slave:

> And the slave of my holy people [that is, a Jewish/Hebrew slave]
> Sustain on his going free
> But forever with the Kushite
> Work at the task.[110]

Joanna Westphal found an intriguing entry relating to the manumission of slaves in the Barbados congregation's minute book. In 1800 a woman named Judith Pereira was removed from the pension list for "having endeavored to emancipate her negro woman." The Mahamad preferred that she donate the slave to the congregation or sell her and donate the profits. She evidently promised to comply, as six months later Pereira was reinstated on the list on condition that she "gives a deed to her nieces for her negro slave."[111] As mentioned in many of the essays in this volume, control over the manumission of slaves constituted a common strategy in societies with numerous slaves. As of 1713 masters in the French Caribbean islands needed written permission from the governor general in order to free a slave.[112] Perhaps the attitude of the Sephardic leaders on Barbados reflected the positing of a positive commandment of eternal servitude of non-Jewish slaves. Yet the invocation of this attitude out of halakhic sources served as little more than a homegrown justification for the imitation of the de facto racialized practices of Caribbean Christian slaveholders. When it is said, therefore, that Jewish slaveholders did things "Jewishly," we see that this often signified far less than it purported.

NOTES

    1. Jacob Barnai, "The Jews of the Ottoman Empire in the Seventeenth and Eighteenth Centuries," in *Moreshet Sepharad: The Sephardi Heritage*, ed. Haim Beinart (Jerusalem: Magnes Press / Hebrew University, 1992), 147.

    2. Meir b. Shem Tov Melamed, *Mishpat Tsedek*, vol. 1 (Salonika, 1615), responsum no. 52. The hardline position of Melamed, shared by other Sephardic rabbis in the eastern Mediterranean area, drew on an opinion expressed anonymously by the Mishnah to the effect that all contracts executed in non-Jewish courts were valid, despite the use of non-Jewish witnesses, *except* for writs of divorce and manumissions of slaves (Mishnah Gitin 1:5).

    3. Avraham b. Eliezer ha-Levi, *Eyn Mishpat* (Salonika, 1897), responsum no. 45.

    4. Aharon b. Hayyim Avraham ha-Cohen Perahya, *Mateh Aharon* (Amsterdam: Moshe b. Avraham Mendes Coitinio, 1703), pt. 1, responsum no. 32. The immersion conducted here was for the sake of manumission or conversion to full Judaism. Another immersion was required by Halakha when a slave was first acquired in order to make the slave minimally Jewish.

5. Hasdai b. Shmuel ha-Cohen Perahya (1605?–1678), *Sefer Torat Hesed* (Salonika, 1733), responsa no. 49 and 50.

6. Shmuel b. Moshe de Medina, *Sh'elot u-Teshuvot*, vol. 1, pt. 2 (Yoreh De'ah) (Salonika, 1797), responsum no. 194.

7. David ibn Zimra, *Sh'elot u-Teshuvot mi K'Y* (Bnei Brak: Eit Sofer, 1975), pt. 4, responsum no. 1157.

8. Mordehai ha-Levi (Egypt, seventeenth century), *Sh'elot u-Teshuvot Darhei No'am* (Yoreh De'ah), responsum no. 9; Yosef David, *Sefer Beit David* (Salonika, 1740), responsum no. 123; Ha-Cohen Perahya, *Sefer Torat Hesed*, responsum no. 44.

9. Ruth Pike, *Aristocrats and Traders: Sevillan Society in the Sixteenth Century* (Ithaca, N.Y.: Cornell University Press, 1972), 182.

10. Shlomo b. Yosef Amarillo, *Kerem Shlomo* (Salonika, 1719), responsum no. 16.

11. Fernand Braudel, *The Mediterranean and the Mediterranean World in the Age of Philip II* (New York: Harper and Row, 1973), 2:754–755. Braudel was citing Christoval de Villalon, *Viaje de Turquía . . .* (1555; reprint, Madrid: Espasa-Calpe, 1919).

12. Ovadia Salama, "Slaves in the Ownership of Jews and Christians in Ottoman Jerusalem [Hebrew]," *Cathedra* 49 (1989): 71.

13. David, *Sefer Beit David*, responsum no. 127. See also Ibn Ezra, who expressed the same opinion (commentary to Lev. 25:26).

14. Avraham b. Moshe de Boton, *Lehem Rav* (Izmir: Avraham b. Yedidiah Gabai, 1660), responsum no. 44.

15. Ibid.

16. Ibid. Other complexities enter the narrative but stand beyond the scope of this discussion. The confused rabbinic court in Ferrara turned to R. Boton for help, hence the case's appearance in the responsa of the latter.

17. Ibid., 27a.

18. See the comments of Yvonne Seng on the closely parallel contemporary Ottoman world: "Slaves, we find, . . . took on the familial identity, professions, and communities of their masters." Yvonne Seng, "A Liminal State: Slavery in Sixteenth-Century Istanbul," in *Slavery in the Islamic Middle East*, ed. Shaun E. Marmon (Princeton, N.J.: Markus Wiener, 1999), 37.

19. Contrast this with the turbulent sexual and romantic, but rarely marital, relationships between servants and masters in eighteenth-century France. Sarah Maza, *Servants and Masters in Eighteenth-Century France: The Uses of Loyalty* (Princeton, N.J.: Princeton University Press, 1983).

20. Hayyim Moshe b. Shlomo Amarillo, *Sh'elot u-Teshuvot Diber Moshe* (Salonika, 1742), pt. 1, responsum no. 57.

21. David, *Sefer Beit David*, responsum no. 125.

22. See Orlando Patterson's essay in this volume, "Three Notes of Freedom: The Nature and Consequences of Manumission."

23. Amarillo, *Kerem Shlomo*, responsum no. 16.

24. Hayyim Benvenisti, *Sh'elot u-Teshuvot Ba'ei Hayyei* (Jerusalem, 1970; photo reprint of Salonika, Greece, 1791), pt. 1 (Yoreh De'ah), responsum no. 229.

25. Medina, *Sh'elot u-Teshuvot*, pt. 2, responsum no. 195.

26. Ibn Zimra, *Sh'elot u-Teshuvot*, pt. 4, responsum no. 1360.

27. Shlomo b. Avraham ha-Cohen, *Sh'elot u-T'shuvot Maharshakh* (Salonika, 1594), pt. 1, responsum no. 8.

28. E. Leigh Gibson, "The Jewish Manumission Inscriptions of the Bosporan Kingdom" (Ph.D. diss., Princeton University, 1997), 201. According to Gibson, this practice was adopted from "the [local] pagan practice of freeing slaves in a religious setting" (251).

29. David, *Sefer Beit David*, responsum no. 125.

30. Shmuel b. Moshe Kalai, *Mishpetei Shmuel* (Jerusalem, 1970; reprint of Venice, 1599), responsum no. 93.

31. Meyer Fortes, "Ritual and Office in Tribal Society," in *Essays on the Ritual of Social Relations*, ed. Max Gluckman (Manchester: Manchester University Press, 1962), 86.

32. David b. Hayyim ha-Cohen, *Sh'elot u-Teshuvot ha-Radakh* (Ostraha, 1834), responsum no. 9.

33. Perahya, *Mateh Aharon* 1:74a (responsum no. 32).

34. Cited in Hayyim Motziri, *Sh'elot u-Teshuvot B'er Mayyim Hayyim* (Salonika, 1794), pt. *Yoreh De'ah*, responsum no. 14.

35. Perahya, *Mateh Aharon*, pt. 2, responsum no. 51.

36. Sommi, Leone de, *A Comedy of Betrothal (Tsahoth B'dihutha D'Kiddushin)*, trans. Alfred S. Golding (Ottawa: Dovehouse Editions, 1988), 117 (act 4, scene 7). For the Hebrew, see J. Schirmann, ed., *The First Hebrew Play: The Comedy of Betrothal by Yehuda Sommo (1527–92) (Leone Sommo de Portaleone) Edited from Three Mss.*, 2nd ed. (Jerusalem: Tarshish/Dvir, 1965), 76.

37. Jacob Katz, *Exclusiveness and Tolerance: Studies in Jewish-Gentile Relations in Medieval and Modern Times* (West Orange, N.J.: Behrman House, 1961), 41.

38. Yehuda Aryeh Leib b. Yehoshua Heshke, *Lev Aryeh* (Wilhelmsdorf, 1674), 93a (parshat be-Ha'alot'ha).

39. Yitshak b. Eliahu Shangi, *Sh'elot u-Teshuvot B'erot ha-Mayyim* (Salonika, 1755), pt. "Even ha-Ezer," responsum no. 65.

40. R. Ya'akov b. Avraham de Boton, *Eidot be-Ya'akov* (Salonika: Avraham b. David Nahman and Moshe Kanfilias, 1720), responsum no. 8. A similar case: Ha-Cohen Perahya, *Sefer Torat Hesed*, responsum no. 44.

41. Israel Abrahams, *Jewish Life in the Middle Ages* (Philadelphia: Jewish Publication Society of America, 1911), 99.

42. Again, the "origin" of this choosing not to convert slaves can be found in both Jewish and non-Jewish discourse. Dutch colonists, for instance, rarely propagated Calvinism among their slaves, whether in Brazil, Suriname, or Curaçao, preferring even to have them practice Roman Catholicism. In Curaçao the Dutch allowed Spanish Catholic priests to function.

43. David Pardo, *Compendio de dinim que todo Israel deve saber y observar* (Amsterdam, 1689); the first edition of the *Shulkhan Arukh* (Cracow, 1578–1580), section 267, Laws of Slaves.

44. R. Selomoh de Oliveyra (d. 1658), *Darhei ha-Shem* (Amsterdam: David de Castro Tartas, 1683); Jósef Franco Serrano, *Los cinco libros de la sacra ley* (Amsterdam: Mosseh Dias, 1695), section in back, Dinim tocantes â los Preceptos siguientes; R. Moshe b. Ya'akov Hagiz (1672–1751?; Jerusalem, Amsterdam), *Sefer Eleh ha-Mitsvot* (Amsterdam, 1713); R. Binyamin Rafael Dias Brandon, *Orot ha-Mitsvot* (Amsterdam: Jan Janson, 1753); R. Avraham Gabay Yzidro, *Yad Avraham: Ve-Hu Hibur ha-Azharot* (Amsterdam: Leib b. Moshe Zusmans / Jan Janson, 1763). The last author served as gabay in Suriname and rabbi in Barbados. Selomoh Levy Maduro, *Brit Yitshak* (Amsterdam: Gerard Johan Janson / House of Mondui, 1768). Maduro lived in Curaçao.

45. Jonathan Israel, "Menasseh ben Israel and the Dutch Sephardic Colonization Movement of the Mid-Seventeenth Century (1645–1657)," in *Menasseh ben Israel and His World*, ed. Yosef Kaplan, Henry Méchoulan, and Richard H. Popkin (Leiden: E. J. Brill, 1989), 106.

46. Haskamah 32 (dated 5409/1649); translated in Arnold Wiznitzer, *The Records of the Earliest Jewish Community in the New World* (New York: American Jewish Historical Society, 1954), 69.

47. This trajectory stands both in accord with and in contrast to the "converso" belief described by Miriam Bodian about the "religio-ethnic defining power of circumcision" when it came to the masters themselves. Miriam Bodian, *Hebrews of the Portuguese Nation: Conversos and Community in Early Modern Amsterdam* (Bloomington: Indiana University Press, 1997), 97–98. In their case the Amsterdam "rabbis frequently cooperated in making circumcision a precondition for full acceptance in 'Portuguese' communities" (ibid., 112). At the same time it is possible that the very sacramental and salvational status accorded to circumcision in some "crypto-Jewish" circles precluded its being shared with others deemed unworthy, such as black and mulatto slaves. Rabbi Saul Levi Morteira compared circumcision to the possession of a certificate of *hidalguía* (nobility). See Levi Morteira, *Tratado da Verdade da Lei de Moisés*, trans. Hermann Prins Salomon (Coimbra, Portugal: Por ordem da Universidade, 1988), 899.

48. Wilhelmina C. Pieterse, ed., *Livro de bet haim do kahal kados de bet yahacob: Original Text* (Assen, Netherlands: Van Gorcum, 1970), 45.

49. "Libro dos termos da ymposta da naçao," 20 Tamuz 5387 (1627), Archive of the Portuguese Jewish Community of Amsterdam, Gemeentearchief Amsterdam (hereafter cited as GAA), sec. 334, no. 13, fol. 42.

50. Robert Cohen, *Jews in Another Environment: Surinam in the Second Half of the Eighteenth Century* (Leiden: E. J. Brill, 1991), 161.

51. Ernst van den Boogaart, "Colour Prejudice and the Yardstick of Civility: The Initial Dutch Confrontation with Black Africans, 1590–1635," in *Racism and Colonialism: Essays on Ideology and Social Structure*, ed. Robert Ross (The Hague: Martinus Nijhoff, 1982), 45n37; Eli Faber, *Jews, Slaves, and the Slave Trade: Setting the Record Straight* (New York: New York University Press, 1998), 16, citing Johannes Menne Postma, *The Dutch in the Atlantic Slave Trade, 1600–1815* (Cambridge: Cambridge University Press, 1990), 10.

52. Escamoth (n.d. [1640]), GAA, sec. 334, no. 19.

53. "Livros dos Acordos da Nacao e Ascamot," GAA, sec. 334, no. 19, fol. 173.

54. B. N. Teensma, "The Brazilian Letters of Vicent Joachim Soler," in *Dutch Brazil*, vol. 1, *Documents in the Leiden University Library* (Rio de Janeiro: Editora Index, 1997), 61.

55. "Livros dos Acordos da Nacao e Ascamot," 24 Nisan 5407 (1647), GAA, sec. 334, no. 19, fol. 224.

56. "Livros dos Acordos da Nacao e Ascamot," 9 Sh'vat 5418 (1658), GAA, sec. 334, no. 19, fol. 426; cited also in Yosef Kaplan, "The Portuguese Community in Amsterdam in the Seventeenth Century: Between Tradition and Change (Hebrew)," *Reports of the Israeli National Academy of Sciences* 7, no. 6 (Jerusalem: Israeli National Academy of Sciences, 1986), 168.

57. Colin A. Palmer, *Slaves of the White God: Blacks in Mexico, 1570–1650* (Cambridge, Mass.: Harvard University Press, 1976), 54.

58. In 1555 the first Mexican Ecclesiastical Provincial Council declared Indians, mestizos, mulattos, descendants of Moors, Jews, and people sentenced by the Inquisition "inherently unworthy of the sacerdotal office." The Third Provincial Council (1585) relaxed this somewhat, admitting "Mexicans who are descended in the first degree from Amerindians, or from Moors, or from parents of whom one is a Negro." By implication full-blood Indians and blacks

remained unacceptable for admission. All from C. R. Boxer, *The Church Militant and Iberian Expansion, 1440–1770* (Baltimore: Johns Hopkins University Press, 1978), 15–16.

59. Ibid., 9.

60. The communal ordinances of the Sephardic congregations in Morocco, for instance, made no mention of issues related to the burial or ritual participation of slaves. See Shalom Bar-Asher, ed., *The Taqanot of the Jews of Morocco: A Collection of Communal Ordinances from the 16th to 18th Century as found in "Kerem Hemer" II by Avraham Ankawa* (Jerusalem: Zalman Shazar Center / Hebrew University, 1977).

61. Brion Davis, "Jews in the Slave Trade," *Culture Front* 1, no. 2 (Fall 1992): 42–43.

62. In Livorno, for example, rabbis were intentionally kept away from cases of merchant dispute (Bernard Dov Cooperman, e-mail to author, November 1999).

63. Humphrey E. Lamur, "Slave Religion on the Vossenburg Plantation (Suriname) and Missionaries' Reaction," in *Caribbean Slave Society and Economy: A Student Reader*, ed. Hilary Beckles and Verene Shepherd (New York: New Press, 1991), 287.

64. J. D. Eisenstein, "The Development of Jewish Casuistic Literature in America," *Publications of the American Jewish Historical Society* 12 (1904): 144.

65. On the segregation of Calvinism and slaves, see Cornelis Ch. Goslinga, *The Dutch in the Caribbean and on the Wild Coast, 1580–1680* (Assen, Netherlands: Van Gorcum, 1971), 368–369; R. A. J. van Lier, *Frontier Society: A Social Analysis of the History of Surinam* (The Hague: Martinus Nijhoff, 1971), 72–74; Rosemary Brana-Shute, "The Manumission of Slaves in Suriname, 1760–1828" (Ph.D. diss., University of Florida, 1985), 256–258.

66. J. Hartog, *Curaçao: from Colonial Dependence to Autonomy* (Aruba: De Wit, 1968), 148.

67. Isaac S. Emmanuel and Suzanne A. Emmanuel, *History of the Jews of the Netherlands Antilles*, 2. vols. (Cincinnati: American Jewish Archives, 1970), 1:146.

68. Jacob Rader Marcus, *The Colonial American Jew, 1492–1776*, 3 vols. (Detroit: Wayne State University Press, 1970), 1:200.

69. Emphasis added; Levy Maduro, *Brit Yitshak*, 15b–16a.

70. He did so by conflating the cessation of Canaanite slave laws with the time universally assigned to the end of *Hebrew* slaves, the point at which the jubilee year supposedly was no longer observed (because of the destruction of the Jerusalem Temple, the absence of the twelve tribal representatives, etc.). Levy Maduro's view went counter to that of Maimonides, who specifically distinguished between the laws pertaining to Hebrew slaves—dependent on the Temple, the jubilee—and the "eternal" laws pertaining to Canaanite slaves. Maimonides, *Mishneh Torah*, Laws of Slaves 5:17.

71. On the Maduros of Curaçao, see Isaac S. Emmanuel, *Precious Stones of Curaçao: Curaçaon Jewry 1656–1957* (New York: Bloch, 1957), 209–213. One Samuel Levy Maduro served as *hazan* in the early eighteenth century. Emmanuel and Emmanuel, *Jews of the Netherlands Antilles*, 2:553.

72. Emmanuel and Emmanuel, *Jews in the Netherlands Antilles*, 2:653.

73. Unfortunately, I have been unable yet to find any pertinent evidence from seventeenth-century Suriname.

74. Cohen, *Jews in Another Environment*, 159.

75. Brana-Shute, "Manumission of Slaves," 260.

76. *Historical Essay on the Colony of Surinam, 1788*, ed. Jacob R. Marcus and Stanley F. Chyet, trans. Simon Cohen (Cincinnati and New York: American Jewish Archives / KTAV Publishing House, 1974), 71. The name is probably a mistake for de Britto, a prominent Sephardic planter family.

77. Among the library's holdings: the talmudic tractates Kidushin, Gitin, Ketubot, and Yebamot (among others); a commentary on the Shulkhan Arukh (though in bad condition {*mal tratado*}); and perhaps most crucially, three different multivolume editions of the Shulkhan Arukh itself. Records of Jurators of Surinam; Portuguese Jewish Communion [*sic*] / Archief der Nederlandsch-Portugeesch-Israelietische Gemeente in Suriname, Algemeen Rijksarchief, The Hague, no. 25 (American Jewish Archives; hereafter cited as AJA) microfilm reel 67h, fols. 48–49.

78. P. A. Hilfman, "Notes on the History of the Jews in Surinam," *Publications of the American Jewish Historical Society* 18 (1909): 185, provided a list of the rabbis serving in Suriname until 1750.

79. Richard D. Barnett, "The Correspondence of the Mahamad of the Spanish and Portuguese Congregation of London during the Seventeenth and Eighteenth Centuries," *Transactions of the Jewish Historical Society of England* 20 (1959/1961): 17.

80. Brana-Shute, "Manumission of Slaves," 180, 202, 187. She did not compare the manumission rates of Jewish versus non-Jewish owners.

81. Ibid., 33, 340 (table VII:2).

82. Saul S. Friedman, *Jews and the American Slave Trade* (New Brunswick, N.J.: Transaction Press, 1997), 68. He was basically quoting from Emmanuel and Emmanuel, *Jews in the Netherlands Antilles* 1:79.

83. Joanna Westphal, "Jews in a Colonial Society: The Jewish Community of Barbados, 1654–1833" (master's thesis, London University, 1993), 52.

84. Wilfred Samuel, "A Review of the Jewish Colonists in Barbados in the Year 1680," *Transactions of the Jewish Historical Society of England* 13 (1932/1935); Bertram Wallace Korn, "Barbadian Jewish Wills, 1676–1740," in *A Bicentennial Festschrift for Jacob Rader Marcus*, ed. Bertram Wallace Korn (Waltham, Mass.: American Jewish Historical Society / KTAV Publishing House, 1976).

85. Frederick P. Bowser, "The Free Person of Color in Mexico City and Lima: Manumission and Opportunity, 1580–1650," in *Race and Slavery in the Western Hemisphere: Quantitative Studies*, ed. Stanley Engerman and Eugene D. Genovese (Princeton, N.J.: Princeton University Press, 1975), 334.

86. See Willem Wubbel Klooster's essay in this volume, "Manumission in an Entrepôt: The Case of Curaçao."

87. Maimonides, *Mishneh Torah*, Laws of Slaves 6:4; Karo, Shulkhan Arukh, Yoreh De'ah, sec. 267:77–78.

88. Cohen, *Jews in Another Environment*, 305n39. I have not yet found this crucial document. Brana-Shute, "Manumission of Slaves," 101, 107–111. Later legislation made manumissions increasingly formal, time-consuming, costly, and difficult (116–172).

89. Ibid., 108.

90. Ibid., 111. As she showed, worries about the economic self-sufficiency of those to be freed fueled this and later efforts to limit and regulate manumission (118–119).

91. Ibid., 256.

92. Ibid.

93. Document of March 11, 1711, parish of St. Michael, excerpted in Zvi Loker, ed., *Jews in the Caribbean: Evidence on the History of the Jews in the Caribbean Zone in Colonial Times* (Jerusalem: Misgav Yerushalayim, 1991), 194.

94. Brana-Shute, "Manumission of Slaves," 377. In Barbados, however, manumission by means of a last will "was relatively infrequent"; see Jerome S. Handler and Arnold A. Sio,

"Barbados," in *Neither Slave nor Free: the Freedmen of African Descent in the Slave Societies of the New World*, ed. David W. Cohen and Jack P. Greene (Baltimore: Johns Hopkins University Press, 1972), 225.

95. Brana-Shute, "Manumission of Slaves," 193.

96. Ibid., 373.

97. Microfilm reel 67a, fols. 74–75, AJA.

98. Microfilm reel 67a, fol. 643, AJA. At the same time Gabay Farro issued explicit instructions to the executor of his estate about maintaining his plantation, Gosen (Goshen), with "50 good slaves" (ibid., fol. 642).

99. Will of Elias Valverde (July 3, 1739), in Samuel, "Jewish Colonists in Barbados," 89.

100. Will of Moseh Hamis (Gago) (March 26, 1684), in ibid., 72.

101. Will of Mozes Castello (June 16, 1729), in Korn, "Barbadian Jewish Wills," 307.

102. Will of Miriam Arobas of St. Michael (July 31, 1733), in ibid.

103. Will of David Pintto, Paramaribo (June 14, 1765), microfilm 67a, frame 353, AJA. Pintto also ordered his heirs or estate executors to buy "a Black newly off the boat" for the free black woman Adjuba, "in compensation for the good services he had from her."

104. Will of Ishak de Semuel de Meza (May 1, 1769), microfilm reel 67a, frame 893, AJA.

105. See, for instance, the widow B.H. da Costa, who freed a five-year-old mulatto girl, Cornelia, daughter of her black slave Janica. Cornelia was required to live with the widow until reaching the age of fifteen. Brana-Shute, "Manumission of Slaves," 333. As Brana-Shute points out, the condition was likely to have been met in any case since Janica remained a slave in the same household.

106. Will of Samuel Carrilho and Ribca Gaba⌣ Faro (June 28, 1767), microfilm reel 67a, frames 614–615, AJA.

107. Order of Sarah, widow of Jah: R' de Meza (March 8, 1769), microfilm reel 67a, frame 845, AJA. Keeping families together constituted the early policy practiced in Suriname. Brana-Shute, "Manumission of Slaves."

108. The 1713 codicil of Daniel Ulloa stated that if his daughter "has no children, the slaves are to revert after her death to Sarah's siblings and their heirs and assigns" (Korn, "Barbadian Jewish Wills," 306), while the 1733 will of Miriam Arobas specified that should any of her children "die before reaching the age of twenty-one and without issue, the slave bequeathed to that child are to be divided equally among the other children named, and their heirs and assigns" (ibid., 307). Similar clauses can be found among Surinamese Jews as well, for instance, in the will of Abraham da Costa (August 12, 1768), microfilm reel 67a, frame 777, AJA.

109. Yzidro had been in Suriname since at least 1735 or so, when his name was mentioned as a teacher in the Jodensavane community (microfilm reel 67h, frame 143, AJA). He had been born in Spain, fled to England and studied in Amsterdam with David Israel Athias, before leaving for the Caribbean. His wife came from the Sephardic community of Bayonne, France. Loker, *Jews in the Caribbean*, 83nn1–2.

110. Gabay Yzidro, *Yad Avraham*, 4b. My translation ignores the rhyme scheme. Yzidro substituted, no doubt based on his experience in plantation slave societies, the traditional term "Canaanite" slave with "Kushite."

111. Entries of September 22, 1800, and March 10, 1801, Minute Book of the Mahamad and Adjuntos 1791–1808 (MS 328), Lauderdale Road Synagogue, London; cited in Westphal, "Jews in a Colonial Society," 54.

112. David Brion Davis, *The Problem of Slavery in Western Culture* (Ithaca, N.Y.: Cornell University Press, 1966), 263.

MARY CAROLINE CRAVENS

Manumission and the Life Cycle of a Contained Population

—ɯ—

The VOC Lodge Slaves at the Cape of Good Hope, 1680–1730

INTRODUCTION

In 1680 the Vereenigde Oost-Indische Compagnie (VOC; the Dutch East India Company) completed construction of a large windowless building at the entrance to the company's lush gardens in the center of Cape Town. This building, the slave lodge, would house the company's slave labor force for the next 115 years.[1] A contemporary description notes that it stood "just in front of" the garden and was "a building of one story, about 30 feet high, flat-roofed, 77 paces long and 46 deep, where dwell a great number of the slaves of the Hon. Company."[2] The lodge's slave force, the largest single holding in the history of the Cape of Good Hope, included from three hundred to five hundred men, women, and children at any one time during the period in question.[3] The lodge slaves fulfilled the company's diverse labor needs. Most, men *and* women, performed manual labor, working on the construction and maintenance of the company garrison, the "castle"; stevedoring for the ships in the port; and removing waste from the streets. Others worked in the company gardens or as domestic servants. A few were artisans: carpenters, blacksmiths, coopers, nurses, and masons, for instance, learning trades that allowed them to replace European craftsmen who were eager to go into the interior to claim land and higher status for themselves.

The lodge slaves were necessary to the efficiency and economic success of the VOC operations at the cape, but little direct evidence survives concerning their daily life experience. Various travelers' accounts and journals note the presence of these company slaves, and the slave lodge appears on most eighteenth-century maps and views of Cape Town. These men and women left permanent marks on the city, having been responsible for the construction of a large number of civic buildings, including their own lodge. Their existence is not doubted, but it was a silent one. No slave narratives have survived from the lodge, leaving these men, women, and children without a voice in the narrative historical record.

Because of this silence most cape slave historians have turned to the more fully described slaves of the settlers, leaving the lodge slaves at the periphery or out of their work altogether. Because of its demographically, architecturally, and geographically contained nature, however, the slave lodge population provides an opportunity for an analysis and reconstruction of aspects of slave life not covered by the narrative record and so ignored by many historians of New World as well as cape slavery. Demographic analysis through the calculation of fertility, mortality, and rate of union, and of age, sex, and racial composition of the population, further illuminates our picture of these slaves' material conditions of living and social as well as biological life experience. As Barry Higman noted, "Slaves' manipulation of their material conditions of life had a significance for their patterns of fertility and mortality which remains ambiguous and inadequately understood. But the parameters were always set by the masters."[4] The integration of demographic evidence in the reconstruction of the lodge slaves' social experience exposes social ties crossing the boundary between slavery and freedom, indicates certain unofficial factors contributing to patterns of manumission, and suggests legal agency among some subgroups of the general lodge population.

The integration of demographic evidence in the reconstruction of social experience is not really new. Rates of fertility, mortality, and nuptiality have informed historians' views of European societies from as early as the eighteenth century.[5] The use of these methods of analysis depends entirely on the availability of vital registration data, accounts of births, unions, and deaths. For populations before the institution of comprehensive vital registration or censuses, as in the case of the European populations mentioned above, records of baptisms, marriages, and burials have provided good substitutes.

In the nineteenth century, especially as the Atlantic slave trade began to end, most colonial governments registered their slave populations more carefully. Some valuable demographic analysis has come out of this. Barry Higman's study of slaves in the British Caribbean area, for example, analyzes demographic features as evidence of the variable material condition of life across that region.[6] This type of study has not often been possible for preliterate African and New World populations, nor for early slave populations in many other parts of the world. Patrick Manning's study of the effects of the Atlantic slave trade on African slavery illustrates some of the difficulties. Because no record survives at all of the demographic lives of these populations, Manning had to make large assumptions and use broad estimates, backward projections, and simulated models to complete his analysis.[7] The lodge slaves, as a well-documented early slave population, represent an exception to these problems.

Demographic Historiography of the Cape and of Slavery

For the world's European populations, historical demographers have found evidence readily available in parish church records or county courthouse vital registers. Although limited demographic analysis of cape slaves has been incorporated in various histories of the colony, most demographic studies concerning South Africa have also concentrated on the European or "white" population, for which a great deal more evidence survives.[8] Certain demographic studies of other slave populations provide better models for this study. Barry Higman's analysis of British Caribbean slave populations provides the most comprehensive example, using demographic evidence to look at variations in slave life experience.[9] James Trussell and Richard Steckel have looked at the onset of menarche and at the age of first birth for slave women, and at the implications of that data with regard to natalist policies among slave owners.[10] Herbert Klein and Stanley Engerman studied the possible effects of lactation practices on the fertility of slave populations, comparing the United States with the British West Indies.[11] Alida Metcalf's study of colonial Brazilian society uses quantitative analysis as a "framework for qualitative analysis of other sources."[12] Demographic composition and dynamics are powerful tools in the analysis of social experience. They describe in biological terms marriage and child bearing (in this case, a transformation of slave woman from unsexed laborer to mother and/or wife), the hardship of everyday life and the toll it took, legal rights, and social mobility. In the interest of the variety of aspects of slave social experience which can be examined in the light of demographic evidence, this project offers a demographic profile of the lodge with a particular emphasis on patterns of manumission.

Comparative Context

The slave lodge was a rather atypical slave structure. The population size was fairly constant throughout the period of slavery at the cape, largely because of the stability of the VOC's labor needs. The company never became directly involved in the Cape's rapidly expanding agricultural sector (the primary reason the settlers' slave labor needs grew so rapidly) but limited its operations to urban administrative and commercial port activities. The Cape Colony differed from most colonial territories in the Atlantic world in that it was directly administered by a commercial institution, the VOC, rather than by the government of a mother country. This affected both policy and its enforcement. VOC policies were fairly strictly enforced upon the lodge slave population, intended as an example to the settler slaveholders at the cape, although they tended not to follow it closely. Strict enforcement of VOC policy among lodge slaves helps reveal underlying patterns as they diverge from those the policy would predict.

Because the VOC was a commercial institution rather than a private slave owner, the ways in which slaves entered and exited other slaveholdings did not apply to lodge slaves. Not only did these slaves avoid transfers by inheritance or auction because of an owner's death, but company policy forbade that they be sold out of the lodge at any time or for any reason, except for transactions involving subsequent manumission for marriage.[13] Their vital statistics also remain uncomplicated by issues of entailment or migration by an owner. Escapes from the lodge, another conceivable way of leaving it, were too rare to be significant to the analysis. According to Robert Ross, it was the free burghers (former servants of the company), not the company, who had a problem with runaways at the cape, with the exception of one incident involving seven Angolan slaves who escaped only two and a half months after their arrival in 1658.[14] The only ways out of the lodge population were manumission, although that was also somewhat rare, and death; the only ways in were to be born to a lodge slave mother or imported, for which purpose the company had its own slaving ships.[15]

Only a few other slave populations came close to this degree of containment. The slaves on the religious estates of early colonial Brazil, the Araçariguama *fazena*, for example, were equally protected from sale, or division by inheritance, by the religious code and the institutional nature of their ownership. The Indian and African laborers on these estates generally worked three days for the Jesuit or Dominican brothers of the estate in return for land and housing. This protected arrangement ended when the Jesuits were expelled, however.[16] The better known population of company slaves based in the Dutch West India Company's Castle at Elmina on the West African coast even more closely resembled the population of the lodge.[17] The Elmina slaves performed roughly the same occupations, received similar rations and accommodation, and were recorded with similar Dutch.[18] Population size was also similar; Elmina had 348 slaves in residence in 1703, compared to the slave lodge's 369 in 1693.[19] Unlike Elmina the cape had a permanent European settler population, and it functioned as a commercial way station rather than a point of origin or destination. This insulated the lodge slaves from the larger slave trade to the west. Entry and exit of the lodge population were limited and consequently easily documented, thereby presenting a unique opportunity to analyze the dynamics of a more or less circumscribed slave population.

Institution of Slavery at the Cape and the VOC Slave Lodge

The VOC established its "refreshment station" at the Cape of Good Hope in 1652 purely as a commercial enterprise, not a settlement colony. The supplying of ships had become more difficult, due to both a shortage of produce from the restricted settlement and the refusal of wary indigenous Khoisan pastoralists to trade livestock to the Dutch. The company released a few of its servants from shipping duties and granted them land on condition that they maintain market gardens to increase the supplies. From the outset, largely because of the availability of "free" land, the settlement experienced a labor shortage.[20] By

1658 Jan van Riebeeck, company governor at the cape, had decided on the basis of his knowledge of the company's experiences in Batavia and Ceylon that the introduction of slaves would be the most efficient answer to the colony's labor needs.[21] While van Riebeeck's primary intention was for the free burghers to use the slaves in their agricultural production, the company also maintained a population of slaves.

The first company slaves were housed in the fort, or castle. When that became crowded and inconvenient, the slaves lived in a lodge built near the VOC gardens and enlarged in 1669. In 1679 fire destroyed the enlarged version and an entirely new two-story, flat-roofed, windowless lodge was built by the slaves themselves, across from the company hospital and at the entrance to the gardens.[22] By 1680 all company slaves, with the exception of those placed at government posts in the outlying districts (about 15 percent), lived in this single building in Cape Town; the lack of windows, save a few two-inch slits to let in some light, were as likely a reflection of the company's shame as of a need for security. This lodge remained relatively unchanged throughout the tenure of slavery at the cape, except for an extension and restoration in 1751.[23]

The internal division of space seems to have varied during the lodge's use as a slave residence, but most reports include descriptions of separate quarters for "the Lodging of each Sex" and for "married" couples, separate rooms set aside as an infirmary for the ill, a "strong prison where the drunken, the disobedient, etc. are confin'd and punish'd," and a schoolroom for the children.[24] A closed central courtyard provided a place for roll call, work assignment, meals, and other mass meetings and was also at one time reported to have held pigs. The building still stands today, currently housing the South African Museum. Today it is a striking white with dark green shutters for the many large windows which have been added. The museum chronicles a history of the Cape Colony from its European beginning in 1652, displays cases full of the produce of the cape, the type of cargo that was shipped through, the furniture and household implements used by the settlers, and the clothes they wore. The dank basement has been completely filled in with cement, the courtyard with lush greenery, and the upper rooms with sunlight, leaving very little of the atmosphere that must have been the lot of the buildings' former inhabitants, who had been circumscribed architecturally as well as demographically.

Almost all of the men, women, and children who lived in the lodge were slaves. Lunatics from the cape settler population and political criminals sent from the company's eastern possessions were kept in the lodge and treated as the slaves were, except that their stays there were temporary. Aside from these few, no Europeans lived there. The VOC officers in charge of the slave labor force, the Fiscal, the commissioner of slaves, and two upper foremen, lived outside the walls. One of them, the *opziender,* was responsible for daily roll call and locking the door every evening.[25] The slave lodge population itself *was* first divided by sex, socially as well as spatially. At the top of the hierarchy were the *mandoors,* male slave overseers of other slave men, and a *matres* (matron), who served the same function for the lodge women. The next divisions were along lines of descent, those slaves with a European parent having advantages over those born of two slave parents. Slaves who were born in the lodge, even those who had two slave parents, had real biological as well as social advantages over those who had been imported. The more creolized or naturalized to the cape environment and society a slave was, the better chances he or she would have both for advancement within the lodge and for manumission out of it. This picture of lodge experience can be tested with demographic evidence concerning sex and descent composition, compiled and calculated from VOC and Dutch Reformed Church records of the lodge slaves.

SOURCES

The Dutch in the seventeenth century, claiming both the largest merchant marine and the Western world's center of insurance and finance in Amsterdam, were meticulous record keepers.[26] This is illustrated by the lengths to which they went in keeping track of their trade in slaves. For example, in Curaçao the West India Company maintained a complicated practice of branding slaves first with Arabic numerals from 1 to 100 and later with the letters A to Z, according to the ships on which and the years in which they arrived at that particular slave trading depot. Under this system complete records might be more easily kept.[27] For the Caribbean trading entrepôts the extent and variety of surviving ledgers made by the Dutch is equally indicative of Dutch record-keeping propensity: detailed lists of incoming and outgoing ships, accounts of slaves sold, ships' manifests, invoices, bills of lading, inventories of forts and batteries, muster rolls of garrisons and poll tax lists of citizens, their families, and slaves—all for the seventeenth century.[28]

The cape itself had been involved in Dutch record keeping long before the establishment of a settlement there. Peter Kolb wrote in 1704 of this early seventeenth-century VOC practice:

> Every commander going out was provided with a square stone, upon which at his Departure from the Cape, he caus'd the ship's Name, his own Name, and the Names of the principal officers to be fairly cut, together with the day he arrived there, and the Day he departed. This stone, with such inscriptions, was buried in a certain place without the Fort, and under it was put a tin box seal'd up, containing letters from the Captain and others to the Directors of the Company together with such other letters as any persons on board should think for to send to Europe. This stone and box were taken up by the next Dutch East India ship that pass'd by in her return and by her convey'd to Holland.[29]

The VOC kept good records of its operations, the slave lodge being no exception. Official correspondence from the period, however, indicates that VOC record keeping at the cape was not quite up to the standards of at least one company inspector. In a memorial to Governor Heer van Assenburg on April 19, 1708, inspector Heer Simons wrote:

> The reason why I have been unable to investigate in how far [sic] the orders of the Company regarding slaves have been complied with here, is that it has been neglected to record them by name in the Company's books, in which should be added their age, and by what ship they arrived here, and in what year, which should be done with those next received, and in the presence of the Independent Fiscal, who should be warned for this the day before, since this is specially ordered in the Instructions, and when asking him to do this, a nominal roll of these slaves should always be sent to him, with an indication of where they will by employed in the service of the Hon. Company, so that he can perform his duty.[30]

Even so the records were remarkably complete by any other standards. The officials took complete censuses of the VOC slaves in 1693 and again, in 1714, kept lists of slaves arriving on company ships as well as records of all deaths and manumissions. Complementing the company records, the Dutch Reformed Church in Cape Town kept records of all baptisms performed there, including those of the company's slaves. From these documents it is possible to reconstruct a fairly complete demographic profile of the lodge community and, through that profile, reconstruct the life-cycle dynamics of this slave population. The first step to understand this population necessarily involves such a demographic reconstruction, an establishment of the parameters of the constituents. The movements of these women and men in and out of the state of slavery—as well as their patterns of forming unions, giving birth, and dying— are aspects of slave life at the cape not apparent in the narrative record, which concentrates on their behavior (and even more on that of settlers' slaves) toward masters and travelers, occupational functions, and criminal activity rather than on their personal lives.

The 1693 and 1714 Censuses

The 1693 census was actually a set of two censuses taken nearly a year apart. The first, taken in January, enumerated the 371 lodge slaves.[31] The second, taken in December, added 57 company slaves residing in outlying districts.[32] Because the censuses were taken at different times, a few slaves (usually male) appeared in both and so were counted twice because they were moved to company frontier outposts between January and December.[33] A few company slaves possibly never were recorded because of moves in the opposite direction, although a move in that direction was not as likely. The 1714 census, taken in August of that year, was a single census recording the 466 occupants of the lodge.[34]

These censuses recorded each slave's name, racial descent, occupation, and approximate age for infants, except for a group of infants born between 1690 and 1692, for whom the precise birth years are recorded. The fifteen infant girls from this group, for whom the exact ages were given, form a "core" sample of mothers for this study. Their children later appeared in the baptismal register.

Death Registers

The death registers for lodge slaves record the name, date of death, and age at death for each slave.[35] For example, Elizabeth, a three-year-old "school maiden" and the daughter of Maria Blom, died on December 20, 1719.[36] These records contributed to the analysis in two ways. First, as in the case of Elizabeth van Maria Blom, they eliminated certain slaves from the "potential mothers" category. Second, for slaves dying at ages well into or past motherhood, such as Jacomintje, who died in 1719 at the age of fifty, the recorded ages provided a means for calculating mothers' birth dates.[37] In addition the death registers allowed the calculation of mortality rates for potential mothers— taken to be women of child-bearing age, roughly fourteen to forty-five—among the company slave population. Mortality rates can tell us something about the harshness of conditions under which eleven slaves lived. The points during their life-cycles at which they died as well as the rates at which they died also sometimes suggest likely causes of death.

Manumissions

The Netherlands rose to commercial prominence in a seventeenth-century world centered on Calvinist theology. Calvinism conveniently tolerated capitalist practices and significantly influenced many commercial institutions.[38] The Dutch directors and local cape officers of the VOC were strict Calvinists, and this identity was manifest in their policies. Any slave born into the "household" of the lodge, according to VOC policy, was to be baptized within eight days of birth and, when old enough, educated in rudimentary Christian principles.[39] These Christian slaves were considered members of the "household" of the lodge and in accordance with that status could not be sold or given away. While some members of the Synod of Dordt, which ruled on many of these religious issues in 1618, believed that baptized slaves should enjoy equal rights, including liberty, with all other Christians, the official decision was that they could remain enslaved but could not be sold.[40]

A principal inconsistency between this scheme for lodge slave treatment and Calvinist doctrine was the nightly sanctioned prostitution of the lodge women. For an hour each evening the "Calvinist" local officials of the VOC threw open the lodge doors to soldiers of the garrison, passing sailors (the "lords of six weeks"), and any of the local male population. Perhaps surprisingly, the money changing hands during these transactions ended up in the hands of the lodge slaves, although often those of the male slaves rather than the women.[41] Before 1688, when the company assisted the immigration of several Huguenot refugee families in a final attempt to implement free labor, the lodge slave women outnumbered all cape settler women put together. In effect the lodge became a brothel, and the company slave women, prostitutes. As slave status passed through the maternal line, all of the children produced by these unions were enslaved from birth, regardless of paternity.

Settler-slave unions accounted for approximately half of the slave lodge population's fertility between 1680 and 1730, while the internal sexual activity of the lodge population accounted for the rest.[42] Hendrik Adriaan Van Reede, a company commissioner who visited the cape in 1685, was deeply shocked by the number of slaves visibly of Dutch paternity he found in the lodge. He left behind a detailed set of instructions and recommendations for dealing with this problematic (for the Calvinist officials) group of approximately five dozen slaves. His proposals for dealing with this problem of "enslaving members of one's own nation" included providing them with education, decent training in trades, and special, more liberal provisions for manumission.[43] Provisions for manumission included thirty years (twenty-five for those of European descent) of faithful service, the ability to speak Dutch, confirmation in the Dutch Reformed Church, and between 100 and 150 florins (women had to pay more because of a greater outlay for their clothing on the part of the company). According to these terms, and consistently with attitudes throughout the Atlantic world, manumission was to be considered "a favor, not a right."[44] The general idea was that many of such freed slaves, especially men, would then provide a source of artisans upon which the company could draw. Artisans were in short supply at the cape in this period.

The majority of manumissions involved racially mixed children and their mothers.[45] This leads to speculation about the concern of settler fathers/husbands regarding their enslaved family members. What types of relationships were forged through lodge brothel activity? The shortage of women at the cape in this early period of its history makes it more likely that some of these unions, rather than being merely supplemental, were the only unions in which some of the men were involved. They therefore might have been more likely to result in matrimony, providing that the man in question could afford to manumit his bride. A slave known only as Manda Gratia exemplifies this process. A lodge slave on the 1714 census, she is recorded later as having married a settler named Guilliam Frisnet and gradually managed to free many of her children born prior to the marriage.[46] This case provides some evidence of successful company policy as well, in that one of her freed sons joined the company as a sailor.[47] Yet a slave first had to be manumitted before she was allowed to marry. The cost of this was prohibitive because it included not only the purchase of the slave's freedom but also some additional reimbursement of the company for that slave's education and upbringing.[48] Consequently, regardless of the relationships developed, few could afford such manumissions and instead continued visiting the lodge as they liked. For slaves who were not of the preferred marriageable category and who did not meet age or descent requirements, there was one other option. They could, if they could afford it, replace themselves with another slave. Demographic analysis of manumissions indicates that this almost never happened.

Baptisms

Perhaps the most important source of data for the period covered by this study is the baptismal records.[49] These are complete records of all baptisms of slaves, Europeans, and free people in Cape Town for the period 1680–1730. VOC baptismal policy on this matter was handed down from the governor general and the Council of Batavia: "All slaves of the person with whom they live, whether the owner or not, are to be baptized and must be obliged to educate them in the Christian religion; this being chiefly founded upon the example of the Patriarch Abraham, in whose faith all who were in his house were circumcised, and the observance has been accordingly followed here. . . . You may therefore take this regulation for your guidance, and if you proceed in that holy work, there, as is done here, you will do well and act the part of a Christian."[50] According to this policy, which was based on the decisions made during the Synod of Dordt in 1618, all slaves born in the slave lodge *had* to be baptized. This is an interesting counterpoint to Frank Tannenbaum's contention that most Protestant groups did not generally baptize their slaves while Catholics did.[51]

The VOC's mandatory baptismal policy, combined with confidence in Dutch bureaucratic diligence, allows us to assume that all slaves born in the lodge were recorded in this baptismal register during the period in question. The baptismal records are a valuable font of information about the slave population at the cape during the VOC's administration of the colony, 1652 to 1795. The registers of 1,265 slave baptisms provide names, birth dates,[52] rough ages (that is, "child" or "adult"), racial descent, and sometimes parents' and owners' names and places of origin. For example, the slave Margreta Geertruij, a "half breed" child from the Cape owned by the VOC, was baptized on February 18, 1714, the daughter of the VOC slave Manda of the cape and an unknown father. The settler fathers of children born into the lodge often absented themselves or were too ashamed to claim their mixed descent offspring for whom they were not held legally accountable, while settler fathers of privately owned slaves (although fewer of these were baptized to begin with) were more often recorded in the baptismal records because the parentage generally was of common knowledge. Of 1,125 slave baptisms, 767 were of VOC slaves and 358 of privately owned slaves.[53] Because the mother of each slave was recorded in the baptismal record, it was possible to reconstitute families of

77 mothers and 220 children. Most newly imported mothers likely were not present as children in these baptismal registers and therefore had to be excluded from parts of the demographic analysis.

METHODOLOGY: FAMILY RECONSTITUTION

The French *annalistes* Marcel Fleury and Louis Henry pioneered the method of "family reconstitution" in the 1950s. They devised a system of family cards, on each of which all available information about a male-female couple and their children (in the case of this project, a mother and fifteen children without the father generally made up a family) from a variety of historical sources could be recorded. This allowed for the demographic study of populations during periods of their history before regular censuses. Church records, private family records, and other such sources could now be used in the study of historical demography.

This project combines the sources described above, carefully linking slaves by listed parentage, origin, and in some cases only by name, in the reconstitution of seventy-seven mother/children families, tracking their births, child bearing, manumissions, and deaths, in order to discover the average life expectancies of lodge slaves in terms of these events. The chief flaw found in the family reconstitution method in other studies is its inability to take into account the effects of migration on the population.[54] In the case of the lodge population, imports take the place of immigration and manumissions that of emigration, and since both of these were recorded as well as births or deaths, this problem could be overcome for the purposes of this study.

A few difficulties with family reconstitution remained for the project. In the cases of more completely recorded names, the linkage of mothers with children was unambiguous. Mothers with prevalent names such as Maria or Helena were often recorded without specific information concerning matronym or patronym, and linkages involving these women were more difficult to make.[55] The integrity of these linkages was based on common origin and owner for mothers as well as demographically possible ages and intervals for birth, a biologically likely interval being somewhere between eighteen months and three years.[56] The corruption of pronunciation and. then spelling of less familiar names, especially African, Indian, and Indonesian, between baptism and adulthood also hindered linkage. In addition all slave mothers who married Europeans disappeared from the record, often before the end of their motherhood, substantially lowering the average apparent completed family size (total number of children per mother) for the lodge population as a whole. Identification and exclusion of such subsequently manumitted mothers corrects for this distortion.

ANALYSIS: SLAVE LODGE POPULATION COMPOSITION

Sex

One of the most striking characteristics of the lodge population was its sex ratio. Unlike any other colonial slave population, or early settler population, for that matter, the lodge had a rough equality of numbers between men and women from the beginning. In fact, in the late seventeenth century, the lodge held more women than men; the ratio was 88 men to 100 women in 1693.[57] By the second decade of the eighteenth century this had shifted in favor of men, though it was still substantially lower than other early slave (and settler) populations. The ratio was 159 to 100 in 1714.[58] By comparison the cape settlers' slaves had a more typically disparate sex ratio until early in the nineteenth century, reaching levels as high as 398 to 100 in 1738.[59] The relatively balanced sex ratio in the lodge was apparently due much more to chance and to the abilities and preferences of suppliers than to any policy or control on the part of the company. The only evidence of any preference on the part of the company was the requests made to the slave traders for male laborers.[60]

Age

While most slaves imported to the cape were adults, there are a few instances, especially in the beginning, of slaves being brought to the cape as children. The VOC ship, the *Voorhout,* picked up 50 slaves "reportedly all boys and girls under sixteen" at St. Augustine's Bay, Madagascar, in 1677.[61] Another company ship, the *Amersfoot,* brought 174 slaves to the cape in 1658, the majority of whom were children.[62] In 1693 the age breakdown of the slave lodge was 72 percent adults (those at least sixteen years old) and 28 percent children, of whom 16.5 percent were school-aged (five to sixteen years) and the remaining 11.5 percent infants (birth to five years). This had not changed significantly by 1714, when 80 percent were adults, 15.2 percent children and 4.8 percent infants. The lodge maintained, throughout the period under study, a significant number of younger residents, enough to establish a school for them after 1685. Many of these were born into the lodge, which as time went on created a population increasingly creole (locally born) and therefore generally more resistant to disease. By 1693, in fact, after only thirty-five years of slavery, 95 percent of the lodge children were creole, already fully one-quarter of those being of part settler descent.[63]

Origin

The appeal of lodge slaves to their European brothel clientele varied directly with the degree of somatic compatibility in their appearances, which was directly related to descent. Settler-descended slave women, because of their more European appearance, were generally the most preferred. Slaves of mixed descent were most likely to be born at the cape, where the potential European fathers were. Geographic origin and descent, therefore, were important to mothers' fertility. Of the 1,265 slave mothers recorded in the baptismal registers,

616 were lodge mothers. Of those, 290, or 47 percent, were creole slaves. As for the rest, the overwhelming majority came from neighboring Madagascar, and the remaining few from the Indian Subcontinent, the Indonesian archipelago or other parts of Africa.

The origins of slave men were similar in distribution but slightly greater in diversity. Just over half had been born at the cape, with a significant percentage of those foreign born coming from Madagascar. The remainder came from as far and wide as Angola, Guinea, the Indonesian Archipelago, the Indian subcontinent, and China.

POPULATION DYNAMICS

Slave Marriage and the Rate of Union (Nuptiality)

After birth and death, marriage (or union) is the most important vital event in the constitution of population dynamics. Slaves at the cape could not marry among themselves until 1826 legislation provided for it.[64] "While the majority of lodge slaves were baptized Christians," Robert Shell notes, "most of the other Christian rites, including that of marriage were withheld. Slaves had first to be manumitted in order to be married."[65] This was not a frequent occurrence. Although actual rates of marriage can be calculated through a study of manumission records, the nuptiality rate is not useful for this study. Instead, for slaves the rate of sexual union is more appropriate to the demographic analysis. Of fifteen (1693) core potential slave mothers, seven subsequently appear as mothers in the baptismal registers. This would indicate a low rate of union. However, when the very high mortality rate, infant mortality, and rates of miscarriage are taken into consideration, it seems more likely that many of the remaining eight either died before they had the chance to give birth or gave birth to children who died even before they could be baptized.

Infertility also affects the calculation of the rate of union. James Trussell, Jane Menken, and Susan Watkins have established that diet was not likely to affect reproductive health absolutely, although it could significantly affect the age of onset of menarche, the age at which slaves could begin bearing children.[66] Lodge rations were nearly equivalent to those of the garrison.[67] Sexually transmitted diseases were certainly present at the cape during this period as well and often made victims infertile. However, since having a venereal disease resulted in corporal punishment, few admitted to it.[68] Consequently the effects of STDs are difficult to quantify. The available data indicates a rate of union for female lodge slaves of approximately 50 percent. But consideration of all these other factors suggests a much higher rate of union for those who survived.

Mortality

The mortality rate of this particular slave population was high, as was true for many newly arrived populations, slave and free.[69] From the very beginning high mortality was a significant problem in the maintenance of the VOC slave force. Mortality rates on the slave trading ships as well as among slaves recently landed were extremely high. Of the 257 slaves arriving on the *Voorhout* in 1676, 92 were dead within only three months. Of the 119 slaves landed from the *Soldaat* in 1697, over half were dead within the year.[70]

If they survived the first year of arrival slaves were then faced with the daily perils of climate, fatigue, and, most of all, disease. Regular smallpox epidemics struck at the cape; the first documented occurred in 1713 and killed more than half of the lodge slave population.[71] These epidemics were not rare and would have substantially affected the long-term mortality rates as well as those for the years in which they occurred.

The eight core potential mothers from the 1693 census missing from the baptismal registers must either have been infertile or died young. In the light of the death and manumission documentation, narrative evidence of generally high mortality and the impossibility of recovering information on other reasons for not bearing children, such as infertility rates, it is likely that many of the remaining eight died before reaching the age of motherhood. For a few of them, death before motherhood can be inferred. The slave Cleopatra, for example, born in 1691, did not live to be included in the 1714 census in which all company slaves were included.[72] She could not have left the lodge except by manumission or death, and she was not manumitted. So the core mothers likely had a mortality rate of over 50 percent. This high mortality rate significantly affected this analysis as it drastically depleted the supply of "potential mothers" (female children who survived to adulthood). The majority of women in this population died in the first few years of life. The highest period of mortality was between birth and age 5, long before child-bearing age. After this, mortality dropped but was followed by a slow but steady climb in female mortality until the age of 30.[73] The average age at death for women was 26.8.

The death registers demonstrate that mortality rates for men were even higher. Mortality for men was highest between the ages of 25 and 35 (48.4 percent of deaths occurred in this interval). Aside from that they followed much the same pattern as women, a peak in early childhood followed by a fall during school years and a subsequent gradual rise to the end.[74] The average age at death for men was 26.3.

Slave lodge mortality was largely seasonal as well. Most deaths occurred during the damp cape winters. The period of lowest mortality was the spring and earlier summer; deaths were fewer as the weather became warmer. These high death rates as well as their seasonality suggest that slaves were likely exposed to the elements in their work and possibly even in their sleep. With no central heating, scarce fire for fear of arson, and no sunlight, the lodge was probably a very cold and damp place to be in the winter. These conditions were probably similar to those of many colonial armies at the time. Such soldiers had also been brought far from home, performed highly stressful work during the day, and retired to damp, cold, crowded barracks by night. Mortality was high for these men as well. Historians and demographers looking at slightly later periods for which births and deaths in the lodge were faithfully recorded and enumerated for each year have noted that, regardless of when the deaths occurred, births never even came close to making up for them, making the lodge a "demographic sinkhole."[75] Births are not enumerated for each year during the period in question, but the situation was not likely any different (save an even greater deficit of births) than in later periods.

Manumissions

The demographic record does vaguely reflect company policy on manumission outlined above in that it does show preference for slaves with certain profiles. But it is not a direct reflection of that policy. For instance, from 1680 to 1730 the company manumitted only 21 lodge slaves, coming to a rate of 4.2 slaves per year. This comes to a rate of 1.02 per thousand slaves, much lower than most other Atlantic world slave populations, even for the seventeenth century, and significantly lower than other Dutch Atlantic populations such as those reported by Willem Klooster in this volume.[76] This rate is also lower than the rate among the cape settler population.[77]

Consistent with the social hierarchy at the cape and within the lodge, all but one of the slaves manumitted had some settler parentage. The exception, a cook from Ceylon named Pintura, was manumitted in 1686 well into adulthood.[78] His manumission could have been a result of the company's no longer being willing to take care of a slave past his prime, or he could have been one of those rare cases, achieving manumission by replacing himself with another slave. Otherwise, the pattern of manumission diverges from a reflection of company policy, which would have meant a preponderance of slaves aged between forty and fifty years. Of these early manumissions, nine were men and twelve women, and eleven of the total were under the age of fourteen. While manumissions from the lodge in this period were hardly frequent, patterns to those that did occur are recognizable. These patterns favored children, women, and above all, slaves of settler descent.

The reasons for the lower rate of manumission and the failure of the pattern directly to reflect company policy were intimately connected to the very high rate of mortality in the lodge discussed above. Most lodge slaves were unlikely to live long enough to meet the age/term of labor qualifications outlined by Van Reede. In addition to this, and the difficulty of coming up with the money required for freedom, there was the frequency of settler fathers' refusal to recognize their enslaved offspring, making it more difficult for some slaves to prove their qualification for manumission under the more generous terms set for settler-descended slaves.

Fertility

During this period, long before the abolition of the oceanic slave trade in 1807, female slaves were not generally valued in their capacities as reproducers of the slave population. They were valued as laborers, just as were their male counterparts.[79] The lodge slave women, however, were in a slightly different situation from the rest of the cape slave female population. Because they functioned partly as prostitutes as well as laborers, the lodge women were in some way valued for their sex. This recognition of their sex gave them a way out of the lodge which was not open to men. If a lodge slave had a child by a European settler, this father occasionally officially recognized the child and bought his "wife" from the company to manumit and marry her. As residents of an informal brothel, therefore, female lodge slaves had a reason to want to have children which did not apply to the rest of the cape slave women. Fertility rates for the set of reconstituted families from the baptismal register yield a fertility rate of 3.1 children per lodge slave woman listed as a mother in the baptismal register. Mothers of slave descent had an average of 3.6 children, and mothers of part settler-descent an average of 2.5 children. The unexpectedly lower rate for the more somatically compatible (from the brothel clients' point of view) slaves is deceptive as it does not follow the mother through possible manumission and therefore represents only her fertility during her term of slavery. The general rate is lower than that of the white population given by Guelke. This could be due to records of motherhood being cut short by manumission, to high mortality, to high rates of miscarriage, to venereal disease–induced infertility, or to late age at first birth because of postponed onset of menarche.[80]

Age at First Birth

Demographers from Aristotle to Thomas Malthus to the present have recognized the importance of age at first birth to the demographic dynamics of any society.[81] Today it is the key index of the "demographic transition" whereby a society moves from one demographic regime (early marriage and many children) to another (late marriage and few children). Relief and aid organizations such as the World Bank and the International Monetary Fund use age at first birth or marriage in the formation of their policies toward developing countries, many of which by most estimations have such high fertility rates, even with dropping mortality, that they are said not yet to have made the "demographic transition."[82] In a study for the World Bank concerning African fertility rates, Charles Westoff concluded that raising the age at marriage among African populations would fundamentally lower the fertility rate.[83] John Hajnal and Ansley Coale have both emphasized the importance of marriage-age patterns in their demographic studies of European populations.[84]

Age at first birth would have affected profoundly total fertility of the lodge population as well. Unfortunately, evidence concerning this index has not been well preserved in the historical record. For the first period this variable was calculated from a group of thirty mothers for whom both a birth date and a reliable series of children could be recovered using all the described sources together. The average age at first birth for the general lodge population was 16.6. It was lower, 16.1, for the mixed descent women, and higher, 17.7, for all other slave women. This was perhaps due to the formers' earlier initiation into the evening brothel because of higher demand. Ages at first birth for lodge slaves in general were lower than for the European population as described by Guelke, 18.8 years of age.

This age at first birth can be compared with a later one for South African slaves as well as with one for cape European women at this time. Auction records for the settlers' slaves (1823–1830), recopied by the British colonial government in 1830 in accordance with slave registration legislation preparatory to Emancipation, preserved extensive age and birth information for both mothers and their children. The age at first birth for slave mothers born after 1805 was 17.6.[85] The age at first birth for European women in the same period "lay no higher than 25," according to Robert Ross.[86]

Conclusion

The infant mortality rate in the slave lodge is impossible to recover for this period as deaths were not consistently recorded until later in the eighteenth century (nor were rates of miscarriage and perinatal mortality),[87] although as for any "pre-transitional" population, they are likely to have been high. Life expectancy at birth estimated from censuses and available death records was 7.25 years for women and 7.94 years for men. For those slaves who were born and who lived long enough to be baptized (8 days), the next hurdle was the first five years of childhood. Life expectancy for children 1–4 for those surviving to the beginning of this period was 9.0 further years for women and 8.84 further years for men. Surviving this period, barring a smallpox or other epidemic, meant a good chance of surviving to adulthood or the age of child bearing.

Maternal mortality (dying because of complications of pregnancy or childbirth) is also hard to recover as the diagnosis of cause of death was not highly sophisticated even in Europe at this time. Mortality would not only have reduced fertility figures but also limited the completed family size (total number of births) for each woman. Lodge slave women had active reproductive lives if they were members of the tiny group who did survive to the age of motherhood. Most had at least one child by the age of sixteen and a half. Although the survival rate of their children would be no higher than it had been for their own generation, they did give birth to large numbers, sometimes as many as seven. As compared to the European women in Cape Town during this period, the slave women of the VOC lodge were having fewer children even though first children for slaves were coming sooner than those for European women. Of the children the cape women had, fewer survived in the slave than in the free population. This was consistent with the experience of other slave populations.

These extremely high rates of mortality for both infants and adults had a significant impact on manumission rates. Manumission was rare to begin with: Women had a 0.16 percent chance of manumission at an average age of 15.44, men a 0.09 percent chance at an average age of 16.04. Still, lodge slaves were manumitted according to identifiable patterns. Gender helped shape patterns of manumission. Women's chances of manumission were higher than men's; 63 percent of manumissions were of women. Slave men, not bearing children, had fewer demographic markers by which to enter Dutch record books. Yet what demographic reconstruction is possible adds to our knowledge of their lives. Their demographic composition is nonetheless important to an analysis of their social experience because, according to their sex and in some cases their descent, they did have a better chance of advancement within the VOC hierarchy.[88] On the other hand, the demographic record also makes clear that, as in the case of Dutch Suriname as well as in many of the other cases in this volume, gender put them at a disadvantage in terms of manumission.[89]

Origin also helped shape manumission patterns. Consistent with company policy, creoles were far more (95 percent of manumissions) likely to be manumitted than foreign-born slaves. Finally, age, though not so consistently with company policy, affected manumission patterns. Fifty-one percent of manumissions were of children under the age of fourteen. Because of social and biological ties to those in the freed world, children often had a better chance than their parents of escaping slavery before death.

The lodge slaves who lived past childhood had lives about which we know comparatively little. We cannot reconstruct their thoughts. Some aspects of slaves' fertility and mortality will never be fully understood without narrative records. Demographic evidence, however, can contribute to a reconstruction of the aspects over which policy had more influence. The parameters set by the VOC in its slave lodge are thus reflected in the demographic record, reconstructed from the careful records kept by the Dutch of their labor force. The slaves' mortality tells us of the harsh material conditions of life under which they lived. The profile of their manumissions tells us that this rare event was only likely for a small group of specific sex, age, appearance, and/or descent. Sex and descent were also especially important in the internal hierarchy of the lodge. The slaves higher and earlier fertility than the settler population tells us that no social constructs, such as marriage, postponed their unions and so limited their fertility. Disease and death comprised the limits on fertility.

Demographic evidence also helps uncover aspects over which the company had little influence. The same socially unlimited fertility contributed to the development of social patterns, further limiting company control. Divergence from patterns predicted by company policy reflected in the demographic record tells us about uncontrolled factors such as gender and fertility contributing to patterns of manumission and hint at the development of slave agency, both through the exploitation of social ties with free people and freed people and, rarely but surely, through the legal exercise of learned rights.

NOTES

1. VOC control of the cape ended in 1795, when the British took possession of the colony. Although slaves still lived in the lodge up until their official emancipation in 1827 (seven years before the rest of the cape slaves), the British did not rely on this labor force as the Dutch had. The former company slaves, which were given over to the British along with control of the colony, still performed domestic labor and some artisanal work, but for the most part the lodge gradually became, in effect, an old-age home for them.

2. François Valentijn, *Description of the Cape of Good Hope with Matters Concerning It* (1704; reprint, Cape Town: Van Riebeeck Society, 1971–73), 1:101.

3. James Armstrong and Nigel Worden, "The Slaves," in *The Shaping of South African Society, 1652–1840,* ed. Richard Elphick and Hermann Giliomee (Middletown, Conn.: Wesleyan University Press, 1989), 123.

4. Barry Higman, *Slave Populations of the British Caribbean, 1807–1834* (Baltimore: Johns Hopkins University Press, 1984), 396.

5. David Yaukey, *Demography: The Study of Human Population* (Prospect Heights, Ill.: Waveland Press, 1985), 187.

6. Higman, *Slave Populations*, 1.

7. Patrick Manning, *Slavery and African Life: Occidental, Oriental and African Slave Trades* (Cambridge: Cambridge University Press, 1990), 39, 57, and chap. 3, nn. 2, 8.

8. The disparity in evidence between white, European and "nonwhite," non-European populations may have had more to do with civic status than with color in this period. For example, Ross was able to include "free blacks" in his analysis of the eighteenth-century Cape population. Robert Ross, "'White' Population of South Africa in the Eighteenth Century," *Population Studies* 29, no. 2 (1975): 217–330.

9. Higman, *Slave Populations*.

10. James Trussell and Richard Steckel, "The Age of Slaves at Menarche and Their First Birth," *Journal of Interdisciplinary Studies* 8, no. 3 (Winter 1978): 477–505.

11. Herbert Klein and Stanley Engerman, "Fertility Differentials between Slaves in the United States and the British West Indies: A Note on Lactation Practices and Their Possible Implications," *William and Mary Quarterly*, 3rd ser., 35, no. 2 (1978): 357–374.

12. Alida Metcalf, *Family and Frontier in Colonial Brazil: Santana de Paraíba, 1580–1822* (Berkeley and Los Angeles: University of California Press, 1992), 13.

13. A. Hulshof, ed., "H. A. van Reede tot Drakesteijn, Journaal van zijn verblijf aan de Kaap," by H. A. van Reede tot Drakesteijn, *Bijdragen en Medede van Het Historisch Genootschap* 62 (1941): 213–214.

14. Robert Ross, *Cape of Torments: Slavery and Resistance at the Cape* (London: Routledge and Kegan Paul, 1983), 11–12.

15. The manumission rate for the entire period of slavery at the cape was 0.17 percent; less than one lodge slave per year obtained freedom this way. For the period in question, the rate was actually an even lower 0.10 percent.

16. I am grateful to Judy Bieber-Freitas for suggesting this comparison and directing me to these references. Metcalf, *Family and Frontier in Colonial Brazil,* 132, 182; Stuart Schwartz,

"Indian Labor and New World Plantations: European Demands and Indian Responses in Northeastern Brazil," *American Historical Review* 83, no. 1 (1978): 43–79. Schwartz used baptismal records for Indian slaves in Brazil in similar ways to this study.

17. Paul E. Lovejoy, *Transformations in Slavery: A History of Slavery in America* (Cambridge & New York: Cambridge University Press, 1983), 131.

18. Johannes Postma, *The Dutch in the Atlantic Slave Trade, 1600–1815* (Cambridge: Cambridge University Press, 1990), 72; "Instructions for the Slave Supervisor at Elmina," in Postma, *Dutch in the Atlantic Slave Trade,* Appendix 21, 402.

19. Slave census (Lodge), "Generale Opneming en monster rolle van'd Comp: Soo slaven als bandieten," Dutch East India Company Archives/Algemeen Rijksarchief, the Hague (hereafter VOC), 4030: folios 359–367 (January 1, 1693); Slave census (Elmina), "Opnemingh van Compagnies Groot en kleen vee, mitsgaders der materialen, bouw gereedschappen en andere goederen in 1693 bevonden," VOC, 4032: folios 65–73 (December 31, 1693); Postma, *Dutch in the Atlantic Slave Trade,* 72.

20. Leonard Guelke and Robert Shell describe this "Wakefieldian effect" occasioned by large quantities of accessible "free" land; see Guelke and Shell, "An Early Colonial Landed Gentry: Land and Wealth in the Cape Colony 1682–1731," *Journal of Historical Geography* 9, no. 3 (1983): 265–286.

21. Nigel Worden, *Slavery in Dutch South Africa* (Cambridge: Cambridge University Press, 1985), 6.

22. Victor de Kock, *Those in Bondage: An Account of the Life of the Slaves at the Cape in the Days of the Dutch East India Company* (London: Allen and Unwin, 1950), 76.

23. Ibid.

24. Peter Kolb, *The Present State of the Cape of Good Hope,* trans. Guido Medley (1731; rpt., New York: Johnson Reprint Company, 1968), 352; De Kock, *Those in Bondage,* 37. This imposed internal division of space in the slave lodge paralleled the Dutch endeavor to stamp order onto the very plan of Cape Town. For a lucid discussion of these spatial "artefacts of domination," see Martin Hall, "High and Low in the Townscapes of Dutch South America and South Africa: The Dialectics of Material Culture," *Social Dynamics* 17, no. 2 (1991): 41–75.

25. Armstrong and Worden, "Slaves," 127; De Kock, *Those in Bondage,* 36.

26. Postma, *Dutch in the Atlantic Slave Trade,* 9.

27. Ibid., 52.

28. I am grateful to Neil Kennedy for suggesting the comparison and for bringing these documents to my attention. The St. Eustatius Historical Museum is one repository of such documents. Facsimiles may be found there, and the originals are located at Algemeen Rijksarchief, The Hague, the Netherlands.

29. Kolb, *Present State of the Cape of Good Hope,* 18–19.

30. Valentijn, *Description of the Cape* 1:213.

31. Slave census, "Generale Opneming en monster rolle van'd Comp."

32. Slave census, "Opnemingh van Compagnies Groot."

33. Matching based on name and origin indicates that nine slave were counted both in Cape Town and in the districts. This was only 2.3 percent of the total slave force and so does not substantially affect analysis.

34. Slave census, Attestatiën, "Verklaring na gedane monsteringe bevonden te hebben onder te naeme 's Comp: leijfeijgenen," C336: 457–475 (August 31, 1714), Cape Archives Depot, Cape Town, South Africa (hereafter cited as Cape Archives Depot).

35. This project incorporated death registers from the years 1719, 1720, and 1721. Death registers: Attestatiën, C338: 525–526, 779; C339: 55, 171–172, 247, 335, 663, 779, Cape Archives Depot.

36. Death register, C338: 597, Cape Archives Depot.

37. Death register, C338: 525, Cape Archives Depot. Because the registers contain both the ages at death and the date of death, a simple subtraction gives the birth year of the slave.

38. Postma, *Dutch in the Atlantic Slave Trade*, 8.

39. De Kock, *Those in Bondage*, 102; Robert C.-H. Shell, "Religion, Civic Status, and Slavery, from Dordt to the Trek," *Kronos* (November 1992): 6–7.

40. Shell, "Religion, Civic Status, and Slavery," 4.

41. Robert C.-H. Shell, *Children of Bondage: A Social History of the Slave Society at the Cape of Good Hope, 1652–1838* (Hanover, N.H.: Wesleyan University Press), 285–287.

42. Baptismal registers, Kaapstad Doopboek GR 1 1/1, 8/1–2, Dutch Reformed Church Archives (Cape Archives Depot). This accounting of fertility results from an analysis of the recorded descent of every lodge slave baby appearing in the baptismal record during the period.

43. Hulshof, "H. A. van Reede tot Drakesteijn," 210–214.

44. Anna J. Böeseken, ed., *Belangrike Kaapse Dokumente: Memoriën en Instructiën 1657– 1699*, 2 vols. (Cape Town: South African State Archives, 1967), 1:206–207, 217.

45. Accounts of the manumission of company slaves were kept in several places: Hendrik Carel Vos Leibraandt, *Requesten (Memorials) 1715–1806*, 5 vols. (Cape Town: South African Library, 1989; reprint, Cape Town: Cape Times, 1905); "Transporter en Schepen kennis," vols. 1–60, Deeds Office, Cape Town, South Africa; Anna J. Böeseken, et al., eds., *Suid-Afrikaanse Argiefstukke: Resolusies van die Politieke Raad (1652–1732)*, 8 vols. (Cape Town: Cape Tunes, 1957–75).

46. Slave census, C336 (1714): 471, nos. 388, 245, 267, Cape Archives Depot.

47. Shell, *Children of Bondage*, 288.

48. Böeseken, *Memoriën en Instructiën*, 1:206–207, 217.

49. Baptismal registers, Kaap Notule 1665–1694, GR 1 Vol. 1; Kaapstad Doopboeke 1695–1712, GR Vol. 8/1; Kaapstad Doopboeke 1713–1742, GR 1 Vol. 8/2, Dutch Reformed Church Archives (Cape Archives Depot).

50. Donald Moodie, comp., *The Record or a Series of Official Papers Relative to the Condition and Treatment of the Native Tribes of South Africa* (Cape Town: Balkema, 1960), 273n1.

51. Frank Tannenbaum, *Slave and Citizen: The Negro in the Americas* (New York: Knopf, 1946), 62–63, 82–90, 102.

52. Baptismal dates for children can be roughly equated with birth dates because of company baptismal policy concerning slaves.

53. Baptismal registers, Kaapstad Doopboek GR 11/1, Vol. 8/1–2, Dutch Reformed Church Archives (Cape Archives Depot).

54. See Sune Akerman, "An Evaluation of the Family Reconstitution Technique," *Scandinavian Economic Historical Review* 25, no. 2 (1977): 160.

55. Slave names, as recorded by the Dutch, could have as many as four parts. First was the Christian or given name; if the slave was baptized, this was usually a Western name. If not, many of the lodge slaves kept preenslavement names, whereas settler owners more often changed the names of their slaves to something more familiar to themselves. The company, for the most part, did not change these names, so that many indigenous names survived in the lodge. The second name was the matronym, indicating the slave's mother. The third part was the patronym, naming the slave's father, and the fourth, the toponym, indicating place of birth

or known origin. For example, Christijn Pietersz van Maria van de Caap would be Christijn of parents Maria (a slave) and Pietersz (likely a cape settler) born at the cape. Slave names varied in their degree of incorporation of all these parts although slaves, with more common given names such as Jan or Maria more likely to have a greater number of further modifiers in order to differentiate them from others. For further information on slave naming at the cape, see Armstrong and Worden, "Slaves," 121; also see Shell, *Children of Bondage,* chap. 8.

56. Yaukey, *Demography,* 171.

57. Slave census, "Generale Opneming en monster rode van'd Comp."

58. Attestatiën, C336: 457–475 (August 1714), Cape Archives Depot.

59. Armstrong and Worden, "Slaves," 133.

60. Ibid., 124.

61. James C. Armstrong, "St. Augustines Bay and the Madagascar Slave Trade in the Seventeenth Century," unpublished ms., 1982, Overseas Operating Division, Library of Congress.

62. Ross, *Cape of Torments,* 11.

63. Slave census, "Generale Opneming en monster rolle van'd Comp."

64. Shell, "Religion, Civic Status, and Slavery," 28.

65. Ibid., 9.

66. James Trussell, Jane Menken, and Susan Watkins, "The Nutrition Fertility Link: An Evaluation of the Evidence," *Journal of Interdisciplinary History* 11, no. 3 (Winter 1981): 425–441.

67. Valentijn, *Description of the Cape,* 243.

68. Robert Shell, "Tender Ties: The Women of the Cape Slave Society," in *Collected Seminar Papers: The Societies of Southern Africa in the Nineteenth and Twentieth Centuries,* vol. 17 (London: Institute of Commonwealth Studies, University of London, 1992), 15.

69. Philip Curtin, *The Atlantic Slave Trade: A Census* (Madison: University of Wisconsin Press, 1969), 275–286; Philip Curtin, *Death by Migration: Europe's Encounter with the Tropical World in the Nineteenth Century* (Cambridge: Cambridge University Press, 1989), 16–20; Philip Curtin, *The Rise and Fall of the Plantation Complex* (Cambridge: Cambridge University Press, 1990), 81.

70. Armstrong and Worden, "Slaves," 126.

71. Ibid.

72. Slave census, C336: 457–475 (August 31, 1714), Cape Archives Depot.

73. Death registers, C338: 525–526, 597–598, 779; C339: 55, 171–172, 247, 335, 663, 779, Cape Archives Depot.

74. Ibid.

75. Shell, *Children of Bondage,* chap. 6. See also Armstrong and Worden, "Slaves," 126.

76. Rosemary Brana-Shute, "Approaching Freedom: The Manumission of Slaves in Suriname,1760–1828," *Slavery and Abolition* 10 (3): 66–93; also see Brana-Shute's essay in this volume, "Sex and Gender in Surinamese Manumissions."

77. Shell, *Children of Bondage,* 383.

78. Böeseken, *Resolusies,* 3:136.

79. Claude Meillasoux, "Female Slavery," in *Women and Slavery in Africa,* ed. Claire C. Robertson and Martin A. Klein (Madison: University of Wisconsin Press, 1983), 49–66.

80. R. J. W. Burren, M. J. R. Healy, and J. M. Tamrer, in a study on the age at menarche among South African Bantu schoolgirls living in the Transkei reserve in the 1950s, concluded that nutrition, while it did not induce infertility, did significantly contribute to the postponing

of child-bearing capability. "Age at Menarche in South Africa Bantu Schoolgirls Living in the Transkei Reserve," *Human Biology* 33 (1961): 259.

81. Charles Emil Strangdand, *Pre-Malthusian Doctrines of Population: A Study in the History of Economic Theory* (1904; reprint, New York: Augustus M. Kelley, 1966), 26.

82. The raising of the age at marriage (considered equivalent to age at first birth and with historical data certainly easier to recover in most societies) is the first step in that transition to a stable fertility rate (replacement fertility is 2.1 children per woman).

83. Charles F. Westoff, "Age at Marriage, Age at First Birth and Fertility in Africa," *World Bank Technical Paper No. 169*, 22.

84. John Hajnal, "Age at Marriage and Proportion Marrying," *Population Studies* 7 (1955): 111–132; Ansley Coale, "Age Patterns of Marriage," *Population Studies* 25 (1971): 193–214.

85. Slave Office, 10118 (Cape Town, February 17, 1834), Cape Archives Depot.

86. Robert Ross, "The Age at Marriage of White South Africans, 1700–1951)," in *African Historical Demography II: Proceedings of a Seminar Held in the Centre for African Studies, University of Edinburgh, 24th and 25th April 1981* (Edinburgh: Centre for African Studies, University of Edinburgh, 1981), 490. Data for Europeans is taken from Leonard Guelke, "The Anatomy of a Colonial Settler Population: Cape Colony 1657–1750," *International Journal of African Historical Studies* 21 (1988): 468. Slaves: 1675–1730 (N = 30), 1823–1830 (N = 73); data for calculation for slaves for the second period is taken from Slave Office 10118 (Cape Town, February 17, 1834), Cape Archives Depot.

87. Deaths occurring in the weeks before and just after birth.

88. It would be possible to break this data down according to Dutch-recorded categories of descent, although because of the relatively small size of the population, it would mean dealing with very small numbers.

89. Brana-Shute's essay in this volume, "Sex and Gender in Surinamese Manumissions."

Evelyn P. Jennings

Paths to Freedom

—✺—

Imperial Defense and Manumission in Havana, 1762–1800

After the German scientist and traveler Alexander von Humboldt visited Cuba in 1803, he penned the following observation about the possibilities for Cuban slaves to achieve freedom:

> In no part of the world, where slavery exists, is manumission so frequent as in the island of Cuba; for Spanish legislation, directly the reverse of French and English, favors in an extraordinary degree the attainment of freedom, placing no obstacle in its way, nor making it in any manner onerous. The right which every slave has of seeking a new master, or purchasing his liberty, if he can pay the amount of his cost; the religious sentiment that induces many persons in good circumstances to concede by will freedom to a certain number of negroes; the custom of retaining a number of both sexes for domestic service, and the affections that necessarily arise from this familiar intercourse with the whites; and the facilities allowed to slaveworkmen to labor for their own account, by paying a certain stipulated sum to their masters, are the principal causes why so many blacks acquire their freedom in the towns. . . . The position of the free negroes in Cuba is much better than it is elsewhere, even among those nations which have for ages flattered themselves as being most advanced in civilization.[1]

For studies of Cuba, the main components of Humboldt's observation and interpretation of manumission on the island have shaped discussions about the nature of enslavement in Cuba to the present day—its relative uniqueness, its distinctly urban manifestation, the importance of domestic service and skilled occupations, Iberian laws and religious institutions that favored freedom, a diverse economy that supported practices like hiring out and self-purchase in installments (*coartación*), and the resultant large free population of color.[2] Contemporary observers such as Humboldt and later scholars of slavery have also found value (though animated often by different interests) in a conceptual framework that compared the development and practices of slave societies in different settings.[3]

In a number of ways Cuba does provide a unique case through which to examine manumission in the Atlantic world. Different from the main sugar islands of the Caribbean, Cuba developed not one but two distinct slave systems over the colonial period. The first, prominent from the sixteenth through most of the eighteenth century, was based largely in Havana and tied to imperial service and commerce. The second system was based on plantation production of export commodities like sugar in the countryside and dominated the Cuban economy from the late eighteenth century until final abolition in 1886.

Humboldt visited the island just as Cuba was being transformed from an imperial service to a plantation economy at the beginning of the nineteenth century and his observations on manumission seem more closely tied to the earlier slave system. Echoing Humboldt, Cuban historian Manuel Moreno Fraginals noted this "peculiar" colonial development created conditions in Havana favorable to manumission—a high demand for slaves and a perennial labor shortage—especially in civil and military construction. In this setting the practice of hiring out and *coartación* benefited both owners and slaves, though unequally.[4]

Research to date outlines several trends in manumissions in Cuba over the entire colonial period. First, most manumissions were not "free" grants of liberty but grants of freedom for payment, as slave owners could both recoup their investment and salve their consciences by facilitating self-purchase. Second, women, both African born and creole, predominated in all types of manumissions—free grants and purchases.[5] Both these findings suggest that enslaved women found the paths to freedom in colonial Cuba more open than did enslaved men. The findings also suggest that state service, which employed far more men than women, was a less reliable road to freedom than work in the private sector.

Despite the importance of imperial service over hundreds of years to the development of slavery in Cuba, few studies have examined the Spanish colonial state as a slave owner and employer in detail.[6] This essay will explore the possibilities for manumission open to slaves working in the defense sector of Havana in the late eighteenth century, a time when Spain's rule in the Caribbean was severely challenged. This case raises several questions with which to test some of the generalizations about manumission in Cuba noted above: Did Spanish traditions and laws also favor freedom for slaves in state service? What kinds of occupations in state service might offer paths to freedom for state slaves? Did the acquisition of skills for slaves in state service increase opportunities for achieving freedom? How important was state service to overall patterns of manumission in Havana between 1762 and 1790? Though a complete investigation of manumission among state slaves in the defense sector remains to be done, the evidence presented here will sketch out a broad outline of possible answers to these questions, an outline that suggests patterns of manumission often in contrast to those observed in the private sector.

SPANISH LAW AND MANUMISSION

The Spanish Crown had a long history of owning and employing slaves in defense construction and military service on the peninsula and in its New World colonies. The monarch himself owned slaves, known as *esclavos del Rey,* who served the Crown in myriad employments throughout the empire. For major state projects such as fort construction, galley service, or work in royal mines, the king would assign contingents of Crown slaves and also hire privately owned slaves, convicts, and free workers.[7]

As Spain's empire crossed the Atlantic, sub-Saharan Africans, enslaved and free, were involved in all of the major expeditions of the conquest era, as servants and auxiliaries in battle.[8] Once settlements were established enslaved Africans were called upon to help defend communities like Havana in a variety of ways. They were members of crews that built and repaired fortifications, stood watch, and fought invaders. Such service could occasionally bring rewards that included manumission, most often for extraordinary service in battle.[9]

Research to date does indicate that Spanish traditions and laws supported freedom for slaves who rendered extraordinary service to the state. A legal framework for the operation of the institution of slavery had been in place in Castilian law since the promulgation of the code known as the Siete Partidas in the thirteenth century.[10] The portions of the code governing slavery and the philosophy behind those regulations guided Crown policy for centuries. Even after new slave codes were produced in 1789 and 1845 in response to the growth of plantation economies in the Spanish Caribbean, the Siete Partidas' juridical framework continued to shape interactions in Spain and its colonies among slaves, their owners, and the state.[11] Though it is unlikely that the Siete Partidas was transferred in toto to Spanish America, evidence of the application of its main principles is extensive enough to argue for its importance over the entire colonial period up to abolition in Cuba in 1886.[12]

The Siete Partidas characterized slavery as an institution with deep historical roots but also one that was evil and against natural reason.[13] In some measure the code was a theoretical work that tried to bridge the contradiction between the slave as mere chattel and the slave as a human being with a soul, capable of attaining salvation and deserving of mercy.[14] Recalling the value placed on liberty by the "ancients," the code declared that "all the laws of the world always aided freedom,"[15] yet the power to free a slave rested mainly with the state and slave owners, less frequently with slaves themselves.

The Siete Partidas did recognize that some slaves deserved freedom on their own for their good works ("por las bondades que facen"), often by performing specific acts of service to the state, which would then grant their freedom and compensate their owners. Such acts of service included denouncing a virgin's rapist and reporting counterfeit money or army deserters. For a slave who discovered treason against the king or his realm, no compensation had to be paid.[16] Such a policy reinforced desirable loyalty toward the Crown and the empire by slaves but cost the state little as it remained a rare and individual reward for extraordinary service.

The code also recognized a slave's access to freedom through self-purchase since "servitude is the worst thing in the world that is not a sin." With this path to freedom, slaves could exercise the initiative by beginning self-purchase, entrusting money toward their price to a third party. When the full price had been set aside, this party was to buy the slave from the master to set him or her free.[17] It was stipulated that the slave could take the third party to court if the agreement was not carried out.[18] The Siete Partidas hedged the leveling possibilities of such policies by emphasizing the origin of the power to free. Slaves who were freed had to continue to love and honor their former masters, never being disrespectful to them or defaming or attempting to litigate against them for past wrongs. Masters were permitted to rescind freedom if the freed tried to dishonor them.[19]

The importance of self-purchase by slaves to the historical development of Cuba is supported by numerous examples over the colonial period though gaps in our knowledge of the practice remain.[20] The practice also evolved to include other customary features including self-purchase by installments or *coartación*, which created a group of enslaved people that had an intermediate status between enslavement and freedom.[21] Once the slave had made the initial payment on her or his freedom, the price could not be changed. His or her new status as a *coartado/a* (one whose enslaved status had been "cut" by a payment toward freedom) allowed the slave to look for a new owner with or without cause. When a *coartado/a* was sold, the new owner was only entitled to the portion of the *coartado/a*'s labor that had not yet been paid for by the slave.[22] Many authors point to this practice as crucial to the more open and fluid character of urban enslavement in Cuba, some claiming it was unique to the island.[23] However, recent work suggests it was more widely practiced in New World colonies.[24] Considerable evidence exists, then, to support Humboldt's contention that Iberian law and custom supported manumission, especially when slaves were willing and able to pay for it. He may have overstated the ease with which slaves could achieve freedom as ample evidence also exists of some owners' resistance.[25] The sizable free population of color in Cuba by the late eighteenth century (19% of the island's total population in 1792), however, attests to the society's relative openness to manumission and the vigor of Cuban slaves in pursuing it.[26]

Paths to Freedom in State Service

Havana's vulnerability to attack as a Caribbean port necessitated the emergency recruitment of blacks, both enslaved and free, to defend against corsairs in the earliest days of settlement, though it is not clear how many might have been freed for this service.[27] As the Spanish Crown began to invest more resources in fortifying the city after the institution of the fleet system in the mid-1500s, the state increased its resort to service and labor by the enslaved in imperial defense over the next two hundred years. The main sites of this service and labor were in Havana's six stone forts built between the 1550s and 1780.[28] Most occupations in the state's fort projects tended to require minimal skills and considerable coercion of workers. Though the projects did employ a few free workers, the labor force was most often composed of Crown and hired slaves, convicts, and tributary Amerindians (in the sixteenth century).[29] On the other hand the other major state enterprise in Havana, shipbuilding, required more skilled workers and recruited mostly free laborers: shipwrights from vessels in port, local ironworkers, along with some Crown slaves and hired slaves whose salaries approximated those paid to free laborers such as carpenters and caulkers.[30]

The Crown's defense strategy of land fortification supplemented with a small Spanish garrison and local militia units was reasonably successful in protecting Havana from the late 1500s onward until Spain's entrance into the Seven Years' War as France's ally. The British mounted a massive expedition in June 1762 that laid siege to Havana and occupied the city for eleven months. A close look at the labor and service slaves performed during the siege and after Spain reclaimed the island in June 1763 and the responses of state officials to that service highlights the range of possibilities for manumission for slaves in the king's service.[31]

Both Britain and Spain recruited enslaved blacks to serve in this conflict. British commanders purchased slaves in Martinique and some of the smaller islands, along with a group of slaves commandeered in Jamaica for the Havana campaign.[32] On the Spanish side wealthy landowners donated some of their slaves to defend the city, some of whom manned the artillery in the El Morro fort, transported batteries to hills surrounding Havana, and fought along with free militiamen of color, dying by the hundreds according to English sources.[33] Spanish officials also tried to purchase slaves through traders in Jamaica with little success because of the disruptions of the war.[34]

The Spanish captain general Prado fearing that an increasing number of privately owned slaves might defect to the British if offered their freedom to do so, decided to preempt such an outcome. He granted freedom to twelve or thirteen slaves who had voluntarily left the El Morro fort to engage an English advance force on June 26.[35] Seeing that many more slaves had willingly taken up arms, Prado also formed a company of approximately one hundred black volunteers under two white commanders who distinguished themselves and were granted their freedom.[36]

In total the Spanish state rewarded 164 slaves who fought during the siege. The process and terms under which they were rewarded is worth examining in some detail for the insights they give to the blendings of gratitude, paternalism, and calculation imbedded in Spanish officials' decisions and the possibilities of freedom available to slaves for military service in the wake of the worst threat to Spanish sovereignty in eighteenth-century Cuba.

When Prado granted full freedom to the 118 slaves mentioned above, he pledged to compensate their owners with two hundred pesos and four reales each.[37] Lacking the names of some meritorious slaves and their owners in the chaos of the siege and its aftermath, Prado was unable to fully reward all deserving slaves and compensate all their owners. Among the instructions given to the new captain general, the Count of Ricla, before he landed in Cuba to retake the plaza from the British in June 1763, was Prado's request that he complete the task of rewarding these slaves and satisfying their owners. The king added the authority for Ricla to extend liberty to other slaves who could verify their equally distinguished bravery and service.[38] These instructions confirm the importance high Spanish officials attached to both extraordinary service by slaves in wartime and to the property rights of their owners. Despite military defeat, occupation, and substantial losses of revenue and resources, the king, the disgraced Prado, and his overburdened successor Ricla were all committed to just compensation for both groups.[39]

Ricla began a wide-ranging inquiry to find slaves deserving of reward and to determine what the state owed their owners. He issued a proclamation ordering all the slaves freed by Prado and their owners to present themselves at the city's government offices. Those slaves who still lacked their letters of freedom would receive them. Ricla also requested the appearance of any other slaves who had been badly wounded defending the city along with their owners. This review identified ten additional slaves worthy of reward. But Ricla's call to request reward for service produced so many enslaved petitioners that he decided to appoint Field Marshall O'Reilly to continue the review and judge the merits of the slaves who came forward. O'Reilly decided that twenty-three more slaves had in fact been injured during the siege and deserved their freedom.[40]

Because of the importance the state attached to loyal service by slaves, Ricla made the review process, the announcement of the judgments, and the conferment of rewards public events. One hundred fifty-one slaves were declared "free of all subjection, captivity, and servitude"[41] and given individual letters of freedom; their manumission was announced publicly in a list of all their names posted in the market square. Ricla ordered the freedmen to appear in government offices to be informed of his decision, be recognized, and have their prices determined. He also issued a proclamation that all other slaves did not merit freedom or reward and were to be returned immediately to their owners' control. The captain general was clearly not prepared to free all slaves who had been wounded or served in some capacity during the siege, only those whose service or loss had been deemed extraordinary.[42]

Still, the public character of these rewards induced even more slaves to come forward to claim recognition of their service and Ricla felt compelled to investigate their claims carefully. From this newest group Ricla identified thirteen more, four of whom he granted full liberty for having been incapacitated in the siege.[43]

Interestingly he chose another six slaves for a partial grant of freedom for reasons that are worth quoting in full: "Six [others] . . . not entirely disabled by different wounds and blows and having them appraised I assigned to those who were not *coartados* half of their value so that in this part they would be free, thus providing that their owners, conforming to the custom of this Country, would enjoy from them only half of their service."[44] Here we see the new captain general adapting the Cuban variant of *coartación* to extend the king's grace of manumission beyond only the most deserving of his enslaved subjects. Like slaves in the private sector who enjoyed partial freedom proportionate to the amount of their price already paid, these slaves could now control half their time and labor for lesser but still exemplary service to the king. To the remaining three slaves who were *coartados*, Ricla awarded thirty pesos each. At current slave prices of two hundred to three hundred pesos this award represented 10–15 percent of their total value, which they could use toward their full liberty if they chose.[45]

The paternalism of the state also extended to care for three slaves who, though having gained their freedom through their exemplary service and sacrifice, were so badly maimed as to be "incapable of seeking their sustenance." Ricla felt that since they "had been in the service of the King and the *Patria*, I not only gave them their aforesaid liberty, but at the same time in order be a greater stimulus to others, and prize to these [slaves] I conferred upon them one real per day for reason of their disabilities."[46] Again, these public awards were designed to highlight the Crown's gratitude and generosity by turns, to be just as well as expedient in encouraging the loyalty and sacrifice of Cuba's slaves at a moment when Spanish officials fully expected imminent resumption of war with England. Thus 155 slaves received full freedom; 3 of these were also awarded a maintenance allowance because of the severity of their injuries. Six slaves received half-freedom and 3, a cash reward.

Ricla ended his letter to the minister of the Indies also outlining various provisions for slave owners. He expressed his intention to pay owners whose slaves had died in the siege of Havana as well as those whose slaves had been freed by the state. Some owners demonstrated their loyalty by renouncing compensation, ceding to the king their slaves' value. Other owners preferred that the state repay them either with new slaves or cash.[47]

These awards show Spanish officials' perception of slaves as human beings and subjects deserving of mercy and reward for sacrifice and as property whose value could be minutely assessed, possessed, and compensated. What was unusual about the Cuban case was the acknowledgment by all parties—slaves, slave owners, and the state—that slaves could control at least a portion of their value through their own initiative in specific circumstances, in this case through *coartación* and through military service.

Another point of note here is that all the slaves rewarded after the siege belonged to private owners. State priorities and the possibilities for freedom among its own slaves were often different from those exhibited toward privately owned slaves in state service. Recruiting enslaved fighters and auxiliaries in wartime from the private sector necessitated the provision of tangible rewards to both owners and their slaves as Spanish officials clearly realized. Recruiting labor for defense construction after 1763 came to rely on state slave ownership, which was a very different matter.

As Spanish officials in Cuba faced the debacle of the British siege and occupation and the likelihood that war would resume shortly, the Crown developed a massive plan to refortify the city, a plan which included the construction of three new forts and numerous repairs to existing fortifications and the city wall. The urgency and size of these projects necessitated resorting to the only avenue of labor recruitment that could produce thousands of workers over a very few years, direct purchases from the transatlantic slave trade.

In developing a new defense plan for Havana, Bourbon officials recognized that a shortage of workers had stymied Prado's efforts to secure the city before the British siege. Thus Ricla arrived in 1763 with wide powers from the Crown to recruit enslaved labor for fort construction directly from Africa or even through markets in foreign colonies like Jamaica.[48] During the last seven months of 1763 Spanish officials purchased 795 African slaves. In 1764 and 1765 the Crown's slave purchases grew to 1,967 and 1,436 people respectively for a total of 4,198; only about 400 of these newly purchased slaves were women.[49] The state's contracts also included provision for more slaves to be imported for private sale. In 1764 alone a total of 7,255 slaves were legally disembarked in Havana.[50]

By March 1765 there were more than two thousand workers employed in Havana's fortification projects. The vast majority were recently arrived Africans, royal slaves who accounted for 54–67 percent of the total workforce over the year. A much smaller group of creole king's slaves comprised only 0.5 percent of the total workforce. Privately owned slaves constituted another 2.7 percent and free workers of color averaged 1.9 percent of the total. The only other group whose numbers averaged in the hundreds was convicts, who accounted for 19–29 percent of the total in 1765.[51]

The most intense phase of the fort projects spanned the years 1764 through 1769 and the bulk of the work involved unskilled, backbreaking labor— digging and hauling earth, quarrying and transporting stone, and manning the ovens to produce lime and charcoal. There was some specialization of tasks among the fort workers. On the one hand the state tried to reduce potential losses from slaves' flight by confining the transport of materials around the fort sites to convicts. On the other hand certain skilled jobs, such as carpentry or fascine making, remained the province of small groups of king's slaves. The majority of royal slaves in the fort projects, however, did unskilled construction work.[52]

Royal slaves were the largest contingent of workers in the initial phase of fort building from 1763 and 1765, with the highest yearly total of 1,967 reached in 1764. By 1765 officials were already becoming concerned about the overwhelming expense involved in so many large and complex projects. The punishing work regimes had led to high incidences of disease, injury, and death among royal slaves, so the king ordered the Intendant in Havana to begin selling off unskilled slaves to raise money for the fort works.[53] After 1765 the proportion of king's slaves to convict laborers began to decline until by 1769 convicts outnumbered slaves.

For the more than four thousand state slaves purchased from 1763 to 1765, fort construction imposed work regimes that were unusual in Cuba before the plantation era. Slave and convict brigades of about one hundred men each were mustered out under military guard; royal slaves were branded with the letter of their assigned garrison. Housing was makeshift and cramped even by plantation standards; mobility outside of work hours was restricted to the fortification sites themselves, except perhaps on holidays.[54] The possibilities of enjoying the comforts of family life were few as the sex ratio of male to female slaves on the fort projects of the 1760s was 9.8 to 1.

These miserable conditions also meant that few opportunities existed for enslaved fort workers to pursue the paths to freedom open to other slaves in Havana as most were removed from the open and fluid urban milieu that favored freedom through hiring out and domestic service. Recently arrived, the overwhelmingly male workforce had little access to urban networks of friends and family that aided other Havana slaves in developing strategies and resources to purchase freedom. Nor were relationships with white military guards likely to produce free grants of manumission. Even with the few skilled royal slaves who worked at the fort sites the Crown remained keen to retain those with important skills while divesting itself of the unskilled as expenses mounted. Hundreds had been sold off by the late 1760s and by 1772 the number of royal slaves at the fort sites stood at 423, down from the highs of 1,100 to 1,900 in the mid-1760s. Once sold, if these slaves remained in Havana at other urban occupations they might have enjoyed greater opportunity to pursue their freedom, but while they belonged to the king their chances for freedom remained slight.[55]

As the Crown's experience with fort building in Havana showed, large-scale resort to state slavery over the long term was rare in the Spanish empire. The expense of purchasing and maintaining large numbers of royal slaves was prohibitive. Therefore after the extremity of the immediate post-occupation moment of the 1760s, the Spanish state most often used its control of criminal justice to recruit convicts as forced laborers for public works. Royal slaves were much more likely to be trained for specific tasks and retained. There were some possibilities to achieve freedom for these specially trained royal slaves, but the Crown often granted them privileged status instead in hopes of keeping them in the king's service. A case in point was the enslaved artillerymen of Havana.

Although armed corps of slaves in actual combat were rare in the Spanish empire, especially after the conquest period, the militarization of Havana that followed the British occupation included the creation of an elite corps of king's slaves assigned to the city's artillery companies. As part of the army and militia reorganization undertaken after 1763, the Spanish reestablished the two artillery companies that had defended Havana before the occupation and a group of Crown slaves was assigned to this company.[56]

By late spring of 1765 the king had approved the purchase of one hundred royal slaves to serve the new artillery brigades in various capacities.[57] This plan included the state's purchase of an additional one hundred female slaves to marry the artillerymen and establish families. In a blend of self-interest and paternalism the Crown took pains to provide better housing, religious instruction, and rewards for devoted service to these two hundred slaves. The intendant asked the king's permission to exempt them from the church fees charged for marriage and baptism since they were under the special protection of the captaincy general and the intendancy. The artillerymen were to have special uniforms with the insignia of the artillery corps and a pair of shoes, markers of their higher status, as the fortification workers usually labored barefooted.[58]

Housing constructed by the state for the artillery company's royal slaves was considerably better than that endured by the king's slaves working on the fortification projects. Each married couple and their children were considered a separate family and were not obliged to share their quarters with others. The artillery's commissary provided daily rations to all family members. The entire family was also entitled to medical attention in the royal hospital and medicines from the military pharmacy throughout their lives.[59]

The wives were to be allowed time to earn money for their own use, in part to lessen the state's burden in providing their daily rations. Between February

1767 and May 1773 the wives of the artillery company's slaves were paid 3,376 pesos and 7 reales for making clothes for royal laborers in the Arsenal.[60]

Couples who produced offspring in their first year of marriage would be rewarded with a payment of four pesos. Children born in the second year of marriage would garner two pesos. The children of these king's slaves were to be educated in a useful trade, with the boys given preference in filling vacancies in the artillery company when possible. All children would become, of course, property of the king. The regulations of the artillery company also made provision for the granting of manumission to its slaves. If a family produced twelve children, the couple, but presumably not the children, would be emancipated. Extraordinary service in time of war could also bring manumission.[61]

The Intendant saw a number of advantages for the state in the formation of this special company of slaves. A well-trained group of artillerymen would supplement regular soldiers who were often in short supply. Their offspring increased royal assets while family ties and relative privilege would help assure the artillerymen's obedience and loyalty.[62] The considerable investment and care taken to establish this corps of slaves suggest that the state highly valued their skills and planned to keep them as a permanent part of that company.

The number of king's slaves in the artillery company reached about two hundred in 1768.[63] Their numbers were augmented with royal slaves from the fort works through the 1770s as needed to alleviate what seems to have been a perennial shortage of people trained in the use of cannons.[64]

By 1784 the numbers of king's slaves in the artillery company had fallen somewhat to 144 people, 70 men and 74 women. Records enumerating enslaved artillerymen also suggest an aging population—12 male slaves under fifteen years old, 31 between fifteen and sixty years of age, and 27 over sixty years old. Although no marital status is listed for any of the residents of the company in 1784, the close correspondence in the numbers of men and women among the enslaved points to the maintenance of family groups in the second generation of the slaves living in the artillery company almost twenty years after its creation.[65]

LATE-EIGHTEENTH-CENTURY MILITARY CAMPAIGNS

By 1770 there had been significant improvement in the defenses of Havana both in the reorganization of its armed defenders and its fortifications.[66] The outbreak of armed rebellion against British rule in North America in 1776 emboldened Spain to shift from a predominantly defensive posture to an offensive one, targeting British outposts around the Caribbean. Cuba provided crucial support for the Spanish victories in the northern Caribbean theater as part of the overall Bourbon strategy of creating scattered diversions for the British around the fringes of their empire to prevent them from concentrating their forces against any one threat.[67] Unlike the extraordinary resort to state enslavement that refortified Havana after 1763, the gulf campaigns showed Spain's more common strategic, but limited, use of slaves in military service. Spanish commanders brought in veteran soldiers from around the empire, disciplined militias from colonies like Cuba, and recruited Native American fighters among allies in the gulf region.[68]

Slaves were members of most of these expeditions but their numbers seem to have been small and they were rarely, if ever, officially armed. Alejandro O'Reilly's 1769 expedition to New Orleans to quell rebellion and reestablish Spanish rule listed only four slaves among its personnel destined to work in the troop hospital.[69] The larger expeditions against Mobile in 1779 listed a group of 100 *negros gastadores*, with hatchets and machetes, along with 24 slaves. The term *gastadores* suggests a measure of coercion though the documents called them volunteers, so they were most likely not enslaved. The assault on Pensacola in 1781 also included a similar group of 102 fort workers as auxiliaries to the troops.[70]

By the time that cycles of warfare engulfed the Caribbean after 1791, Spain was again on the defensive, forced into more extensive reliance on enslaved fighters and the reward of freedom for military service. When Spain intervened to retain the plantation system on Hispaniola in 1793, Spanish officials extended the precedent of negotiating with and recruiting rebellious slaves to fight in the king's name. Even before an official declaration of war, both the French and Spanish governments had authorized their representatives on Hispaniola to seek out the support of black rebel fighters. Starving and ill-equipped slaves were offered their freedom along with uniforms and rations to fight for Spain. The Spanish were also able to outflank French Republican commanders in recruiting black leaders such as Jean François, Georges Biassou, and for a time, Toussaint-Louverture.[71] Rather than the groups of perhaps several hundred slaves employed in earlier conflicts, the rebel armies numbered in the thousands by the mid-1790s.[72]

Such an expedient was necessary in part due to the decline of the Spanish army in Cuba. By the time Revolutionary France declared war on Spain in March 1793, the regular army in Cuba had fallen in both numbers and quality. Commanders in Cuba were unable to recruit sufficient numbers of soldiers on the island, or in places like the Canaries. Spain itself could offer few replacements as peninsular troops were fighting the Revolution in Europe.[73]

Spanish officials in Santo Domingo expressed considerable unease about the necessity of relying so heavily on both the fighting skills and loyalty of black rebels. By January 1794 the Spanish captain general in Santo Domingo was reporting that most of the men under arms were "undisciplined" free mulattos and blacks or untrained and insubordinate black slaves. He also feared that these fighters might, at some point, change sides if they perceived some advantage in doing so.[74] The rebel leaders, Jean François and Biassou, remained in

Spanish employ, but Toussaint skillfully played all the European participants before he finally left Spanish service and declared for France in the spring of 1794.[75]

With Spain's defeat and withdrawal from the conflict in the summer of 1795, Spanish officials were forced to undertake delicate negotiations to reward their allies. They had to develop a plan to resettle Jean François and Georges Biassou, their soldiers, and their families somewhere in the Spanish empire. The Crown took its responsibility to these allies seriously, but officials in the Caribbean were forced to carefully balance reward for service with concerns about potential disruptions in colonies like Cuba where plantation slavery was growing.

The Spanish governor in Santo Domingo advocated the immediate abolition of the black fighters' units and titles. The black soldiers and their families, on the other hand, wanted to retain their units, titles, pay, and rations and be given land to resettle as a group in their own town.[76] When a contingent of black soldiers arrived in Havana's port with their leaders and families, the Cuban captain general Las Casas vehemently opposed allowing their disembarkation stating, "Every colonist imagines his slaves will rebel and the colony will be totally destroyed the moment these individuals arrive. Wretched slaves yesterday, they are today the heroes of a revolution, triumphant, wealthy, and decorated."[77]

Despite opposition from the governors of its Caribbean colonies, the Spanish state reciprocated the loyalty and preserved the freedom of the black troops from Hispaniola. Since Jean François and his entourage of 790 people would likely have been dangerous examples of black self-liberation in the growing plantation regime in Cuba, this group ultimately sailed for Cádiz, Spain, where Jean François remained in the king's service until his death. Georges Biassou, resettled in Florida and fought again for the king in campaigns against Spain's Native American enemies. When Biassou died in 1801, he was buried in St. Augustine with full military honors. The rest of Spain's black allies were sent to fringes of the empire to which the metropolis hoped to attract settlers, like Trinidad, Panama, and Honduras.[78] As historian Jane Landers has noted, slaves were among the most loyal of Spain's auxiliaries in wartime. They could trust the Crown's willingness to grant freedom and other rewards for devoted military service and uphold those rewards despite hostility and discrimination from white officials and from soldiers, even in the charged moment of the Haitian Revolution.[79]

CONCLUSIONS

Returning to the questions posed at the beginning of this essay, several points emerge on the possibilities of achieving freedom for slaves in state service. Clearly, Spanish traditions and laws created an institutional framework and supported attitudes permitting slaves to pursue their freedom. Spain's long history of reconquest on the peninsula and conquest in its vast empire privileged military prowess and service, even by slaves, over almost any other occupation, except a religious vocation. To defend its far-flung empire Spain had to rely, more than any of its European rivals, on the military employment of the enslaved.[80]

Spanish law and custom saw slavery as unnatural and recognized freedom as a legitimate goal for all slaves. Law codes and Crown directives also defined slaves as human beings, subjects, laborers, and property simultaneously. Colonial officials had to try to judge the merits of slaves' service to the state weighing the relative importance of each of those attributes in a given historical moment. Thus the Crown could use the possibility of granting of freedom as a tool to recruit defenders for the empire and as a reward for service. Such tools would only have the desired result if slaves had a reasonable expectation of enjoying those rewards. The evidence presented here from the period of the British occupation and its aftermath suggests that slaves could hold out such hopes.

We should not, however, romanticize unduly Spanish willingness to reward slaves' state service with freedom. These rewards were extended to very few enslaved fighters in the period under review here, even though the empire faced its most dire threat to sovereignty before 1898. Spanish officials took their charge seriously; they wanted to reward those slaves they saw as deserving and to encourage continued loyalty and sacrifice by slaves. They also sought to minimize costs to the state and to slave owners. Only when certain slaves had run extraordinary risks and suffered debilitating injuries would the king's grace free them.

The black troops who allied with Spain in Hispaniola represent a case in which many of the former slaves and their leaders had liberated themselves by force of arms rather than petitioning the king for the favor of manumission. Spanish officials were forced to recognize their freedom, albeit grudgingly in some cases. Yet even at this historical moment when the dangerous potential of rebellion and self-liberation by the enslaved for slave societies was clear, Spain fulfilled its obligations to its allies, though it avoided settling them in the growing plantation colony of Cuba.

The fort works, on the other hand, were a virtual dead end for most of the slaves owned and employed there by the state, and the unskilled had the fewest opportunities to achieve freedom in late-eighteenth-century Havana. Here the Crown was interested in slaves' labor and little else. Work conditions were harsh and often fatal. Access to the kinds of resources needed to pursue self-purchase were minimal at best and the state quickly divested itself of such a large and expensive slave workforce long before any could accumulate monies toward their price. Though the work of the royal slaves in building the fortifications of Havana was crucial to the city's defense, manual labor in the king's service brought few rewards.

For skilled royal slaves like those assigned to the city's artillery company, the state seems to have discouraged the pursuit of freedom by instead granting privileges. After the considerable expense to purchase, outfit, house, and train this group of slaves, the state hoped to enjoy the benefits of their training, service, and offspring for many years.

Alexander von Humboldt's contention that the Spanish placed "no obstacle" in freedom's way nor made "it in any manner onerous" is too generous a reading of the state's practice toward the slaves in its service. What is more striking is the willingness of slaves to serve the king bravely in battle and to vigorously pursue even this narrow path to freedom.

NOTES

1. This English translation is taken from Alexander von Humboldt, *The Island of Cuba: A Political Essay*, ed. Luis Martínez Fernández (Princeton, N.J.: Marcus Weiner, 2001), 136. For an excellently edited edition in Spanish with an extensive introductory study, illustrations, and appendices, see Humboldt, *Ensayo político sobre la isla de Cuba,* ed. Miguel Ángel Puig-Samper, Consuelo Naranjo Orovio, and Armando García González (Junta de Castilla y León: Ediciones Dos Calles, 1998), 192.

2. The bibliography on each of these points is extensive, but most begin with Frank Tannenbaum, *Slave and Citizen: The Negro in the Americas* (New York: Knopf, 1947), which relied heavily on Humboldt's conclusions about the importance of access to manumission to the character of Cuban slavery and the importance of Iberian law and traditions in ameliorating the most dehumanizing aspects of plantation slavery. The validity of Tannenbaum's thesis continues to be debated in conferences and in print. For conferences, see "Comparative Slavery in the Atlantic World, 1500–1825: The Tannenbaum Thesis Revisited," Workshop of the Atlantic History Seminar, Harvard University, November 6, 2004. In print, see Alejandro de la Fuente, "Slave Law and Claims-Making in Cuba: The Tannenbaum Debate Revisited," *Law and History Review,* Summer 2004, http://www.historycooperative.org/journals/lhr/22.2/forum_fuente.html/ (accessed December 16, 2006), and responses to this article by María Elena Díaz, "Beyond Tannenbaum," and Christopher Schmidt-Nowara, "Still Continents (and an Island) with Two Histories?" and de la Fuente's reply "Slavery and the Law: A Reply," in the same issue. On the free population of color, see Franklin W. Knight, "The Free Colored Population in Cuba during the Nineteenth Century," in *Slavery Without Sugar: Diversity in Caribbean Economy and Society Since the 17th Century,* ed. Verene A. Shepherd (Gainesville: University Press of Florida, 2002), 224–247.

3. Comparative explorations of slavery over time and place in order to challenge received "truths" and generate new questions and perspectives can be powerful. See also the *American Historical Review*'s forum, "Crossing Slavery's Boundaries," 105, no. 2 (April 2000): 451–484, which contains the David Brion Davis article, "Looking at Slavery from Broader Perspectives" (452–466) and responses from Peter Kolchin, Rebecca Scott, and Stanley Engerman.

4. Manuel Moreno Fraginals, "Peculiaridades de la esclavitud en Cuba," *Islas* 85 (1986): 3–12.

5. Alejandro de la Fuente, "A alforría de escravos em Havana, 1601–1610: Primeiras Conclusões," *Estudos econômicos* 20 (January–April 1990): 139–159, examined eighty-three cases of manumission in the first decade of the seventeenth century. Moreno Fraginals,

"Peculiaridades," 7. Moreno examined a random sample of 1,320 letters of freedom from Cuban notarial records of the eighteenth century (no more specific dates are given) of which 80.3 percent were purchased rather than free grants. He also noted that "many more" women than men achieved their freedom, that women achieved their freedom at younger ages (forty-two years as opposed to forty-eight for men), and that women were more likely to be freely granted their liberty (25%) than men (10%). For the period 1790–1880 see Laird W. Bergad, Fe Iglesias García, and María del Carmen Barcia, *The Cuban Slave Market, 1790–1880* (Cambridge: Cambridge University Press, 1995), 122–142, 145. The authors compiled statistics from Cuban notarial records on a total of 23,045 slave sales, extracting data on 3,438 *coartado* sales (sales of slaves who had already made partial payment toward their freedom). They found the "overwhelming majority of *coartados* were female," or 68 percent of all registered *coartados* (123).

6. The most notable exceptions to this are Francisco Pérez Guzmán, *La Habana clave de un imperio* (Havana: Editorial de Ciencias Sociales, 1997), and Francisco Pérez Guzmán, "Modo de vida de esclavos y forzados en las fortificaciones de Cuba: Siglo XVIII," *Anuario de estudios americanos* 47 (1990): 241–257; Jane Landers, "Transforming Bondsmen into Vassals: Arming Slaves in Colonial Spanish America," in *Arming Slaves from Classical Times to the Modern Age*, ed. Christopher Leslie Brown and Philip D. Morgan (New Haven, Conn.: Yale University Press, 2006): 120–145; and María Elena Díaz, *The Virgin, the King, and the Royal Slaves of El Cobre* (Stanford, Calif.: Stanford University Press, 2000).

7. Ruth Pike, *Penal Servitude in Early Modern Spain* (Madison: University of Wisconsin Press, 1983) and Ruth Pike, "Penal Servitude in the Spanish Empire: Presidio Labor in the Eighteenth Century," *Hispanic American Historical Review* 58, no. 1 (1978): 21–40, both discuss state slaves and convicts in state enterprises.

8. On the peninsula most slaves were Muslims from North Africa, though cities like Seville had sizable populations of sub-Saharan Africans by the sixteenth century. Peter M. Voelz, *Slave and Soldier: The Military Impact of Blacks in the Colonial Americas* (New York: Garland, 1993), 11–14. See also 19–20, footnotes 4–7, which contain useful bibliography on the use of blacks, enslaved and free, in the conquest of the expanding Spanish empire. More recently see Landers, "Transforming Bondsmen into Vassals," 120–124, on the heterogeneity of the early modern Spanish army in Europe and in the composition of conquest expeditions.

9. Voelz, *Slave and Soldier*, 24; Landers, "Transforming Bondsmen into Vassals," 123, 125–126; Díaz, *Virgin*, 258, 297, on military service and manumission among the *cobreros* of eastern Cuba.

10. Virtually all authors who write on slavery in Spain or its colonies treat the Siete Partidas as the general legal framework for slavery under Castilian rule in both areas. See Tannenbaum, *Slave and Citizen*, 45–53; Herbert Klein, *Slavery in the Americas* (Chicago: University of Chicago Press, 1967), 59–66; and more recently De la Fuente, "Slave Law and Claims-Making in Cuba."

11. De la Fuente, "Slave Law and Claims-Making in Cuba" and "Slavery and the Law: A Reply."

12. De la Fuente, "Slave Law and Claims-Making," para. 40.

13. Partida IV, título 5 and título 21, ley 1, in Jerry R. Craddock, John J. Nitti, and Juan D. Temprano, eds., *The Text and Concordance of Las Siete Partidas de Alfonso X*, microfiche based on edition of the Real Academia de la Historia, 1807 (Madison, Wisc.: Hispanic Seminary of Medieval Studies, 1987).

14. See the discussion on this question throughout David Brion Davis, *The Problem of Slavery in Western Culture* (1966; reprint, New York: Oxford University Press, 1988), for example, 58–61 and 98–106, 251.

15. Partida III, título 5, ley 4, in Craddock, Nitti, and Temprano, *Text and Concordance.*

16. Partida IV, título 22, ley 3, in ibid.; Voelz, *Slave and Soldier,* chap. 23, 431–450, contains examples from sixteenth-century Cuba along with many from other Spanish and European American colonies into the nineteenth century

17. Partida IV, título 2, ley 8, in Craddock, Nitti, and Temprano, *Text and Concordance.*

18. Partida III, título 2, ley 8, in ibid.

19. Partida IV, título 21, ley 9, in ibid.

20. For the sixteenth century see María Teresa de Rojas, "Algunos datos sobre los negros esclavos y horros en la Habana del siglo XVI," in *Miscelánea de estudios dedicados a Fernando Ortiz por sus discípulos, colegas y amigos . . .* (Havana: Sociedad Económica de Amigos del País, 1956), 1275–1287. For the early seventeenth century see Alejandro de la Fuente, "A alforría de escravos em Havana, 1601–1610"; for the eighteenth and nineteenth centuries see Moreno Fraginals, "Peculiaridades," 6–8, and Bergad, Iglesias García, and Barcia, *Cuban Slave Market,* 122–142. For royal slaves in eastern Cuba in the seventeenth and eighteenth century, see Díaz, *Virgin.*

21. On the evolution of *coartación* see Manuel Lucena Salmoral, "El derecho de coartación del esclavo en la América española," *Revista de Indias* 59, no. 216 (1999): 357–374. The author argues that in Spanish America generally the term *coartación* initially meant all manumissions by self-purchase or outright grant by owners. He contends that Bourbon commercial reforms, which raised duties paid on slave purchases, led to a shift in the meaning of *coartación.* After 1768 the term was most often restricted to meaning payments in installments by slaves toward their full freedom.

22. De la Fuente, "Slave Law and Claims-Making," paras. 45–46.

23. In addition to Humboldt see the comments by the editor of the English translation of his *The Island of Cuba,* John Thrasher, 212–213, and the sources cited in footnote 19. Also the now dated Hubert H. S. Aimes, "Coartación: A Spanish Institution for the Advancement of Slaves into Freedom," *Yale Review* 17 (February 1909): 412–429. Aimes's evidence is drawn mostly from the eighteenth and nineteenth centuries, after the practice had been codified into law. Klein, *Slavery in the Americas,* 196–200, also has evidence mostly from the eighteenth and nineteenth centuries, adding sources such as newspaper advertisements giving a slave's price reduced by the portion he or she had already paid. Bergad, Iglesias García, and Barcia, *Cuban Slave Market* again use evidence mostly from the nineteenth century. See especially 133–141. These authors have argued that the practice of *coartación* was unique to Cuba.

24. For evidence that partial freedom and *coartación* existed in other Iberian slave societies, see Lucena Salmoral, "Derecho de coartación," or Douglas Cole Libby and Clothilde Andrade Paiva, "Manumission Practices in Late Eighteenth Century Brazilian Slave Parish: São José d'El Rey in 1795," *Slavery and Abolition* 211 (April 2000): 96–127. For evidence from the colony of New Netherland under the Dutch and New York under the English, see Edgar J. McManus, *A History of Negro Slavery in New York* (1966; Syracuse: Syracuse University Press, 2001), 13 and 141–148.

25. De la Fuente, "Slave Law and Claims-Making," paras. 49–50.

26. Knight, "The Free Colored Population in Cuba," 227, table 10.1, which also shows that the proportion of free people of color fell to between 15 and 16 percent during the height of slave importations to the island from the 1790s to the 1860s. Later in the two decades before final abolition the percentage of free people of color in the Cuban population rose to 20 percent in 1877 and 32.5 percent by 1887.

27. Voelz, *Slave and Soldier,* 24, cites five such instances against French and English corsairs in sixteenth-century Cuba—1555, 1558, 1566, 1567, and 1582—several of which recruited two hundred to three hundred slaves and free blacks. See also Landers, "Transforming Bondsmen to Vassals," 122–124.

28. The three forts built in the sixteenth century are los Castillos de: la Real Fuerza, los Tres Reyes del Morro, and San Salvador de la Punta. The three forts built after the British occupation of 1762–63 are los Castillos de: San Carlos de La Cabaña, Santo Domingo de Atarés, and El Príncipe. See Tamara Blanes Martín, "Fortificaciones habaneras: La defensa de La Habana del siglo XVI a la primera mitad del XIX," in *La Habana: Puerto colonial (Siglos XVIII–XIX),* ed. Agustín Guimerá and Fernando Monge (Madrid: Fundación Portuaria, 2000), 154–164. Another important state enterprise on the island was the Havana shipyard, which began constructing ships for the Spanish fleets in the second half of the sixteenth century. Its labor recruitment practices differed significantly from those of the fort projects. For more detail on the shipyard, see Evelyn Powell Jennings, "War as the 'Forcing House of Change': State Slavery in Late-Eighteenth Century Cuba," *William and Mary Quarterly,* 3rd ser., 62, no. 3 (July 2005): 417–420, 422–423.

29. José Félix Martín de Arrate, *Llave del Nuevo Mundo antemural de la Indias occidentales* (1761; reprint, Havana: Comisión Nacional Cubana de la UNESCO, 1964), 55; Renée Méndez Capote, *Fortalezas de la Habana colonial* (Havana: Editorial Gente Nueva, 1974), 10, 23–24; Pérez Guzmán, *Habana,* 15.

30. Levi Marrero, *Cuba, economía y sociedad,* vol. 2 (Madrid: Editorial Playor, 1974), 204–205, lists daily wages in shipbuilding from 1589 to 1592 for carpenters at 295 maravedís (mvs), caulkers at 282 mvs, and slaves at 282 mvs.

31. With the Treaty of Paris signed in February 1763, ending the Seven Years' War, Spain recovered Havana at the cost of transferring control of western Florida and control of the Honduras coast to Britain. France compensated its Spanish ally for these losses with the colony of Louisiana.

32. Daniel E. Walker, "Colony versus Crown: Raising Black Troops for the British Siege on Havana, 1762," *Journal of Caribbean History* 3, nos. 1 & 2 (1999): 74–83; Guillermo Calleja Leal and Hugo O'Donnell, *1762, La Habana Inglesa: La toma de la Habana por los ingleses* (Madrid: Ediciones de Cultura Hipánica, 1999), 66–67, 113,146, 149.

33. *Authentic Journal of the Siege of Havana by an Officer* (London: T. Jeffrys, 1762), 18, 30. The author of this journal remarked of the defenders of El Morro that "the fire of the enemy was rather superior to ours, as they were very brisk in remounting their canon [*sic*], and had many slaves at work" (25).

34. Calleja Leal and O'Donnell, *1762,* 91, which notes only about twenty-five slaves purchased through these efforts.

35. There is a small discrepancy on the exact number. Conde de Ricla to Julián de Arriaga, Minister of the Indies and Navy, May 13, 1763, legajo 1212, Santo Domingo (hereafter cited as SD), Archivo General de Indias (hereafter cited as AGI), mentions twelve. Conde de Ricla to Julián de Arriaga, November 1763, legajo 1212, SD, AGI, mentions granting freedom to thirteen slaves in this group. Landers, "Transforming Bondsmen into Vassals," 128, mentions a similar incident with a group of twenty slaves though it is unclear if this was the same event. Perhaps those freed were the survivors of this charge.

36. Again there is a small discrepancy in the numbers. Ricla to Arriaga, May 13, 1763, mentions 100. The November 1763 letter mentions 105 freed. See also Celia María Parcero Torre, *La pérdida de la Habana y las reformas borbónicas en Cuba 1760–1773* (Valladolid: Junta

de Castilla y León, Consejería de Educación y Cultura, 1998), 155, which says this was a company of musketeers.

37. Ricla to Arriaga, November 1763, legajo 1212, SD, AGI.

38. Julián de Arriaga to Conde de Ricla, May 13, 1763, legajo 1212, SD, AGI.

39. The Spanish lost 3.4 million pesos in cash and goods and almost 20 percent of the Spanish fleet that had been stationed in the harbor when the siege began. For estimates of monetary losses, see Parcero Torres, *Pérdida de la Habana,* 182. On the portion of vessels lost to the navy, see Ovidio Ortega Pereyra, *El Real Arsenal de La Habana* (Havana: Editorial Letras Cubanas, 1998), 24.

40. Ricla to Arriaga, November 1763, legajo 1212, SD, AGI.

41. This phrase appears in most declarations of manumission and letters of freedom.

42. Ricla to Arriaga, November 1763, legajo 1212, SD, AGI.

43. Ibid.

44. Ibid. My translation.

45. John Robert McNeill, *Atlantic Empires of France and Spain, Louisbourg and Havana, 1700–1763* (Chapel Hill: University of North Carolina Press, 1985), 44, discusses both official prices and those of slaves imported illegally.

46. Ricla to Arriaga, November 1763. My translation.

47. Ibid.

48. March 29, 1763, legajo 1211, SD, AGI.

49. A summary of expenses for July 1763–December 1772, legajo 2129, SD, AGI; Pablo Tornero Tinajero, *Crecimiento económico y transformaciones sociales* (Madrid: Ministerio de trabajo y seguridad social, 1996), 36.

50. Gloria García, "El mercado de fuerza de trabajo en Cuba: El comercio esclavista (1760–1789)," in *La esclavitud en Cuba* (Havana: Editorial Academia, 1986), 135.

51. A series of summaries of fort workers from March 9, 1765, to October 27, 1765, legajo 1647, SD, AGI.

52. For a more detailed examination of the labor force in fort construction from 1763 to 1790, see Evelyn P. Jennings, "State Enslavement in Colonial Havana, 1763–1790," in *Slavery without Sugar: Diversity in Caribbean Economy and Society Since the 17th Century,* ed. Verene A. Shepherd (Gainesville: University Press of Florida, 2002), 152–182.

53. A summary of fort expenses from May 27, 1764 to December 31, 1772, legajo 1647, SD, AGI, mentions "the growing number of dead . . . and the deserters" as a cause of rising expenses. Pérez Guzmán, *Habana,* 55, reproduces a document listing the deaths in one royal hospital from April to October 1764 at 529. Thirteen royal slaves were convalescing and 33 convict laborers had died during the same period.

54. Letters from Arriaga, December 22, 1763, and April 25, 1764, legajo 1647, SD, AGI, and Pérez Guzmán, "Modo de vida," 246–253.

55. Pérez Guzmán, *Habana,* 67, estimates that 75 percent of the African slaves sold from state military projects were sold to work in sugar plantations, tobacco farms, and the civil and religious construction projects on the island after 1765.

56. For a thorough study of this military reorganization, see Allan J. Kuethe, *Cuba, 1753–1815: Crown, Military, and Society* (Knoxville: University of Tennessee Press, 1986).

57. Notice of purchase, February 26, 1766, 2344, no. 6, Secretaría y Superintendencia de Hacienda (hereafter cited as SSH), Archivo General de Simancas (hereafter cited as AGS).

58. *Reglamento para el govierno militar, politico, y económico de la Compañía de Artillería compuesta de negros de S.M. y sus familias* (Havana: D. Blas de los Olivos, 1768), 2, in part 2, box

1, folder 20, José Escoto Archive, Houghton Library, Harvard University. See also Sherry Johnson, "'Señoras en sus clases no ordinarias': Enemy Collaborators or Courageous Defender of the Family?" *Cuban Studies / Estudios cubanos* 34 (2003): 27–28.

59. *Reglamento para el govierno,* 5–6.

60. Arriaga to Altarriba, May 18, 1773, copy, 1153, Papeles de Cuba (hereafter cited as PC), AGI, noted the king's approval of allowing the slaves more use of this money. On work outside the barracks see Johnson, "'Señoras no ordinarias,'" 27.

61. *Reglamento para el govierno,* 3, 5, 8–9.

62. February 26, 1766, 2344, no. 6, SSH, AGS.

63. In AGI, 2122, SD contains a series of charts recording the slaves housed in the Quartel de San Isidro for January–July and September–December 1768, and 1371, PC, contains a chart from December 1784.

64. November 7, 1777, Consejos, 20892, Archivo Histórico Nacional (hereafter cited as AHN), in a packet of materials defending the Marqués de la Torres during his tenure as captain general.

65. Summary of black artillery workers and their families in Havana, December 31, 1784, legajo 1371, PC, AGI.

66. Kuethe, *Cuba,* 24–49.

67. Thomas E. Chávez, *Spain and the Independence of the United States: An Intrinsic Gift* (Albuquerque: University of New Mexico Press, 2002), 10 and 15–16.

68. Many sources discuss aspects of the Spanish alliances with Native American groups in the North American Southeast in this period. For examples see Kuethe, *Cuba,* 100–101. See John Caughey, *Bernardo Gálvez in Louisiana, 1776–1783* (Berkeley and Los Angeles: University of California Press, 1934), 153–157, on Gálvez's Manchac expedition, which included 160 friendly Indians. Eric Beerman's *España y la Independencia de Estados Unidos* (Málaga: Editorial Arguval, 1992), 55–56, discusses 400 Choctaw natives who fought for the Spanish in the early 1780s.

69. *Reglamento* explaining the Havana treasury's obligation to pay for the slaves' maintenance and clothing, February 23, 1770, legajo 1223, SD, AGI.

70. For the 24 slaves on the Mobile expedition, Kuethe, *Cuba,* 104. For the listing of 100 *negros gastadores,* also for Mobile, see no. 63, 1247, PC, AGI. For the Pensacola expedition and its 102 black workers, see Kuethe, *Cuba,* 107–110. In both instances Kuethe lists these laborers as "fort workers" and does not elaborate on their status.

71. David Geggus, *Slavery, War, and Revolution* (Oxford: Clarendon Press, 1982), 103.

72. David Geggus, "The Slave Leaders in Exile: Spain's Resettlement of Its Black Auxiliary Troops," in *Haitian Revolutionary Studies* (Bloomington: Indiana University Press, 2002), 179–180. Geggus cites figures from about five thousand troops to a high of fourteen thousand, which he says is most likely an exaggeration.

73. Kuethe, *Cuba,* 140–145.

74. Letter from Joaquín García, expediente 5, nos. 19, 24, 25, 7159, Guerra, AGS.

75. David Geggus, "The 'Volte-Face' of Tousssaint Louverture," in *Haitian Revolutionary Studies* (Bloomington: Indiana University Press, 2002), 119–136.

76. Landers, "Transforming Bondsmen into Vassals," 132.

77. Quoted in Geggus, "Slave Leaders in Exile," 182–183.

78. Ibid., 182–203; and Landers, "Transforming Bondsmen into Vassals," 132–135. For more on Spanish officials' reaction to Haitian soldiers asking to relocate in Cuba and the possible involvement of some of them in the Aponte Rebellion of 1812, see Matt D. Childs, *The 1812 Aponte Rebellion in Cuba and the Struggle against Atlantic Slavery* (Chapel Hill: University of North Carolina Press, 2006), 163–167.

79. Landers, "Transforming Bondsmen into Vassals," 137.

80. Ibid., 120.

JOHN F. CAMPBELL

How Free Is Free?

—∿∿—

The Limits of Manumission for Enslaved Africans in Eighteenth-Century British West Indian Sugar Society

The slaves who most commonly gain a manumission here from their owners, are
1. Domesticks, in reward for a long and faithful course of service. 2. Those, who
have been permitted to work for themselves, only paying a certain weekly or
monthly sum; many of them find means to save sufficient from their earnings, to
purchase their freedom. 3. Those who have effected some essential service to the
public, such as revealing a conspiracy, or fighting valiantly against rebels and
invaders. They have likewise generally been requited with an annuity, from the
public treasury, for life.

E. Long, "Freed Blacks and Mulattos," in *Slaves, Free Men, Citizens* (1973)

Edward Long's 1754 summation of the avenues available to enslaved people for
manumission in the British West Indies identified three main groups of
enslaved beneficiaries. The first comprised those who rendered "domestic" services; the second, those who sought self manumission through the hiring out
of their skills or through astute marketing of their meager commodity assets;[1]
and the third group consisted of those enslaved people who had turned their
backs on their black brethren and chosen instead to undermine resistance
strategies by becoming informants for the white managerial class.

While categories two and three were open equally to both male and female
enslaved people, category one, that of "Domesticks," was usually dominated by
females. This domination by female recipients arose from the "reward" context
manumission assumed when offered by white male sugar management for
enslaved women's more intimate "domestic" services. Category two, that of
enslaved "skilled" workers, also provided additional benefits to plantation
management. These benefits amassed as these enslaved people secured much
more than their value for their "masters," through the hiring out of their particular skills. Category three, which comprised "those who have effected some
essential service to the public," was also invaluable to white society.

Their importance was based on the security input they gave to slave society—an important input especially in slave societies like Jamaica, where the seething enslaved community at times outnumbered the whites by as much as sixty to one on some estates.[2] In this context white society was only too happy to reward deserving informants with the "gift" of manumission. Indeed, while manumission offered "freedom" to the enslaved person, in many cases it ultimately provided planter management with a more than commensurate benefit.

Edward Long's summation of the main manumission categories thus reflected white sugar management's broad aims of gender exploitation, profit maximization, and colonial security, which taken as a whole sought more to buttress the hegemony of white plantation society than it sought to ease the conditions of the enslaved Africans and their descendants. By noting that the third category of manumitted people had earned an annuity for life, Long also highlighted the partial solution to a dual concern that confronted white society over manumission. This concern arose over the way white society was expected to interact with the new "freedmen" and how these "freedmen" were to subsist as nonworkers within a society that traditionally saw their worth only in terms of their productive capacity within the sugar monoculture.

These concerns were highlighted by the first significant set of manumission candidates coming off of the sugar estates in the eighteenth century. These had been old or infirm people who had been more liabilities than assets to the plantations' work regime. Their manumission was then a simple way for the planters to avoid the cost of their upkeep. This early practice of manumission was frowned upon, not because it led to increased hardships for this vulnerable group of people but because they became nuisances to white civil society as they wandered around waiting to die. As a consequence colonial assemblies quickly drafted laws which insisted new manumittees be granted "pensions" from the estates that manumitted them.[3] These laws were intended to take the pressure off of the community's general resources and to curb the number of people subsequently manumitted. With stringent manumission laws in place by the mid-eighteenth century, therefore, the second concern, subsistence of manumitted people, was resolved. However, the first all important issue of their "freedman" status was never adequately resolved and continued to form the basis of antagonistic black/white relationships throughout the entire period of slavery and beyond. In light of this fundamental problem of social definition, why then was the practice of manumission continued?

This essay argues that the "freedom" offered to enslaved Africans through manumission was, in practice, limited, and as such, its continued use within British West Indian sugar society during the eighteenth century never really contradicted the de facto functioning of the slave society. Indeed, the practice of manumission was perhaps more beneficial to white male sugar management than it was for the few enslaved people who actually "benefited" from it.

THE BASIS OF MANUMISSION

Stinchcombe defines manumission as "the establishment of a former slave as free by a governmental act initiated by the property owner."[4] Such a definition, while accurate in accounting for the bureaucratic process, only allows a de jure understanding of manumission within British West Indian sugar islands. For a more complete understanding of how manumission worked in practice, it would be necessary to look at specific cases and analyze the "freedoms" it actually gave. Perhaps the first limited aspect of manumission stemmed from the fact that it was legally initiated by the property owner and not the enslaved person. As such the granting of manumission always remained a discretionary act dependent on the will of white sugar management.

This meant that although an enslaved person could in theory have "earned" the right to manumission or had secured his manumission price, the actual act itself still needed the consent of white management, a consent which white management sparingly gave. Indeed, one example of one institutional brake to management's "discretion" arose from the constant need of sugar plantations for more field labor. These labor demands stemmed from periodic inadequate supplies of laborers because of the exigencies of warfare and supply-related problems on the West African coast. They were also due to extremes of the tropical weather which ensured that there were always more tasks at hand than the available labor supply could handle at any given time. Simon Taylor,[5] for example, summed up all that could go wrong for sugar management's labor supply on an average production day. Having just visited his sugar plantation, he reported in October 1767 that "the Negroes had been very sickly, but were then on the mending hand but even then there were 36 in the Hott House & 21 in the Yaws which is a very great drawback on the Estate especially as there had been a very great flood in May which had laid almost every part of the Estate under Water and Caterpillars had very much hurt the young rattoons near the Riverside."[6]

In order to make up for the damage caused by the floods and for other maintenance work on the estate, he diverted already scarce labor from the production and preparation of sugar. At the end of the exercise he lamented to his absentee landlord, Chaloner Arcedeckne, about the lack of labor he had at his disposal for accomplishing the many tasks he had to do.

Simon Taylor's preoccupation with the estate's labor supply was typical of most managerial correspondences of eighteenth-century sugar managers. They were always complaining of the lack of labor and how this forced them to adopt expensive labor expansive strategies such as "jobbing"[7] to compensate. Their labor woes were further compounded by the lack of local reproduction of the enslaved people, their high mortality rate, and finally, the loss of the sugar estates' productive capacity because of the demands made on its labor force for hurricane repair and the colony's many military and social building works.

From the outset, therefore, one notes that during the eighteenth century the practice of manumission in British West Indian sugar colonies operated in the constant shadow of the particular sugar colony's need for estate labor. Over time the higher manumission rates were exhibited by those colonies whose land fertility had been exhausted and the immediate demand for labor lessened.[8] In a still highly productive colony like Jamaica, which was in its "golden age" from the mid–eighteenth century, there were always labor demands that set limits on the manumission level.

Jamaica thus offers a typical case study of how planter inspired manumission operated within an "active" sugar colony. In this context we see firsthand how manumission in practice was not such a contradictory end for white profit maximizing sugar management even though they often complained of the lack of labor. Taylor's estate correspondences, for example, do not include many cases of enslaved manumissions. In fact, his only reference in forty-one years of plantation correspondences on the Golden Grove estate concerned one long overdue case. This case, based on a sexual relationship between the plantation's doctor and an enslaved woman, is revealing as it highlights an institutional limit to manumission that is not immediately apparent from Edward Long's account or from definitions like Stinchcombe's.

CATHERINE'S LIMITS

Doctor Collins had been the plantation doctor on the Golden Grove plantation in Jamaica during the mid–eighteenth century. During his tenure he had secured the affections of a comely enslaved woman named Catherine. Their union was productive, and over the years Catherine bore him three sons Johnny, Edward, and Isaac. As a plantation doctor serving a large parish, Collins's place with Catherine was not permanent, and he eventually left the estate and was replaced there by another doctor, Hayward. But Collins never forgot Catherine and the children whom he had by her, and on his death he directed the executor of his will, one John Archer, to use £350 pounds from his estate to manumit Catherine and the children he had made with her.

In 1771 Simon Taylor, the Golden Grove sugar manager, wrote to his absentee employer on this manumission matter. He pointed out that "one Dr. Collins, who I believe formerly lived at Golden Grove, kept a woman belonging to you named Catherine, and had by her three sons, whose names are Johnny Chaplin, Edward Kidvallide Collins & Isaac Collins. He left Archer his executor, and money in his hands to buy the freedom of these people. He gave himself no trouble about it in his life, but by his will he mentioned it, and desires they may be bought."[9]

Taylor's letter to Arcedeckne drew attention to the fact that following Collins's death, Archer, his executor, "gave himself no trouble" about the manumission of Catherine and her children. Only on the death of John Archer in 1771 do Archer's executors in turn bring the matter of Catherine and her children's manumission to the attention of the Golden Grove management. Even so, Simon Taylor, being already harassed by the labor shortages on the estate, was willing to ignore the matter as he had other more "productive" matters to be concerned with. However, his interest in Catherine's case was stimulated by the absentee's mother, Mrs. Arcedeckne, who, being resident on the island, had taken a personal interest in the matter. As Taylor apologetically confessed to his absentee, "she [Arcedeckne] seems anxious about the matter for the children to be free."[10]

Even with the interest of the matriarch on the side of the enslaved woman, nothing more was done on the matter. Two more written directives from the various executors appear in 1773 and 1776, which stipulated the terms of the will and reminded the Golden Grove management that the terms of the manumission were for "the Freedom of a Sambo Woman Slave named Catherine . . . & her three Children . . . provided the said Freedom or Manumission can be purchased for the Sum of three Hundred & fifty pounds of Current Money of Jamaica . . . out of my (Dr Collins) Estate for that purpose & . . . during the term of her (Catherine's) natural Life an Annuity or yearly sum of Twelve pounds Current Money of Jamaica."[11]

In spite of the detailed manumission reminders in the intervening years following Taylor's first mentioning of the matter to Chaloner, nothing still was done in terms of Catherine's and her children's manumission. In fact, by 1776 Mrs. Arcedeckne had passed on, and it seemed that the matter of Catherine's manumission would now also remain a dead letter. But Catherine, desperate for the manumission that was given her and her children so long ago, forced a new manumission appeal to the absentee. To this end she located one of her former white owners and persuaded him to pen on her behalf a stirring emotive appeal to Chaloner Arcedeckne stating that she was now "growing in years" and, out of respect for his own late mother's wishes, Chaloner should see to have her manumitted. To this latter end he reminded Chaloner that "your late dear Mother, . . . often promise[d] that she would use her endeavour, that Catherine & her children should have their Freedom."[12]

It was now five years since the death of Collins's executor, and an additional indeterminable number of years since the death of Collins himself. The matter was allowed to rest for a further seven years, and it was only when Taylor was temporarily away from the estate because of ill health that another mention was made of the matter in 1783 by his proxy, Timothy Penny. Why then had the Golden Grove management ignored the manumission of this enslaved woman and her children even though adequate provisions had been made for it by the doctor's will?

In 1771, when the matter was first mentioned, the Golden Grove estate was experiencing its customary labor shortage. In this context it is understandable why the usually forceful Taylor could have acquiesced on the issue of the manumission of Catherine. Additionally, at this time Catherine was still a viable working asset, and her manumission would not have served any beneficial purpose to the estate. It would have only benefited her and her children. By 1783, however, things had changed. For one, the correspondences now refer to Catherine as "aging," while at the same time the estate would now benefit from manumitting her for the sum set aside for the purpose.[13] As profit maximizing entrepreneurs Taylor and his compatriots sought to derive as much utility as possible from each unit of often scarce labor. Manumission aided this project only insofar as it allowed them to purchase younger more productive labor. Manumission, while promised to Catherine, was perhaps never granted her or was granted to her at a time when the personal utility to be derived from her freedom was in decline, a telling comment on how white planter management viewed the rationale underlying "manumission."

The long time lag involved in actually manumitting an enslaved person was also a convenient legal device facilitated by most manumission bequests. As Catherine's bequest demonstrated, the legal wording of many of these manumission documents stated that it was up to the executor and the owner of the enslaved person to decide whether or not the terms and remuneration of the bequest were adequate. As it offered no limitations on the period of "consideration," an open ended situation in favor of white sugar management was often created.

This lack of prompt action (if any at all) on manumission bequests brings into question how "free" these de jure manumitted people were. Clearly in these cases, the promises of manumitted freedom, even though stated in a will or in correspondences, were often never de facto benefits that effected the lives of the candidates in the manner that they were supposed to.

We can only speculate as to whether or not Catherine and her children were ever manumitted, but as her case illustrates, the promise of manumission, so routinely touted as one of the few "benevolent" actions of planter management, often became no more than just that—a promise. How "free" then, for Catherine, was her manumission? Perhaps if this case were isolated, one would overlook this consideration. However, sad to say, Catherine's case was not isolated. Another infamous planter adventurer, Thomas Thistlewood, in his diaries also inadvertently writes of the oftentimes hollow impact of the manumission process.

JOHN AND PHIBBAH

Thomas Thistlewood, who resided in Jamaica from 1750 till his death in 1786, tried his hand at pen keeping and sugar management and, during his involvement in these activities, was able to record his numerous sexual adventures with enslaved women.[14] Within the large number of alleged escapades he noted his favorite sexual partner, an enslaved woman named "Phibbah," who subsequently became his "wife." With her he had a son in April 1760, a mulatto boy named John Thistlewood.[15] Thomas readily admitted paternity of the boy and, in a manumission entry dated May 3, 1762, had the boy manumitted.[16] However, about a year later, on April 12, 1763, Thistlewood noted in his diaries that to date he had only been given a "receipt for John's manumission" as it had "not been recorded yet."[17] Five months later and a full seventeen months after he had sought to have the boy manumitted he still had not succeeded in procuring John's manumission papers.[18] This example again illustrates that even in the best of times, when plantation management had a vested interest in speeding up the manumission process, the length of time between the actual receipt of official manumission through the procurement of the papers and the promise of manumission was often a long and drawn out affair. In the interim, no doubt, the manumitted "candidate" (especially if an adult) would have acknowledged it in his best interest to remain a model enslaved person.

The case of Phibbah, the mother of Thistlewood's mulatto son, is also illuminating. She became Thistlewood's "wife" in 1753 with his move as overseer to the Egypt Sugar Estate.[19] By mid-June 1757 Thistlewood was again on the move, this time to the Kendal estate. By now things between him and Phibbah had advanced to the point where he wished to take her with him. To this end, Thistlewood made offers to purchase or hire Phibbah from her owners, Mr. and Mrs. Cope. However, Mrs. Cope refused to entertain any such deal.[20] Not until ten years later, in November 1767, was Thistlewood finally allowed to hire Phibbah from Mr. Cope, and she came to live with him at Breadnut Island Pen.[21]

This new "living in" arrangement worked quite satisfactorily for Thistlewood, and while he openly continued having sexual relations with other women, Phibbah remained monogamous to him. Indeed, prior to his having her personally established in his home, she had clearly shown her preference for others, and it is perhaps only with his being able to guarantee her "home stability" that was she now prepared, in return, to be monogamous.[22] As such, her manumission was perhaps not necessary while he was alive as he was guaranteed her fidelity, and besides, her owners felt that she was more profitable to them while rented out to Thistlewood.[23] Of importance to us is her eventual manumission through Thistlewood's will.

Thistlewood died on November 30, 1786, and in his will left provisions for Phibbah to be manumitted. However, as in the case of Catherine on the Golden Grove estate, Phibbah was also not immediately manumitted. In fact, she was only manumitted six years later in November 1792.[24] At that time she was an old woman with poor eyesight and gastric and dental ailments. As these examples demonstrate, manumission, although granted at times when the enslaved person could have benefited from it, was often not actually given to them at that point.

Additionally, by manumitting these enslaved women, usually at the death of their white "husbands," their good behavior was ensured during the lifetime of their "husbands." Insofar as male plantation management was concerned, the promise of manumission often served far more effectively as a control device for their "relationships" than actual manumission would. These considerations thus bring us to question the underlying motives for manumission and, by so doing, help explain the often lackadaisical approach toward granting it.

Manumission became a tool of control which, when properly dangled by sugar management, ensured greater submission of the often "own minded" enslaved women. This control was furthered when, as stated by Long, a fixed sum of money was bequeathed to the manumitted person for life to be drawn on an annual basis. This is an interesting manumission clause because, in addition to providing some form of sustenance to the manumitted person, it also limited her ability to move far from the confines of the estate.

While it was true that manumitted people were often free in theory to go where they liked, in practice this was not so. Just as the system of apartheid in South Africa set rigid limitations to the movement and enjoyment of people with black skins, so too did plantation society set limits to the movement of manumitted people. An immediate disincentive to their exhibiting a freedom to move around arose from the precarious nature of their "paper" freedom. In this sense a lost manumission paper, or one that was callously destroyed by a vindictive or labor-starved white manager, meant that the manumitted freedom was at an end unless it could be otherwise proven. In this case, as Cox argued, the fear of being mistaken for slaves in rural areas forced skilled free people of color to gravitate to towns while the continued dependency by rural manumitted people on estate labor forced others to remain close to the plantation.[25] The point is that for equally valid reasons freed people of color were not as free to move about as their status should have allowed them. As such, former enslaved person were well advised to stay within the proximity of bona fide witnesses willing to vouch for their free status. Thus the manumitted person, in practice, was confined to a limited geographical area. This point was further concretized as most manumissions had a yearly stipend attached to them that warranted physical presence for collection.[26]

In most cases, and certainly by the mid-eighteenth century, it became a pre-requisite that the manumitted person be provided with a pension to ensure that he or she did not depend on the funds of the state. Although a practical consideration, it also facilitated another, more sinister managerial aim of plantation society. For it ensured that the manumitted person in order to collect her pension would remain in proximity to the estate, thereby serving as a living example of planter "manumission." This was important because manumitted people, few as they were, were needed to serve as tangible proof to the rest of the enslaved people of what could be achieved if they were good "slaves." Geographical mobility would defeat this aim of plantation management.

Clearly, then, the terms of the manumission document sought not to grant to the enslaved person total freedom but only a limited freedom from the regimented work on the estate. In addition, the extent to which she would be free was dependent on the extent to which there were other economic activities available to her outside of the plantation.

THE PROBLEM OF FREEDOM

But what then of those enslaved people who had actually received their manumission papers? How free were they? By manumitting their mixed-race offspring, plantation management was also encouraging a social practice of miscegenation which sought to concretize the point of lighter skin color being beneficial to the freedom project. Manumission in this regard was more than just a paternal instinct; it also buttressed the idea of white supremacy within the color-based social order. Indeed, the limited "paternalistic" thrust inherent in this avenue of manumission came from the fact that the manumitted person remained always at a disadvantage within a society that, though it had changed his legal status, had not changed the all-important color of his skin.[27] Manumission in this case was more a matter of "up and out" of the social order rather than "up and in" as in Africa.[28] This is the critical point. What was the worth of manumission in a society that understood social relations and status, primarily in terms of skin color? To be manumitted in such a society, ironically, meant to become only part of another alienated group.

Manumitted people in the context of the slave system were less "free" as true people in terms of their identity. This was so as they saw their freedom as a means of becoming more accepted into white society. Thus a breed of "mimic men" developed. Mary Prince,[29] for example, the first enslaved Caribbean Indian woman to write her autobiography, noted that the free colored people she came into contact with had often taken on airs and had isolated themselves from the rest of the enslaved community. She wrote of Martha Wilcox, who was a hired mulatto woman working in the Wood household and "such a fine lady she wanted to be mistress over me. I thought it very hard for a colored woman to have rule over me because I was a slave and she was free . . . she was a saucy woman, very saucy; and she . . . rejoiced to have power to keep me down. She was constantly making mischief; there was no living in for the slaves—no peace after she came."[30]

In this sense the freedom bestowed on these manumitted people, because of social conditioning, contributed to their alienation from the rest of the enslaved class. Freedom was a freedom that left one not free to be oneself, and Mary Prince wondered how "free" really the mulatto woman was.

In this context one notes the use white society made of the testimonies of the "properly" acculturated "free" black population in the aftermath of the 1817 Rebellion in Barbados. From the recorded testimonies it was clear that the free people had, parrot like, provided testimony that buttressed the belief of white society that the rebellion was due to the enslaved people being stirred up by their misunderstanding of the Registration Ordinance. Further, the testimonies of these "witnesses" all claimed that the enslaved people had been well treated and humanely kept.[31] As a reward the free colored population were given further "incentives" after the inquest.

Clearly here was a role for manumitted people of color within white society. Their role was to act as models for the rest of the enslaved community and to buttress white society whenever necessary. Manumission was therefore a viable and important tool of black acculturation that white society depended upon. Indeed, the societal benefits derived from it more than made up for any marginal cost associated with granting freedoms to token enslaved people. Even growing up as a free manumitted person did not necessarily mean that the person was "free," as the case of Thistlewood's manumitted son, John, illustrated.

As a lad of seventeen John Thistlewood had been serving an apprenticeship with a Mr. Hornby and had been absent from the place of his apprenticeship without permission of the master. Hearing this news Thistlewood immediately "had him put in the bilboes when he came from muster & kept him in all night."[32] The next day Thistlewood had John returned securely bound with ropes to Hornby. The same treatment was also meted out to the recaptured enslaved man Jimmy, who was also returned to Hornby under the same guard together with John. Clearly, then, for all his manumitted status, John was still fundamentally considered, and punished, like other enslaved people.

But this was not just an isolated case of an irate father responding to the misadventures of his mixed-race offspring. In general white society exhibited a low toleration threshold for the manumitted person. This is not to be confused with the fact that, as Long stated, white society appreciated them for their economic worth[33] and their strength in terms of deficiency ratios. But that was as far as it went. White society did not find it right to allow them the real freedoms to "life and liberty" that a free man should enjoy. Manumitted people were thus less free to exhibit the freedom that their manumission had allegedly procured for them.

FURTHER LIMITS TO THE MANUMISSION PROMISE

In 1810 Mary Prince returned to Bermuda, and through the cultivation and sale of produce, she began to save for manumission.[34] Eighteen years later she still had not saved enough to manumit herself, and so as an enslaved woman she accompanied her owners to London.[35] This observation on Mary Prince illustrates two other aspects of the manumission process. First, that while it was true that the system allowed the opportunity for a minority of enslaved people to conduct business to save toward their manumission, this in itself did not mean success in their businesses or the attainment ever of the required funds for self-purchase. Second, as in the case of Prince and in most examples of manumission, when manumission eventually came, the manumitted people were usually not fit enough to enjoy it to the fullest. Mary Prince, for example, when she had secured her quasi-freedom in London, was already severely crippled and almost blind.

White society itself also generated negative blocks to the attainment of manumitted freedom. As Moira Ferguson points out in the case of Mary Prince's owners, "The Woods evaluated Mary Prince's desire to leave them and find another master who would manumit her as a reflection on the quality of their ownership. So they compelled her to remain their slave in order to protect themselves from a moral judgement about the quality of servitude in their house-hold."[36]

White owners themselves thus placed hurdles in the path of the enslaved's access to the legal "option" of manumission. This is taken to an extreme in plantation managers like Thistlewood, who also made demands on the meager earnings of the enslaved population through loans or through charging them for goods and services they used or for tasks unsatisfactorily performed.[37] Lurking in the background of all these human activities too was the weather, which, particularly in sugar islands like Jamaica, devastated both land and limb and no doubt terminated many other manumission hopes through loss of life and the added expenses of survival.

Negative white attitudes and the vagaries of nature apart, for manumission to succeed it had to take into account the human dimension of "the enslaved people as people."[38] To manumit an enslaved woman while keeping the rest of her family enslaved was often a hollow accomplishment. It meant freedom for the individual, but in a real sense he was still enslaved, by association, with the ongoing pain and suffering of his spouse and offspring. How free was this type of manumitted "freedom"? Indeed, as in the case of Phibbah, Thistlewood had only manumitted her son while her daughter remained enslaved.

Certainly, then, in light of these many considerations and hurdles that still confronted manumitted people, manumission was perhaps not intended as an end in itself. Other reasons may thus offer better justifications for enslaved manumissions by white sugar society.

THE MANAGERIAL SIDE OF MANUMISSION: CONTROLLING SEXUALITY

Manumission buttressed the sexual impropriety of the sugar estates. Long's mention of the rightness of manumitting enslaved "domesticks" reflected a deviously veiled planter agenda. Beckles argued that these "domesticks" often became domestics in name only and were usually mistresses or hired sex slaves.[39] Sexual practices like these not only advocated the right of the master to have control of the enslaved woman's body in the field but also extended his rights to her body within the house. However, these arrangements, while providing white male management a preferential access to the sexuality of the enslaved women, did not guarantee management's exclusivity of it—a sore point that harbored ill on the male ego and necessitated action.

To this end an illustrative incident occurred in Kingston during the first half of 1768 and was reported by Simon Taylor in his daily account of the colony's sugar business. According to him two counselors, Bayly and Kennion, were involved in a fracas over a quadroon girl.[40] Apparently, she had chosen to allocate her sexual favors between the two white men, and their subsequent fighting over her had caused quite a stir in Kingston. The reason for their animosity toward each other centered on who had the proper "right of possession" of the enslaved girl. It is clear from Taylor's account of the fracas that the girl was legally "owned" by Bayly. However, even though she was "owned" by him, her sexuality, as far as she was concerned, was obviously not controlled by him.

Hillary Beckles elaborated on the (ab)use made of enslaved women's sexuality during the period of enforced labor. He also identified the association between sexuality and manumission in the prostitution taverns of British West Indian sugar society where enslaved women were offered the boon of freedom as an incentive for maintaining their "enthusiasm." As he concluded in these cases, manumission was an appropriate incentive for them as "freedom was a legal status not easily rejected."[41] While it is true that countless enslaved women were violated under these conditions, many enslaved women, far from being only victims, also used their sexuality to better their positions.

Long, for example, wrote, "In regard to the African mistress, . . . her dexterity consists in persuading the (white) man she detests to believe she is most violently smitten with the beauty of his person . . . and, by this stratagem, she is better able to hide her private intrigues with her real favourites."[42] While Long could be faulted for his racial bias, examples of male "cuckolding" by enslaved women abound throughout the plantation literature. Hall cites Thomas Thistlewood and the problems he had keeping his favorite mistresses faithful to him. He also points to other cases where the enslaved women had the better of many of the white estate managers. White plantation management, then, while in a position to abuse enslaved women's sexuality, were generally not in a position to control it. In this regard enslaved plantation women were free to engage in other sexual liaisons with other men both black and white.

The move to "wifedom" and the associated manumission or promise of manumission that often came with it sought, in a real way, to restrict the enslaved woman's sexuality. For she now had a legal sponsor or "husband," who in wanting to reserve her favors for his exclusive use took her off the sex "market." This end was achieved as the enslaved woman now had the hope of manumission dangled before her and so would make every effort to ensure that this desired hope was achieved even if it meant fidelity—a fidelity, Long was clear to point out, they were expert in showing. While fidelity to their "husbands" was a desired end of white management, it was oftentimes not the only end. This point is exemplified in the case of the wife of Sampson.

When Sampson, the overseer on the Amity Hall estate, decided to "marry" his black mistress in Jamaica in 1818, the terms of the manumission document prepared for her were very clear. In addition to stating that she and her children were under "bond of Thomas Sampson," it also stated that she and her children were also the "property of Amity Hall." In a strange twist then, her annuity was to be matched by the estate itself.[43] As such she was now indebted both to the estate and to Sampson for her "freedom." In ways like this we see collusion between male absentees and local white male management in buttressing a practice that benefited primarily their ends rather than that of the manumitted person's. In this case the estate benefited as her labor would still be around the estate, and Sampson benefited as he now had an "obedient" wife.

The practice of allowing white employees to purchase/manumit enslaved women and their mulatto children was also a mark of favor done in order to maintain harmony between owners (usually absentees) and local managers. As Lord Barham told one of his managers, "I have to confess very strong objections to sell my slave in whatever case—but I should be sorry to let the opportunity escape of expressing my regard for you and opinion of your services."[44] In this context manumitted freedom was dependent more on providing an incentive to the white worker than it was intended as a reward for the enslaved person who was manumitted. Attitudes like these most definitely shaped the degree and type of "freedom" that was on offer.

As incidents like these illustrate, manumitted women were now legally bound to their benefactors as their papers clearly identified who had manumitted them and were paying their pensions. And by manumitting an enslaved woman or by promising to manumit her, white management not only made her freedom dependent on them but also made her more "monogamous."[45] In this case institutional practices like manumission supported this move toward curtailment of the woman's sexual freedom. Again, the question could be asked of these women after manumission: How free is free?

Indeed, the Barbadian legislature clearly summed up the ego-based phole-centric reasoning that underlay manumission when they debated the continued status of female enslaved manumission in the colony. Beckles notes:

> In 1774, a bill was introduced into the Assembly aimed at curtailing the number of females being manumitted. It was designed to raise the manumission fee to £100, but was rejected on the grounds that slave owners should not be deprived of the right to assist the "most deserving part" of their slaves—the females who have generally recommended themselves to our "kindest notice." It was defeated by a vote of eleven to five; opposition was led by Sir John Gay Alleyne who argued that female slaves who gave their loyalty, love and service to masters should not be denied the opportunity to gain freedom.[46]

Manumission during the period of British West Indian slavery was the practice of granting legal freedom to a very small group of enslaved Africans and their enslaved descendants. This numerically small group, in the anglophone Caribbean, hardly affected the ranks of enslaved people as had the large numbers of manumitted people within Greek slavery. Indeed, in many cases, the promise of manumission rather than the benefits of the act itself became the closest that many of these enslaved people came to receiving their "freedom." While many writers have argued that manumission was a widespread practice in the anglophone Caribbean during the period of enslavement, I have argued that its impact was negated because of its operation as a managerial and social conditioning tool. These concerns overshadowed any context of planter benevolence it may have had and meant that the freedom derived from it would be a limited one.

Even in the best of times manumission was a lengthy and drawn-out process which was seldom reflected by the manumission request carried in wills or noted in plantation papers. Too often have researchers viewed *the provisions of* manumission within wills and legacies as *proof of* manumission. Often, because of the high demand for plantation labor and the gross indifference of white plantation management, manumission was a dead letter in the lives of the vast majority of enslaved people.

Ultimately the practice of manumission in white plantation society respected white rights of ownership and pleasure and the exigencies of plantation labor above the rights of the enslaved person. These factors, not any sense of misguided passion or loyalty, determined who eventually was manumitted and when they would be so. These considerations prompted my query: How free is free? The point is that within a society that saw the natural inequality of the races, the manumitted person would never automatically belong to the "free" society by virtue of a legal device.

Perhaps a necessary corollary to manumission concerns the related avenue of the subsequent level of social "absorption." For this determined not only the extent to which the manumitted person would be an equal (or not) but also determined the means he or she would have to enjoy freedom within the society. In the British West Indies, as the struggle of the coloreds right through to the nineteenth century demonstrated, proper enjoyment of manumitted freedom was never the case, nor, as I contend, was it ever a desirable goal underlying planter sponsored manumission in these societies.

NOTES

1. The usual means to saving enough for manumission through the "commodity" route came through the marketing of crops obtained from the gardens of the enslaved people or through sales of animals they owned.

2. Craton points out that by 1780 the population ratio had stabilized "to around 10:1 overall but being up to six times as high on the estates and those farthest inland." M. Craton, *Empire Enslavement and Freedom in the Caribbean* (Kingston: Ian Randle, James Curry, Markus Wiener, 1997), 165–166.

3. In 1739, for example, the manumission fee in Barbados had been legally set at fifty pounds plus an annuity of four pounds in local currency; the annuity was insisted upon by poor law officials as one way to prevent slave owners from freeing old and infirm people who could not reasonably be expected to earn their subsistence.

4. A. L. Stinchcombe, *Sugar Island Slavery in the Age of Enlightenment: The Political Economy of the Caribbean World* (Princeton, N.J.: Princeton University Press, 1995), 139–140.

5. Simon Taylor was born in Jamaica in 1740 and owned four plantations in addition to those he managed for absentee owners such as Arcedeckne. For a detailed insight into his career and plantation interests, see Betty Wood and T. R. Clayton, "Slave Birth, Death and Disease on Golden Grove Plantation, Jamaica, 1765–1810," *Slavery and Abolition* 6, no. 2 (September 1985): 99–121.

6. Simon Taylor to Benjamin Cowell, October 3, 1767, Vanneck (Arcedekne) Papers (hereafter cited as Vanneck Papers), 2 boxes, Jamaican Estate Records 1765–1810 (hereafter cited as JER).

7. "Jobbing slaves" were gangs of enslaved people usually owned by another planter or overseer and rented out to estates as and when they were required.

8. One also notes an overall increase in manumission rates occurring in all islands on the eve of emancipation.

9. Taylor to Arcedeckne, Kingston, December 3, 1771, Vanneck Papers.

10. Ibid.

11. Extract of will dated May 24, 1773, and contained in Timothy Penny to Chaloner Arcedeckne, February 6, 1783, Vanneck Papers.

12. Extract of letter dated October 31, 1776, and contained in Timothy Penny to Chaloner Arcedeckne, February 6. 1783, Vanneck Papers.

13. The usual practice was to manumit aged enslaved people when their utility was low and their purchase price could be used to finance the purchase of younger workers. For an example of this reasoning, see Hibbert & Taylor to Sir Hugh Smyth, August 19, 1797, A CWO 16 (27), 117(a), County Council Record Office, Bristol (hereafter cited as BCCRO); see also Fearon to Penhryn, October 25, 1805, UNW: Penhryn MS. 1366, University of North Wales.

14. Shepherd points out that "his physical and sexual abuse of enslaved women leaves us in no doubt about his attitude toward them" and he "like other white men, seemed to have believed that one advantage of coming to the island was the chance of sexually exploiting many black and coloured women." Verene A. Shepherd, "Gender and Representation in European Accounts of Pre-emancipation Jamaica," in *Caribbean Slavery in the Atlantic World*, ed. V. A. Shepherd and H. M. Beckles (Kingston: Ian Randle, 2000), 706.

15. D. Hall, *In Miserable Slavery: Thomas Thistlewood in Jamaica 1750–86* (Kingston: University of West Indies Press, 1999), 94.

16. Ibid., 314.

17. Ibid., 129.

18. Ibid.

19. Ibid., 32, 51. This followed his separation from his first "wife" Jenny.

20. Ibid., 79.

21. Ibid., 146.

22. Ibid., 250, 302. Thistlewood did note that he suspected her of having a tryst with Egypt Lewie in May 1777 and, later, in January 1785 with "Strap." However, the illicit context of these episodes clearly implied that she was not entitled, as he was, to outside affairs.

23. No doubt the Woods used Phibbah's involvement with Thistlewood to keep him involved with the management of their affairs as well.

24. Hall, *In Miserable Slavery*, 314.

25. E. L. Cox, *Free Coloreds in the Slave Societies of St. Kitts and Grenada, 1763–1833* (Knoxville: University of Tennessee Press, 1984), 29–32.

26. Even in the later acquired British territories like Grenada, new legislation was quickly introduced to bring them up to par with the other islands' legislation in this regard. For example, a 1764 law stipulated that people manumitting enslaved people by last will were to pay an additional one hundred pounds for each manumission. See Cox, *Free Coloreds*, 33–37. In Antigua during the eighteenth century the law required "landless manumitted people 'to enter themselves into the service of some family'" (Edward Long, "Freed Blacks and Mulattos," in *Slaves, Free Men, Citizens*, ed. D. L. Landros Comitas [New York: Anchor, 1973], 321). Jamaica had perhaps the most elaborate laws, and from 1711 it passed legislation for the entire group of free colored people that set severe restriction on them. D. Hall, "Jamaica," in *Neither Slave nor Free: The Freedmen of African Descent in the Slave Societies of the New World*, ed. D. W. Cohen and J. P. Greene (Baltimore: Johns Hopkins University Press, 1972), 197–198.

27. The newly liberated manumitted person entered at the bottom of an already existing social hierarchy, which was itself highly stratified according to skin color and wealth. K. Watson, *The Civilised Island Barbados: A Social History 1750–1816* (Bridgetown: Caribbean Graphic Production, 1979), 105.

28. J. L. Watson, *Asian and African Systems of Slavery* (Berkeley and Los Angeles: University of California Press, 1980), 10.

29. Mary Prince was born about 1788, and her autobiography was published as M. Prince, *The History of Mary Prince: A West Indian Slave Related by Herself*, rev. ed. (Ann Arbor: University of Michigan Press, 2000), 1,4.

30. Ibid., 79–80.

31. See, for example, the testimonies of Jacob Belgrave, a "free" mulatto; Thomas Harris, a "free" man of color; William Yard, a "free" black man; and Thomas Brewster, a "free" colored man, cited in *The Report from a Select Committee of the House of Assembly {Appointed} to*

Inquire into the Origin, Causes and progress of the late Insurrection, Barbados House of Assembly (1818), 38–40.

32. Hall, *In Miserable Slavery,* 251, 261, where in addition to being put in the bilboes and tied, John was also "pretty well flogged" and denied the use of his shoes.

33. Long pointed out that they also provided a source of skilled apprentices who would undercut the exorbitant prices charged by white tradesmen.

34. Prince, *History of Mary Prince,* 9.

35. Ibid., 21.

36. Ibid., 18.

37. See, for example, Saturday May 19, 1781, where he forced his enslaved people to pay for limes he thought they had stolen. See also February 10, 1784, where he also made the estate's fisherman, Dick, pay him for "bringing such bad fish." For references, see Hall, *In Miserable Slavery,* 284, 298.

38. Hall rightly stressed this point in his "People in Slavery," in *Inside Slavery: Process and legacy in the Caribbean experience,* ed. H. M. Beckles (Kingston: Canoe Press, 1985), 13.

39. Beckles, "Property Rights in Pleasure," 694.

40. Simon Taylor to Chaloner Arcedeckne, July 25, 1768. Vanneck Papers.

41. Beckles, "Property Rights in Pleasure," 697.

42. Long, "Freed Blacks and Mulattos," 87–88.

43. Correspondences of Amity Hall, Vere and the Bogue Pen, Jamaica, May 20, 1818, 304 / Box 42, Surrey Record Office, Surrey.

44. Barham to White & Webb, July 1, 1804, Bodl. MS. Clarendon dep. c. 357, Bodleian Library, University of Oxford.

45. As Beckles demonstrated in his analysis of late-eighteenth-century Barbadian slave prostitution, there was less availability of women becoming slave prostitutes when their status changed to being "mistresses" or "married." Beckles, "Property Rights in Pleasure," 697.

46. Ibid., 699–700.

Willem Wubbo Klooster

Manumission in an Entrepôt

—ᴧᴧ—

The Case of Curaçao

The tiny island of Curaçao, with a surface area of merely 178 square miles, occupied a special place in the economy of the early modern Caribbean. Conveniently located off the Venezuelan coast, Curaçao provided a concentration of supply and demand, assuring buyers from all nationalities that the products they sought were available. The Curaçaoan entrepôt attracted merchants from every part of the Caribbean and was a transit point for trade with the Dutch Republic, whence large amounts of American produce were sent. The island became a distribution center for African slaves, who initially were not imported for domestic purposes but for reexport to Spanish America. Starting in the late seventeenth century, an increasing number remained on the island, where they worked for individual whites or the West India Company. This essay tries to establish the frequency, reasons, and consequences of their manumission.

Curaçao's economic base differed sharply from the typical New World colony where everything revolved around the cultivation of cash crops. No crops were grown on a large scale; an official late eighteenth-century report only refers to the production of corn to feed the slaves and the cattle and mentions an extremely modest output of sugar and cotton. The combination of a rocky soil and extended droughts defeated any attempt to produce crops for the European markets. The majority of the slaves were, nonetheless, put to work on so-called plantations, all of which were originally owned by the West India Company. Toward the end of the seventeenth century, private plantations started multiplying, and by the time the West India Company was abolished in 1791, few "company blacks" remained. By then most slaves worked for wealthy Protestants and Jews. Rural slaves predominated slightly in 1789 (57.9 percent), and more clearly in the nineteenth century (on average 68.4 percent between 1816 and 1863).[1] While the lives of these slaves somewhat resembled those of rural slaves elsewhere in the Caribbean, there were also pronounced differences. Actual agricultural labor only took up six months, while specific cleaning and repairing tasks were carried out in the other half of the year.[2] Management was not very market-oriented, as exemplified by the custom to sell slaves individually rather than en bloc when a plantation was put up for sale.[3] While field slaves predominated, there were plenty of women with only domestic chores, working as laundresses, seamstresses, or vendors. Many male slaves were artisans; among them we find carpenters, shoemakers, masons, and tailors.

The size of slave gangs employed in and around the elite's country houses was correspondingly small. In 1735 the average master owned fewer than four slaves. Most owned one or two, while only eight slaveholders possessed more than fifty.[4] Three decades later at least two planters each had two hundred slaves at work,[5] but the basic pattern had not changed, and by 1863, the year of Dutch emancipation, most slaveholders still owned fewer than five slaves.

The limited importance of slave labor was borne out in 1775, when for the first time in many years a slave ship arrived from West Africa. Instead of importing the 238 bonded Africans, the authorities instantly resold them to Saint-Domingue.[6] No slave ship would sail into Willemstad again,[7] but enslaved Africans continued to be exported—officially more than 4,000 in the period 1816–1847.[8] Curaçao's slave population had grown rapidly throughout the eighteenth century, reaching 12,864 by 1789, or 61.3 percent of the island population. Political turmoil—the constant changing of the guards in the wake of the French Revolution and especially the long British occupation— and repeated economic setbacks led to a marked decline of the overall island population. Numerous slaves left with their masters for other Caribbean islands. The number of slaves had been halved by the middle of the nineteenth century, and when the Dutch government finally abolished the "peculiar institution" in 1863, 6,684 private and 67 government slaves remained.[9]

Curaçao had a distinctly urban character. The city of Willemstad, with its districts of Otrabanda, Pietermaai, and Scharloo, provided for numerous economic opportunities as well as social and cultural interaction between various ethnic and social groups. A common trait of nonclassical plantation societies such as Curaçao is the relative freedom of slaves. Female slaves in early Spanish Hispaniola, for example, could make a living in urban marketplaces. Scores of slaves in the Dutch colony of New Netherland worked independently, and their counterparts in Curaçao were likewise allowed to work on their own, returning to their masters at regular intervals to bring back a share of the income they had earned.[10] Others worked semi-independently, earning money to supplement the livelihood provided by the master by chopping wood, selling the products of their provision grounds, or burning lime and selling it downtown.[11]

What set Curaçao apart from most non-Dutch colonies was the large number of slave fishermen and sailors.[12] These slaves earned a salary on board private vessels and those of the West India Company. The muster of one company ship, the *Erffstadhouder,* included an Irish captain, a white Curaçaoan quartermaster, three white Curaçaoan sailors, one sailor born on Aruba, one on Bonaire, and seventeen slave sailors, of whom twelve had been born on the island itself and five in West Africa. Each sailor, irrespective of his legal status, earned ten pesos per month.[13] Of all possible professions, that of sailor undoubtedly lent slaves most freedom of movement. This life seemed so attractive to some Africans that they borrowed letters of freedom from other sailors, which allowed to them to sail on one of the merchant vessels leaving Willemstad every day. This practice was outlawed more than once by a regulation which permitted free blacks and mulattoes only to be recruited with the permission of their masters.[14] Some slave sailors abused this freedom by running away; sailors constituted one-sixth of the runaways in the eighteenth century.[15] Part of the sailors' ordeal was the risks involved in the contraband trade, in which the Curaçaoan sloops and schooners routinely participated. Seizure by Spanish coastguard vessels might result in the auctioning off of the ship, the trade goods, as well as the black crew members slaves and freedmen alike, who were often taken for human cargo.[16]

Running away was more common than what might be expected because of Curaçao's reputation of being a mild slave regime. Just between 1759 and 1766, 380 slaves deserted their masters.[17] Running away in Curaçao meant stealing a boat or canoe and rowing to the Venezuelan coast. Was life that miserable? Apparently it was for some West India Company slaves, as appears from a survey of their way of death, which was drawn up midway through the eighteenth century. The slaves invariably did jobs to which the white islanders had an aversion. Eight slaves died after lugging very heavy stones and one was killed hoisting a crane. One slave drowned after the boom of a company sloop swept him overboard, while another one fell off a high scaffold while painting. Exhaustion killed two slaves, and two others probably contracted pneumonia after standing too long in the water during dredging operations. One slave was beaten to death by the master to whom he had been lent, and two slaves, finally, protested against the tasks which had been assigned to them by hanging themselves.[18]

Curaçao, for all its social control, also had its cases of extreme white violence against blacks. Planter Jan Hendriks, for instance, took the law into his own hands in 1749, after slaves of the West India Company plantation Hato had set out for the government buildings with drums and other instruments to wish Governor Faesch a happy Pentecost. While waiting to be ferried to the old part of town, they diverted themselves with music. Hendriks became so annoyed over this that he broke up the "orchestra," wounding many slaves, of whom three were left behind in a serious condition. Hendriks dragged one slave to his house, where he gave him another beating.[19] In another incident Pieter François Diedenhoven was disgruntled about the alleged theft by a young female slave from another planter. He had her tied up and dragged from his plantation, one hour from town, to Willemstad. In his house he had her whipped for so long that two surgeons bandaged her for three weeks. The girl was probably an invalid for the rest of her life.[20]

Although neither Hendriks nor Diedenhoven obviously had to fear sharp punishment, the matter was taken to court in both cases. Hendriks was fined six thousand pesos, and Diedenhoven apparently came off with an even smaller fine but still raised a hue and cry over it. During the hearing of his case he made it clear that he had put out eight hundred thousand guilders at interest on Curaçao and that he would ruin the island if he were condemned. Since it is unlikely that he was ever forced to pay, this case smacks of class justice,[21] all the more because slaves could expect severe penalties even if they were arrested for misdemeanors. A black who stole four and a half pesos from the Poor Relief Fund in 1732 was condemned to stand in a public square for a whole day with a rope around his neck. Subsequently, he was to be branded and whipped.[22]

Was manumission a realistic alternative to running away for those slaves who longed to be free? Manumission in the Dutch plantation society of Suriname has been described as "a happy incident, not a prospect."[23] Was it similar in an entrepôt? We would be in the dark here if it were not for a very accurate census taken in 1789. Assuming that the slave population remained constant in the remainder of the century, we can estimate that the manumittees constituted over 0.5 percent of the slaves in the late eighteenth century, significantly higher than in Suriname, where the rate was under 0.2 percent.[24] By the middle of the nineteenth century the manumission rate had gone up in a spectacular way to 1.2 percent.[25]

Manumission was usually initiated by the slaveholder, who set a slave free either directly or as a testamentary disposition. In a third of the cases (32.9 percent) loyal service was listed as the reason, while one in fourteen slaves (7.3 percent) was manumitted for affection. It is difficult to determine whether the use of phrases such as "loyal service" and "affection" was merely rhetorical, although it is clear at times that an emotional bond had been forged between manumittor and manumittee. One widow explained her motive to set free a slave girl as being "for love and respect of my religion, since she has received Holy Baptism and I myself am the witness."[26]

Women were twice as likely as men to be manumitted for their loyal service. The reason frequently was gratitude for their services as wet nurses, which was explicitly mentioned in some manumissions.[27] There is no proof that many slave women obtained manumission through concubinage,[28] even if the scores of mulattoes show that the phenomenon of concubinage was widespread. In general more women were manumitted than men: 60 percent of all of manumittees were female (among blacks, 65 percent; see table 1), which is not particularly different from what we know about other slave societies. One explanation for the higher incidence of female manumissions can be ruled out: They were not of lesser value. In case of self-purchase or if a third party freed a slave, the prices paid for adult men and women were remarkably similar: 263 pesos for men, 257 for women, and the manumission of a girl even required a larger amount of cash than that of a boy (table 2).[29] These data seem to point to an equally valued economic contribution of females. The larger number of female manumissions, however, undercuts that thesis.

Flight was not an option for most female slaves. The care of children prevented many from even trying, although there are examples of women escaping with infants clasped to their breasts. Of the ninety recorded female runaways in the eighteenth century, eight escaped with a total of fifteen children. The overwhelming majority of runaways (84.4 percent) were black males,[30] precisely the category that was underrepresented among the manumitted. Black men were not only less fortunate than black women, who were occasionally given their freedom by way of thanks for loyal service, they were also less likely than mulattoes to obtain their freedom in other legal ways. In a society where skin color correlated with social standing, black men found themselves at the bottom of the social ladder. See table 3.

The proposition that "slave laws were harsh and barriers to the manumission of slaves particularly strong" in Dutch America,[31] certainly does not apply to Curaçao. What is more, the relatively high frequency of manumission could reinforce a very positive view of Curaçaoan slavery, with its mild labor regime, semi-independence, and high degree of social control. Such a representation would stretch the truth, however, as even contemporaries noted. In a report of 1791 two commissioners of the Dutch States General observed that the relative freedom of Curaçaoan slaves should not be mistaken for happiness. On the contrary, slaves in the Dutch colonies in Guiana were actually better off, considering the completely inadequate food supply in Curaçao.[32]

Protracted droughts occurred almost as often as not; the years 1697, 1701, 1707, 1709–1712, 1717–1722, 1747, 1763–1764 and 1770–1771 stood out as extremely dry,[33] and settlers were driven to despair: "In the absence of rain we are suffering here such a severe drought that there is hardly any water to get hold of for the people to drink, while all the crops are shriveling in the fields and the cattle are on the verge of extinction for lack of food and because of the scorching heat of the day, and for not having any liquid to quench their thirst."[34] In the summer of 1779 supplies were so limited that there were daily bereavements among the slaves and the poor free population. A merchant staying on the island reported in a letter that the local flour supply would only be sufficient for the next two days. One loaf of bread cost six times as much as in Amsterdam. Whites feared a slave uprising if the two ships that had been long awaited would not arrive within three or four days.[35] The slaves themselves were not inclined to start a rebellion; they preferred to escape from Curaçao.

Nearby Coro in Venezuela exerted such an attraction that in 1774 alone, another year of near-famine, 140 slaves managed to reach this town.[36] They arrived in a place that had seen wave after wave of Curaçaoan slaves wash ashore. More than 400 of the 2,000 inhabitants of the parish of Santa Ana de Coro were runaways from the Dutch island.[37]

Even in prosperous times slave food left much to be desired. The notion that Curaçao's slave diet was rich in protein, consisting of corn, fruit, meat, and fish,[38] can be dismissed. The slaves ate little else than corn bread. Nor, for that matter, did the poor whites eat fresh fruit or meat.[39] As paltry as the slave diet was, many a master made drastic cutbacks in times of economic decline. A prominent reason for slaveholders to manumit their slaves was to rid themselves of the responsibility for the slaves' livelihood. Once again Curaçaoan slavery proved to be different from those New World colonies, where the production of staples predominated. In those societies slaves were essential, whereas in Curaçao they were more often "luxury servants": In the manumission letters, for instance, reference is made to several violinists, a French horn player, and an oboist.[40]

Manumission was often a mixed blessing. All of a sudden the released slave was forced to make a living by himself. Especially to domestic slaves the newly gained status must have appeared as a punishment. The slave had become a burden because of age, sickness, or a physical handicap. Planters often saved first on slave provisions, when an economic recession hit, although this did not automatically mean they proceeded to manumission. Some masters did not take such a drastic step, preferring to give their slaves two or three weekly days off, during which time these were supposed to fend for themselves. While this measure relieved the planters of the task to feed their slaves, it led to a rise in criminal activity on Curaçao, since the few days a week proved insufficient for the slaves to make a living in a legal fashion. Many engaged in the theft of sheep and goats.[41]

For the longest time the colonial government did not take any steps to impose restraints on this practice. In 1762 it was decided that for every manumitted male slave over sixty years of age and every female over fifty, one hundred pesos had to be paid to the colonial treasury.[42] But this stipulation was revoked after only one year. A more permanent measure was imposed under the Batavian Republic in 1804. It prescribed that any manumission had to be publicly announced six weeks ahead of time, and that the slaveholder was bound to provide for the manumitted. This promptly led to an increase of underhanded manumission, which was soon outlawed.[43] Numerous masters henceforth chose to sell "redundant" slaves abroad.[44]

The practice of manumission was not limited to these arbitrary acts on the part of the masters. As indicated above, a slave could purchase his or her own freedom and a third party could pay for it. The price of freedom varied widely.

The average fee was 218 pesos, but while one slave needed only 10 pesos, others had to pay over 1,000 pesos.[45] The average price of manumission was by far the highest in the booming decade of the 1740s, suggesting a correlation with economic prosperity. However, whether in prosperous times or not, some slave groups were at a disadvantage. Slave sailors were not likely to ever amass enough money to pay for their own freedom, but self-employed slave artisans and porters stood a better chance.[46]

Purchase frequently occurred in installments and was spread out over many years. Miriaantje, a woman of mixed Indian and black parentage, paid a first installment in 1763 to her mistress, Rachel Bueno Vivas, but was not released until 1785. The mulatto woman Sica paid for her freedom in 1748, in 1755, and again in 1764, when she was released after her final installment.[47] Mothers with children under sixteen years of age were usually emancipated along with their children, but except for the sucklings these did not get a free ride. The price for a manumission of a mother with one child was 375 pesos, only slightly less than the combined fees for an average woman and an average child. A letter for a woman with two children was, however, relatively cheap: 395 pesos. The emancipation of a woman along with her offspring was not the rule, and in many cases the enfranchised slave woman subsequently worked for several years to pay for the freedom of her children. (Step)fathers, incidentally, almost never appear in the documents as payers.[48]

It was common for slaveholders to attach conditions to freedom, whether it was granted or purchased. Continued service was often demanded, and little changed for former slaves who were required to stay with their master or mistress for the rest of their lives.[49] The mulatto tailor Jean Pierre had to promise continued service, making and repairing clothes for Curaçao's fiscal agent for the duration of the latter's stay on the island.[50] Maria Martha was set free, provided that she serve her master's family on their voyage to Holland. Her emancipation only took effect after her return.[51] In addition to a payment of seven hundred pesos, mason Juan Andrees had to teach his craft to two or three slave boys until they were skilled in their trade.[52] When Roelof Meyboom manumitted Fortuyn (a.k.a. Juan Bastiaan), he required him to bring four pitchers of corn every week to "the old Negress Sebel."[53] In a few isolated cases a slave was set free in exchange for the services of a new slave. It is unclear how these new slaves appeared on the scene.[54] An 1832 law finally stipulated that slaveholders could no longer require the continued personal service of a manumitted person.

A special type of manumission, solely for form's sake, occurred in the middle decades of the eighteenth century, as Spanish coastguard vessels stepped up their activities against Dutch merchantmen. Black crew members were more likely to be arrested than their white colleagues, and languished in prisons in Cartagena, Caracas, and Havana. Producing a letter of freedom proved the way out of this ordeal, provided that the prisoner would be reenslaved upon his return to Curaçao.[55]

The comparatively large number of manumissions created a sizable group of free blacks and mulattoes. While there were only 48 of them in 1717, making up 5.6 percent of the population, in 1742 their number had increased to 540, and in 1789 to 3,714, or 17.7 percent of the population, a higher percentage than anywhere in the Caribbean. In 1750 the rapid growth of the free black and mulatto population induced the government to make planters pay one hundred pesos to the West India Company for the manumission of every male slave under the age of sixty and every female under fifty. Although the measure was rescinded within two years, the increase of this group did not halt. Between 1817 and 1833 they surpassed the slave population, making up 43.5 percent of all Curaçaoans in the latter year. It was the free blacks who dominated within this group: In 1719 they accounted for 77.1 percent, in 1742, 74.1 percent, and in the period from 1741 to 1830, nearly twice as many blacks as mulattoes were manumitted.[56]

For both women and men there was little change after they obtained their letter of manumission. Near the Ascension plantation one observer came across "a hamlet of free blacks, being several straw huts on a barren soil, where nothing grew. The planters, who were [traveling] with us, complained on that occasion about the inconvenience caused by these free blacks: their numbers were steadily rising, and they lacked any regular means of existence, so that many of them lived by stealing, or purchasing stolen goods."[57] Their large numbers notwithstanding, the freedmen had difficulties finding a niche in the island's economy. In rural districts they often ended up on the same plantations and performing the same chores as slaves. In 1789, 1,097 lived in the countryside, but many more— 2,617—dwelled in Willemstad, making a living as artisans and sailors. Their lives were hardly different from those of semi-independent slaves, since legally they were still not the equals of whites. Retail trade, for instance, was a possible line of work, but complaints from less affluent whites, who viewed the free blacks and mulattoes as rivals, led in 1749 to a prohibition for the latter to keep a shop in town, although they could continue their commercial dealings in their homes and take merchandise to town during the daytime.[58]

Yet in another respect the freedmen played a vital role: as soldiers. As early as 1676 the directors of the West India Company suggested that the numerous slaves imported in Curaçao would make excellent military men. They advised the governor to have them exercise "in the European fashion," since many of them, especially those from Angola, had fought in wars in their own country and knew how to handle a gun.[59] It was not the slaves but the free black and mulatto militia, which was assigned an important task in maintaining public order. When a slave ran away (and when it was clear that he or she had not escaped to Venezuela), the master called at the governor, appealing to him to send the militia to catch the fugitive. This "hunt" sometimes lasted for a week or two, during which time the militiamen were allowed to visit all plantations.[60]

The social position of the freedmen was obviously inconsistent with their indispensability as soldiers. This was shown, for instance, toward the end of the eighteenth century. In 1796 fear of a British invasion led to the formation of four National Guard artillery companies. Since many blacks and mulattoes had gained experience on board merchant vessels with the use of guns against pirates and coast guards, they were placed in these companies. Among the officers, *mustiezen* and other "people of color" actually predominated, to the utter dismay of white islanders.[61]

There was a relatively high incidence of manumission in Curaçao. The economic system can explain why: the absence of a factory-style production of cash crops, which was characteristic of other New World colonies. A Curaçaoan slave was less a capital good than in Suriname and more a luxury servant, sometimes even a form of conspicuous consumption. That made him expendable in times of economic adversity, which in Curaçao often entailed a food crisis. Many owners would proceed to manumission in order to relieve themselves of the concern for slave provisions. Another unofficial, blatantly illegal form of manumission also existed: The slaveholder would send his slaves on a food hunt for their own expense two or three days a week. The poor soil and the lack of rainfall, factors that helped Curaçao become an entrepôt, provided for less harsh working condition than elsewhere and a more lenient manumission policy, thus making for a precarious livelihood for its enslaved population.

TABLE 1. Manumission in all age groups according to gender, 1741–1863

	Men (%)	Women (%)
1741–50	53.3	46.7
1751–60	49.1	50.9
1761–70	37.9	62.1
1771–80	34.5	65.5
1781–90	30.7	69.3
1791–00	33.2	66.8
1801–10	29.7	70.3
1811–20	41.4	58.6
1821–30	38.0	62.0
1831–40	44.0	56.0
1841–50	39.1	60.9
1851–60	42.7	57.3
1861–63	47.1	52.9

Source: Calculated on the basis of T. van der Lee, *Curaçaose vrijbrieven 1722–1863: Met indices op namen van vrijgelatenen en hun voormalige eigenaren* (The Hague: Algemeen Rijksarchief, 1998).

TABLE 2. The price of manumission (in pesos)

	1741–50	1751–60	1761–70	1771–80	1781–90	1791–00	Average/ decade
Men	307	268	211	271	254	265	263
Women	298	225	248	260	279	230	257
Boys	101	126	100	123	165	145	127
Girls	153	93	125	128	144	166	135
Overall	286	204	184	200	231	203	218

Source: Calculated on the basis of T. van der Lee, *Curaçaose vrijbrieven 1722–1863: Met indices op namen van vrijgelatenen en hun voormalige eigenaren* (The Hague: Algemeen Rijksarchief, 1998).

TABLE 3. Manumission according to ethnicity (in percentages)

	Blacks	Mulattoes	Mustiezen	Sambos
1741–50	64.8	29.7	3.5	2.0
1751–60	71.3	22.6	11.7	3.6
1761–70	53.0	35.2	8.6	3.3
1771–80	45.8	33.7	13.5	7.0
1781–90	56.8	26.2	11.2	6.1
1791–00	47.4	30.4	12.4	8.0
1801–10	54.0	24.8	9.3	14.6
1811–20	57.0	25.0	5.0	14.0
1821–30	32.3	42.9	16.5	12.0

Source: Calculated on the basis of T. van der Lee, *Curaçaose vrijbrieven 1722–1863. Met indices op namen van vrijgelatenen en hun voormalige eigenaren* (The Hague: Algemeen Rijksarchief, 1998).

Note: Mustiezen were the offspring of whites and mulattoes, sambos of blacks and mulattoes.

NOTES

1. In 1789, 5,419 slaves were recorded in Willemstad, against 7,445 in rural districts. Raad van Coloniën, 120, Nationaal Archief, The Hague (hereafter cited as NA). "Generaal rapport over Curaçao en onderhorige eylanden," Bijlage no. 16: Opgave der huizen van particulieren; W. E. Renkema, *Het Curaçaose plantagebedrijf in de 19e eeuw* (Zutphen: De Walburg Pers, 1981), 121. See for the early history of slavery on the island, Han Jordaan, "The Curaçao Slave Market: From Asiento Trade to Free Trade, 1700–1730," in *Riches from Atlantic Commerce: Dutch Transatlantic Trade and Shipping, 1585–1817*, ed. Johannes Postma and Victor Enthoven (Leiden: Brill, 2003), 219–257.

2. Humphrey E. Lamur, "Demographic Performance of Two Slave Populations of the Dutch Speaking Caribbean," in *Caribbean Slave Society and Economy: A Student Reader*, ed. Hilary Beckles and Verene Shepherd (Kingston: Ian Randle, 1991), 209–220, 216.

3. Renkema, *Het Curaçaose plantagebedrijf*, 123.

4. H. Hoetink, "Surinam and Curaçao," in *Neither Slave nor Free: The Freedmen of African Descent in the Slave Societies of the New World*, ed. David W. Cohen and Jack P. Greene (Baltimore: Johns Hopkins University Press, 1972), 59–83, 66.

5. Governor Jean Rodier and the Council of Curaçao to the WIC, Chamber of Amsterdam, December 14, 1767, and Governor Jean Rodier to the WIC, Curaçao, October 3, 1769, Nieuwe West-Indische Compagnie (NWIC) 318 and 319, NA.

6. Governor Jean Rodier to the WIC, Chamber of Amsterdam, Curaçao, January 10, 1775, NWIC 1166, fol. 17, NA; cf. J. de Veer and Michiel Römer to the WIC, Curaçao, May 1, 1786, NWIC 613, fol. 1034, NA.

7. The last documented slave ship reached Willemstad in 1775, although possibly another three hundred were landed there before 1795.

8. Renkema, *Het Curaçaose plantagebedrijf*, 119.

9. Ibid., 118.

10. Cf. John Thornton, *Africa and Africans in the Making of the Atlantic World, 1400–1680* (Cambridge: Cambridge University Press, 1992), 178; L. Virginia Gould, "Urban Slavery—Urban Freedom: The Manumission of Jacqueline Lemelle," in *More than Chattel: Black Women and Slavery in the Americas*, ed. David Barry Gaspar and Darlene Clark Hine (Bloomington: Indiana University Press, 1996), 298–314, 300, 302. For ethnic interaction in Curaçao see Linda M. Rupert, "Trading Globally, Speaking Locally: Curaçao's Sephardim in the Making of a Caribbean Creole," in *Jews and Port Cities, 1550–1990: Commerce, Community, and Cosmopolitanism*, ed. David Cesarani and Gemma Romain (London: Vallentine Mitchell, 2005), 109–122.

11. Albert Kikkert, "Economische toestand op Curaçao, Boanire en Aruba," in *Breekbare Banden: Feiten en visies over Aruba, Bonaire en Curaçao na de Vrede van Munster, 1648–1998*, ed. Maritza Coomans-Eustatia, Henny E. Coomans, and To van der Lee (Bloemendaal: Stichting Libri Antilliani, 1998), 164.

12. Interrogation of Samuel Levi Maduro, Puerto Cabello, September 6, 1730, Santa Domingo 781, Archivo General de Indias.

13. The year was 1758: NWIC 601, fol. 953, NA.

14. Wim Klooster, "Subordinate but Proud: Curaçao's free blacks and mulattoes in the eighteenth century," *New West Indian Guide* 68, nos. 3–4 (1994): 283–300, 285.

15. Field slaves made up one-fourth of the runaways. Ibid., table 1.

16. From 1730 to 1737 at least fifty-one Curaçaoan blacks and four mulattoes were seized off the Venezuelan coast by the Compañía Guipuzcoana. Oud Archief Curaçao 806, 622ff., NA.

17. Cornelis Ch. Goslinga, *The Dutch in the Caribbean and in the Guianas 1680–1791* (Assen, The Netherlands, and Dover, N.H.: Van Gorcum, 1985), 248.

18. Appendices to Governor Isaac Faesch to the WIC, Curaçao, April 15, 1752, NWIC 598, fols. 1053–1057, NA.

19. Undated memorandums of governor Isaac Faesch and disposition of Jan Hendriks, November 16, 1749, NWIC 597, fols. 66–90, NA.

20. Fiscal P.Th. van Teijlingen to the WIC. Curaçao, December 29, 1786, NWIC 614, fols. 2721–2723, NA.

21. Diedenhoven was indeed extremely wealthy. Eleven years later, he was still worth two hundred thousand pesos. A.A. Lutter, "De 25e penning op Curaçao anno 1797," *De Indische Navorscher* 5, no. 4 (1992): 161–164.

22. Goslinga, *Dutch in the Caribbean*, 246.

23. Gert Oostindie, *Roosenburg en Mon Bijou: Twee Surinaamse plantages, 1720–1870* (Dordrecht: Foris Publications, 1989), 168.

24. One in 494 females was manumitted in Suriname in 1826, and 1 in 1,004 males. Rosemary Brana-Shute, "The Manumission of Slaves in Suriname, 1760–1828" (Ph.D. diss., University of Florida, 1985), 223.

25. This was the sequence: 1844: 0.8%, 1845: 0.8%, 1846: 0.9%, 1847: 1.0%, 1848: 0.7%, 1849: 0.8%, 1850: 3.8%, 1851: 1.5%, 1852: 1.0%, 1853: 0.9%, and 1854: 1.1%. Calculated on the basis of T. van der Lee, *Curaçaose vrijbrieven 1722–1863: Met indices op namen van vrijgelatenen en hun voormalige eigenaren* (The Hague: Algemeen Rijksarchief, 1998), 396–449; and Renkema, *Het Curaçaose plantagebedrijf*, 118 (table 5.1, right column).

26. Van der Lee, *Curaçaose vrijbrieven*, 247 (September 27, 1791).

27. Ibid., 228 (July 28, 1786), 301 (November 21, 1800).

28. Claire Robertson, "Africa into the Americas? Slavery and Women, the Family, and the Gender Division of Labor," in *More than Chattel: Black Women and Slavery in the Americas*, ed. David Barry Gaspar and Darlene Clark Hine (Bloomington: Indiana University Press, 1996), 3–42, 24–25.

29. This was not uncommon; in colonial Sabará, Brazil, women paid a higher price than men. Kathleen J. Higgins, "Gender and the Manumission of Slaves in Colonial Brazil: The Prospects for Freedom in Sabará, Minas Gerais, 1710–1809," *Slavery and Abolition* 18 (1997): 1–29, 8.

30. List of slaves belonging to the citizens of Curaçao that fled to Coro or other places, Curaçao, July 7, 1775, NWIC 1166, fol. 124ff, NA.

31. David Eltis, *The Rise of African Slavery in the Americas* (Cambridge: Cambridge University Press, 2000), 81–82.

32. By contrast a Swiss traveler thought in 1782 that the Curaçaoan slaves were better fed and clad than slaves in the French and British colonies. Justin Girod-Chantrans, *Voyage d'un suisse dans différentes colonies d'Amérique pendant la dernière guerre* (Neuchatel: Société Typographique,1785), 99.

33. Isaac S. Emmanuel and Suzanne A. Emmanuel, *History of the Jews of the Netherlands Antilles*, 2 vols. (Cincinnati: American Jewish Archives, 1970), 1:64; Governor Jean Rodier to the Chamber of Amsterdam of the WIC, Curaçao, January 9, 1764, NWIC 604, fol. 425, NA.

34. Pieter Kock Jansz to the directors of the Middelburgse Commercie Compagnie, Curaçao, October 8, 1763, Middelburgse Commercie Compagnie, 56.2, 185, Archief Zeeland, Middelburg.

35. Mark Häberlein and Michaela Schmölz-Häberlein, *Die Erben der Welser: Der Karibikhandel der Augsburger Firma Obwexer im Zeitalter der Revolutionen,* Studien zur Geschichte des Bayerischen Schwabens, vol. 21 (Augsburg: Bernd Wissner, 1995), 55.

36. Governor Jean Rodier to the WIC, Chamber of Amsterdam, Curaçao, January 10, 1775, NWIC 1166, fol. 17, NA.

37. Obispo Mariano Martí, *Documentos relativos a su visita pastoral de la diócesis de Caracas (1771–1784): Providencias* (Caracas: Academia Nacional de la Historia, 1969), 62.

38. Cf. Lamur, "Demographic Performance," 217.

39. Deposition of Apero van der Houwen, commissioner of the slave trade, Curaçao, February 11, 1683, NWIC 617, fol. 261, NA; Coenraad de Termeijer to Joan Coijmans, Josua van Belle, Hendrick Staats, and Manuel Belmonte, Curaçao, April 18, 1687, in *Pertinent en Waarachtig Verhaal van alle de Handelingen en Directie van Pedro van Belle ontrent Den Slavenhandel, ofte, het Assiento de Negros, eerst door D. Juan Barosso y Posso, bij zijn overlijden door*

D. Nicolas Porsio, en daar na door Balthasar Coijmans met den Koning van Spangien aangegaan, zoo in Spangien, de West-Indijes, als op Curaçao: Dienende Tot onderrichtinge van alle die gene, die bij het voorsz. Assiento, ofte de Compagnie van Coijmans en Van Belle tot Cadix, eenigsints zouden mogen wezen geinteresseert (Rotterdam: Reinier Leers, 1689), Appendix, 59; Han Jordaan, "De veranderde situatie op de Curaçaose slavenmarkt en de mislukte slavenopstand op de plantage Santa Maria in 1716," in *Veranderend Curaçao: Collectie essays opgedragen aan Lionel Capriles ter gelegenheid van zijn 45–jarig jubileum bij de Maduro & Curiel Bank N.V.,* ed. Henny E. Coomans, Maritza Coomans-Eustatia, and Johan van 't Leven (Bloemendaal: Stichting Libri Antilliani, 1999), 473–501, 486–487; Commissioners of the Council of Curaçao, J. G. Pax and Nathaniel Ellis, to governor Isaac Faesch and Council, Curaçao, September 24, 1753, NWIC 599, fols. 912–913, NA.

40. Van der Lee, *Curaçaose vrijbrieven,* 291 (June 21, 1799), 282 (June 1, 1798), 214 (February 21, 1783).

41. Governor Jean Rodier to the WIC, Curaçao, August 14, 1770, NWIC 607, fols. 616–617, and July 22, 1771, NWIC 608, fols. 300–301, both in NA. In 1789 Curaçao had 31,401 sheep and 9,201 goats. Joh. Hartog, *Curaçao: Van kolonie tot autonomie* (Aruba: De Wit, 1961), 1:372.

42. Goslinga, *Dutch in the Caribbean,* 555.

43. T. van der Lee and J.Th. de Smidt, "Inleiding," in Van der Lee, *Curaçaose vrijbrieven,* 5–6.

44. Renkema, *Het Curaçaose plantagebedrijf,* 140.

45. Van der Lee, *Curaçaose vrijbrieven,* lists some cases of 1,000 pesos and more: 75 (December 3, 1750): 1,000 pesos; 154 (March 22, 1774): 1,100 pesos; 166 (January 16, 1776): 1,125 pesos; 199 (June 18, 1781): 1,236 pesos and 4 reales; 245 (May 28,1791): 1,100 pesos; and 263 (January 29, 1795): 1,000 pesos. With one exception, these manumissions concerned girls and women. No manumission prices were listed after 1811.

46. Renkema, *Het Curaçaose plantagebedrijf,* 132.

47. Van der Lee, *Curaçaose vrijbrieven,* 221, 121.

48. There was one notable exception. Van der Lee, *Curaçaose vrijbrieven,* 195 (January 30, 1781). In one instance a son paid for his mother. Ibid., 293 (September 11, 1799).

49. Ibid., 70 (February 7, 1749), 105 (July 17, 1758), 122 (November 16, 1764), 125 (August 5, 1765), 128 (April 22, 1766), 130 (August 21, 1767), 132 (February 15, 1768), 146 (March 31, 1772), 189 (March 23, 1780), 318–319 (December 9, 1803).

50. Ibid, 201 (August 23, 1781).

51. Ibid., 108 (August 29, 1759).

52. Ibid., 59 (May 25, 1747).

53. Ibid., 219/134 (August 28, 1783).

54. Ibid., 95 (July 22, 1756), 116 (December 12, 1760), 126 (August 26, 1765), 222 (March 1, 1785).

55. Ibid., 24 (August 14, 1742), 35 (October 16, 1742), 43 (September 15, 1744), 57 (April 29, 1747), 63 (December 14, 1747), 80 (May 4, 1752), 83 (January 16, 18, and 30, 1753), 84 (March 27 and 30, April 9 and 12, 1753), 85 (May 5 and 9, 1753), 86 (September 1 and 4, 1753), 87 (September 4 and 20, October 4, 1753), 93 (August 6, 1755).

56. J. H. J. Hamelberg, *De Nederlanders op de West-Indische eilanden* (1901; reprint, Amsterdam: S. Emmering, 1979), 178; Hoetink, "Surinam and Curaçao," 71. In 1719 there had been only 37 free blacks and 11 free mulattoes; in 1742, 400 and 140, respectively. NWIC 574, fol. 461, and NWIC 590, fols. 445–451, NA.

57. G. B. Bosch, *Reizen in West-Indië,* 2 vols. (1829–1836; reprint, Amsterdam: S. Emmering, 1985), 1:181.

58. Klooster, "Subordinate but Proud," 289.

59. Directors of the West India Company to Governor Joan Doncker, Amsterdam, November 13, 1676, NWIC 467, fol. 19, NA.

60. Gerret Specht, captain of the citizens, to the WIC, Curaçao, January 21, 1767, NWIC 318, NA.

61. Johan Rudolph Lauffer to the Comittee Regarding the Colonies and Possessions of the Batavian Republic in America and the Guinea Coast, Curaçao, August 21, 1797, West-Indisch Comité, NA. *Mustiezen* were the offspring of whites and mulattoes.

ROSEMARY BRANA-SHUTE

Sex and Gender in
Surinamese Manumissions

—ww—

In Suriname the majority of the slaves manumitted were female—regardless of
changes in economic, political, demographic, legal, and bureaucratic conditions. Historians accept that in American (New World) societies, a slave's
"lighter" phenotype, urban domicile, and ability to compensate an owner positively affected a slave's chances for manumission. However, although in many
American societies females were (as in Suriname) manumitted in much greater
numbers than males, about two females for every male, there has been little
attention paid to explaining this phenomenon. This essay is meant to encourage a discussion of the ways in which gender appears to have influenced patterns of manumission.

The manumission experience of female slaves, as a group, differed from that
of male slaves, just as other aspects of slavery did. Whereas slaves are often
referred to by skin color in studies of American slave societies, they are frequently referred to as "slaves," neutered, as if a slave's sex was of little importance. A deeper understanding of the practice of manumission can provide a
particularly useful way to view how gender intersects with race and other variables. The Suriname records show how manumission documentation can offer
more data on women, children, and slave families than we generally find available, particularly in Caribbean records. Manumission records can also throw
much needed light on relationships between free people and slaves, on how males
and female slaves differentially experienced slavery and interacted with free people, and on how a society's view of the different nature of males and of females
(gender) allowed either more or fewer opportunities for slaves, depending on
their sex and age as well as their color, skills, patrons, and other variables.[1]

After placing Suriname within the broader spectrum of New World
colonies, I summarize the legal basis for manumission in the eighteenth and
early nineteenth centuries. The broad patterns of manumission, and the important role of slaves, especially females, in attaining their own freedom is clear
but needs to be understood in light of two important developments of the
second half of the eighteenth century: the growth of the capital city of Paramaribo and the emergence of a prominent group of free "colored" and free

black residents.[2] Finally, I discuss why gender is an important component in understanding manumission.

THE COLONIAL CONTEXT

The focus in this essay is a 70-year period in the middle of the 196 years when Suriname was an Amsterdam-dominated, export-oriented plantation colony on the coast of northeastern South America. Exploiting enslaved African labor, in 1760 its economy was booming, with about five hundred large plantations exporting sugar, coffee, indigo, cacao, and hard woods. As such, Suriname much more closely resembled Barbados, Saint-Domingue, South Carolina, and Jamaica than it did the Dutch colonies of the Antilles.[3] The population of the colony is estimated at fifty thousand to fifty-eight thousand, with the free population (of all races) no more than 5 percent of the total in 1738 and 15 percent in 1830.

The distribution of that population changed over time. Whereas Paramaribo probably had fewer than fifty houses in the early eighteenth century, by midcentury the city was emerging as a handsome capital. By 1787 Paramaribo was home to 19 percent of the colony's inhabitants, a figure that rose to over 25 percent within fifteen years. By the end of slavery in 1863 more than one-third of the entire colonial population lived in this primary city. Concomitant with the growth of the town was the emergence of a free colored and free black population that by 1811, half a century before the end of slavery, already outnumbered the white population.

This shift in residential patterns reflected a growing decline of the plantation system beginning in the 1760s and accelerating by the 1790s. Moreover, almost the entire free "colored" (mixed race) and free black population resided in Paramaribo, the majority of whom were most probably women and creole (locally born) children. In contrast, until the nineteenth century the plantations were overwhelmingly male, adult, and African. As planters moved to spend more and more time in town after 1760, it appears that many of the slaves they brought with them were creole (locally born) and/or female slaves, intensifying the trend of a greater density of Europeans, women, children, and free people of color in Paramaribo than in rural areas.

MANUMISSION AND THE LAW

It was not until 1733, sixty-six years after the Dutch conquered Suriname, that the planters' own elected, representative body, the Court of Policy and Criminal Justice, decided to forbid the customarily private practice of freeing slaves. This new legislation laid the foundation for the state's regulation of manumission.[4] The court declared that no slaves would be considered legally free without a guarantee that the manumitted person would never resort to public charity. Permission to manumit would not be forthcoming unless that future self-sufficiency was guaranteed by the manumitters and supported by a financial pledge or bond, a requirement that was increasingly enforced over the years. Owners were legally obliged to educate the manumitted in Christianity (although there is little evidence that this was ever enforced, or undertaken voluntarily, before the 1830s). For their part, manumitted people had to continue to "respect" their former owners and provide financial support for them if they became destitute. And they were allowed to marry or cohabit "among themselves or with others," but definitely not with "persons who are in slavery," a particularly onerous provision that was frequently disobeyed. Mates, or spouses in a conjugal although not legal sense, appear in the manumission records, evidence that common-law marriage ties were maintained in spite of provisions designed to separate the manumitted from the enslaved.[5]

Why the court issued this decree in 1733 is unclear, although it is clear that this legislation was intended to control both the manumitters and the emerging manumitted—though a very small group. Also clear is that the court wanted to ensure that the colonial treasury would never have to expend a florin on any of the manumitted, making the manumitted the only people in the colony's history who were forbidden to become poor and needing of charity. The court was interested in compliance (order) from all residents, whatever their color and sex. In that it made no distinctions. It is important to note, however, that almost all the provisions of the legislation are aimed at the owner, who had to apply to the court for the legal recognition of a slave's change from slave to free status. Without that permission, the manumission would remain illegal, and the would-be manumitted subject to confiscation by the government.

The direction of manumission legislation did not change until fifty-five years later, when dramatically, in 1788, the court decided manumission was an eminently taxable transaction. With the introduction of the tax came the first legal distinction between male and female slaves, as the rates were based on age and sex. Slave men over the age of fourteen were to pay one hundred florins; women and all children under the age of fourteen were levied fifty florins for their letters of manumission.[6] Male slaves who could not pay the newly required tax could choose to serve in the militia for three years without pay. No similar provision of labor in lieu of money was available to women and children.

In 1804 the sex-based differential in manumission taxes for males and females was ended when the court increased the taxes for both adult males and females to a uniform five hundred pounds, an increase of 500 percent for males and 1,000 percent for females.[7] The court councillors knew that they could collect these heavy taxes, as many slaves and free residents valued manumission and would continue to pay the higher costs for letters of freedom. Although legally always more comfortable grouping women, children and other "minors" together, adult women (aged fourteen and over) were removed, for tax reasons only, from the category of children.

MANUMISSION PETITIONS AS SOURCES

The printed primary and secondary sources on Suriname are almost totally silent about both manumission and those topics crucial to understanding manumission: the growth of the urban sector; free blacks and free coloreds, and children. The only printed primary sources are the collected decrees (*plakaten*) issued by the planter-elected Court of Policy and Criminal Justice on a wide range of issues, including manumission. From the first manumission decree (1733) regulating manumission until the end of slavery itself in 1863, any free resident of the colony who wished to manumit a slave legally was required to petition the Court of Policy and Criminal Justice (Hof van Politie en Crimineele Justitie). These letters of petition (*requesten*), local and personal in quality and origin, only needed to satisfy the court that all the legal conditions had been met. This is a boon for historians, as most of these petitions have survived, centralized in the correspondence received and registered by the secretary of the court (and not scattered in church registered and private wills). Moreover, the petitions are letters which provided more information than the court needed, leaving a body of evidence about the legal, social, and economic aspects of manumission that affected individuals, families, and estates.

An initial systematic sample (one in every three years) yielded 943 petitions within which were requests for 1,346 slaves, a sample size estimated to include at least a third of all manumissions in Suriname between 1760 and 1826.[8] The statistical figures cited here are based on that sample. (My own records now include almost every case of manumission, about 4,000, covering 1740 to 1830. A few initial years are closed to researchers, but probably total no more than 20 petitions). The broad patterns of manumission (numbers over time, duration of process, court decisions, age groups, color, sex, occupation, etc.) were analyzed as appropriate. Details about slave and free families, including the names of everyone involved, were collected, and wherever possible these names have been traced and linked over time in a variety of records in order to understand the social relationships that ultimately led to manumissions.

The petitions make clear that manumission was not just a legal event but a social process. As manumissions were not distributed randomly among the slave population, the researcher has to ask why particular slaves were "chosen" to be freed. Understanding that a legal manumission was the consequence of an owner agreeing to allow a slave to become free, the question is, how did this decision come to be taken? What was unique about a particular slave and/or a particular owner that permitted this manumission? The questions themselves suggest that counting the numbers (frequencies) of manumission is unlikely to yield an adequate explanation, particularly as statistical data are based on only select information and are likely to describe trends over time without necessarily explaining why changes occur. This suggests that we need to explore what happened before the actual legal act of manumission freed a slave. In other words manumission may be better understood if approached as a process which developed slowly in the interstices of daily life where blacks and whites, free and slave, rich and poor, male and female came into personal contact, a social process of creating relationships that could lead to a legal escape from slavery to freedom. Seen in this light the actual legal change in social status from enslaved to free is a legal event, countable but not understandable without knowledge of what transpired between slaves and owners. Moreover, it becomes clear that although the court had the last word on manumissions, it rarely denied a petition. The real problem for slaves was getting owners to agree to a manumission in the first place, before a petition was ever even penned.

The value of the petitions (before fill-in-the-blank application forms were designed in the early nineteenth century) is that they recount how this individualization occurred and the nature of the interactions and negotiations that preceded manumissions. Slaves, not owners, emerge as perhaps the most resourceful and dynamic agents in the process, not as solitary, passive entities accepting freedom when and if it was bestowed. Just because most of the petitions were written by white notaries and lawyers, one should not assume that owners were the active parties or even the initiators of the process. Many petitions detail the roles played by slaves in the personal world of the owners, demonstrating that the slave was both an active and interactive individual and clearly a contributor toward his or her own freedom, and that of enslaved kin. A study of manumission petitions suggests a prerequisite to all manumissions: the individualization of the slave. So long as a slave was perceived by an owner as just a slave and not as an individual (however unequal in status), there would be no manumission. The mechanisms varied by which this individualization occurred; kinship and/or personal and intimate contacts on a regular and usually protracted basis between slave and owner were the most common conditions to move owners to manumit. I return to this later to suggest how and why women were often better able to facilitate this "individualization."

ACTUAL MANUMISSION PATTERNS

The actual trend for manumissions was very different from what might have been anticipated. The more stringent the laws became, the greater the number of slaves were in fact freed. Moreover, a summary of actual decisions rendered by the court in response to petitions submitted by private citizens during the period 1760 to 1826 supports the notion that the legal event was anticlimactic. Table 1 shows the number of slaves for whom petitions were submitted. The court granted freedom outright to over 99 percent of slaves nominated for manumission and denied only five slaves (less than 0.5%) their freedom during the twenty-three sample years.[9] This suggests that the process whereby slaves were found worthy for freedom did not take place at court. Instead, the decision to manumit was made between owner and slave before pen was ever put to paper to petition the court. The very low incidence of denials by the court should not camouflage the real impediments to manumission which made the chances of ever having a request submitted in one's behalf very poor in the first place. Between 1760 and 1827 legal manumissions freed on average less than 1 percent of the slave population.

Table 1 also illustrates that there were four years in which the number of slaves to be manumitted as a result of petitions was extraordinarily high: 1787, 1802, 1808, and 1827. What these years illustrate is that many slaves were living "as free" illegally or were in arrangements with their owners that included some agreement that they were (quasi-)free. What happened in these years was that the court announced it was either initiating or raising taxes on each manumission. Once announced, owners and their agents scrambled to submit petitions. The large number of manumission requests reflect postponed manumissions that were flushed out in reaction to impending radical changes in the colonial administration. The year 1787 was the last chance for those who wished to manumit slaves, including slaves interested in purchasing their freedom, before the transaction was taxed for the first time. The years 1802 and 1808 were similarly uncertain for potential manumitters and slaves: Much higher taxes were to be collected in 1803. In 1808 owners perhaps feared that the British-imposed abolition of the slave trade to Suriname would lead the court to prohibit manumissions in order to ensure planters replacement slaves (which never did happen). In the 1820s the government moved to close loopholes in law enforcement and tax collections, and in 1827 there was a virtual stampede to manumit before the new law forbidding the manumission of "slaves [living] without masters" became effective. These peaks are evidence that manumissions were hurried when greater barriers to freedom loomed.

Given the increased financial and legal burdens involved in manumitting a slave, which were substantial, it is clear that only very determined, and adequately financed, individuals would free slaves. This includes slaves themselves, who worked to buy their own freedom where possible and to find free people who would act in their behalf to facilitate a manumission.

PROFILE OF MANUMITTED SLAVES

The sex and color of slaves were the only indelible and immutable external characteristics they possessed, and they are the characteristics most consistently noted in the petitions. Of the 1,340 slaves in the sample whose sex is known, 837, or 62.5 percent, were female. Table 2 illustrates a strong and persistent pattern that females were favored for manumission over males during the twenty-three years sampled.[10] This finding is consistent with other studies of American slave societies. Herbert S. Klein's recent survey of New World slavery noted that "all recent studies have found that approximately two-thirds of the manumitted were women (from 60–67%)."[11]

The majority of females in the petition process is more striking than at first glance might indicate: "Until 1735, more than 70% of the total [slave] imports to Suriname were male. . . . Even after the planters began more seriously to encourage breeding as a replacement strategy in the period after 1735, the proportion of female imports did not rise above 40%."[12] In 1830 the first year for which published population figures are available that differentiate by sex, 48.6 percent of the slave population of 48,784 were female.[13] If the population was similar in 1826, the closest year for which there is full manumission data, then each female manumitted in 1826 represented 1 in 494 female slaves; each male freed in the same year represented 1 in 1,004 male slaves. The odds favoring females in the manumission process would have been even greater in the earlier years when the sexual balance was more disproportionately male. Also, many of these males were children, not adult males who negotiated their own manumissions.

Of the 1,231 slaves for whom color is known, almost 40 percent were black or of purely African ancestry. On the other hand, about 60 percent of the slaves in the sample were of mixed race, almost 54 percent of whom were mulattos, clearly indicating that those whose ancestry included some European admixture were favored over blacks. How much so is evident when we compare these figures with the percentage of slaves of mixed ancestry in the total slave population. In 1805 colored slaves constituted 2.6 percent of the slave population, while in 1830 they constituted 6.6 percent of that total.[14] Whereas coloreds constituted about 60 percent of all manumitted slaves during the 1760–1836 period, they were most likely never more than 7 percent of the slave population. Nonetheless, the majority of slaves of mixed race were never manumitted.

Color was clearly a strong predictor of which slave was more likely to be freed, but the data in table 2, categorizing the manumitted by color and gender, indicate that the sex of a slave made a difference: Colored males were favored for freedom over colored females, but black females had the edge over black males. On the face of it, a slave's color appears to have been a more important factor than his or her sex. However, it is not a single variable but a cluster of traits that is crucial. In this case, sex, color, age, and kinship should be the cluster we look at, mainly because the petitions suggest that most of the colored slaves manumitted were children of both sexes, many too young to negotiate their own freedom.[15]

In order to consider the extent to which being female (or male) was (dis)advantageous in negotiating a manumission, we need to know the age (group) to which a slave belonged, and the nature of his or her relationship of the owner and to the other slaves manumitted on the same petition. Unfortunately, the manumission requests from Suriname are poor sources for the specific ages of slaves advanced for manumission. Some of this missing data is currently being constructed from other sources, so that finer calculations may be possible at a future date and that an explanation advanced to explain the social factors behind the different patterns of manumission for males and females of varying color.

Meanwhile, age categories were constructed from social and economic indicators found in the petitions (such as motherhood and occupation) for 76.7 percent (1,032) of the slaves. The evidence suggests that very old slaves were rarely manumitted, probably because owners would have had to guarantee their support in addition to paying taxes. The overwhelming majority of those freed were children and young adults (76.7% of the 1,032 for whom we can assign an age category).[16] This indicates that owners were freeing slaves of an age when their economic productivity would have been greatest, and when the owner was also paying a higher fee to the court. If economic considerations were uppermost in the minds of owners, it seems likely that an owner would have freed a slave before or after that slave reached a productive age. The petitions suggest that other motives, discussed below, were more important.

I would suggest that one aspect of color that is often undiscussed is that mixed racial ancestry also suggests a greater likelihood that the slave is a creole. Of the 1,346 slaves who appeared on the petitions, 60.1 percent were racially mixed, so we may assume that most if not all were creoles. This is not surprising, as those born and/or raised and socialized locally would presumably have learned the preferred codes of deference, the local creole language, possibly Dutch or another European language widely spoken in the colony, and other social and economic skills that would have facilitated getting the positive attention of local free people. Newly imported ("saltwater") adult slaves would have been less deft linguistically and socially in European(ized) households, especially in town, and therefore less able to initiate or sustain and develop the kinds of long term personal relationships with free people that might be parlayed into successful negotiations for freedom.

Of the total 1,346 slaves in the manumission petitions, only 256 (19%) were cited as coming from plantations, although the numbers of slaves who had some experience with plantation life is probably much higher. In Suriname slaves generally were considered to be part of a plantation's moveable property, and early in the colony's history the practice had evolved to leave slaves with plantations when the estates were sold (similar to serfs on medieval estates). For at least the first hundred years of the plantation colony, it was also common practice that slave families not be separated or sold apart, although how family was defined is open to controversy.[17]

At least 135 of the 256 slaves we know came from plantations were freed with family members. Ninety-six of those 135 were members of two-generational family units (almost all mothers with children), and an additional 11 were part of three-generational families (grandmother, daughter, and her children), all being freed together. The remaining 28 were freed in one-generational kin groups of two to five siblings per group. Even among the 121 slaves who were freed without kinsmen, one notices frequent references to a kinsman who was already free. Kinship, especially the mother-child bond, was repeatedly noted, perhaps an indication that plantation owners and administrators were still cognizant of the need to minimize the separating of families.

Slaves were often moved to and from Paramaribo to deliver cargo, work on fortifications, learn a skill, or accompany owners as household servants. As planters grew more conscious, in the last quarter of the eighteenth century, in particular, of the difficulty of reproducing the slave population naturally, enslaved pregnant women were increasingly moved to town where they could be more closely monitored until they gave birth, a sex-related public policy if ever there was one.[18] Although the impending delivery made these women potentially more valuable to the owner, the urban context provided opportunities, particularly social ones, that could facilitate a manumission. Important here would be the increased opportunities to meet free people of all colors (potential patrons) and learn the political ropes of town life (such as the function of lawyers). The opportunities to work as domestic servants, street hawkers, and skilled and semiskilled labor to be hired out also were greater in town than in rural areas. This movement of pregnant women also increased the concentration of women in the city. Almost none of the slaves who purchased their own freedom came from plantations, according to the petitions, so being in town was an important advance step to freedom.

Darker slaves had a better chance at manumission in the urban area; conversely, lighter color increased one's chances for freedom more in plantation areas than it did in town.[19] Black males had a particularly poor chance of manumission in the plantation area; more than nine black females were freed for every one black male there, whereas only 2.1 females were freed in town for each black male. Explaining this pattern necessitates a certain amount of speculation. The key to the manumission of the majority of plantation slaves was kinship. A majority of slaves were freed in groups with (some of) their kin. A number of others were freed alone as individuals, but by kin who were already free. Of those freed with kin, a clear pattern emerges of mothers freed with their children, almost all with mothers darker than their children. As might be anticipated a larger number of their owners identified themselves as plantation directors or administrators who purchased these particular people from an estate with the specific intent to free them. This does not prove their paternity, although most of these owners were probably white males, and the children of the women freed were almost all lighter than their mothers. Within this pattern there is little room for black males—unless they were the children of a woman being freed.

THE CHANGING PROFILE OF THE MANUMITTERS

Many New World slave studies have noted that frequently the manumitted were women and children, and that lighter phenotypes were favored over those who were black. Almost all such studies cite examples of white fathers freeing their colored children, often implying, intentionally or otherwise, that manumission was a white man's reward for sexual favors granted him by a black woman. That implication of sex-for-manumission has retarded an understanding of manumission, if unintentionally; sexuality muddied the waters of interpretation. Was manumission a form of prostitution that had to be condemned, ignored in embarrassment, or explained away as a necessary evil produced by the existence of slavery?

The first problem in dealing with this scenario is the assumption that a white man having sex with a black or colored enslaved woman was so extraordinary as to induce him to manumit her in gratitude. There is no reason to assume that sexual intimacy was such a rare and idealized prize in Suriname, or in Europe or anywhere in the Atlantic world in the late eighteenth and early nineteenth century that a male property owner would return the favor by (1) freeing that slave woman from all future labor for (and sexual intimacy with) him, (2) relinquishing the right to sell her for her market value, and (3) incurring very large legal costs in pursuing her legal manumission.

Moreover, the sheer power of owners over all slaves' bodies—their property—was intensified by the customary right of owners to use their female property sexually as they wished. After all, it was the manumitted who were proscribed in law from consorting with slaves (on pain of flogging and reenslavement); similar laws were never issued to restrain male owners who could and did use their female slaves as they wished. Colonial laws regulated the physical abuse of slaves with the whip, not sex. In any case male sexual behavior (provided it was not homosexual) was not regulated as was female behavior. Sexual relations with black or colored women who were slaves was, to most whites, a question of sex with females of no public respectability. White males were in the "regrettable" position of having a need for whom no "suitable" white women were available as a preferred alternative.[20] If fault was attached, it was to "circumstances" or sex ratios out of their control. As such the law would neither punish white males for (ab)using their class and racial power over female slaves, nor protect females of a degraded caste or sex. Gratitude by white men was never required. Power relations between owners and slaves were such as to necessitate no repayment ever, whether or not sexual relations occurred willingly.

A second problem with citing manumission as the reward for sexual intimacy was the existence of many colored slaves who were never freed, the consequence of the disinterest or inability of fathers to manumit. In fact, it appears that even those of mixed race who were freed were always a small minority of those who remained in slavery.

However, another way to approach the issue is to note the propensity of authors to imply or assume that the manumitters were in fact white males. A study of the manumission petitions in Suriname, however, indicates that one of the major changes to occur during the 1760–1826 period is that white males were an increasing minority as manumitters.[21] Whereas almost all owners in the early years of the sample were white males, by the early nineteenth century the majority of owners were female (of all colors) and colored and black freedmen. The belief that manumissions were essentially the humane acts of white men freeing their mistresses and/or their colored offspring distorts the reality. The documentation suggests that this image of white male manumitters has camouflaged the increasing importance of both females and freedmen as manumitters in many places besides Suriname. It may also emerge that the image of manumission as white male noblesse oblige may have been an intentional whitewashing, and romanticizing, of sexual behavior that would have been otherwise increasingly inexcusable to informed Europeans in the metropole, particularly as the issue of abolition evolved into a public discourse to which both men and women were privy.[22]

What is particularly interesting to consider is that despite the changes over time in the sex and race of owners, the pattern of a high percentage of women freed continued, even with female owners. This suggests we need to rethink the motivations of owners, among other factors, to understand why owners as a group favored females for manumission.[23]

MOTIVATIONS FOR MANUMITTING

Historians have used two approaches to determine why some slaves were manumitted. The first relies on what manumitters themselves stated as their motives, and the second deduces general macro-patterns from demographic and economic profiles in order to establish or strongly suggest both motives of owners and profiles of slaves who were manumitted. A combination of the two approaches, however, can suggest underlying relationships and motives that may not be immediately obvious.

As historians have moved away from the juridical and cultural argument of Frank Tannenbaum,[24] they have come increasingly to minimize the importance of affection, humaneness, and gratitude as prime movers in facilitating manumissions. In contrast, historians increasingly explain manumissions in terms of economic self-interest. As a result, the stated motives of slave owners have been only briefly addressed, as if they were of minor consideration or so biased as to make acceptance of those motives impossible. For example, when writers noted that an owner had claimed he or she was freeing a slave because of a Christian duty, they often have been able to cite that the owner also received payment for that same slave's freedom. The impression left is that owners were self-serving and therefore unreliable in their own self-assessments. Similarly, a stated motive that freedom was being extended in grateful recompense for long service has been often discounted by historians as self-serving and hypocritical, if not false. The seeming inconsistencies should not be resolved necessarily in favor of one or other rationale. An owner cruel to most of his slaves could still free some; accepting payment does not disqualify the important act of permitting a manumission in the first place.

The words "affection" and "gratitude" as reasons for manumitting a slave—almost always a female—were real, although these terms should be used with caution and circumspection. It is clear from numerous archival sources, such as the journals of the governors, wills, and the petitions themselves, that even white masters recognized profound human qualities in their "chattel." Slaves were recognized as being part of and having families. Individual slaves were recognized for their skills and talents, both mechanical and emotional. Recognizing these human, individual qualities toppled neither the legal matrix nor colonial customs built on human slavery. It is a condition of inconsistency that most lived with and rationalized, if unconsciously. Slaves had no rights as a result of any affection, gratitude, or esteem an owner might develop. Manumission was a privilege of the owner to withhold or bestow, never the right of the slave to claim.

Many cases suggest that some owners were dependent on the very slaves they were freeing. The willingness to manumit a slave from his or her "birthright" may well have derived from an owner's feelings of affection, but the conditions masters occasionally (but rarely) tried to impose on that freedom indicate that owners were afraid they would be abandoned by those they were freeing. In one case an owner apparently was still afraid that his slave would leave him once he freed her, even after thirty loyal years in his service and her promise to stay with him. (Think of the interdependencies of thirty years together.) In all the cases where owners tried to limit future freedom, usually by conditioning the manumission with a requirement that the slave continue to live with the owner, every one indicated a close relationship between the owner and the slave, a relationship that was interdependent and cooperative, even if unequal. Almost all of these cases involved slaves, both male and female, who were directly involved in the personal or intimate aspects of the owner's life as a nurse, housekeeper, personal servant, companion to the owner's children, or co-worker.

The most frequently cited reason for initiating a manumission was the owner's statement that he or she wished to reward a slave for trustworthy service and because the owner felt an affection for that particular slave. For whatever reason, in 1808 Hecquet de Berranger manumitted the black woman Regine because "of love for her, I wish to give her freedom."[25] When Harmanus Cordova chose to free his black female slave Cerie in 1760, he noted that she had worked loyally not only for him but for his parents, and that she had nursed them and him during serious illnesses. He approached the court to grant her freedom "out of her slavery and birthright."[26] A simple and straightforward petition, Cordova's reasons are replicated in the other petitions that state recompense for trustworthy service.

The nature of the services performed by these slaves all appear to have been personal and even intimate, although not all sexual. What emerges from the records is a pattern of affection for and dependence on those slaves who nursed owners and their kinfolk through serious illnesses. For the black Cecelia and the mulatto Jeanneton, Jacobus Saffin requested freedom and volunteered to pay all the necessary court costs and to continue to support both women, not only for loyal service but also for the exceptional care they gave to his wife in her final illness. In addition to that nursing, after his wife's death these two slaves had managed his household and taken care of his three motherless children. He decided to free them, both in gratitude to them and "to the encouragement of his other slaves."[27]

The second most frequently stated motive for a manumission was self-purchase, although this is likely to be an under reported occurrence. Of the 310 slaves freed for whom motives were stated, 89 were freed because they bought themselves from their owners. Of these 89 slaves, 58 were female and 31 were male, almost a perfect representation of each sex's appearance in the entire manumission sample, although males were rarely freed for this reason before the nineteenth century. Self-purchase was also a mechanism used by free coloreds and free blacks to reunite some of their kin, although only if owners cooperated. Self-purchase was and is commonly defined as a slave paying an owner in cash or in kind for his or her freedom. There were other forms of self-purchase, however. Surely the long and "loyal" years of personal and domestic service provided by many of the manumitted, most of them women, also should be considered as payment. This is not being sentimental. Recognizing the effort slaves put into getting owners to develop some fondness and care for them was a full-time, long-term proposition without guaranteed results, and there is no need to grant manumitters more credit than is due them.

Of the archival sample of 1,346 slaves, fully 1,143, or 85 percent, were freed during the lifetime of their owners, indicating that most owners chose to directly assist in the freeing of slaves while they were still alive and could have continued to enjoy their services. In fact, the use of a testament to free a slave decreased over time, while self-purchase and freeing slaves during the lifetime of the owner increased. Interestingly, those who used wills were increasingly free coloreds and free blacks. This was a wise move on their part, as it precluded the involvement of the state and creditors deciding who got whatever estate there was. For many of those free coloreds and free blacks, their estates were used to buy kinsmen from others and then to free them or used to free their own mothers, sons, daughters, grandchildren, and other relatives who were still slaves and property of the deceased's estate.

The reason given for 67 manumissions was that the slave was related by kinship to the owner. Of these, 64 were consanguineous ties, while 3 were mothers of the owners' children. These archival data indicate that only 7 of the 67 slaves related to their owners were freed by white males who acknowledged their paternity; the remaining 60 were freed by colored and black kinsmen and women. Only 7 slaves were freed by a total of 5 white men who acknowledged their paternity.[28] Although this is probably a great underestimate of paternity, it is likely that fewer than 300 slaves out of 1,346 could have been the children of the white owners manumitting them.

There is another way to understand kinship besides a direct bond between owner and slave, and that is recognition on the part of owners (of all colors) that individual slaves were members of families. In the cases of over 53 percent of the 1,346 slaves freed, other family members were also mentioned. The importance of manumission in reconstituting families outside of slavery is probably one of the least appreciated aspects of the process. The pervasive references to family—and the stories recounted in the petitions themselves—clearly demonstrate that reconstituting families was a major motivation for manumitting a slave, particularly among free coloreds and free blacks. In part this also explains why they were buying slaves: Some were family members. Even if never freed, kin owned by their relatives were secure from that pervasive fear of being sold away from family. Sometimes a former owner was able to forward that goal. The freedwoman Maria van Sebastiaan Pelserius inherited her brother and sister from her late former master. The freedman Frederik Ulrici inherited his mother from the late J. F. Ulrici in 1780. In 1799 he finally applied for her letter of freedom because of "sentiments of gratitude for all the efforts and care of this black woman, his mother."[29] In many cases reunion was only possible when one free colored or free black was able to purchase kinsmen and perhaps then manumit them. There must have been tremendous tension between wanting to legally manumit and permanently secure a kinsman's future on the one hand and to save the manumission costs for another kinsman or loved one, or even for the costs of living, on the other hand.

The importance of gender also emerges from a closer look at manumission in Suriname. Nearly all studies of New World slavery have noted the preponderance of females among the manumittees, but the next conclusion has rarely been drawn: Manumission is largely a gender-related phenomenon. Females were freed in much greater number than males, and this generally was the case elsewhere in the circum-Caribbean and Latin America.[30] Females were perceived as less threatening, and their access to free people was often eased by the fact they were women. To handle laundry, infants and young children, sustained nursing of the young, old and infirm, kitchen chores and food preparation, and other activities that belong largely to the private and domestic "women's" sphere, females were favored overwhelmingly to males. Here one sees most clearly that a perception of what is appropriate to a sex ("naturally") prepares the path for the role a person would be most likely to play. None of this negates the evidence that women poisoned and robbed owners, committed arson, ran away, or otherwise begrudged owners their dominance. The pattern is clear, and that should suggest the gender needs the attention in future slave studies that people gave it in life.

GENDER AND STATE-INITIATED MANUMISSIONS

There is one major exception to the predominance of females in the manumission records, and it occurred outside of the normal process of private petitions. Nonetheless, it supports the importance of considering gender in acquiring freedom. The court did employ its power to impose manumissions when owners themselves did not wish to free slaves. The circumstances that dictated this rare event arose with a resurgence of maroon attacks in 1765. To deal with the emergency the court took the unusual step in 1772 of authorizing the purchase of an initial contingent of some three hundred skilled, healthy, and trustworthy male slaves to assist local citizen militias. Some of the slaves were purchased on the slave market and from urban slaveholders, most from plantations. These men were organized under white volunteer officers into a new military unit, the Korps Zwarte Jagers (Corps of Black Hunters). In return for faithful service they were promised their freedom and a plot of land on the edge of Paramaribo.[31] This appears to have been by far the largest number of slaves freed in any year since the colony's establishment, making the court the most important manumitter in Suriname, a somewhat ironic circumstance in the face of the court's increasing restrictions on manumissions.[32] These manumissions did not follow normal (petition) procedures through private individuals and were not a feature of the entire period under study. The case of the Black Hunters only underscores the importance of gender, however, as those men were chosen first and foremost because of a preconceived sex role: Only men could fight. When it came to questions of defense and soldiering, males had the edge in being manumitted; when it came to personal and domestic access and relationships, women were favored. Where whites were forced to turn to their slaves to protect their colonial investments by arming slaves to aid them against enemies and domestic maroons, male slaves were liberated—because they were males and only males were considered ("naturally") for military duties.

Even a consideration of the males freed by the regular petition process bears this out. Of these 503 males, the majority (269) were described as the "child of" a particular woman, as if an appendage of the woman named. For most if not all of these 269, a major factor for these males being manumitted was the mother who bore them, and the costs many of these mothers paid for their freedom. It was her ability to get the owner to agree to a manumission that was singularly important.

CONCLUSIONS

Women constituted the large majority of those freed. That should not be surprising, but the reason seems to be not so much a question of sex as of gender. Although black and even colored slave women worked in the fields along with men, when it came to running a household it was almost always a woman, whether in town or on a plantation. Europeans generally saw domestic duties (other than pater familias), especially food preparation and child care, as appropriate for women. This is a view that was probably in conformity with general perceptions that may have been retained from West Africa. Often (perceived as) more vulnerable and dependent, especially if they had young children, females (and/like children) were relegated to roles within the personal or domestic sphere where owners and slaves came into more regular and personal contact, which in turn provided opportunities for social maneuvering that could become the basis for a manumission.

Finally, it may be worth considering whether a preoccupation with race and (bad) race relations in slave studies has not helped to divert attention from other social divisions such as gender within American societies (a division, I suspect, that slavery intensified). Likewise, the emphasis on antipathy between groups of different phenotypes (white vs. colored vs. black) has camouflaged a reality for many slaves and freed people: multiracial and multishaded families and kin groups. If a mother was black and her children mulatto, does it increase our understanding to separate them by color as if they were antithetical and unrelated? Multiracial (and in Suriname, multireligious and multiethnic) families and households became increasingly common, certainly in town, during the period of slavery. Women appear central to this development, and manumission records can provide an entry into the complexity of these relationships and family realities.

TABLE I. Total number of slaves for whom manumission requests were decided by the court, by year

Year	Number of slaves	Number of requests
1760	22	10
1763	7	5
1766	39	25
1769	32	21
1772	31	15
1775	50	22
1778	20	11
1781	52	34
1784	51	31
1787	88	61
1790	37	26
1793	37	25
1796	62	39
1799	127	99
1802	161	120
1805	46	29
1808	91	71
1809	93	64
1811	76	59
1813	68	51
1814	54	38
1815	64	46
1817	52	40
1818	41	38
1819	70	51
1820	77	62
1821	52	44
1822	53	46
1823	61	48
1824	57	52
1825	85	66
1826	73	52
1827	373	269
1828	13	10
Total	2,315	1,680

Source: Hof van Politie, Requesten.

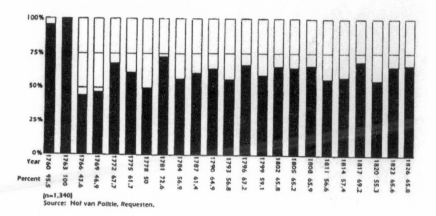

Source: Hof van Politie, Requesten.

FIG. 1. Slaves for Whom Manumission Was Adjudicated: Percentage of Females by Year

TABLE 2. Gender and color of slaves manumitted, 1760–1826

	Male (%)	Female (%)	(M:F)
Black	146 (11.9)	341 (27.8)	1:2.3
Karboeger	30 (2.41)	49 (4.0)	1:1.6
Mulat	201 (16.4)	282 (23.0)	1:1.4
Mesties	68 (5.5)	94 (7.7)	1:1.4
Kasties	11 (0.9)	3 (0.2)	3.7:1
Indian	0 (0.0)	4 (0.3)	0:4
Total	456 (37.1)	773 (63.0)	

Source: Hof van Politie, Requesten.

Note: N = 1,229. Total percentage is over 100 because of rounding to one decimal place.

NOTES

1. There is a new and rapidly growing literature on New World slavery, especially studies on women, that explores this difference, although gender and manumission are still understudied. Among the newest publications is *More than Chattel: Black Women and Slavery in the Americas*, ed. David Barry Gaspar and Darlene Clark Hine (Bloomington: Indiana University Press, 1996), which includes one article on manumission by L. Virginia Gould, "Urban Slavery— Urban Freedom: the Manumission of Jacqueline Lemelle," and an introductory essay on gender by Claire Robertson, "Africa into the Americas: Slavery and Women, the Family and the Gender Division of Labor." This volume has the best bibliography available to date, except for the Dutch colonies that are not represented.

2. The term "colored" is used here as it appears in the primary sources (*kleurling*), referring to people of mixed racial ancestry. The term "mulatto" is more specific, referring to ancestry that is specifically half-European and half-African. "Colored," however, can refer to any degree of racial mixture.

3. The neighboring Guiana riverine colonies of Demerara, Essequibo, and Berbice, which today make up Guyana, were also Dutch plantation colonies until 1815.

4. The court determined that "the frequent manumission of slaves and mulattos" generated a problem that required regulation. What the court meant by "frequent" is unclear. Koulen notes that in 1738 there were only 598 free coloreds and free blacks, about 1 percent of an estimated slave population of 50,000–55,000. However, these 598 were already almost 22 percent of the total free population of the colony, including whites. Paul Koulen, "Schets van de Historische Ontwikkeling van de Manumissie in Suriname, 1733–1863," unpublished Kandidaatsskriptie geschiedenis, Universiteir van amsterdam, 1972, 1, 7n. Given the small number of free nonwhites, and that the large majority was probably women and children, white fears of this group would seem exaggerated.

5. The early laws of Suriname have been compiled in *West Indisch Plakaatboek: Plataten, Ordonnantien en Andere Wetten, Uitgevaardigd in Suriname, 1667–1816*, 2 vols., ed. J. A. Schiltkamp and J.Th. de Smit (Amsterdam: S. Emmering, 1973) (hereafter cited as *Plakaatboek*).

6. *Plakaatboek* 2:892 (February 11/28, 1788).

7. *Plakaatboek* 2:977 (July 11, 1804). For all children under the age of fourteen the sum was raised to £250, an increase of 500 percent.

8. In order to satisfy both an interest in the quantitative and qualitative patterns and subtleties involved in the manumission process, it was decided to sample by year. The first year chosen at random was 1796. Thereafter, every third year was chosen as a sample year, working through the years before and after 1796 until the archival evidence became unavailable. All cases of manumission decided in the samples years were studied. For a full explanation of the sampling methodology used, see Rosemary Brana-Shute, "The Manumission of Slaves in Suriname, 1760–1828" (Ph.D. diss., University of Florida, 1985), 19–34. The original sample is currently being expanded to include all cases of manumission from 1760 to 1828 in order to link both slaves and free people by names and trace them, when possible, over time into freedom and through future generations. The names will allow an integration of manumission data with court cases, tax lists, and wills and probate records. Most pre-1760 archival records are closed to researchers, although eight years between 1740 and 1759 have been added to date.

9. A detailed analysis of the legal process is in Brana-Shute, "Manumission of Slaves," 176–219. The court's final decisions remain unclear regarding 36 slaves. The slaves purchased and freed in return for their services in the Corps of Black Hunters, discussed at the end of this essay, are included only in figure 1, where the sharp peak for 1772 that rises to 331 represents the actual number of slaves freed in that year when those on regular petitions (represented by the peak rising to 50) are augmented by this batch manumission. The specific case of Mariana van Pinto, who fought first for her own manumission and then for her sons, is in R. Brana-Shute, "Legal Resistance to Slavery in 18th Century Suriname," in *Resistance and Rebellion in Suriname: Old and New*, ed. Gary Brana-Shute, Studies in Third World Societies no. 43 (Williamsburg, Va.: College of William and Mary, 1989), 119–136.

10. The only exceptions occurred in 1766 and 1769, but the difference in slaves freed is only a total of seven males.

11. Herbert S. Klein, *African Slavery in Latin America and the Caribbean* (New York: Oxford University Press, 1986), 227.

12. Richard Price, *The Guiana Maroons: A Historical and Bibliographical Introduction* (Baltimore: Johns Hopkins University Press, 1976), 12, primarily citing data from Johannes Postma, "The Dutch Participation in the African Slave Trade: Slaving on the Guinea Coast, 1675–1795" (Ph.D. diss., Michigan State University, 1970).

13. R. A. J. Van Lier, *Frontier Society: A Social Analysis of the History of Surinam*, 2nd ed., KITLV translation series no. 14 (The Hague: Martinus Nijhoff, 1971), 74; A. F. Lammens, *Bildragen tot de Kennis van de Kolonie Suriname, Tijdvak 1816–1822*, ed. G. A. de Bruijne, Bijdragen tot de Sociale Geografie en Planologie no. 3 (Amsterdam: Geografisch en Planologisch Instituut, Vrije Universiteit, 1982), 10.

14. W.O., 1/149, fol. 243, National Archives of the U.K.: Public Records Office, London; Van Lier, *Frontier Society*, 98.

15. In fact, statistical data on manumission are too often presented as tables of frequencies by sex, then another by color of slave freed, then another by residence, and so on, as if sex, color, and age in particular are traits that occur independent of each other.

16. This conforms with patterns of other American societies. See Klein, *African Slavery in Latin America and the Caribbean*, 227.

17. Price, *Guiana Maroons*, 19–20; Van Lier, *Frontier Society*, 154–155. Van Lier suggests that planters may have changed this practice after the 1773 crisis, although this is open to question.

18. J. G. Stedman, *A Narrative of a Five Years' Expedition Against the Revolted Negroes of Suriname in Guiana on the Wild Coast of South America from the Years 1772 to 1777* (1796; reprint, Barre, Mass.: Imprint Society, 1971), 1:161; Albert Von Sack, *A Narrative of a Voyage to Surinam*, 115; Price, *Guiana Maroons*, 12.

19. B. W. Higman found the same patterns held for the British Caribbean urban areas. B. W. Higman, *Slave Populations of the British Caribbean, 1807–1834* (Baltimore: Johns Hopkins University Press, 1984), 382–383.

20. There are two journals written by white men in the tropics, one in Suriname and one in Jamaica, which deal openly, if romantically in Stedman's case, with liaisons they had with enslaved women, and whose behavior would support this interpretation. The former is Stedman's *Narrative of a Five Years' Expedition,* and the latter is that of Thomas Thistlewood, edited and abridged by Douglas Hall in *In Miserable Slavery: Thomas Thistlewood in Jamaica, 1750–86,* Warwick University Caribbean Studies Series (London: Macmillan. 1989).

21. Figures and rough population estimates do not adequately indicate the relatively very poor economic position of free coloreds and blacks, which minimized their ability as a group to pay the costs required in manumitting. this is not surprising, given the lack of schooling and access to jobs traditionally held by whites, especially in the eighteenth century. Moreover, free blacks and coloreds competed with slave labor and European males who mustered out of the military to set up as civilians in the colony. Consider also that the majority of free coloreds and free blacks were female: In 1805, 67.5 percent of the free colored and black group was female; in 1830, 63.9 percent was female. the economic opportunities of the entire group of free coloreds and free blacks were lessened as these females had an even more limited range of economic opportunities than men, although perhaps a greater opportunity in an expanding city to work at lower pay as domestics, housekeepers, cooks, nurses, laundresses, and other similarly "female" jobs. The majority of market and street vendors were also female. for the

time period studied here, the majority of coloreds and blacks were female, and one effect was the limitation of options for them to secure financial independence because they were female. For many, it is likely that change would come in the following generations, when their male children could begin to compete more publicly (in business, the professions, and real estate), the direct consequence of their mothers having been manumitted.

22. Although it was not explored in this essay, there is, interestingly, the existence of a body of literature in early modern Europe that equates, by analogy, women and slaves, marriage and slavery, and husbands and owners, a body of literature that might be fruitfully mined for what it will tell us about how European men and women might have differentially viewed both themselves and slaves. A closer look at the primary sources for slave societies in the Americas is likely to yield many texts that suggest an equation of the condition of slavery with being female.

23. Of the 1,346 slaves nominated for manumission through the petition process during the years sampled, we only know the sex of the owners of 992 (73.5% of the total). Of these 992, 40.6 percent were freed by female owners. The remaining 59.4 percent were freed by male owners. Of the 1,346 slaves presented for manumission, at least 23.3 percent had black or colored owners. For 981 slaves we know the owners' sex and color. At 48.7 percent, fewer than half of the manumitting owners were white. Of the 981 owners for whom both sex and color are known, 59.6 percent were male (of which 81.7% were white and 18.3% were black or colored). The 40.4 percent of the owners who were female were more evenly divided between white women (53.3%) and black or colored women (46.7%). Whereas white males were more than double the white females manumitting, the opposite is true among colored and black owners; women freed 63.4 percent and men freed 36.6 percent of all the slaves freed by colored and blacks, almost mirroring their presence as manumittees. These figures are a sum total of the entire sample. The percentages vary over time, however, so that by the end of the sample period white males are a minority of the manumitters and females and freedmen are the majority. Too often statistical data on manumission fails to follow variables over time to see the changes that occur. See also Rosemary Brana-Shute, "Liberating Women: Female Manumitters in Late 18th and Early 19th Century Suriname," in *Differentiating Caribbean Womanhood*, ed. Jacquelin Stevens, Working Paper No. 3, Centre for Gender and Development Studies (Mona, Jamaica: University of the West Indies, 2000), 38–48.

24. Frank Tannenbaum, *Slave and Citizen: The Negro in the Americas* (New York: Vintage, 1946).

25. Hof van Politie, Requesten, 503 (1808), 29, ARA. For 116 slaves, this was the reason given.

26. Hof van Politie, Requesten, 383 (May 6, 1760); Notulen, 62 (May 19, 1760), ARA.

27. This is the only case in which an owner indicated he or she understood the importance of manumission as an incentive to trustworthy behavior on the part of slaves, although many must have know that manumission was an alternative to overt rebellion. Hof van Politie, Requesten, 408 (1772), 207, ARA.

28. The 67 slaves cited as kin to their owners constitute only 5 percent of the entire sample of 1,346 slaves, but 21.6 percent of those 310 slaves freed for an explicitly stated reason. The figure is probably a severe underestimate, mainly because there was no requirement that motive, including kinship, be stated. Also not included in this count are those cases where parents and siblings aided their relatives into freedom by serving as "street guardians" and bondsmen. Nor are adoptions of slave children by free coloreds and blacks included. Even the seven cited here are only presumed to have been white, for lack of data to confirm their color.

29. Hof van Politie, Requesten, 469 (1799), 4; Hof van Politie, Requesten, 538 (1799), 1, ARA.

30. Higman, *Slave Populations*, 383. This pattern continued through the 1820s and changed only as emancipation approached. In Suriname we would probably have to look at the 1850s for comparable data. For Latin America see the bibliography and appropriate sections in Klein, *African Slavery in the Caribbean and Latin America*.

31. This section of Paramaribo is still known today as Free Man's Ground (*Sranan*: Frimangron). The Black Hunters are famous in Surinamese history for their effectiveness as soldiers and for their red headgear, for which they were called the *Redi Moesoe* (Red Berets) in the creole language of Sranan Tongo or Neger Engels. John Stedman's account describes them at length.

32. "Boni-Oorlog" and "Redi-Moesoe," in *Encyclopedie van Suriname*. A list of 116 slaves with skills and prices noted is in Resolutien en Notulen van Gouverneur en raden, 364 (July 15), ARA.

Mariana L. R. Dantas

Child Abandonment and Foster Care in Colonial Brazil

—ᘯᘯ—

Expostos and the Free Population of African Descent in Eighteenth-Century Minas Gerais

The baptism and marriage records of colonial Minas Gerais contain frequent references to expostos or engeitados, people who at some point in their childhood had been abandoned by their original parents and raised by foster parents. Among these expostos historians have found many people of African descent, described as pretos (blacks) or as pardos, mulattos, or cabras (mixed race). The presence of these "nonlegitimately white" children caused, at times, some embarrassment to the institutions in charge of providing for their care and support. Evidence from the documents of colonial Brazil shows that at many different locations and moments in their histories, these institutions expressed doubts about whether these children should be given the same care and attention dispensed to white expostos. According to their arguments, by doing so they were encouraging promiscuity among women of African descent by helping them dispose of the fruit of their sins. The fact that some of these children were actually, as they later discovered, the offspring of slave women generated further uncertainty as to what treatment should be dispensed to these expostos. When providing for them, these institutions had to face the possibility that they unknowingly might have been helping slave mothers to free their children to the detriment of their masters' property. Finally, because foster parents were entitled to a stipend or salary to compensate for their expenses in the support of the child, these institutions often suffered financial difficulties. Thus the possibility of denying support to those abandoned children suspected to be of African descent would decrease the costs incurred by them.

Individuals of African descent also appear in documents referring to expostos as foster parents. Whether they took in these children as an act of charity or were attracted by the promise of financial compensation is a question that cannot be easily answered. The significant presence of widows and single women among these foster parents, the majority of whom were of African descent, is a strong indication of the latter. Living in an environment that offered few opportunities for financial success, these women welcomed the money they were able to earn raising these children. Furthermore, if they decided to adopt the child or simply keep it as an *agregado* (dependent) after the completion of its upbringing (when the child reached seven years of age), they would be able to count on his or her labor to increase the household's income. Using data collected from baptism and marriage records, account books of the municipal council of Sabará, and inventories, I discuss the effects the practice of abandonment could have on the lives of some of these individuals.

The presence of people of African descent among abandoned children and foster parents deserves special attention from scholars interested in the history of this group in colonial Brazil. What the documents relevant to the phenomenon of expostos show is that the system of assistance to these children also allowed individuals of African descent to improve the lives of their offspring and often their own as well as, in some cases, obtain freedom for their enslaved children. But more important, they illustrate how people of African descent, despite at times claiming ignorance of the law and customs of the "white," were able to perceive in them certain contradictions and opportunities that they could explore to suit their own purposes. In a context where these individuals had very few rights recognized and enforced, it was necessary for them to find indirect ways to have their interests satisfied. As demonstrated by other essays in this volume, the struggle of individuals of African descent, slave or free, with a restrictive environment was not a preserve of those living in colonial Brazil. In various places throughout the Americas—and at different times—learning local customs, laws, and legal procedures could mean the difference between enslavement and freedom. Furthermore, by employing these customs and laws they were reinforcing their right to participate in them.[1]

Manumissions: A Conditional Freedom

In colonial Brazil, furthermore, Minas Gerais stands out for the size of its slave population and, furthermore, for its population of free "black" and "mixed-race" people. Although the practice of manumitting slaves was widespread in the Portuguese colony of Brazil, it has been argued that the economic and social organization of the *capitania* of Minas Gerais allowed slaves to obtain their freedom more frequently there than elsewhere. The main difference was that slaves there had easier access to some sort of income, allowing them to purchase their freedom. Thus the gold rush, the development of towns, and the demand for labor and consumable goods created an environment financially advantageous to industrious slaves.[2] In fact, it was not rare for slaves to be able to administer their own labor, which their masters permitted in exchange for part of their profit. According to the will of Sebastião Pereira de Aguiar, made in 1716, three of his slaves were working under such an agreement: The slaves were allowed to have and administer their own property (in this case, land and farm animals) as long as de Aguiar received half of the product of their labor.[3] This type of arrangement provided slaves with more autonomy to insert themselves successfully in the local economy. Raising animals and producing foodstuff is only one example of an economic activity pursued by slaves. Throughout the documentation of colonial Minas Gerais, one can find them as peddlers, *faiscadores* (panners for gold), craftsmen, or simply hired out as unskilled labor. Masters also benefited from these arrangements; they not only shared in the fruit of their slaves' work but also, by having slaves in these circumstances provide for themselves, had the additional advantage of incurring fewer expenses with the slaves' support.[4]

The need to provide for themselves as well as to satisfy their masters' demands for their part of the bargain made life difficult for many slaves. As Russell-Wood points out, some slave women in Minas Gerais resorted to prostitution in order to meet the share demanded by their masters.[5] Evidence from letters of freedom show, however, that there were slaves successful enough to buy not only their freedom but also the freedom of a child or spouse. Retail licenses issued by the municipal council of Sabará to street vendors, storekeepers, butchers, and so on are yet another source of evidence of successful slaves. For three consecutive years, from 1797 to 1799, Izabel, crioula, a slave of Doña Josefa da Costa Moreira, was granted a license to carry on sales in the neighborhood of Pompeu and was always listed as a slave. But in 1800 her name appears as Izabel da Costa Moreira, crioula forra (manumitted black).[6] It seems safe to conclude that through her occupation as a street vendor Izabel managed to save enough money to buy her freedom.

Mineiro society also afforded slaves the opportunity to forge personal liaisons which could increase their chances of gaining freedom. The predominance of small slaveholdings, the rather tight concentration of the population in mining districts, and the high level of miscegenation allowed slaves to develop closer relationships with their masters and members of the free population.[7] Examining various letters of freedom registered in the notorial offices of Sabará, I have found some instances of masters manumitting their slave children or, in some cases, their slave mistresses.[8] Children born of a slave mother and a free father who was not the mother's master also had their freedom purchased by their fathers. Other relatives that appear in these documents are grandparents, children, grandchildren, and—in the case of the manumission of Angélica, mulatta, slave of André de Barros Rego—her sister Ana.[9] Godparents also played an important role in the manumission process of their grandchildren, by either purchasing their freedom or helping them with the costs of manumission.[10] In the specific case of the slave girl Sabina, her godfather was actually her master. He granted her and her mother their freedom on the grounds that the former was his *afilhada* (goddaughter) and the latter his *comadre* (the mother of his goddaughter). Sabina had to comply, though, with one condition: She would have to stay with her godfather and his wife until she married or reached the age of fifty, thus allowing the couple to look after her and protect her from a "life of vice."[11]

Personal connections also favored slaves who were not able in the specified period of time to come up with the amount their masters required for their manumission. The case of Antônio, a slave of André Machado da Cunha Guimarães, is an example of how slaves who were given the chance to purchase their freedom were not always able to comply. According to Guimarães's will, Antônio should be given his letter of freedom as soon as he finished paying the installments imposed by his master's will, a common form of negotiating freedom called *coartação*.[12] Because he did not have the means to fulfill the terms of this *coartação,* he informed the Orphans Court that he wished to give up his status as a *coartado*.[13] In cases similar to Antônio's, knowing someone who could lend the amount required for manumission or who could simply vouch for the *coartado* could be vital to the successful conclusion of the slave's negotiation of his or her freedom. The slave Jacinto, for example, obtained his letter of freedom after his father's *compadre* (the godfather of one's child) paid Jacinto's master, the reverend priest Miguel Eugênio da Silva Mascarenhas, half the value of his *coartação*.[14]

Finally, it is important to keep in mind that masters did not necessarily feel obliged to grant a slave his or her freedom. Many, for example, appreciated the economic benefits of the practice. The administrative board of the vínculo do Jagoara, while considering the offer made by some slaves who wished to purchase their manumission, managed to put in writing what many masters thought of the option of selling slaves their freedom: "It seems . . . in the interest of freedom and also of the 'vínculo' . . . to provide a letter of freedom to all who require it and pay the amount for which they were appraised, and with it buy new slaves who will be able to work more intensively. And it would even be an opportunity to slowly renew the slave force and avoid in the future the problem imposed by older slaves."[15] Getting rid of older or insubordinate slaves by selling them their freedom was certainly a convenient solution for some; it relieved masters of future problems with their slaves while allowing them to purchase new hands. According to the letters of freedom some slaves even saved their masters the trouble of buying a substitute by handing their owners another slave individual in order to obtain their manumission.[16] However, in the case of young productive slaves already trained to perform the work required of them, such transactions might not have seemed compensation enough. Masters would lose a valuable hand and be left with a new slave who needed to be trained and disciplined. When confronted with a master's refusal to negotiate their manumission, some slaves would attempt to get help from other sources, including the church (mainly through a brotherhood), governors, or even the king.[17] That was the course of action adopted by the brotherhood of Saint Gonçalo Garcia in the town of São João del Rei. In 1786 representatives of that brotherhood petitioned the queen, Doña Maria I, requesting the power to induce masters to sell them their slave brothers so they could obtain their freedom.[18] To justify the righteousness of such a measure, they offered a long description of the many cruelties practiced by slave masters, including that of forcing slave women into concubinage and then maintaining their offspring as slaves. The governor of Minas Gerais advised the queen not to favor this request as it would cause uneasiness among slave owners and cause loss to their property. However, he suggested she could grant them permission to buy their brothers in the specific cases that a master's cruelty could be proven. Despite all these difficulties the letters of freedom contain evidence that many slaves did manage to buy their freedom while they were still young and productive. Without knowing more about the lives of these slaves and their relationships with their masters, it is hard to determine what inspired their owners to free them. It seems fair to suggest, though, that slaves' power to negotiate with their masters the terms of their freedom would be an important part of it all. In this sense the type of relationship established between them would surely influence the outcome of negotiations.

The act of being manumitted and the possession of a letter of freedom did not always mean that the now former slave was free to enjoy his life in whatever manner he or she found fit. It was common for masters to impose certain conditions on their slaves' freedom.[19] The most frequent one was the obligation to serve them while they were alive; until his or her master's death, therefore, the slave would only have the promise of freedom to enjoy. Some masters chose to impose more utilitarian conditions. Manuel João de Miranda, for example, would grant his slave Rita de Miranda her freedom as long as the man she intended to marry, Manuel Dias, repaired his (the master's) tools and made him mining and farming tools. Joana Felix de Jesus declared that her slave Thomás could only enjoy his freedom after paying for her funeral expenses.[20] Conditions such as these were imposed even when slaves had already paid for their freedom. Masters made it clear that if slaves did not comply with their demands, the process of manumission would be cancelled. Furthermore, according to Portuguese law a master who had freed a slave could revoke the decision if the master thought that particular slave was treating him or her with ingratitude.[21]

The conditions imposed by masters and the threat of having their manumission revoked were not the only obstacles that kept freed slaves from fully enjoying their freedom. As argued in a petition presented to the king by the free "blacks," "mulattos," and other "mixed race persons" of the four *comarcas* of Minas Gerais, they constantly had to deal with abuses and injustice from the white population.[22] Their main complaint referred to the way they were cheated in their commercial businesses by white people who would take advantage of their "illiteracy and ignorance of the law." The whites would not settle their debts in due time and would often forge documents that altered the terms of a transaction causing confusion over who owed whom. Furthermore, the petitioners claimed that it was often useless to bring their cases to local courts where white people had more influence. They also complained that some white men would denounce freed women of African descent for crimes they did not commit in order to avenge these women's refusal to accept their sexual advances. In order to redeem the situation the petitioners asked the crown to provide them with a "black" or "mulatto" man from Portugal, knowledgeable and experienced in judicial matters, who would serve as their attorney. I did not find any mention of the crown's answer to this request. The fact that such a magistrate did not exist in any of the towns of Minas Gerais suggests that the petition was not taken into consideration—another example of the government's negligence where issues affecting the free population of African descent of Minas Gerais were concerned.

Free people of African descent were thus constantly confronting the limitations of their freedom, represented either by the conditions imposed by their former masters or by the abuse suffered at the hands of white authorities and white individuals. It is not difficult to imagine that under such circumstances slaves were constantly trying to procure a less conditional freedom. Thus when we see a slave or a free mother of African descent choosing to abandon her child, we must not discard the possibility that by doing so she was trying to provide it with a better life.

Providing for the Abandoned

The presence of abandoned children in colonial Minas Gerais should not come as a surprise. The widespread practice of concubinage, the high rate of illegitimacy among the newly born, and the poverty experienced by many led mothers desperate to protect their honor and family integrity, or simply lacking the means or the desire to support a family, to abandon their children. The fate of many of these children was to die of cold and hunger and, in some cases, be attacked by wandering animals. Others who were found in time were, in accordance with Portuguese law, reported to the municipal councils, the institution that was legally responsible for them, which would find them a wet nurse or a foster family. Those in charge of the child would then receive a predetermined stipend from the council to help with the child's support.[23] In Portugal as well as in Salvador and Rio de Janeiro from the beginning of the eighteenth century on, the responsibility for the well-being of foundlings had been placed in the hands of the Santa Casa da Misericórdia. This institution ran the "house of the expostos" where a turning wheel was installed; mothers would place their babies on the wheel and someone inside the house would collect them. This system allowed a mother to leave her child in a place safer than the middle of the street or other deserted locations, while still allowing her to keep her identity unknown. Working for the house of the expostos were wet nurses who looked after the child until an outside wet nurse or family was accepted to take care of it. The Santa Casa da Misericórdia also provided foster parents with a certain amount of money intended to compensate for their expenses with the child.[24]

In Minas Gerais during the eighteenth century houses of expostos similar to the ones administered by the Santa Casa de Misericórdia did not exist. Only in 1831 would the first foundling wheel (*roda dos expostos*) of the province be installed in Vila Rica.[25] Children were placed at the doorsteps of private houses or of the municipal council. Those who found the children were supposed to report the foundling to the officials of the municipal council, who would then register them. If the same people who reported the child did not want to look after it, the council would then find it a wet nurse or foster parent. The stipend provided these foster parents seems to have varied from place to place and throughout the eighteenth century. According to Russell-Wood, during the first half of the eighteenth century the city council of Salvador paid wet nurses 2$000 réis quarterly, while the Santa Casa da Misericórdia paid them 2$000 a month.[26] In the city of Mariana, according to Laura de Mello e Souza, the council provided foster parents with a monthly stipend of 3$600 until 1759, and of 2$400 after that date.[27] In Sabará between 1782 and 1808 a foster parent received on average 14$400 per year from the council.[28] The variations in the stipend paid to foster parents did not prevent the institutions supporting expostos from making similar complaints that such expense represented a heavy strain on their financial stability. In the case of Sabará the accounts books of the council show that the care for expostos could represent from 12 to 25 percent of the institution's annual expense (table 1.)

TABLE 1. Annual expense with support for expostos

	1782	1786	1789	1798	1805	1808
Total amount	928$800	594$400	568$800	544$771	679$575	501$600
Percentage of total annual expense	25	13	16.7	14.8	14.3	12.4

Source: Códices 66; 75; 84; 88; 97; 99; 125, Câmara Municipal de Sabará, APM.

In accordance with the Portuguese law that allowed municipal councils to establish temporary taxes (*fintas*) to help cover the cost of assisting expostos, the municipal council of Sabará created, in 1794, a new tax of 2$400 réis per year on the sale of *cachaça* (a strong alcoholic beverage derived from processing sugar cane).[29] This tax affected every street vendor, storekeeper, or tavern keeper carrying a license to sell *cachaça*. Ironically, one of these license holders, Thomázia Rocha do Sacramento, a street vendor, was herself the foster parent of an exposto. In that year taxes were collected from 337 license holders, representing an increase of 808$800 réis to the town's income.[30] By the end of 1794 the council had published an announcement summoning all foster parents to attend, with documents in hand, a meeting at the council for the distribution of the money collected.[31] Since each foster parent would receive 14$400 réis for a year's worth of care for an exposto, this amount would allow for the support of fifty-six abandoned children, a rather low number in comparison to other locations.[32]

Municipal councils in Minas Gerais could not avoid the responsibility of taking care of expostos; nevertheless, they did try to present alternatives that would reduce the cost of providing for these children. In a petition sent by the municipal council of the city of Mariana to the king of Portugal in 1763, councilors complained that the number of expostos had increased considerably because women of African descent, slave and free, were also abandoning their children. According to the petitioners, the main reasons for this were that through abandonment "mulatto and negro [children] do not endure the infamies of being of such low sphere" and "incur fewer life risks." Also, "mulatto and black tramps abandon [their children] . . . in order to maintain themselves apt and free to continue carrying on the same offenses to God." And finally, because "being many of these slaves, [they cover] their stomachs and then [have the children] abandoned with the purpose of making them free."[33] The councilors required the king of Portugal to order that all abandoned children who were not legitimately white be subjected to the disposition of the council. The council would provide for their upbringing until the age of seven, after which time they would be employed in whatever way necessary to compensate the council for its expenses. They believed that if this were the case, slave and free mothers of African descent would be discouraged from abandoning their children, the latter for not wanting to see them treated in such a fashion and the former because they would prefer their own masters to own their children. The Overseas Council denied the request. It replied that the city representatives' intention to keep the abandoned "black" and "mixed race" children as slaves was scandalous and in disagreement with the true objectives of such a Catholic and pious institution. The procedure recommended by the king's counselors was to keep freed and slave women under close surveillance, obliging them to report their pregnancies and afterward the development of their babies.[34]

One might say that the city representatives of Mariana certainly tried to present a good case for enslaving nonwhite expostos. They appealed to two issues that had on many other occasions inspired the Crown to take action: the threat to miners' property in slaves, essential to the well-being of the mineiro economy, and the religious morality of the king's subjects, endangered, apparently, by the promiscuity of women of African descent. But they underestimated the Crown's concern for the well-being of these children. On one hand reports of bodies of children found in the streets of colonial towns, many times half-eaten by dogs or pigs, inspired the crown's sensibility. The fact that many of these children died without having been baptized was also of concern to Catholic monarchs all over Europe, who believed it was a moral and civic responsibility to provide for these children.[35] Thus even though the possibility of enslaving children of African descent might discourage mothers from abandoning them at the door steps of the council or of private houses, it would not solve the general problem of abandonment—as babies could still be left in fields and squares—or of infanticide. On the other hand, as the issue of slavery was beginning to be reconsidered in Europe, the Portuguese government also started to revise its position on the institution within the metropolitan area. In 1773 a law was passed granting freedom from then on to all children born of slave mothers as well as to all people whose slave ascendancy went back to their great-grandmothers. Taking this into consideration, it seems possible to suggest that the king and his counselors would be somewhat averse to the idea of condemning children of unknown origin to a life of captivity. In fact, in 1775, seven years after this petition was presented to the Overseas Council, the Crown issued a decree reinforcing the right of expostos of African descent to be raised as free individuals; based on the "privilege of ingenuity," they were to be considered freeborn.[36] Because expostos had no parents, the condition of slavery could not be passed on to them.

Laws and royal decrees did not prevent, however, some foster parents from selling children placed in their care into slavery. Also, some masters, learning of the abandonment of a female slave's child, would attempt to retrieve it even though the law guaranteed its right to freedom. Even when these children were not submitted to slavery per se, some experienced at the hands of their foster parents the same treatment usually reserved for slaves: hard labor, inadequate feeding and clothing, and domestic violence. The recurrence of death, disappearance, or signs of ill treatment among the expostos was probably what motivated the council to verify every year that the child was alive and well before paying for its stipend.[37] Finally, as the document described above points out, the position of the municipal council was not always one inspired by the desire to protect and provide for these children's needs. The fear that council officials might claim the child to be the property of some slaveholder or dispose of them in unsatisfactory ways after they came to age was probably what induced some foster parents to declare the children as white despite doubts and disagreements of others. Thus when Thereza de Nogueira registered the exposto Francisco, she declared him white, although, according to the officer of the council, he was registered on his baptism record as a "light mulatto." By doing so Thereza was not only preventing suspicions from arising that Francisco might be the child of a slave mother but was allowing him to be raised and known as a white child.[38]

All these problems, however, did not discourage mothers of African descent from depositing their children at the doorsteps of the municipal councils and private homes of the citizens of Minas Gerais. Unfortunately, there is no way of knowing which of these children were the sons and daughters of slaves. The petition described above and evidence presented by other studies strongly suggest that this might have been the case for some of the "black" and "mixed race" children named in the documents. Still, where free mothers of African descent were concerned, they may have abandoned their children because of their inability to take care of them because of poverty, disease, or the desire to provide them with a better home. The rather prejudicial implication made by the city representatives of Mariana that "black" and "mulatto" women abandoned their children because they were eager to maintain themselves "apt and free" to pursue their "offenses to God" can be dismissed by evidence presented by recent studies of the Mineiro society. It has been shown that households composed of single mothers and their offspring were fairly common among women of African descent and rarer in the case of white women.[39] It can be argued, then, that "black" and "mulatto" single mothers hesitated less often to assume responsibility for their illegitimate children than did their white counterparts. Furthermore, the attitude of the council, qualifying the behavior of women of African descent as offensive to religion and morality while providing assistance to white children, many of which were the fruit of illegitimate sexual liaisons, illustrates perfectly the type of double standards faced by slaves and freedpeople. Councilors were ready to assist white expostos and help preserve the honor of white women and their respective families at the expense of "black" and "mulatto" children.

However demeaning to women of African descent, the council's explanation for the abandonment of these children did strike a plausible key. By abandoning their children some of these mothers might actually have intended to spare them the "infamies of being of such low sphere." Although the council seems to be referring to the place these children would occupy in the social hierarchy of the colony, there is still another possible reading of this comment. As pointed out by Orlando Patterson in his work, enslaved individuals who managed to obtain their freedom were not always able to break free from certain ties of dependency to their masters or other members of the free population or even overcome the submissive role society imposed on them. In some cases this status was passed on to the next generation.[40] Some of the ways in which slaves obtained their manumission in Minas Gerais (through *coartação,* accepting conditions imposed by their masters, or borrowing money from someone) placed individuals in the same position described by Patterson; in these cases to achieve finally the status of free could be a long and difficult transition. Furthermore, if these quasi-libertos had children before becoming fully free, there was a great chance that these children would inherit the obligations that tied their parents to their masters or creditors and they might, in fact, be considered slaves.[41] Given these circumstances, it is not farfetched to assume that the desire to spare their children from suffering the consequences of their own deficient freedom might have led *coartado* mothers and indebted parents to abandon them.

EXPOSTOS AND FOSTER PARENTS

Different historians have pointed out that, according to documents referring to expostos in Salvador and Rio de Janeiro, white children were abandoned more frequently than those of African descent, and as a consequence white mothers practiced abandonment more often than their slave or freed counterparts. The evidence I have gathered for the town of Sabará and parishes of Antônio Dias and Ouro Preto in Vila Rica seems to reproduce the pattern found for Salvador and Rio de Janeiro. However, the great number of expostos whose color or origin was not mentioned makes it difficult to make a more accurate assessment.

Unfortunately for the historian, the omission of one's color is rather common in colonial Mineiro documents. Whether this was a result of the impossibility of being precise about one's racial background, as widespread miscegenation generated a great variety of skin colors, or of the irrelevance of this information to whomever was making the registration, or yet because people simply chose to omit such information, one cannot know for sure. In the case of documents referring to expostos another possible explanation for these omissions, as mentioned before, is that when foster parents registered a foundling with council officials they intentionally tried to prevent these children from being registered as "black" or "mulatto." It has been argued that Minas Gerais offered freed individuals more laxity than other slave societies in the Americas.[42] That does not mean, however, that these individuals did not suffer to some extent the stigma of being African or of African descent. The incident involving Doña Thereza Damiana de Azeredo and the lay brotherhood of Nossa Senhora do Carmo in Sabará, formed by white prominent inhabitants of the town and with strong excluding rules, is a good example of how one was never totally dissociated from his or her origins.[43] Doña Thereza was married to Antônio José de Almeida Lobo, a brother of the Irmandade do Carmo, and by marriage had been accepted as a member. However, because of accusations that she carried the "infamy of being a mulata," her right to be a member was questioned. A board of brothers was put together to evaluate Thereza's situation but, unfortunately, I was not able to find more information on the case.

However, it seems clear from the language used in the document that being a "mulata" was not a trait the brothers of N. Sra. do Carmo really appreciated; moreover, it qualified as a reason to consider the cancellation of someone's affiliation to the brotherhood.

In an attempt to fill the gap left by the documents containing information on expostos, I have examined some population data from Sabará. According to the population map of 1776, the number of free children of African descent between the ages of zero and seven in Sabará was 726, representing 34 percent of the total population of children in that age range (table 2).[44] When slave children are added to this share, the percentage increases to 84. White children corresponded to 16 percent of that segment of the population. This means that, in theory, if the proportion of white expostos to those of African descent

TABLE 2. Age distribution by gender, color, and civil status in four parishes of Sabará, 1776

Male inhabitants

Age	< 7 N (%)	7–15 N (%)	15–60 N (%)	60–90 N (%)	> 90 N (%)	Total
Whites	211 (17)	172 (22)	644 (12)	201 (28)	3 (25)	1231
Free mulattos	233 (19)	183 (24)	339 (6)	70 (10)	1 (8)	826
Slave mulattos	314 (26)	128 (16)	370 (7)	33 (4)	0 (0)	845
Free blacks	135 (11)	135 (17)	620 (12)	109 (15)	8 (67)	1007
Slave blacks	338 (27)	161 (21)	334 (63)	317 (43)	0 (0)	4162
Total	1231 (100)	779 (100)	5319 (100)	730 (100)	12 (0)	8071

Female inhabitants

Age	< 7 N (%)	7–14 N (%)	14–40 N (%)	40–90 N (%)	> 90 N (%)	Total
Whites	145 (15)	111 (13)	356 (13)	130 (13)	4 (14)	746
Free mulattos	248 (27)	226 (28)	462 (17)	164 (17)	5 (18)	1105
Slave mulattos	203 (22)	170 (21)	435 (16)	96 (10)	0 (0)	904
Free blacks	110 (12)	113 (14)	328 (12)	242 (25)	19 (68)	812
Slave blacks	229 (24)	197 (24)	1113 (42)	345 (35)	0 (0)	1884
Total	935 (100)	817 (100)	2694 (100)	977 (100)	28 (100)	5451

Source: "Mapa de População de 1776 das Freguesias da Comarca do Rio das Velhas," doc. (112)11, Coleção do Arquivo Histórico Ultramarino, APM.

Note: The four parishes are Freguesia de N. Sra. da Conceição, Freguesia de N. Sra. do Pilar de Congonhas do Sabará, Freguesia de Santo Antônio do Rio Acima, and Freguesia de Raposos.

were equal to the proportion observed for the general population of children discussed above, for every white foundling there would be two or more of African descent (assuming that some slave children were also abandoned). The data available on births in Sabará in 1772, drawn from another population map, offers an even higher figure.[45] In that year 85 white children and 308 "black" or "mixed race" children were born. Thus for every potential white exposto there were 3.6 potential expostos of African descent. Also, the numbers referring to white women and women of African descent, slave and free, within the average child-bearing age (fourteen to forty) in 1776 show that for every potential white mother in Sabará there were 6.5 of women African descent. Although most of what we can do with this information is speculate, the fragmentary state of the data collected from the documents does not leave us with much choice. Considering the probabilities derived from the statistical information presented above, it seems safe to presume that more expostos in Sabará were actually of African descent than the documentation initially suggests.

At the same time the proportion of free adults of African descent (people above fourteen/fifteen years of age) to that of white adults (at a ratio of 1.8:1) suggests that statistically there was a higher probability that people of African descent would take in an abandoned child than would white people. Although these numbers cannot prove much, they suggest that among fosters parents whose color was not specified in the documents, more were probably of African descent than not.

I would like to turn now to other aspects of the practice of child abandonment and foster care revealed by the information gathered from the historical documents. According to the population map of 1776 there were, in Sabará, more male children between the ages of zero and seven than female children (at a ratio of 0.76 girls for every boy). Yet the data collected on expostos (table 3) shows that more girls were abandoned than boys (the ratio here being 1.29 girls for every boy). The difference observed could be explained by the higher mortality rate of young boys; the numbers of the population map of 1776 suggest that for every three boys aged zero to seven, one would die before reaching the next age group. Thus male children abandoned at an early age had a greater chance of dying during their stay with a foster family than did female children. However, the data on girls aged seven to fourteen and boys aged seven to fifteen shows that the ratio of girls per boy within that segment of the population is 1.1:1, still lower than the one found for expostos. Based on this analysis, it seems possible to suggest that there was a tendency in these locations to abandon girls more often than boys.[46] A possible explanation for this behavior would be that male children were considered more essential to the household. Thus families or single mothers confronted with the impossibility of raising more than one child would tend to abandon a daughter rather than a son. Another possibility is that parents or single mothers who felt they could not provide their daughters with an adequate dowry would try to place them with families of greater means to allow them to contract a good marriage, one which could improve their social standing. The common practice among testators in colonial Minas Gerais to bequeath money to the dowries of abandoned and orphan girls as a form of charity explains further why parents might have been inclined to abandon their daughters.[47]

The number of foster parents of African descent in the sample also deserves a closer analysis. The information gathered on these individuals shows that among those who had their "color" declared, "black" and "mulatto" people seemed to predominate; the ratio of white foster parents to those of African descent being 1:2.7. Furthermore, within this group women seemed to offer themselves as foster parents more often than men. In fact, some men were only registered as the foster parent of the exposto because of their position as head of the household. In this sense it is interesting to examine separately the data collected from the census of 1804, as that document contains more detailed information on households which accommodated expostos. Thus among the sixty-two expostos found in Antônio Dias and Ouro Preto in 1804, thirty-six were in the care of women, all of which were either single (eighteen), widows (sixteen), or had an absent husband (two);[48] six of these women were declared to be of African descent (two widows, three single women, and one with an absent husband). That women would become foster parents more frequently than men can simply be explained by the fact that, after all, they were the ones able to fulfill the council's need for wet nurses. However, the economic aspect of the "job" is also relevant. The fact that many of these women were alone suggests that, when confronted with the prospect of having to provide for themselves, they might have considered the adoption of an exposto as a means to secure a more stable income. The example of Clara Maria da Conceição indicates that this actually was the case for some women. Clara's husband died in 1776, leaving her with a small estate in the parish of Curral del Rei (where they planted manioc and produced flour), four slaves (all between the ages of thirty and forty), and a few items of furniture.[49] To support herself and her five-year-old daughter, Clara would have to keep the property productive, which meant overseeing the slaves or hiring someone to do it. But it seems she found another means of support. By the end of the eighteenth century we find her petitioning the municipal council of Sabará for the stipend owed her for the "many expostos . . . [she] was put in charge of raising."[50]

Finally, observing the relations between children and foster parents in table 3, it seems fair to suggest that no specific pattern of adoption was practiced in that context. Children of different "color" seemed to have been placed with foster parents also of different "color" quite randomly. However, to come to such conclusion, it is necessary to examine certain cases separately.

TABLE 3. Expostos and foster parents by color and gender: Sabará, Antônio Dias, and Ouro Preto, 1750–1808

Foster Parents		White		Black		Mixed race		Unspecified		Total
		F	M	F	M	F	M	F	M	
White	F	2	_	_	_	2	_	1	_	5
	M	2	3	_	_	1	_	1	2	9
Black	F	1	_	1	_	1	_	4	4	11
	M	_	_	_	_	_	_	1	_	1
Mixed	F	1	5	_	_	_	2	4	6	18
	M	2	1	_	_	1	2	2	_	8
Unsp.	F	3	5	1	_	2	2	26	14	53
	M	8	1	_	_	4	3	31	28	75
Total		19	15	2	_	11	9	70	54	180

Source: Paróquia de Sabará: Livro de Assento de Casamentos, 1758–1800; Paróquia de Sabará: Livro de Assento e asamentos, 1800–1848; Paróquia de Sabará: Livro de Batismos, 1732–1780; Paróquia de Sabará: Livro de atismos, 1776–1800, Cúria Metropolitana de Belo Horizonte; H. G. Mathias, *Um recenseamento na capitania de Minas Gerais, Vila Rica—1804* (Rio de Janeiro: Ministério da Justiça, Arquivo Nacional, 1969).

The first element of the identity of these foster parents to which I would like to draw attention is their social and economic status. As I argued above, the promise of financial compensation led many individuals of meager means to offer to take in expostos. However, the presence among these foster parents of some people with significant slaveholdings,[51] and of André Francisco Braga and the *alferes* Francisco da Costa Pereira—both declared by the municipal council of Sabará as *abastados* (wealthy) in 1756—suggest that some abandoned children were actually taken in by families with enough resources and prestige to allow them to enjoy a better social position.[52] Eufrásia, a "mulata" who had been abandoned at the house of Manuel André dos Reis, a storekeeper, in 1779, seems to have enjoyed this luck. Not only was she adopted by the family with whom she stayed until her marriage in 1795, but she married into a white family.[53] Furthermore, in the case of some foster parents of African descent, the fact that they either had an *ofício* (trade) or a business suggests that these children were not necessarily left in the hands of idle people whose sole interest was to live on the stipend received.[54] Manuel Lopes Natividade, a tailor and shop owner of unspecified color, and João Baptista Tavares, a "mulato" barber, for example, though they might have welcomed the stipend they received as the foster parents of Joaquina and Emerenciana, certainly did not rely on it to support their household.[55]

Evidence from the data collected shows that in some cases foster parents were actually related to the abandoned children they adopted. For example,

Quitéria Maria de Jesus, a "mulatto" widow, was raising two expostos. One of them, Marco Pereira, was her grandson. Marcus Coelho Neto, a drummer in the local militia, was also raising an exposta whom he declared to be his grand-daughter.[56] The most intriguing example, though, is that of the João Ferreira de Azevedo, a mulatto, and the exposta Joana. According to her baptism record, Joana had been abandoned at the house of Ferreira de Azevedo who not only took her in but also became her godfather. Years later, when Ferreira de Azevedo died, he declared having a daughter named Joana who was thirteen years old. The fact that both his goddaughter and his daughter had the same name and were of the same age suggests that they were actually the same person.[57] If that was the case, we can only speculate how he came to take care of his child in the condition of a foster parent. However, the reason why he became her godfather was probably very simple. Having in mind the implications of godparentage in the context of colonial Brazil it is not difficult to interpret Ferreira de Azevedo's decision. One might say that the relationship between a godfather and a godchild implied almost the same notions of dependency and responsibility as that of a father to a child. By becoming her godfather he could publicly assume responsibility over her well-being without having to assume his paternity.[58]

Among the data on expostos collected from baptism records (corresponding to 25 abandoned children) in seven cases the foster parent was also the godfather of the child, and in one case the same was true for the godmother. Unfortunately, as had been the case with João Ferreira, I could not gather further information on these people. Again, one can only speculate what relationship really existed between them and these children. Of course the possibility that their actions were inspired by charity must be taken into account. By baptizing an exposto as a godparent a foster parent would not only be strengthening the connection between them but also demonstrating a stronger sense of commitment to the child's well-being. The majority of the expostos, however, had someone else for a godparent besides his or her foster parent. Manuel, for example, who was placed under the care of Almázia Nunes Pereira, a "black" freed slave, had as his godfather Diogo de Andrade. Andrade was an apothecary who was also listed as one of the *abastados* of Sabará. The fact that he became Manuel's godfather suggests some connection between himself and Almázia, and even between himself and Manuel. Andrade could have been related to Manuel by blood (maybe even be his father). As a godfather he could participate in the boy's upbringing without arousing suspicions of a possible blood relation. Another possibility was that Almázia, having some kind of personal connection to Andrade, asked him to baptize Manuel as the godfather. Manuel would then be able to enjoy the benefits of being related to someone with the social and financial means to provide for his needs in times of distress.[59]

CONCLUSION

Slaves adopted various strategies to attempt to gain freedom. The different negotiations described in the letters of freedom exemplify only a few of these strategies; running away was another solution adopted by many slaves. Freedom, however, did not always turn out to be what these individuals might have expected. The status of a liberto, not to mention that of a runaway, often did not allow these individuals to achieve the same privileges or social standing available to the freeborn. Furthermore, in a society strongly marked by social discrimination, free individuals of African descent unable to attain financial stability frequently found themselves dependent on others who could provide for their social and economic well-being. The development of such ties of dependency placed many of these individuals in a situation that could closely resemble slavery. It is therefore natural that slaves seeking their manumission or that of their children, as well as free people of African descent, would attempt to develop strategies that would allow them to fully enjoy their freedom. When one considers the practice of child abandonment it seems clear that slave and freed mothers, even those of African origin, by observing the actions of other women could quickly appreciate how the system of assistance to expostos worked and what abandonment could mean for their own children. The same can be argued for foster parents of African descent interested in increasing the income of their households and in achieving financial independence. As Russell-Wood pointed out in his study of expostos, households of free "blacks" or "mulattos" in colonial Bahia generally incorporated members of the extended family, godchildren, and in some cases even the children of neighbors.[60] The possibility of continuing this practice with the added advantage of receiving a stipend for it was not overlooked by the free "blacks" and "mulattos" of colonial Minas Gerais.

Two petitions concerning the manufacture of soap in the colony presented to the Overseas Council by the municipal councils of Mariana and São José del Rei offer yet another example of slaves' strategies to break free from their masters. According to a royal decree passed by Dom João V in the late 1760s, subjects of the crown living in the Brazilian colonies were no longer allowed to manufacture soap; it was to be purchased either directly from Portugal or from the hands of contractors. In Minas, however, there were no soap contractors: the local production of soap was mainly in the hands of slaves or of scattered individuals who made it their livelihood. The king's decree would cause many to lose their business and means of support, and force all the inhabitants of Minas to use soap imported from Portugal. Considering that in 1760 imported soap cost sixteen times more than its locally made equivalent it is not difficult to understand why this decree would potentially upset the Mineiros.[61] Yet this did not seem to be the councilors' main concern. According to the document produced by the municipal council of Mariana, the "people of these Minas are suffering from continuous and inevitable embarrassment and aggravation. They are exposed to the penalties imposed by the said decree without having transgressed its determinations. And they are losing part of their slaves all because many slaves in order to avenge themselves will place amounts of locally made soap in their master's home and then denounce their masters for possessing illegal soap. Other slaves will manufacture soap and sell it publicly so as to suffer the penalty of deportation and thus cause their masters to lose them."[62] In their own petition requesting the king to annul the prohibition on the manufacture of soap, the councilors of São José del Rei argued that slaves "always serve [their masters] involuntarily and are only interested in the freedom that they await." Thus, they implied, to obtain freedom slaves would denounce and harm even innocent people.[63] Apparently this law was only enforced for a short period; the price lists produced by the inspector of the Câmara Municipal de Ouro Preto after 1768 continued to include both Portuguese and locally made soap. Though I do not have evidence that any slave was actually deported for having committed the crime of selling soap, what is of relevance in this document is the council's description of how slaves, learning the terms of this new law, used it to attack their masters and attempt to gain freedom.

The petitions related above, in conjunction with the discussion on child abandonment, point to the fact that slaves and free people of African descent were very much aware of the practices, customs, and laws that regulated colonial Mineiro society. Furthermore, the benefits that could be gained by employing them did not remain unexplored. Individuals of African descent, slave or free, were an intrinsic part of the societies that developed in the Americas. By participating in the same practices and customs observed by free members of these communities, and by exploring the existent laws to fulfill their own interests, they were constantly claiming their right to be included in these societies and to enjoy the various privileges available to others.

NOTES

1. For other works in this volume that address similar issues, see the essays by Keila Grinberg, Beatriz Gallotti Mamigonian, and Scott Hancock.

2. A. J. R. Russell-Wood, *The Black Man in Slavery and in Freedom in Colonial Brazil* (New York: St. Martin's Press, 1982); Luciano R. Figueredo, *O Avesso da Memória* (Rio de Janeiro: Ed. José Olympio, 1995); Eduardo Paiva, *Escravos e Libertos nas Minas Gerais do Século XVIII* (Belo Horizonte: Annablume, 1995); K. Higgins, *"Licentious Liberty" in a Brazilian Gold-mining Region* (University Park: Pennsylvania State University Press, 1999).

3. Testamento de Sebastião Pereira de Aguiar, October 26, 1716, códice 1.1, p. 12, Cartório do Primeiro Ofício, Museu do Ouro de Sabará / Arquivo Casa Borba Gato—Minas Gerais (hereafter cited as MOS/ACBG.)

4. Such arrangements between masters and slaves were also common in the context of other slave societies. Historians Ira Berlin and Philip Morgan have provided us with excellent discussions of this phenomenon or, as they have called it, the "slave economy"; see I. Berlin

and P. Morgan, "The Slaves' Economy: Independent Production by Slaves in the Americas: Introduction," *Slavery and Abolition* 12, no.1 (May 1991): 1–27.

5. Russell-Wood, *Black Man*, 122.

6. Registro de Licença para Lojas e Vendas, códice 101, 1797–1805, Câmara Municipal de Sabará, Arquivo Público Mineiro (hereafter cited as APM). It is worth noting that after 1804 no more reference was made to either her status or color.

7. See Russell-Wood, *Black Man*; Paiva, *Escravos e Libertos*; Luciano Figueredo, *Barrocas Famílias: Vida Familiar em Minas Gerais no Século XVIII* (São Paulo: Editora Hucitec, 1997); and Julita Scarano, *Devoção e Escravidão* (São Paulo: Companhia Editora Nacional, 1976).

8. It was very rare for masters to assume the paternity of slave children in letters of freedom. However, in some cases I was able to confirm the master's paternity through their wills and inventories where, in accordance with the last wishes of the testator, these children were declared as their own and listed as heirs. See inventories of José Affonso, 1751, doc. (13)6; João da Costa Lima, 1761, doc. (23)2; André Machado da Cunha Guimarães, 1763, doc. (23)7; Antônio Duarte Couzinha, 1782, doc. (52)5, Cartório do Segundo Ofício, MOS/ACBG.

9. Carta de alforria, April 8, 1773, Livro de Notas L. 63:171, MOS/ACBG.

10. In the process of my dissertation research, I have collected a sample of 488 letters of manumission issued between 1757 and 1807, among which 17 referred to manumissions sponsored by a godfather, a godmother, or both. For a more lengthy study of manumissions in colonial Sabará, see Higgins, *"Licentious Liberty."*

11. Carta de Alforria, August 5, 1796, Livro de Notas L82, MOS/ACBG. Stuart Schwartz and Stephen Gudeman in their study of godparentage in Bahia report not having found any case where a master might have been a godfather to a slave. In general, according to baptism records, this seems to have been the case in Sabará too. In this specific case one wonders if Bento de Faria Sodré was not actually the biological father of Sabina. See S. Gudeman and S. Schwartz, "Purgando o Oecado Original: Compadrio de Batismo e Escravos na Bahia do Século XVIII," in *Escravidão e Invenção da Liberdade: Estudos sobre o negro no Brasil,* ed. J. J. Reis (São Paulo: Brasiliense, 1988).

12. It is common to find in wills and inventories masters granting slaves the right to be manumitted as long as they pay their heirs the amount for which they were evaluated within a specified time limit. This type of manumission was called, in the Brazilian context, *coartação*. The impossibility of meeting the deadline would mean the loss of the opportunity to become free. For a discussion of the *coartação*, see Higgins, *"Licentious Liberty"*; Paiva, *Escravos e Libertos*; Laura de Mello e Souza, "Coartação: Problemática e Episódios Referentes a Minas Gerais no séc. XVIII," in *Norma e Conflito: Aspectos da História de Minas no Século XVIII,* by Laura de Mello e Souza (Belo Horizonte: Editora UFMG, 1999), 151–174. See also Laird W. Bergad, "Coartación and Letters of Freedom," in *The Cuban Slave Market, 1790–1880,* by Laird W. Bergad, Fe Iglesias García, and María del Carmen Barcia (Cambridge: Cambridge University Press, 1995), 122–142.

13. Inventory of André Machado da Cunha Guimarães, July 7, 1773, Cartório do Segundo Ofício, MOS/ACBG.

14. Carta de alforria, September 9, 1807, Livro de Notas L.89, MOS/ACBG.

15. "Petição da Mesa Administrativa do Vínculo do Jagoara ao Rei D. João VI," August 29, 1805, doc. (177)24, Coleção do Arquivo Histórico Ultramarino, APM.

16. In my sample, mentioned above, sixteen manumissions were obtained in such a manner.

17. For a longer discussion of petitions to the crown, see Silvia Hunold Lara, *Campos da Violência: Escravos e senhores na capitânia do Rio de Janeiro, 1750–1808* (Rio de Janeiro: Paz e

Terra, 1988), 237–293; A. J. R. Russell-Wood, "'Acts of Grace': Portuguese Monarchs and their Subjects of African Descent in Eighteenth-Century Brazil," *JLAS* 32 (2000): 307–332; Maria Beatriz N. da Silva, "A Luta Pela Alforria," in *Brasil: Colonização e Escravidão* (São Paulo: Ed. Nova Fronteira, 1999), 296–310.

18. "Representação da Irmandade de São Gonçalo Garcia, da Vila de São João del Rei," August 22, 1786, doc. (125)20, Coleção do Arquivo Hitórico Ultramarino, APM.

19. See Russell-Wood, *Black Man*; Higgins, *"Licentious Liberty"*; Souza, "Coartação."

20. Carta de alforria, July 13, 1757, Livro de Notas L2, MOS/ACBG-MG; Carta de alforria, August 1, 1808, Livro de Notas L89, MOS/ACBG-MG.

21. See Ordenações Filipinas, livro 4, título 63: "Das doações e alforrias que se podem revogar por causa de ingratidão," facsimile of the 1870 ed. (Lisbon: Fund. Calouste Gulbenkian), 867.

22. "Requerimento dos crioulos pretos das Minas da Vila Real de Sabará, Vila Rica, Serro do Frio, são José e São João pedindo que se lhes nomeie um procurador para os defender das violências de que são Vítimas," October 14, 1755, doc. (68)66, Coleção do Arquivo Histórico Ultramarino, APM.

23. On abandoned children in colonial Brazil, see A. J. R. Russell-Wood, *Fidalgos and Philanthropists: The Santa Casa de Misericórdia of Bahia, 1550–1755* (Berkeley and Los Angeles: University of California Press, 1968); Renato P. Venâncio, *Famílias Abandonadas: Assistência a Crianças de Camadas Populares no Rio de Janeiro e em Salvador—séc. XVIII e XIX* (Campinas: Papiro, 1999); Laura de Mello e Souza, *Norma e Conflito: Aspectos da História de Minas no Século XVIII* (Belo Horizonte: Editora UFMG, 1999), 47–77; Maria Beatriz N. da Silva, "O Problema dos Expostos na Capitânia de São Paulo," *Anais do Museu Paulista* (1980/81): 147–158.

24. On the role of the Santa Casas da Misericórdia in the care for expostos, see Russell-Wood, *Fidalgos and Philanthropists*; Venâncio, *Famílias Abandonadas*. For studies of similar institutions in Europe, see Joan Sherwood, *Poverty in 18th Century Spain: The Women and Children of the Inclusa* (Toronto: University of Toronto Press, 1988); Rachel G. Fuchs, *Abandoned Children: Foundlings and Child Welfare in Nineteenth-Century France* (Albany: State University of New York Press, 1984). According to Fuchs, a mechanism correspondent to the foundling wheels of the Santa Casas da Misericórdia already existed in 1180 in a Montpellier hospital for abandoned children called the *tour*. For a more general study of abandoned children and mechanisms of assistance, see John Boswell, *The Kindness of Strangers: The Abandonment of Children in Western Europe from Late Antiquity to the Renaissance* (New York: Pantheon Books, 1988).

25. Souza, *Norma e Conflito*, 65.

26. Russell-Wood, *Fildalgos and Philantropists*, 299. The réal (plural réis) was the Portuguese monetary unit in the eighteenth century. One thousand réis was usually written "1$000."

27. Souza, *Norma e Conflito*, 58.

28. "Livro de Receita e Despesa da Câmara," Códices 66 (1782), 75 (1786), 84 (1789), 88 (1792), 97 (1808), 99 (1798), 125 (1805), Câmara Municipal de Sabará, APM.

29. Ordenações Filipinas, livro 1, título 88, sec. 11, and livro 1, título 66, sec. 40.

30. Códice 93, 1794, Câmara Municipal de Sabará, APM.

31. Códice 92, 1794–1796, Câmara Municipal de Sabará, APM.

32. According to Renato Venâncio, 1,594 children were abandoned to the care of the Santa Casa da Misericórdia in Rio de Janeiro between 1801 and 1810, and 1,079 in Salvador, meaning that an average of more than 100 children per year were added to the list of expostos provided for by those institutions. Venâncio, *Famílias Abandonada*.

33. "Petição da Câmara Municipal de Mariana, March 16, 1763, doc. (81)20, Coleção do Arquivo Histórico Ultramarino, APM.

34. The crown here was merely reinforcing an existing decree, passed in Mariana in 1748, which determined that all pregnant women who were not married would have to report the baby to the council within twenty days of its birth. Those who did not comply would be fined fifty oitavas (60$000), which would be used to provide for the support of the exposto. Document, cited in Figueredo, *Barrocas Famílias,* 125. The attitude of the Portuguese Crown was not unprecedented. According to Rachel Fuchs, in 1556 King Francis I of France issued an edict obliging pregnant women to declare their condition to the local magistrate. It was assumed that the shame of public exposure would discourage women to engage in premarital sex and thus help control the increase of illegitimate children. Fuchs, *Abandoned Children,* 5.

35. Venâncio, *Famílias Abandonadas*; Sherwood, *Poverty in 18th Century Spain*; Boswell, *Kindness of Strangers.*

36. "Alvará de 31 de Janeiro de 1775," cited in Venâncio, *Famílias Abandonadas,* 131; Lara, *Campos da Violência,* 249. One must keep in mind that the word "ingenuity" in English and ingenuidade in Portuguese, derived from the Latin word *ingenuus* (native, inborn, freeborn), had in the eighteenth century the meaning of "the condition of being freeborn." *The Oxford Dictionary of English Etymology,* ed. C. T. Onions (Oxford: Clarendon Press, 1966), s.v. "ingenuity"; *Diocinário Etimológico da Língua Portuguesa,* ed. J. P. Machado (Lisbon: Ed. Confluência, 1967), s.v. "ingenuidade." It is interesting to observe that, as the Portuguese lexicographer Antônio de Moraes e Silva points out, the word *ingênuo* (ingenuous) was used in the end of the nineteenth century in Brazil to refer to the children of slaves born after September 28, 1871, that is, after a law granting freedom to every child born of a slave mother was passed in Brazil. *Grande Dicionário da Língua Portuguesa,* ed. A. M. e Silva (Lisbon: Ed. Conluência, 1949), s.v. "ingêneo."

37. Although I have not encountered examples of this in the documentation I have consulted, I am relying on evidence presented by secondary sources: Russell-Wood, *Fidalgos and Philantropists*; Venâncio, *Famílias Abandonadas*; Mary Karasch, *Slave Life in Rio de Janeiro, 1808–1850* (Princeton, N.J.: Princeton University Press, 1987); and Souza, *Norma e Conflito.*

38. Livro de Receita e Despesa da Câmara Municipal de Sabará, recibo no. 35, 1798, Códice 99, Câmara Municipal de Sabará, APM. The fact that these children were registered by the municipal council based on the declarations of those who found them and took them in suggests that it would not have been difficult to conceal their "color" from council officials. In fact, many did not even have their color registered. Furthermore, examples where the exposto was declared as "appearing white" suggests that, when in doubt, both foster parent and, sometimes, officers of the council chose to declare the child as white.

39. See Figueredo, *Barrocas Famílias*; Figueredo, *O Avesso da Memória*; M. del Priore, *Ao Sul do Corpo: Condição Feminina, Maternidades e Mentalidades no Brasil Colônia* (Rio de Janeiro: Ed. José Olympio, 1993); D. Ramos, "From Minho to Minas: The Portuguese Roots of the Mineiro Family," *Hispanic American Historical Review* (November 1993): 639–662.

40. Orlando Patterson, *Slavery and Social Death: A Comparative Study* (Cambridge, Mass.: Harvard University Press, 1982), 240–261. Also see Orlando Patterson's essay in this volume, "Three Notes of Freedom: The Nature and Consequences of Manumission."

41. In the case of *coartado* slaves or of conditional manumissions, it was the norm that any child born of a female slave before she had settled her debt or fulfilled the terms of her freedom would be considered a slave.

42. Russell-Wood, *Black Man*; Higgins, *"Licentious Liberty."*

43. Document transcribed in Zoroastro Vianna Passos, *Em Torno da História do Sabará* (Rio de Janeiro: Ministério da Educação e Saúde, 1940), 106.

44. This particular document was chosen for the information it provides on different age groups.

45. This was the only document I was able to find containing information on birth distribution by racial group for Sabará. "Relação Abreviada das pessoas existentes nas freguesias da Comarca de Sabará, 1772," doc. (104)61, Coleção do Arquivo Histório Ultramarino, APM.

46. A similar pattern was observed by Venâncio for the first half of the nineteenth century, but not for the eighteenth century. *Famílias Abandonas,* 47.

47. On the issue of dowries in colonial Brazil, see Muriel Nazarri, "Parents and Daughters: Change in the Practice of Dowry in São Paulo (1600–1770)," *HAHR* 70 (1990): 639–665; Alida Metcalf, *Family and Frontier in Colonial Brazil: Santana de Paraíba, 1580–1822* (Berkeley and Los Angeles: University of California Press, 1992), 87–119.

48. H. G. Mathias, *Um recenseamento na capitania de Minas Gerais, Vila Rica—1804* (Rio de Janeiro: Ministério da Justiça, Arquivo Nacional, 1969).

49. Inventário de Manuel da Rocha Dantas, September 1, 1776, Cartório do Segundo Ofício, doc. (50)5, MOS/ACBG.

50. Document, cited in Silva, "O problema dos expostos."

51. In the context of the specific locations from which the data on expostos were collected, marked by urbanization and the presence of small properties, I am considering any slaveholding with more than eight slaves as above average.

52. Códice 84, Câmara Municipal de Sabará, APM; "Relação de Homens Abastados das comarcas de Minas," July 24, 1756, doc. (70)40, Coleção do Arquivo Histórico Ultramarino, APM.

53. Códices 66, 1779, Câmara Municipal de Sabará, APM; Códice, 93, 1794, Câmara Municipal de Sabará, APM; Assento de Casamento, September 1, 1775, Paróquia de Sabará: Livro de Assento de Casamentos, 1758–1800, 252, Cúria Metropolitana de Belo Horizonte.

54. Within my sample I found thirty-seven foster parents who either carried a trade or business or held a position within the local bureaucracy or the militia.

55. Códice 66, 1779, Câmara Municipal de Sabará, APM; Códice 84, 1789, Câmara Municipal de Sabará, APM.

56. Mathias, *Recenseamento na capitania de Minas Gerais,* 45, 80.

57. Inventário de João Ferreira de Azevedo, October 24, 1794, doc. (67)6, Cartório do Segundo Ofício, MOS/ACBG; Certidão de Batismo, 3/19/1780, Paróquia de Sabará: Livro de Batismos, 1776–1800, 21, Cúria Metropolitana de Belo Horizonte.

58. For a discussion on godparentage, see Russell-Wood, *Black Man*; Gudeman and Schwartz, "Purgando o Pecado Original"; and Figueredo, *Barrocas Famílias.*

59. Certidão de Batismo, January 30, 1780, Paróquia de Sabará: Livro de Batismos, 1776–1800, 18, Cúria Metropolitana de Belo Horizonte; "Relação de Homens Abastados das comarcas de Minas," July 24, 1756, doc. (70)40, Coleção do Arquivo Histórico Ultramarino, APM.

60. Russell-Wood, *Fidalgos and Philantropists.* Data from the census of 1804 for Vila Rica sustains such observation. See Mathias, *Recenseamento na capitania de Minas Gerais.*

61. "Pauta de preços para estes dous meses de novembro e dezembro, 1760," Câmara Municipal de Ouro Preto, microfilm 29, Arquivo Público Mineiro.

62. "Representação dos oficiais da câmara de Mariana," December 31, 1767, doc. (91)85, Coleção do Arquivo Histórico Ultramarino, APM.

63. "Representação dos oficiais da câmara de são José," April 23, 1767, doc. (92)56, Coleção do Arquivo Histórico Ultramarino, APM.

Manumission, Gender, and the Law in Nineteenth-Century Brazil

—ɯ—

Liberata's Legal Suit for Freedom

About 1790 José Vieira, resident of the area of Desterro, located in the south of the Brazilian colony, bought Liberata, then a ten-year-old mulatta. Shortly thereafter he began to pursue her until she consented to have sexual relations with him in exchange for a promise to free her.

Three years later Liberata and Vieira had a son, baptized as a free person with the name of João. After this Liberata suffered such persecution from Vieira's family that when their second son was born, she found it preferable to baptize him as a slave without declaring his paternity. From that point she began to demand from her master the liberty she had been promised. Vieira then promised her that when he died he would free her in his will, but she no longer believed him. She wanted to change her life and began a romantic relationship with a free mulatto, José, and approached the parish priest to intercede with Vieira so that he would free her in exchange for 115$200 réis.[1] José wanted to buy Liberata's freedom so that she could marry him. However, Vieira did not consent to the amount, thereby prohibiting her from marrying.

Liberata went to the municipal court of Desterro and in July 1813 filed an action for her liberty against Vieira, in which the custodian requested that Liberata be freed based on the "sacred laws" of the empire, arguing that she was being kept in a private prison and suffering daily abuse from her owner.[2] But Vieira did not respond to the requests of the court. Instead, he preferred to defend himself by trading slaves with his stepson Floriano José Marques. Thus Marques became the legal owner of Liberata, which meant that the promises of freedom that Vieira had made were now worthless.

Faced with this situation Liberata's custodian adopted a new strategy based upon information Liberata had given him, that of accusing José Vieira of killing his grandchildren, the illegitimate children of his daughter. Vieira had killed four newborn babies, either throwing them into the sea or burying them on his property, out of fear of damage to his reputation. The accusation achieved results: One month later, Liberata withdrew the allegations and was granted her freedom.

This is the first part of a very long freedom suit found in the Rio de Janeiro National Archives, in the section on the city's court of appeals. Along with the wealth of details and the remarkable story, a reading of this process gave me the distinct impression that this was a relatively common case. The atrocities of José Vieira aside, what appeared routine was the private resolution of the question of liberty. Although begun by legal action, the case was resolved through an agreement between a slave and her owner, with the approval of a lawyer. This was not, however, what was revealed by the many of the other legal actions in pursuit of liberty.

FREEDOM SUITS IN NINETEENTH-CENTURY BRAZIL

Knowledge of the existence of freedom suits, such as those which had existed in Brazil, is not new. Sílvia Lara mentions them in her book about slavery in Campos in the colonial period. Peter Eisenberg, writing about the transition from slavery to free labor in Pernambuco, emphasized the importance of his study as a way to better understand the effectiveness of the laws concerning manumission. Lenine Nequete analyzed these documents from a legal point of view in *O Escravo na Jurisprudência Brasileira* (*The Slave in Brazilian Jurisprudence*). Also, the books of Sidney Chalhoub and Hebe Mattos, which addressed the strategies of obtaining freedom in the last decades of the slave labor regime in Brazil, are today essential reading.[3]

When Sidney Chalhoub published his *Visões da Liberdade* (*Visions of Freedom*), the first work based on a study of a large number of these sources, one of the central concerns of Brazilian historiography about slavery was to emphasize the humanity of the slaves, presenting their everyday actions and strategies to achieve freedom from a master's domination. Searching for sources that would provide more knowledge about the lives of slaves, their personal and day-to-day relations with masters and free people, Chalhoub was interested in revising the already traditional interpretation that the behavior of slaves could be understood only in terms of the duality of passivity and rebellion.[4] Hebe Mattos, in *Das Cores do Silêncio* (*About the Colors of Silence*), also contributed to refuting the idea that slaves, if they did not participate in a rebellion, could do little to change their status. In his analysis freedom suits are used to demonstrate the growing fragility of the policy of a master's dominion, from the moment that slaves—represented by lawyers—defended their right to be freed in the courts, breaking the bonds with the slave owners to whom until then they had owed obedience.

The work of Chalhoub and Mattos provided a body of evidence of the role of such legal actions in the process of delegitimizating slavery in nineteenth-century Brazil. It is clear from this work that legal actions challenging established customs and redrawing the relationships between slaves and slave owners were a resource used by slaves and lawyers, starting in the 1850s, to apply pressure to free slaves and to promote civil rights and even general emancipation. This article will, through a discussion of the freedom suit pursued by the slave Liberata, analyze the possibilities of obtaining freedom in Brazil through lawsuits in the nineteenth century, especially in the period prior to the abolition of the Atlantic slave trade in 1850.[5] The fact that many slaves managed to free themselves through legal processes such as these shows that the Brazilian Empire intervened effectively in changing the condition of these people.

It is known that recourse to the courts on the part of slaves was a relatively common practice in Brazil, at least during the nineteenth century. While researching the Rio de Janeiro Court of Appeals in the National Archives, I found a drawer called "Slaves" consisting of a total of 671 documents, 291 criminal processes and 380 freedom suits, all of which occurred in Brazil between 1808, when Dom João VI and the Portuguese court moved to Rio de Janeiro, and 1888, when slavery was abolished in Brazil.[6] Although it is not known when such lawsuits first occurred in Brazil, the documentation found makes it clear that they occurred during the entire nineteenth century, increasing in number over this time (see fig. 1).

It is also known that these legal processes occurred throughout the country, but especially in the southeastern and southern regions (see fig. 2).[7] In fact, Chalhoub and Mattos's studies concentrate on southeastern Brazil, the wealthiest and most populous area at the time, suggesting that proximity to the principal urban centers facilitated access to the information and individuals necessary to undertake the legal process of obtaining freedom. In addition, the majority of slaves who became involved in freedom suits were native born and maintained some form of relationship with their masters as well as maintaining some sort of stable family ties; this evidence suggests that lasting relationships with the master and with one's own family were a key factor in the success of slaves' attempts to win their freedom.

Judging by the arguments submitted by slaves and found in the freedom suits, slaves brought cases against their masters to the court for a wide range of reasons. In the case of Liberata the principal reason was the refusal of her owner to allow the purchase of her freedom, causing her to endure continual violence. But in other cases the reasons included any of the following: the failure of a master to grant promised letters of manumission, the refusal of beneficiaries to uphold a master's will granting freedom to the decedent's slaves, the allegation that the slaves already had lived as freedmen and were defending themselves against an attempt by a former master or another person to reenslave them (these cases were known as *manutenções de liberdade,* "maintenance of freedom"), and cases in which the masters themselves claimed that their slaves were living unlawfully as freedmen (*manutenções de escravidão,*

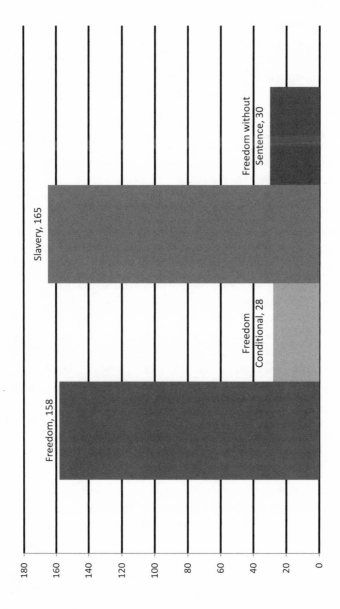

Fig. 1. Occurrence of Freedom Suits in Nineteenth-Century Brazil

"maintenance of slavery"). Other arguments were the "free womb," in which slaves claimed to be the descendants of a free woman, generally an indigenous woman, and were therefore unlawfully enslaved; cases involving the purchase of freedom, either by the slaves themselves or by a third party; the claim to have arrived in Brazil after the Atlantic slave trade had been outlawed, which meant that those slaves recently arrived were to be immediately freed; and accusations of violence on the part of the master, including the employing of slaves as prostitutes. The last two arguments directly address contemporary legislation. When arguing that they had arrived after the Atlantic slave trade was abolished, slaves might be referring to either the law of November 7, 1831, which although never effectively put into practice instituted that "all slave entering the lands or ports of Brazil, coming from overseas, shall be free," or the law of 1850, which actually succeeded in ending Brazil's participation in the Atlantic slave trade (see table 1).[8]

The first two alleged motives in table 1, "letter granting freedom" and "maintenance of freedom," which together represent 47.75 percent, or almost half, of the cases, reflect how the slaves depended on their owners to obtain freedom. The letter granting freedom expressed the will of the owner to free his or her slave (although after his or her death), and maintenance of freedom cases involved slaves who had been free for some time and who, under the threat of some conflict and aware of the possibility of being brought back into slavery, asked for protection. These two motives show that the manumission

TABLE 1. Arguments used in freedom suits, Rio de Janeiro, 1806–1888

Arguments	Number of suits	%
Letter granting freedom	126	31.50
Maintenance of freedom	65	16.25
Purchase of freedom	55	13.75
Maintenance of slavery	45	11.25
"Free womb"	43	10.75
Violence	16	4.00
Arrival after the end of the slave trade	11	2.75
Unspecified	39	9.75
Total	400	100.00

Source: Rio de Janeiro Court of Appeals, National Archives–RJ.

Note: Data presented in this and in the following tables refer to all freedom suits the appeals of which were heard in the court of appeals in the nineteenth century. During this period there were three similar courts in Brazil: Bahia, Pernambuco, and Recife. In 1874 more were established in Porto Alegre, Ouro Preto, São Paulo, Goiás, Mato Grosso, Belém, and Fortaleza. Before that time, the court in Rio de Janeiro had served the entire central-southern region of Brazil. Prior to that appeals went to the House of Appeals in Lisbon.

also meant, in a good share, a reinforcement of slavery, by propagating among the slaves the idea that good behavior and submission could result in future freedom. In short the main motives cited by the slaves involved in the suits show that manumission, even through freedom suits, was a powerful tool for reinforcing the ideology and power dynamics of slavery in Brazilian society.

However, those cases are not enough to explain all meanings that freedom suits had in nineteenth-century Brazil. All other cited motives, particularly the ones of self-purchase (13.75% of the cases), show that the slaves had a certain degree of autonomy. To buy their freedom, they had to have some money. To prove the descendence of someone illegally enslaved (10.75%) or the arrival in Brazil after the end of the slave trade (2.75%), these slaves had to have good sources about their situation, which could only be achieved through contacts with other slaves, freedmen, and freemen, mainly in large cities. Furthermore, the motives that underwent a substantial increase in frequency were the purchase of freedom and the "free womb," numerous cases of which appear after 1860. This shift in motives proves that during the final crisis of the slavery regime manumission assumed new meanings and increasingly became a political force of opposition to slavery. This transformation in the meaning of manumission helps explain why legal suits increased rapidly after Brazil gained its independence, and even more so after the end of the Atlantic slave trade in 1850.

TABLE 2. Freedom suits, Rio de Janeiro, 1806–1888

Period	Number of suits	%
1806–1822	12	3
1823–1850	107	26.75
1851–1870	201	50.25
1871–1888	80	20
Total	400	100

Source: Rio de Janeiro Court of Appeals, National Archive–RJ.

Note: The temporal delineations are based on the year of Brazil's independence (1822), the date which marked the end of the Atlantic slave trade (1850), the promulgation of the Free Womb Law (1871), and the abolition of slavery (1888). The year 1806 was the first in which freedom suits were brought forth in the Rio de Janeiro Court of Appeals.

Until the independence of Brazil in 1822, only 12 freedom suits reached the court of appeals. Even though this number may seem suspect—for with the arrival of the Portuguese royal family in 1808, although judiciary institutions were installed in Rio de Janeiro, several documents were lost—in the period between the Brazilian emancipation and the end of the slave trade, the number of freedom suits rose substantially. In only twenty-seven years 107 suits were decided. The number of suits dramatically increased after the banning of the slave trade in 1850. In the period from the end of the trade until the Free Womb Law, the slaves sought their freedom through the courts, giving a political meaning to the suits and fighting for the end of slavery. The sudden decrease in the number of suits after 1871 is a matter of controversy; while it is clear that the decline is due to the promulgation of the Free Womb Law, historians disagree about the full effects of the law on the suits. The law instructed judges in how they should decide these types of proceedings; they were to practice "administrative" judgment, granting liberty to those capable of proving their right to it and denying it to those unable to give evidence supporting their demands. This reasoning allowed for the majority of cases to be resolved akin to the lower courts.[9]

While Brazilian slaves did not participate directly in the associated conflicts surrounding independence,[10] many Brazilian slaves realized the possibilities of relating political liberty to the end of slavery.[11] After the closing of the Atlantic slave trade, the number of freedom suits increased substantially. The ban on slave imports led to a great boom in the internal slave traffic and had an enormous demographic and social impact on the Paraíba Valley region, where most of the freedom suits originated. Before 1850, for example, at least half of the slaves were Africans. Ten years later, only 20 percent of the slave contingent was composed of laborers born in Africa. This process of creolization of slave society, combined with the growth of the internal market, made domestic and communal relationships among slaves of the larger plantations very important. Such relations governed the possibility of gaining access to the world of free people and thus obtaining freedom.

The increase in the number of freedom suits in the nineteenth century, however, does not form sufficient grounds for an application of Ira Berlin's hypothesis regarding the relation between the occurrence of manumissions and the development of the slavery society in the United States to the situation in Brazil.[12] As the Brazilian pattern of freedom suits demonstrates, with even those dating prior to the eighteenth century, the practice of appealing to the courts to secure freedom dated back to the period of Portuguese rule.[13]

There have so far been no studies of the occurrence of freedom suits in other Portuguese colonies. There are, however, indications that such suits existed in the Portuguese empire since at least the sixteenth century, as can be seen in *Pranto do Clérigo* (The Priest's Lament) by Henrique da Mota, in which a "female black slave reacts to the accusations of his master and to the punishment of 'dripping' (a frequent punishment in which drops of boiling fat and melted lead rained down on a person), by threatening to appeal to the judge (which the priest opposes, as to him the slave, that . . . does not deserve such a privilege)."[14] Thus even taking the period of slavery as a whole, while manumission continued to be both an indication of slavery's strength, and while that strength ebbed and flowed depending on the period, slaves used freedom suits also as a means of opposing slavery throughout the Brazilian slavery regime.

This pattern was possibly due to the concepts of justice current under the Iberian absolutist regimes. With the king in the position of mediator of potential conflicts, the maintaining of social order was linked to the king's capacity to place himself above the rest of society.

The issue becomes more complex when the records of the court of appeals are considered and when the judge's initial verdict was modified. In some cases the judge granted liberty and the court of appeals later denied it; in other cases, while the judge decided the slave had no right to freedom, later the court of appeals granted it. Significantly, the latter cases were far more common than the former, as shown in table 4: 36 percent of the cases decided in favor of the maintenance of slavery in the lower court were later modified, whereas only 21 percent of the opposite occurred. Additionally, 79 percent of the cases which were decided for the freedom were confirmed by the court of appeals, whereas it happened only in 64 percent of the suits in which the result was the confirmation of slavery. The conclusion is that the Rio de Janeiro Court of Appeals liberated more slaves than the primary judges did, as it was more likely to modify sentences which had been in favor of slavery than those in favor of freedom.

This was the surprise that the beginning of Liberata's story hid. Many of the problems between slaves and masters were resolved through the intervention of the state rather than through private agreements between the parties. Thus freedom lawsuits should be considered an effective mechanism that slaves could use to achieve their freedom against the will of their owners. This conclusion goes against an idea common to Brazilian historiography that the Brazilian state did not interfere in the master-slave relationship and did not free slaves without the consent of their owners.[15] On the contrary the Brazilian state during the nineteenth century effectively contributed to the liberation of particular slaves, even in opposition to the will of the slave owners.

TABLE 3. Results of freedom suits, Rio de Janeiro, 1806–1888

Sentence	Number of suits	%
Freedom	158	39.50
Conditional freedom	28	7.00
Slavery	165	41.25
Unspecified	49	12.25
Total	400	100.00

Source: Rio de Janeiro Court of Appeals, National Archive–RJ.

TABLE 4. Rulings in freedom suits in the appeals process, 1806–1888

Initial verdict	Appeals		Total	
	Upheld	Overturned		
Freedom	133 79%	36 21%	169 100%	
Slavery	108 64%	60 36%	169 100%	

Source: Rio de Janeiro Court of Appeals, National Archive–RJ.

Note: Regarding requests for special consideration directed to the king or the emperor of Brazil, see A. J. R. Russell-Wood, *Black Man in Slavery and Freedom in Colonial Brazil* (London: Macmillan and St. Anthony's College, 1982); Arno Wehling and Maria José Wehling, "Cultura Jurídica e Julgados do Tribunal da Relação do Rio de Janeiro: A invocação da boa razão e o uso da doutrina: uma amostragem," in *Cultura Portuguesa na Terra de Santa Cruz,* ed. Maria Beatriz Nizza da Silva (Lisboa: Editorial Estampa, 1995), 235–248.

Note: These are suits that abruptly end before any resolution is reached or suits in which the final pages are missing.

This does not mean, however, that the state or its agents had acted in accordance with abolitionist principles. The court of appeals decisions do not reflect a commitment to abolition. The results of table 4 represent the entire course of the nineteenth century, including time periods when abolition was not an important political or social issue, as it became in the later years of the century. Even further, as the suits took place in Rio de Janeiro, the capital of the empire, the attorneys and magistrates who participated in them were often deeply engaged in imperial politics.[16] However, precisely for being situated in Rio de Janeiro, far from the site where these suits had begun, these judges were also removed from the pressure exerted by the slave owners. The judges of lower courts were not only acquainted with the people involved in the lawsuit but were also part of the same milieu. In Rio de Janeiro judges had more autonomy to decide cases based on the law and on jurisprudence. An analysis of the attorneys' performances in the Rio de Janeiro Court of Appeals confirms this hypothesis.

The existence of abolitionist societies and of attorneys willing to take the struggle to court was of fundamental importance in assuring the slaves success. In Brazil the presence of abolitionist attorneys in the final part of the period of slavery, most notably beginning in 1865, was apparent in the documentation of the suits.[17] But in the situation prior to 1865 attorneys involved in freedom suits were not necessarily interested in contributing to the end of slavery. From the twenty-six attorneys who took part in more than five suits, none defended only slaves or masters, and all of them were sometimes successful, sometimes not. It is also important to note that judges, not attorneys themselves, determined who would represent the slaves since attorneys could not freely choose their clients. It is thus unclear the degree to which an attorney's performance reflected abolitionist sentiment.

This data gives new meaning to the attorneys' participation in freedom suits: Instead of acting according to their political convictions about slavery, they acted according to professional criteria, trying to be consistent in their arguments, no matter who they were defending. Therefore, even after the changes that took place because of the end of the Atlantic slave trade, and with the exception of the last years of the slavery regime,[18] attorneys generally treated the freedom suits as they would do in any other case, sometimes defending masters, sometimes slaves, sometimes winning, sometimes losing and utilizing arguments which might quickly and easily win them their particular case, while rarely advocating a general emancipation.[19] As a result slaves' victories in freedom suits throughout the nineteenth century were not the result of the abolitionist efforts of their lawyers. The verdicts demonstrate the degree to which the upper echelons of the state had the ability to interfere in the outcomes of the lawsuits.

THE LEGACY OF LIBERATA

Liberata's lawsuit allows still other analyses. As in many other cases, this process reveals an essentially feminine story: A slave is seduced by her owner in exchange for the promise of liberty and, upon realizing that the promise would not be kept, resolves to pursue liberty through legal action.

In general there was little difference between the number of male and of female slaves who pursued freedom suits, as can be seen in the fig. 2. Of a total of 1,206 slaves who initiated freedom lawsuits in the Rio de Janeiro Court of Appeals, 52.62 percent were men and 46.38 percent were women, and the percentage of sentences decided in favor of liberty had the same distribution.

Similarly, men and women were equally involved in different types of processes, as can be seen in fig. 3, and were part of individual, family, and collective actions.[20]

Although these data point to similarity of genders in terms of initiating a freedom suit and in achieving freedom, the reasons given by men and women in these actions were generally very different. These data contradict the general pattern of manumission in Brazil and in the Americas, two-thirds of which, according to Higgins, Karash, and Brana-Shute, are considered to have benefited women, mainly those slaves in urban areas. As for these freedom suits, there is no noticeable difference between men and women in their seeking court action to obtain freedom. But a closer look at these data does confirm the general tendency for women to be granted freedom. After all, as freedom suits are a very peculiar means of obtaining freedom, what is noteworthy here, as the authors mentioned have underscored, are the different reasons that make a female slave or a male one turn to the court to solve their conflicts. Men were more likely to obtain freedom by purchasing it, as well as to file freedom suits to solve problems concerning their own value. Conversely, women generally filed suits when they realized the agreements they had with their masters were not respected, agreements referring to household duties and errands, or to consensual relationships the slaves had with their masters.

Liberata's case is a good example: beyond the fact that the course of her life was specifically that of a woman, it was the fact that she had had sexual relations and children with her master that allowed the destiny of her other children to be changed.

In 1835, more than twenty years after failing to win the freedom lawsuit brought by Liberata, her two youngest children, José and Joaquina, went to the court at Desterro to request that the case be reopened so they could prove that they were Liberata's children and thus illegally enslaved. José and Joaquina argued that during their mother's lawsuit, they were sent to an orphan's home and then, when Liberata won her freedom, their birth certificates were torn up and they were sold as slaves. At the end of a three-year legal process the custodian of Liberata's children finally managed to convince the tribunal that the sale had been illegal and that the slaves in question really were children of Liberata.

The end of the process is truly surprising: Twenty years after the initial action had been archived, the only ones who had remained slaves managed to revive the story of their mother and win their freedom. It was Liberata's trajectory and the fact that she had sought help in the courts of justice that allowed her children to obtain freedom.

Thus the analysis of Liberata's freedom lawsuit is important to a deeper understanding of the role of the condition of women and of the state in contributing to freedom for slaves in Brazil in the nineteenth century. After all, if on the one hand her trajectory is specifically a woman's story, on the other she acted like countless other slaves, both men and women, taking her private disputes with her owners to be resolved in the courts of justice, as an example of what was a common practice of appealing to the state as a way to resolve private conflicts.

In this sense, as demonstrated by Whitman, Jennings, and Meisel, we must emphasize that although the state did not always respond the way slaves and freedmen who appealed to it would have expected, it was seen as a legitimate recourse for them to obtain freedom and to change their legal status. Several were the countries that were unarguably committed to the question of freedom, even if it was not in the best interest of their fellow men.[21]

Although there were moments when the states were more or less active, as in the flow of independence processes, mainly in the cases of Brazil and the United States, it is important to note that for these slaves to seek the state to try to solve their private conflicts was a due form. If this per se does not change

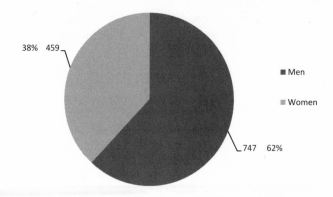

FIG. 2. Gender Division among the Slaves that Initiated Freedom Suits in Nineteenth-Century Brazil

Note: Between 1865 and 1870 seven appeals originating in the extreme southern regions of Brazil were directed to Rio de Janeiro, all of them concerned with the same issue: Slaves had gone to the province of Uruguay, which had been free of slavery since 1840, and upon return to Brazil had attempted to reclaim their liberty based on the law of 1831. The same local lawyers appear in all of the cases. See cases number 11.689, box 3679, Pelotas, 1865; number 12.126, box 3694, Pelotas, 1867; number 13.194, box 3680, Uruguaiana, 1868; number 13.196, box 3685, Uruguaiana, 1868; number 12.465, box 3683, Bagé, 1868; number 13.794, box 3690, Alegrete, 1869; number 3221, group 216, Uruguaiana, 1870, Rio de Janeiro Court of Appeals, National Archive–RJ.

the character of the states—especially in the case of the Brazilian state, which, generally speaking, keeps supporting patriarchal practices and the power of slave masters over the slaves—at the same time, it enables us to have a much more comprehensive view of the complex relationships governing slave masters, slaves, and agents of the state and also because it demonstrates that the interests of the state and those of the oligarchies were not always in accordance with one another.

But what is perhaps more important than the considerations that can be raised about the character of those states in the Americas that nurtured slavery from the eighteenth to the nineteenth century and along the current century is the fact that the situations brought about herein, such as is the case of Liberata, as well as of freedom suits in general, were made possible because the slaves themselves took the first steps to obtain freedom. If manumission already demonstrates how autonomous many slaves came to be, freedom suits are a much more vehement demonstration of how certain slaves in urban areas managed to establish social relationships with other slaves, freedmen, freemen,

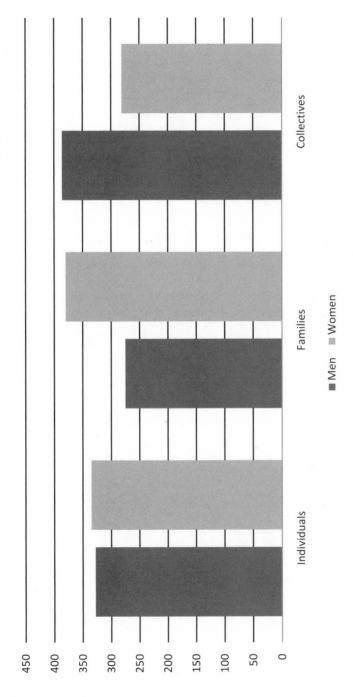

Fig. 3. Relationship Gender—Type of Freedom Suit

and mainly with powerful landowners who gave them the opportunity to file suits in courtrooms.

Moreover, before a freedom suit could be initiated, the slave had to have access to a free man willing to sign a petition on his behalf, had to hire a lawyer to act on his behalf, and in some cases, the slave had to pay for the costs of the proceedings. If they were the "social dead," as defined by Patterson, no slave would have been able to behave likewise.[22] In this sense I shall conclude this essay underlining the fact that, although freedom suits stand for a pathway to slave resistance, they did not represent an exception to an oppressive and violent system. Urban slavery in Brazil was oppressive and violent, but resources such as freedom suits were part of its structure and as such were utilized by slaves who were aware of the possibilities of freedom, who knew the law and— why not—who knew their rights.

NOTES

1. Réis was the name of the Brazilian currency at this time.

2. Trial number 1337, Box 214, Desterro, Tribunal da Relação, National Archives–Rio de Janeiro.

3. Sílvia H. Lara, *Campos da Violência: Escravos e senhores na Capitania do Rio de Janeiro, 1750–1808* (Rio de Janeiro: Paz e Terra, 1988); Peter Eisenberg, *Modernização sem Mudança: A indústria açucareira em Pernambuco, 1840–1910* (Rio de Janeiro: Paz e Terra; Campinas: Editora da Unicamp, 1977); Lenine Nequete, *O Escravo na Jurisprudência Brasileira: Magistratura e ideologia no Segundo Reinado* (Porto Alegre: Revista dos Tribunais, 1988); Sidney Chalhoub, *Visões da Liberdade: As últimas décadas da escravidão na Corte* (São Paulo: Companhia das Letras, 1990); Hebe Mattos, *Das Cores do Silêncio: os significados da liberdade no Sudeste escravista—Brasil século XIX* (Rio de Janeiro: Nova Fronteira, 1998).

4. As an example of the historiography that subscribe to this dualism, see Fernando Henrique Cardoso, *Capitalismo e Escravidão no Brasil Meridional: O Negro na Sociedade Escravocrata do Rio Grande do Sul* (São Paulo: DIFEL, 1962); Jacob Gorender, *O Escravismo Colonial* (São Paulo: Ática, 1971). For an analysis of this historiographical movement, see Ciro Flamarion S. Cardoso ed., *Escravidão e Abolição no Brasil—Novas perspectivas* (Rio de Janeiro: Jorge Zahar Editor, 1988).

5. As the freedom suits express a form of conflict between masters and slaves, they provide a means of evaluating some of the factors responsible for the decline of slavery. Among these factors are the existence of established communities of freeborn and freed Africans and their descendants, slaves' involvement in diverse economic activities, and the social role of attorneys, jurists, judges, and the state as a whole in defining the status of those individuals who argued that they were not, or at least were no longer, slaves. Those are the themes primarily addressed by the most recent historiography concerning freedom suits in United States. See, for example, Kimberly Hanger, *Bounded Lives, Bounded Places: Free Black Society in Colonial New Orleans, 1769–1803* (Durham, N.C.: Duke University Press, 1997); Stephen T. Whitman, *The Price of Freedom: Slavery and Manumission in Baltimore and Early National Maryland* (Lexington: University Press of Kentucky, 1997); and Patience Essah, *A House Divided: Slavery and Emancipation in Delaware, 1638–1865* (Charlottesville: University Press of Virginia, 1996).

6. In the Rio de Janeiro National Archives the section referring to the court of appeals are organized in alphabetical order according to the name of the author of the process (combining both criminal and civil cases). The processes related to slaves are collected in a separate drawer.

7. This could be explained by the fact that until 1874, the Rio de Janeiro Court of Appeals collected the cases that had their decisions appealed in courts located in the South and Southeast of the country. The actions originating in northeastern Brazil, after having their decisions appealed, were forwarded to the Bahia Court of Appeals in Salvador.

8. See *Coleção das Leis do Império do Brasil* (Rio de Janeiro: Typographia Imperial, 1831).

9. See Mattos, *Cores do Silêncio*, 207; Keila Grinberg, *Liberata—a lei da ambiguidade: A sações de liberdade da Corte de Apelação do Rio de Janeiro no século XIX* (Rio de Janeiro: Relume Dumará, 1994), 25; Eduardo Spiller Pena, "Resenha de Liberata: A lei da ambiguidade," *Afro-Ásia* 17 (1996): 237–243.

10. In Brazil conflicts relating to the proclamation of independence occurred only in the province of Bahia, where the local government was forced to flee and the city of Salvador became isolated. See Kátia M. de Queirós Mattoso, *Bahia, Século XIX: Uma Província no Império* (Rio de Janeiro: Nova Fronteira, 1992).

11. In reference to the political climate during the period of independence, see Lúcia M. B. Pereira das Neves, "Corcundas, constitucionais, pés-de-chumbo: A cultura política da Independência (1820–1822)" (Ph.D. diss., University of São Paulo, 1992) and Gladys S. Ribeiro, "A liberdade em construção: Identidade nacional e conflitos antilusitanos no Primeiro Reinado" (Ph.D. diss., Unicamp, 1997).

12. *Macmillan Encyclopedia of World Slavery*, s.v. "Manumission: United States."

13. Studies of the seventeenth and eighteenth centuries in Brazil support this claim. See John Monteiro, *Negros da Terra: Índios e Bandeirantes nas Origens de São Paulo* (São Paulo: Companhia das Letras, 1995); Lara, *Campos da Violência*; Eduardo França Paiva, *Escravos e Libertos em Minas Gerais: Estratégias de Resistência Através de Testamentos* (São Paulo: Annablume, 1995).

14. Maria do Rosário Pimentel, *Viagem ao Fundo das Consciências: A Escravatura na Época Moderna* (Lisbon: Colibri, 1995), 57.

15. *Liberdade* means "Freedom," and *Escravidão* means "Slavery."

16. Suits with unspecified results or those suits which were later brought before the Supreme Court for later appeals are excluded from this total.

17. *Escrav. Para Liberd* means the sentences changed from slavery to freedom, and *Liberd. Para Escrav* means the sentences changed from freedom to slavery.

18. This argument was developed in an article by Manuela Carneiro da Cunha, "Sobre os silêncios da lei: Lei costumeira e positiva nas alforrias de escravos no Brasil do século XIX," in *Antropologia do Brasil: Mito, história, etnicidade* (São Paulo: Brasiliense/EDUSP, 1986), 123–144.

19. For a profile of the judges occupying positions tied to the Central Powers during the nineteenth century, see Mattoso, *Bahia, Século XIX;* and Eduardo Spiller Pena, "Pajens da Casa Imperial: Jurisconsultos e Escravidão no Brasil Imperial" (Ph.D. diss., UNICAMP, 1998).

20. After 1870 some of the attorneys were clearly abolitionists. Luiz Gama was one of them who, during the last decades of slavery, actively pursued the cause of abolition, defending innumerous slaves, including those in rural regions, in freedom suits. See Elciene Azevedo, *Orfeu de Carapinha: A trajetória de Luiz Gama na Imperial Cidade de São Paulo* (Campinas: Unicamp, 1999).

21. This same general opinion was shared by the judges who took part in the cases. While it would be impossible to compile a model of judges' behavior similar to that of the attorneys, as verdicts were made by panels composed of six or seven judges whose votes were not recorded separately, in the majority of sentences the justification for liberty lay in the recognition that a particular slave crossed the boundary separating slavery from liberty.

22. *Homens* means "Men," and *Mulheres* means "Women," in a total of 1,206 slaves (*escravos*).

23. The freedom suits could be indivduals (*individuais,* as shown in the graphic), or initiated by one slave, familiar (*familiares*), initiated by one slave in the behalf of his or her family, or collective (*coletivas*), initiated by a group of slaves, normally members of different families.

24. Stephen Whitman, "Manumission and Black Apprenticeship in Maryland, 1770–1870," paper presented at the From Slavery to Freedom: Manumission in the Atlantic World conference, College of Charleston, Charleston, S.C., October 4–7, 2000; Evelyn Jennings's essay in this volume, "Paths to Freedom: Imperial Defense and Manumission in Havana, 1762–1800"; Seth Meisel, "Military Manumissions in Early Republican Argentina," paper presented at the From Slavery to Freedom: Manumission in the Atlantic World conference, College of Charleston, Charleston, S.C., October 4–7, 2000.

25. Orlando Patterson, *Slavery and Social Death: A Comparative Study* (Cambridge, Mass.: Harvard University Press, 1982); Orlando Patterson, "Slavery: The Underside of Freedom," *Slavery and Abolition* 5 (1984): 87–104.

Beatriz Gallotti Mamigonian

Conflicts over the Meanings of Freedom

—ᴥᴥ—

The Liberated Africans' Struggle for Emancipation in Brazil, 1840s–1860s

On November 24, 1857, at the police department of the city of Rio de Janeiro, the African Carolina Conga appeared before Dr. Izidro Borges Monteiro, the Chief of Police. Asked whether she had requested or asked someone to request her emancipation, she responded that when she was at the plantation she received from little mistress D. Amalia, the daughter of the late Mr. Aureliano, a letter hidden in a sugar tin brought to her by crioulo Jacintho, a slave of the plantation, and having it read by Antonio de tal, she realized the letter advised her to run away so that the little mistress could obtain her manumission, and that when she came to Niterói with her sick daughter, she received a message from the little mistress brought by one pardo man from D. Clara's household where the little mistress lived, telling her to find a way to escape to her house so that she [the mistress] could arrange for her manumission and that she, in fact, ran away one night with her daughter Eva to D. Clara's house, where the little mistress lived and from there they embarked on a boat at night that reached Santa Luzia beach [in Rio de Janeiro], from where they went to rua das Marrecas to the house of Mr. Pedro de Alcântara, with the pardo Belmiro, who had been a servant of the late Mr. Aureliano and now lived at D. Clara's house; he had been waiting for her at Santa Luzia beach.

"Interrogation of the African Carolina Conga,"
November 24, 1857, Arquivo Nacional–Rio de Janeiro

The woman who undertook the dramatic escape described above operated under the codes of slavery but was not legally a slave. Carolina had been brought to Brazil from west-central Africa in 1834. The slave ship that brought her was captured by Brazilian authorities and condemned for illegal slave trading under the international agreements for the abolition of the Atlantic slave trade. Carolina and the other nearly three hundred enslaved Africans who were on board the *Duquesa de Bragança* were, following the agreements, emancipated and put under the care of the Brazilian government for a term of apprenticeship that was to last fourteen years. They belonged to the special legal category of *africanos livres* (liberated Africans), that is, those who were neither slave nor free.[1] After completing their apprenticeships they still had to petition the Brazilian government for what they considered would be *plena liberdade* ("full freedom"). Indicating that liberated Africans saw their terms of service as slavery, liberated African Carolina declared she was seeking *alforria* ("manumission").

Carolina Congo had served her compulsory term at the Paquequer tea plantation near Rio de Janeiro, where she worked with other liberated Africans and with slaves. The plantation belonged to Aureliano Coutinho, the minister of justice in the early 1830s, who had been directly in charge of the administration of the liberated Africans; it had been sold to a medical doctor, José Francisco Frongeth, who obtained permission to keep the liberated Africans under his responsibility. Carolina had served for more than twenty years when the daughter of Aureliano, Amália Guilhermina, helped her to obtain her final emancipation in 1857. She had had four children and was married to Domingos, a slave of Frongeth's plantation. Her case reveals many aspects of the daily lives of liberated Africans and their relationships with slaves and free people, but more than that, it illustrates quite dramatically the liberated Africans' struggle for their final emancipation, which involved petitioning the Ministry of Justice, presenting supporting documents, proving themselves worthy of "full freedom," and sometimes having their hopes for autonomy frustrated. I address the petition process from the point of view of the individual liberated Africans in an attempt to uncover through the direct testimony of their petitions the meanings they gave to their terms of service and to their emancipation. Moreover, I discuss how the application of the decrees regulating liberated African emancipation was related, on the one hand, to the changes in slave-master relations and manumission practices in the nineteenth century and, on the other, to the emerging debate over slave emancipation in Brazil.

THE LIBERATED AFRICANS AND BRAZILIAN SLAVERY IN THE 1830S AND 1840S

British pressure for the abolition of the Atlantic slave trade imposed significant changes on the Brazilian slave system in the nineteenth century. High mortality rates and negative or low natural increase in the slave population made for a sustained demand for African slaves. Ever since the transfer of the Portuguese royal court to Rio de Janeiro in 1808, this demand had increased; the coffee boom in the Paraíba Valley in the 1830s and 1840s made the slave trade reach unprecedented numbers. Yet Portugal and Great Britain signed a treaty for the abolition of the slave trade in 1815 and measures for the suppression of the trade were put in place. Independent Brazil was forced to sign a similar treaty in 1826; under the Anglo-Brazilian treaty that went into force in March 1830, all of the Brazilian slave trade was prohibited, and bilateral tribunals were to adjudicate the apprehensions made by Brazilian or British naval authorities. Mixed Commission courts were set up in Freetown, Sierra Leone, and in Rio de Janeiro to judge the seized slave ships; they were also responsible for emancipating the slaves found on board the ships condemned for illegal slave trading.[2]

The Mixed Commission court sitting in Rio de Janeiro between 1830 and 1845 was responsible for the emancipation of more than four thousand Africans, who following the instructions included in the bilateral agreements were put under the guardianship of the Brazilian government.[3] According to the regulations the *africanos livres* were to be employed "as servants or free laborers" for fourteen years before being granted "full freedom."[4] The labor experience of the liberated Africans in Brazil in the 1830s and 1840s reflected the transformations in Brazilian slavery: Not only were they employed as slaves, but their release from guardianship became more difficult than it had been for the Africans emancipated by the Anglo-Portuguese court in 1821.

The prohibition of the slave trade to Brazil, inscribed in the Anglo-Brazilian treaty that came into force in March 1830 and in the Brazilian law of November 7, 1831, was the key factor for the changes. As a result of the prohibition, and given the sustained labor demand, particularly from the coffee regions, slave importation rose dramatically in the years leading up to 1830, and slave prices rose too. Manumission rates declined, and conditions shifted: while the majority of manumissions between the last decades of the eighteenth and first decades of the nineteenth century were paid for by the slaves, after the 1830s fewer slaves could pay their market prices, and the path to freedom involved more negotiation for free or conditional manumission.[5] Moreover the prohibition was not sufficient to stop the slave trade. It continued despite the repression and brought 760,000 slaves to Brazil illegally between 1830 and 1856. The liberated Africans were therefore only a small portion of the Africans who were imported to Brazil in the nineteenth century.[6]

To serve their terms of apprenticeship, liberated Africans were distributed among private individuals and public institutions, mainly in the city of Rio de Janeiro. A close look at their labor experience reveals that they lived and worked alongside private slaves at their hirers' houses or crown slaves at the public institutions and were treated as slaves in many ways: Liberated Africans could not be bought or sold, but the transfer of their "concessions" was often a monetary transaction; they were often hired out or put *ao ganho* to hire themselves out in the streets of Rio and never kept their earnings; and they were not trained to take on skilled occupations.[7] Until the 1860s the children of liberated Africans inherited the ambiguous status of their parents instead of being considered free.[8] Moreover, in the late 1840s Brazilian authorities changed their policy and did not recognize liberated Africans' right to "full freedom" after fourteen years of service. In other Atlantic territories where this category existed, with the exception of Cuba, the treatment of the liberated Africans was adjusted to new ideas on free labor during the nineteenth century, and the terms of apprenticeship were shortened.[9] In Brazil, much like in Cuba, the presence of liberated Africans among the slaves, particularly the newly arrived Africans, was resented by masters and avoided by the authorities whenever possible. Thus they were kept under increased control.

Every attempt by liberated Africans to assert their different status was repressed as "insubordination." Some cases were dealt with as part of the daily problem with discipline, such as that of Jacinto, who served at the House of Correction and, reprimanded by the overseer of liberated Africans for speaking to him without removing his hat, responded by saying "he would not doff his hat to the emperor himself, much less to an overseer," reacted violently to an attempt to punish him, and was taken to trial.[10] Other complaints were formal and addressed to the Curator of liberated Africans, to judges of orphans, or to senior administrators. In those cases the liberated Africans stressed their free status, demanded better treatment, or complained that their term of service had expired. Still, their acts were considered "insubordination." The best documented case of the liberated Africans' formal struggle to have their rights enforced is that of a group of Mina (West African) men who served their first fourteen years at the Navy Arsenal in Bahia. When they complained to the president of the province of Bahia that their terms of service had been completed and demanded their final emancipation, they were transferred to Rio de Janeiro. Some of them were taken to the Iron Foundry of Ipanema, where, within a month of their arrival, they presented a petition to the local judge in the nearest city. In truncated but emphatic wording the Mina liberated Africans made clear that they knew they were free, that they had already completed the agreed upon period of service, and that they would no longer submit to the conditions under which they were held. Once more the reaction, in the name of "order and subordination," was to remove them from the group of liberated Africans in which they could instill undesirable ideas and send them elsewhere.[11]

As a result of their ambiguous status liberated Africans were seen by Brazilians as standing at the bottom of the social scale, a perception well illustrated by a list of "best and worst things" published in 1849 by the Bahian humorous newspaper *A Marmota* in which "not being a slave" ranked best and "being a liberated African" ranked worst of all things. The justification given was that liberated Africans "could not free themselves."[12]

THE ABOLITION OF THE SLAVE TRADE AND THE DECREE OF 1853

After the expiration of the Anglo-Brazilian treaty and the closure of the Mixed Commission courts in 1845, the Brazilian government came under renewed naval and diplomatic pressure from the British to curb the slave trade. Between 1846 and 1850 the illegal slave trade to Brazil reached unprecedented numbers: On average, more than fifty thousand African slaves were imported per year.[13] Under the Aberdeen Act passed in the British Parliament in 1845, the Brazilian slave trade was declared piracy and Brazilian slavers were liable to be seized and taken to British courts. Incidents with British cruisers in Brazilian waters ignited public opinion and raised a diplomatic crisis in 1850. Amid fears of major slave unrest—a massive plot to poison slave masters had been discovered in the Paraíba Valley in 1848–49—and an epidemic of yellow fever, both of which were associated with the continuation of the illegal trade, the Brazilian government issued new legislation and engaged seriously in the repression of the slave trade.[14]

Approximately five thousand Africans were seized and emancipated during this new phase. Yet the new policy for their distribution for service reflected new times, as liberated Africans seized in the late 1840s and early 1850s were no longer given to private individuals; they all served public institutions in Rio de Janeiro and preferably in the provinces, where new laborers were needed and they could be closely watched. The Africans who had been emancipated in the 1830s and early 1840s were mostly scattered in the city of Rio under little or no control from their hirers until then but would soon be "recalled" to the House of Correction, a prison workhouse that centralized their assignment for service.

The year in which the Brazilian government decreed the emancipation of the liberated Africans, 1853, was a critical one for convincing the public of the government's will to abolish the trade. The news of the importation of nearly five hundred slaves into the southern part of Rio de Janeiro province prompted severe repression by the government, and the debates surrounding what was called "the Bracuhy affair" dominated newspapers and political tribunes early in 1853. The event raised the issue of whether it had been appropriate for the police to search for newly imported Africans inside the plantations, fueling thoughts of emancipation among the predominantly African slave population.[15] By then the existence in the country of hundreds of thousands of African slaves imported since the trade had been prohibited in 1830 had become a legal problem. One contemporary interpretation of the Brazilian law for the abolition of the trade passed in November 1831 proclaimed that those Africans should be considered "free Africans," having the same status as those liberated by the Mixed Commission or by local authorities. Many times the imperial government had to reassure the planters that the measures taken to enforce the 1850 law for the abolition of the slave trade would not threaten their "right" to the African slaves imported previously.[16]

Pressure from British foreign representatives regarding the Africans liberated by the extinct Anglo-Brazilian mixed commission had been mounting. As cosignatories of the treaties and comembers of the mixed commission, the British felt responsible for the fate of the Africans emancipated by the court. While trying to control the Brazilian administration's handling of the liberated Africans, British officials always insisted on the observance of the limit on the term of apprenticeship set in the bilateral agreements. A new phase of the British pressure on the Brazilian government over the issue of the liberated Africans had been instituted in 1850, when Lord Palmerston instructed James Hudson, the British chargé d'affaires in Rio de Janeiro, to suggest the establishment of a mixed commission to investigate the cases of Africans suspected of being imported during the illegal phase of the slave trade and declare whether they should be freed. Palmerston equated the right to freedom of the Africans who had been liberated by the mixed commission between 1831 and 1845 to that of those imported illegally during that period. He wanted to extend "liberated African status" to those illegally held in slavery. Needless to say the Brazilian government adamantly refused such cooperation, considering it an inadmissible intervention in national affairs.[17] Brazilian ministers had known for a long time that under the excuse of protecting the Africans emancipated by the mixed commission, the British Foreign Office advocated abolitionist principles that threatened the maintenance of the slave system in the country. Deflating British excuses for interfering in those matters was probably one of the expected side effects of the 1853 decree emancipating liberated Africans. It did not work that way; rather, it fueled diplomatic pressure and brought the issue to public debate.

Pressure from the liberated Africans had also been mounting before December 1853. Even if the level of awareness of their status and rights was not uniform, the Ministry of Justice records show that in the late 1840s and early 1850s more liberated Africans were prepared to voice their complaints than before. At the time of their arrival they had participated in a formal ceremony of emancipation before a judge or before the mixed commission members, during which they had been given Brazilian names, and had their body marks, signs, ages, and ethnic origins recorded. Subsequently, at the time of their distribution to hirers or institutions, they had been told the conditions and duration of their service and shown their letters of emancipation issued by the mixed commission or by the judges of orphans.[18] Those who had been first emancipated in the early 1830s and distributed for service after 1834 completed their fourteen-year terms of service in 1848 and in the following years and became increasingly restless and unruly, to the point that their hirers preferred not to keep them. Such was the case of Maria Rebola, emancipated from the ship *Angélica* and granted to hirer Francisco do Rego Quintanilha in January 1836. Since 1851 Quintanilha complained that her conduct had become "very bad, beyond the superlative." She no longer obeyed his orders; she worked only for herself as a washerwoman, no longer for the hirer's family; and she accused her hirer of "stealing her services."[19] Like her there were countless other liberated Africans who refused to obey their hirers or administrators after their term of service expired and who claimed their final letters of emancipation. It was after taking into consideration British pressure and liberated African unrest, and after consulting the Council of State, that Minister of Justice Nabuco de Araújo issued a decree offering emancipation to the liberated Africans who had worked for private hirers for fourteen years in December 1853.

THE PETITION PROCESS

> I deemed advisable . . . to order that the free Africans that have served private
> persons for a term of fourteen years be emancipated when they so request, with
> the obligation, however, that they reside in that place designated by the Govern-
> ment and that they take a salaried occupation.
>
> Decree no. 1303 of 28 December 1853

News of the decree reached the liberated Africans and their hirers through the newspapers. News gradually spread among those involved with the admin-istration of the liberated Africans and among the Africans themselves."[20] The decree issued on December 28, 1853, offered emancipation to the liberated Africans who had served private hirers for fourteen years, but it required those entitled to that right to come forward to claim it through petitions to the emperor. The legislation that had regulated their assignment for service since 1834 had not fixed a limit on the term of service for liberated Africans because it was based on the premise that they would be sent back to Africa. The admin-istration had been working since then under the assumption that there was no fixed time limit on their compulsory service when, in fact, the new decree only reiterated the duration of the term of service that had actually been established by the royal decree of 1818. Nevertheless, the decree made an important dis-tinction between the liberated Africans who had served private hirers and those who served in public institutions, favoring the first group and denying the right to emancipation of the second. It also made emancipation conditional on the emancipated Africans' obligation to establish residence wherever they were designated by government officials and to be employed in salaried positions. The analysis of the liberated Africans' petitions and of the records of their han-dling by the long line of government officials in charge of their evaluation reveals that liberated Africans, their hirers, and some officials adopted strate-gies and arguments used in the negotiations between masters and slaves for individual manumission (only adapted to the liberated Africans' distinct sta-tus). But more than that, it also exposes a key moment in the history of Brazil-ian slavery when the government, at first reluctant to admit the expediency of liberated Africans' collective emancipation, shifted to full support for this policy in 1863–64, when "the liberated African question" threatened to accelerate slave emancipation.

When Anna Benguela stated that she "had already acquired the knowledge necessary to live on her own and gain her subsistence as a freedwoman," she argued that she wanted to be emancipated because she "was not yet free." Her case and many others demonstrate that liberated Africans felt their term of service to be like slavery for a limited time. This argument was also used by another liberated African woman, Maria Cabinda, when she claimed her right to be emancipated: she stated that "the term of her captivity had expired."[21] In collective petitions, liberated Africans also compared their situation to slavery. The liberated Africans from the House of Correction complained to their curator that they lived in "quasi-slavery" and had no other guarantee of their freedom than the legislation that protected them.[22] It is clear that liberated Africans associated with slavery the strict control to which they were subjected and expected their emancipation to deliver them "full freedom."

Many liberated Africans associated their final emancipation with manumission, dependent upon the good will of the hirer/master or upon monetary compensation. Plácido Cabinda, for example, worked "ao ganho" as a bricklayer, paid a weekly sum to his hirer, and believed in his hirer's promise that she would free him when she died. Beliza, from the gunpowder factory, petitioned for her emancipation and offered to give a slave to take her place or to pay the sum corresponding to her value. Custódia Rebola, too, offered to pay the sum corresponding to the time she had left to serve.[23]

Because they were formal procedures followed when one wanted to prove his or her right to freedom, liberated Africans' petitions can be compared to freedom suits. During the judicial process, slaves remained in deposit away from their masters and depended on the help of curators and on the testimony of people with whom they were familiar. So did the liberated Africans while their petitions were analyzed. Unlike freedom suits, though, the petitions of liberated Africans were administrative procedures handled by the Ministry of Justice and did not involve legal arguments by lawyers and judges; the process revolved around the application of the 1853 decree only. The key evidence for obtaining emancipation through the Ministry of Justice decree was a certificate of the term of service. It consisted of a copy of the liberated African's record of concession to a private hirer or to an institution, clearly stating the time elapsed since the beginning of his or her service. This certificate was attached to the petition for emancipation addressed to the emperor and delivered to the Ministry of Justice. Sometimes letters of reference from persons for whom the liberated African had worked were attached to the petitions as well, to testify to the African's good behavior and rectitude.

The judicial proceedings of freedom suits and the administrative proceedings of the petitions for emancipation were very different.[24] Once received by the section of the ministry that handled issues related to the slave trade and liberated Africans, the petition followed a long course, during which it received information from the judge of orphans, the curator of liberated Africans, the director of the House of Correction, and the chief of police. An interrogation of the liberated African by the subdelegate of police was part of the proceedings. It was intended to verify the identity of the African in question and to determine whether there was any third-party interest involved in the emancipation process.[25] Each of these authorities determined whether the liberated African deserved emancipation.

Different government officials dealing with the petitions had different ways of considering whether a liberated African deserved emancipation. The judge of orphans and the curator checked the identity of the liberated African against the register and testified to the length of the term he or she had served. They were always in favor of emancipation if the African had served for fourteen years, regardless of the place of employment. The chief of police gathered information from the hirer, from the director of the House of Correction where the African had been put in deposit, and from supervisors of the liberated African's work. He looked for evidence of obedience, ability to support oneself through regular work, and in particular for solid indications of the "regular conduct" of the African. The chief of police never failed to mention to his superiors whether the African had drinking or gambling habits. The Ministry of Justice officials who dealt with the petition and summarized it for the minister agreed with the opinion given by the chief of police, whether it supported emancipation or not. The minister of justice always had the last word, either denying emancipation or issuing notices of emancipation to the judge of orphans and the chief of police.[26]

All the petitions centered their justification on the fact that the liberated African had completed (and often surpassed) the term of service and that, by virtue of the legislation, he or she should be emancipated. However, the wording of the liberated Africans' petitions also included many arguments raised to convince government officials that the petitioner was worthy of emancipation. In this liberated Africans proved once again that they played by the slave code. Demonstrating obedience and respect for the hirers or superiors, proving to have the ability to support oneself through regular work, or showing oneself to be married or to have children to support were some of the common strategies. Dionísia Bié, for example, argued that she was "tired of serving" and wanted to live with her two sons, whose father, named José Guedes, presumably a free man, intended to provide them with "education, moral and religious instruction."[27] Hipólito Angola presented proof that he had secured a contract to work as a house servant for 96$000 réis per year for a widow living in Gamboa, D. Polucena Roza dos Prazeres.[28] Idalina Umbuí had served at the Misericórdia Hospital and at the Pedro II Hospice and petitioned for emancipation under the argument that she "had acquired illnesses resulting in having her lungs affected, a disease that she cannot treat in reclusion," adding that she intended to work as a house servant for one "honest person with the means to give her treatment and see to her total recovery."[29] The Africans were responding to the expectations of the government officials who handled their cases, for whom those worthy of emancipation "besides having completed the term of service, should have good behavior and be able to conduct themselves regularly without any control."[30]

As in the slaves' freedom suits, in the petition process the liberated Africans benefited from outside help at different stages of the process. It was common for liberated Africans to resort to the use of proxies to write their petitions and follow them through the intricacies of the imperial bureaucracy. The Africans probably paid for this service from their earnings. Unlike judicial procedures, the petition processes did not require the liberated Africans to have curators to represent them or lawyers to defend them. Liberated Africans' petitions could be written by anyone who formulated them in the accepted format and were usually done by professionals who announced their services as proxies in the yearly city directory, *Almanak Laemmert*, just under the lawyers' listing.[31] At times hirers paid the proxies to help the Africans or wrote the petitions themselves. Ninety percent of the petitions were made in the name of the liberated Africans by proxies or by the Africans themselves, but a few were handled by hirers or other curators, in their own names, claiming emancipation for the liberated Africans.[32] Significantly, in 262 cases of emancipation consulted, 4 were either written or signed by the liberated Africans themselves. In a few other cases the Africans were able to write but preferred to have the petition written by someone else.[33]

Liberated Africans sought help from their hirers and from other persons willing to support their emancipation claims. Support could come in the form of letters attesting to the good conduct of the liberated African, written by their hirers or by persons for whom they had worked; in the form of testimonies; in the form of guarantees of protection or employment; and also in the form of an engaged participation on behalf of the Africans. Prisca Benguela, for example, received support from the person who rented her services from her hirer. Manoel Antônio Gonçalves de Mello wrote her petition and testified on her behalf, attesting that she had served him as wet nurse for his daughter and always behaved well. At that point Prisca was making use of a form of help accepted by the Ministry of Justice clerks and, at the same time, trying to avoid the negative impact the testimony of her hirer could have on her claim. Rosa Lúcia de Jesus, dreading the idea of losing the income she earned from Prisca's services, declared that the African had a very irregular conduct, saying "there was hardly a week when she does not get drunk more than once and hardly a month when she does not run away from home." Prisca's first petition

had already been turned down by ministry officials because it had been prepared by a proxy but paid for by a Portuguese man, Joaquim José, possibly her
mate, who appeared as a party interested in her emancipation.[34]

The case of Carolina Conga, whose interrogation opened this chapter,
demonstrated that the African woman benefited from a more engaged type of
help than the one usually found in the petition cases. Carolina worked at a tea
plantation in Petrópolis that had belonged to Aureliano Coutinho, the minister of justice in the 1830s. In her interrogation at the police department in
November 1857, she recounted that one day at the plantation she received,
hidden in a sugar tin, a letter from Amália Guilhermina ("little mistress"), the
daughter of the late Coutinho, encouraging her to run away to Niterói to procure her emancipation. Carolina was helped by an "underground network" of
people arranged by "little mistress" to convey the liberated African woman and
her daughter to Rio de Janeiro, where she found refuge at the house of João
Pedro de Alcântara. Operating under the accepted codes of slavery, which protected slaves from ill-treatment and brutal masters, Amália Guilhermina petitioned on behalf of Carolina, asking for her emancipation and accusing her new
hirer, a Doctor Frongeth, of intentionally keeping Carolina in servitude; she
instructed the African woman to raise the issue of the ill-treatment she suffered
on the plantation. Carolina was sent to the House of Correction to await a decision on her petition, and her daughter was sent to stay with her mother's pro-
tector. The African woman was quickly emancipated.[35] The clandestine
execution of this operation demonstrates the difficulties that faced liberated
Africans who wanted to petition for emancipation against the will of their hirers or who lived outside of Rio de Janeiro. The quick solution to her case
should be attributed to the powerful intervention of Coutinho's daughter in
the process. Amália Guilhermina had already helped liberated African Delfina
the previous year, by declaring that she might contract Delfina's services once
the African woman received her emancipation.[36]

Certain hirers or protectors—ministers, councilors of state, senators, senior
government officials—had a powerful influence over the proceedings at the
Ministry of Justice and could speed up or block petition processes easily. This
is a sign that the social hierarchy among hirers interfered with the liberated
Africans' access to final emancipation. But even the hirers who did not have a
high standing in the social hierarchy were influential in the outcome of the
petitions, because hirers could attest before the ministry that the liberated
Africans, once emancipated, would behave as they were expected, that is, like
obedient freedpersons. The most feared consequence of liberated African emancipation for the hirers was the breakup in their authority over the emancipated
African in question, over the other liberated Africans they might have under
their service, and also over their slaves, who might think they were entitled
to the same rights (and they often were). The government tried to avoid this

consequence; that is probably why the petition process in many ways resembled a negotiation for manumission, in which the hirers/masters played such an important role. Because liberated Africans and slaves coexisted in the same city, often in the same households, and slavery depended upon the acceptance by the slaves of the legitimate authority of the masters over them, deciding who had and who had not the right to freedom as a liberated African held much importance for the maintenance of slavery in those turbulent times.

OBSTACLES ON THE WAY TO FINAL EMANCIPATION

Despite expectations from liberated Africans and hirers, the government was not guided solely by the logic that applied to individual manumissions. Neither a combination of good conduct, ability to support oneself, and obedience nor hirers' guarantees seemed to have ensured the emancipation of the liberated Africans filing petitions. In fact a very close look at the documentation belies the appearance of faithfulness in the government's offer of emancipation to the liberated Africans. There were traps in the course of the petition process. The recurrence of petitions by liberated Africans who complained that they had been waiting for a positive response to their request for months; the repeated denial of emancipation to the Africans serving in public institutions; and the appeals by liberated Africans who did not receive their final letters of emancipation point to the existence of a higher policy for the emancipation of the liberated Africans, one that took into account their collective impact over the slave population. This policy changed between 1853 and 1864, though.

The petitions from liberated Africans serving in public institutions were repeatedly turned down in the 1850s, even if they had completed and often surpassed the fourteen-year term of service, on the grounds that they were not entitled to the right to emancipation decreed in 1853. Liberated African Lino, for example, had been serving the Municipal Police Corps since December 1835 when he wrote by himself a petition in November 1856 saying that "his term had expired" and that he had behaved well during his term of service, spending it "without committing a single fault." Lino had probably been brought to the service of the Permanentes as a young boy, and in his twenty years of service there he must have learned how to read and write. Demonstrating that the level of adaptation to the country and the ability to support oneself or to defend one's own freedom was not sufficient to guarantee the right to final emancipation. Minister of Justice Nabuco de Araújo denied Lino's request four months later because "he was employed in a public institution."[37] Likewise petitions from liberated Africans serving at the other public institutions in the city were repeatedly turned down. Tertuliano and Catarina, married liberated Africans serving at the War Arsenal in Rio de Janeiro, had been serving since 1839 and 1836, respectively, yet had their "full freedom" denied in 1857 because "their services belonged to a public institution."[38] The same happened to two other couples serving at the War Arsenal: Onofre and Suzana and Hilário and Carolina.[39] The liberated Africans in public service knew that their mates in the service of private hirers had been receiving their emancipation. They all had been making associations between their term of service and captivity, but for those in the public service it must have seemed that effectively there was no way out.

The restrictions imposed by the Brazilian government were not exclusively aimed at liberated Africans in public service. Up to that time liberated Africans working for private hirers had a better chance but no guarantee of obtaining their letters of emancipation in a short time. Because it was required that liberated Africans be placed in the House of Correction while waiting for their petitions to go through the ordinary steps—and the House of Correction was the center for the distribution of liberated African laborers to ministries, to institutions, and to the provinces—the liberated Africans waiting for emancipation were caught in this system and ended up being sent to work in institutions, delaying considerably their emancipation The trap lay in the fact that the Africans' subsequent petitions were turned down because they were seen as "belonging" to the institutions they were temporarily serving. The case of Ignácio Oanba is emblematic. He was first emancipated in 1839 and served hirer Joaquim Cândido Soares de Meirelles until 1856, when he and his fellow liberated Africans were placed at the House of Correction to wait for emancipation. His fellows were emancipated while he was transferred to the Misericórdia Hospital and received his emancipation only in 1864.[40] Minas Quelimane fell into the same trap. Having served private hirers for fourteen years, he was sent to the House of Correction in 1855 when his hirer died, and from there transferred to work at the Medical School, then at the Misericórdia Hospital. He repeatedly petitioned to receive his letter of emancipation, which he believed had been issued in 1855, but by then he was seen as a servant of the public institutions and therefore not eligible for emancipation.[41]

In November 1859 the right to emancipation of the liberated Africans serving in public institutions was discussed in the justice section of the Council of State. Councilors admitted that the only reason the liberated Africans working in public institutions should have been excluded from the emancipation offered in the 1853 decree was the government's need for their labor, but they expressed their belief in the equality of rights between the two groups and advised the government to extend the decree's provisions to those serving in institutions. Their instruction reveals the type of emancipation favored by those statesmen:

If the government of His Imperial Majesty is resolved to exempt itself from the obligation it contracted to re-export those Africans, it is fair that the aforesaid decree should be extended to those who serve in public institutions. If, however, the number of those Africans is large, the section thinks it would be convenient to adopt some measures to subject them to the inspection of some authority and to disperse them, for example, through some colonies, for the rapid introduction of so many free blacks in the same place where they lived, if not entirely as slaves but at least subject to a certain regimen does not fail to bring inconvenient [consequences]. What is certain is that, in all fairness, being free, they cannot be perpetually subjected to a guardianship so close to slavery, in the expectation of a reexportation that becomes a true fraud.[42]

The councilors of state admitted the similarity between the guardianship of the liberated Africans and slavery and agreed that they should be finally granted release from guardianship, or final emancipation, but did not favor their autonomy. They recommended not only a gradual emancipation but also a controlled one: The Africans were to be dispersed throughout colonies in the interior, inspected by some authority that would evaluate the potential danger of their release. Again, there is one element left unsaid. What inconvenient consequences would arise from the release from guardianship of the liberated Africans at the places where they had been serving for at least fourteen years? Who could be bothered by their freedom? The councilors were making an implicit reference to the Africans who had been kept in illegal slavery and whose rights were increasingly associated with those of liberated Africans. Liberated Africans' full freedom, like their guardianship, was to be limited and controlled because they carried the status that should be, but was not, extended to all illegally imported Africans.[43] The Council of State extended the right to emancipation to the liberated Africans working in public institutions but confirmed the policy followed by the Ministry of Justice in previous years: liberated Africans' emancipation should be gradual and their freedom limited.

Elusive Emancipation

What happened to the liberated Africans after the Ministry of Justice issued the notices of emancipation is the untold story of their emancipation. Compiled data refers to the dates when the notices were issued, that is, when the minister of justice had accepted their petitions. True emancipation may have been close or still quite distant. The notice ordered the judge of orphans to issue a letter of emancipation to be sent to the chief of police, who was to deliver it to the liberated African after determining his or her place of residence. The recurrence of petitions by Africans who had had their notices issued but had not received their letters of emancipation calls attention to the existence of a hidden policy in the

Ministry of Justice for the administration of the liberated Africans who were entitled to emancipation.

Narcizi Cassange petitioned in December 1855 and again in January 1856 to receive her letter of emancipation, which had already been issued and had sat in the office (or most probably in the drawers) of Rio de Janeiro's chief of police. She had been first emancipated in 1835 from the *Rio da Prata* and had served private hirers for twenty years. While she was in deposit at the House of Correction, she had been sent to work at the division of the Misericórdia Hospital, which took care of foundlings. In the petition she entered in January 1856 she was careful to attach a copy of the Ministry of Justice notice dated July 30, 1855, that ordered her letter of emancipation issued, yet her request was not granted. She was officially emancipated but had no right to receive her letter.[44] Cases such as Narciza's, that of deliberate withholding of the liberated Africans' letters of emancipation by the chief of police, multiplied in 1856 and 1857, demonstrating a change in the ministry's policy regarding the emancipation of the liberated Africans.

It emerged from the correspondence exchanged between the police and the Ministry of Justice on the subject of the repeated complaints from the liberated Africans that the order to retain the letters of emancipation had come from the Ministry of Justice itself. In effect the chief of police declared that he withheld the letters after he had received the order from the Ministry of Justice, dated September 9, 1855, to "stop the delivery of letters of emancipation to liberated Africans and the shipment of liberated Africans to the provinces until further notice."[45] As a consequence of that order, all liberated Africans who were waiting for emancipation or who had already had their notices of emancipation issued could not receive their letters. The distribution of the liberated Africans placed in the House of Correction to the various public institutions in need of labor continued, now with a growing number of Africans, since those working for hirers continued to be placed at the House of Correction to wait for emancipation, and those at the service of the institutions were repeatedly denied emancipation. Not surprisingly, the liberated Africans were increasingly restless by the late 1850s and hardly pleased the administrators of the public institutions, who returned to the House of Correction the liberated Africans deemed "incorrigible" and asked for "well-behaved" and "obedient" ones.[46]

The policy regulating the emancipation of the liberated Africans by the Ministry of Justice combined labor and social control considerations and arrived at its most "polished" format after the recommendations of the councilors of state clearly separated the legal freedom of the liberated Africans from their autonomy. By 1861 the Ministry of Justice had found the way to handle the liberated Africans who were waiting for emancipation: the procedure was to remove them all to the House of Correction and add their names to a list of

Africans who were waiting for emancipation. They would be emancipated when the ministry determined where they would be sent.[47] The assignment of liberated Africans in groups to work in the provinces, very common in the 1850s, would now be extended to "emancipated" Africans.

In apparent contradiction to the new policy, the chief of police received emphatic orders to let the emancipated Africans know that they were then completely free and that they could contract their labor freely and work for whomever they chose.[48] The combination of these orders can be seen in the cases of Bento, Firmo, Epifânio, Joaquim, Policarpo, and Paulo, whose notices of emancipation had been issued in September 1860 and, who one year later were still at the House of Correction. In October 1861 they were issued letters of emancipation stating that they were completely free and that they "could" contract their services to councilor Sinimbu, who was moving to the northeastern province of Alagoas. On the same date correspondence was sent to the president of the province announcing that the Africans would arrive there under contract to Sinimbu and were to be put under government protection. It is clear that the emancipated Africans had no choice in their "voluntary engagement" to go to Alagoas.[49]

Once set the procedures for emancipation remained unchanged after 1861. The chief of police, when assigning places of residence for the liberated Africans, was guided by the Ministry of Justice's direction to send them away from the city of Rio de Janeiro. Individually they were given their letters on the condition that they live somewhere else in the province of Rio de Janeiro; in groups they were sent to distant provinces as laborers in public works, military colonies, or new companies. The presidents of the provinces received the "emancipated" Africans with instructions to keep them under surveillance and were responsible for assigning them for service. This could hardly be considered "full emancipation" by any standard.

The government's concern with the impact of the "emancipated" Africans on other liberated Africans and on slaves emerged in the cases of Delfina and Carolina, the two liberated African women who had once served the late minister Aureliano Coutinho and had received help from his daughter Amália in their petition process. In February 1857 the minister's widow, the Viscondessa de Sepetiba, petitioned the Ministry of Justice to have Delfina, who had already been emancipated, arrested in the House of Correction or sent to another province, for Delfina "had been around her house trying to seduce the other liberated Africans who had also been entrusted to her husband and also the couple's slaves to run away or give themselves to debauchery, just like she has done."[50] Apparently she had her wish granted, and Delfina was probably taken temporarily to the House of Correction as an intimidation measure. The woman soon regained her cherished mobility and kept contacting her old mates: in November of that year she visited Carolina at the same prison deposit and gave Carolina news from her daughter.

Carolina herself, emancipated in the beginning of 1858, raised concern in the police department when she asked for authorization to live in Petrópolis. At the police department voices were raised against such an authorization, for "there seems to be a well-founded fear that she intends to live in Petrópolis, where the plantation where she once worked is located, with the intention to seduce the other liberated Africans living and working there to run away, give up their services and come to hire themselves out in this Court [Rio de Janeiro]." The police authorities and the hirers were obsessed with the idea that the liberated Africans, once fully emancipated and finally free from control, would be a very bad example to the liberated Africans still in service and to the slaves. Their ability to lead autonomous lives, supporting themselves by hiring out their services in the streets of Rio de Janeiro, was not praised; on the contrary, it was held against them. However, Carolina wanted to return to the place where she had established her relationships. She had family members in the Paquequer plantation; she was married to Domingos, a slave of Frongeth's, and had two small sickly daughters who lived with her in addition to the two others apprenticed to seamstresses in Niterói. She had been the plantation's cook and presumably felt part of a community of slaves, liberated Africans, and free people of color (such as the pardo Belmiro, who helped her in the secret night passage across Guanabara Bay) who had worked for the Sepetibas and now served Frongeth at the Paquequer plantation. Even if she applied to live in Petrópolis, saying that she had a contract to work for Francisco de Mello Franco, it was clear that it was a personal reason that made her want to go back. Demonstrating that not even after their second emancipation would liberated Africans be free of government control, the authorization for her to live in Petrópolis was granted, but the police department in that city was to be advised through the president of the province of Rio de Janeiro to "have her under their eyes" and not to issue her an authorization to be near the district where the plantation was located.[51]

For numerous liberated Africans the petition process culminated not in uncontrolled autonomy but in involuntary engagement and transfer to another province. Hirers such as the Viscondessa de Sepetiba knew the imperial government was sending liberated Africans away from Rio de Janeiro and wanted potentially dangerous Africans such as Delfina to be sent along. To remove somebody from the place where he or she had formed relationships had long been a form of punishment for criminals, and it appears that the hirers perceived the transfer to faraway provinces to be a form of punishment for the liberated Africans' "disobedience" or "insubordination." The involuntary transfer to the frontier provinces may, in fact, have been used as a threat to liberated Africans who were inclined to claim more independence and autonomy than

their hirers and the society at large were willing to afford them. For the imperial government, sending "emancipated" Africans to the provinces not only
served the function of "removing them from the theatre of their vices" but also
provided frontier projects with much-needed labor. That policy was widely
adopted in the early 1860s; liberated and "emancipated" Africans were sent to
the northern provinces of Pará and Amazonas and also to the Native Indian settlements in the western frontier of Paraná.

The slow progress and the biases in the process of liberated-African emancipation can be attributed to labor considerations but were also related to the
imperial government's concern with social control, particularly in Rio de
Janeiro. Census data show that the slave population in the capital of the
empire had peaked in 1849, with 78,000 slaves, who comprised 38.3 percent
of the total population of 205,000 people, and afterward steadily declined in
absolute and relative numbers until slave emancipation in 1888.[52] Sidney
Chalhoub has suggested that besides the pull factors that attracted slaves to
the coffee regions, such as their high market prices, the climate of fear created by slaves who were increasingly defiant of their masters' orders after
1850 was also taken into account by urban slave owners (push factors), who
effectively chose to get rid of their "dangerous slaves."[53] The liberated-
African data support Chalhoub's argument because there was no market for
liberated Africans. They could not be bought or sold, and therefore they
could not be pulled by the plantations, by cities in the interior, or by the
frontier areas. They could only be pushed out of the capital city. The imperial government, like the slave owners, was eager to send the "dangerous"
individuals away from Rio de Janeiro.

However, the fate of the liberated Africans came under public scrutiny
those days, thanks to the indefatigable British minister William Christie and
a number of Brazilian liberal representatives who brought the issue to the press
and to the parliamentary tribunes in 1862. The correspondence on the liberated Africans that passed between the British Foreign Office officials in Brazil
and their superiors in London—and was published in the Blue Books—was
reviewed in articles by liberal deputy Francisco Otaviano in the leading newspaper, *Correio Mercantil*, in 1862, and the governmental dragging out of the
emancipation process was harshly criticized by Senator Jequitinhonha and
Deputy Madureira in the tribunes. The young liberal deputy Tavares Bastos
published an informative series of articles detailing the legislation and acts relative to the government's handling of the liberated Africans over the years that
made clear the fact that the government had unduly evaded giving the liberated Africans their rightful freedom.[54]

Finally, in June 1864 the Ministry of Justice moved to dispense with the
petition process and favor the quick emancipation of all liberated Africans, a
decision ratified in the decree issued months later, in September. The orders

sent to all the provinces where liberated Africans had been in service authorized local judges of orphans to issue letters of emancipation and the chiefs of
police to deliver them, and instructed them to keep registries listing the emancipated Africans and their designated places of residence because "public convenience [required] that the Imperial Government continue to guarantee the
freedom of those *workers*."[55] Even if it was taken under pressure, the decision
to speed up the procedures to grant final letters of emancipation to all remaining liberated Africans proved the government could take decisions that were
contrary to the will of hirers and masters and enforce them. It was the first time
freedom was decreed an unconditional right by the government.

THE "LIBERATED AFRICAN QUESTION" AND SLAVE EMANCIPATION

Scattered evidence attests to the far-reaching impact the measures taken by the
imperial government to guarantee the freedom of the liberated Africans had on
the population at large and particularly on the slaves of every district where
liberated Africans could be found. Since in the popular mind *africanos livres*
comprised all the Africans imported during the illegal slave trade and not only
those who had been captured, local authorities had the difficult task of publi-
cizing the difference, enforcing the official definition of the category, and making sure that all living liberated Africans were emancipated. Already during
the controlled petition process, an emblematic case was brought before the
Ministry of Justice in Rio in 1860, in which two African women and one man
claimed liberated-African status. Laura Benguela, Firmina Congo, and Júlio
Moçambique worked for the same person, the Portuguese merchant José Baptista Martins de Souza Castellões. The investigation conducted during the
process demonstrated that only Laura and Firmina had been freed from seized
slave ships, while Júlio was a slave of Castellões and had been "incited" by the
two female mates to claim liberated-African status.[56] Laura and Firmina's letters of emancipation were issued but should be delivered only to the two liberated African women "on the occasion when, with others, they would be
bound to go away from Rio de Janeiro." Júlio was returned to his master after
going through the petition process with Laura and Firmina. For the Ministry
of Justice, he was not a liberated African but wanted to pass as one.[57]

The executive authorities had been centralizing the processing of petitions
and the emancipation of liberated Africans precisely to maintain control over
who was and who was not considered a liberated African. Only in 1862 did the
Ministry of Justice recognize the right of provincial authorities to judge the
right to emancipation of the liberated Africans who had been emancipated and
distributed for service there.[58] In a hopeless attempt to block a wider interpretation of liberated-African status, the government insisted that the judges had
no power to handle these cases.[59] Already in 1862 news reached the minister
of justice that the municipal judge of Pouso Alegre refused to accept petitions

from liberated Africans for he discovered that the vicar of the parish of Santa Anna de Sapucaí was baptizing Africans imported after 1831 and registering them as free.[60] Likewise, Luiz Gama, who later became an irreducible abolitionist lawyer, would use his experience as a clerk in the police department in São Paulo at the time when liberated Africans received their final letters of emancipation and engaged in defending slaves in their freedom suits. He lost his job at the police department in 1869 for attacking a municipal judge who blocked his action on behalf of the African Jacinto, a runaway slave from Minas Gerais, who claimed he had been brought to the country during the illegal years of the slave trade.[61]

In 1864 and in the following years, as liberated Africans everywhere left their places of employment and moved toward the provincial capitals to be accounted for and to receive their final emancipation, the Ministry of Justice officials strove to compile information that would, for the first time, provide statistics on how many had died, how many were emancipated, and how many were unaccounted for. The register, or *a matrícula geral dos Africanos livres*, would presumably satisfy the British, who had long been asking for a registry, establish which liberated Africans had the right to emancipation and put an end to what was by then referred to as "the liberated African question."

The public learned from the reports of the Ministry of Justice, relative to the activities conducted in 1867 and 1868, that the work on the register of liberated Africans had gathered information on about 11,008 individuals at the last count. Of those listed, 35 percent had died, 26 percent had been emancipated, almost 7 percent had been reexported, almost 2 percent had run away, and 30 percent were unaccounted for.[62] The liberated Africans who had been sent to the provinces figured prominently among those whose fates were unknown. The government never admitted that some of the liberated Africans might have been reenslaved.[63] The issue was treated in a very negative tone: The liberated Africans had been mishandled by the Brazilian government despite the bilateral agreements and national legislation, and they had been reenslaved, had died, and had worked well beyond the prescribed term of service. Those who survived had been emancipated. The public was left with the semblance of a closed question.

Information on the individual fates of the liberated Africans first emancipated in the 1830s from the *Duquesa de Bragança, Continente, Novo Destino, Rio da Prata, Cezar, Angélica,* and *Amizade Feliz* shipments and from small seizures made by local authorities reveals details about the liberated African experience never examined until now. The separation of the liberated Africans by place of service and by gender, and moreover, the calculation of the length of their terms of service until their deaths or emancipation provide a sense of "the liberated African question," perhaps shared by contemporaries close to the issue and felt by the Africans themselves, but never exposed in the official documentation.[64]

The records clearly confirm the changes in the procedures of the Ministry of Justice and the biases in the granting of emancipation to the liberated Africans between 1853 and 1864. It becomes clear that in the first two years after the announcement of the 1853 decree, the Ministry of Justice issued a fair number of notices to all the Africans who, in the officials' opinion, were "worthy" of emancipation. That period was followed by a sharp drop in the granting of emancipation notices, with the clear shift in policy marked by the 1855 orders. A gradual move toward emancipation can be seen in the number of notices issued after the Council of State's decision, in December 1859, but it was actually only in 1864 that unconditional emancipation began. More than a quarter of the liberated Africans in this group were kept by the government until the very end.[65]

Since they were among the first to be affected by the imperial government's rules for distribution issued in October 1834, which were interpreted as not limiting the length of their terms of service, the liberated Africans emancipated in the 1830s, such as Carolina of the Paquequer plantation, had to work the longest terms of service until their emancipation in the 1850s and 1860s. They had all completed fourteen years of service when the decree was issued in 1853, yet most of them worked much longer before receiving their final letters of emancipation. How long they worked depended on their gender and their place of employment. Women received their emancipation first. Among the women working for public institutions, 67 percent of them worked between twenty and twenty-four years and 33 percent worked between twenty-five and twenty-nine years, while 93 percent of the men worked between twenty-five and twenty-nine years and 7 percent worked more than thirty years. A similar gender difference can be found in the sample of 130 male and 103 female Africans emancipated after having worked for private hirers, but in general they worked shorter terms than those in institutions. While 67 percent of the women served terms of fifteen to twenty-four years, 53 percent of the men served between twenty-five and twenty-nine years before receiving their final emancipation.

The figures also show exactly how long each African served in excess of the fourteen years of compulsory service and collectively how they all were held much longer than the period prescribed in the bilateral agreement and in the royal decree of 1818. In other Atlantic territories liberated Africans served alongside slaves and were subjected to poor working conditions as well; compulsory labor during the term of service was not exclusive to Brazil. What sets the Brazilian experience apart is the fact that the Brazilian government extended the already long period of guardianship and compulsory service for liberated Africans far beyond the prescribed term. As it has been shown, the need for coerced laborers in public ventures was a factor, but social control also influenced the government's conservative emancipation policy, as the councilors of state suggested in 1859.

The ghost of an uncontrolled slave emancipation prompted by the extension of liberated-African status to all the Africans imported after the prohibition of the slave trade haunted moderate Brazilians, who never lost a chance to voice their support for the emancipation of slaves but had never concretely adopted measures to effect it until then. In fact, it appears that the agitation surrounding the liberated African emancipation, with the British pressing for the emancipation of all slaves brought into the country by the illegal trade and the slaves ready to assume liberated African status, prompted Emperor Pedro II and eminent lawyer and jurist Perdigão Malheiro to take on themselves the task of proposing gradual measures to effect emancipation. Perdigão Malheiro, as president of the Institute of Brazilian Lawyers, proposed in 1863 the gradual extinction of slavery through the emancipation of newborn slaves, and Emperor Pedro II three months later urged his councilors, as statesmen, to act promptly to solve the problem of slavery before the circumstances surrounding the abolition of the slave trade repeated themselves. In this sense the rupture of diplomatic relations with Great Britain in 1863 and liberated African emancipation in 1864 were measures taken to avoid further British interference in Brazilian slavery matters just as the Brazilian government had expected the abolition of the slave trade in 1850 to be.[66] The "liberated African question" was clearly associated by the British with the right to emancipation of all the Africans brought into the country during the illegal slave trade. This justified the government's preoccupation with presenting the issue not only as separate from the larger and more dangerous question but also as a closed affair.

Perdigão Malheiro did so when he presented his summary of the "liberated African question" in 1867. Deliberately avoided in his 1863 address to his fellows at the Institute for Brazilian Lawyers, the problem of the liberated Africans received due attention in the book-length essay the eminent lawyer published about Brazilian slavery in 1866 and 1867.[67] Malheiro discussed the fate of the group immediately after his observations about the Brazilian government's efforts to suppress the slave trade but tried to dissociate the existence of the category and the responsibility for the Africans from the British, giving emphasis to the Brazilian legislation and administration instead. He wrongly assumed that the bilateral convention of 1826 determined the Africans' reexportation and never openly mentioned the British attempts to transfer the liberated Africans to the British West Indies. In reviewing the handling of the group by the Brazilian government, the lawyer, who claimed he had served temporarily as a curator, admitted that the Africans had been treated as slaves, discussed some of the problems related to their handling by hirers and administrators but chose to concentrate on the measures taken by the Brazilian government for their emancipation. He claimed for the Brazilian government the initiative in emancipating the Africans that Christie had attributed to diplomatic pressure and to Lord Palmerston's speech in Parliament in July 1864.[68] Perdigão Malheiros strove to dissociate the "question of the liberated Africans" from the discussion of the rights of the slaves imported during the illegal slave trade, to present that "question" as closed, and to call for a moderate, well thought out, and prudent solution to the impending question of slavery.[69] The position he represented prevailed, but the "liberated African question" continued to haunt, into the 1870s and 1880s, those who defended the legality of Brazilian slavery and who admitted, at most, a gradual process of slave emancipation.

NOTES

This research was funded by CAPES–Brazilian Ministry of Education. I am grateful to the Manumission Conference participants and to Michael Craton, David Murray, and Eduardo Spiller Pena for their comments on an earlier version of this essay.

1. On the liberated Africans in Brazil see Robert E. Conrad, "Neither Slave nor Free: The *Emancipados* of Brazil, 1818–1868," *Hispanic American Historical Review* 53 (1973): 50–70; and my own dissertation, Beatriz G. Mamigonian, "To Be a Liberated African in Brazil: Labor and Citizenship in the Nineteenth Century" (Ph.D. diss., University of Waterloo, 2002).

2. On the diplomatic struggle for the abolition of the Brazilian slave trade and the treaties and conventions that created the category of liberated Africans, see Leslie Bethell, *The Abolition of the Brazilian Slave Trade: Britain, Brazil and the Slave Trade Question, 1807–1869* (Cambridge: Cambridge University Press, 1970); and Robert E. Conrad, *World of Sorrow: The African Slave Trade to Brazil* (Baton Rouge: Louisiana State University Press, 1986).

3. A Brazilian government internal report obtained by the British Foreign Office in 1865 estimated the number of Africans emancipated by the Anglo-Portuguese mixed commission between 1819 and 1822 and by the Anglo-Brazilian mixed commission between 1830 and 1845 at 4,785; those emancipated by Brazilian authorities between 1844 and 1849 were estimated at 458; and those emancipated after the Brazilian law for the abolition of the slave trade of September 1850 were estimated at 3,430. Although this estimate is very conservative (it calculated the total number of liberated Africans at 8,673, when in 1868 the Ministry of Justice's report listed 11,008 people in the registry of liberated Africans), it provides an idea of the distribution of the emancipations over time. See Hunt to Russell, March 10, 1865, Great Britain, Foreign Office Slave Trade Series (hereafter cited as FO 84), 1244; Brazil, *Relatório do Ministério da Justiça {1868} apresentado à Assembléia Geral Legislativa pelo Ministro de Secretário de Estado José Martiniano de Alencar* (Rio de Janeiro: Typographia Progresso, 1869), 134–135.

4. See Article 7 of the "Regulations for the Mixed Commissions annexed to the Additional Convention to the Treaty of the 22nd January 1815, between Great Britain and Portugal, for the purpose of preventing the Slave Trade," July 28, 1817, reprinted in "Accounts and Papers: Slave Trade—Instructions to Naval Officers," *British Parliamentary Papers* 50 (1844); *Parliamentary Papers on the Slave Trade* 8 (1969); and "Alvará com força de lei de 26 de janeiro de 1818," *Coleção das leis do Brazil de 1818* (Rio de Janeiro: Imprensa Nacional, 1889), 7–10.

5. Manolo Florentino, "Sobre minas, crioulos e a liberdade costumeira no Rio de Janeiro, 1789–1871," in *Tráfico, Cativeiro e Liberdade: Rio de Janeiro, séculos XVII–XIX*, ed. Manolo Florentino (Rio de Janeiro: Civilização Brasileira, 2005), 331–366.

6. David Eltis, *Economic Growth and the Ending of the Transatlantic Slave Trade* (Oxford: Oxford University Press, 1987), Appendix A, 243–244.

7. Beatriz Gallotti Mamigonian, "Revisitando a 'transição para o trabalho livre': A experiência dos africanos livres," in *Tráfico, Cativeiro e Liberdade*, 389–417.

8. Alinnie S. Moreira, "Os africanos livres, suaj prole e as discussões emancipacionistas: As famílias e a administração dos descendentes de africanos lives na Fábrica de Pólvora da Estrela (Rio de Janeiro, 1830–1860)" *Estudos Afro-Asiáticos* 29, 1–2–3 (2007): 161–200.

9. Rosanne M. Adderley, *"New Negroes from Africa": Slave Trade Abolition and Free African Settlement in the Nineteenth-Century Caribbean* (Bloomington: Indiana University Press, 2007); Monica Schuler, "Liberated Central Africans in Nineteenth-Century Guyana," in *Central Africans and Cultural Transformations in the American Diaspora*, ed. Linda Heywood (Cambridge: Cambridge University Press, 2002), 319–352. Liberated Africans elsewhere in the Atlantic served under similar regulations, but their experience varied according to local conditions. See David R. Murray, "A New Class of Slaves," in *Odious Commerce: Britain, Spain and the Abolition of the Cuban Slave Trade* (Cambridge: Cambridge University Press, 1980), 271–297; Ines Roldan de Montaud, "Origen, Evolucion y Supresion del Grupo de Negros 'Emancipados' en Cuba (1817–1870)," *Revista de Indias* 42, no. 167–168 (1982): 559–641; Howard Johnson, "The Liberated Africans in the Bahamas, 1811–1860," *Immigrants & Minorities* 7, no. 1 (1988): 16–40; Alvin O. Thompson, "African 'Recaptives' under Apprenticeship in the British West Indies, 1807–1828," *Immigrants & Minorities* 9, no. 2 (1990): 123–144; Christopher Saunders, "Liberated Africans in Cape Colony in the First Half of the Nineteenth Century," *International Journal of African Historical Studies* 18, no. 2 (1985): 223–239; Christopher Saunders, "'Free, yet Slaves': Prize Negroes at the Cape Revisited," in *Breaking the Chains: Slavery and its Legacy in the 19th Century Cape Colony*, ed. Nigel Worden and Clifton Crais (Johannesburg: Witwatersrand University Press, 1994), 99–115; and John Peterson, *Province of Freedom: A History of Sierra Leone, 1787–1870* (London: Faber and Faber, 1969).

10. The case, from January 1845, is discussed in Thomas H. Holloway, *Policing Rio de Janeiro: Repression and Resistance in a 19th-Century City* (Stanford, Calif.: Stanford University Press, 1993), 215. Apparently, Jacinto received his final letter of emancipation from the judge of orphans so that he could stand trial "as a free man rather than as a legal ward of the state." If the "insolent" Jacinto was the one Jacinto Benguela, from the shipment of the *Duquesa de Bragança* existing at the House of Correction in 1845, he had served for ten years already; see Arquivo Nacional, IJ6 471, Ofícios, relações e processos sobre africanos livres, 1834–1864.

11. The complaint the "Mina" liberated Africans took to the judge of orphans in Sorocaba in 1849 has been transcribed and discussed in Rodrigues, "Ferro, trabalho e conflito: Os africanos livres na Fábrica de Ipanema," *História Social* 4–5 (1998): 29–42. The trajectory of those liberated Africans, from Bahia to Rio de Janeiro, and their relentless struggle for their rights has been addressed in Beatriz Gallotti Mamigonian, "Do que 'o preto mina' é capaz: Etnia e resistência entre africanos livres," *Afro-Ásia* 24 (2000): 71–95.

12. *A Marmota* (Bahia), May 2, 1849, 4. I am grateful to Hendrik Kraay for this reference.

13. Eltis, *Economic Growth*, 243–244.

14. Bethell, *Abolition of the Brazilian Slave Trade*, 327–363; Pierre Verger, *Flux et reflux de la traite des nègres entre le golfe de Bénin et Bahia de Todos os Santos du XVIIe au XIXe siècle*

(Paris: Mouton, 1968), 381–393; Sidney Chalhoub, "The Politics of Disease Control: Yellow Fever and Race in Nineteenth Century Rio de Janeiro," *Journal of Latin American Studies* 25, no. 3 (1993): 441–463; Dale Graden, "An Act 'Even of Public Security': Slave Resistance, Social Tensions, and the End of the International Slave Trade to Brazil, 1835–1856," *Hispanic American Historical Review* 76, no. 2 (1996): 249–282; Jaime Rodrigues, *O Infame Comércio: Propostas e experiências no final do tráfico de africanos para o Brasil (1800–1850)* (Campinas: Editora da UNICAMP/CECULT, 2000); Jeffrey Needell, "The Abolition of the Brazilian Slave Trade in 1850: Historiography, Slave Agency and Statesmanship," *Journal of Latin American Studies* 33 (2001): 681–711.

15. The severe procedures adopted in the repression were discredited only by the failure to prosecute influential planters involved in the case. Martha Abreu, "O caso do Bracuhy," in *Resgate: Uma Janela para o Oitocentos*, ed. Hebe Maria Mattos de Castro and Eduardo Schnoor (Rio de Janeiro: Topbooks, 1995), 165–195.

16. See the speech of the president of the council of ministers, Visconde de Paraná, in the Senate on September 20, 1853. *Anais do Senado do Império do Brasil, 1853*, vol. 2 (Rio de Janeiro: Typographia Nacional, 1826–89), 291. The issue is briefly discussed in Joaquim Nabuco, "O tráfico e a escravidão," in *Um Estadista do Império* (Rio de Janeiro: Topbooks, 1997), 228–229.

17. Palmerston to Hudson, July 5, 1851, in W. D. Christie, *Notes on Brazilian Questions* (London: Macmillan, 1865), 203–205. The issue is discussed in Bethell, *Abolition of the Brazilian Slave Trade*, 381–382 and developed in Beatriz G. Mamisonian, "In the Name of Freedom," *Slavery and Abolition* 30, no. 1 (2009): 41–67.

18. Instructions prescribed that the liberated Africans were to be given tin plaques, which they should have carried around their necks and which would have contained their letter of emancipation with name, number, and marks to identify them as liberated Africans. Only two references have been found to the actual use of those tin plaques. "Instruções," attached to the Ministry of Justice notice of October 29, 1834, and later modified by the imperial decree of December 24, 1835; Joana Maria das Candeias, Pedido de exoneração de responsabilidade sobre o Africano livre Leão Benguela, October 1856, AN, Diversos SDH, cx. 782, Ofícios de Ministros, 1826–1840; Pedidos de cartas de emancipação de escravos, 1854–1857, pacote 2; André Mina, Petição de emancipação, January 8, 1855, AN, Diversos SDH, cx. 82, pc. 3.

19. Maria Rebola, Petição de emancipação, June 17, 1857, AN, GIFI 6D-136. Maria had been working for Quintanilha for twenty-one years when she petitioned for emancipation.

20. Joaquim Benguella, according to his hirer, had seen news in the paper about the decree; Francisco Servulo de Moura, Intervenção em favor de Joaquim Benguela preso na Casa de Correção, July 1855, AN, IJ6 468—Ofícios do Chefe de Polícia e Casa de Correão sobre Africanos, 1834–1864. Priest João José Moreira, the hirer of Florêncio Rebolo, learned from the decree in the paper and wanted the African to be granted emancipation; João José Moreira, Pedido de exoneração de responsabilidade sobre o Africano livre Florêncio Rebolo, 1855, AN, Diversos SDH, cx. 782, pc. 2.

21. Anna [Benguela], Petição de emancipação, March 6, 1843, AN, IJ6 471; Maria Cabinda, Pedido de emancipação, May 15, 1856, AN, Diversos SDH, cx. 782, pc. 2.

22. Figueiredo to Barbosa, July 4, 1853, AN, IJ6 523, Ofícios e processos sobre africanos livres, 1833–1864.

23. Plácido Cabinda, Petição de emancipação, November 9, 1856, AN, Diversos SDH, cx. 782, pc. 3; Beliza, Petiç̃ao de emancipação, April 1856, AN, Diversos SDH, cx. 782, pc. 2–3; Custódia Rebolo, Petição de emancipação, July 6, 1856, AN, Diversos SDH, cx. 782, pc. 3.

24. For a discussion of freedom suits, see Keila Grinberg, *Liberata, a lei da ambigüidade: As ações de liberade da Corte de Apelação do Rio de Janeiro no século XIX* (Rio de Janeiro: Relume-Dumará, 1994).

25. The interrogation was summarily registered. The liberated African was asked his or her name and nation, age, and occupation; whether it was by his or her initiative that the petition was made; and whether he or she had been treated with fairness by the hirer of his or her services. In exceptional cases interrogations were longer and entered into more detail about the relationship with the hirers or about the petition process. See, for example, José Benguela, Interrogation, September 29, 1855, AN, GIFI 6D-136; and Amália Guilhermina de Oliveira Coutinho, Pedido de emancipação para a Africana livre Carolina Congo, December 2, 1857, AN, GIFI 6D-136.

26. The procedures established for the petition process were criticized in the early 1860s by Brazilian deputy Tavares Bastos and discussed in the British House of Commons in 1864. See Aureliano Cândido Tavares Bastos, *Cartas do Solitário*, 3rd ed. (São Paulo: Companhia Editora Nacional, 1938), 122–146; Great Britain, Parliament, *Hansard Parliamentary Debates,* 3d ser., 176 (1864): July 12, 1864.

27. Dionísia [Bié], Petição de emancipação, March 19, 1856, AN, Diversos SDH, cx. 782, pc. 3.

28. Hypolito Angola, Petição de emancipação, August 29, 1856, AN, Diversos SDH, cx. 782, pc. 3. He was going to earn 8$000 per month, while liberated Africans (or slaves) hiring themselves out earned 12$000. Yet it was a much better salary than the hirers of liberated Africans paid to the government for their services, usually fixed at 12$000 per year. See Mamigonian, "Revisitando a 'transição para o trabalho livre.'" For an excellent discussion on the world of masters and servants, see Sandra Lauderdale Graham, *House and Street: The Domestic World of Servants and Masters in Nineteenth-Century Rio de Janeiro* (Cambridge: Cambridge University Press, 1988).

29. Idalina Umbuí, Petição de emancipação, January 5, 1863, AN, GIFI 5E-130. Idalina had been first emancipated in April 1850 from the *Rolha* and had been first assigned to serve at the gunpowder factory. Her final emancipation was issued on June 17, 1863. The fact that she had not completed fourteen years of service was not raised during the petition process.

30. See the various notices sent by the chief of police returning the liberated Africans' petitions properly informed and documented to the Ministry of Justice for their final decision, late in 1854. AN, Diversos SDH, cx. 782, pc. 2–3.

31. This function was called "solicitador de causas." See, for example, the *Almanak Administrativo, Mercantil e Industrial da Corte e Província do Rio de Janeiro para o anno de 1855* (Rio de Janeiro: Laemmert, 1855), 393–396.

32. In a sample of 148 notices of emancipation issued between 1859 and 1862, 90 percent of the petitions had been made in the name of the Africans themselves or by proxies, while only 10 percent of the petitions had been entered by hirers or administrators of public institutions. AN, IJ6 15.

33. See Henrique Rebolo, Petição de emancipação, October 26, 1863, AN, GIFI 5E-130; Ildefonso Angola, Petição de emancipação, April 21, 1863, AN, GIFI 5E-130; Lino Africano livre, Petição de emancipação, November 17, 1856, AN, Diversos SDH, cx. 782, pc. 3; Maria Cabinda, Petição de emancipação, May 15, 1856, AN, Diversos SDH, cx. 782, pc. 2.

34. Manoel Antônio Gonçalves de Mello, Pedido de emancipação para a africana livre Prisca, January 8, 1857, AN, GIFI 6D-136; Prisca Benguela, Petição de emancipação, December 1855, AN, Diversos SDH, cx. 782, pc. 2. Hirers who wished to obstruct the

process of emancipation of the liberated Africans under their service either testified to the bad behavior or misled the bureaucratic searches for the identity of the African in question. Hirer Joaquina Amália de Almeida, for example, testified that she was a poor woman who depended on the work of Dionísia Angola for her living. Dionísia in her second petition unmasked her hirer, saying she had five slaves and earned her living by hiring them out; Dionísia Angola, Petição de emancipação, May 1855, AN, GIFI 6D-136.

35. On the "moral economy" of punishment, see Silvia Hunold Lara, *Campos da Violência: Escravos e senhores na Capitania do Rio de Janeiro, 1750–1808* (São Paulo: Paz e Terra, 1988). Amália Guilhermina de Oliveira Coutinho, Pedido de emancipação para a Africana livre Carolina Congo, December 2, 1857, AN, GIFI 6D-136. Carolina's notice of emancipation was issued on December 11, 1857; she had been first emancipated in 1835, from the *Duquesa de Bragança*.

36. Delfina Bié, Petição de emancipação, November 6, 1855, AN, Diversos SDH, cx. 782, pc. 2.

37. Lino Africano livre, Petição de emancipação, November 17, 1856, AN, Diversos SDH, cx. 782, pc. 3.

38. Tertuliano e Catarina, Petição de emancipação, January 27, 1857, AN, GIFI 6D-136.

39. Hilário 20. e Carolina, do Arsenal de Guerra, Petição de emancipação, June 8, 1856, AN, Diversos SDH, cx. 782, pc. 3; Onofre e Suzana, do Arsenal de Guerra, Petição de emancipação, October 28, 1856, AN, Diversos SDH, cx. 782, pc. 3.

40. Ignácio Oanba, Petição de emancipação, June 10, 1864, AN, IJ6 523, Ofícios e processos sobre africanos livres, 1833–1864; Severino Congo, Paula Congo, Agda Rebola, Sabino Benguela, Carolina Quelimane, Eusébio Benguela, Luiza Samba and Ignacio Oanba, Petição coletiva de emancipação, April 1, 1856, AN, Diversos SDH, cx. 782, pc. 3; Ministério da Justiça, notice of June 17, 1864, AN, IJ6 16, Africanos livres—Registro de avisos a diversas autoridades, 1863–1865. The record of his first emancipation is in AN, cód. 184, vol. 4, Cartas de emancipação de Africanos, 1839–1840, published in a facsimile edition as *Marcas de escravos: Listas de escravos emancipados vindos a bordo de navios negreiros, 1839–1841* (Rio de Janeiro: Arquivo Nacional, 1989).

41. Minas Quelimane, Pedido de entrega de carta de emancipação, January 15, 1856, AN, Diversos SDH, cx. 782, pc. 2.

42. "Resolução de 20 de dezembro de 1859—Sobre os africanos livres que estão em serviço de estabelecimentos públicos," in *Imperiais Resoluções tomadas sobre Consultas da Seção de Justiça do Conselho de Estado*, ed. José Próspero Jehovah da Silva Caroatá (Rio de Janeiro: Garnier, 1884), 842–843.

43. See Beatriz Gallotti Mamigonian, "O direito de ser africano livre: Os escravos e as interpretações da lei de 1831," in *Direitos e Justiças: Capítulos de História Social do Direito no Brasil*, ed. Silvia H. Lara and Joseli Mendonça (Campinas: Editora da Unicamp, 2006).

44. Narciza Cassange, Pedido de entrega de carta de emancipação, January 18, 1856, AN, Diversos SDH, cx. 782, pc. 3.

45. Antônio Thomaz de Godoy to Thomaz Nabuco de Araújo, October 1, 1856, AN, Diversos SDH, cx. 782, pc. 3.

46. The records of the administration of the liberated Africans by the Ministry of Justice between 1859 and 1864 are good indicators of their transfers between public institutions. See AN IJ6 15, Tráfico de Africanos—Registro de avisos a diversas autoridades, 4a seção, 1859–1862, and IJ6 16, Africanos livres—Registro de avisos a diversas autoridades, 1863–1865.

47. Lobato to Chefe de Polícia da Corte, June 4, 1861, AN, IJ6 15, Tráfico de Africanos— Registro de avisos a diversas autoridades, 4a seção, 1859–1862; Lobato to Chefe de Polícia da Corte, December 26, 1861, AN, IJ6, Africanos livres—Registro de avisos a diversas autoridades, 1863–1865.

48. Lobato to Chefe de Polícia, 6/8/1861, and Lobato to Chefe de Polícia, October 5, 1861, AN, IJ6 15, Tráfico de Africanos—Registro de avisos a diversas autoridades, 4a seção, 1859–1862. It is likely that this applied only to liberated Africans with powerful patrons.

49. Lobato to President of the Province of Alagoas, October 31, 1861, and Lobato to Chefe de Polícia, October 31, 1861, AN, IJ6 15, Tráfico de Africanos—Registro de avisos a diversas autoridades, 4a seção, 1859–1862.

50. Viscondessa de Sepetiba, Pedido de recolhimento da Africana emancipada Delfina à Casa de Correção, February 1857, AN GIFI 6D-136.

51. Carolina, Pedido de licença para residir em Petrópolis, January 14, 1858, AN, IJ6 523, Ofícios e processos sobre africanos livres, 1833–1864.

52. Karasch, *Slave Life in Rio de Janeiro, 1808–1850* (Princeton, N.J.: Princeton University Press, 1987), 66.

53. Sidney Chalhoub, *Visões da Liberdade: Uma história das últimas décadas da escravidão na Corte* (São Paulo: Companhia das Letras, 1990).

54. Tavares Bastos, *Cartas do Solitário*, 122–180; Christie, *Notes on Brazilian Questions*, 15, 24–27.

55. See correspondence sent to the provinces of Minas Gerais, Santa Catarina, Bahia, Pernambuco, Amazonas, Mato Grosso, São Paulo, Rio Grande do Sul, Espírito Santo, Paraná, and Ceará between July 16, 1864 and August 2, 1864, AN, IJ6 16, Africanos livres—Registro de avisos a diversas autoridades, 1863–1865. "Decreto n. 3310 de 24 de Setembro de 1864," in *Coleção das leis do Império do Brasil de 1864,* tomo 2 (Rio de Janeiro: Typographia Nacional, 1864), 160–161. Emphasis added.

56. Júlio Moçambique, averiguações sobre sua condição, 1860, AN, GIFI 5E 280.

57. Aviso de emancipação para Laura Benguela e Firmina Conga, September 2, 1861, AN, IJ6 15, Tráfico de Africanos—Registro de avisos a diversas autoridades, 4a seção, 1859–1862; Justiça to Chefe de Polícia, February 1, 1862, AN, IJ6 15, Tráfico de Africanos—Registro de avisos a diversas autoridades, 4a seção, 1859–1862.

58. Until then, petitions from the liberated Africans serving in the provinces went to Rio de Janeiro to be processed, resulting in very long delay for the Africans because their records could not be found in Rio. Lauriana ou Edeltrudes, Petição de Emancipação, February 6, 1860, AN, IJ6 523, Ofícios e processos sobre africanos livres, 1833–1864; Justiça to Chefe de Polícia, February 4, 1862, AN, IJ6 15, Tráfico de Africanos—Registro de avisos a diversas autoridades, 4a seção, 1859–1862; Justiça to Presidente da Província de Pernambuco, July 29, 1862, AN, IJ6 15, Tráfico de Africanos—Registro de avisos a diversas autoridades, 4a seção, 1859–1862.

59. "Aviso de 22 de Março de 1859," in *Coleção de Decisões do Governo do Império do Brasil, 1859* (Rio de Janeiro: Typographia Nacional, 1859), 68.

60. The episode is discussed in Judy Bieber Freitas, "Slavery and Social Life: Attempts to Reduce Free People to Slavery in the Sertão Mineiro, Brazil, 1850–1871," *Journal of Latin American Studies* 26, no. 3 (1994): 597–619; in the context of the application of the law which forbade the illegal enslavement of free people, see 618.

61. Luiz Gama openly publicised this case and his dismissal in the press. On his life, and his literary, political, and abolitionist involvement, see Elciene Azevedo, *Orfeu de Carapinha: A trajetória de Luiz Gama na imperial cidade de São Paulo* (Campinas: Ed. da Unicamp/Cecult, 1999). Jacinto's case is treated in 110–124. In English see Robert Edgar Conrad, *The Destruction of Brazilian Slavery, 1850–1888* (Berkeley and Los Angeles: University of California Press, 1972), 154–155. In the following years many lawyers and judges scattered throughout the country, probably linked by their association with Masonic lodges, would use the defense of the Africans brought during the illegal slave trade as one of their abolitionist strategies. Using the argument with the most destabilizing potential for the legality and legitimacy of slavery, freedom suits based on the 1831 abolition law became more common in the 1870s and by 1883 would be considered by abolitionist judge Macedo Soares as "the most momentous problem of the present time." Antônio Joaquim Macedo Soares, *Campanha Jurídica pela Libertação dos Escravos, 1867–1888* (Rio de Janeiro: José Olympio Editora, 1938).

62. Brazil, *Relatório do Ministério da Justiça apresentado à Assembléia Geral Legislativa pelo Min. José Martiniano de Alencar, 1868* (Rio de Janeiro: Typographia Progresso, 1869), 134–135.

63. Little explanation was provided concerning the reexportation of 748 liberated Africans, or about the emancipation of 354 of them by a notice issued in the 1830s, which presumably benefited those from the shipments of the *Emília* and the *Destemida* who had their fourteen-year term limits observed because they had been assigned for service before October 1834. The notarial records confirm that liberated Africans from the *Emília*, from the *Destemida*, and from other ships captured before November 1831 received their final emancipation before the 1853 decree, for some of the Africans took their final letters of emancipation to be notarized in the 1840s.

64. Tables with information on the liberated Africans of the *Duquesa de Bragança* (1834), *Continente* (1835), *Novo Destino* (1835), *Rio da Prata* (1835), *Angélica* (1835), *Amizade Feliz* (1835), and *Cezar* (1838), and of apprehensions made by local judges between 1835 and 1837 prepared by the ministry of justice probably in 1864 or 1865, contain compiled information on where each liberated African was put to work (name of the hirer or institution) and what became of him/her (death, emancipation, escape, unknown) and when (date of death or emancipation). This data was completed with information gathered from petitions of emancipation and registries of death of liberated Africans. The total number of Africans listed is 955. AN, IJ6 471—Ofícios, relações e processos sobre Africanos livres, 1834–1864. The tables used, relative only to a few of the shipments of liberated Africans, were found among other documents on liberated Africans with no reference to the register or to the rest of the set. Such data represents only a portion of the total number of liberated Africans emancipated in Brazil and calls for further inquiry into the fates of those emancipated in the 1850s and of those handled entirely by the provinces.

65. Ibid.

66. Eduardo Spiller Pena, *Pajens da casa imperial: Jurisconsultos, escravidão e a lei de 1871* (Campinas: Ed. UNICAMP/CECULT, 2001), 273–295; Conrad, *Destruction of Brazilian Slavery,* 70–80; Richard Graham, *Britain and the Onset of Modernization in Brazil, 1850–1914* (Cambridge: Cambridge University Press, 1968), 160–186.

67. Pena, *Pajens da Casa Imperial,* 286. Pena also discusses Perdigão Malheiro's contacts with Tavares Bastos on the subject of gradual abolition.

68. Agostinho Marques de Perdigão Malheiro, *A Escravidão no Brasil: Ensaio histórico-jurídico-social*, vol. 2 (São Paulo: Edições Cultura, 1944), 49–60, 70–75; Christie, *Notes on Brazilian Questions*, 24–25.

69. "Resta somente a magna questão da escravidão existente no Império, e sua consequente abolição: Questão da maior gravidade e ponderação, que cumpre estudar e resolver com o maior critério e prudência." Perdigão Malheiro, *A Escravidão no Brasil* 2: 75; Pena, *Pajens da Casa Imperial*, 288.

Scott Hancock

From "No Country!" to "Our Country!"

—ᘯ—

Living Out Manumission and the Boundaries of
Rights and Citizenship, 1773–1855

During the Revolutionary War and the first decades of the early U.S. Republic, as free people of color sought to define their place in the new nation, they
expressed little connection to an American nationality. But antebellum black
leaders later articulated a powerful vision of Africans as Americans. As slaves
and free blacks had done during the Revolutionary era, they based this African
American identity in part upon a biblical view of human rights and a natural
rights philosophy, but they also buttressed black identity formation by making a rights discourse the fulcrum of their argument for full inclusion in the
polity. Coinciding with the rise of black parades as a public and confrontational
means of asserting African American citizenship, black leaders constructed an
African American identity intimately connected to legal notions of citizenship
and rights stemming from the Declaration of Independence and the Constitution, thereby finding another means of publicly reinforcing to both white
and black Americans an African American identity. Toward the close of the
antebellum era, William C. Nell put the capstone on black self-definition as
African American by constructing a patriotic black heritage.[1]

In the Atlantic world manumission invariably meant that people of color
crossed some kind of legal boundary. When slaves forced their own manumission by running away or rebelling, they violated the law; when slaves achieved
manumission through self-purchase or by general abolition, they acted within
the law. Much of the excellent work on manumission in this volume and elsewhere notes how the law frequently inhibited manumission, how the law's
ambiguities could mask oppression before and after emancipation, and how
slaves struggled against and within the law's often confining apparatus to
achieve freedom and forge some kind of life after manumission. This chapter
complements those studies by following the stories of the manumitted a bit
further by examining how freed people of color, in the wake of emancipation,
used the law and constructed legal beliefs and how their use of the law shaped

their identity in ways that simultaneously birthed new possibilities and aborted others.

This chapter, then, serves as a preliminary model revealing how people of color in one locale engaged with the law—that overarching institution that had the power to enslave and emancipate, to oppress and empower. In the northern United States, site of some of the first emancipations in the Americas, freed people of color eventually used a legal rights ideology—a belief that claiming, possessing, and wielding legal rights held the power to institute fundamental social, political, and economic change for black men and women—to help define themselves as fully American during an era that witnessed virulent challenges to their place in the polity. For these black women and men, manumission meant the opportunity to acquire previously denied rights, rights sometimes gained and later lost but sometimes realized and secured. But fighting to secure those rights and defining themselves in part by the ability to hold those rights also meant that African Americans inserted themselves into a system that often controlled the manner and extent of change. A broad spectrum of responses to the law no doubt existed among freed people of color in other parts of the Atlantic world, all of whom engaged the law at some point simply by crossing the legal boundary from slavery to freedom. Those responses, influenced by the distinct regional and local character of the law and legal systems as well as their own experience and culture, shaped the world in which they and their children would live. In this chapter I examine the process and consequences of the African American response in the northern United States.

Massachusetts slaves sensed in the 1770s that the time was ripe to push for general abolition. Cognizant of revolutionary rhetoric and hopeful that it might provide the impetus for freedom, slaves made out four freedom petitions to the legislature. The first, submitted in January 1773 by slaves in Boston, pointed out that freed slaves would make good subjects, "able as well as willing to bear a Part in the Public Charges," and that despite their bitter circumstances, slaves had already demonstrated their virtue and faith and would continue to do so. In one of the more striking statements the petitioners cried out, "We have no Property! We have no wives! No children! We have no City! No Country!"[2]

Slaves could and did own property, and they could and did have wives and children. The petitioners' plaintive cry was intended to make clear the desperate circumstances engulfing most black men and women. All slaves, regardless of whether or not they owned property or had family, shared a lack of control over their future. The loss of family and property was always a genuine risk should an owner decide to sell a slave south or to the West Indies, a point the third petition, offered in 1774, made clear when the petitioners protested that "we are no longer man and wife than our masters or mistresses thinkes proper" and grieved the loss of children "taken from us by force and sent maney miles from us." The rights of the master to sell his chattel trumped any claims slaves made. And for virtually all black men and women, slave or free, the poignant cry of "No Country!" rang especially true.[3]

In the midst of the revolutionary change in America, the black peoples of Massachusetts found themselves in the midst of revolutionary changes in identity. While white Americans, busy constructing and validating an American identity distinct from English nationalism, "imagined themselves as a separate people," free and enslaved blacks were, in many ways, already a separate people. There was no country with which they identified. In 1778 some Massachusetts whites attempted to ensure black inhabitants' separation from the polity through the fifth article of the proposed state constitution, which excluded free blacks, mulattos, and Indians from voting rights. Though this constitution was voted down—not, however, because of objections to the fifth article—Massachusetts blacks were aware of some whites' attempts to maintain the alienated status of the small black populace. Having little reason to identify with the new nation, many black men and women held onto connections with African homelands, connections that for some were at best tenuous.[4]

Most slaves and free blacks, the majority of whom were at this point second or third generation, had been in New England long enough that identification with African roots was frequently through a generalized and idealized Africa. Some transplanted Africans did retain detailed memories; Belinda, a Boston slave who petitioned for her freedom in 1783, recalled the lush paradise of her childhood: the "banks of the Rio Da Volta . . . mountains Covered with Spicy forests, the valleys loaded with the richest fruits, spontaneously produced; joined to that happy temperature of air."[5] But the memories frequently were painted with broad strokes; often there was no specific detail about ethnic or geographic origin. The petitions of 1774 and 1777 rendered everything African as an inviting paradise, nostalgically recalling Africa as "a Populous Pleasant and plentiful country." The construction of a fondly remembered and generalized paradise called Africa would become a powerful source of identification for many black New Englanders.

Alongside that Africanized identity, black petitioners placed slaves within a broader human family through a blend of a biblical world view and natural rights ideology. In 1774 Cesar Sarter, a Newburyport freedman, called on white colonials to extend "the *natural rights and privileges of freeborn men*" to slaves since he and many other slaves had been born free in Africa. But even those who had been born into slavery should be able to expect "the same *natural rights of mankind*." Sarter stretched the revolutionary rhetoric across the Atlantic, in essence arguing that natural rights knew no geographic or color boundaries. He drove home his point by describing the physical and emotional horrors of captivity and asking if whites could truly claim to be living out "that excellent rule given by our Saviour, *to do to others, as you would, that they should do to you.*"[6]

The first of the four freedom petitions to the Massachusetts legislature used similar strategies by pointing to both public opinion and God who "hath lately put it into the Hearts of Multitudes on both Sides of the Water" to push for black emancipation. The second petition demonstrated that the black petitioners were keenly aware of the arguments white colonials were making in response to Parliament's attempts to reassert its authority over the colonies in the early 1770s. The petitioners expected "great things from men who have made such a noble stand against the designs of their *fellow-men* to enslave them," namely, for them to take the sensible next step and "give us that ample relief which, *as men*, we have a natural right to." This petition also exhibited the lack of attachment these slaves had to the colony. Expressing a desire to "leave the province, which we determine to do as soon as we can," the petitioners planned a return to Africa once they had earned sufficient funds.[7]

These petitioners and other Massachusetts blacks had little cause to invest in the crusade to establish a new nationality. Some whites did argue for the participation of free black men in the polity; one writer pointed out that excluding anyone on the basis of color made no more sense than excluding those "long-nosed, short-faced, or higher or lower than five feet nine." But in addition to making the effort to separate black people from the polity part of the public record by publishing the state constitution's denial of black suffrage, another Boston paper carried an acerbic poem ridiculing black equality. Though the paper printed responses that criticized the public castigation of black people, the responses focused on Africans' equal worth as fellow human beings and did not articulate a vision of an active black citizenry. During that same spring the issue of freeing slaves in order to form a black regiment caused a riot in Boston. Whether or not the disturbance involved slaves is unclear, but black Bostonians surely were aware that these protesters militated against the notion of slave owners giving up their property, even to protect liberty. There was little in the rhetoric of even sympathetic whites to encourage blacks to conceive of themselves as Americans in the face of constant public repudiation of their participation in the polity.[8]

Toward the close of the Revolutionary War, after hundreds of black men had fought against the British to earn freedom, black petitioners still gave little indication that they identified with the new nation. In 1780 seven Massachusetts black men submitted a request to be relieved from tax assessments, arguing that decades of "Long Bondage and hard slavery" had left them in an abject state of having no inheritances or foundation upon which to build an estate. These black men were obviously familiar with the inconsistency of being taxed while the state constitution denied them the vote, yet their appeal pushed not for enfranchisement, but for financial relief. Only a few recently freed blacks had managed to gain even a "small Pittance of Estate . . . through much hard Labour & Industry," and their situation remained so precarious that taxes threatened even this shadow of security. Reminding the legislature of their own revolutionary rhetoric, the petitioners pointed out that no blacks, even those with small estates, shared the "Privilage of freemen of the State having no vote or Influence in the election of those that Tax us," and this despite the record of many black men who "cheerfully Entered the field of Battle in the defence of the Common Cause . . . against a similar Exertion of Power (in Regard to Taxation)." But even after that pointed reminder of how free people of color had been denied the rights white Americans had fought to procure for themselves, the overriding theme of this petition was not a call to an active part in the polity, and there was no claim to the right to vote based on any notion of citizenship or identification with the state or country. The thrust of the petition was simply to be excused from taxation, and the argument was predicated upon the notion that the legislators and white society in general owed something to those of "African extract." In contrast to later arguments made by African Americans, the petitioners did not argue for suffrage because free people of color were citizens and had a certain body of rights; in fact, they did not argue for suffrage at all. The debt arose out of two causes: first, because whites had historically denied slaves economic opportunity and therefore caused the present debilitating state of many freed people; and second, because many slaves and free blacks had aided whites in *their* cause—not blacks' cause—against unfair taxation. In short these men pushed for financial redress, not suffrage or citizenship rights.[9]

There continued to be an absence of identification with the new country in most of the extant writings and speeches by free people of color for the next two decades. In June 1789 the members of Boston's African Lodge of Masons listened to the black minister John Marrant's message to the masonic lodge that fixed his black listeners within a biblical and masonic lineage that stretched back to creation. In Marrant's sagacious rendering masonry became a historical redemptive force: God gifted the Masons with skill and knowledge in order to use them to rebuild the world after the postflood disaster at the Tower of Babel. Placing his audience of black Masons and African Americans in general within a grand context that transcended time and space, Marrant attempted to create a transatlantic and transhistorical bond. He connected African Americans with Africans of the biblical (and therefore also masonic) past and present, and reminded his audience that God had Africans to "stand on the level not only with them, but with the greatest kings on the earth." Marrant then placed his listeners "under a double obligation to the brethren of the craft of all nations on the face of the earth, for there is no party spirit in Masonry." A blend of Christianity, masonry, and African heritage provided the touchstones of identity and the bonds of community in Marrant's exhortations.[10]

The connections to Africa were purposefully aimed at his audience. In contrast to his Boston sermon, in his narrative Marrant nowhere defined himself as African or of African heritage, and he barely referred to any other black people; indeed, were it not for the title identifying him as "A Black," a reader would not know. The only hint of how he thought of his heritage comes near the end of the narrative. Living in London, Marrant "had a feeling and concern for the salvation of my countrymen . . . and had continual sorrow in my heart for my brethren, for my kinsmen, according to flesh," which he interpreted as a call to ministry. This is not to argue that Marrant submerged his African heritage; his narrative, "related" to a white reverend and written with a largely white audience in mind, surely does not tell us everything about how Marrant defined himself. But the narrative's absence of identification with Africa and the subsequent connections to Africa that he made in the sermon suggest that Marrant purposefully summoned images and histories of Africa when preaching to black listeners to weave a transatlantic black identity. When John Marrant spoke of his "countrymen," he did not mean Americans, English, or Cherokee, even though he preached to them all. To him and other black men and women in the North, "countrymen" were black kinsmen.[11]

The lodge's founder, Prince Hall, offered a similar formula of African heritage, Christianity, and masonry in his addresses during annual St. John's festivals. He held up Tertullian, Cyprian, Augustine, and Fulgentius—all leaders of the early church, some rendered as Africans—as examples for emulation. In 1797 Hall reminded the lodge brethren, "We shall call ourselves a charter'd lodge of just and lawful Masons . . . give the right hand of affection and fellowship to whom it justly belongs; let their colour and complexion be what it will, let their nation be what it may, for they are your brethren, and it is your indispensable duty so to do; let them as Masons deny this, and we & the world know what to think of them be they ever so grand."[12] A few years previous Hall had taken a leading role in submitting a petition to the Massachusetts legislature requesting the state's financial aid for an emigration plan of black Bostonians to settle on the west coast of Africa. The petition, signed by seventy-three black men, described Africa as a land "for which the God of nature has formed us; and where we shall live among our equals, and . . . may have a prospect of usefulness to our brethren there."[13]

Themes of identification with Africa and the near-absence of identification with America persisted into the early nineteenth century. In the 1808 pamphlet *The Sons of Africa* an unnamed member of Boston's African Society repeatedly juxtaposed Africa in opposition to other nations, thereby creating and reinforcing a quasi-nationalism for African Americans. Asserting God's creation of all the nations from one blood, the writer noted that "all the Africans, at the present day, seem to be the butt of the nations over which men choose to tyrannise, enslave, and oppress." He later prodded his readers to come up with any legitimate rationale for slavery by asking if "Africans ought to be subject to the British or Americans, because they are of a dark complexion." If Turkey, Spain, or Portugal enslaved Americans, America would rightfully consider those nations as "divested of all humanity," and so "what must be said of America . . . which treats the African in ways similar?" Furthermore, in all references to anything American, the writer uses not the first- but the third-person possessive pronoun: "their," not "our."[14]

The writer of *The Sons of Africa* participated in a process described by historians as the creation of a creolized "Africa" in the minds of African Americans that absorbed original ethnic and cultural distinctives. David Waldstreicher notes that during the late eighteenth and early nineteenth centuries, the "redefinition of Africa as one nation can be seen in virtually all contemporary black writing."[15] This redefinition would have been more pronounced in the North, where public orations and print culture provided forums for black northerners to articulate and disseminate views on slavery, freedom, and the inequities of northern society. When they did so, black speakers and writers almost invariably invoked a representation of Africa in which regions encompassed the entire continent. Nineteen New Hampshire slaves identified themselves as "natives of Africa" who had been betrayed into slavery by "their native countrymen" in a 1779 freedom petition. Jupiter Hammon sanctioned a message in 1786 by identifying himself as a man of "your own nation and colour." Hammon did not mean the United States. Writing from Philadelphia in 1794, Richard Allen and Absalom Jones promised that someday "princes shall come forth from Egypt" to lead African-descended peoples to a promised land. In 1799 Absalom Jones led seventy-three black Philadelphians in a petition to the president and Congress protesting slavery and the slave trade and linked themselves to those of "like colour and national descent." Again, the "nation" was Africa.[16]

Concurrently the public discourse of African Americans betrayed little identification with the American nation during the first two decades of the new republic. Because Africa was a somewhat mythologized homeland and because even those who did desire to return to Africa found it difficult to do so, the cry of "No country!" continued to ring true for most free people of color. James Oliver Horton has noted that most free people of color "identified with the words and the spirit of the Declaration of Independence and the Revolution," but they qualified even the occasional hint of articulating any connection to any form of an American polity. The laws of the African Society did identify its members in 1796 as "We, the African Members . . . true and faithful citizens of the Commonwealth in which we live," and in a qualified but complimentary attitude toward that commonwealth, *The Sons of Africa* noted that "Massachusetts is greatly to be valued for the peculiar advantage which we enjoy, as it respects our freedom." But for the most part, the author credited any benefits of living in Massachusetts to God and not to the benevolence of whites, and even here he continued to juxtapose himself and other free people of color against other Americans by calling blacks "Africans, who inhabit Massachusetts."[17]

Black men and women during and after the Revolution in Massachusetts, and elsewhere in the North, evinced little identification with the new nation. This should not be surprising, especially in light of white Americans' sometimes violent struggles over what it meant to be an American. If, for white Americans, defining the new nation and what it meant to be a citizen of that nation could be heavily contested ground, Africans and their descendants had even greater reasons to be diffident, leery, and even resistant toward partaking in any attempt to sow the seeds of a national American identity among free people of color.

A few decades later the militant David Walker called America his "native land" and declared, "This country is as much ours as it is the whites." In 1832 fellow black Bostonian Maria W. Stewart labeled herself "a true born American" and lectured to black and white Bostonians about the "American free people of color." Later that same year Peter Osborne painted a picture for his New Haven church of African Americans holding "the Declaration of Independence in one hand and the Holy Bible in the other," fighting for "our native country" and thereby fulfilling the mantle laid upon them by their forefathers who had "fought, bled and died to achieve the independence of the United States." The rhetoric of antebellum black leaders contrasted strikingly with the language of their forebears.[18]

Surveying just the first year of the *Liberator* reveals pointed sentiments by African Americans claiming an American identity. A Philadelphia man asserted his identity as an American by noting that his ancestors had been in the colonies since William Penn's time and asking, "Am I now to be told that Africa is my country, by some of those whose birth-place is unknown?" Another "Colored Philadelphian" stated, "We are told Africa is our native country; consequently the climate will be more congenial to our health. We readily deny the assertion. How can a man be born in two countries at the same time? Is not the position superficial to suppose that American born citizens are Africans?" Brooklyn African Americans referred to the "United States of America, our native soil" and called themselves "*countrymen* and *fellow-citizens*" who demanded "an equal share of protection from our federal government."[19]

Another columnist in the *Liberator*, who did not identify him or herself as white or black, suggested a "change of appellation," with the term "Afric-American" being most appropriate, since it "asserts . . . that the colored citizen is as truly a citizen of the United States of America as the white." William Lloyd Garrison asked his "colored" readers for a response, and the only direct response, from a letter writer who did not identify his or her color, rejected the "change of appellation." More telling is the indirect response of African Americans: In the next issue Robert Wood and John T. Hilton, two prominent and activist members of Boston's black community, issued a notice for a meeting about establishing a black vocational college and used the term "Afric-American." Another notice of a meeting in Hartford used the same term, and in the fall, a group of female black Bostonians organized a literary association called the Afric-American Female Intelligence Society of Boston. In December Peter Osborne exhorted his New Haven church to "take courage, ye Afric-Americans!"[20]

Though the individual and corporate identification with the United States became an integral part of northern African American identity, black Bostonians and other free people of color in the north by no means repudiated their African identity. The transatlantic perception combining African heritage and American themes came through clearly in a testimonial dinner in 1828, when David Walker and several other members of Boston's black leadership cadre welcomed the West African Prince Abduhl Rahaman, an escaped slave who had come to Boston in an effort to raise support for gaining his family's freedom from southern slavery. The language of some of the toasts were infused with American notions of "Independence and Liberty" and hopes that "the Spirit of Liberty which pervades our Northern Hemisphere" would spread south and worldwide. Cato Freeman praised Haiti for being "founded on the basis of true republican principles," and Coffin Pitts anticipated the day when "[Christianity], industry, prudence, and economy" would "characterize every descendant of Africa." James G. Barbadoes expressed a similar desire that the "sons and daughters of Africa soon become a civilized and christian-like people." Within these testimonials, given for an African prince they called brother, Boston's black leaders affirmed both their African heritage by labeling themselves "sons and daughters" of Africa, and their American character by defining their hopes for the future with ideological terms that had become central to American identity—republicanism, "Independence," "Equality," and "Liberty."[21]

Claims of an American heritage or identity by free people of color in the late eighteenth and the first years of the nineteenth century were muted or nonexistent, but as the nineteenth century progressed, northern African Americans consciously and stridently laid claim to the American aspects of their heritage. Signal events helped catalyzed this evolution of identification, especially the abolition of the slave trade in 1808, the rise of the colonization movement in the next decade, and attempts in various northern states to pass segregationist legislation. When Congress made the importation of slaves illegal as of January 1, 1808, African Americans finally had some cause to celebrate the nation for something specifically related to an essential part of their identity and heritage—what seemed to be the end of the rape of their homeland. Public gatherings keynoted by orators extolling the virtues and sins of the United States marked what was essentially African Americans' first national day of celebration. The orations "fought American racial injustice while inventing and establishing black nationality."[22]

Other speeches made a more explicit identification with America: at the opening of his speech in 1808, Peter Williams defined himself and his audience both as "Africans, and the descendants of Africans," and as "American[s]." A year later, Joseph Sidney had no trouble using the first possessive pronoun "our" when referring to America and went further not only by identifying with America but also by placing himself and African Americans in general as guardians of America's future through support of the Federalists and opposing "our enemies," the Jeffersonians. On the sixth anniversary of the abolition of the slave trade, Russell Parrott pointed to the War of 1812 as proof that "we are faithful to our country . . . the black bore his part, stimulated by pure love of country." Parrott likely had in mind black sailors who fought in the war, many of whom made clear declarations of what W. Jeffrey Bolster called "a radical African American patriotism" when impressed by the Royal Navy. Several months later, black New Yorkers would express their allegiance and stake their claim as a part of the nation by turning out unbidden to build fortifications in case of a British attack.[23]

Whereas the abolition of the slave trade provided a positive reason for aligning with the American polity, the rise of the colonization movement proved to be a negative force triggering a vigorous assertion of American identity among African Americans throughout the antebellum era. While African Americans continued without reservation to avow an African heritage, the characterization of Africa changed. The orations on the abolition of the slave trade had typically recalled an almost idyllic Africa, but in one of the first responses against colonization, James Forten and Russell Parrott referred in 1817 to "the burning plains of Guinea." Subsequent emigrants confirmed those opinions; in 1833 Joseph Dailey wrote back to Philadelphia describing high death rates among emigrants to Liberia, crowded hospitals, poor agriculture, and corrupt politics. At the same time Dailey referred to America as his "native country." The colonization movement aroused a fierce black American patriotism.[24]

African Americans' assertion of America as a homeland and their claim to a stake in America rested on two intertwined arguments. First, the labor of generations of slaves entitled them to far more than they presently had. Second, they had a right to stay in their homeland and realize a better future—a right conferred by God, by nature, and by legal rights based upon the Constitution. Relying on the law and the Constitution signaled an acceptance of how legitimate change would be accomplished while weakening more radical challenges. Radical challenges, however, such as a separatist movement to establish a black nation within the nation, were not realistic—the threat to white hegemony would have been too great to be ignored. Moreover, if their words are to be believed, most African Americans saw themselves as part of the country and not as a separate nation that happened to exist within another nation. But African Americans' vision and interpretation of the law in general and the Constitution in particular did provide black leaders an effective tool for challenging white hegemony by calling for white Americans to live up to the promises of the revolutionary heritage they so loudly proclaimed.

Black writers and orators interpreted and applied the Declaration of Independence and the Constitution as they saw fit. The Constitution was commonly used against itself, often by privileging the Preamble over the body of the Constitution and sometimes by referring to specific parts. William Howard Day employed both tactics in 1851 when he first quoted from the Preamble to point out that "if it says it was framed to 'establish justice,' it, of course, is opposed to injustice" then supported his position further by using a portion of the Fifth Amendment: "If it says plainly 'no person shall be deprived of life, *liberty*, or property, without due process of law,'—I suppose it means it." At times the Declaration and the Constitution became fused in black rhetoric, as in the case of a black Philadelphian who argued that racist practices were "in direct opposition to the Constitution; which positively declares, that all men are born equal, and endowed with certain inalienable rights—among which are life, liberty, and the pursuit of happiness." Their arguments, at times constructed not from specific articles or amendments but from principles they believed the documents intended to profess, mirrored the broader process of Americans who "commonly spoke in constitutional terms when debating political and social issues." For free black leaders this habit began early on; in a 1797 petition to Congress, four southern black men who had fled to the north referred to "the unconstitutional bondage" they had left behind and called the Fugitive Slave Act of 1793 a "direct violation of the declared fundamental principles of the Constitution."[25]

Interpreting the Constitution as an antislavery document at times put black leaders at ideological odds with one another. In 1844 Massachusetts black and white attendees of the New England Anti-Slavery Convention heard Charles Lenox Redmond criticize the Constitution as an instrument of oppression upon "the few whom it entirely overlooks, or sees but to trample upon." At an Ohio convention H. Ford Douglas offered a fervent denunciation of the proconstitutional positions held by William Howard Day and John Mercer Langston, declaring that "the gentleman may wrap the stars and stripes of his country around him forty times, if possible, and with the Declaration of Independence in one hand, and the Constitution of our common country in the other, may seat himself under the shadow of the frowning monument of Bunker Hill." Langston replied that he hoped black men would do anything "under the Constitution, that will aid in effecting our liberties." But Douglas's repudiation demonstrates how deeply other African Americans had drunk of the Constitutional well; he castigated the thorough identification of other black leaders with American ideals and heritage. That identification fostered support for the Constitution and led the convention to side with Day and Langston. They voted down Douglas's motion to reject the Constitution twenty-eight to two.[26]

The anticonstitutional position of Remond and of his successors like Henry McNeal Turner has been characterized by Mary Frances Berry as a negative view of the Constitution. Berry labels this group as the "blacks-do-not-need-whites-to-succeed" school. On the other hand, antebellum black abolitionists emphasized "Americans' own stated ideals" and often "attempted to identify with those ideals and to insist that the nation should live up to them." Berry notes that the civil rights movement, beginning in the nineteenth century and continuing into the twentieth, "was a distinctly American movement, making appeals to traditional American culture and values." And though, as Peter Hinks points out, Americans, black or white, did not have a monopoly on many of these values, the context within which black leaders worked and the culture and value system they drew from was nonetheless an American one. When Charles Lenox Redmond, speaking before the Massachusetts legislature in 1842, called Boston the "Athens of America," he invoked a republican vision of independence and equality that Americans, black and white, intuitively understood.[27]

African Americans saw themselves as part of that republican vision of America. They called upon federal and state governments to uphold the spirit of the Constitution's preamble to "promote the general welfare, and secure the blessings of liberty to ourselves and our prosperity." According to their interpretation of the Constitution the government ought to serve their interests since they were a part of the sovereign people. In this African Americans differed little from other Americans; Americans had undergone a significant change in their view of the law and government in the nineteenth century, when the traditional view of rights was largely displaced. The traditional view had "emphasized what government could *not* do," but within that older view, which had been essential when an absolute sovereign had the potential to take away established practices, "rights defined as restraint made less sense where the people themselves were sovereign. . . . If the people owned the government, it should serve their interests. So argued those energetic Yankees who called on law to help them modernize the economy, conquer the continent, and exploit its riches." While historian R. Kent Newmyer and the Yankees he describes were concerned with how changes in the law helped to liberate capital, free people of color argued for a government and law that served their civil interests. In Boston Hosea Easton drove this point home. African Americans, he said, "being constitutionally Americans," were depending on "American government, and American manners . . . [and] a withholding of the enjoyment of any American principle from an American man . . . is in effect taking away his means of subsistence; and consequently, taking away his life." African Americans believed that the ability to take complete advantage of the nation's burgeoning economic opportunities was predicated upon a freedom from racial oppression that would begin by achieving equal civil rights.[28]

Legal historian William J. Novak points to the state's crucial role in establishing and regulating public ways and space, noting that there was "nothing *inherently public* about highway or riverway. Publicness had to be constructed and defended in a political and social milieu fraught with conflict and tension." The government ensured the unrestrained movement of capital by ensuring that highways and riverways became public. During the same period, however, there were efforts in Massachusetts to segregate some forms of public transportation, thereby placing some controls on black access to public ways and space. Some whites in the antebellum era sought to limit African Americans' participation in the polity, just as some whites had done so in the Revolutionary era. Limiting or controlling black access to public ways and space held the potential to not only define black citizens as lacking the same rights but also to define them as not being a part of the same American public as whites.[29]

The construction and regulation of public space and ways was integral to the positive vision of the republic and intimately connected to building the social and economic well-being of the nation. Excluding free black men and women from public ways excluded them from that progressive vision of the nation's economic and social life. Likewise, fighting exclusion had broader implications than merely ensuring that black folks could get around on public ways. African Americans claimed full citizenship by insisting on the same rights to public space and ways and argued for inclusion in the progressive vision of the American nation. Their argument stood in dramatic opposition to the weaving of whiteness throughout American identity. Fighting exclusion from schools, transportation, or the militia was, at its root, an ideological challenge to the construction of a white American identity.

Though David Walker and other black leaders unflinchingly concentrated attention on the sins and inconsistencies of the United States, they shared the moral, economic, and political aspirations of most Americans. The point here is not to enter into the well-worn argument about assimilation versus resistance. Certain aspects of African and American value systems could and did coexist; nevertheless, nineteenth-century African Americans expressed these ideals and aspirations in an American context and in American terms. Like many other African Americans, Walker did express corporate ties reaching beyond the shores of the United States, persisting in defining himself as African or of the "African race," and though opposed to emigration held up Haiti for emulation. But these transatlantic connections did not subsume an American identity or Walker's commitment to a system of morals and values accepted by many white and black Americans. Walker "wanted only the

opportunity for his people to participate fully without obstacle in the expanding free labor economy and the culture of Protestant moral improvement."
Celebrating the end of slavery in New York on July 4, 1827, the escaped slave
and entrepreneur Austin Steward exhorted African Americans to inscribe "in
letters of gold upon every door-post—'industry, prudence, economy.'" Samuel
Cornish, cofounder of the nation's first black newspaper, articulated a Jefferson-
ian-like vision of getting black families to establish a literal stake in this country when he ran an ad for the sale of a two-thousand-acre parcel of land along
the Delaware River in New York. For buyers he was looking for some of his
"brethren who are capitalists," who, he hoped, would in turn sell it for a small
profit to black families who would build an African American farming community. Walker, Steward, Cornish, and others connected pursuit of financial
stability to sound morals, education, hard work, and prudence—qualities
inseparable from the overall goal of full equality.[30] But black leaders believed
virtue, frugality, and education would be insufficient to elevate ordinary free
people of color to full social, economic, and political equality without procuring all the rights that God, nature, and the Constitution imparted.

Most African Americans, far from proposing radical change or abandoning
the country, were intimately tied to many of the goals articulated by white
Americans. As Kimberle Crenshaw has pointed out for the twentieth-century
civil rights movement, antebellum black activists called on social and political
institutions to act in the way they were supposed to act according to the Constitution so that African Americans, like white Americans, could realize those
goals. Black New Yorkers, gathering in 1840 for a state convention aimed at
gaining black suffrage, professed themselves "to be American and republican,"
and described the Declaration of Independence and the Constitution as
embodying "the primary ideas of American republicanism." In their estima-
tion the framers of those documents had intended federal and state governments to live up to those ideals by granting and protecting the "republican
birthright" of every individual, black or white.[31]

When African Americans spoke of a "birthright," they infused the term
with multiple meanings. Birthright connoted a stake in America because their
forefathers fought for freedom and implied that an inheritance was due them
because slaves had worked the land. But it also grounded a rights discourse by
focusing on constitutionally defined citizenship by right of birth. During the
plenary address at the 1840 New York convention, published in the *Colored
American* and likely read by Boston's black leaders, Austin Stewart neatly summarized this by asserting, "We *do* regard the right of our birthdom, our service
in behalf of the country, contributing to its importance, and developing its
resources" as sufficient reason to consider African Americans as worthy of
suffrage. Stewart also predicated the right to vote on "still higher ground"—
the "certain peculiar rights" belonging to any being "found endowed with the

light of reason." But though human nature provided the foundation and legitimation for rights, the Declaration of Independence and the Constitution represented the ultimate expression of the "natural and indestructible principles of man," designed to secure "the purest liberty God ever conferred" upon a people.[32]

Making rights rhetoric the heart of the argument for full equality and opportunity was "a way of saying that a society . . . ought to live up to its deepest commitments." The complicating factor is that using rights to achieve the desired goals can be limiting. Crenshaw notes that "demands for change that do not reflect the institutional logic—that is, demands that do not engage and subsequently reinforce the dominant ideology—will probably be ineffective." Because African Americans shared many of the same goals and ideals of other Americans, most had little desire to effect radical change that threatened established institutions (other than slavery) or to challenge an ideology that placed the Constitution and the law as a primary agent of change.[33]

Insights from critical race theory on the possibilities and limitations of twentieth-century rights rhetoric are directly relevant in discussing antebellum black activists. Like their twentieth-century successors, black leaders made claims framed in language of rights rhetoric that Americans of all ranks would recognize. Their claims "reflected American society's institutional logic: legal rights ideology." By talking about legal rights African Americans in both centuries "exposed a series of contradictions," primarily the contradiction between Constitutional promises of citizenship and its attendant privileges, and the systematic denial of those privileges through the practice of racial subordination. But African Americans, beginning in the antebellum era, advanced arguments "as if American citizenship were real, and demanded to exercise the 'rights' that citizenship entailed." This represented an attempt "to restructure reality to reflect American mythology," a mythology that presumed rights undergirded all social and political equality and would also open the doors to economic opportunity. Obtaining full exercise of rights would supposedly make reality fit the mythology.[34]

In order to maintain legitimacy, dominant groups at times open the door for change to subordinate groups. But at the same time "it is the very accomplishment of legitimacy that forecloses greater possibilities. In sum the potential for change is both created and limited by legitimation." By using the Declaration of Independence and the Constitution to legitimate their citizenship, African Americans made legal rights ideology an integral part of their identity. Challenging that ideology would be difficult because it would mean challenging their self-definition. This helps explain why few black leaders advocated rejecting the Constitution.[35]

Incorporating a legal rights ideology into a free black identity may have foreclosed more radical alternatives, such as a "classical" black nationalism.

Wilson Jeremiah Moses defines classical black nationalism as black attempts "to create a sovereign nation-state and formulate an ideological basis for a concept of a national culture." The movement to create a black republic never received broad support in part because an African American identity that rested in part on a vigorous claim to American citizenship, which in turn rested on birthright and the Constitution, undercut classical black nationalism. Part of living out their identity—part of being African American—was fighting for full citizenship rights and making the myth a reality.[36]

The use of legal rights ideology fought racial hegemony that employed racial ideologies to define black people as the "other" who belonged outside the polity. Black people, through word and deed, demonstrated they had the same rights and in a sense constructed a competing legal consciousness—a belief in their ability and right to use the law—against those who sought to use the law to exclude them from the polity through segregationist laws. African Americans exploited weaknesses in the hegemonic function of the law, where the law typically works to protect the dominant social order. But the law had to be perceived as apolitical and impartial in order for citizens to believe that the law was indeed just and equitable, especially during the relatively young years of the republic. The need to appear just meant that the legal rights arguments African Americans made could not be easily discarded but had to be wrestled with. Some legal scholars argue that legal consciousness legitimates hierarchy and hegemony and in this case would have legitimated a white racial hegemony. And black legal consciousness and the wielding of a legal rights ideology that flowed out of that legal consciousness did in some respects validate hegemony by confirming the rule of law, the centrality of rights, and the legitimacy of pursuing change through the law. But black legal consciousness also *challenged* hegemony by articulating a multiracial citizenry, based upon the very legal rights ideology that occupied a central place in American identity, that stood against a growing racialized identity premised on whiteness.

Using legal rights ideology held the potential for radical change in other respects as well. Long before modern debates on the role of the law and government to take active social and economic roles, African Americans like Hosea Easton and others articulated a vision of the law as having a fundamental role in either denying or enabling black men and women to participate in the nation's social, political, and economic future. They participated in the construction of citizenship and a legal rights ideology that made legal rights the fulcrum of progress. And in many respects, later developments proved them correct: the systematic denial of legal rights played a significant role protecting white supremacy and furthering African Americans' ruinous political, economic, and social position.

While free blacks' use of a legal rights ideology may have limited some potential for change, the historical context is crucial: few alternatives existed for African Americans. The law and rights rhetoric offered one of the few possibilities for change. For most free people of color, emigration or the establishment of a classical black nationalism was beyond their means and, more important, beyond their desire. Though the choices free people of color had available to them were limited, the elements of choice and agency remain important. They consciously conceived of themselves as Americans with a legitimate claim to citizenship, and protecting that basic right was crucial in their daily life. Ordinary African Americans who exercised their rights to use the law and the courts in a variety of ways would have suffered had they, unlike their enslaved southern brethren, not been able to take advantage of the guarantees of the fifth through the eighth amendments or been unable to execute writs of *habeas corpus*. A letter written by a black man to the *Liberator* pointed to the consequence of slaves being unprotected by the Constitution: "They are not permitted to testify against a white criminal, in courts of justice; consequently, their persons, property, and lives are at the mercy of every white ruffian, thief or murderer. The question therefore should be quickly settled, whether free colored persons, born or naturalized in this country, are not American citizens, and justly entitled to all the rights, privileges and immunities of citizens of the several states; and whether the Constitution of the United States makes or authorises any invidious distinction with regard to the color or condition of free inhabitants."

A few years earlier a report in *Freedom's Journal* pointed out injustice in the West Indies when a slave managed to publicly identify his assailant shortly before he died from the injuries. The slave's testimony, however, had no legal standing and his murderer was allowed to go free. For free people of color, this story was a vivid reminder of the costs of the denial of citizenship and legal recognition to millions of slaves."[37]

The legal rights ideology had been established and forcefully voiced as a part of African American identity. As noted above, part of that ideology rested on a claim that African Americans belonged because of their birthright. African Americans stretched the concept of birthright to connote their participation in the birth of the country, sealing the argument that they had the right to be Americans. They wedded a constructed memory of black participation in wars for freedom onto their legal rights ideology, ensconcing black self-definition as fully American. This memory centered on black forefathers who came to be seen as having sacrificed as much as, if not more than, white Americans for freedom and rights when they bled and died during the Revolutionary War and the War of 1812 after enduring a past of oppression and for a future that held only uncertain fulfillment of freedom's potential.

A useful silence was an important tool in crafting that heritage. Notably absent in the memorialization of ancestors who fought for freedom was any mention of the ancestors who fought for freedom *from* the Americans by fighting *for* the British, an empire cast by American revolutionaries as the tyrannical enemy of liberty. In the 1850s William Cooper Nell compiled accounts of African Americans who filled a variety of roles during the two wars against the British. Nell proudly recalled John Hancock's presentation of a silk flag to a company of black soldiers from Massachusetts, the Bucks of America, "as a tribute to their courage and devotion in the cause of American Liberty." Nell gathered accounts from a variety of sources to reconstruct the heroic deeds of black soldiers and sailors. Beginning with Crispus Attucks, he crafted a black patriotic tradition by rendering Attucks as a black man who led others into an epic moment that unfolded into a momentous history. Others echoed Nell's narratives. In 1858 at the Convention of Colored Citizens of Massachusetts, the Business Committee described Attucks as "the first martyr . . . ushering in the day which history has selected as the dawn of the America Revolution." The 1859 New England Convention's president reminded the delegates that "some colored men, conscious of their manhood . . . stood side by side with their white fellow-countrymen in the battles that secured the freedom and rights of a common country, felt, demanded and exercised the prerogatives of American citizenship." The terminology is revealing: Whites were not simply fellow soldiers but also fellow *countrymen*, fighting for common cause and country. William Wells Brown neatly intertwined a legal rights ideology and patriotic imagery to remind delegates of their heritage in the face of colonization efforts. "Let us remain here," he proclaimed, "and claim our rights upon the soil where our fathers fought side by side with the white man for freedom . . . and vindicate our right to citizenship, and pledge ourselves to aid in completing the Revolution for human freedom, commenced by the patriots of 1776."[38]

But forgotten were the Boston slaves who petitioned Gen. Thomas Gage in 1774 for weapons and told him that many other black men would fight for the British if they were rewarded with freedom. Their motives were clearly not to fight with "fellow countrymen" or for American liberty. Their own personal liberty concerned these black petitioners far more than any national liberty, and the disorder of war combined with the steady flow of runaways sparked by Lord Dunmore's offer of freedom to slaves who joined the British provided a window of opportunity.[39]

This useful silence regarding the hundreds, perhaps thousands, of slaves who fought against American patriots—perhaps even against black revolutionaries—is all the more striking because Nell's state-by-state account in his 1851 publication skips over Virginia and Maryland, from whence large numbers of slaves absconded. More telling was Nell's expanded 1855 edition, *Colored Patriots of the American Revolution*, which did cover Virginia and Maryland and contained a much lengthier section on South Carolina that included a fictive reconstruction of a story Nell had heard regarding slaves who met to debate killing their owners and fleeing to the British. In the end they showed

their natural love of liberty by deciding to "take their freedom without mur-
dering their masters" if the British came.[40] But within the context of the entire
work Nell's semifictive narrative of this meeting did not weaken his reification
of Revolutionary era black men and women as patriots. Nell never mentioned
the possibility that taking their freedom meant aiding the British against
Americans because that would have undermined his central theme, epitomized
in his title. Nell's labeling black revolutionaries as "colored patriots" aligned
his subjects with the twin causes of liberty in general and American liberty in
particular. His tome had a specific purpose: validating black American citizenship.

This does not undermine the courage and convictions that drove black men
to risk their lives for freedom. Nell's recollections and those of others were
accurate; black men did fight and die in the Revolution. The Philadelphia man
who wrote to the *Liberator*, whose ancestors had been in the colonies since
William Penn, also said he had fought in the Revolution. He typifies the progression of identity for many free people of color. He claimed a Revolutionary
War heritage and an American identity in 1831, but it is questionable if he
conceived of himself quite so distinctly during the war. But over time he came
to think of himself as an American with certain rights, and he metamorphosed
his wartime service into a fight for the right to belong to the American polity.
When he was fighting he was likely fighting for rights, but rights more
broadly defined: the right to be free and to make a life for himself. By 1831 he
had incorporated the right to call himself an American citizen and claim all
attendant rights. Other black soldiers would later note their Revolutionary
War service in terms of fighting for the nation, but it seems more likely that
they too were constructing memories: Many recorded their accounts long after
the war, writing in the context of forging a legal rights ideology and a fight to
define free people of color as Americans. When Nell described black men as
"those who . . . had warm hearts and active hands in the 'times that tried men's
souls,'" he situates black revolutionaries within a distinctly American tradition
by calling forth the image of the grand struggle against British tyranny for the
sake of American liberty. But it was a tradition and identification that probably would have been foreign to those black soldiers who fought for liberty *from*
Americans, the British, or anyone else who stood between them and freedom.[41]

The black patriotism of the antebellum era clearly differed from the patriotism of most antebellum white Americans. Inseparable from the creation of
an African American patriotic tradition was the uncompromising critique of
the national failure of the United States to honor its ideals. African Americans
did not flag in their efforts to keep national exploitation and hypocrisy a public matter. They had "a critical sense of their country's history, their condition
permitting no easy escape into a national folklore." This was the essence of the
qualitative difference: For African Americans, the creation of patriotic heritage
was not easy and not an escape; it was a necessary construction—a resurrection,

perhaps—in order to further ground their right to full citizenship. But it was a construction nonetheless.[42]

Building that black patriotic identity, an identity tied to the struggle for freedom that had come to characterize the nation's founding, an identity wedded to the legal rights ideology articulated by black leaders, anchored free people of color in the North to a distinct black identity. The unflagging and unsparing protest that African Americans promulgated throughout the early era of the Republic flowed from this identity. African Americans had moved from bleakly acute cries of "No Country!" to compellingly resolute declarations of "Our Country!" Vincent Harding notes that one of the "essential questions" raised by the black freedom movement was, "Who were 'we the People of the United States'?" Like Maria Stewart, who proclaimed herself a "true born American," most black women and men had no doubt in their own minds that they belonged. The challenge was making American social and legal institutions recognize what African Americans already knew.[43]

Orlando Patterson has termed manumission a "cultural gift" that is not free but calls for patronage from the manumitted to the manumitter. In many Atlantic world societies this likely described the relationship between freed slaves and former slave owners. In the northern United States it could be argued that state governments and the law made a cultural gift of sorts to slaves by outlawing slavery. But black men and women played a significant role in pushing events along to the point where the ruling powers "gave" them freedom. The concept of manumission as a gift becomes problematic when it is given in part because of the agency of the recipient. The concept of subsequent patronage also becomes problematic in the antebellum north. For African Americans, the "patron" was the law, and in an abstract sense they did exhibit a degree of patronage by reinforcing the law's legitimacy and the institutional logic of legal rights ideology. And yet they made demands on the law. They argued that the law should *serve their interests*, which does not fit into the relationship Patterson describes. Using the law, they claimed an identity as Americans to place demands upon the "patron."

Quce Godshall's story illustrates some of the conceptual themes that complicate Patterson's model. Godshall, an African-born free black man from Salem, Massachusetts, sailed for several months aboard the *Voador* until captured by the British in 1814. Initially taken as a prisoner of war, Godshall was released and returned to Salem. Meanwhile the vessel was taken to Halifax, Nova Scotia, although the British eventually decided to release it. The owners sent a man for retrieval, but the harbor master in Halifax schemed to have the vessel taken and sailed to England. A friend of the owners somehow stumbled across the vessel in Liverpool, informed the owners, who apparently pursued the matter in the courts there, and managed to get one thousand pounds, though they did not regain the *Voador*.

Quce Godshall got word of this. He took the owners to court, demanding $128 in unpaid wages. And he won. Apparently important to the court before deciding in his favor was determining Godshall's citizenry. The court twice specifically defined Godshall as an American, once noting that he was on the *Voador*, which the British considered "as *American* property and Godshall, the seaman who makes the claim for wages, was taken from her as an *American* subject and considered as a prisoner of war," and again stating, ostensibly unconnected from anything else in the proceedings, that it was understood that though he was African-born, he boarded the *Voador* as an American citizen.[44]

In simplest form, for Godshall being an American citizen meant $128. Unlike most white Americans, the claim of American citizenship was a debatable status in many people's minds for black men such as Quce Godshall, but the law could resolve that debate. In his court case it clearly did. Most free people of color would, like Godshall, depend upon the law to define themselves as Americans. Godshall, who probably came to New England via the West Indies, gained manumission in either the West Indies or the United States. He did not patronize the state or the law that manumitted him but used the law to gain what was important to him: $128. In the process the court validated his claim to citizenship, which connected him to a host of other legal rights. This identification was pregnant with possibilities and limitations that could birth new opportunities to exercise freedom and abort other more radical alternatives to suggest how change might occur in the new nation. But with few other alternatives, the legal validation of free people of color such as Godshall as American citizens formed an integral part of their identity.

Quce Godshall and other African Americans may have cut their eyes at anyone suggesting emancipation was a gift of any sort. From slavery to freedom they lived out a complicated relationship with the law, constantly wrestling, giving, and claiming ground, coming under the rule of law and placing demands upon it, all the while hoping to realize for all free people of color the full citizenship rights that the law would not give until a century later, and even then African Americans would see once again the law's ability to both challenge and shield racial hegemony: never a gift but always a struggle.

NOTES

1. On African Americans' use of biblical and natural rights ideologies in Revolutionary era discourse, see Gary Nash, *Race and Revolution* (Madison: Madison House, 1990); Thomas J. Davis, "Emancipation Rhetoric, Natural Rights, and Revolutionary New England: A Note on Four Black Petitions in Massachusetts, 1773–1777," *New England Quarterly* 62 (March 1989): 248–263; Mia Bay, *The White Image in the Black Mind: African-American Ideas about White People, 1830–1925* (New York: Oxford University Press, 2000), 13–37; on black parades and their connection to citizenship and identity, see Shane White, "'It Was a Proud Day': African Americans, Festivals, and Parades in the North, 1741–1834," *Journal of American History* 81 (June 1994): 13–50; and David Waldstreicher, *In the Midst of Perpetual Fetes:*

The Making of American Nationalism, 1776–1820 (Chapel Hill: University of North Carolina Press, 1997), 294–348.

2. Herbert Aptheker, ed. and comp., *A Documentary History of the Negro People in the United States* (New York: Citadel Press, 1951), 1:5–10.

3. Ibid. 1:9.

4. T. H. Breen, "Ideology and Nationalism on the Eve of the American Revolution: Revisions *Once More* in Need of Revising," *Journal of American History* 84 (June 1997): 13–39, 34. The proposed constitution was printed in the *Boston Gazette & Country Journal*, March 23, 1778.

5. Sidney Kaplan, *The Black Presence in the Era of the American Revolution* (Greenwich: New York Graphic Society, 1973), 214.

6. *The Essex Journal and Merimack Packet or The Massachusetts and New-Hampshire General Advertiser*, August 17, 1774.

7. Aptheker, *Documentary History of the Negro People* 1:6–10. On public opinion as a factor in abolition in Massachusetts, see T. H. Breen, "Making History: The Force of Public Opinion and the Last Years of Slavery in Revolutionary Massachusetts," in *Through a Glass Darkly: Reflections on Personal Identity in Early America*, ed. Ronald Hoffman, Mechal Sobel, and Fredrika J. Teute (Chapel Hill: University of North Carolina Press, 1997), 67–95.

8. *Boston Gazette & Country Journal*, March 23, 1778; *Independent Chronicle*, January 5, 29, February 5, 12, 1778; Massachusetts Archives, 199:80–81, 84, Massachusetts State Archives, Boston.

9. Aptheker, *Documentary History of the Negro People* 1:14–16.

10. John Marrant, "You Stand on the Level with the Greatest Kings on Earth," in *Lift Every Voice: African American Oratory, 1787–1900*, ed. Philip S. Foner and Robert James Branham (Tuscaloosa: University of Alabama Press, 1998), 27–38.

11. Henry Louis Gates Jr. and William L. Andrews, eds., *Pioneers of the Black Atlantic: Five Slave Narratives from the Enlightenment 1772–1815* (Washington, D.C.: Counterpoint, 1998), 11, 80.

12. Prince Hall, "Pray God Give Us the Strength to Bear Up Under All Our Troubles," in *Lift Every Voice: African American Oratory, 1787–1900*, ed. Philip S. Foner and Robert James Branham (Tuscaloosa: University of Alabama Press, 1998), 52.

13. Kaplan, *Black Presence*, 207–208. The 1787 petition is reprinted here.

14. *The Sons of Africans: An Essay on Freedom. With Observations on the Origin of Slavery. By a Member of the African Society in Boston* (Boston, 1808), 20–21, 10. Pamphlet located at the Boston Athenæum, Boston, Mass.

15. See Waldstreicher, *In the Midst of Perpetual Fetes,* 320–322; W. Jeffrey Bolster, *Black Jacks: African American Seamen in the Age of Sail* (Cambridge, Mass.: Harvard University Press, 1997), 38–39.

16. New Hampshire slaves' petition in the *Magazine of American History with Notes and Queries* 21 (January–June, 1889), 63; Jupiter Hammon, "An Address to the Negroes in the State of New York," in *Afro-American Religious History: A Documentary Witness*, ed. Milton C. Sernett (Durham, N.C.: Duke University Press, 1985), 34; Richard Allen and Absalom Jones, *A Narrative of the Proceedings of the Black People, during the Late Awful Calamity in Philadelphia, in the Year 1793: And a Refutation of some Censures Thrown upon Them in some late Publications* (Philadelphia, 1794), 24, 28; 1799 petition reprinted in Dorothy B. Porter, ed., *Early Negro Writing, 1760–1837* (Boston: Beacon Press, 1971), 330.

17. James Oliver Horton, *Free People of Color: Inside the African American Community* (Washington, D.C.: Smithsonian Institution Press, 1993), 150; *Sons of Africa*, 14, 17; *Laws of*

the African Society, instituted at Boston, 1796, pamphlet, located at the Boston Athenæum, Boston, Mass.

18. David Walker, *David Walker's Appeal, in Four Articles; Together with a Preamble, to the Coloured Citizens of the World, but in particular, and very expressly, to those of the United States of America* (Boston, 1829), 55. I am using the 1995 edition of the Hill and Wang 1965 reprint, with an introduction by Sean Wilentz. Marilyn Richardson, ed., *Maria W. Stewart: America's First Black Woman Political Writer* (Bloomington: Indiana University Press, 1987), 46; Peter Osborne, "It Is Time for Us to be Up and Doing," in *Lift Every Voice: African American Oratory, 1787–1900*, ed. Philip S. Foner and Robert James Branham (Tuscaloosa: University of Alabama Press, 1998), 124–125.

19. *Liberator*, January 22, March 12, July 3, 1831.

20. *Liberator*, July 16, July 23, August 13, 1831. The lone writer who rejected the suggested term appeared September 24, 1831. Marilyn Richardson notes the 1831 founding of Boston's female literary association in *Maria W. Stewart*, 127; Osborne, "It Is Time for Us," 125.

21. *Freedom's Journal*, October 24, 1828; C. Peter Ripley, ed., *The Black Abolitionist Papers* (Chapel Hill: University of North Carolina Press, 1991), 3:78. According to Ripley's editorial note, the prince, whose full name was Abd al-Rahman Ibrahima, had originally embarked on this tour to promote the American Colonization Society in return for their help in raising funds to free the rest of his family. The *Freedom's Journal* and other African Americans, however, typically portrayed his cause as the emancipation of his family (which was undoubtedly the prince's sole motivation) and neglected to mention the colonization aspect to his northern tour.

22. Porter, *Early Negro Writing*, 35; Waldstreicher, *In the Midst of Perpetual Fetes*, 344.

23. Porter, *Early Negro Writing*, 350, 357, 361, 390; Bolster, *Black Jacks*, 117; Shane White, *Somewhat More Independent: The End of Slavery in New York City, 1770–1810* (Athens: University of Georgia Press, 1991), 150.

24. Porter, *Early Negro Writing*, 267; Ripley, *Black Abolitionist Papers* 3:74–77.

25. Vincent Harding, "Wrestling Toward the Dawn: The Afro-American Freedom Movement and the Changing Constitution, " *Journal of American History* 74 (December 1987): 718–739, 720–721; Philip S. Foner and George E. Walker, eds., *Proceedings of the Black State Conventions, 1840–1865* (Philadelphia: Temple University Press, 1979), 1:262; *Liberator*, February 12, 1831; Donald G. Nieman, *Promises to Keep: African Americans and the Constitutional Order, 1776 to the Present* (New York: Oxford University Press, 1991), 31; Aptheker, *Documentary History of the Negro Peoples* 1:43.

26. Ripley, *Black Abolitionist Papers* 3:442; Foner and Walker, *Proceedings of the Black State Conventions* 1:262–263; Donald G. Nieman, "The Language of Liberation: African Americans and Equalitarian Constitutionalism, 1830–1950," in *The Constitution, Law, and American Life: Critical Aspects of the Nineteenth-Century Experience*, ed. Donald G. Nieman (Athens: University of Georgia Press, 1992), 67–90, 68.

27. Mary Frances Berry, "Vindicating Martin Luther King, Jr.: The Road to a Color-Blind Society," *Journal of Negro History* 81 (1996): 137–144, 141; Peter Hinks, *To Awaken My Afflicted Brethren: David Walker and the Problem of Antebellum Slave Resistance* (University Park: Pennsylvania State University Press, 1997), 110; see also William M. Wiecek, *The Sources of Anti-Slavery Constitutionalism in America, 1760–1848* (Ithaca, N.Y.: Cornell University Press, 1977); Ripley, *Black Abolitionist Papers* 3:368.

28. R. Kent Newmyer, "Harvard Law School, New England Culture, and the Antebellum Origins of American Jurisprudence," *Journal of American History* 74 (December 1987): 814–835, 821; also see James Willard Hurst, *The Law and Conditions of Freedom in the*

Nineteenth-Century United States (Madison: University of Wisconsin Press, 1956); and Morton J. Horwitz, *The Transformation of American Law 1780–1860* (Cambridge, Mass.: Harvard University Press, 1977); Hosea Easton, *A Treatise on the Intellectual Character, and Civil and Political Condition of the Colored People of the United States* (Boston, 1837), 49.

29. William J. Novak, *The People's Welfare: Law and Regulation in Nineteenth-Century America* (Chapel Hill: University of North Carolina Press, 1996), 117.

30. Hinks, *To Awaken My Afflicted Brethren*, 108–110; Austin Steward, "Termination of Slavery," in *Lift Every Voice: African American Oratory, 1787–1900*, ed. Philip S. Foner and Robert James Branham (Tuscaloosa: University of Alabama Press, 1998), 108; Cornish's ads in the *Freedom's Journal*, July 13, 1827, and several other issues. On new perspectives regarding the assimilation versus resistance argument and black New Englanders, see Robert E. Desrochers Jr., "'Not Fade Away': The Narrative of Venture Smith, an African American in the Early Republic," *Journal of American History* 84 (June 1997): 40–66.

31. Kimberle Williams Crenshaw, "Race, Reform, and Retrenchment: Transformation and Legitimation in Antidiscrimination Law," *Harvard Law Review* 101 (May 1988): 1331–1387, 1367; Foner and Walker, *Proceedings of the Black State Conventions* 1:21.

32. Foner and Walker, *Proceedings of the Black State Conventions* 1:21–22.

33. Crenshaw, "Race, Reform, and Retrenchment," 1365–66; Foner and Walker, *Proceedings of the Black State Conventions* 1:21–22.

34. Crenshaw, "Race, Reform, and Retrenchment," 1367–1368.

35. Ibid. For arguments similar to Crenshaw's regarding how the need to legitimate law and legal ideology works both to maintain hegemony while also exposing it to challenges, see Douglas Hay, "Property, Authority and the Criminal Law," in *Albions' Fatal Tree: Crime and Society in Eighteenth-Century England*, by Douglas Hay, Peter Linebaugh, John G. Rule, C. P. Thompson, and Cal Winslow (New York: Pantheon, 1975), 3–64; E. P. Thompson, *Whigs and Hunters: The Origin of the Black Act* (New York: Pantheon, 1975).

36. Wilson Jeremiah Moses, *Classical Black Nationalism: From the American Revolution to Marcus Garvey* (New York: New York University Press, 1996), 2.

37. *Liberator*, January 15, 1831; *Freedom's Journal*, September 14, 1827. On the antebellum environment for African Americans, see Gary Nash, *Forging Freedom: The Formation of Philadelphia's Black Community, 1720–1840* (Cambridge, Mass.: Harvard University Press, 1988); Leonard P. Curry, *Free Blacks in Urban America* (Chicago: University of Chicago Press, 1981); Shane White, "'We Dwell in Safety and Pursue Our Honest Callings': Free Blacks in New York City, 1783–1810," *Journal of American History* 75 (September 1988): 445.

38. William Cooper Nell, *Services of Colored Americans in the Wars of 1776 and 1812* (Boston: Prentiss and Sawyer, 1851), 5–7, 9. This book served as a blueprint for Nell's later book, *The Colored Patriots of the American Revolution, with Sketches of several Distinguished Colored Persons: To which is added a Brief Survey of the Condition and Prospects of Colored Americans* (Boston, 1855); Foner and Walker, *Proceedings of the Black State Conventions*, 99, 208, 212.

39. Sidney Kaplan, "The 'Domestic Insurrections' of the Declaration of Independence," *Journal of Negro History* 61 (July 1976): 249–250; see also Benjamin Quarles, *The Negro in the American Revolution* (Chapel Hill: University of North Carolina Press, 1961) and Benjamin Quarles, *Black Mosaic: Essays in Afro-American Historiography* (Amherst: University of Massachusetts Press, 1988); Sylvia Frey, *Water From the Rock: Black Resistance in a Revolutionary Age* (Princeton, N.J.: Princeton University Press, 1991).

40. Nell, *Colored Patriots*, 250–252.

41. Ibid., 181.

42. Quarles, *Black Mosaic*, 92.

43. Harding, "Wrestling Toward the Dawn," 721.

44. Attorney's papers, Marine & Shipping Cases, 1814–1821, October 29, 1816, Box 1, Folder 1, Andrew Dunlap Papers, Peabody Essex Museum, Salem, Mass.

"If the rest stay, I will stay;
if they go, I will go"

—⁂—

How Slaves' Familial Bonds Affected American
Colonization Society Manumissions

Parents will be torn from their children—husbands from their wives—brothers from brothers—and all the heart-rending agonies which were endured by our forefathers when they were dragged into bondage from Africa, will be again renewed, and with increased anguish. The shores of America will, like the sands of Africa, be watered by the tears of those who will be left behind. Those who shall be carried away will roam childless, widowed, and alone, over the burning plains of Guinea.

James Forten, Chairman, Philadelphia Convention, 1817,
Pease and Pease, eds., *The Antislavery Argument*

African Americans in Philadelphia published the above protest in January 1817, shortly after establishment of the American Colonization Society (ACS). The new organization proposed to send all blacks—slave and free—to Africa. The idea alarmed most free blacks, who feared for their own well-being and as noted above envisioned dire consequences for slave families. But the scheme appealed to many whites, including Henry Clay, John Marshall, Francis Scott Key, and numerous other prominent figures. To advance the movement even further, in August 1817 Robert G. Harper of Maryland penned a public letter which outlined the major arguments in favor of African colonization.

Harper ignored the familial issues raised by the Philadelphians and instead rebutted other objections to the ACS's program. Some free blacks would be reluctant to go to Africa, he admitted, but their hesitancy would dissipate as the advantages of emigration became manifest. Harper then parried a second complaint, predicting that slaveholders would embrace colonization. Burdened with a politically divisive, economically inefficient, and downright dangerous institution, slaveholders would gladly send their bondpeople to Africa, he predicted.

At this point Harper finally addressed the question of how slaves would be affected by colonization. "To the slaves, the advantages, though not so obvious or immediate, are yet certain and great," he declared, and those advantages included removing free blacks who corrupted slaves and thereby compelled masters to employ increasingly harsh punishments to maintain plantation discipline. Harper also contended that colonization would open up the prospect of manumission and would thus provide bondpeople with a "powerful incitement to good conduct."[1]

The notion that slaveholders dangled freedom in order to elicit "good conduct" bears upon a central debate in the historiography of manumission studies. Orlando Patterson, Ira Berlin, Robert Fogel, Stanley Engerman, and several other scholars have contended that manumission stabilized slavery, that the lure of freedom defused bondpeople's discontent.[2] This position has merit, but manumission also disrupted the slave system. Offering freedom might benefit an individual master, for his slaves would be dutiful and productive, but what did his neighbor think of the matter? Equally important, did bondpeople see manumission as stabilizing slavery? Historians have focused almost exclusively upon the emancipators, the views of local observers and slaves being largely ignored.

This oversight has been especially egregious in studies of the ACS. We know a lot about whites' attitudes toward colonization. Several monographs and innumerable articles have examined ACS advocates as well as their abolitionist and proslavery nemeses. Over the last thirty-five years, more scholars have investigated northern blacks' opinions on colonization. Recently, southern free blacks' perspectives have also been the subject of inquiry. But amid the din, slaves' voices are rarely heard.[3]

This essay surveys the factors that bondpeople contemplated when they considered going to Liberia. It suggests that familial considerations were very important to potential slave emigrants. Colonization officials often managed to accommodate slaves' desires to travel with their kin, but success in these matters was no easy feat, and the problem impeded ACS efforts in the South. Making emigration a familial endeavor had two additional consequences for the colonization movement. First, it aided the colonization movement by making ACS manumissions surprisingly conjunctive endeavors, and second, it blurred the distinction between proslavery and antislavery activities.

The ACS and Slavery

During the antebellum era the ACS was saddled with a curious, even contradictory, reputation. William Lloyd Garrison and other abolitionists portrayed the organization as a tool of southern slaveholders, an artifice primarily involved in the removal of free blacks and unruly slaves.[4] In the South, however, colonizationists faced the opposite charge. They were frequently deemed covert abolitionists, intent on destroying slavery and promoting racial equality. ACS leaders replied that they were moderates and that colonization was a compromise program which could unite the nation. They may have been correct, but in holding the middle ground colonizationists remained trapped in the crossfire over slavery.

So although colonization ideology embodied antislavery implications—an America without blacks implied an America without slavery—ACS officials were purposely vague on questions concerning the "peculiar institution." Robert G. Harper's public letter was actually one of the more forthright statements on the subject. In official publications such as the *African Repository* and the organization's *Annual Reports,* ACS officers tended to be more evasive on the slavery issue. Their editorials usually skirted the topic entirely by focusing on the removal of free blacks—a project most northern and southern whites could readily endorse. When ACS leaders did address slavery, they disavowed abolitionism and insisted that the property rights of slaveholders were inviolable.[5]

Still, the organization's antislavery potential was evident, and changes in manumission laws during the early antebellum period increased the likelihood that the ACS would be helping free bondpeople. Among the revisions that southern legislators enacted were requirements that newly emancipated blacks be removed from the state. Virginia first passed such a statute in 1806; South Carolina followed suit in 1820. One by one lawmakers across the South adopted this policy. Some states—such as Maryland, Tennessee, and Louisiana—specifically encouraged emancipators to send freedpeople to Africa. By 1850 only Delaware, Missouri, and Arkansas permitted former slaves to remain in their territories. Freedpeople had to be sent somewhere, and the ACS was ready to carry them to Liberia.[6]

When ACS officials helped effect emancipations, they wanted bondpeople to expressly choose going to Africa over remaining slaves in America. The organization's leaders believed that blacks were qualified to make that decision, for a central tenet of colonization ideology was that African Americans were capable of self-government. Once beyond the shadow of white racism, they argued, blacks' innate abilities would blossom. Colonizationists thus reasoned that slaves should determine for themselves whether they wanted to live in Africa. Accordingly ACS slaveholders gave their bondpeople the choice between freedom in Liberia and enslavement in America. The final decision on emigration, in other words, was the slaves' alone.

LEARNING ABOUT LIBERIA

When contemplating emigration a bondperson had several ways of learning about Liberia. ACS officials were a likely source of information. Occasionally, slaves themselves wrote the organization. One Missouri bondman asked the ACS for additional volumes of the *African Repository,* explaining, "I am a *poor slave* but . . . I Expects to goe to Liberia before long and would like to know all about It."[7] More commonly traveling ACS agents visited potential emigrants and spent many hours in conversation with them. These interactions produced bonds of respect and friendship—the parties often had kind words for each other. Yet as shall be seen, beneath the rosy veneer lay mutual mistrust.

Candid slaveholders also alerted their bondpeople to Liberia's attributes and shortcomings. As Ann R. Page of Virginia readied her slaves for emigration, for example, she told them to expect adversity in Africa. John Hartwell Cocke offered his bondpeople similar advice, as did John McDonogh of Louisiana. Mississippian Edward Brett Randolph likewise warned his slaves that sickness and poverty pervaded Liberia. Although abolitionists alleged that colonizationists cast unprofitable and unwary bondpeople to the wilds of Africa, few ACS slaveholders acted malevolently or improvidently. To the best of their ability, they prepared their bondpeople for freedom in Liberia. To the best of their knowledge they informed their slaves of the colony's imperfections. Most freedpeople suffered anyway, but their misfortunes cannot be ascribed to malicious intentions or cunning deceptions.[8]

Slaves listened to the reports of their owners and ACS officials with suspicion. As one white North Carolinian noted, "They seam [*sic*] to like the news very much yet they fear to emigrate[,] believing that Liberia is not the place that it is said to be." The correspondent continued, noting that "they can not believe that white folks is willing to do as much for them as to carry them to this great place of freedom and happiness."[9] William Starr, an ACS agent who discussed emigration with countless African Americans, encountered skeptical slaves on many occasions. For blacks, Starr lamented, "there is little trust to be placed in a white man."[10]

Robert G. Harper, had anticipated the colonizationists' credibility problem but foresaw a simple solution. "However distrustful of whites, they will confide in the reports made to them by the people of their own color and class," he wrote.[11] Harper had free blacks in mind when he authored that passage, but the point was equally valid for slaves. For bondpeople who were considering emigration, the most trustworthy information came from blacks who had a personal knowledge of Liberia.

As Harper expected, emigrants' testimonials benefited the ACS. The excitement engendered by Sion Harris, a freedman who returned to America to discuss Liberia with blacks, is a case in point. Harris aroused more interest in colonization, claimed Samuel Casseday of Kentucky, "than any ten white men could have done in double the time."[12] In many ways the ACS came to rely on emigrants' accounts of Liberia. When ACS agent R. W. Bailey was escorting one Virginia freedman to port, he wrote that the man's family and friends had been trying to dissuade him from emigrating. Such opposition would not last long, contended Bailey: "If he gives a good report of the country, others will follow from this section."[13] William Starr, the aforementioned ACS agent who bemoaned slaves' incredulity, even considered paying David Wiles, a Liberian colonist who was visiting Virginia, five dollars for every black that Wiles convinced to emigrate.[14] That the financially troubled ACS would contemplate such a scheme suggests how influential emigrants' statements were on the colonization movement.

Glowing accounts of Liberia could win over skeptical slaves, but critical correspondence could deter potential emigrants from moving to Liberia. William H. Ruffner of Virginia explained to ACS officials that the tribulations of one freedman, Samuel Harris, had "scared nearly all of my emigrants." Even Harris's wife was now refusing to leave. "I still believe that some will go this fall from here," predicted Ruffner, "but how many will depend principally on Harris['s] next letter."[15] William Kennedy's slaves were equally anxious about emigrating after they received distressing news from Liberia. Between 1852 and 1853 Kennedy sent fifty-five bondpeople to Africa, many of whom died. The survivors informed Kennedy's remaining slaves that they should stay in Tennessee until Liberia had more doctors and better houses. The bondpeople wavered with indecision. "Sometimes they determine to go & at other times they decline," wrote Kennedy. "I do not know what they will eventually do." Ultimately only one more of his slaves went to Liberia.[16]

Emigrants knew that their opinions were affecting slaves' decisions about going to Africa. Consequently, those who liked Liberia felt obliged to pen letters which disputed the disapprobatory accounts of other colonists. When Moses Jackson wrote disparagingly of Liberia, for example, Nelson Sanders retorted that Jackson's allegations were outright lies. Another emigrant, Seaborn Evans, had little patience for lackadaisical Liberians who deceived blacks back in America. "It is true Some people come to this country [and] . . . Say they cannot live here," Evans wrote to his former master, "but it is nobody but the lazy people who had the overseer to drive them in America, and the misfortune is that they have no overseer to drive them here." One of Robert E. Lee's former bondmen, William C. Burke, knew many blacks that had emigrated on the recommendation of colonists, only to be disappointed with their new home. Burke had witnessed this so many times that he refused to offer advice on the subject. Slaves may have been suspicious of whites' accounts of Liberia, but emigrants' contradictory descriptions did little to clarify the conditions in the colony.[17]

FACTORS IN SLAVES' DECISIONS CONCERNING EMIGRATION

When bondpeople contemplated moving to Africa, they could consult a variety of sources, including their owners, ACS officials, and previous colonists. After listening to these myriad reports, what issues figured most prominently in their decision? Many were concerned about mere survival in Liberia. Their apprehension was justified, for the "African fever" took the lives of thousands of emigrants.[18] Moreover, some slaves suspected that diseases weren't the only agents of death in Africa. In 1855 two bondpeople wrote the ACS that they had heard that "the negroes in Liberia was killing one another and Eating [the victims]." The epistlers themselves were undeterred, but when other members of their party learned of the terrible tales, it "fritened some of them almost to death."[19] Stories about sickness and cannibalism, along with rumors of ferocious animals and conflicts with the natives, could give pause to the most stalwart would-be emigrants.

Those who were unswayed by Liberia's dangers still faced the question of how they were going to support themselves in the colony. The ACS promised a parcel of land to new arrivals, but there were few dray animals to till the soil. Some engaged in *petit* trade, but commerce was dominated by wealthy free blacks who had emigrated in the 1820s. Simply securing a livelihood was difficult, which letters from Liberia made abundantly clear. After legal fees consumed the money that Capt. Isaac Ross had left his former bondpeople, for example, an embittered Peter Ross suggested that emigrants supply themselves with as many domestic, mechanical, and agricultural tools as possible. "They will need them," Ross wrote from Liberia, "for they cannot be got here." Another freedman, Charles Jefferson, explained the consequences of emigrating without provisions. "We were sent away poor & necked," Jefferson wrote to James Haynes, "and today we remain poor."[20] Following the colonists' advice proved difficult. Although some freedpeople accumulated property while slaves and others inherited money from deceased owners, most emigrated with few possessions and suffered accordingly.

Some bondpeople seemed unconcerned with the material hardship that awaited them in Liberia and instead saw emigration as a missionary endeavor. Washington Watts McDonogh, for example, went to Africa in 1842 with hopes of Christianizing the native population. Unlike other members of his party who settled in the coastal town of Monrovia, McDonogh trekked one hundred miles inland to Settra Kroo. There McDonogh began his work among "ignorant" and "superstitious" Africans. Five years later his religious fervor had not diminished. "I am still among the heathens," McDonogh wrote his former owner, "trying to teach them the ways of God." Another freedman, James P. Skipwith, was less enthusiastic about proselytizing but urged his fellow colonists to maintain their spirituality. "We have to carry our tools all day," he exhorted, "& and our Bibles at Night." Like Skipwith, most emigrants sailed to Liberia with few provisions but plenty of faith.[21]

Slaves thus mulled over a variety of issues when debating whether they would go to Liberia. They weighed their desire for freedom against their chances for survival and advancement in the impoverished colony. The evangelical among them also considered the prospects of successful missionary work. All of these issues played a role in slaves' decisions. But perhaps their greatest concern was whether they would emigrate with their families.

EMIGRATION AS A FAMILIAL ENDEAVOR

When Francis Gideon of Fulton County, Georgia, died in 1855 his will gave his bondpeople the option of remaining slaves in America or emigrating to Africa. Few of his slaves expressed clear preferences on the matter. Three bondwomen—Sucky, Martha, and America—absolutely refused to go to Liberia. But Charles preferred to emigrate. The others offered ambiguous responses, explaining that their final decision would depend on the others' answers. Washington announced that he would "stay or go with the old ones." Sarah would likewise "either stay or go as the rest do." Dennis concluded, "If the rest stay, I will stay; if they go, I will go."[22] As these statements suggest, familial considerations were arguably the preeminent factor in slaves' decisions concerning emigration. If bondpeople were going to journey to Liberia, they wanted to sail with their kin.

ACS officials in Washington, D.C., came to realize that Liberian emigration would be a familial endeavor. This awareness is evidenced by the terminology they employed in a file titled "Applicants for Emigration to Liberia." In this lengthy document there are hundreds of familial references: "a family of 16, freed by will," "a family of 5 servants," "5 slaves freed, a family," "a coloured family left free," "man, wife, and 7 children (slaves)," "a family of 6 slaves," and so on.[23] Even at this preliminary stage, when ACS officers were merely identifying prospective colonists, the role that families would play in Liberian emigration was apparent.

Those slaves who eventually went to Africa often did so with several family members. ACS ship registers testify to this custom. The ship registers sometimes specified the relationships among the passengers. In such cases spousal and parental connections are usually noted; more distant kin are occasionally recorded as well. When the exact nature of the relationship is not indicated, the grouping of the passengers connotes consanguinity. Emigrants with shared surnames are almost invariably listed together, with middle-aged passengers coming first (often one male and one female), followed by children in descending order of age. A more detailed analysis of the ship registers will further elucidate the familial relations among ACS emigrants, but even a cursory review suggests that freedpeople traveled with their kin.[24]

Demographic evidence corroborates this conclusion. Consider the manumitted emigrants' sex ratio. Men outnumbered women, but not by much (48 percent to 42 percent, with 10 percent unknown).[25] There are several possible explanations for the small imbalance. First, some slaveholders may have emancipated more males than females, believing the former to be better suited to the rugged demands of a settler society. Second, it is possible that women were more likely to decline offers of freedom in Liberia, since females could not easily resign their child-rearing responsibilities. A third explanation rests on the fact that there were usually more bondmen than bondwomen on large plantations, and preliminary research indicates that ACS masters were often large slavehold-ers.[26] Whatever the reason for the slight preponderance of males, the fairly even sex ratio provides further evidence that emigration was a familial enterprise.

Another demographic characteristic—age distribution—also affirms this view. Nearly one-third of the manumitted emigrants were under the age of ten. ACS slaveholders were not so malicious as to exile young slaves to Africa, and colonization officials were not so foolish as to transport helpless children to their problem-plagued colony. Liberia, in other words, was not an orphanage for castoff slave youth. Rather, these children went to Africa with their parents or older kin, who were presumably among the 29 percent of freedpeople between the ages of twenty and thirty-nine. Historian Tom W. Shick arrived at the same conclusion nearly forty years ago: "The even sex ratio and the age distribution," Shick wrote in 1971, "indicates a pattern of family emigration."[27]

Shick also argued that familial bonds influenced the political and commercial development of Liberia. "The rapid rise of an elite in Monrovia, especially in economic affairs," Shick explained in *Behold the Promised Land,* "was partially due to the vitality of family relations." Other scholars noted the same phenomena. In fact, nepotism prevailed into the twentieth century. "To understand Liberian politics," George Dalton contended in 1961, "knowledge of kinship connections among high government officials is more useful than knowledge of the Liberian constitution." While a detailed analysis of the economic and political history of Liberia is beyond the purview of this essay, the existing literature on the subject clearly demonstrates that familial relations shaped the settlement and growth of Liberia.[28]

The extent of familial cohesion should not be overstated. Moving to Africa required separation from relatives, and the exact relationship between emigrants is not precisely understood. Nevertheless, freedpeople who made the transatlantic voyage were generally not bereft of kin. Ship registers and ACS officials' writings both indicate that emigrants traveled in family units. Demographic statistics provide further evidence on this matter, as do the patterns of economic and political development in Liberia. Emigration to Liberia was a familial enterprise. And making it so had several important ramifications for the colonization movement.

FAMILIAL EMIGRATION IMPEDES THE COLONIZATION MOVEMENT

Accommodating slaves' wishes to journey with their kin became a recurrent problem for colonizationists. A master may have wanted to liberate a bondman, but the bondman's wife or children might have been free blacks who refused to emigrate. Or they could have belonged to a slaveholder who was disinclined to grant them freedom. Such situations were not uncommon. Bondpeople's desire to go to Africa with their family thus impeded the colonization movement.

ACS leaders in Washington, D.C., received countless letters which chronicled how slaves' familial affinities impaired efforts to transport bondpeople to Liberia. In 1847, for example, R. A. Winnell of Virginia wrote that his father had manumitted a servant, "one of the most correct men I have ever known." "The only difficulty in his way of remaining in Liberia," Winnell warned, "is that of being separated from his wife and children, who are in the service of others." The Rev. J. Packard found himself in an analogous situation the following year. The minister intended to send his cook to Liberia, assuming that "the whole matter was settled." But the cook's husband, who was owned by another individual and who had also planned on emigrating, began to have doubts. As Packard remarked flatly, "Of course, this has changed the aspect of things as to my cook." Even if the couple decided to go to Liberia, Packard lamented, their current indecision would prevent them from sailing anytime soon.[29]

Sometimes colonizationists learned of slaves' demurrals at the moment of embarkation. "After staining every nerve, up to the last hour, [and] making all necessary arrangements," Rev. G. W. Leyburn wrote to William McLain, "the wife of the free man who was to go today refuses to go [and] everything falls apart." Leyburn claimed he had anticipated this contingency and received assurances that the man would emigrate. "But it seems she proved to be the "*better half.*"[30] Several years later, a much wiser and more experienced Leyburn calmly reported that he was unsure whether all of Sally Price's bondpeople would emigrate, noting that several were related to people who remained in bondage.[31] Yet whether Leyburn (or any another ACS supporter) responded with anger or equanimity, the basic problem remained unresolved. Simply put, slaves' familial demands vitiated the colonization movement from start to finish.

In addition to letters other sources show the ways in which familial considerations hindered the ACS. In the document titled "Applications for Emigration to Liberia," for example, one entry notes that a Georgia woman and her six children were scheduled to emigrate in December 1852. One month before the embarkation, the woman "got married & [now] will not go." A similar scenario unfolded in Alabama two years later. A black family was ready to sail on April 1, 1854. The date of departure was later crossed out, and in its place was written, "Probably never—woman will not go."[32] For ACS officials, such disappointments seemed never-ending.

Already beleaguered by the logistical and financial problems, as well as by the constant vituperation of abolitionists and proslavery ideologues, colonizationists occasionally voiced their frustration over slaves' intractability. "Alas! What a changeable set the blacks are!" wrote Alexander M. Cowan after several bondpeople reneged on their promises to emigrate. In like fashion, ACS agent William Starr lashed out, "I am convinced there is no relying on the word of a darkie at all."[33] Coordinating expeditions thus vexed the society's agents. Fulfilling slaves' familial wishes, in particular, proved especially troublesome. Yet the agents often overcame these obstacles and made Liberian emigration a familial undertaking. One of the keys to their success was their ability to promote cooperation between slaveholders.

FAMILIAL EMIGRATION AIDS THE COLONIZATION MOVEMENT BY ENCOURAGING CONJUNCTIVE MANUMISSIONS

Manumission is a private act with social consequences. If slavery constitutes "social death," as Orlando Patterson suggests, emancipation entails granting "social life." A social nonentity joins the community, thereby changing that community and raising questions about the status and rights of the newly freed. ACS advocates hoped to circumvent these issues by sending freedpeople to Liberia. Blacks would be liberated, but they would not become members of society. As it turned out, colonization did little to mitigate the social impact of manumission. In fact, the ACS's program may have exacerbated the problem, for transporting freedpeople to Africa often required communal collaboration.

Manumission has traditionally been seen as an exceptional act performed by an intrepid individual. Most historians have contended that slaveholders emancipated a special bondperson whose diligence and loyalty—or paternity—entitled him or her to freedom. But southern whites were so defensive about slavery, the orthodox interpretation follows, that even these seemingly innocuous liberations occasioned ostracism. As Ira Berlin argued in *Slaves Without Masters,* slaveholders who freed their bondpeople incurred "the cold stare and angry words of their neighbors, as well as the lasting enmity of their heirs."[34] In short, southerners who trod the road of manumission walked in solitude.

Traditional accounts tend to overlook how African American families influenced manumission. Herbert Gutman, O. Vernon Burton, and other scholars have demonstrated that bondpeople's familial affinities transcended plantation confines, state lines, and even regional boundaries.[35] These family bonds turned ACS manumissions into conjunctive affairs. Slaveholders did not always trek the road of manumission alone; many were joined by others of like minds and on occasion travelers with dissimilar views as well.

The issue can be studied statistically by calculating how often two or more ACS slaveholders freed bondpeople at the same time and from the same county.[36] I call such events "conjunctive emancipations." Conjunctive emancipations do not reveal every nuance involved in sending black families to Africa. Sometimes neighboring slaveholders manumitted bondpeople simultaneously simply because it was convenient to do so. Conversely, there were occasions when slaveholders in distant counties worked together, each liberating different members of a black family. Conjunctive emancipation statistics fail to account for these scenarios and thus should be seen only as a rough measure of cooperation among ACS slaveholders.

Even with these shortcomings in mind, the frequency of conjunctive emancipations suggests that traditional notions about solitary liberators are not entirely accurate. On seventy-nine separate occasions, multiple slaveholders freed bondpeople at the same time and from the same county. In one remarkable instance a dozen individuals from Somerset County, Maryland, sent slaves to Liberia. All totaled, 41 percent of ACS slaveholders were involved in conjunctive emancipations. Southerners who manumitted bondpeople may have endured "the cold stare and angry words of their neighbors," as Berlin contended. But for a sizable minority of them a fellow emancipator was nearby to offer words of consolation and encouragement.

Slaves' desire to emigrate with their kin provided the impetus for conjunctive emancipations. For example, when William Foote of Alexandria County, Virginia, died, he willed that two of his slaves, Aaron and Robert Carroll, be sent to Liberia. Richard C. Mason liberated Robert Carroll's wife and three children, his only regret being that he could not afford to pay their passage to Liberia. Similarly, after Martha Gibbs of Jefferson County, Virginia, liberated two female slaves, Rebecca Hunter obliged the bondwomen by freeing another family member, Richard Hinch. In the same manner the testamentary emancipation of James H. Terrell's sixty-eight slaves touched off a small flurry of manumissions and slave "purchases." Four county residents freed slaves who were related to the Terrell party, and three other slaveholders sold bondpeople to Terrell's executors so that they could emigrate with their family. Colonizationists were not always successful in securing the liberty of freedpeople's kin, but conjunctive emancipations did occur with remarkable frequency.[37]

Even slaveholders who disavowed colonization at times accommodated the ACS. In 1854 the heirs of Robert Stuart freed Edmund Brown, who set about trying to liberate various family members so that they could accompany him to Africa. Capt. Hugh Adams manumitted Brown's wife and three of his children. Brown himself managed to purchase four more kin. But Brown's activities became the subject of controversy. Local bondpeople began to inquire whether they too could have these opportunities. Not surprisingly, some slaveholders believed Brown's conduct was setting a dangerous precedent. Among those who felt this way was a Mr. Stuart, who refused to sell Brown's son, Moses. After a little cajolery, Stuart agreed to sell Moses for eight hundred dollars. The matter was far from settled, though. Moses had a wife, whose owner demanded five hundred dollars. Even for an industrious and enterprising man like Brown, procuring these sums would have been impossible without aid from the ACS. A local minister begged colonization officials for help. "I do hope that Moses and Martha will not be left," wrote Rev. James Paine; "if so, I fear their fate is forever sealed." Although Stuart had agreed to sell Moses, the monies, in the end, could not be raised. On November 6. 1854, Brown left for Liberia without his son and daughter-in-law.[38]

A comparable affair occurred in Georgia later that year. The Hon. C. Hines emancipated a large family that was to be sent to Liberia. But the patriarch of the clan, Harry Bacon, was owned by another man, Thomas Mallard. Bacon was purportedly worth fifteen hundred dollars, but Mallard asked one thousand dollars for the bondman. ACS officials still thought Mallard a bit avaricious, but the slaveholder protested that he was being as charitable as his circumstances would permit. "I have a large family to provide for," he explained, "and it would not be doing justice to them to give Harry [Bacon] away because he wants his freedom." Mallard nevertheless agreed to drop the price for Bacon another one hundred dollars. With the help of special donations, colonization officials managed to purchase the bondman, who sailed with his family for Liberia in January 1855. One senses that ACS leaders had been through this sort of thing before. Shortly after buying Bacon, William McLain expressed relief that Mallard was unaware that the funds were being raised by emergency contributions. If Mallard had known, McLain speculated, "he would have stuck us for another hundred dollars."[39]

That the ACS would have difficulties obtaining the freedom of slaves like Moses Stuart and Harry Bacon is not surprising. What is instructive about these stories is that slaveholders like Stuart and Mallard, who clearly disfavored colonization, accommodated ACS efforts to secure the liberty of certain bondpeople. Slaves' familial demands thus had a paradoxical effect on the colonization movement: As noted above, they impeded the ACS. But they also aided the organization by drawing in slaveholders who were otherwise indifferent— or even hostile—toward colonization. Such slaveholders probably had little doubt that colonizationists hoped to end slavery, but other southerners may have been less sure, for ACS activities could not always be pigeonholed as either "antislavery" or "proslavery" endeavors.

FAMILIAL EMIGRATION OBFUSCATES ANTISLAVERY
AND PROSLAVERY ACTIVITIES

As previously noted, some antebellum observers asserted that the ACS was a proslavery façade while others insisted that it was an abolitionist cabal. Modern historians have generally adopted this polarized framework. Early Fox, Frederic Bancroft, Phillip Staudenraus, and many other scholars have contended that the ACS was a conservative antislavery organization. Amos Beyan and a few others still argue that colonizationists reflected slaveholders' interests. After 180 years of debate, the ACS's relationship with slavery is still a matter of dispute.[40]

Which view is more accurate? Aggregate emigration statistics do not provide a clear answer. On one hand, free blacks—and especially southern free blacks— were overrepresented in the emigrant population. During the antebellum period approximately 12.5 percent of the African American population was free. Yet nearly 40 percent of the antebellum Liberian colonists were free blacks, and the large majority (75 percent) of these individuals were from southern states. On the other hand, colonizationists labored for the emancipation of slaves and eventually secured the freedom of nearly six thousand bondpeople. Was colonization an antislavery enterprise? The society's mixed record precludes a definitive answer.

Firm conclusions are difficult to draw because the frame of reference—"proslavery" versus "antislavery"—is conceptually flawed. A closer look at the emigration data suggests that colonization activities defy dichotomization. The reason, once again, stems from the familial nature of ACS emigration. Some members of a black family could be free while others were enslaved. When they emigrated together it muddled the ACS's relationship with the "peculiar institution."

It was not uncommon for free blacks and manumitted emigrants to move to Liberia together. Approximately 25 percent of the time, when a group of emigrants left a county, the party consisted of some combination of free blacks, former slaves, or "purchased" emigrants.[41] In such cases the company's members were often related by blood or marriage. The heterogeneity of emigrant parties made it difficult to discern whether the ACS was strengthening slavery (by removing free blacks) or eroding the institution (by liberating bondpeople).

The distinction would have been lost on ACS agent Thomas C. Benning, who reviewed hundreds of application for transport to Liberia. Benning always accepted slave emigrants, regardless of whether their owner could pay for their passage and support. Yet he knew that free blacks might want to join the company. Benning was reluctant to take on older, poorer individuals. "But when they are connected with a family," he admitted, "I do not feel at liberty to decline taking them."[42] In this fashion slave manumissions encouraged free black emigration.

The process worked in the opposite manner, too, with slaveholders liberating bondpeople so that they could depart with their free black kin. John L. Andrews of Riceboro, Georgia, freed Ephriam Andrews, a thirty-year-old wheelwright, who then journeyed to Liberia with his free wife and children. Another Georgian, R. B. Haveland of Augusta, manumitted Jack Harris, a twenty-five-year-old druggist, who emigrated with his wife and her family, all of whom were free. James H. Carney of Norfolk, Virginia, likewise emancipated Mingo Carney, so that the latter could emigrate with his free wife and seven children. Similarly, a Mrs. Hunter of Portsmouth, Virginia, manumitted Lydia Amboy, who sailed to Liberia with her free husband and two sons. In the process of gathering emigrants, colonizationists frequently traversed the boundary that separated the bonded from the free.[43]

Proslavery apostles were rightly concerned about the ACS's plans for slavery. Colonization ideology certainly portended the demise of black bondage, and the ACS actively countenanced slave manumissions. Yet the threat was muted by the simultaneous departure of free blacks. Was the ACS helping or hurting slavery? It was difficult to say, for heterogeneous emigrant parties did not fit conventional "antislavery" and "proslavery" categories.

ACS leaders originally failed to consider how slaves' opinions might affect the colonization program. Once the organization began transporting blacks to Africa, though, its officials learned that familial considerations were central to slaves' decisions regarding emigration. This concern, we have seen, affected the ACS in several important ways. Slaves' familial demands impaired the society's efforts to send blacks to Africa; they also aided the organization by prompting conjunctive manumissions and obfuscated "proslavery" and "antislavery" activities, for related free blacks and manumitted emigrants sailed to Liberia together.

NOTES

1. William H. Pease and Jane H. Pease, *The Antislavery Argument* (New York: Bobbs-Merrill, 1965), 28, 29.

2. Ira Berlin, *Slaves Without Masters: The Free Negro in the Antebellum South* (New York: New Press, 1974), 149; Robert William Fogel and Stanley L. Engerman, *Time on the Cross: The Economics of American Negro Slavery* (New York: Norton, 1974), 150–151.

3. Recent books on the African colonization movement include Marie Tyler-McGraw, *An African Republic: Black and White Virginians in the Making of Liberia* (Chapel Hill: University of North Carolina Press, 2007); Eric Burin, *Slavery and the Peculiar Solution: A History of the American Colonization Society* (Gainesville: University Press of Florida, 2005); Emma J. Lapansky-Werner and Margaret Hope Bacon, *Back to Africa: Benjamin Coates and the Colonization Movement in America, 1848–1880* (University Park: Pennsylvania State University Press, 2005); Claude A. Clegg III, *The Price of Liberty: African Americans and the Making of Liberia* (Chapel Hill: University of North Carolina Press, 2004); Kenneth C. Barnes, *Journey of Hope: The Back-to-Africa Movement in Arkansas in the Late 1800s* (Chapel Hill: University of North Carolina Press, 2004), and Richard L. Hall, *On Afric's Shore: A History of Maryland in Liberia, 1834–1857* (Baltimore: Maryland Historical Society, 2003). See also Philip J. Staudenraus, *The African Colonization Movement, 1816–1865* (New York: Columbia University Press, 1961). The abolitionist critique of colonization is thoughtfully reviewed in George M. Fredrickson, *The Black Image in the White Mind: The Debate on Afro-American Character and Destiny, 1817–1914* (New York: Harper & Row, 1971), 1–42. For proslavery opinions, see Douglas R. Egerton, "Averting a Crisis: The Proslavery Critique of the American Colonization Society," *Civil War History* 43, no. 2 (June 1997): 142–156. Southern free blacks' attitudes are discussed in Marie Tyler McGraw, "Richmond Free Blacks and African Colonization, 1816–1832," *Journal of American Studies* 21, no. 2 (Aug. 1987): 207–224. Slaves' views are addressed in two collections of letters, namely, Bell I. Wiley, ed., *Slaves No More: Letters from Liberia, 1833–1869* (Lexington: University of Kentucky Press, 1980), and Randall M. Miller, ed., *"Dear Master": Letters of a Slave Family* (Ithaca, N.Y.: Cornell University Press,

1978). See also Randall M. Miller, "Home as Found: Ex-Slaves and Liberia," *Liberian Studies Journal* 6, no. 2 (1975): 92–108.

4. William L. Garrison, *Thoughts on Colonization* (1832; reprint, New York: Arno Press, 1968), 13.

5. See, for example, American Colonization Society (ACS), *The Annual Reports of the American Society for the Colonizing the Free People of Colour of the United States* (1819; reprint, New York: Negro Universities Press, 1969), 2:7–9.

6. Berlin, *Slaves Without Masters*, 138–139.

7. Titus Shropshere to William McLain, May 21, 1848, Reel 55, Records of the American Colonization Society, Library of Congress, Washington, D.C. (hereafter cited as RecsACS).

8. C. W. Andrews, ed., *Memoir of Ann R. Page* (1856; reprint, New York: Garland, 1987), 53, 58; Miller, *"Dear Master,"* 35; John T. Edwards, ed., *Some Interesting Papers of John McDonogh* (McDonogh, Md.: Boys of McDonogh School, 1898), 49–50; *Niles' Weekly Register* 49, no. 1 (November 21, 1835): 195.

9. Edward Mayo to William McLain, April 20, 1855, Reel 76, RecsACS.

10. William Starr to William McLain, April 30, 1855, Reel 76, RecsACS.

11. Pease and Pease, *Antislavery Argument*, 31.

12. Samuel Casseday to William McLain, December 5, 1848, Reel 57, RecsACS.

13. R. W. Bailey to William McLain, September 23, 1848, Reel 56, RecsACS.

14. William Starr to William McLain, June 2, 1855, Reel 76, RecsACS.

15. William H. Ruffner to "My Dear Sir," May 20, 1848, Reel 56, RecsACS. See also William H. Ruffner to "Dear Sir," September 16, 1848, Reel 56, RecsACS.

16. William E. Kennedy to William McLain, November 8, 1854, RecsACS, Reel 74; William E. Kennedy to William McLain, March 29, 1855, Reel 75, RecsACS.

17. Moses Jackson to Elliot West, March 22, 1846, in Wiley, *Slaves No More*, 257; Nelson Sanders to Susan Fishback, January 5, 1848, in Wiley, *Slaves No More*, 258; Seaborn Evans to Josiah Sibley, November 5, 1856, in Wiley, *Slaves No More*, 270; William C. Burke to William McLain, July 31, 1858, in Wiley, *Slaves No More*, 205.

18. Antonio McDaniel, *Swing Low, Sweet Chariot: The Mortality Cost of Colonizing Liberia in the Nineteenth Century* (Chicago: University of Chicago Press, 1995), 104.

19. Eve and Samuel Gideon to "Dear Sir," March 30, 1855, Reel 75, RecsACS.

20. Peter Ross to Robert Carter and John Ker, March 23, 1848, in Wiley, *Slaves No More*, 158; Charles Jefferson to James Haynes, March 2, 1858, in Wiley, *Slaves No More*, 278.

21. Washington Watts McDonogh to John McDonogh, December 28, 1845, in Wiley, *Slaves No More*, 138, and Washington Watts McDonogh to John McDonogh, November 13, 1847, in Wiley, *Slaves No More*, 147; James P. Skipwith to Berthier Edwards, May 31, 1860, in Wiley, *Slaves No More*, 95.

22. Francis H. Core to "Dear Sir," January 13, 1855, Reel 74, RecsACS.

23. "Applications for Emigration to Liberia," Reel 314, RecsACS.

24. For a discussion of similar lists found in the federal census returns, see Orville Vernon Burton, *In My Father's House Are Many Mansions: Family and Community in Edgefield, South Carolina* (Chapel Hill: University of North Carolina Press, 1985), 168.

25. Emigration figures are drawn from my database of all the African Americans who went to Liberia between 1820 and 1860. This database was compiled primarily from three sources: first, U.S. Congress, *Roll of Emigrants that have been sent to the colony of Liberia, Western Africa, by the American Colonization Society and its Auxiliaries, to September, 1843, & c.*, 28th Cong.,

2nd sess., S. Doc. 150; second, ship registers printed in the *African Repository*; and third, handwritten passengers lists in Reel 314, RecsACS.

26. Brenda E. Stevenson, *Life in Black & White: Family and Community in the Slave South* (New York: Oxford University Press, 1996), 181; Herbert Gutman, *The Black Family in Slavery and Freedom, 1750–1925* (New York: Vintage Books, 1976), 38, 43.

27. Tom W. Shick, "A Quantitative Analysis of Liberian Colonization from 1820 to 1843 with Special Reference to Mortality," *Journal of African History* 12, no. 1 (1971): 47.

28. Thomas Shick, *Behold the Promised Land: A History of Afro-American Settler Society in Nineteenth Century Liberia* (Baltimore: Johns Hopkins University Press, 1980), 44–45; George Dalton, "History, Politics, and Economic Development in Liberia," *Journal of Economic History* 25, no. 4 (December 1965): 589.

29. R. A. Winnell to "The American Colonization Society," December 15, 1847, Reel 54, RecsACS; J. Packard to William McLain, August 11, 1848, Reel 56, RecsACS.

30. G. W. Leyburn to William McLain, August 29, 1848, Reel 56, RecsACS.

31. Rev. G. W. Leyburn to "My Dear Sir," February 9, 1855, Reel 75, RecsACS.

32. "Applications for Emigration to Liberia," Reel 314, RecsACS.

33. Alexander M Cowan to William McLain, September 23, 1848, Reel 56, RecsACS; William H. Starr to William McLain, April 30, 1855, Reel 76, RecsACS.

34. Ira Berlin, *Slaves Without Masters*, 141. See also Carl Degler, *The Other South: Southern Dissenters in the Nineteenth Century* (New York: Harper & Row, 1974); Merton L. Dillon, *Slavery Attacked: Southern Slaves and Their Allies, 1619–1865* (Baton Rouge: Louisiana State University Press, 1990), 177–179; Stanley Harrold, *The Abolitionists and the South, 1831–1860* (Lexington: University Press of Kentucky, 1995).

35. In addition to Gutman, Burton, and Brenda E. Stevenson, all cited above, see also Ann Patton Malone, *Sweet Chariot: Slave Family and Household Structure in Nineteenth Century Louisiana* (Chapel Hill: University of North Carolina Press, 1992); John Blassingame, *The Slave Community: Plantation Life in the Old South* (1972; rev. ed., New York: Oxford University Press, 1979); and Deborah Gray White, *Ar'n't I a Woman? Female Slaves in the Plantation South* (New York: Norton, 1985).

36. By "at the same time" I refer to slaveholders whose bondpeople sailed to Liberia on the same ship.

37. Dr. R. C. Mason to Rev. William H. Starr, October 9, 1854, Reel 74, RecsACS; William H. Starr to William McLain, October 10, 1854, Reel 74, RecsACS; Rebecca Hunter to William McLain, April 24, 1855, Reel 76, RecsACS; *African Repository* (January 1857): 21–23.

38. Rev. James Paine to J. W. Lugenbeel, October 14 and 16, 1854, both in Reel 74, RecsACS; *African Repository* (December 1854): 379.

39. C. Hines, C. C. Jones, and Edward Harden to Unknown, November 20, 1854, Reel 74, RecsACS; C. C. Jones to William McLain, December 28, 1854, Reel 74, RecsACS; Thomas Mallard to Mr. C. Hines, December 28, 1854, Reel 74, RecsACS; William McLain to J. W. Lugenbeel, December 30, 1854, Reel 74, RecsACS.

40. Early Lee Fox, *The American Colonization Society* (Baltimore: Johns Hopkins University Press, 1919), 49, 181; Frederic Bancroft, "The Colonization of American Negroes, 1801–1865," in *Frederic Bancroft: Historian*, ed. Jacob E. Cooke (Norman: University of Oklahoma Press, 1957), 147–258; Staudenraus, *African Colonization Movement*, vii–viii; Amos Beyan, *The American Colonization Society and the Creation of the Liberian State* (Lanham, Md.: University Press of America, 1991).

41. "'Purchased' slaves" refers to bondpeople whose freedom was bought, either by themselves or by someone else.

42. Thomas Benning to "Rev & Dear Sir," June 10, 1848, Reel 55, RecsACS.

43. John L. Andrews to "Dear Sir," November 7, 1854, Reel 74, RecsACS; "List of Emigrants by the Barque *Baltimore*," Reel 314, RecsACS; "Emigrants by the *Linda Stewart*," Reel 314, RecsACS; "Emigrants by the *Liberia Packet*" (tenth voyage), Reel 314, RecsACS.

Eva Sheppard Wolf

Manumission and the Two-Race System in Early National Virginia

—⚹—

Students of slavery know that in most slave societies freeing individual slaves served to support the institution of slavery. Apparently the negation of slavery, manumission was in fact an intrinsic part of the system, in part because it defined a slave owner's power—the power to free as well as the power to hold a slave—and in part because manumission, as a reward for good behavior, provided slaves a legitimate, peaceful, path to freedom that could serve as an incentive to slaves to behave well and not to resist their enslavement. In these societies freed slaves could be integrated into a free population that was not necessarily racially distinct from the slave population, though the process of integration might take generations.[1] As Thomas Jefferson observed, "Among the Romans emancipation required but one effort. The slave, when made free, might mix with, without staining the blood of his master."

Slave societies in which slavery coincided with a binary racial system of white versus black, such as colonial British North America, were generally hostile to manumission, however, since freeing even a few black slaves would threaten the racial system that undergirded and justified not only slavery but the entire social order. To Jefferson, writing shortly after Independence, manumission in Virginia would require a "second" and "necessary" step beyond the granting of freedom: The slave "is to be removed beyond the reach of mixture," so that the races might remain distinct and pure.[2]

Virginians after the American Revolution behaved in ways that began to disrupt the Anglo-American pattern, and in the process to challenge the racial basis of freedom in the United States. Between 1782, when an act of the legislature made it possible for owners to free their slaves without the special approval that had been necessary previously, and 1806, when the legislature amended the law to require newly freed slaves to leave Virginia, white and black Virginians freed about ten thousand slaves. The 1782 law was partly a response to Quaker petitions requesting permission to free slaves, and partly a product of the legislature's own movement, probably influenced by Revolutionary ideology, to loosen the restrictions on manumission.[3] Acts of manumission between 1782 and 1806 added to the small number of free blacks who lived in Virginia before the Revolution, creating a newly vibrant free black population that, while only a small percentage of the total population in Virginia by 1800, was concentrated in urban areas where their numbers seemed, to white observers, significant. The growth of the free black population together with the acts of manumission themselves challenged the congruence between race and slavery that had been essential to an American racial and political ideology in which all whites were understood to share equally in freedom in part *because* all blacks were slaves.[4] New patterns of behavior offered a vision of a more racially flexible social order and of a more complex and varied slave system than had existed in the colonial period. But such a vision proved terrifying to most white Virginians.

Ultimately it was this—white Virginians' fears that disrupting the binary race-slavery system (black/white equals slave/free) that had been created in the colonial period would promote social instability, or worse, lead to race war— that put an end to Virginia's experiment with manumission. The 1806 law, which caused a precipitous drop in the annual number of slaves freed, came as a response to fears of social unrest and mass slave insurrections, which ran particularly high after the 1800 discovery of a conspiracy by a Richmond-area slave, Gabriel, to seize the state capital and end slavery in Virginia.[5] In Virginia, then, cultural and racial factors more than economic ones dictated the laws regarding manumission.

OVERVIEW OF MANUMISSION IN VIRGINIA

In the period during which manumission in Virginia was legally feasible, there were two main patterns of manumission. Until the mid-1790s manumission in Virginia was primarily a response to the religious and secular arguments against slavery that had been part of the Revolution's Enlightenment ideology. John Teackle of Accomack County, for example, declared in his 1787 deed of manumission to twenty-two slaves that he was "deeply impressed with the fullest Sensibility of the Equal Rights of Human Nature to the Enjoyment of Personal Liberty."[6] Manumission as a protest against slavery was highly unusual for slave societies, and in America seems to have occurred almost exclusively in the upper South in the first decade after the American Revolution.

The second pattern, which dominated after the mid-1790s, aligned more closely with patterns of manumission in other slave societies. In this period most manumittors freed their slaves for other, individual, and even idiosyncratic reasons. Anna Maria Andrews freed Major in 1800 "in consequence of a Suit in the District Court . . . instituted by major for his freedom against me," while in 1802 William Ball freed his slave Luke, "the late Stage Driver," for his "many faithful services."[7] Slave owners in this second period also utilized manumission as an incentive, a reward to faithful slaves that might motivate others to work faithfully. In addition, the role blacks played in manumission increased over time; a significant proportion of the manumissions that took place after the mid-1790s were cases in which slaves purchased their freedom or free black Virginians manumitted family members. By the turn of the century manumission had become less a reflection of Revolutionary-era antislavery thought than a regular, if infrequent, aspect of Virginia slavery, reflecting both its complexity and its potential for change.

A detailed look at the practice of manumission between 1782 and 1806—who freed whom, when, and why—illuminates this complexity, demonstrates the changing meaning of manumission over time, and points to the unrealized potential of manumission to alter both race and slavery] in Virginia. This study is based on 359 emancipating documents (260 deeds and 99 wills) filed in eight Virginia counties that stretched from the Tidewater region, where slavery had grown up in the colonial era, to the western frontier beyond the Allegheny mountains.[8] Together, the proportion of slaves in the eight counties approximated the proportion in Virginia as a whole, about 40 percent, while the variations among the counties reflected the diversity of Virginia's communities. One county, Chesterfield, included the urban center of Manchester (now part of Richmond), but most of the counties, like most of Virginia, comprised rural communities whose economies were primarily agricultural. The total population of the counties composed about one-ninth of the Virginia population in 1800, and the citizens of those counties freed about twelve hundred slaves, as recorded in the county deed and will books (see table 1). There is good reason to believe that the number of acts of manumission found in the deed and will books is nearly complete, since freed slaves needed legal documentation in order to prove their status. An act of manumission that did *not* find its way into the historical record hardly would have counted as manumission at all, since it would have left the freedperson vulnerable to reenslavement. In addition, the free black registers compare well to the manumission records; for almost all the free blacks who claimed to have been emancipated, either a deed or will of emancipation could be found in the county records.

While 10,000 slaves freed between 1782 and 1806 sounds like a lot, only a small portion of the Virginia slave population, which stood at and nearly 350,000 by 1800, ever saw freedom. And while many of Virginia's white citizens fretted over the growth of the free black population, free blacks never formed more than 3 percent of the state's population, though in some cities they made up more than 10 percent of the population. Moreover, the annual proportion of slaves freed in Virginia, about one-tenth of 1 percent, put Virginia's manumission rate among the lowest of all slave societies.[9]

TABLE 1. Slave and free black population of the eight counties in 1800
compared to the total population of Virginia

County	Slaves, 1800	Free blacks, 1800	Total county pop., 1800	% of slaves	% of free blacks	Num. of slaves freed 1782–1806[a]
Accomack	4,429	1,541	15,693	28.2	9.8	809
Botetourt	1,343	116	9,825	13.7	1.2	31
Charles City	3,013	398	5,365	56.2	7.4	90
Chesterfield	7,852	319	14,488	54.2	2.2	149
Fauquier	8,754	131	21,329	41.0	0.6	43
Lancaster	3,126	159	5,375	58.2	3.0	18
Mecklenburg	8,876	553	17,008	51.0	3.3	76
Wythe	831	11	6,380	13.0	0.2	3
Total in eight counties	38,024	3,228	95,463	39.8	3.4	1229
Total in Virginia	346,968	20,507	886,149	39.2	2.3	8,000– 11,500

Sources: U.S. census, 1800; deed and will books for the eight counties.
[a]The number is approximate because wills of emancipation do not always detail the number of slaves freed; the given numbers are probably within 3 percent of the actual number freed.

IDEAS ABOUT SLAVERY AND FREEDOM IN DEEDS AND WILLS OF EMANCIPATION

The 1782 law that allowed private manumission made provisions for determining who had been legally emancipated by requiring former slaves to have a copy of the document that freed them and carry that document with them if they traveled out of their home county. Legal instruments of emancipation had to be written, ordinarily either in the form of a deed or a will, and proved in court and entered into the county record books.[10] It is there in the county records that manumission documents survive, deeds and wills authored by a wide range of slaveholding Virginians, including women, illiterate people, wealthy planters, and middling slaveholders. While wills of emancipation rarely included more than a phrase or two setting a particular slave or group of slaves at liberty, deeds of manumission sometimes contained long, detailed explanations of why an owner had decided to free his or her slaves. In addition, deeds of manumission were relatively rare, unfamiliar, and innovative legal documents in late-eighteenth-century Virginia. Thus unlike most legal papers, which were so formulaic as to leave little room for an individual's voice, deeds of manumission with their variations and idiosyncrasies revealed the ideas and motives of individual Virginia manumittors.

The personal expressions sometimes found in deeds of manumission resulted in part from the form of the documents. Like other deeds, deeds of manumission transferred property from one party to another in exchange for valuable consideration—a quid pro quo that completed a contract and made the transfer binding. A deed transferring land, for example, might read "in consideration of the sum of £150, I do hereby grant the following tract of land." Similarly, Richard Ames's deed of manumission to Luke read "by *Considerations* of right Justice and Duty [I] do hereby manumit liberate and set free my negroe man Slave Luke."[11] Because those who drafted deeds of manumission modified the ordinary form of deeds to suit the new purpose and often left in the formulaic phrase, "in consideration of," many manumittors were moved to articulate just what freedom had been granted *for*. Like Ames, who freed Luke for an intangible consideration—right, justice, and duty—George Corbin freed his slaves for abstract values. He freed his slaves "for divers good Causes and Considerations . . . but more Especially from Motives of Humanity, Justice, and Policy."[12]

Given the traditional function of deeds as instruments transferring property, it is not surprising that the main idea about slavery embedded in deeds of manumission was that slavery was a legitimate relationship of possession. Virginia emancipators had a specific understanding of what that meant. Owning another person was more to them than simply possessing "right, title, and interest" in a slave. To George Herndon, for example, who emphasized in his deed of manumission that he was "legally possessed" of his three slaves, relinquishing ownership entailed "quit[ting] claim unto . . . their *persons* as well as their *Services* and *estate*."[13] Herndon and others understood that slavery was literal ownership of another person's body that consequently included whatever was (re)produced by that body, be it labor or children. By transferring the property value of a slave from the owner to the slave himself, deeds of manumission underscored the notion that slaves had no claim to their own bodies while free people were, both legally and metaphorically, self-possessed.

Since possession of a slave's body entitled slave owners, they thought, to control over the slave's mind as well, emancipation endowed slaves with the ability to, as Thomas Crippen put it, "be at their own Disposal and liberty to act for themselves as any other free People without the le[as]t hindrance or molestation of me or any other person." Caleb Bradford also spelled out (if awkwardly) the idea that emancipation meant relinquishing power and control as well as ownership when he wrote in 1802, that "Annes Negro the *property* of me Caleb Bradford I this Day Mancipates her and Declares her to be a free woman and that I have no *Command* of the sd Negro from this the 27th day of December 1802."[14]

Manumission, by turning slaves into free people—property into thinking, self-possessed persons—also marked the moment when they entered the social body, even if black people were not citizens according to Virginia's laws.[15] As Bridgett James explained in her deed of manumission to her slave Liddia, the "Introduction of the above Mentioned Negron [*sic*] into Society, Make a Sec'd Name Necessary for the distinction from the Negrons, who have been or may be hearafter [*sic*] Liberated." To emphasize that freed blacks had undergone a deeply meaningful transition, some manumittors bestowed symbolic surnames on the slaves they freed, such as Joy, Jubely, Planter, or Godfree.[16] While it is generally assumed that slaves took on the last names of their owners, most slaves had, took, or were given surnames which differed from their manumittor's last name. Furthermore, at least some freed slaves changed their names, asserting their independence by choosing surnames different from the ones imposed by their former masters.

The words manumittors used in deeds of manumission also highlighted the transitional nature of emancipation. Moving from slavery to freedom was, according to most white Virginia manumittors, an essential change, an alteration of basic nature rather than a simple change in role. Slaves in their minds were not once-free people who had been enslaved and were now being returned to liberty, as Enlightenment philosophers such as Montesquieu might have it. Rather, white Virginia manumittors viewed slavery as an inborn, natural status, a belief that was one of the basic assumptions of deeds of manumission. Frequently, when manumittors or their lawyers could come up with no other definition of the freedom that they were granting to their slaves, they simply declared them "to all intents and purposes free as if they were born free."[17] Because most manumittors did not see emancipation as restoring slaves to their original state of liberty but as altering their natal status, deeds (and wills) of emancipation generally turned rather than *re*turned slaves into free people.

Indeed, most white manumittors never questioned the premises upon which slavery rested: that their slaves were born as unfree people outside society who were first and foremost property over which owners had ultimate power. To nearly all of the men and women of the late eighteenth century who held (and in this case freed) their slaves, the idea of owning other people was not troublesome. The vast majority of manumittors asserted possession of their (soon-to-be-former) slaves without apparent thought. Over and over again in their deeds of manumission to their slaves, slave owners referred to the people they were freeing as "my negro woman," "my negro man," or "my several negroes." Even in the very act of setting them free, of giving up possession, most manumittors still unreflectively called their slaves "mine." Sometimes they continued to do so even after their slaves had gained freedom. In his will

Ezekiel Tatham gave five acres of land, a cow, and a calf to "*my negro* Mathew *that* once was a slave to me but is now free." In continuing to think of Mathew as a possession and an object, referring to her by means of the impersonal pronoun "that" and calling her "my negro," Tatham demonstrated that it was even harder for white people to liberate themselves from the reflexes of slaveholding than to free their slaves.[18]

AGGREGATE PATTERNS IN MANUMISSION

While most manumittors shared common ideas about the nature of slavery and the nature of freedom, manumission itself had different meanings over time. Manumission started out as a rare but unequivocal response to antislavery ideology, but by the mid-1790s it resulted from various, even contradictory, motives. Manumission on the eve of the 1806 law was a regular part of a stable system of slavery in Virginia rather than a challenge to it.

One important variable was the annual number of slaves freed, which is shown in graphs 1 and 2, and in table 2. The heavy lines in the graphs showing the annual number of manumission documents filed each year can be read as an indicator of annual changes in emancipation behavior—how many people freed slaves.[19] Significantly, the patterns of manumission for deeds and wills differed. The number of people who freed slaves by deed varied significantly over time. Few did so in the early 1780s; more did in the early 1790s; and the number of manumissions by deed dropped at the end of the decade before rising in 1805 and 1806 in response to legislative discussions about banning manumission altogether and the final passage of the 1806 law forbidding subsequently freed slaves to remain in the state.[20] While as a society white Virginians made the decision to limit the number of free blacks and to try to exclude them from the commonwealth with the 1806 amendment, in their local communities individual Virginians chose *not* to force their freed slaves to leave the state and acted in relatively large numbers to emancipate them before the statutory change, a disjunction that revealed the inherent tensions and contradictions in slavery. Emancipation by will showed a more stable pattern than emancipation by deed. It was also uncommon in the 1780s but reached a steady, low level by around 1792 and did not change in response to the impending 1806 law. Comparing the graphs, one can see that the proportion of emancipations by will versus by deed grew over time: more and more of the people who freed slaves did so upon their deaths, by means of a will, rather than during their lifetimes by deed.

The variations in manumission over time show that there was no initial rush to free slaves, as one might expect if, in the heat of the Revolutionary-era antislavery movement, there were great pent-up demand for the ability to manumit. The four individuals who wrote deeds of manumission and the single person who freed a slave in his will in 1782 hardly qualify as a groundswell.

TABLE 2. Slaves Freed by Deed and by Will in Eight
Virginia Counties, 1782–1806

Year	Slaves freed, deeds	Number of deeds	Average number freed per	Slaves freed, wills	Number of wills	Average number freed per	Total of slaves freed	Total of documents
1782	55	4	13.8	1	1	1.0	56	5
1783	12	3	4.0	0	0		12	3
1784	0	0		0	0		0	0
1785	16	5	3.2	4	2	2.0	20	7
1786	4	1	4.0	1	1	1.0	5	2
1787	97	6	16.2	0	0		97	6
1788	31	10	3.1	4	3	1.3	35	13
1789	49	12	4.1	9	1	9.0	58	13
1790	129	30	4.3	1	1	1.0	130	31
1791	34	13	2.6	8	3	2.7	42	16
1792	16	5	3.2	20	6	3.3	36	11
1793	54	13	4.2	18	7	2.6	72	20
1794	28	9	3.1	7	3	2.3	35	12
1795	12	3	4.0	20	8	2.5	32	11
1796	35	12	2.9	8	4	2.0	43	16
1797	10	8	1.3	13	6	2.2	23	14
1798	10	10	1.0	10	3	3.3	20	13
1799	17	6	2.8	17	7	2.4	34	13
1800	32	12	2.7	14	6	2.3	46	18
1801	10	5	2.0	22	7	3.1	32	12
1802	10	6	1.7	20	6	3.3	30	12
1803	27	16	1.7	17	6	2.8	44	22
1804	26	13	2.0	17	5	3.4	43	18
1805	56	17	3.3	32	9	3.6	88	26
1806	177	41	4.3	19	4	4.8	196	45
Total	947	260	3.6	282	99	2.9	1,229	359

Sources: Deed and will books for Accomack, Botetourt, Charles City, Chesterfield, Fauquier, Lancaster, Mecklenburg, and Wythe counties, 1782–1806

In the late 1780s manumission by deed became more common, reaching its high point in 1790, *after* Quakers had generally forced compliance with anti-slavery practices within their ranks, *after* Methodists had begun to back away from their strict antislavery policy, and *after* Baptists had also softened their stance against slavery. In fact, the decade of the greatest number of people who freed slaves was not the 1780s, shortly after the law was passed, but the 1790s, by which time antislavery sentiment in Virginia was apparently in decline. Even the Haitian Revolution, thought to have crushed antislavery sympathies in the southern states, seems to have had only a temporary effect, if any, on the rate of manumission. Though the number of emancipations dipped a bit in 1791 and 1792 relative to the spike in 1790, manumission continued at a low level, and manumission by will rose significantly only after 1791.

The number of slaves each manumittor freed compared to the number he or she owned corresponds to these temporal shifts. Most early manumittors who wrote deeds of manumission liberated all of their slaves; from 1782 to 1791 the proportion who did so was nearly 70 percent. But from the early 1790s a much smaller share of those who freed slaves by deed emancipated all their slaves, only about 40 percent from 1792 to 1806. Overall, about half of the cases of manumission by deed represented the slaveholder's total divestiture from slavery.[21] Slightly more than one-third of those who emancipated slaves in their wills freed the entirety of their slave property. In general, then, about two-thirds of the time people who freed slaves upon their deaths did not free all they slaves they had owned; although there were variations from year to year in this proportion, there was no discernible pattern to the fluctuations in the percentage of slaves freed.[22]

The reasons manumittors gave for freeing their slaves help clarify the transformations in manumission over time. Because emancipators rarely if ever explained why they freed slaves in their wills, this information comes exclusively from deeds of manumission. From 1781 to 1793 nine out of ten of the manumittors who gave specific reasons for freeing their slaves (by deed) cited either secular or religious antislavery ideology or a combination of both. Biblical injunctions often found their way into deeds of manumission in the form of the Golden Rule, especially in deeds authored by Quakers. Mecklenburg County Quakers Thomas Durham Madkins and James Williams, for example, both wrote that they were "fully persuaded that freedom is the natural Right of all mankind & that it is my duty to do unto other as I would desire to by done by in the Like Situation."[23] Non-Quakers also combined "the Laws of Religion" with those of "Morality" to determine that "God Originally distributed equally to the Human race the unalienable right to the enjoyment of Personal Liberty."[24]

Manumittors cited antislavery arguments only rarely after the early 1790s. In deeds written from 1794 on, slightly more than half the manumittors freed slaves for reasons that were either pecuniary or specific to the slaves involved.[25] For example, Hardyman Irby purchased Eliza in 1797 with the understanding that "part of the consideration of which purchase is that the said slave is to have her freedom at the end of five years from this date together with all her future increase."[26] Martha Turpin purchased Anica with the intention "to liberate and legally set her free, so soon as her services should have reimbursed me in one half of her purchase money," an obligation apparently met by 1804, when Turpin manumitted Anica.[27] In Anica's case it seems Turpin acted as a third party to help Anica obtain her liberty. Hardyman Irby's manumission of Eliza, along with similar cases, shows that slavery in Virginia was not always seen as perpetual. Though it was rare in Virginia, some slave owners acquired new slaves as temporary servants whom they intended to free after a specified period of time. Were it not for the 1806 law that curtailed manumission, it is likely that these sorts of manumisisons would have increased, especially in regions where slavery was becoming less important to the economy, such as on the Eastern Shore. Slavery there might have evolved to resemble the system in neighboring Maryland, where, particularly in Baltimore, owners engaged in what might be called term slavery—buying slaves for specific terms of service rather than for life, since as described by T. Stephen Whitman it seemed less expensive to guarantee a slave's freedom after a certain number of years than to risk his running away.[28]

Another common reason owners freed slaves after the early 1790s was as a reward for their loyal service, a common form of manumission in most slave systems. Henry Custis, for example, freed Babel in consideration of his "faithful performance," and William Chilton similarly freed George "in consideration of the honesty and general good conduct of my negro man Slave George."[29] It is likely that Babel and George knew at some point that they might be emancipated if they were loyal, and behaved accordingly. Perhaps the slaves also saw, even if their owners did not, that there was some irony in rewarding excellence in slavery with freedom from slavery, in stating that a person was so good at being a slave, so humble, obedient, and loyal, that he deserved liberty.

A significant number of the manumissions that took place after the middle of the 1790s resulted from the actions of African Americans—an expression of antislavery sentiment to be sure, but not a reflection of whites' commitment to universal liberty. One of the surprises of this study, in fact, is the relatively large number of slaves who were able to buy their freedom; about one-twelfth of the acts of manumission in the eight counties occurred when slaves or parties acting on their behalf purchased themselves from their owner. Almost all of the Virginia slaves who bought their freedom did so after the mid-1790s, indicating that it took more than a decade after the passage of the manumission law for slaves to gain the knowledge and the funds with which to purchase

TABLE 3. Manumission by Self-Purchase

Year of deed	Slave's name	Sex of Slave	Amount Paid	Payer	County
1787	Derry	m	£50	slave	Botetourt
1790	Durham	m	£14	Walter Bayne, Esq.	Accomack
1796	Duke	m	£40	slave	Lancaster
1796	Tom Jesup	m	£50	slave, by subscription	Lancaster
1797	Frank	m	£40	slave	Accomack
1797	Holly	m	£80	Sam Moody	Chesterfield
1798	James	m	£60	slave	Accomack
1800	Fanny	f	£37	Robert Pollock	Chesterfield
1800	Fanny	f	£40	slave	Fauquier
1801	Thomas Kirk	m	£60	slave	Fauquier
1802	Solomon Downing	m	£40	slave	Accomack
1803	Robin	m	£75	slave, partial credit given	Accomack
1803	Patty	f	$100	slave?	Chesterfield
1804	Solomon	m	£88	slave, on credit	Accomack
1805	Caleb	m	£80	slave, on credit	Accomack
1805	Patience	f	£76, 10s	her husband Stephen Neelab	Accomack
1805	Beckey	f	£62, 10s	slave and her husband, free negro Cuffee	Chesterfield
1805	Chriss Laws	f	$100	slave	Lancaster
1806	James	m	£100	slave, through his wife Dority Hill	Accomack
1806	Davy	m	£70	slave?	Fauquier
1806	Westley, Lewis, and William	mmm	$100	slaves?	Fauquier

their liberty. Indeed, the amounts they paid for their freedom were often substantial, ranging from fourteen to one hundred pounds (see table 3).[30] Judging from information contained in deeds of manumission as well as other evidence, slaves who purchased themselves from their owners shared certain characteristics. They were independent and willful yet respectful of their masters. Many were skilled and had probably been allowed to hire themselves out and earn their own wages, thus acquiring the requisite cash to buy themselves. Most were men. In cases of self-purchase the impetus for manumission lay primarily with the slaves themselves and their determination to break free of their bondage. Nevertheless, they could not have done so without the aid of sympathetic whites. Owners sometimes allowed slaves to purchase themselves for less than market value, and it was not unusual for a slave to receive help in purchasing his freedom either from his master, in form of credit, or from other whites who gave money or loans. In the case of Tom Jesup in Lancaster County, members of the community even raised a subscription to help Jesup purchase his freedom.[31]

Several African Americans also acted as manumittors. Usually they were free black men who purchased and then liberated their wives and children. One example is Reubin Howard, freed in 1790 by the Methodist preacher Edward Mitchell. By 1799 Howard had purchased "a Negroe Woman Slave named Minta Howard & her Child Named Reubin." Although Reubin Howard did not state explicitly that Minta Howard was his wife and Reubin his child, their names indicate they formed a family. Borrowing language from contemporary secular antislavery thought, and perhaps suggested to him by white friends or lawyers, Howard freed Minta and Reubin "being fully Satisfyed that liberty is the birthright of all persons whatsoever." Howard's deed reflected his continuing relationship with his former owner Edward Mitchell who witnessed it, and the deed indicated his own humble station and lack of literacy as it was signed only by his mark.[32] More unusual was Mary Griffin's liberation of Cyrus Rose Arrow in 1804, a man she, a "free woman," had purchased a few days before. The deed of manumission was witnessed by two men who, like Griffin, signed with their marks, which was unusual for whites of that era but common for former slaves. While the evidence is sparse, it is almost certain that Mary Griffin and the two witnesses were all free blacks, part of a community that cared about helping other African Americans gain their freedom, and that they worked together to effect Cyrus Arrow's liberty and to welcome him to the local free black community.[33]

Slaves around the turn of the century also took advantage of the courts to obtain their liberty; several deeds from that period resulted from suits for freedom brought by slaves against their owners. There were only a few of these cases, but they demonstrated that slaves could have a sophisticated understanding of the law and of how to use the court system to gain emancipation.

The slave George, belonging to Maryland resident Thomas Wood Potter, brought a suit claiming that Potter had violated the law against importing slaves into Virginia when he sent George to work there, and that George should therefore be free as the law dictated for illegally imported slaves. Potter freed George "in consideration of the past Services of the said George as alas to prevent further Litigation concerning his claim to freedom."[34] It is likely that slaves such as George were aided in their quest for liberty by antislavery activists, inspiring a 1795 law designed to limit the number of freedom suits by subjecting those found "aiding, abbetting, or maintaining any person in the prosecution" of an unsuccessful suit to a steep fine of one hundred dollars.[35]

SEX AND AGE OF FREED SLAVES

In rural areas freed slaves were slightly more likely to be male than female. Fifty-six percent of the slaves freed in the eight counties were men or boys (57 percent of those freed by deed, 54 percent of those freed by will, where sex could be determined), and the sex ratio seems to have changed little if any over time. In urban areas, however, the ratio was reversed, with more women freed than men.[36] The relatively even sex ratios of freed slaves show that manumission did not result primarily from concubinage, in which male owners freed female slaves, nor did owners disproportionately free their less valuable female slaves.

The reason for the predominance of men among freed slaves in rural areas results in part from the larger number of men who were able to buy their freedom. But it seems that male slaves were somehow better able to convince their masters they deserved freedom even in cases that did not involve an exchange for money. An unruly slave, or one who ran away often (usually male), might prove such a burden to his master that the owner would agree to free him after a certain number of years of good service, as happened occasionally in Maryland.[37] Owners also may have calculated that their male slaves could more easily support themselves as rural laborers than women could.

The different pattern in urban areas may be explained by a corollary of the above principle. In towns there were jobs in which freed women might be employed and by which they might make a living, as domestic servants or laundresses, for example, so there was less resistance among whites to freeing them. The slight majority of women among freed slaves in towns probably resulted, in part, from the relatively high percentage of emancipators in those areas who were free blacks, as was the case in Norfolk.[38] Free black men were better able to raise the funds to free their enslaved wives than free black women were to emancipate their slave husbands.

The average age at which slaves were emancipated, about twenty-six years, shows manumittors sometimes freed valuable slaves in their prime. At the same time the number of freed slaves who were over forty, nearly one-eighth of the slaves whose ages could be determined (in both deeds and wills), suggests that sometimes owners did manumit older slaves of little value, in part to be rid of the responsibility of caring for them.[39] One important variation in the ages of freed slaves also indicates economic considerations did play some role in manumission. Slaves freed in the Piedmont area, where tobacco production was central to the economy, were slightly older, though most were still freed before the age of 30.[40] Men tended to be slightly older at the time of their emancipation than women, 26.8 versus 25.1 years old for slaves freed by deed, but this is probably an artifact of the different ages of majority for males and females. (In Virginia white men were considered to be legally of age when they reached 21, and white women when they were 18. The manumission law followed this custom, outlawing manumission for male slaves under 21 and female slaves under 18.)

Delayed Emancipation and Strategic Manumission

One common form of manumission in Virginia, delayed manumission, shows how the promise of freedom could be used as an incentive. More than half of the slaves freed in Virginia did not actually attain their liberty until months or years after the emancipating document had been drafted. In Virginia as elsewhere, manumission thus served primarily to *support* the system of slavery rather than to weaken it, even though any individual act of manumission was an implicit challenge to the idea that all blacks should be slaves.

Although one might expect fewer delayed emancipations in wills than in deeds, since the deceased emancipator himself gained no additional benefit by keeping the slaves in bondage, delayed emancipation was more common in wills. About two-thirds of the slaves freed by last will and testament were not freed immediately, and the length of the delay ranged from one to thirty-three years. About half of slaves freed in deeds were held as slaves past the date of the deed, with an average (mean) of about nine years before freedom would commence. This often resulted from the statutory provision against freeing children; owners would draft a deed but set the date of freedom at time of the slave's majority. But in a number of cases, slaves were held in bondage until the age of thirty or thirty-five, or their freedom was put off until the death or marriage of the emancipators' heirs.

Showing that one would, at some future date, relinquish ownership of one's slaves was important within some religious groups. In Accomack County, where Methodism took strong hold and the antislavery commitment of the church lasted longer than elsewhere in Virginia, Methodist quarterly meetings required their members to produce certificates of emancipation for their slaves, even after the national church had dropped similar requirements. Many Methodists, including the preacher Griffin Callahan, submitted documents that delayed the emancipation for significant periods of time, allowing the slave owners simultaneously to remain in good standing with the local church and to continue to benefit from their slaves' labor.[41]

It appears that the main function of delayed emancipation in wills was to allow slaveholders to balance their desire to reward their slaves with their duty to provide for their descendants. Negotiating among the interests of descendants and slaves could result in elaborate provisions. William Wilkinson, for example, freed all of his slaves in his last will and testament. He directed that the slave boy George and girl Hannah were to serve his son until the slaves reached thirty-five years of age respectively. Other child slaves were similarly devised to Wilkinson's children until the slaves reached thirty-five, by which time most of their productive years would be past. Wilkinson's adult slaves Harry and Sarah were to be hired out for four and two years respectively. Wilkinson willed that the profits from their hire be divided among his daughters. It was likely that the female slaves would have children while still in bondage, but Wilkinson did not specify whether those children would also be freed, so they probably were not.[42] Wilkinson knew that it cost money to raise slaves, and probably wanted to ensure that his heirs would recuperate the cost of bringing the slaves up. In addition, many of the people who freed slaves in their wills freed the younger slaves only, which may have been a way to divest slowly from slave owning.

Sometimes owners made clear that delayed emancipation was a bargain, a promise of eventual liberty in exchange for years of good, loyal, and honest service from one's chattels. Ann Muir, for example, freed her slaves in 1806 "for and in consideration of the tenderness which she bears toward her . . . negroes after they the said negroes do serve for the term of years respectively as hereafter specified." She promised them "freedom from slavery *upon the express condition* that the said negroes herein named do first serve myself and my heirs . . . [for] that portion of their time respectively before which period they are hereby intended to be and go free." Muir then laid out a schedule of manumissions by which some slaves might not be free until 1849. Until that time they would remain as slaves to Muir, and after her death, they would serve Muir's sister and nephews.[43] In an even more explicit exchange of freedom for good service, Foxhall Sturman promised to free a slave he had inherited from his father in one year "if the said negro Cupid shall well and truly perform the duties & services of a Servant to the said Sturman for the full end and term of Twelve months."[44] Cupid apparently did fulfill his obligation, and was freed in 1805.

If delayed manumission, with its implicit and sometimes explicit exchange of good service for freedom, could actually bolster a master's command over his or her slave, the mere hope that exemplary behavior might be rewarded with liberty could similarly encourage slaves to be loyal and dutiful. Richard Drummond Bayly, who freed his slave Caleb in 1805 understood this.[45] As a member of the state legislature from Accomack County, he participated in an 1805 debate over whether to prohibit manumission entirely. Bayly wrote to his friend John Cropper that the proposed ban "appears to be a most cruel Law which neither the Safety nor the policy of the state will warrant. To forever shut the door of the hope of freedom against this unfortunate portion of the human species, To say that no Servant however meritorious his conduct may be shall be freed by a master, carries to my mind horror and injustice in the very idea." Bayly also objected to a ban on private emancipation in Virginia because it would interfere with the property rights of slave owners. But his final and most passionate argument rested on the principle that the possibility of freedom strengthened a master's command over his slaves. If manumission were outlawed, then slaves' hope for being free would be crushed, making them restless and even dangerous. He asked, "Will not such a law [banning manumission] make servants relax in their endeavour to please when they know that the great Reward which probably prompts them to the faithful discharge of their duty can never be bestowed upon them? Is it not Sir the idea of being at some future period free (althou' the hope frequently proves elusive) which makes them in some measure contented with their condition and proves a security for the peace of families? And Sir will not the withdrawing of this only hope from their minds instead of returning or of preventing accelerate & bring forth all the horrors of domestic insurrections? Freedom is the ardent wish of all mankind."[46] Since the discipline of slavery could be enforced either through the threat of physical harm or the promise of reward, and since "freedom is the ardent wish of all mankind," liberty was the ultimate promise one could make to a slave in order to extract dutiful and loyal service.

VARIATIONS AMONG COMMUNITIES

In spite of the potential of manumission to be used as an instrument of control, freeing slaves in a society dedicated to and dependent on slavery was a bold and even radical act. Though the number of people who did so was not overwhelming, about one or two individuals per county per year, many would not have freed slaves at all were it not for particular factors that encouraged it in their respective communities. The county communities examined in this study varied significantly in economy, culture, population, and geography and were dispersed among all four of Virginia's main regions (Tidewater, Piedmont, Valley, and Trans-Allegheny).

Although several factors shaped the patterns of manumission, one broad generalization holds true: a greater proportion of slaveholders freed slaves in the older eastern counties and a smaller proportion in the rapidly growing western regions and the area south of the James River. About four times the proportion of slaveholders freed slaves in Accomack, Charles City, and Chesterfield counties, all old Virginia communities, than in the more recently settled Fauquier, Mecklenburg, and Tazewell. Taken together, the average number of slave owners who freed slaves each year was tiny, about one-quarter of 1 per-cent.[47] Peter Albert found similar regional variations, with more manumissions in the southern Tidewater, slightly fewer in the northern Tidewater, "and still less in the fall zone and Piedmont." He also noted rising numbers of emanci-pations in the larger towns after the 1780s.[48]

In part the regional variations resulted from the greater presence of anti-slavery groups and religious organizations in some Tidewater counties, and the relatively lesser importance of slaves in the declining Tidewater versus rising Piedmont economies. But another factor was at work as well: the eastern coun-ties were at a later stage of social development and had stable, well-connected communities. Since, as demonstrated below, manumission often took place within groups, older counties were more likely to have the kind of cohesive communities that could both enforce manumission and integrate freed slaves.

Other more specific and local, even idiosyncratic, factors shaped the details of manumission in each county. One-sixth of the manumissions (by deed) in Chesterfield County, for example, took place in its urban center at Manchester. Here the urban environment encouraged manumission, especially because it allowed slaves like Patty to raise the cash—one hundred dollars in her case—necessary to buy their freedom. Another group of manumittors in Chesterfield was a group of four people, possibly all Baptists, who freed twenty-seven slaves between 1789 and 1793. First to manumit was Martin Baker, who freed Amy, Caeser, and Joe on Christmas Day, 1789. Six months later, John Baker, proba-bly Martin's brother, and Thomas Bridgewater wrote identically worded deeds, both of which were witnessed by Martin Baker. And Bridgewater, John Baker, and Baptist Deacon Reuben Winfree together freed a single slave a few years later. It is clear that the two Bakers, Winfree, and Bridgewater formed a com-munity that reinforced their commitment to the idea that "all men by nature are equally free," as they all stated in their deeds of manumission. Other than these individuals, few people who freed slaves in Chesterfield expressed anti-slavery sentiment, especially after 1793, when most people who freed slaves freed only a single individual. In addition no one freed any slaves by deed before 1788 or by will before 1785.[49]

In Charles City County, which had no urban center, a large portion of the manumittors were either Quakers or Methodists. Even so, none of them freed any slaves until 1791, when Quaker Samuel Hargrave freed five slaves, "being fully persuaded that freedom is the natural right of all mankind, and being desirous of doing to others as I should be done by." Hargrave and another Quaker, John Crew, both freed slaves on several occasions. Methodist ministers Benjamin Dancy and John Bowry also freed slaves in Charles City County. Dancy freed all of his, but Bowry freed only one. Their example seems not to have been followed by many of their congregants. Few others freed any slaves, and those who were not Quakers generally freed only one or two slaves. One exception is Richardson

Walker, who died without a wife or children and left his entire estate to his slave Abigail and her three daughters, all of whom he freed. It is quite possible that Abigail's daughters were his daughters, too.[50]

The factors shaping manumission in Lancaster were similar. There was a cluster of manumissions in 1790, the year Methodist minister John Dogget and three others freed some of their slaves. Dogget also witnessed one other deed in 1798. The other seven people who freed slaves in that county either freed a small number of slaves in their wills, or set their slaves free in exchange for cash payments. No one in Lancaster freed more than three of his slaves, and none appears to have freed all his slaves.

In Mecklenburg, Botetourt, and Wythe counties, all newly settled regions, there were few manumittors. Many of the people who freed slaves could be identified as Quakers or were associated with Methodists. Fauquier County, in the northern Piedmont, had a relatively large number of manumittors, but none of them expressed antislavery sentiment, and most of them freed only one slave.

In some ways the pattern in Accomack was similar to the other counties, but because there were so many slaves freed there, Accomack deserves special attention. Proportionally, Accomack County had about the same number of manumittors as Charles City or Chesterfield County. As in Charles City and Mecklenburg, a small group of manumittors could be identified as Quakers who generally freed all of their slaves in the 1780s and early 1790s.[51] A much larger group were Methodists, who like Methodists in Lancaster, Mecklenburg, and Botetourt freed their slaves from the 1790s through 1806. And as in Chesterfield, a few manumittors were also Baptists. The striking difference in Accomack, however, is the large number of slaves freed by the average manumittor, and the relatively high proportion who freed all their slaves. In addition there was a large group of county elites, many of whom were Episcopalian, who freed significant numbers of slaves, while in other counties manumittors fell into two broad groups—either they were members of marginalized or alternative religious groups, such as Quakers, Methodists, and Baptists, who freed many slaves, or they freed only one or two slaves for special or idiosyncratic reasons.

The prominent Accomack citizens who emancipated slaves had multiple connections to one another that seem to have helped promote manumission. On a single day in September 1787 four of Accomack's leading citizens together emancipated eighty-seven slaves. Three of them, Charles Stockly, Col. William Parramore, and John Teackle were judges on the county court, and Parramore and Teackle were at different times members of the Episcopalian vestry. They, along with George Corbin, all cited natural rights philosophy in their deeds of manumission, declaring "the Equal right of Human Nature to Personal liberty." Parramore, who was active in the Methodist church, was likely the instigator, influencing his friends and peers who in turn witnessed additional deeds of manumission and were related to other emancipators.[52] Corbin, for example, may have influenced his nephew, John Cropper Jr., to free his sixteen slaves in a 1794 deed in which he stated that "all men by Nature are equally free." John Cropper was in turn connected with other Accomack County emancipators, including John S. Ker, a wealthy merchant whose large Federalist-style mansion currently serves as home to the Eastern Shore of Virginia Historical Society. Ker was a cousin of Cropper's second wife, and he freed all twenty-eight of his slaves shortly before his death in 1806. For years, he said, his mind had been "much exercised on the Subject" of the "evils of Slavery." Thomas Evans, another friend of General Cropper's, and like Cropper a Federalist delegate to the Virginia House of Delegates, freed three slaves in 1791.[53] Like Cropper, many of Accomack's manumittors had served in the army or navy during the Revolution, and the politicians among them were Federalists.[54]

Something unusual happened on Virginia's Eastern Shore: The ideals of the Revolution—devotion to liberty and the equal rights of all people—took deep root. For men such as Cropper the experience of fighting for those ideals affected their daily lives, shaped their values, and encouraged them to emancipate their slaves. The difference between Accomack and elsewhere can be explained in part by the accidental collection of powerful personalities such as Cropper, Corbin, and Ker. In addition, the Eastern Shore is both culturally and geographically separate from the rest of Virginia. And certainly the influence of Methodism and the small number of Quakers in the county played an important role. But Methodists in other places did not free as many slaves as in Accomack. And in other counties Revolutionary War veterans and local elites, such as George Hancock in Botetourt County (future father-in-law to explorer William Clark), did not usually free all of their slaves. Hancock freed two, whom his father had intended to liberate, "in consideration of their faithful services."[55]

More important, the economic conditions in Accomack County provided the basis for the culture of manumission that evolved there. The relatively small percentage of slaves (compared to other Tidewater communities) and their peripheral role in an economy no longer dependent on plantation agriculture made it easier for slave owners to free them. If economic factors were not sufficient in themselves to foster manumission—Lancaster County, with a similar economy, did not see many emancipations—they were certainly necessary. The decreasing economic importance of slavery provided a substrate upon which other factors, such as religion, politics, and local culture operated.

Implicit in the discussion above is that religious communities were important loci of manumission, as historians have traditionally understood. But the common belief that most manumittors were Quakers is not supported by the available evidence since Methodists and Baptist preachers formed a large number of Virginia emancipators. Indeed, only one quarter of those whose religion could be identified were Quakers.[56] Perhaps so few manumittors were Quakers because by the 1780s few Quakers owned slaves, but this argument is not entirely convincing, since the Friends knew it was illegal to free slaves before 1782, and that any illegal emancipation could be challenged in court. In fact, it was to enable themselves to free slaves legally that they had lobbied for the 1782 law. It is more likely that the findings simply reflect the dearth of substantial Quaker communities in Virginia. The Virginia Friends had been a small group who lost members during the Revolutionary era with their strictures against military service and slaveholding, lost more members to migration westward in the late eighteenth and early nineteenth centuries, and had almost disappeared in Virginia by the mid–nineteenth century.

Most of those identified as Quakers resided in three of the counties under study: Mecklenburg, Charles City, and Accomack. They account for most of the manumissions in Accomack in 1782–83, and in Mecklenburg and Charles City throughout the 1782–1806 period, but especially in the early 1790s. The Quaker deeds in these counties shared common language, sometimes even identical phrases, suggesting that individual Quakers brought examples of deeds with them if they traveled to other meetings. Indeed, it was the very cohesiveness of the Quaker sect and the intensity of the Quaker commitment to community that pushed many of them to act on their beliefs and free their slaves. Daniel Mifflin, for example, witnessed eight deeds of manumission in addition to freeing his own slaves. Perhaps inspired by the example of his son, antislavery activist Warner Mifflin, Daniel Mifflin seems to have been a local leader in the cause of emancipation, influencing fellow Quakers, and perhaps even some non-Quakers, to set their slaves at liberty.[57] But not all Quakers were so moved, Quaker records contain numerous instances of Friends who were dismissed out of the meeting, or expelled, for failure to emancipate their slaves.[58]

A similarly small group of manumittors could be identified as Baptists, and most of those were ministers whose names were found in surviving Baptist Association records and in secondary sources.[59] Additional Baptists who freed slaves may go unrecognized because the Baptist church records of this period are scanty and rarely include full membership lists. The predominance of ministers among those identified as Baptists is probably not, however, merely an artifact of the remaining evidence. Because the Baptist church did not force its members to free their slaves, those who did so were among the most religious and devoted members of the church, many of whom were probably preachers.

About half of those whose religious affiliation could be identified were members of the Methodist church, many of them in Accomack County, and seven were ministers.[60] Once again, the ardent nature of religious leaders, such

TABLE 4. Manumittors as a proportion of all slaveholders, 1782–1806

County	Number of deeds of manumission	Number of individuals who freed slaves by deed	Number of individuals who freed slaves by will	Approximate number of slaveholding heads of household in county	Proportion of manumittors (deeds) to slaveholding households	Proportion of manumittors (wills) to slaveholding households	Proportion of all manumittors to slaveholding households	Approximate annual rate of manumitting
Chesterfield	32	29	13	410 (1790)	7.1%	3.1%	10.2%	0.41%
Accomack	149	146	64	2025 (1800)	7.2%	3.2%	10.3%	0.41%
Charles City	19	17	6	249 (1795)	6.8%	2.4%	9.2%	0.39%
Botetourt	9	10	2	284 (1787)	3.5%	7.0%	4.2%	0.18%
Lancaster	8	8	4	305 (1790)	2.6%	1.3%	3.9%	0.16%
Fauquier	18	20	4	946 (1800)	2.1%	0.4%	2.5%	0.10%
Mecklenburg	14	12	6	724 (1790)	1.6%	0.8%	2.4%	0.10%
Tazewell/Wythe	1	1	0	81 (1810)	1.2%	0.0%	1.2%	0.05%
Total	250	243	99	5024	4.8%	1.9%	6.9%	0.28%

as Edward Mitchell of Botetourt County, is evident. Mitchell stated his motivation for freeing his fourteen slaves in 1790 clearly, declaring that "it is contrary to the Principals of Christianity to hold our Fellow Creatures in Bondage." Judging from the shared texts of the deeds, Mitchell influenced his brother Samuel and at least one other Botetourt resident to free their slaves in 1791 and 1805.[61]

Within all religious groups a few leaders, usually ministers, served as centers around which manumission took place. They witnessed deeds of manumission, provided examples by freeing their own slaves, and in some communities preached against slavery. Perhaps it is only coincidence, but nearly half of all the manumittors who could be identified as preachers (five of eleven) freed slaves in the single year of 1790. Assuming that when religious leaders freed slaves at least some of their congregants followed suit, the cluster of ministers who manumitted slaves in 1790 accounts for the spike in the number of slaves freed by deed in that year.[62] The act of emancipation took leadership and initiative that ministers especially could offer. And because manumittors often acted in groups, a strong individual personality, a tightly knit religious community, or a few energetic free blacks could greatly affect the patterns of manumission in a county.

CONCLUSION

That manumission in Virginia had several meanings resulted in part from the transience of Revolutionary-era antislavery sentiment; manumission changed from being primarily a reflection of that sentiment in the 1780s to a mirror of slavery's diversity and complexity by the turn of the century. Perhaps more important, manumission and its consequences paved the way for changes in the meaning of freedom, slavery, and race, even though Virginians chose not to take the newly opened path. In the absence of the 1806 law that curtailed manumission in Virginia, slavery in those parts of the state where the plantation economy was waning, the Eastern Shore and northern Tidewater, might have evolved toward the system that developed in Baltimore and its environs. There manumission and term slaves—slaves who would labor for a defined term of service before receiving their freedom—became common in the early nineteenth century.[63] The continuation of manumission in Virginia, even at the low rate of the late 1790s, would have added steadily to the free black population, challenging more with each additional free black person the racial basis of freedom. It might have forced Virginians to reconceptualize their ideas about the connections between race and liberty. Making freedom multiracial would have been a healthy development, not just for nineteenth-century Virginia but for twentieth-century America, as well.

It was precisely white Virginians' fear of such an innovation that put an end to the Old Dominion's experiment with manumission. Because the American idea of freedom was absolute and did allow for inequalities in the rights of free people, and because white Virginians did not believe whites and blacks could cohabit equally in the same society, a large number of free blacks who did *not* have the same rights as other free (white) people would destroy the very meaning of freedom for *all* Virginians.[64]

Opponents of manumission expressed clearly their conviction that whites and blacks could not and ought not live together as free people in their arguments against manumission after the discovery of Gabriel's 1800 plot to take Richmond. A group of citizens from the Tidewater county of King and Queen referred to the recent conspiracy when they asserted in a petition to the Virginia House of Delegates that it was "notorious that the Law for Freeing Negroes hath tended to bring upon us our Disturbed & Distressed Situation." In their view blacks must remain enslaved and separate from whites because if free they might mix with whites, and "commixture to our minds is abhorrent."[65] In legislative debates a few years later over whether to ban manumission, one delegate asserted that manumission was dangerous because slaves who see "others like themselves free . . . will repine"; free blacks who "obtain some education . . . can thus organize insurrection" and "will, no doubt, unite with the slaves" in any rebellion.[66] Two fears were at the center of whites' anxiety about free blacks: sexual mixture that would diminish the division between the races, and the violent retribution of all blacks, slave and free, against all whites.

Of course there was a flaw in the logic that impelled Virginians to reject manumission and cast out free blacks, recognized by state delegate John Minor, who pointed out during the 1806 debate over manumission that free blacks did *not* tend to ally with slaves, and that it was not in their interest to foment race war. Minor suggested that public safety would be better served by allowing some slaves to be freed, and splitting the black population into two classes. "'Divide and conquer' is as true in policy as it is as a military maxim. The free blacks are sureties for the slaves. It will be their interest to give information of insurrection." Minor pointed out that Gabriel and his followers had been slaves: "In the late insurrection one free black only was accused and he was acquitted."[67]

In most slave societies the master class has seen it Minor's way, believing that both manumission and freed slaves could help control the enslaved population. Manumission could provide an incentive to good behavior, and freed slaves, often viewed as the most loyal subjects because of what they owed to their masters (liberty), could help control those still enslaved.[68] That Virginians saw it otherwise demonstrates how their obsession with race and their fear of free blacks shaped both manumission and slavery in the Old Dominion and marked it as different from most other slaves regimes.

Virginia stands out in two other ways. Virginia manumittors granted freedom to men more often than women, while the opposite was the case elsewhere, suggesting that perhaps freedom in Virginia was gendered—male—as well as racialized. But the most remarkable aspect of manumission in Virginia, especially given the intensity of the cultural commitment to white liberty there, is the number of antislavery manumissions that took place in the state. Particularly in the Atlantic world, where manumission was almost always coupled with a strong slave system, freeing slaves because of commitment to

TABLE 5. Deeds freeing slaves by year, 1782–1806			TABLE 6. Wills freeing slaves by year, 1782–1806		
Year of deeds	Slaves freed	Number	Year of wills	Slaves freed	Number
1782	55	4	1782	1	1
1783	12	3	1783	0	0
1784	0	0	1784	0	0
1785	16	5	1785	4	2
1786	4	1	1786	1	1
1787	97	6	1787	0	0
1788	31	10	1788	4	3
1789	48	10.9	1789	9	1
1790	129	30	1790	1	1
1791	34	13	1791	8	3
1792	16	5	1792	20	6
1793	54	13	1793	18	7
1794	28	9	1794	7	3
1795	12	3	1795	20	8
1796	34	11	1796	8	4
1797	10	8	1797	13	6
1798	10	10	1798	10	3
1799	16	5	1799	17	7
1800	31	11	1800	14	6
1801	10	5	1801	22	7
1802	10	6	1802	20	6
1803	27	16	1803	17	6
1804	26	13	1804	17	5
1805	56	17	1805	32	9
1806	171	35	1806	19	4

antislavery principles was unusual. The few people who did so were almost unique in that context.

And so we are left with several contradictions. The home of some of the most radical acts of manumission in the Atlantic world—manumission as an indictment of slavery—was also home to some of the most conservative ideas about freedom, unyielding to change even in the face of change. Virginia slave owners freed slaves regularly even as they expressed terror about the growth of a free black population. And manumission in Virginia served both to support the system of slavery and to undermine slavery's racial basis.

NOTES

1. Orlando Patterson, *Slavery and Social Death: A Comparative Study* (Cambridge, Mass.: Harvard University Press, 1982), 340–41, and passim.

2. Thomas Jefferson, *Notes on the State of Virginia,* 2nd American ed. (Philadelphia: Mathew Carey, 1794), 209–210. For more on the relationship between race and the status of freed slaves, see Patterson, *Slavery and Social Death*; and Carl Degler, *Neither Black nor White: Slavery and Race Relations in Brazil and the United States* (New York: Macmillan, 1971; reprint, Madison: University of Wisconsin Press, 1986), 83–92.

3. Eva Sheppard Wolf, *Race and Liberty in the New Nation: Emancipation in Virginia from the Revolution to Nat Turner's Rebellion* (Baton Rouge: Louisiana State University Press, 2006), 28–35. The law limited manumission to healthy, sane, adult slaves under age forty-five, unless former masters promised to maintain any aged or ill slaves they freed.

4. See Edmund Morgan, *American Slavery, American Freedom: The Ordeal of Colonial Virginia* (New York: W. W. Norton, 1975), and Degler, *Neither Black nor White,* for two cogent articulations of this argument. Also see Joanne Pope Melish, *Disowning Slavery: Gradual Emancipation and "Race" in New England, 1780–1860* (Ithaca: Cornell University Press, 1998), for the relationship between race and freedom in New England.

5. Douglas Egerton, *Gabriel's Rebellion: The Virginia Slave Conspiracies of 1800 and 1802* (Chapel Hill: University of North Carolina Press, 1993).

6. Deed of John Teackle to slaves (September 24, 1787), Accomack Co. Deeds 6 (1783–1788), Library of Virginia, Richmond (hereafter cited as LVA).

7. Deed of Anna Maria Andrews to Major (November 4, 1800), Accomack Co. Deeds 10 (1800–1804), LVA; deed of William Ball to Luke (November 27, 1802), Chesterfield Co. Deeds 16 (1802–1805), LVA.

8. Two unpublished studies of Virginia manumission are Theodore Stoddard Babcock, "Manumission in Virginia 1782–1806" (master's thesis, University of Virginia, 1973); Peter Joseph Albert, "The Protean Institution: The Geography, Economy, and Ideology of Slavery in Post-Revolutionary Virginia" (Ph.D. diss., University of Maryland, 1976), chap. 7.

9. Wolf, *Race and Liberty in the New Nation,* 44–47, 76; Patterson, *Slavery and Social Death,* 271–75.

10. William Waller Hening, *The Statutes at Large; Being a Collection of all the Laws of Virginia from the First Session of the Legislature, in the year 1619*, 13 vols. (Richmond, Va., 1809–23; facsimile reprint, Charlottesville: University of Press of Virginia, 1969), 11:39–40 (1782).

11. Deed of Richard Ames to Luke (April 21, 1806), Accomack Co. Free Negro and Slave Records, Manumissions 1783–1814, LVA.

12. Deed of George Corbin to slaves (September 25, 1787), Accomack Co. Deeds 6 (1783–1788), LVA.

13. Deed of George Herndon to slaves (March 17, 1806), Fauquier Co. Deeds 16 (1804–07), LVA. Emphasis added. The analogy between slaves and other types of property, particularly land, is clear in deeds such as Herndon's, especially as he gave up the right, title, and interest he held in his slaves in exchange for one hundred dollars, just as one would relinquish right, title, and interest in a piece of land in exchange for money or other valuable consideration.

14. Deed of Thomas Crippen to slaves (November 2, 1782), Accomack Co. Deeds 5 (1777–1783), LVA; deed of Caleb Bradford to Annis (December 27, 1802), Accomack Co. Deeds 10 (1800–1804), LVA.

15. In 1779 Virginia law defined citizens as all "white persons born within the territory of this commonwealth." While 1783 and 1786 laws eliminated the word *white* and replaced it with *free*, black Virginians could not vote even if they held property, and the definition of citizenship did not touch on the legal status of emancipated slaves. Hening, *Statutes* 10:129 (1779), 11:323 (1783), 12:261 (1786). Patterson discusses manumission as a symbolic rebirth, returning the alienated slave to the social body, in *Slavery and Social Death,* chap. 8.

16. Deed of Bridgett James to Liddia (May 26, 1789), Accomack Co., Free Negro and Slave Records, Manumissions 1783–1814, LVA. "Planter" is from deed of John Teackle to slaves (September 24, 1787), Accomack Co. Deeds 6 (1783–1788), LVA; "Godfree" is from deed of George Corbin to slaves; "Jubely" from deed of Thomas Ames to slaves (January 8, 1793), Accomack Co. Deeds 7 (1788–1793), LVA; and "Joy" is from deed of Thomas Cropper to slaves (December 25, 1792), Accomack Co. Deeds 7 (1788–1793), LVA.

17. Deed of Richard M. C. Chichester to slaves (April 29, 1806), Fauquier Co. Deeds 16 (1804–1807), LVA.

18. Deed of Ezekiel Tatham to Mathew (July 20, 1790), Accomack Co. Deeds 7 (1788–1793), LVA; will of Ezekiel Tatham (January 27, 1791), Accomack Co. Wills, 1788–1794, LVA. Emphasis added. Mathew was indeed female; Tatham had freed "my negro woman Mathew" for the purpose of "doing Justice to Humanity."

19. The graphs do not, however, represent the annual number of people who gained their freedom, since slaves "freed" by a deed or will in the given year may not have actually received their freedom for several months or even years; delayed manumission was a common phenomenon and is discussed further below in the essay. Peter Albert's study revealed a similar pattern: The annual number of emancipations by deed spiked briefly in 1782–83, declined for a few years, and then rose to a high point in 1800 before turning down again after the turn of the century. The number of emancipations by will per year rose gradually from 1782 to 1795 and maintained a steady level until 1806. Overall, the era of the greatest number of emancipations was the 1790s. See Albert, "Protean Institution," chap. 7.

20. I have used the year in which deed and wills were written rather than the date at which they were recorded in court to trace the trends in manumission. The date at which the document was drafted more accurately reflects changes in sentiment regarding emancipation of slaves

21. I used tax and census records to determine the number of slaves a manumittor held. Because the records are imperfect and often do not include women or itinerants, I had to leave a number of manumittors out of this calculation.

22. I used information contained in the wills themselves to make this determination, since they generally listed all important property, including any slaves *not* freed.

23. Deed of Thomas Madkins to slaves (April 14, 1783), and deed of James Williams to Sarah (August 12, 1783), Mecklenburg Co. Deeds 6 (1779–86), LVA. There were eleven

deeds using these words, three from Mecklenburg County and eight from Charles City County, representing the acts of eight individuals (Thomas Madkins wrote two deeds of manumission, and Samuel Hargrave wrote three). I have been able to verify seven of these individuals as Quakers.

24. Deed of Abel Teackle to slaves (January 1, 1791), Accomack Co. Deeds 7 (1788–93), LVA.

25. Of all the documents, including those which gave no reason for freeing slaves, the proportion of antislavery deeds was 47 percent from 1782 to 1793 and 23 percent from 1794 to 1806.

26. Deed of Hardyman Irby to Eliza (November 23, 1797), Charles City Co. Deeds 4 (1789–1802), LVA.

27. Deed of Martha Turpin to Anica (December 4, 1804), Chesterfield Co. Deeds 17 (1805–1808), LVA.

28. T. Stephen Whitman, *The Price of Freedom: Slavery and Manumission in Baltimore and Early National Maryland* (Lexington: University Press of Kentucky, 1997), chap. 3.

29. Deed of Henry Custis of Bayside to Babel (December 28, 1794), Accomack Co. Deeds 8 (1793–1797), LVA; deed of William Chilton to George (April 24, 1804), Fauquier Co. Deeds 15 (1801–1804), LVA.

30. Wolf, *Race and Liberty in the New Nation,* 68. I would like to be able to compare the price they paid for themselves to the average market price. But because price varied widely according to age and skill level, information about the slaves I rarely have, this is difficult. One intriguing bit of evidence is that Solomon had been valued at seventy-five pounds in Abel West's estate but purchased himself a few months later for eighty-eight pounds; Valuation of Abel West's estate, August 6, 1804, Accomack County Wills, 1804–06, LVA. Other prices seem low and suggest some owners helped their slaves out by offering them a discount on their self-purchase.

31. Deed of Thomas Gaskins to Tom Jessup (April 17, 1796), Lancaster Co. Free Negro and Slave Records, Emancipation Deeds, LVA.

32. Deed of Edward Mitchell to slaves (October 25, 1790), Botetourt Co., Emancipation of Slaves, LVA; deed of Reubin Howard to Minta and Reubin (January 11, 1799), Botetourt Co. Deeds 6 (1796–1799), LVA.

33. Deed of Thomas M. Bayly to Mary Griffin (November 5, 1804), and deed of Mary Griffin to Cyrus Rose Arrow (November 16, 1804), Accomack Co. Deeds 11 (1804–1807), LVA. It is clear that Mary Griffin was African American or else there would have been no reason to identify her as free.

34. Deed of Thomas Wood Potter to George (January 4, 1794), Accomack Co. Deeds 8 (1793–1797), LVA.

35. Samuel Shepherd, *The Statutes at Large of Virginia: From October Session 1792, to December Session 1806, Inclusive, in Three Volumes, (New Series,) Being a Continuation of Hening* (Richmond, Va.: Printed by Samuel Shepherd, 1835–36; reprint, New York: AMS Press, 1970), 1:364. For more discussion of freedom suits, see Michael L. Nicholls, "'The Squint of Freedom': African-American Freedom Suits in Post-Revolutionary Virginia," *Slavery and Abolition* 20 (1999): 47–62.

36. The pattern was similar in the counties studied by Peter Albert in "Protean Institution," 289–290. Tommy Bogger and Suzanne Lebsock also found more women freed in urban areas: Bogger found that 62 percent of the adults manumitted in Norfolk were women, and Lebsock found three-fifths (about 60 percent) of the adults freed by whites in Petersburg were women. Tommy L. Bogger, *Free Blacks in Norfolk, Virginia, 1790–1860: The Darker Side of*

Freedom (Charlottesville: University Press of Virginia, 1997), 13; Suzanne Lebsock, *The Free Women of Petersburg: Status and Culture in a Southern Town, 1784–1860* (New York: W. W. Norton, 1984), 95. My own study includes the towns of Manchester in Chesterfield County, and Warrenton in Fauquier County, but there were so few emancipated slaves in those two towns that my data are inconclusive.

37. Whitman, *Price of Freedom,* chap. 3. Gerald Mullin shows that in eighteenth-century Virginia men ran away more often than women . Gerald W. Mullin, *Flight and Rebellion: Slave Resistance in Eighteenth-Century Virginia* (London: Oxford University Press, 1972).

38. Albert, "Protean Institution," 279; Bogger, *Free Blacks in Norfolk,* 12–17.

39. The average age of newly freed slaves was about twenty-six years for slaves freed by deed and twenty-seven for slaves freed by will. Albert gives a distribution of ages which shows that most slaves were under thirty at the time of their freedom. Albert, "Protean Institution," 286–288.

40. Ibid., 282–286.

41. Kirk Mariner, *Revival's Children: A Religious History of Virginia's Eastern Shore* (Salisbury, Md.: Peninsula Press, 1979), 96–97.

42. Will of William Wilkinson (December 29, 1804), Accomack Co. Wills, 1804–1806, LVA. The courts decided differently on such matters, for it was not clear whether such slaves were legally free after the deed or will was written. See Wolf, *Race and Liberty in the New Nation,* 152–155.

43. Deed of Ann Muir to slaves (April 29, 1806), Accomack Co., Deeds 11 (1804–1807), LVA. Emphasis added. Will of Ann Muir (May 30, 1806), Accomack Co. Wills, 1806–1809, LVA.

44. There were several transactions around Cupid's manumission. Sturman sold Cupid to two others, Richard Baker and Bernard Roe, for one dollar. Baker and Roe promised that Cupid would serve Sturman for one year, and if he did so well he would be freed. Indenture between Sturman, Baker, and Roe (May 17, 1804), Fauquier Co. Deeds 16 (1804–1807), LVA.

45. Caleb bought his freedom for eighty pounds, which was secured to Bayly by bond. Bayly trusted Caleb to raise the funds at some future date. Deed of Richard D. Bayly to Caleb (November 19, 1805), Accomack Co. Deeds 11 (1804–1807), LVA.

46. Richard Drummond Bayly to John Cropper, January 6, 1805, John Cropper Papers, Virginia Historical Society, Richmond.

47. Wolf, *Race and Liberty in the New Nation,* 76.

48. Albert, "Protean Institution," 293.

49. Martin Baker to slaves (December 25, 1789), Chesterfield Co. Deeds 11 (1779–1791), LVA; deed of Thomas Bridgewater to slaves (June 9, 1790), Chesterfield Co. Deeds 11 (1779–1791), LVA; deed of John Baker to slaves (June 9, 1790), Chesterfield Co. Free Negro and Slave Records, LVA; deed of Thomas Bridgwater, Reuben Winfree, and John Baker to William (February 22, 1793), Chesterfield County Deeds 13 (1793–1796), LVA.

50. Will of Richardson Walker (September 22, 1793), Charles City Co. Wills 1 (1789–1808), LVA.

51. Unfortunately, Accomack County's meeting records are not extant; but some of the Quakers there have been written of and identified in other sources.

52. Parramore was a member of the vestry of the then-Anglican church in 1780, but a few years later he played host to Methodist leader Francis Asbury on his 1783 trip through the Eastern Shore. St. George's Parish Vestry book, 1763–1787, photostat, LVA; Kirk Mariner, *Revival's Children,* 21. John Teackle was a member of the Episcopal Vestry in 1810, shown in St. George's Parish, Accomack County, *Records, 1793–1841* (photocopy, 1979), 22, Eastern

Shore Public Library. The deeds are deed of John Teackle to slaves (September 24, 1787), deed of George Corbin to slaves (September 25, 1787), deed of William Parramore to slaves (September 24, 1787), and deed of Charles Stockly to slaves (September 27, 1787), Accomack Co., Deeds 6 (1783–1788), LVA. Though the deeds were written on different days, they were all entered in court on September 27, 1787.

53. Deed of John Cropper to slaves (December 31, 1794), Accomack Co. Deeds 8 (1793–1797), LVA; deed of John S. Ker (March 4, 1806), Accomack Co. Free Negro and Slave Records, Manumissions 1783–1814, LVA; deed of Thomas Evans (December 27, 1791), Accomack Co. Deeds 7 (1788–1793).

54. Anthony Iaccarino suggested Federalist ideas were more consonant with antislavery beliefs than Republican thought was. See Anthony Alfred Iaccarino, "Virginia and the National Contest over Slavery in the Early Republic, 1780–1833" (Ph.D. diss., University of California at Los Angeles, 1999), 56–57, 99.

55. Deed of George Hancock to Will and Hannah (December 15, 1797), Botetourt Co. Deeds 6 (1796–1799), LVA.

56. About a third of those who freed slaves in deeds of manumission could clearly be identified as a members of a particular religious group.

57. Two of the deeds were written by the same person, and one was written by a free black man who bought and then emancipated his wife and child. Thus there were six white individuals whose deeds Mifflin witnessed. Four of these were likely to have been Quakers. The other two may have been Quakers, but the circumstantial evidence is quite scanty. Mifflin himself freed ninety-one slaves in 1775 under the influence of his son Warner Mifflin.

58. See William Wade Hinshaw, *Encyclopedia of American Quaker Genealogy* (Ann Arbor, Mich.: Edwards Brothers, 1936–50).

59. Four were definitely members of a Baptist church, two others were probably members, and circumstantial evidence suggests about seven to eight others were affiliated with the Baptists.

60. This proportion may significantly overestimate the proportion of all manumittors who were Methodists, for Accomack had more manumittors than other counties, and evidence from that region may distort the totals. In Mecklenburg and Botetourt counties as well, however, Methodists seem to have formed a significant proportion of manumittors.

61. Deed of Edward Mitchell to slaves (October 25, 1790), Botetourt Co. Emancipation of Slaves, LVA; deed of James Wright to slaves (September 13, 1791), Botetourt Co. Deeds 4 (1788–1793), LVA; deed of Samuel Mitchell to James Rideout and Charlotte (December 31, 1805), Botetourt Co. Deeds 9 (1805–1809), LVA. And as noted above, Edward Mitchell witnessed the deed of his former slave Reubin Howard, who freed his family in 1799.

62. I do not know why so many ministers should have freed their slaves in that year. Nothing I have read so far in the secondary literature makes 1790 a particularly strong year for manumission.

63. Whitman, *Price of Freedom*.

64. Carl Degler's argument about the absolute nature of American freedom has influenced my thinking here. Degler, *Neither Black nor White.*

65. Legislative Petition of King and Queen Co. (December 2, 1800), LVA.

66. *Virginia Argus,* January 17, 1806.

67. Ibid.

68. Patterson, *Slavery and Social Death,* 340–341.

SEAN CONDON

The Slave Owner's Family and Manumission in the Post-Revolutionary Chesapeake Tidewater

—ʍ—

Evidence from Anne Arundel County Wills, 1790–1820

In the half-century following the American Revolution, thousands of enslaved men, women, and children living on the lands surrounding the Chesapeake Bay gained their legal freedom through manumission. Recent scholarship, focused on the northern half of the region, has argued convincingly that manumission can be understood best as another arena of conflict and compromise between slave and master. The changing nature of slavery in much of Maryland, and especially in the city of Baltimore, including the need for greater slave mobility and the increased likelihood of successful escape, meant that slaves were in a better position to bargain or buy their way out of enslavement and into nominal freedom. As a result slave owners paradoxically used manumission as a strategy for securing labor by exchanging perpetual ownership for an increased assurance that they would have a relatively dependable worker for a period of years.[1] Surpassing an older focus on individual slave owners acting alone,[2] this literature emphasizes the changing relationship between slave and slave owner. By doing so it recaptures much of the drama and conflict of the manumission process, and the meaning of this process for those affected by it.

Certainly the causes and meanings of individual acts of manumission must be located first and foremost in the relationship between master and slave, and Orlando Patterson is correct when he argues that in most slave societies the process of manumission "became an intrinsic part of the process of slavery."[3] But in most corners of the Atlantic world, and certainly in the post–Revolutionary War Chesapeake, manumissions did not occur every day. Rather, manumissions were noteworthy and unusual acts that not only restructured the relationships of individual masters and slaves but also affected, and were in turn shaped by, the families of slave and master, neighbors, and larger communities both real and imagined. This essay considers just one of these larger contexts by examining how family connections and considerations affected slave owners' decisions to manumit. As Walter Johnson has shown, the relationships between the members of white slaveholding families were profoundly affected in myriad ways by slavery, so it is likely that the act of manumission would also affect these relationships.[4] And in the antebellum period, as slavery came to be perceived as a peculiar institution in a bourgeois world, its effect on family relationships and morals was a perennial topic of debate. While there are many ways to address questions of family relationships and identity and their impact on slavery, this essay examines manumission by will in one representative county, Anne Arundel in Maryland, largely through slave owner wills,[5] to assess the importance of the slaveholder's family in the manumission process.[6] Contemporary observers often argued that manumission, and especially manumission by last will and testament, was undertaken by individuals seeking to quiet their consciences at the expense of their children's economic well-being. The evidence from Anne Arundel County wills suggests otherwise. Testators with children or grandchildren were much less likely to manumit their slaves than their counterparts who did not have children, and if they did emancipate, it was likely to be selective, greatly delayed, or hedged with other qualifiers. Furthermore, the patterns of manumission, combined with the way slave owners authored their wills, suggest that parents and grandparents who did manumit usually considered the perceived needs of their offspring before manumission. These strategies, at least in Anne Arundel County, centered on efforts to secure the labor of bondservants for the benefit of the slave-owning family in a time and place where the institution of slavery was undergoing profound change.

Located on the state's lower Western Shore immediately to the south of rapidly growing Baltimore, Anne Arundel County remained predominantly rural throughout the period. County residents continued to produce tobacco in large quantities, while wheat and other grains grown for export, and vegetables, fruit, meat and wood produced for the growing urban market in Baltimore changed but did not completely transform, the county's economy.[7] The county grew very slowly in the decades following the Revolutionary War, from slightly more than 22,500 people in 1790 to roughly 27,200 by 1820. Slaves made up almost 45 percent of the county's population in 1790, and 40 percent three decades later. Through manumission legally free blacks were the only portion of the county's population that experienced significant growth. In 1790, 804 legally free blacks were enumerated, and the population grew to 3,382 by 1820, an increase of more than 400 percent.[8] Like other areas in the post-Revolutionary Chesapeake, roughly equal numbers of men and women were manumitted. As others have shown, this pattern in the Chesapeake differs from the manumission pattern elsewhere in the Americas, where females comprised 60 to 65 percent of those freed by manumission. While manumission by deed had been available to slave owners and slaves throughout the eighteenth century in Maryland, manumission by will was not made legal until 1790. The 1790 law required that at the time of their release manumitted slaves were to be less than fifty years old and be able "to work and gain a sufficient maintenance and livelihood." The law prohibited manumissions if they were executed to the detriment of a testator's or testatrix's creditors or drawn up during an owner's last illness. In 1796 the maximum age for manumission was lowered from fifty to forty-five, and the final illness restriction was eliminated.[10] As table 1 shows, more manumissions occurred in every decade through the 1810s.[11] Because the total slave population of the county did remain rather stable during this period, the annual rate of manumission increased throughout the period under consideration. The rate for the 1780s was two slaves manumitted for every thousand per year, jumping to six per thousand in the 1790s, seven per thousand the decade after that, and eleven per thousand the second decade of the century. This rate of manumission, especially after 1790, is much closer to rates found for Spanish America and Brazil than for the U.S. South in the late antebellum period.[12]

TABLE 1. Manumissions in Anne Arundel County, Maryland, 1780–1819

Decade	Slaves freed by deed	Slaves freed by will	Percentage freed by will	Total
1780–89	215	—	—	215
1790–99	448	125	21.8	573
1800–09	630	235	27.2	865
1810–19	858	308	26.4	1,166
Total	2,151	668	23.7	2,819

How did the age and composition of a slave owner's family affect his or her decision to emancipate slaves? Contemporary opponents of manumission implicitly argued that one's family made no difference because those interested in manumission were acting without taking their families into consideration. In 1790 a letter to the *Annapolis Maryland Gazette,* written by "A True Friend to Union," argued that emancipation would lead to economic ruin for a great many families. The danger identified by "True Friend" concerned the long-term ramifications of the act of manumission: "A man dies, for instance, possessed of several slaves. He gives his land to a son or sons, but having daughters to provide for, he leaves each of them a number of Negroes, according to his circumstances, for the support of those daughters. Their hire, with the industry of their mistresses, yields a competency for the support of all. Some of the girls have their education to finish. Take away their support, and you leave them to the world as beggars."[13] In a 1789 speech arguing for the legalization of manumission by will, William Pinkney noted the objections to a liberalization of manumission laws and attempted to refute each one. Pinkney hoped to dispel the argument that "testators may impoverish their families by inconsiderate manumissions in their last sickness. They may be frightened by preachers, refined moralists, and others, when the mind is easily alarmed and incapable of its usual resistance." Pinkney did not deny that this is what would happen; rather, he argued that substantive justice often involved sacrifice, an argument that likely reassured few opponents of manumission. As long as the owner was of sound mind and he gave his consent to manumissions, it did not matter how the person was convinced to relinquish his slaves, as long as fraud was not involved: "Should he reduce his family to beggary by it, I should not be one to repine at the deed. I should glory in the cause of their distress, while I wished them a more honest patrimony."[14]

Despite these contemporary assumptions, the evidence contained in Anne Arundel County wills suggests that slave-owning fathers and mothers were less likely to manumit slaves and more likely to delay freedom or encumber it with restrictions than their counterparts who did not have children. In table 2, which includes the 328 wills probated in Anne Arundel County from 1794 to 1818 where the decedent mentioned at least one slave, we can see that certain family relationships did condition the pattern of manumission.[15] The "At least one slave manumitted" column includes the 155 wills where at least slave was manumitted, and it includes ten wills that were conclusively linked to manumission deeds. This table distinguishes among decedents who mentioned children, decedents that mentioned at least one grandchild, and decedents that mentioned neither children nor grandchildren.[16]

TABLE 2. Manumissions in wills that mention slaves in Anne Arundel County, Maryland, 1794–1818, by the mention of children and grandchildren

Slave owner's family	No manumission	At least one slave manumitted	Total number
At least one child, no grandchildren mentioned	63.3%	36.7%	147
At least one grandchild mentioned	50.7%	49.3%	71
No children or grandchildren mentioned	31.8%	68.2%	110
Total	52.7%	47.3%	328

Of the 110 testators who mentioned at least one slave but did not mention any children or grandchildren, nearly two out of every three freed at least one slave in their wills. Of the 147 who mentioned children but not grandchildren, only one-third manumitted at least one slave. The likelihood that a parent manumitted slaves increased if that parent mentioned at least one grandchild—as the table shows, the rate of manumission increased from 37 percent to more than 49 percent. Why would grandparents be more likely to manumit than parents? It is probable that many parents whose children had reached adult-hood and had children of their own had already passed property to those children, even if they maintained legal control until the time of their death.[17] It may be the case that providing for children was considered more essential than providing for grandchildren. Men were also less likely to manumit if they were survived by a widow: Roughly 25 percent of married men in this sample manumitted at least one slave, while 40 percent of men not mentioning a surviving spouse freed at least one slave.[18]

Not only did decedents with children manumit less often than those who did not, they were also more likely to delay the freedom of slaves. Tyler Baldwin's will, probated in 1795, provides an example of a slave-owning parent who freed his slaves but did so in a way that would not seriously affect his sons' patrimony. An apparent widower, Baldwin mentioned three children in his will. The oldest child, a married daughter, received only a horse from her father. Baldwin left the bulk of his estate to his two young sons. He directed his real and personal property to be liquidated for their support, and he wanted his three slaves to benefit them as well, although he made manumission part of the equation. Jacob was to receive his freedom four years after the making of the will, if he paid Baldwin's estate fifty pounds within that time, with the money expressly going to "support my two children."[19] Baldwin's two other slaves, twelve-year-old Jim and a woman Nann, were "to go with my children towards there [sic] support and education" until they each reached the age of fifty, at which point they were to be freed.[20] Overall, of the slave owners like Tyler Baldwin who had children and who manumitted at least one slave, 84.8 percent of the slaves freed (or 162 of 191) were granted delayed manumission; that is, they were supposed to receive their freedom at some point often far into the future. Of those who freed slaves and did not have any direct descendants, slightly less than 50 percent of all slaves manumitted (49.8%, or 155 of 311) were granted a delayed manumission.[21]

Along with being more likely to delay manumission, slave-owning decedents with children and grandchildren also tended to selectively manumit rather than free all of their slaves. Caleb Dorsey, who died in 1795, provides one graphic example. At the time of his death Dorsey owned forty-five slaves. He distributed forty-three of those slaves to five sons, four daughters, two grandchildren, and his wife Rebecca. Only two of the slaves, Peter and Dick, both aged forty-five according to Dorsey, were to serve Rebecca for three years, and then they were to be emancipated.[22] How well did Caleb Dorsey exemplify Anne Arundel slave-owning parents as a whole? One test compares wills where manumissions were clearly selective and wills where testators unambiguously freed all of their slaves. In the Anne Arundel sample there are twenty-nine wills where it is clear that one or more slaves were freed while others were not, and nineteen wills where it is clear that the testator freed all of his or her slaves.

Of the twenty-nine *selective* manumissions, people who were parents or grandparents authored twenty-three, or nearly 80 percent. Of the nineteen *complete* manumissions, only six, or less than one-third, were authored by parents or grandparents.

In addition to being selective and delaying manumission more frequently than their counterparts without offspring, there were other ways that slave-owning parents attached strings to the gift of freedom. Slave owners with families were more likely to require that any children that enslaved women bore prior to that woman's eventual freedom would have to serve long periods in slavery themselves. Achsah Howard's will, probated in 1799, is illustrative. Along with granting land to her two daughters, Howard also distributed nine slaves among two sons and two daughters. Four of the slaves were men, and none of those four were freed. Howard's three enslaved women were to be granted their freedom, if and when they reached the state-mandated maximum age of forty-five. The two children mentioned, as well any children born to the women before they reached the age of forty-five, would themselves have to remain enslaved until the age of forty-five until they were to achieve their legal freedom.[23] Occasionally, slave-owning parents would offer gradual emancipation to female slaves but explicitly deny freedom to any children born prior to the woman's freedom. Mary Scott died in 1804 and bequeathed three male and three female slaves to a son and two grandchildren. All six of the slaves were to be free when they reached the age of thirty-five, but Mary added further instructions: "I also give and bequeath all the children which the said Negroes may have until they arrive at the age mentioned unto the said David Scott to be subject to his will and disposal forever."[24] The frequency with which these kinds of instructions were left and their level of detail almost suggest that slave-owning parents were attempting to calibrate the size of their children's labor force. Occasionally, the tension between granting freedom and providing for offspring led to gifts of dubious benefit and legality. William Fennell's 1802 will granted one slave to each of his four children and one to his granddaughter. Fennell did free an enslaved woman named June, who was to be "free and at full liberty" at his death. For Fennell, "full liberty" no doubt meant something different than it did to June, for he immediately followed this emancipation with the following instructions: "If she should have any children after her freedom to be equally divided between my Daughters Ruthey, Patience and my Grandson Joseph Lowery."[25]

Given these patterns it is not surprising that some people living in the post–Revolutionary War Chesapeake realized that not having to provide for dependents could make one more prone to free his or her slaves. A trial in 1831 suggests that at least one enslaved man who wanted to seize freedom believed this phenomenon happened often enough to use it in crafting a plausible narrative of freedom. The man was captured with what proved to be a forged certificate of freedom, which read: "Know all men by this present that the said negro boy was the property of my onkle, Richard Johnson, living near the mouth of Monocosa. He deceased 1821. He died without any airs. He never was married. Therefore he maid all his negroes free by his will and testament."[26] The wording of this document suggests that if a slave owner did not have children, it was expected that he or she would free their slaves. This is not to say that slave owners without children invariably freed their slaves, or that slave-owning parents never manumitted any slaves. What these previous patterns suggest is that when slave-owning parents freed some or all of their slaves in their wills, these provisions were not divorced from considerations of their families.

Turning from the quantitative pattern to the structure of the wills themselves, it appears that single people who manumitted slaves in their wills were generally less concerned about what happened with the balance of their property, while slave-owning parents were likely to consider manumission as part of a larger strategy of family provision for the future. For example, the only relative mentioned in Joshua Merriken's will was his mother, so it is likely that he died unmarried and relatively young. His will simply granted freedom to "Negro man Jack," and then gave the rest of his property to his "loving mother Elizabeth."[27] For slave-owning parents, manumission typically was subordinated to other considerations in their wills. The vast majority of fathers followed the same general formula. First they distributed their land (if any), then their slaves, then other personal property. If manumissions were included, they either came at the end of the will, or as the decedent specified which heir would receive which slaves. When Zachariah Duvall and Nicholas Gassaway executed their wills in the fall of 1805, both were landowners and slave owners and both were married with children. Duvall was the father of three sons and two daughters, while Gassaway had three underage sons. Both men began their wills with bequests of land to their wives: Duvall's wife was granted all of his land during her widowhood, while Amelia Gassaway was given 360 acres of land for her use until she died. Both men provided equal or roughly equal portions to their children (or at least to their sons). Gassaway's youngest son Berry was to receive the dwelling plantation in Anne Arundel County, while the other two sons, Hanson and John, were to split Gassaway's other lands. Duvall wanted his land and his personal estate "to be valued by two proper men of my children's choosing and if either of them has more in value they are to pay the others until each is made equal." The personal estate of Duvall was to be divided by his two daughters, while Gassaway's sons each received feather beds, two slaves, and some individual horses. At this point Gassaway's will ends, while Duvall makes provisions to free seven slaves ranging in age from sixteen to four, when each arrived at the age of thirty-one.[28] Duvall's bestowal of freedom was not prefaced by any statement regarding slavery, and it was subordinated to the rest of his instructions. While Duvall placed his manumission near the end of his will, other parents like Ruth Dorsey integrated delayed manumission into their bequests to offspring. Dorsey did not have any land to bequeath, but she granted six silver spoons to her son Johnsa, clothes to her daughter Ruth, and a slave to each of three grandchildren. Then she mentioned that man Jim should be sold for four years and then freed, and the money raised should go toward the maintenance of her son Levin, who was given the bulk of Dorsey's estate. Dorsey then continued on with her bequests to other family members.[29]

Of course, even with this subordination or integration of manumission into the rest of a will, testators often betrayed some concern that specific items in their will would not be carried out by their families or executors. Sometimes manumission by will has been portrayed as the simplest method of emancipation: the owner retained use of the slave until death, and then the slave received his or her freedom.[30] However, when the slave owner is conceptualized as a mother or father expected to provide for his or her children, the process of manumission by will becomes a much more complicated and uncertain enterprise. Anne Arundel testators often realized as much and employed many different strategies to deal with this uncertainty. Some, like Benjamin Carr, who freed one slave in his 1796 will, requested that a separate deed of manumission be filed in order to guarantee that the manumission would be carried out.[31] Others tried to make gifts and other bequests conditional on carrying out the provisions of a manumission. William Armiger promised all of his personal estate to his sons Leonard and Benjamin if they followed through on his instructions to "discharge my negro woman Priscilla by manumission from all claims of service and right of property from all manner of persons whatsoever."[32] Other people attempted to penalize offspring who tried to avoid manumitting a slave or slaves bequeathed to them. Samuel Musgrove granted eight slaves to six different children and grandchildren, and each slave was promised freedom at some point in the future, most of them at age thirty. Musgrove firmly advised at the end of his will, "I order none of the above mentioned negroes be sent or sold out of the state and if contrary to this my will any of them is sent or sold out of the state I hereby set him or her so sent free."[33] While obviously intended as a stern warning to his offspring, it is unclear how such a provision could ever be enforced. When Sarah Gray freed her slaves at her death, she admonished her grandchildren that "no heir or representative of mine shall have or exercise any sort of authority or mastership over them or any of them" after they were freed. A few testators mentioned their desire to free some slaves, but left the final decision up to those who survived them. For example, in 1793, Joshua Yates stated, "It is my wish and desire that all my Negroes should become free at the death of my said wife. This, however, to be entirely at her pleasure and discretion."[34]

These requests, pleadings, and occasional threats suggest that a decision to manumit slaves in a will could lead to severe family conflict.[35] Family members who felt snubbed by the provisions of a will had many options, options which often jeopardized promises of freedom. Thomas Boone freed two slaves in his will, but his relatives tried to prove that he was not competent when the will was made. At a hearing to determine Boone's competency one deponent bitterly exclaimed that he "was acquainted with the said Thomas Boone from his infancy, that he . . . never did think the said Boone very capable of managing his affairs as other men did, that he was a soft-headed man."[36] If a husband's will granted less than the dower right, then a wife could refuse the will's provision and claim her dower right. In one case the widow's claim of dower meant that there was not enough personal property left to pay the estate's debts, so she was able to claim that person as a slave for life.[37]

In some cases the actions of slave owners were constrained by prior instructions left by other family members. In 1801 county resident Mary Ann Wood died, leaving a personal estate valued at $959.60. Fourteen slaves were listed in the inventory, comprising $872 of the total estate value. Wood was seventeen years old and single at the time of her death, survived only by her widowed mother. She bequeathed her land to her mother and her personal property to a cousin, and she willed that all of her slaves were to be free, except Nanny, who was to serve Wood's mother until her death. However, strings had been attached by Mary Ann's father, Zebedee, who had died more than thirteen years earlier. Zebedee's will granted all of his property, real and personal, to Mary Ann, who was his only daughter, but he added that if Mary Ann were to die without issue, then all of the property descended to Zebedee's widow, who was to hold onto the property until death or remarriage, and then the property was to go to Zebedee's brother and sisters. Since Mary Ann died without heirs, and because her mother had remarried in the meantime, Zebedee's heirs and his widow seized the slaves. At least one slave, Grace, petitioned the county court for her freedom, and it was granted. But seven years after Mary Ann Wood's death, the judgment in favor of Grace's freedom was overturned by the court of appeals, and she was reenslaved.[39]

Despite the fact that a slave owner's decision to manumit could spark conflict within the family left behind, it does seem clear that most slave-owning parents who manumitted slaves did so in ways that recognized the assumed needs of their families. There are many possible ways that family connections could have led to the decision to manumit, and the wills themselves provide important clues. In a few cases slave owners were carrying out the requests of kin who had wished that certain slaves be freed. Some antislavery voices suggested that slave owners should free slaves in order to prevent the evils of slavery from corrupting their children, and it is possible that other slave owners may have sought to distance their families from the institution in order to take advantage of other economic opportunities that may have appeared more promising than slave-powered agricultural enterprises. However, as the evidence below shows, neither diversification nor a desire to inculcate certain values in their children appears to have been a driving force behind slave owner family strategies. Rather, it was the relative instability of slavery in the county following the Revolution—including the ramifications of moving away from tobacco as the primary crop, and the greater slave mobility and avenues for slaves to obtain their freedom—that made manumission one possible strategy to actually secure for a term of years the labor of perpetual bondservants for the future benefit of the slave-owning family.

In a few cases strong family connections actually served as a motive for manumission: a handful of slave owners stated that they were freeing slaves to fulfill the wishes of a deceased loved one. Richard Sprigg, one of the wealthiest men in the county, at his death in 1798 willed dozens of slaves to his four daughters and several granddaughters. Five of his slaves were freed, and he noted that this selective emancipation was in memory of his wife: "And whereas I have heretofore been requested by my faithful friend and wife (whose memory is and ever will be dear to me) to manumit some of our slaves for their faithful services. I do therefore in consideration thereof and that my own mind most cheerfully assent to such request." Sprigg manumitted four brothers: Daniel, a shoemaker, Ned, a carpenter, Charles and David, house servants, and "yellow woman Bet and her youngest child Charles."[40] In 1790 Sarah Chew made out a will which requested her executor should file a deed freeing boys John and William when they reached the age of twenty-one. This act, she said, was "agreeable to the dying request of my late dear son Samuel Chew."[41]

Another possible way that manumission might have been part of a family strategy is as a response to the moribund agricultural economy of the post-Revolutionary Chesapeake. While many sought relief from the relative economic doldrums by seeking lands west of the Appalachian mountains, some families tried to lessen their reliance on tobacco and slavery but still remain in the region. Phillip Hamilton has recently argued that immediately following the Revolutionary War, St. George Tucker began stressing to his children "to rely on their talents and abilities rather than on patrons and connections with the declining landowning elite. He also drilled into them the importance of professional training, preferably in the law, as a way to support a family free from dependence on the land."[42] Others in Virginia also attempted to diversify away from slavery, but for the most part those who stayed generally followed the trajectory mapped out by James Madison. Theoretically opposed to slavery, Madison did attempt in the 1790s to diversify, including an attempt at land speculation in New York. But by 1820 Madison wrote in response to a young correspondent that in terms of economics, maintaining a slave-labor plantation was preferable to any other option then available in the state, whether stocks or bonds, cultivating the land with hired labor, or renting the land out to others.[43] In Maryland, at least in the northern part of the state, opportunities to pursue other options might have been greater. Christopher Phillips's recent work suggests that in the Baltimore area, planters appeared to have turned away from slave owning as a way to build capital: "Inheritance patterns in probate records during the late eighteenth and early nineteenth centuries suggest that planters consciously stopped bequeathing slaves to their surviving loved ones; instead, they often left instructions to the executors of the estates to sell them and invest the proceeds in enterprises offering more secure returns."[44] Phillips argues that the increased ability of slaves to "steal themselves" away to free-soil areas made depending on slave labor less reliable than other forms of investment.

Anne Arundel is an important case to examine because it was in close proximity to Baltimore, and within the growing city's economic and cultural orbit. But unlike Baltimore, Anne Arundel had long been a predominantly slave-labor county, where tobacco remained an important crop. It appears that diversification did become an option in Anne Arundel, but manumission does not appear to have been an important part of that particular strategy. During the colonial period in the Chesapeake there was an extreme reluctance to liquidate estates even to make a division of assets easier, or to ensure equality of shares. In addition rarely were children granted cash instead of land or chattels. Lois Carr argues that testators were very interested in maintaining the productive elements of the family estate: "Chesapeake planters evidently put great value on keeping land and slaves in the family."[45] In the postwar years testators became much more willing to liquidate the estate, either to provide for more equal shares, or to invest the proceeds in a different resource. Of the 328 slave owners who left wills, slightly more than 12 percent wanted the bulk of their property liquidated and distributed. But slave owners who did not manumit were twice as likely to liquidate land and slaves as those who did manumit. Likewise, 3 percent of slave-owning testators directed that land or slaves be converted into stock or other intangible assets; again, it appears that slave owners who did not manumit were roughly twice as likely to diversify their family fortunes. Most of those who owned bank stock or other intangible assets seem to have considered them in addition to, not in place of, an investment in slaves. Upton Scott of Annapolis, who died in 1814 married but childless, granted the bulk of his property to the children of his deceased nephew. Four of these children received gifts of cash while three received a number of slaves as well as shares of stock. When investment in stocks became an alternative to a continuation of slave owning, the actual transition often had very negative ramifications for the slaves affected. Roger Ditty died in 1804, and he wanted his real estate sold when his youngest child reached adulthood, and the proceeds shared equally by all of his children. He also wanted all of his personal property (including slaves) to be sold and the proceeds put toward the purchase of bank stock for the benefit of his underage children.[47] Eleanor Browning died in 1814 and granted the bulk of her property to her niece Eleanor Councilman. Included in that bequest, Councilman received two of Browning's three slaves, Frisby and Nan Williams, who were both to be sold and the money raised was to be converted into bank stock for her niece.[48] In sum, diversification toward intangible assets was taking place, but it was not strongly connected with manumission.

Associated with economic diversification was a potential change in economic mindset, namely, a viewpoint which argued, or at least suggested, that slave-owning parents would support their children more effectively by not allowing them to become slave owners.[49] Cynthia Lynn Lyerly argues that one of the biggest obstacles faced by antislavery Methodists "was southerners' sense of obligation to their children. Custom and duty required that parents leave their children an inheritance." Slave owners would claim that they had not chosen slavery, and they could not give it up without endangering the economic well-being of their children. Lyerly argues that Methodists developed an argument that parents should "free their children from the pollution of slavery. Instead of passively viewing slavery as a burden passed on to innocent children, Methodists urged parents to . . . break the baneful cycle for the rising generation. . . . Since Methodists connected slavery to related sins of pride, greed, lust and cruelty, emancipating patriarchs were removing their descendants from a context of perpetual temptation."[50]

Is there evidence in Anne Arundel wills that suggests that slave-owning parents were interested in providing a "more honest patrimony" as a strategy for economic success? While there is no overall pattern suggesting that those parents interested in inculcating capitalistic values were more likely to manumit, some wills do hint that manumission could be used in new economic strategies. Frederick Grammar's 1818 will promised freedom to Frank Tucker on the first day of January, 1821, with a couple of conditions. First, Tucker had to "behave himself well and faithfully." Second, once "free" Tucker had to remain in the employ of Grammar's nephew Gottleb "as long as my said nephew shall carry on the business or occupation of a baker in the city of Annapolis." The nephew was to pay Tucker eight dollars a month and provide him with a suit of summer clothes once a year.[51] While a unique (and not quite legal) effort to make his nephew an employer rather than a slave owner, Grammar's concern over proper capitalistic values seems to start and finish with Frank Tucker, not his nephew.

A more compelling case might be the will authored by Helen Weedon. An owner of six slaves, Weedon also owned enough personal property for her estate to be in the top 35 percent of estates in a sample taken from the county from 1800 to 1816. Weedon wanted her land (which amounted to one hundred acres) and her personal property sold and the money divided by her two youngest sons, Cloudberry and Lemuel. Two of Weedon's slaves were to be freed, and the others appear to have been sold. In addition, the youngest son, Lemuel, was to be schooled for two years and then bound as an apprentice "to some respectable mechanick to learn some good trade whereby he may be qualified and enabled the more easily to attain a livelihood when he comes of age."[52] Weedon's will does suggest that she was trying to alter the trajectory of at least one son's life, but it appears that the sale of some slaves rather than wholesale manumission was the engine behind this transformation. Anne Arundel seems to fit a pattern of the larger Chesapeake: The Methodist critique of slavery became absorbed by the dominant slave-owning culture. Slave-owning parents wishing to inculcate traits helpful in a market society found that their desire to hold onto slaves strengthened, not weakened, over time. As David Allmendinger shows this was certainly the case for agricultural reformer and proslavery apologist Edmund Ruffin. Allmendinger argues convincingly that Ruffin developed a plan not only designed "to pass the family fortune down the line to the next generation; here was the man with the values of Franklin, using inheritance to instill the virtues of industry and hard work."[53]

So it appears that if there was a long-term family strategy attached to manumission in Anne Arundel County, it was not strongly connected either to a strategy of diversification away from land and slaves or one explicitly concerned with the moral character of the rising generation. A much more common phenomenon was the effort of dying slave owners to maintain continuity in their estate after their death, as Stephen Whitman has recently argued.[54] The death of an owner was often one of the most traumatic events in the life of a slave, for families and friends might be separated as an estate was divided among the heirs or if slaves were sold to satisfy the claim of creditors. This perennial fear of slaves in the United States mixed with more local changes increased both the motive and the opportunities of slaves to become legally free. One of those developments—the growth of a large city like Baltimore with a large and growing free black population and a great need for labor—created a haven that could provide a cover for runaway slaves from neighboring rural counties. And potential escapees from slavery could also head to the "free state" of neighboring Pennsylvania. The postwar period also greatly increased the threat of forced migration of slaves out of the state; and through manumissions and freedom suits, many local slaves were living evidence that legal freedom was a definite possibility. Whitman argues that slave owners would provide for delayed manumissions in their wills hoping this concession "would induce their slaves to continue to give them reliable service and later provide income-generating labor for their heirs."[56] While the opportunities for slaves were greater in the city than in the countryside, what Whitman found in Baltimore can also be seen in Anne Arundel County. When granting slaves to young children, whether they were sons and daughters or nieces or nephews, slave owners were very likely to grant delayed freedom and direct that the money raised be given to the child for his or her maintenance. Tyler Baldwin's will, discussed above, is a good example. Baldwin's two sons received more than twelve pounds per year for four years from Jacob, and because of the relatively limited term of service, Jacob had a powerful incentive to turn over the fruit of his labor during that time.

This strategy of manumission as insurance seems to have been most pronounced on estates where tobacco production had been abandoned. Nearly every account of manumission in the post-Revolutionary Chesapeake has mentioned the depression in the tobacco economy as an important contributing factor in the increase in manumissions. When tobacco was the main or at least significant crop, steady labor was required for most of the year. Wheat, on the other hand, required labor inputs only at planting and harvest. Given the seasonal labor requirements of the two crops, tobacco planters could introduce wheat agriculture into the crop mix without substantially altering their labor requirements. If, however, tobacco production was abandoned in favor of wheat and other grains, then those in control of the land would be better off hiring seasonal labor for planting and harvest instead of purchasing slave laborers.[57] There are two potential problems with this argument, however. First, while it does explain how a landholder should behave if he or she did not already possess laborers, it is unclear how it would affect those who already owned slaves. Mary Jeske's work on Carrollton Manor tenants in nearby Frederick County shows that both tobacco production and slaveholding declined in the years following the Revolutionary War. Jeske argues that the primary reason for this decline was the gradual replacement of tenants of English descent who had migrated from southern Maryland with tenants from German communities migrating from Pennsylvania. Tenants who already owned slaves made the transition from tobacco to wheat without immediately changing their source of labor. The proportion of English decedents who owned slaves declined after 1800, not due to manumission, but to the fact that "once grain production dominated the manor, those who did not already own slaves were probably less likely to acquire them."[58] The second reason that the transformation from tobacco to wheat might not mean a drastic reduction in the labor force was that individuals who made the switch from planter to farmer would be able to provide other tasks to keep their labor force occupied. When wheat was combined with corn production, it kept laborers occupied for much of the growing season, and the growth of urban areas like Baltimore created markets for garden crops.[59] Thus it is important to point out that an abandonment of tobacco did not automatically lead to a need to reduce the size of one's labor force.

The movement away from tobacco suggests two main possible strategies. One, slave owners who did not grow tobacco had a reduced need for enslaved laborers and used manumission (or sale) as one way to reduce the size of their labor force.[60] And two, a movement away from tobacco production required a more flexible labor force, and this flexibility required, or at least suggested, the use of manumission as an incentive or as insurance. This need for "flexibility" manifested itself in several ways. First, the wheat harvest required intensive amounts of labor for only a short period of time, making slave hiring much more widespread. As Sarah Hughes has argued: "Hiring was a means of adjusting a labor system initiated when tobacco was the profitable staple crop to the needs of the smaller grain-livestock farms of the late eighteenth century. The hire of slaves introduced flexibility in allocating workers in a diversified rural economy with low profit margins."[61] Also, relative to tobacco cultivated largely by hoe and human power, wheat culture and general farming utilized the plow and animal power and created the need for "smaller groups of strong, specialized, highly trained workers."[62] Along with learning new skills, many slaves had to become more mobile in order to ship and mill wheat, market garden crops, and transport lumber to urban markets.[63] These changes allowed many slaves to earn more outside the narrow confines of the tobacco plantation and made much of the day-to-day supervision of slaves more difficult than it had been when tobacco was the focus of agricultural enterprise.[64]

The possible impact of a more mobile, skilled, and less supervised labor force is at least suggested by a comparison of the family structures and the evidence of economic activity among those testators who manumitted at least one slave. Table 3 shows the results of linking 184 slave owner wills to estate inventories for the years 1800 to 1816. Estates are placed into one of three categories. To be included in the first category, "Farms with evidence of tobacco production," estates had either at least one hogshead of tobacco, a mention of tobacco in the field, or hanging to be cured. "Farms with no evidence of tobacco production" are inventories where farming tools were present but no tobacco is mentioned (crops other than tobacco are usually but not always mentioned). The third group, "Nonfarms," are inventories where no farming implements or crops were present. Controlling for other variables, testators with children or grandchildren were usually much less likely to manumit slaves than were testators who had no children. What this table suggests is that parents on non-tobacco-producing farms appear to have been more likely to manumit slaves than parents on tobacco farms. In addition testators who were not on farms and who manumitted slaves were much more likely to not have children or grandchildren. This may be because slave labor might have been an even more important part of their estates: without farm crops, these enslaved laborers might have been the main or the sole source of income. These numbers suggest that slave-labor farms not producing tobacco might have been more willing to turn to manumission to safeguard a portion of their labor force for surviving family members.

TABLE 3. Manumission rate by evidence of tobacco production, controlling
for the presence of children, Anne Arundel County, Maryland,
wills and inventories, 1800–1816

Estate type	Wills in which children are mentioned	Wills in which no children are mentioned
Farms with evidence of tobacco production (N = 73)	13.4%	50.0%
Farms with no evidence of tobacco production (N = 83)	43.9%	50.0%
Nonfarms (N = 28)	38.5%	66.7%

John Boone's case shows how manumission could be used to increase the
flexibility of labor while also ensuring that that labor would be there when the
family needed it. The estate's inventory, recorded in October 1807, found
wheat, corn, and rye but no evidence of tobacco production. Boone granted his
land to his wife during her life and then to two of his children to share. Boone
distributed ten slaves among his wife and his three children. All of the slaves
were to be free at different points in the future, and the children of the six
female slaves were themselves to serve until age thirty-five. Three of the slaves
had actually been manumitted by other people, and they had been either
bequeathed or purchased by Boone to work on his farm. Boone's family had a
flexible labor force, one that could be hired out with less risk of running
away.[65] Even more flexibility would be achieved if adult women continued to
live near their term-slave offspring after they themselves reached freedom.
Levin Warfield died in 1812 and provided for the freedom of all seven of his
slaves. Frank was to serve Warfield's executrix for two years for the support of
Warfield's underage children, "and if he shall serve faithfully and truly until
next Christmas come two years then he is to be free." Other slaves were to gain
freedom from fourteen to twenty-five years into the future, including Hen,
who was to serve for fourteen years "the highest bidder among [Warfield's
nine] children," who was also to receive "all the increase of her body until each
shall arrive at the age of thirty and then be free."[66]

The movement away from tobacco also tended to mean a need for fewer
laborers overall. It appears that some may have used delayed manumission in
an effort to recalibrate their labor force. To see how this recalibration might
have worked, it is instructive to examine the case of John Henry Maccubbin.
Maccubbin's will, authored a few months before his death in 1802, granted
freedom to all the slaves in his estate. Twenty-four slaves were counted in his
inventory, and all but three were bequeathed to Maccubbin's only son, also
named John Henry (three enslaved girls were bequeathed to three friends of
the family). Maccubbin was unusually generous in that he granted immediate
freedom to his enslaved man Robert and gave Robert "200 acres lying on the

north side of back creek and adjoining the land of William Gooding." Maccubbin granted delayed freedom to his entire labor force, but the ages when freedom would be achieved were much younger than the maximum limit of forty-five years; enslaved men were to receive their freedom at the age of thirty, and women had to serve until the age of twenty-five. Even with this relatively early age at freedom, the Maccubbin slaveholdings would not be drastically reduced for a long period of time. Assuming for the moment that none of the slaves died before they came of age, the Maccubbin estate would still have twenty slaves after Maccubbin's death, sixteen slaves five years later, thirteen in 1824, and eleven a full fifteen years after the execution of the will.[67] These calculations do not even take into account any children born to enslaved women with time left to serve.

Of course, providing positive incentives like manumission in the face of greater slave mobility and widened avenues of freedom was not the only possible response. Many slave owners instituted more rigorous and methodical regimes of supervision and used interstate sale as a powerful disciplinary weapon. County resident Gassaway Rawlings placed a number of advertisements for runaway slaves in local newspapers in the years between the Revolutionary War and the War of 1812, and many of these advertisements, like the one for Henny in 1783, stated that the slave would try to pass for free, "as several have been lately set free in the neighborhood."[68] Along with the complications caused by manumission, other postwar developments also affected Rawlings's efforts to keep his slaves working for him. In June 1803 twenty-two-year-old York left him, and along with "try[ing] to pass as a free man," York would try to make it to Baltimore, "as he frequently said that all that went there could get employed as a hireling."[69] In 1809 Ben Tuck escaped from Rawlings and was believed to be somewhere in the local area, but given Tuck's family connections and work history, it could have been any one of a number of places. Before being purchased by Rawlings, Tuck had been owned by Benjamin Stewart, who had rented him out to a Captain Leonard. Tuck's relations were "living at the different quarters of the Mr. Stewarts"; his mother lived at Bridge Mill Quarter, and he had a wife who lived at Mr. Claggetts near Queen Anne.[70] Rawlings died in 1812, and the language of his last will betrays a determination that the Rawlings family would continue to be slave owners despite the efforts of slaves themselves to make manifest a quite different destiny. Of the twenty slaves he owned, he bequeathed twelve, including Ben Tuck, to his grandson William Gassaway Sanders. He gave and bequeathed the twelve "unto my grandson . . . and his childrens children and their great great grandchildren as long as any of them shall be found alive."[71]

Reactions such as Rawlings's are reminders that manumission was far from the only tool available to slave owners. The evidence from Anne Arundel County wills as a whole makes it clear that close family connections, especially the presence of children, served to limit the decision to manumit as well as the terms of freedom. However, these patterns, combined with the way slave owners authored their wills, suggest that when parents and grandparents did manumit they usually considered the perceived needs of their offspring before manumission. And in Anne Arundel these considerations appear to have centered on efforts to safeguard a reliance on coerced labor for the future of the family-farm enterprise. It would be fruitful to investigate how family ties and family expectations influenced the pace and pattern of manumission in slave societies elsewhere in the Atlantic world. Scholars have long noticed that manumission rates in the antebellum U.S. South were among the lowest in the Atlantic world,[72] and arguments have usually focused on either the structural or cultural factors behind this low rate of manumission. Investigations of manumission from the context of the family might be one way to integrate structural and cultural determinants of the manumission process while recapturing more of the drama of manumission acts in specific parts of the Atlantic world.

NOTES

1. T. Stephen Whitman, *The Price of Freedom: Slavery and Manumission in Baltimore and Early National Maryland* (Lexington: University Press of Kentucky, 1997); Christopher Phillips, *Freedom's Port: The African American Community of Baltimore, 1790–1860* (Urbana: University of Illinois Press, 1997), 30–56; Billy G. Smith, "Runaway Slaves in the Mid-Atlantic Region During the Revolutionary Era," in *The Transforming Hand of Revolution: Reconsidering the American Revolution as a Social Movement,* ed. Ronald Hoffman and Peter J. Albert (Charlottesville: University Press of Virginia, 1995), 220; Ira Berlin, *Generations of Captivity: A History of African-American Slaves* (Cambridge, Mass.: Belknap Press of Harvard University Press, 2003), 66, 119.

2. Most interpretations have stressed religion; for example, Kenneth L. Carroll, "Religious Influences on the Manumission of Slaves in Caroline, Dorchester, and Talbot Counties," *Maryland Historical Magazine* 56 (1961): 176–197; for the impact of a "modernizing" impulse, see William W. Freehling, *The Road to Disunion: Secessionists at Bay, 1776–1854* (New York: Oxford University Press, 1990), 200–201; and for guilt, see Charles Grier Sellers, "The Travail of Slavery," in *The Southerner as American,* ed. C. G. Sellers (Chapel Hill: University of North Carolina Press, 1960), 40, 42, 55, 61.

3. Orlando Patterson, *Slavery and Social Death: A Comparative Study* (Cambridge, Mass.: Harvard University Press, 1982), 340.

4. Walter Johnson, *Soul by Soul: Life Inside the Antebellum Slave Market* (Cambridge, Mass.: Harvard University Press, 1999), 89–116.

5. Wills cited in this study were culled from microfilm copies of Anne Arundel County Register of Wills. Originals and microfilm copies are in Maryland State Archives, Annapolis, Md. (hereafter cited as Md. Arch.)

6. In consideration of space this essay deals only with slave-owning families. Equally important to an understanding of manumission is a consideration of the family of enslaved men, women, and children and their myriad efforts to affect the manumission process. For a powerful introduction to this critical part of the equation, see the chapter on "Black Family Strategies," in Whitman, *Price of Freedom.*

7. Economic activity in the county is based on my reading of probate inventories and administration accounts; also see Richard S. Dunn, "Black Society in the Chesapeake, 1776–1810," in *Slavery and Freedom in the Age of the Revolution,* ed. Ira Berlin and Ronald Hoffinan (Charlottesville: University Press of Virginia, 1983; reprint, Urbana: University of Illinois Press, 1986), 48–76.

8. Bureau of the Census, *First Census of the United States,* vol. 9, *Maryland* (Washington, D.C.: Government Printing Office, 1907); Ira Berlin, *Slaves Without Masters: The Free Negro in the Antebellum South* (New York: Pantheon, 1975; reprint, New York: New Press, 1992), 146.

9. Patterson, *Slavery and Social Death,* 263–264.

10. *Laws of Maryland . . . in the Year of Our Lord One Thousand Seven Hundred and Ninety* (Annapolis, Md.: Frederick Green, 1791), chap. 9; *Laws of Maryland . . . in the Year of Our Lord One Thousand Seven Hundred and Ninety-Six* (Annapolis, Md.: Frederick Green, 1797), chap. 67, sec. 23.

11. While manumissions in the county did drop off somewhat in the 1820s, this particular pattern seems to go against two of the trends believed most responsible for the explosion of manumissions in the post-Revolutionary Chesapeake: the objections to slavery made by evangelical religious, especially itinerant Methodists, and the economic downturns of the 1790s. For the Methodists, see Donald G. Mathews, *Slavery and Methodism: A Chapter in American Morality, 1780–1845* (Princeton, N.J.: Princeton University Press, 1965); for the economic doldrums of slave owning in the 1790s, see Eric Robert Papenfuse, "From Recompense to Revolution: Mahoney v. Ashton and the Transfiguration of Maryland Culture, 1791–1802," *Slavery and Abolition* 15 (December 1994): 46, 59; Robert William Fogel and Stanley L. Engerman, *Time on the Cross: The Economics of American Negro Slavery* (Boston: Little, Brown, 1974; New York: Norton, 1989), 87–88. The timing of manumission activity in Anne Arundel differs for that of Virginia.

12. Patterson, *Slavery and Social Death,* 273.

13. *Annapolis Maryland Gazette,* November 11, 1790.

14. *Speech of William Pinkney, Esq., in the House of Delegates of Maryland, at Their Session in November, 1789* (Philadelphia: Joseph Crukshank, 1790), 18; for a general discussion of the tension between the freedom to manumit and the well-being of the family, see Thomas D. Morris, *Southern Slavery and the Law, 1619–1860* (Chapel Hill: University of North Carolina Press, 1996), 378–379.

15. This paragraph and the accompanying table began with an examination of all 604 wills probated in the county between 1795 and 1818. However, for the purpose of comparing those who manumit with those who did not, I selected only the 327 wills where the testator mentioned at least one slave. Because decedents were often not specific about the type of property they bequeathed (for example, "I split my personal estate equally with all of my children"), this selection strategy undoubtedly undercounts the number of slave owners who made wills and therefore overestimates the rate of manumission in wills. However, for the purpose of comparing emancipators and nonemancipators, the omission of slave owners who did not mention slaves at all should not skew the results.

16. This seems like a reasonable way to separate parents from nonparents. It is unlikely that many parents would author an entire will without mentioning their offspring at least briefly, if only to tell them they were to receive nothing. There are many cases where token amounts are provided, and it seems unlikely that one would bequeath their property to friends and distant relatives without mentioning why they were not granting at least something to a child.

17. Carole Shammas, Marylynn Salmon, and Michel Dahlin, *Inheritance in America from Colonial Times to the Present* (New Brunswick, N.J.: Rutgers University Press, 1987), 283n4.

18. This group can be further broken down into widowers (those who mentioned children but not a wife) and single men (those who mentioned neither spouse nor children). As expected, in these wills single men had a higher manumission rate than widowers.

19. Anne Arundel County (hereafter cited as A. A. Co.) Wills, vol. JG 1 (1788–1797), MSA CM 122–25, Md. Arch., 404–405; Jacob was able to pay the money to Baldwin's estate on time. See A. A. Co. Administration Accounts, vol. JG (1797–1802), MSA C 29–5, Md. Arch., 104: The money was received by Baldwin's executor "of negro Jacob who was left free under the will upon paying the same."

20. Fifty years of age was the oldest age a slave could be legally freed in the state until 1796, when the maximum age was lowered to forty-five; see note 7 above.

21. Of course, manumission by will was by definition a delayed manumission, for almost all "immediate" manumissions were to take place at the testator's death, not when the will was drawn up. One mitigating factor was that in Anne Arundel, the majority of wills were signed within nine months of death. Joan Cashin's study of antebellum southern men's wills found that the typical authors wrote wills a year and a half prior to death. See Cashin, "According to His Wish and Desire: Female Kin and Female Slaves in Planter Wills," in *Women of the American South: A Multicultural Reader,* ed. Christie Anne Farnham (New York: New York University Press, 1997), 93. At least one sensational newspaper account suggested that a will promising freedom at the death of the owner was an incentive for an enslaved woman to poison members of the slave owner's family in order to obtain her freedom; see *Annapolis Maryland Gazette,* April 27, 1797.

22. A. A. Co. Wills, vol. JG 2 (1797–1813), MSA CM 122–6, Md. Arch., 45–47.

23. Ibid., 85–89.

24. Ibid., 266–267.

25. Ibid., 205–206.

26. Helen Tunnicliff Catterall, ed., *Judicial Cases Concerning American Slavery and the Negro* (Washington, D.C.: Carnegie Institution, 1926; reprint, New York: Negro Universities Press, 1968), 4:78.

27. A. A. Co. Wills, vol. JG 1 (1788–1797), MSA CM 122–5, Md. Arch., 623–625.

28. A. A. Co. Wills, vol. JG 2 (1797–1813) MSA CM 122–6 Md. Arch., 355–357, 377–79.

29. A. A. Co. Wills, vol. JG 1 (1788–1797), MSA CM 122–5, Md. Arch., 63–64.

30. Michael P. Johnson and James L. Roark, *Black Masters: A Free Family of Color in the Old South* (New York: Norton, 1984), 31.

31. A. A. Co. Wills, vol. JG 1 (1788–1797), MSA CM 122–5, Md. Arch., 588–591.

32. A. A. Co. Wills, vol. JG 2 (1797–1813), MSA CM 122–6, Md. Arch., 7–9.

33. Ibid., 12–14.

34. Ibid., 10.

35. For a powerful example from Virginia in the post–Revolutionary War period, see James H. Kettner, "Persons or Property? The Pleasants Slaves in the Virginia Courts, 1792–1799," in *Launching the "Extended Republic": The Federalist Era,* ed. Ronald Hoffman and Peter J. Albert (Charlottesville: University Press of Virginia, 1996), 136–155.

36. A. A. Co. Wills, vol. JG 2 (1797–1813), MSA CM 122–6, Md. Arch., 139.

37. Thomas Harris and Reverdy Johnson, *Reports of Cases Argued and Determined in the Court of Appeals of the State of Maryland, in 1820, 1821, 1822, and part of 1823* (Annapolis, Md.: Jonas Green, 1825), 5:59.

38. A. A. Co. Inventories, vol. JG 5 (1799–1804), MSA CM 105–8, Md. Arch., 290.

39. See Catterall, *Judicial Cases* 4:61, and Thomas Harris Jr. and Richard W. Gill, *Reports of Cases Argued and Determined in the General Court and Court of Appeals of the State of Maryland, in 1806, 1807, 1808, & 1809* (Annapolis, Md.: Jonas Green, 1826), 2:356–59; will in A. A. Co. Wills, vol. JG 2 (1797–1813), MSA CM 122–26, Md. Arch., 135–137.

40. The value of Sprigg's estate placed him in the top 15 percent of a sample of Anne Arundel testators. See A. A. Co. Inventories, vol. JG 5 (1799–1804), MSA CM 105–8, Md. Arch., 41; A. A. Co. Wills, vol. JG 2 (1797–1813), MSA CM 122–26, Md. Arch., 62–65; Sprigg's wife, Margaret (Caile) Sprigg, did sign a will immediately prior to her death in 1796 which was not presented to the county (because wives could not legally leave wills at that time) but which was used by her husband almost verbatim when he made out the manumission portion of his will, see Kenneth Stampp, gen. ed., *Records of Ante Bellum Southern Plantations: From the Revolution Through the Civil War* (Frederick, Md.: University Publications of America, 1985–2000), series M, pt. 2, reel 13, sec. 17, frames 1043–1045.

41. A. A. Co. Wills, vol. JG 1 (1788–1797), MSA CM 122–5, Md. Arch., 220–222.

42. Phillip Hamilton, "Revolutionary Principles and Family Loyalties: Slavery's Transformation in the St. George Tucker Household of Early National Virginia," *William and Mary Quarterly,* 3d ser., 54 (1998): 540.

43. For Madison's efforts to explore other options, see Drew R. McCoy, *The Last of the Fathers: James Madison and the Republican Legacy* (New York: Cambridge University Press, 1989), 232–233; for Madison's advice in 1820, see Robert McColley, *Slavery and Jeffersonian Virginia* (Urbana: University of Illinois Press, 1964), 184.

44. Phillips, *Freedom's Port,* 28; for another important statement concerning the alternative to tobacco agriculture and "gentry culture" posed by Baltimore, see Charles G. Steffen, *From Gentlemen to Townsmen: The Gentry of Baltimore County, Maryland, 1660–1776* (Lexington: University Press of Kentucky, 1993).

45. Lois Carr, "Inheritance in the Colonial Chesapeake," in *Women in the Age of the American Revolution,* ed. Ronald Hoffman and Peter J. Albert (Charlottesville: University Press of Virginia, 1989), 169–70.

46. A. A. Co. Wills, vol. JG 3 (1813–1820), MSA CM 122–7, Md. Arch., 39–42.

47. Ibid., 282–284.

48. Ibid., 62–63.

49. See Jan Lewis, *The Pursuit of Happiness: Family and Values in Jefferson's Virginia* (Cambridge: Cambridge University Press, 1983), 152–168.

50. Cynthia Lynn Lyerly, *Methodism and the Southern Mind, 1770–1810* (New York: Oxford University Press, 1998), 135–136.

51. A. A. Co. Wills, vol. JG 3 (1813–1820), MSA CM 122–7, Md. Arch., 230.

52. A. A. Co. Wills, vol. JG 2 (1797–1813), MSA CM 122–6, Md. Arch., 571–576.

53. David F. Allmendinger Jr., *Ruffin: Family and Reform in the Old South* (New York: Oxford University Press, 1990), 84; also see Claudia L. Bushman, *In Old Virginia: Slavery, Farming, and Society in the Journal of John Walker* (Baltimore: Johns Hopkins University Press, 2002).

54. Whitman, *Price of Freedom,* 105, 108–109; for postmortem disruptions on one county estate, see description of Doughregan Manor after the death of Charles Carroll of Carrollton

in John Hope Franklin and Loren Schweninger, *Runaway Slaves: Rebels on the Plantation* (New York: Oxford University Press, 1999), 17–19.

55. See Brenda E. Stevenson, *Life in Black and White: Family and Community in the Slave South* (New York: Oxford University Press, 1996), 213–220; Peter Kolchin, *American Slavery, 1619–1877* (New York: Hill and Wang, 1993), 125; Cheryll Ann Cody, "Naming, Kinship, and Estate Dispersal: Notes on Slave Family Life on a South Carolina Plantation, 1786–1833," *William and Mary Quarterly,* 3d ser., 39 (1982): 192–211.

56. Whitman, *Price of Freedom,* 105.

57. When tobacco was the primary crop, slave labor was less costly than short-term free labor because tobacco required almost constant attention during the growing season. Wheat, on the other hand, required roughly one-third the worker-days required for tobacco cultivation. Given the going rate for day labor and the average cost per year of slave labor, Carville V. Earle estimated the wheat farmer's labor costs was 30 percent less if he or she used wage rather than slave labor in the Chesapeake. See Earle, *Geographical Inquiry and American Historical Problems* (Stanford, Calif.: Stanford University Press, 1992), 226–242. Lorena Walsh argues that the collapse of the French tobacco market in the mid-1790s led many Maryland slave owners to do two things that reduced the number of enslaved laborers needed: one, many moved away from tobacco, and they often plowed up extra acres for wheat without any fallow period or fertilizer, which led to fairly extensive erosion; two, they started putting more acreage in pasture and hay to support draft animals: "This further reduced the acreage available for market crops and thus labor needs. Once they could count on animal power, planters needed fewer hoe hands." See Walsh, "Rural African Americans in the Constitutional Era in Maryland, 1776–1810," *Maryland Historical Magazine* 84 (1989): 337–338.

58. Mary Clement Jeske, "Autonomy and Opportunity: Carrollton Manor Tenants, 1734–1790" (Ph.D. diss., University of Maryland, 1999), 13, 162, 196.

59. Lorena S. Walsh, "Work and Resistance in the New Republic: The Case of the Chesapeake, 1770–1820," in *From Chattel Slaves to Wage Slaves: The Dynamics of Labour Bargaining in the Americas,* ed. Mary Turner (Bloomington: Indiana University Press, 1995), 97–122.

60. Gregory Stiverson hypothesizes the effect that switching completely from tobacco to wheat as the primary crop, given typical land and slaveholdings and concludes that "switching away from tobacco because wheat culture would have required that they either purchase more land, sell some of their slaves, or devise alternative forms of employment for their laborers." Stiverson, *Poverty in a Land of Plenty: Tenancy in Eighteenth Century Maryland* (Baltimore: John Hopkins University Press, 1977), 101–102.

61. Sarah S. Hughes, "Slaves for Hire: The Allocation of Black Labor in Elizabeth City County, Virginia, 1782 to 1810," *William and Mary Quarterly,* 3d ser., 35 (1978): 260–261; also see Jonathan D. Martin, *Divided Mastery: Slave Hiring in the Old South* (Cambridge, Mass.: Harvard University Press, 2004).

62. Lorena S. Walsh, "Slave Life, Slave Society, and Tobacco Production in the Tidewater Chesapeake, 1620–1820," in *Cultivation and Culture: Labor and the Shaping of Slave Life in the Americas,* ed. Ira Berlin and Philip Morgan (Charlottesville: University Press of Virginia, 1993), 197.

63. Ira Berlin, *Many Thousands Gone: The First Two Centuries of Slavery in North America* (Cambridge, Mass.: Belknap Press of Harvard University Press, 1998), 267–268.

64. This is not to deny that there were economies of scale in wheat production based partly on the increased productivity of a harvest conducted by gang labor. However, other than harvest the multitude of tasks on a farm were not likely to be performed by large groups of laborers

working in unison. Instead, many different tasks might be performed at the same time. For the economy of scale in the wheat harvest, see James R. Irwin, "Exploring the Affinity of Wheat and Slavery in the Virginia Piedmont," *Explorations in Economic History* 25 (1988): 302–303; for the difficulty of supervision on small, mixed farms vis-à-vis tobacco farms in the upper South, see Fletcher M. Green, ed., *Ferry Hill Plantation Journal, January 4, 1838 to January 15, 1839* (Chapel Hill: University of North Carolina Press, 1961).

65. A. A. Co. Inventories, vol. JG 6 (1805–1808), MSA SC 105–9, Md. Arch., 362.

66. A. A. Co. Willis, vol. JG 2 (1797–1813), MSA CM 122–6, Md. Arch.

67. Ibid.

68. For the first example, see *Annapolis Maryland Gazette,* March 27, 1783.

69. *Annapolis Maryland Gazette,* June 23, 1803.

70. *Annapolis Maryland Gazette,* October 18, 1809.

71. A. A. Co. Wills, vol. JG 2 (1797–1813), MSA CM 122–6, Md. Arch., 543–545[?].

72. Frank Tannenbaum, *Slave and Citizen: The Negro in the Americas* (New York: Knopf, 1947).

ELLEN ESLINGER

Liberation in a Rural Context

—〰—

The Valley of Virginia, 1800–1860

Richard Wade's classic work *Slavery in the Cities*, published in 1964, contended that urban settings were antithetical to slavery, but it also showed that slavery could be an extremely adaptable, complex institution.[1] Slaves were more difficult to supervise in the anonymous, crowded conditions of an urban setting. Southern cities also created numerous wage-earning opportunities, providing in many cases for eventual self-purchase and the manumission of kin as well as the acquisition and enjoyment of property. Wade and historians who followed in his wake found in municipal records a precious extra layer of documentation that allowed for the exploration of southern black community life with an unprecedented level of detail.[2]

Comparable rural studies face greater challenges and therefore remain fewer in number.[3] Much work remains to be done. Before historians can truly appreciate what urban life meant for people of color, we need to better understand the rural context—not just plantation studies but of broader community life. Too much about what historians understand and assume is based on fascinating but narrow urban experiences.

Manumission is a natural place to begin. If cities offered superior opportunities for achieving manumission, what did rural people face? What follows is an initial attempt to examine manumission in the Shenandoah Valley of Virginia, particularly Rockbridge and Augusta counties between 1800 and 1860. The antebellum valley was a fairly discrete rural region removed from the shadow of neighboring metropolises. Its economy was dominated in this period by mixed farming, agricultural processing, and small towns. Especially important, the historical records are unusually complete.

Rockbridge and Augusta formed a pocket of noticeable prosperity in antebellum Virginia. Neither, however, owed its prosperity to tobacco or other agricultural staples associated with slave labor. In 1860 Augusta County led the entire state in the aggregate cash value of farmland and value of farm implements and machinery. It was the state's premier county for milch cows and butter. Augusta also produced more corn than any other Virginia county. The most important commercial crop was wheat, which not only provided farmers with a good livelihood but also supported a number of local processing industries. After 1855 a railroad line provided enhanced access to commercial markets. Rockbridge County also had a thriving economy, although its prosperity was based as much on industry as on agriculture. Whereas Augusta County produced more wheat, Rockbridge County had more gristmills. Distilling and lumber were also prominent local industries in Rockbridge and fostered related production of staves, barrels, and wagons. Several extractive industries also thrived: iron, cement, and stone. In addition, Lexington, the county seat, benefitted from two educational institutions, Washington College and Virginia Military Institute. Although Rockbridge was unable to attract a railroad connection, a canal extension to the James River along the county's southern border provided improved access to Richmond and other markets. By midcentury the prosperity of Augusta and Rockbridge counties had attracted confectioners, photographers, and cigar makers. The area was distinguished for its economic good health.[4]

Slaves and free blacks had been present almost from the very beginnings of agricultural settlement.[5] Their numbers, however, increased slowly during the eighteenth century. In 1800 the federal population census counted 1,070 slaves and 97 free people of color in Rockbridge County. Augusta County had 1,946 slaves and 95 free people of color. Slaves and free people of color together accounted for about one-quarter of the population in Augusta, but only half that in Rockbridge. The black population grew significantly during the antebellum period. By 1860 Augusta County, with its railroad and better access to other parts of Virginia, included 5,616 slaves and 586 free blacks. Rockbridge County, smaller and somewhat isolated yet equally prosperous, included 3,985 slaves and 422 free blacks. The proportion of blacks in relation to the white population was 28.8 percent in Augusta and 34.3 percent in Rockbridge, but the proportion of free blacks had grown very little and remained minuscule at about 3 percent throughout the county, with a slightly greater concentration in the two county seats, Staunton and Lexington. Although the upper valley's black population was modest in size and residentially scattered across the countryside, slavery was firmly entrenched both economically and ideologically.[6]

Little is known about the slaves and free people of color who resided in Rockbridge and Augusta counties during the early nineteenth century. Extremely few individuals can be identified in earlier local records.[7] Nearly all appear to have originated from eastern Virginia, across the Blue Ridge Mountains. Some free blacks were descended from families that had been free during the colonial period, but the greater number had achieved freedom following the American Revolution. The fight for independence had sensitized many Americans to the inconsistency of republicanism and slavery, and although

Virginia did not abolish slavery, it did ease the laws regulating manumission in 1782.[8] Many recently freed people of color seem to have settled in the Shenandoah Valley for the same reason as many of their white neighbors, as part of a broad westward migration taking place throughout much of the seaboard states. Others, the majority, had been manumitted locally. But in a region where the slave population was comparatively small, manumission was not a frequent occurrence.

As a result of legislation passed in 1793 and 1834 that prohibited the entry of free blacks from other states, the upper valley's free black population was composed almost entirely of Virginia natives. Sixteen of 450 former slaves identified as resident in Rockbridge or Augusta counties between 1800 and 1860 can be traced back to specific Virginia counties east of the Blue Ridge Mountains. Another 15 can be traced to western Virginia counties, usually neighboring sections of the Shenandoah Valley. Six came from out of state, including 2 from Ohio and 1 from Louisiana.[9] Local authorities were aware that these latter individuals were from out of state and therefore in violation of Virginia law, but court records indicate that this law was seldom enforced during the early decades of the nineteenth century. The greater number, approximately 400 of the 450 former slaves, were not newcomers but manumitted locally. Most manumissions involved a small number of slaves, no doubt a result of the region's dispersed pattern of ownership.[10] Adult manumissions favored men over women, indicating that concubinage played a minuscule role in the upper valley.[11] At least 30 slaves (7.5 percent) were manumitted by kin. Approximately 95 (24 percent) were manumitted through the wills of five individuals, as part of a large group. All of these wills were recorded after 1820, three of them after 1850.[12] Thus some patterns of manumission in this corner of the upper South do not conform to those found elsewhere. It may well be that the upper Valley of Virginia was exceptional, but with such a small number of recorded manumissions these two western Virginia counties more likely represent variation well within the normal range.

Patterns of manumission in Rockbridge and Augusta counties during the first quarter of the nineteenth century resembled those found elsewhere in Virginia in several significant ways. People were manumitted through both deed and will, although manumission was perhaps not as frequent an event as it was east of the Blue Ridge Mountains, where the slave population was always much larger. An estimated one-third of the free black adults present in 1830 probably had begun life as a slave, a proportion that gradually declined over the next several decades.[13] Although the upper valley's free black population grew during the early nineteenth century, mainly because of to natural increase and immigration, it nonetheless remained numerically quite small and less the subject of white hostility. According to a spokesman for African colonization shortly before the Nat Turner Rebellion, "The free colored persons of the

County are so few in comparison of its total population and so dispursed [*sic*] in their ordinary pursuits that they neither manifest the qualities nor occupy the posture wh. in other places have made them the objects of popular prejudice and apprehension."[14] Whether the upper valley's free black population was actually better or better off is very questionable, but there is no disputing that their subsequent treatment followed the same unhappy direction as elsewhere in the South. By the 1850s blacks other than slaves were seen as a dangerous nuisance and local authorities sought to control what they perceived as a rapidly growing problem.

The primary tool for achieving this goal was state law. Freedom for Virginians of color was governed by an increasing number of statutes in the nineteenth century.[15] For former slaves, one of the most important pieces of legislation was a requirement that they leave Virginia within twelve months of manumission. This law, passed in 1806, as well as many other laws regarding people of color, was not rigorously enforced until after midcentury. Nonetheless, most former slaves departed as required. A small number sought permission to remain in Virginia, usually to be near enslaved kin. For example, Jack Paul had been emancipated in the will of his mistress in 1827 but petitioned the Virginia legislature for permission to remain because his wife, "to whom he is sincerely & faithfully attached," remained a slave under another master. Paul did not ask to remain permanently but only long enough to earn the money necessary to free her. Former slave Walter Smiley's family faced possible separation for a different reason. Smiley's wife and children were free, but he lacked the monetary resources to move them out of state. Smiley had been manumitted by deed in 1818 and went to Ohio in an effort to comply with the 1806 removal law, but he returned to Rockbridge County and successfully petitioned for an exemption.[16] For families like these, freedom presented a dilemma.

Obtaining permission to remain was not easy. Successful petitioners were nearly all older people, able to provide positive character recommendations from former owners as well as other reputable members of the community. Those slaves freed by wills, without the patronage of their former master, labored under a distinct disadvantage in their appeals.[17] Explicitly or implicitly the white patrons also offered assurances that the former slave would not be disruptive or become a public burden. Permission to remain involved petitioning the state legislature for a specific legislative enactment; after that date a law passed in 1815 allowed county and municipal courts to grant local exemptions. In neither Rockbridge nor Augusta do records indicate that local authorities pursued violators of the 1806 law until after midcentury, but they did consider petitions critically.

As the political climate deteriorated, local courts were increasingly determined to keep the free black population from growing. Fewer petitions from former slaves succeeded. Moreover, permission to remain was at the pleasure of the court and could be rescinded. The court of Augusta County did this at least once, for habitual drunkenness, in 1856. The change in atmosphere was also evident in the free papers issued by the court to former slaves, which after around 1856 usually included an explicit statement that the bearer lacked permission to remain in Virginia.[18] Most former slaves did not petition for permission to remain, but it is unclear whether this reflected their own preference or a perception that they lacked the necessary qualities for a positive consideration. Violators of the 1806 law were rarely prosecuted, but they may have been informally threatened with proceedings if they did not depart as required.

Manumission was regulated in other ways as well. Virginia slaves could be manumitted through deed or will, but only those who were able to provide for their own support.[19] Thus manumitted slaves had to be between the ages of twenty-one and forty-five. The upper limit was often ignored in the valley. Poor birth records may have been a factor, but there was apparently little public concern so long as the former slave was fit enough to be self-sufficient and not likely to become a public charge. Thus Rockbridge County Overseers of the Poor summoned William Block "to shew cause why he shall not be compelled to support a negro woman named Nancy—emancipated by him, since she arrived at the age of 45." Yet Franky Brown of Augusta County was manumitted through a will in 1813, aged about sixty, and Bob Lawrence was manumitted in 1848 around age sixty-eight. Perhaps significantly, both individuals were manumitted with younger kin who presumably were being counted on for support.[20] They were nonetheless manumitted contrary to Virginia law.

At the other end of the age spectrum, individuals manumitted as children often had to wait years before tasting freedom. When a Rockbridge County woman named Hannah was freed by the will of David Templeton in 1825, for example, her three children were to remain in servitude to a man named Nathan Carpenter until age twenty-one.[21] Some newly freed parents thus faced a cruel dilemma—remaining in the vicinity contrary to the 1806 law or abandoning their children. No instance can be found in either Rockbridge or Augusta counties where parents were expelled and forced to leave small children behind, unless other circumstances also existed such as criminal charges. Authorities also do not appear to have applied this law to free black fathers liberating enslaved children. Separation was nonetheless a genuine concern for most newly freed families.

Freeborn children of color could also find themselves in temporary bondage. A significant number of free black families were poor, especially those in which the father was enslaved. When a family, black or white, appeared unable to adequately provide for children, county overseers of the poor interceded to assure that the children were physically and morally cared for by placing the child in another household. In the best scenario the child would learn a skill and break out of poverty. Free children of color, however, were usually bound to menial work.[22] In both Rockbridge and Augusta counties boys were much more likely to be apprenticed as farmers and waiters than as blacksmiths or wheelwrights. Although the legal status of bound apprentices was much different than that of slaves, daily living conditions were probably quite similar. Apprenticed children were certainly very vulnerable. Local magistrates might not remove a child from an abusive master until several months had gone by. A few instances also occurred where the master moved away from the county and, although it was not supposed to be done, took his apprentice too. By the time a child reached adulthood his or her free birth might become difficult to prove should a master refuse to acknowledge it. Even when properly released from their indenture, apprentices of color might be mistaken as slaves because of their previously unfree status and racial identity. The risk was especially high where the child was an orphan or apprenticed at a younger age. Former apprentices of color were usually careful to register with local authorities, as Virginia law required, and their papers seldom omitted a specific reference to having been indentured.[23]

Some slave owners attempted to bypass the legal restrictions on manumission through various sorts of special arrangements granting quasi-freedom. As elsewhere in the South, some valley slaves lived comparatively independently of masters, hiring themselves out and paying their masters some agreed upon fee. This practice allowed slaves to keep surplus earnings as well as to find housing closer to family members.[24] One former Rockbridge County slave was described as having "been actually free for some time, his master holding only a pro-forma ownership over him until recently when he has been fully emancipated."[25] William Miller's will manumitted his slaves but in a way which attempted to keep mothers and small children together. If at the time of his death Virginia allowed former slaves to remain in the state, a woman named Becky was to be manumitted, but if not she was to remain with his son William Miller Jr. and receive wages as a hired servant with her two youngest children, Mary and Joseph. William was to give them "comfortable boarding and lodging" until age twenty-one then free them with two suits of clothing. According to the will of Alexander Paxton, executors were to sell all of his slaves at private sale except for one named Ailsey, who was to be manumitted "in consideration of her uniform good conduct and faithful attention to me during my sickness." If the government would not grant her an exception and let her remain in the state, "I revoke the provision of my will, setting her free, and I direct my executor to hire her out from year to year, to such person in the county as she may choose to live with, and to apply her hires to her personal comfort. Under no circumstances is she to be sold."[26] Such practices sometimes blurred an individual's legal status.

Black slave owning also created situations of quasi-freedom. The purchase of a slave did not legally require that the deed be recorded with the local court, so it is impossible to determine the true extent of black slave owning. In most cases it is probably safe to assume that manumission followed closely after purchase. A free black tenant named Patrick Henry, for example, had bought his wife Louisa in 1815 and the following year proudly manumitted her for "her extraordinary and meritorious zeal in the prosecution of my interest, her constant probity and extraordinary deportment subsequent to her being recognized as my wife."[27] Legally Louisa Henry was subject to the 1806 law requiring former slaves to leave Virginia within twelve months or else face reenslavement. This law was seldom enforced in the early nineteenth century, however, and families such as the Henrys were left in peace.

After the Nat Turner Rebellion in 1831, the tolerance was generally lower and likely contributed to increased slave owning by fellow blacks. The upper valley claimed at least six black slave owners during the antebellum decades. Census records indicate that in all cases it was a wife and children being held in bondage. Had they been manumitted, the family faced separation or relocation out of state. The latter required considerable resources, and the financial burden of redeeming kin from bondage no doubt seriously depleted resources.[28] Other families took on loans, which required repayment before creditors would allow manumission. Those few black slave owners who died locally and left wills manumitted family members and provided directions for liquidating the estate. Their strategy for keeping the family together had operated as long as it could under Virginia law, and now the survivors prepared to leave as required.

Meanwhile, however, enslaved kin enjoyed considerable freedom. One of the more extraordinary examples is that of the Howard family of Lexington. Reuben Howard, born free, lived with his second wife and children in a small brick house. Reuben Howard was expelled from Virginia in 1856 on suspicion of circulating abolitionist literature. For reasons that are unclear but may have entailed an effort to avoid a distressed sale of his house and lot, Milly and the children remained in Lexington and supported themselves by taking in laundry. Although Milly Howard and her children did not attain freedom until 1863, under the terms of her husband's will, census enumerators had counted her and the children as free in 1850 and again in 1860.[29] In terms of daily living they probably enjoyed the same freedoms as Reuben Howard and other freeborn people of color. Upon manumission, however, they needed to be prepared to relocate.

Members of the white community strongly encouraged former slaves to consider emigration to Liberia. Local auxiliaries of the American Colonization Society had appeared by 1830 in both Rockbridge and Augusta counties. The activity level varied over time, peaking in the early 1830s and again in the early 1850s, encouraged by subsidies from the Virginia legislature. As else-where in the South, the main target was the free black population, but the colonization movement also produced a number of manumissions in the upper valley region. On the one hand some masters viewed Liberia as a means for escaping slave owning without earning the disapprobation of their white neighbors for adding to the local free black community. On the other hand prospective emigrants with enslaved kin manipulated local white interest in colonization in order to reunite their family. More than half of all known emigrants from Rockbridge and Augusta counties were former slaves.[30]

The Nat Turner Rebellion in 1831 greatly increased interest in African colonization. In late 1831 the Rockbridge County chapter sought transportation for an elderly man named Robert Allen, his wife, and their child. The wife and child had been emancipated specifically to enable them to go to Liberia. The husband had already earned part of the money necessary for their purchase, and local whites supplied the rest (other offspring remained enslaved). The Rockbridge Colonization Society helped with the purchase and planned to supply the cost of transportation and initial support because the members believed that sending a known local figure to report back would aid in removing "the fears & suspicious of our coloured people respecting the colonization scheme." Robert Allen got part of his family manumitted in exchange for a promise to help convince the Rockbridge County free blacks to emigrate.[31]

The situation in neighboring Augusta County was similar. The auxiliary's secretary, a man named William Clark, claimed in 1832, "Numerous applications have recently been made to me, by the coloured persons, for information relative to their getting conveyed by the Parent Society to Liberia." In addition two whites were willing to manumit five slaves, making a total of twenty-three potential emigrants. All were characterized as having good qualities as colonists—young, moral, industrious. Moreover, wrote Clark, "I think it would be an advantage to the cause of colonization, & perhaps promote emancipation, were these persons to be accommodated. No emigrants have gone to Liberia from this part of the country." Sending this group might induce others to follow. The Augusta auxiliary pledged one hundred dollars of assistance.[32]

Clark's brief reference to emancipation is significant. Augusta County had prepared a petition to the Virginia state constitutional convention just a few years earlier, in 1829, proposing the adoption of some reasonable "system of emancipation." The main argument was one of "political wisdom and safety." Slavery was "productive, perhaps of a few transient benefits, but certainly of an infinity of evils, now pressing down upon us, portending general desolation in future." Slave labor was less efficient than free labor, a "source of endless vexation and misery within the houses and of waste and ruin on the farm." It also fostered idleness in white youth and encouraged industrious members of the white population to migrate westward to better prospects. The Augusta petition failed completely at the state level but reveals that a local ambivalence toward slavery existed well into the nineteenth century, independent of moral or humanitarian concerns.[33]

Local interest in Liberia, both black and white, tapered off after the mid-1830s until around 1850, when the American Colonization Society convinced the Virginia legislature to subsidize the transport of free blacks to Liberia. In Virginia as elsewhere in the South, the white population had become much more defensive about slavery. One result was an interest in expelling the free black population. Some Virginians were ready to support expulsion from the state, but popular sentiment in the valley did not go this far. Strong persuasive pressure, however, seemed acceptable. Society agent Rufus W. Bailey, who resided locally in Augusta County, believed that with support from local authorities he could eliminate the entire free black population. Those too poor to move or to leave on their own could go to Liberia all expenses paid. They were told that in Liberia they would be given land to farm, their children would receive a free education, and they would be treated as respectable and valued citizens. For a brief time Bailey's plan seemed feasible. Emigrant lists for the period 1850 to 1855 include 109 individuals from Rockbridge or Augusta County. Although the main target was the free black population, no fewer than 58 of the emigrants were former slaves.[34]

Some former slaves chose Liberia voluntarily, but in other cases migration to Liberia was required by the terms of manumission. In 1839, for example, William Hamilton of Rockbridge County stipulated in his will that two young sisters "shall each become free at the age of twenty one years provided they are then willing to go to the colony of Liberia on the coast of Africa or any other country out of the United States where they can be free." If they chose not to leave they were to serve his heirs as servants until age twenty-six and then be manumitted. If they had any children before that time, however, the children were subject to the same conditions. Not only did Hamilton make liberty conditional, but his plan subjected mother and child to possible separation under the 1806 Virginia law.[35]

As white residents of the upper valley became more apprehensive about the growing free black population intermingling with local slaves, emigration to Liberia as a condition for manumission became noticeably more common. The 1854 probate records for the estate of Robert Stuart include a notation that the "slave Edmon[d] aged 55 years was emancipated by the legatees for the purpose of going to the Republic of Liberia, if he fails to go he yet belongs to the estate." Likewise, the will of Thomas Dixon, also recorded in 1854, manumitted a woman named Fanny "provided she is willing to go to Liberia or in case she has no wish to go, she shall have the privilege of choosing her own master's home." The coercive aspect of such manumissions had limitations; the American Colonization Society did not desire unwilling colonists for its grand mission. A majority of the Virginia legislature felt similarly in 1837 when John Bridger of Augusta County submitted a petition that "being upwards of fifty years old, is totally adverse to spending the remainder of his days in Liberia."[36] Few individuals, however, could challenge conditional manumissions. Many probably found themselves in the position of the slaves of a Mr. Bell of Augusta County, who as he neared death "proposes to his slaves 17 in number to free them & aid them to settle in Liberia. They *declined*, but asked for their *liberty* & Ohio. He offered them Liberia or slavery . . . and no other alternative." The Bell slaves thereupon opted for Liberia.[37]

The colonization movement also produced a secondary set of manumissions. Numerous advertisements for slave sales or runaways demonstrate that Valley slave owners were not inhibited from separating family members across huge geographical distances within the United States. The prospect of separating families across an ocean, however, evoked more humane responses. The foremost impediment to emigration to Liberia, for free blacks and slaves alike, was the separation of families. Colonizationists therefore often had to persuade slave owners not otherwise inclined to deprive themselves of useful servants. Furthermore, because earning the money to liberate kin was difficult, sympathetic whites often donated funds.

Even when successful the typically small size of valley slaveholdings often required cooperation from several masters. The man Edmond mentioned above is a good illustration. Edmond had been pursuing the idea of Liberia for some time before his manumission in 1853. He left with nine members of his family almost exactly one year later. His wife, Fanny, and the three younger children were emancipated by their master, an elderly man who had already sent one slave to Liberia.[38] Edmond, who called himself Edmond Brown, had "by persevering personal application, succeeded in raising a sufficient amount of funds" to enable him to purchase two grown daughters and two grandchildren (for $900), as well as a grown son (for $775). A Princeton, New Jersey, woman had given $275, but most of the donations were probably local. Edmond's son, Moses Brown, did not sail with the family but remained behind until he could buy his wife, who was owned by a different master. This took another year, but had he relied solely upon his own earnings it would have taken much longer.[39] Likewise, a man only recently liberated in Augusta County "is now employed in soliciting donations to enable him to purchase his wife, who is a slave."[40] White enthusiasm for colonization thus provided local blacks with a special opportunity to fund manumission.

Liberia appealed for similar reasons to some of the area's free blacks. One of Lexington's more prominent members of the free black community, a man named John V. Henry, bought his wife and children out of slavery, but Liberia offered an opportunity to reunite even more kin. Henry had migrated to the valley as a young man from the Virginia Tidewater county of Westmoreland.

Although he had been born free, several of his brothers had begun life as slaves. Brother Patrick Henry apparently came to the Shenandoah Valley first, about 1814, followed soon by John V., Duncan, and Williamson. All except Duncan are known to have married enslaved women. By 1840 John V. Henry had found steady employment at Washington College in Lexington. He was able to manumit his wife and three children in 1845, and the local court allowed an exception to the 1806 removal law. About five years later he led his family to Liberia. Joining them was an adopted son, William Henry, and a nephew named Patrick Henry (both born free).[41] Five years later William J. Henry, Woodrow Henry, and Robert Henry also went to Liberia. Their relationship to John V. Henry is unclear, but they had been manumitted by the will of a woman named Sarah Price, the same individual who had owned Williamson Henry's wife, Mary, and emancipated three of their children in 1844.[42] John V. Henry had been able to earn enough to buy his immediate family, but the state subsidies and local white enthusiasm for Liberia offered a chance to reunite his extended family as well. Moreover, kin from elsewhere had preceded them to Liberia. Shortly after their arrival both John V. Henry and one of his daughters wrote back that they were healthy and doing well.[43] Unfortunately he sickened soon thereafter and died.

Liberia was an important destination for the valley's former slaves, but a much greater number apparently headed for the free states. Although Pennsylvania was close, Ohio was a more common destination. Former slaves Walter Smiley and John Beale successfully petitioned for permission to remain in Virginia, but only after going to Ohio and then returning to be with their families left behind in Rockbridge.[44] In her will widow Agnes Reid bequeathed various bonds to "Betty Reid of Ohio, formerly my slave." Likewise, Jacob Judy bequeathed to Archy Walters, "a free man of colour now residing in the state of Ohio and formerly a slave manumitted by me the sum of $300." Martha Porter stipulated that her slaves Daniel and Henry should go with her nephew to Ohio and remain with him and then be manumitted upon reaching the age of twenty-one.[45] Local colonization agent Reverend Rufus W. Bailey, who resided in Staunton, reported in 1850 that a "number of the families . . . have taken a notion to go to *Ohio*, & some have actually started."[46] Most of these were free born people of color, eligible for the legislature's recent appropriation to underwrite the cost of emigration to Liberia. Although northern racism placed limits on black freedom, Ohio seemed preferable when compared to the high mortality rate among Liberian emigrants.[47]

How did manumission in the upper valley compare with experience elsewhere, particularly urban places? The historical literature suggests that manumission occurred more frequently in cities than in the countryside. Various factors have been suggested. The difficulty of supervising urban slaves may have encouraged owners to take the final step and relinquish their slave property entirely. Cities may have offered better wage-earning opportunities, making it easier for people of color to accumulate the money to purchase and manumit. This may have been particularly true for women and skilled artisans.[48] The historical literature has also suggested several more general patterns, such as a tendency over time to manumit a few favorite or meritorious slaves rather than to abandon slavery altogether. This may account for the greater proportion of women among manumissions, and of mulattos rather than blacks. As southern antislavery sentiments declined in the nineteenth century and manumission became less common, more of those manumissions that did occur were the result of purchase at full value. This favored skilled slaves who could command better wages. Elderly slaves past their productive prime figured more prominently as well.[49] Unfortunately, economic and other differences varied so greatly across the South that efforts at regional comparisons are probably futile except at the most general level.

Compounding the problem are local peculiarities and lapses in government records. Virginia law required that newly free people be provided with a copy of the "instrument of emancipation," with the clerk's seal, paid for by the manumitter. Yet many manumission records are impossible to locate, even in a place like the Valley of Virginia, where the black population was smaller and easier to trace. An unknown number of former slaves left no trace in court records. No deed of emancipation or registration can be found for Archy Walters, for example, manumitted by a Rockbridge County resident named Jacob Judy. Some former slaves must have had nothing more than privately issued testaments of their free status. Such papers, of course, offered inferior protection, but the master who provided them suffered no inconvenient travel to the county court and no recording fees. Slaves about to be manumitted could not readily make such a demand.[50] Unfortunately, although detailed community studies are good at uncovering omissions and gaps, the true nature of the problem remains unknown.

Even if we could be confident that nearly all manumissions were recorded, many do not include the full terms of the transaction. The standard pattern in upper valley deeds is a simple reference to "motives of benevolence." For some masters, this expression signified an outright gift, but for others it conceivably expressed a mere cooperation with self-purchase at full market value. Even in the rare instances where purchase money is listed, seldom is it possible to determine how that price compares to the slave's open market value. Thus efforts to analyze opportunities for self-purchase and consider the extent of black agency in manumissions can only go so far. Again, the problem surely operated also in cities and elsewhere and undermines efforts at comparison.

With these limitations in mind, the picture of manumission that begins to emerge in the two rural counties of the Valley of Virginia follows many of the general patterns detected in cities but also suggests some local peculiarity. The prominence of African colonization is particularly striking and, given the risks involved, suggests that perhaps people of color did indeed face extra challenges in rural communities. With one or two hundred free black adults scattered across a countywide area, finding a suitable spouse of free status must have been difficult. Intermarriage with slaves was probably very common. Thus manumission was a key concern for many families of color, free and unfree. Moreover, unskilled agricultural labor perhaps made it harder to earn the necessary money for redeeming family members versus the greater number of wage-earning opportunities available in cities. The white people of the valley also seem to have been more ready to manumit slaves when Liberia was the destination, especially when immediate family members were involved. Colonization thus presented a special opportunity for manumission. Ultimately, of course, high mortality rates made Liberia unattractive.

At least four hundred men, women, and children nonetheless found freedom in this small corner of Virginia. It is possible that further research may yet reveal more about how the prospects for manumission in Rockbridge and Augusta counties, with their lower slave population, compared with other settings. Even if such comparisons remain elusive, the initial impression from these two counties indicates that manumission in rural settings responded to conditions that may have been different yet probably no less complex than those operating upon manumission in southern cities.

NOTES

1. Richard Wade, *Slavery in the Cities: The South, 1820–1860* (New York: Oxford University Press, 1964).

2. Ira Berlin, *Slaves Without Masters: The Free Negro in the Antebellum South* (New York: Random House, 1974); Claudia Goldin, *Urban Slavery in the American South 1820–1860* (Chicago: University of Chicago Press, 1976); Leonard P. Curry, *The Free Black in Urban America, 1800–1850: The Shadow of the Dream* (Chicago: University of Chicago Press, 1981); Michael P. Johnson and James L. Roark, *No Chariot Let Down: Charleston's Free People of Color on the Eve of the Civil War* (Chapel Hill: University of North Carolina Press, 1984); Suzanne Lebsock, *The Free Women of Petersburg: Status and Culture in a Southern Town, 1784–1860* (New York: Norton, 1984); Marie Tyler-McGraw and Gregg D. Kimball, *In Bondage and Freedom: Antebellum Black Life in Richmond, Virginia* (Charlottesville: University Press of Virginia, 1988); T. Stephen Whitman, *The Price of Freedom: Slavery and Manumission in Baltimore and Early National Maryland* (Lexington: University Press of Kentucky, 1997); Christopher Phillips, *Freedom's Port: The African American Community of Baltimore, 1790–1860* (Urbana: University of Illinois Press, 1997); Tommy L. Bogger, *Free Blacks in Norfolk, Virginia: The Darker Side of Freedom* (Charlottesville: University Press of Virginia, 1997); James Sidbury, *Ploughshares into Swords: Race, Rebellion, and Identity in Gabriel's Virginia, 1730–1810* (Cambridge and New York: Cambridge University Press, 1997); Thomas Ingersoll, *Mammon and Manon in Early New Orleans: The First Slave Society in the Deep South, 1718–1819* (Knoxville: University of Tennessee Press, 1999); Midori Takagi, *Rearing Wolves to Our Own Destruction: Slavery in Richmond, Virginia, 1782–1865* (Charlottesville: University Press of Virginia, 1999).

3. See John Mack Faragher's discussion of rural community studies in *Sugar Creek: Life on the Illinois Prairie* (New Haven, Conn.: Yale University Press, 1986). Notable studies of rural African American community life in the antebellum South include Orville Vernon Burton, *In My Father's House Are Many Mansions: Family and Community in Edgefield, South Carolina* (Chapel Hill: University of North Carolina Press, 1985); Brenda Stevenson, *Life in Black and White: Family and Community in the Slave South* (New York: Oxford University Press, 1996); Reginald Dennin Butler, "Evolution of a Rural Free Black Community: Goochland County, Virginia, 1728–1832" (Ph.D. diss., Johns Hopkins University, 1989); Melvin Patrick Ely, *Israel on the Appamattox: A Southern Experiment in Black Freedom from the 1790s through the Civil War* (New York: Knopf, 2004).

4. U.S. Census Office, *Agriculture of the United States in 1860; compiled from the original returns of the eighth census under the direction of the Secretary of the Interior, under the direction of Joseph C. G. Kennedy, superintendent of census* (Washington, D.C.: Government Printing Office, 1864), 154–161; U.S. Census Office, *Manufactures of the United States in 1860; compiled from the Original Returns of the Eighth Census, under the direction of the Secretary of the Interior* (Washington, D.C.: Government Printing Office, 1865), 605–606, 629.

5. For the region's development in the eighteenth century, see Warren R. Hofstra, *The Planting of New Virginia: Settlement and Landscape in the Shenandoah Valley* (Baltimore: Johns Hopkins University Press, 2004); Robert Mitchell, *Commercialism and Frontier: Perspectives on the Early Shenandoah Valley* (Charlottesville: University Press of Virginia, 1977); Nathaniel Turk McCleskey, "Across the First Divide: Frontiers of Settlement and Culture in Augusta County, Virginia," (Ph.D. diss., College of William and Mary, 1990); William Couper, *History of the Shenandoah Valley*, 3 vols. (New York: Lewis Historical Publishing, 1952); John W. Wayland, *Twenty-five Chapters on the Shenandoah Valley* (Strasbourg, Va.: Shenandoah Publishing, 1957); Samuel Kercheval, *A History of the Valley of Virginia*, 4th ed. (Strasbourg, Va.: Shenandoah Publishing, 1925).

6. U.S. Census Office, *Return of the Whole Number of Persons within the Several Districts of the United States, According to "An Act Providing for the Second Census or Enumeration of the Inhabitants of the United States"* (Washington, D.C.: Duane, 1801); U.S. Census Office, *Population of the United States in 1860; compiled from the original returns of the Eighth Census* (Washington, D.C.: Government Printing Office, 1864).

7. But for a fascinating exception, see the story of Edward Tarr in McCleskey, "Across the First Divide."

8. David Brion Davis, *The Problem of Slavery in the Age of the American Revolution, 1770–1823* (Ithaca, N.Y.: Cornell University Press, 1975); Douglas R. Egerton, *Gabriel's Rebellion: The Virginia Slave Conspiracies of 1800 and 1802* (Chapel Hill: University of North Carolina Press, 1993); Eva Sheppard Wolf, *Race and Liberty in the New Nation: Emancipation in Virginia from the Revolution to Nat Turner's Rebellion* (Baton Rouge: Louisiana State University Press, 2006).

9. The 450 former slaves were identified from the black registers, deed books for Rockbridge and Augusta counties, and the American Colonization Society Papers, Library of Congress, Washington, D.C. The extant portions of the Rockbridge County free black register are in two volumes. One volume, encompassing the period 1805 to mid-1831, may be found in the Andrew Reid Record Book, Manuscripts and Rare Books Department, Swem Library, College of William and Mary. A second volume, dating from mid-1831 to mid-1860, is in the Special Collections of the Library of Virginia, Richmond. The register for Augusta County exists as two volumes, one for the county court and one for the Hustings Court of Staunton,

and has been published. They have been published in Katherine G. Bushman, comp., *The Registers of Free Blacks 1810–1864, Augusta County, Virginia and Staunton, Virginia* (Verona, Va.: Mid-Valley Press, 1989).

10. In 1850, for example, 81 percent of Rockbridge County's slave owners held fewer than ten slaves. W. Fitzhugh Brundage, "Slavery in Antebellum Rockbridge County," Northen Fellowship Research papers, 1983, typescript, Special Collections, James Graham Leyburn Library, Washington and Lee University, Lexington, Va.

11. Of the adults manumitted in Rockbridge and Augusta counties between 1800 and 1860, men numbered 118 to only 85 women. Elsewhere the ratio was reversed. See Berlin, *Slaves Without Masters*, 151.

12. In Augusta County the manumitters were John Lawrence, Sam McCune, Elizabeth Via, and Samuel Black; Bushman, *Registers of Free Blacks,* 28–30, 49, 63, 87–88. Esther Paul manumitted a woman and her ten children. Rockbridge County Will Books, Lexington, Va.

13. Derived from the free black registrations for individuals listed as household heads in 1830 and 1850 on the federal population census. Bushman, *Register of Free Negroes*; Rockbridge County Free Black Register, 1805–1831 and 1831–60; Bureau of the Census, *Fifth Census of the United States,* 1830, Manuscript Population Schedule, Augusta and Rockbridge counties, Va.; Bureau of the Census, *Seventh Census of the United States,* 1850, Manuscript Population Schedule, Augusta and Rockbridge counties, Va.

14. The Managers of the Rockbridge Colonization Society, n.d., James McDowell Papers, Southern Historical Collection, University of North Carolina (hereafter cited as McDowell Papers). This document was probably written between 1828 and 1830. See also Ralph R. Gurley to James McDowell Jr., March 18, 1830, McDowell Papers.

15. June Purcell Guild, *Black Laws of Virginia: A Summary of the Legislative Acts of Virginia concerning Negroes from Earliest Times to the Present* (1936; reprint, New York: Negro Universities Press, 1969); Philip J. Schwarz, *Slave Laws in Virginia: Studies in the Legal History of the South* (Athens: University of Georgia Press, 1996). As other historians have amply demonstrated, these statutes were selectively administered. Nonetheless, they were available to local authorities and applied when advantageous.

16. December 29, 1827 and December 11, 1822, Rockbridge County Deed Book L:378, Rockbridge County Courthouse, Lexington, Va. (hereafter cited as Rockbridge County Deed Book); Virginia General Assembly, Legislative Petitions, Rockbridge County, Library of Virginia, Richmond.

17. See the difficulty encountered by John Beale, manumitted in the will of James Templeton, December 8, 1825, Virginia General Assembly, Legislative Petitions, Rockbridge County, Library of Virginia, Richmond. When Beale approached members of the county court for help in petitioning the legislature, he was told it was "inexpedient" since his master was deceased and therefore unable to attest to Beale's good character. Butler found similar conditions in Goochland County in "Evolution of a Rural Free Black Community," 353–357.

18. Bushman, *Register of Free Negroes.*

19. Benjamin Joseph Klebaner, "American Manumission Laws and the Responsibility for Supporting Slaves," *Virginia Magazine of History and Biography* 63 (1955): 443–453.

20. Entry dated June 23, 1817, Rockbridge County Court Order Book 36:272, Lexington, Va.; Bushman, *Register of Free Negroes,* 105 and 49.

21. December 8, 1825, Virginia General Assembly, Legislative Petitions, Rockbridge County, Library of Virginia, Richmond. Hannah's husband remained enslaved to another local master.

22. Berlin, *Slaves Without Masters*, 226–227. Males served until age twenty-one and females to eighteen in Virginia during the nineteenth century, the same for whites.

23. See, for example, the free black registration of a young man named William Gowin, which states that he was "born of a free mulatto women, and was bound out by the overseers for the Corporation of Staunton." Bushman, *Register of Free Negroes*, 107.

24. Clement Eaton, "Slave-Hiring in the Upper South," *Mississippi Valley Historical Review* 46 (1960): 663–678; Loren Schweninger, "The Underside of Slavery: The Internal Economy, Self-Hire, and Quasi-freedom in Virginia, 1785–1865," *Slavery and Abolition* 12 (1991): 1–22; J. Susanne Simmons and Nancy T. Sorrells, "Slave Hire and the Development of Slavery in Augusta County, Virginia," in *After the Backcountry: Rural Life in the Great Valley of Virginia, 1800–1900*, ed. Kenneth E. Koons and Warren R. Hofstra (Knoxville: University of Tennessee Press, 2000), 169–184.

25. James McDowell to Ralph R. Gurley, October 25, 1831, American Colonization Society, Domestic Letters, Library of Congress (hereafter cited as ACS Papers).

26. Rockbridge County Will Books 9:431–432; Rockbridge County Will Books 10:376–377.

27. Rockbridge County Will Books 4A:191–192.

28. Other investigations of black slave ownership indicate that in most cases the subjects were kin relations, but not necessarily. See Carter G. Woodson, "Free Negro Owners of Slaves in the United States in 1830," *Journal Negro History* 9 (1924): 41–85; John H. Russell, "Colored Freemen as Slave Owners in Virginia," *Journal Negro History* 1 (1916): 233–242; Philip J. Schwarz, "Emancipators, Protectors, and Anomalies: Free Black Slaveholders in Virginia," *Virginia Magazine of History and Biography* 95 (1987): 317–338; Michael P. Johnson and James L. Roark, *Black Masters: A Free Family of Color in the Old South* (New York: Norton, 1984), and "Strategies of Survival: Free Negro Families and the Problem of Slavery," in *In Bondage and in Sorrow: Women, Family, and Marriage in the Victorian South, 1830–1900*, ed. Carol Bleser (New York: Oxford University Press, 1991), 88–102. In Virginia a law passed in early 1832 prohibited free blacks from purchasing slaves "other than his or her husband, wife or children." See *Acts passed at a General Assembly of the Commonwealth of Virginia, begun and held at the Capitol, in the city of Richmond* (Richmond, Va.: Printed by Thomas Ritchie, 1832), 21.

29. Rockbridge County Will Books 17:307–308; January 12, 1856, Virginia General Assembly, Legislative Petitions, Rockbridge County, Library of Virginia, Richmond.

30. "Register of emigrants, 4 March 1835 to 3 July 1857," ACS Papers. Of all manumissions in Rockbridge and Augusta counties between 1800 and 1860, about 11 percent emigrated to Liberia.

31. Henry Ruffner to Ralph R. Gurley, September 16, 1831, and James McDowell to Ralph R. Gurley, October 25, 1831, ACS Papers.

32. William Clark to Ralph R. Gurley, June 27, 1832, ACS Papers.

33. Significantly, the existence of this petition is known because of its reproduction in a neighboring newspaper, the *Winchester Republican*, July 31, 1829. The Valley of Virginia has long flattered itself as having been opposed or at least ambivalent to slavery. See Joseph A. Waddell, *Annals of Augusta County, Virginia* (1886; reprint, Harrisonburg, Va.: C. J. Carrier, 1972), 414–415.

34. R. W. Bailey to William McLain, May 14, 1850, and "Register of Emigrants, 4 March 1835–3 July 1857," ACS Papers. Bailey's tenure as an ACS agent discussed in Ellen Eslinger,

"The Brief Career of Rufus W. Bailey, American Colonization Society Agent in Virginia," *Journals of Southern History* 81 (2005): 39–74.

35. Will of William Hamilton (April 26, 1839), Rockbridge County Will Books 8:162.

36. Rockbridge County Will Books 13:47–48 and 80; Virginia General Assembly, Legislative Petitions, Augusta County, January 1, 1837.

37. R. W. Bailey to William McLain, October 14, 1850, and October 31, 1850, ACS Papers.

38. Rockbridge County Deed Books AA:118.

39. *African Repository* 30 (1854): 354; Rockbridge County Deed Books EE:54. The annual rate of hire for an adult male slave was about one hundred dollars during this period.

40. *African Repository* 13 (1837): 258.

41. *African Repository* 26 (1850): 106. The parents of William and Patrick are unknown, although John V. Henry's brother Patrick can be safely eliminated.

42. *African Repository* 31 (1855): 379; Rockbridge County Deed Books Y:115. Williamson Henry and the three children, manumitted in 1844, do not appear to have gone to Liberia. Mary Henry, his wife, apparently died in slavery.

43. *Staunton Spectator*, June 26, 1850.

44. Virginia General Assembly, Legislative Petitions, Rockbridge County, December 11, 1822, and December 8, 1825.

45. Rockbridge County Will Books 8:122 and 10:490–491 and 500–401.

46. R. W. Bailey to William McLain, May 29, 1850, ACS Papers.

47. R. W. Bailey to William McLain, June 26, 1850, ACS Papers.

48. Berlin, *Slaves Without Masters*, 150–153; Lebsock, *Free Women of Petersburg*, 95; Bogger, *Free Blacks in Norfolk*, 13–14; Sidbury, *Ploughshares into Swords,* 210–211; Whitman, *Price of Freedom*, 94–96; Phillips, *Freedom's Port*.

49. Berlin, *Slaves Without Masters*, 150–153.

50. The only evidence of Walters's emancipation is a bequest some time later in Jacob Judy's will. Will of Jacob Judy (January 31, 1848), Rockbridge County Will Books 10:490–491. See also Whitman, *Price of Freedom*, 98.

Contributors

ROBIN BLACKBURN is professor of social history at the University of Essex and Distinguished Visiting Professor of Historical Studies at the New School in New York. Until 1999 he served as editor of *New Left Review*. He is the author of *The Overthrow of Colonial Slavery, 1776–1848* (1994), the award-winning study *The Making of New World Slavery: From the Baroque to the Modern, 1492–1800* (1997), and *The Rise and Fall of New World Slavery* (2007).

DEBRA G. BLUMENTHAL is associate professor of history at the University of California, Santa Barbara. She received her Ph.D. in medieval history from the University of Toronto in 2000. She has been a fellow of the Center for the Study of Cultures at Rice University, the National Endowment for the Humanities, and the Radcliffe Institute for Advanced Study. Her publications include *Enemies and Familiars: Muslim, Eastern and Black African Slaves in Late Medieval Iberia* (2009) and "La Casa dels Negres: Black African Solidarity in Late-Medieval Valencia," in *Black Africans in Renaissance Europe*, ed. K.P. Lowe and Thomas Earl (2005).

ROSEMARY BRANA-SHUTE is associate professor of history at the College of Charleston in South Carolina. A founder of the Program in the Carolina Lowcountry and the Atlantic World, she served as associate director and codirector of the program. She received her Ph.D. in Latin American history from the University of Florida (1985). She compiled *A Bibliography of Caribbean Migration and Caribbean Immigrant Communities* (1983) and coedited *Crime and Punishment in the Caribbean* (1980) and *Money, Trade, and Power: The Evolution of Colonial South Carolina's Plantation Economy* (2001). She has published articles on slavery and manumission, including the entry on manumission for *A Historical Guide to World Slavery*, ed. Seymour Drescher and Stanley Engerman (1998). She is at work on a monograph on manumission in Suriname from 1730 to 1830.

ERIC BURIN is associate professor of history at the University of North Dakota in Grand Forks. He received his Ph.D. from the University of Illinois, Urbana-Champaign. Among his publications are his articles on the American Colonization Society, which have appeared in the *Liberian Studies Journal* and *Pennsylvania Magazine of History and Biography,* and his book *Slavery and the Peculiar Solution: A History of the American Colonization Society* (2005).

JOHN F. CAMPBELL, a graduate of the University of the West Indies and the University of Cambridge, where he read for his Ph.D. in history, has been a temporary lecturer in the Department of History at UWI's Mona Campus since 2000. Among his publications are "Reassessing the Consciousness of Labour and the Role of the 'Confidentials,' 1750–1834," *Jamaican Historical Review* (2001) and "'Always Free': West African Continuities and the Limits to Enslavement on Eighteenth Century Atlantic World Sugar Plantations," *HUArchivesNet: The Electronic Journal of the Moorland-Spingarn Research Center,* Howard University.

SEAN CONDON received his Ph.D. from the University of Minnesota, and currently he is assistant professor of history at Merrimack College in North Andover, Massachusetts. His research focuses on slavery and abolition in Revolutionary America, and he has recently published articles in the *Maryland Historical Magazine* and *Historical Methods.*

MARY CAROLINE CRAVENS is currently a law clerk for the Honorable Stanley F. Birch of the U.S. Court of Appeals for the Eleventh Circuit. At the conclusion of her clerkship, she plans to return to teaching. She received her J.D. as a Wade Scholar from the Vanderbilt University Law School, where she was editor in chief of the *Vanderbilt Journal of Transnational Law.* She received her Ph.D. in history from Johns Hopkins University in 1999, where she taught African and Latin American history before attending law school. She has received a number of awards for graduate student projects.

MARIANA L. R. DANTAS received her Ph.D. from Johns Hopkins University. Her work and research interests focus on the history of the African diaspora and African slavery in the early modern Atlantic world. She is the author of "Homens do Ferro e do Fogo: Escravos nas fábricas de ferro de Maryland no período Colonial," *Revista da Sociedade Brasileira de Pesquisa Histórica* (2000); "'For the Benefit of the Common Good': Regiments of Caçadores do Mato in Minas Gerais, Brazil," *Journal of Colonial History and Colonialism* (2004); and the forthcoming "Inheritance Practices among Individuals of African Origin and Descent in Eighteenth-Century Minas Gerais, Brazil," in *Freed Slaves: Integration and Exclusion,* ed. Marc Kleijwegt. She is currently revising her book manuscript, "Black Townsmen: A Comparative Study of Slaves and Freed Persons in Baltimore, Maryland, and Sabará, Minas Gerais, 1750–1810."

ELLEN ESLINGER is professor of history at DePaul University. She received her Ph.D. in history from the University of Chicago in 1988. She published *Citizens of Zion: The Social Origins of Camp Meeting Revivalism* in 1999 and edited the collection *Running Mad for Kentucky: Frontier Travel Accounts* in 2004.

KEILA GRINBERG (Ph.D., history, 2000) is associate professor of history at Universidade Federal do Estado do Rio de Janeiro, Brazil, and researcher of the National Council for Scientific and Technological Development (CNPq) in Brazil. A specialist on slavery, freedom, and the law in the Americas, she has authored several books, chapters, and articles, including *Slavery, Freedom and the Law in the Atlantic World* (with Sue Peabody, 2007) and "Slavery, Liberalism and Civil Law: Definitions of Status and Citizenship in the Elaboration of the Brazilian Civil Code (1855–1916)," in *Honor, Status, and the Law in Modern Latin America,* ed. Sueann Caulfield and others (2005).

SCOTT HANCOCK, currently associate professor of history and Africana studies at Gettysburg College, examines the impact of African Americans' engagement with the law in the North from the mid–seventeenth century to just before the Civil War. He is particularly interested in how interacting with the law in a variety of ways, from small disputes in lower courts to using constitutional law and legal ideologies, affected the formation of black identity over the course of two hundred years. Some of his most recent work has appeared in the anthologies *Slavery, Resistance, Freedom* (2007) and *We Shall Independent Be* (2008).

EVELYN P. JENNINGS is associate professor and holds the Margaret A. Vilas Chair of Latin American History at St. Lawrence. She received her Ph.D. from the University of Rochester in modern European and Atlantic history in 2001. Her dissertation examined state enslavement in colonial Havana, Cuba, between 1760 and 1840. She has published several articles, including "War as the 'Forcing House of Change': State Slavery in Late-Eighteenth-Century Cuba," *William and Mary Quarterly* (2005). She is working on a monograph titled "Constructing the Empire in Havana: State Slavery in Defense and Public Works, 1763–1840."

WILLEM WUBBO KLOOSTER is associate professor of history at Clark University, where he has taught since 2003. He has been a Fulbright Fellow, an Alexander Vietor Memorial Fellow, an Inter-Americas Mellon Fellow at the John Carter Brown Library, a Charles Warren Fellow at Harvard University, and a postdoctoral Fellow in Atlantic History at the National University of Ireland, Galway. Since 2001 he has been an editor, with Benjamin Schmidt, of Brill's Atlantic World book series. Klooster is the author or coeditor of six books, including *Revolutions in the Atlantic World: A Comparative History* (2009) and *Illicit Riches: Dutch Trade in the Caribbean, 1648–1795* (1998).

BEATRIZ GALLOTTI MAMIGONIAN received a Ph.D. from the University of Waterloo and is a professor of history at the Universidade Federal de Santa Catarina in Brazil. Her research interests focus on the impact of British abolitionism on the Brazilian slave system throughout the nineteenth century and its human consequences. She is completing a book manuscript on the fate of the Africans who were emancipated in the course of the suppression activities in Brazil. She is the coeditor (with Karen Racine) of *The Human Tradition in the Atlantic World* and *The Human Tradition in the Black Atlantic* (both forthcoming, Rowman and Littlefield). In collaboration with Brazilian colleagues, she is also organizing a book on the social history of slavery and freedom in southern Brazil.

ORLANDO PATTERSON is John Cowles Professor of Sociology at Harvard University. His academic interests include the culture and practice of freedom; the comparative study of slavery and ethnoracial relations; the sociology of underdevelopment with special reference to the Caribbean; and the problems of gender and familial relations in the black societies of the Americas. He is the author of numerous academic papers and five major academic books, including *Slavery and Social Death* (1982), *Freedom in the Making of Western Culture* (1991), and *The Ordeal of Integration* (1997). The author of three novels, he has published widely in journals of opinion and the national press, especially the *New York Times*. He is the recipient of many awards, including the National Book Award for Nonfiction, which he won in 1991 for his book on freedom, and the Distinguished Contribution to Scholarship Award of the American Sociological Association; and he was cowinner of the Ralph Bunche Award from the American Political Science Association for the best book on pluralism.

WILLIAM D. PHILLIPS JR. is professor of history at the University of Minnesota and was director of its Center for Early Modern History from 2001 to 2008. He received his Ph.D. in history from New York University in 1971. Among his publications are *Enrique IV and the Crisis of Fifteenth-Century Castile, 1425–1480* (1978), *Slavery from Roman Times to the Early Transatlantic Trade* (1985), and *Testimonies from the Columbian Lawsuits* (2000). With Carla Rahn Phillips he published *The Worlds of Christopher Columbus* (1992). Their *Spain's Golden Fleece* (1997) received the Leo Gershoy Award from the American Historical Association.

JONATHAN SCHORSCH is an assistant professor in the Department of Religion at Columbia University. He received his Ph.D. in history from the University of California, Berkeley, in 2000. He is the author of *Swimming the Christian Atlantic: Judeoconversos, Afroiberians and Amerindians in the Seventeenth Century* (2008) and *Jews and Blacks in the Early Modern World* (2004).

RANDY J. SPARKS is professor and chair of the Department of History at Tulane University. He received his Ph.D. from Rice University in 1988. He taught previously at the College of Charleston, where he was one of the founders of the Program in the Carolina Lowcountry and the Atlantic World and served as codirector and co-associate director of the program. He is coeditor with Jack P. Greene and Rosemary Brana-Shute of *Money, Trade, and Power: The Evolution of Colonial South Carolina's Plantation Society* (2001) and with Bertrand Van Ruymbeke of *Memory and Identity: Minority Survival among the Huguenots in France and the Atlantic Diaspora* (2003). He is the author of *On Jordan's Stormy Banks: Evangelical Religion in Mississippi, 1773–1876* (1994) and, most recently, *The Two Princes of Calabar: An Eighteenth-Century Atlantic Odyssey* (2004).

EVA SHEPPARD WOLF is associate professor of history at San Francisco State University. She received her Ph.D. from Harvard University in 2000 and is the author of *Race and Liberty in the New Nation: Emancipation in Virginia from the Revolution to Nat Turner's Rebellion* (2006). She is currently at work on a microhistorical account of an antebellum Virginian free black family.

Index